social work

third edition

social work

an introduction

Elizabeth A. Ferguson
Castleton State College

J. B. Lippincott Company
Philadelphia • New York • Toronto

HV
40
.F4
1975

ISBN 0–397–47322–2
4 6 8 9 7 5 3

Library of Congress Cataloging in Publication Data

Ferguson, Elizabeth A.
   Social work.

   Includes bibliographies.
    1. Social service. I. Title.
HV40.F4 1975   361   74-19123
ISBN 0-397-47322-2

contents

introduction ...1

1 *social work in the 1970s ...5*

2 *programs of income maintenance ...61*

3 *services to families ...109*

4 *services to children ...163*

5 *services to the aging ...235*

6 *services for health and mental health ...277*

7 *social work in corrections ...355*

8 *social work with selected disabilities ...403*

9 *community organization and planning ...459*

10 *social work issues ...499*

index of authors ...541

index of subject matter ...551

preface

Since the first edition of this book in 1963, the field of social work has changed with bewildering rapidity. The first edition coincided with an unprecedented and long-overdue concern with social justice, individual rights, and support of social work activities. The 1970s are witnessing a reaction against the activities of the preceding decade, reflected in a withdrawal of federal funding for social work education, new restrictions on agency budgets and staffs, and growing hostility to recipients of service. In this decade, also, the baccalaureate social worker (BSW) has attained professional status and may be expected to constitute the principal service delivery staff in a wide variety of human services.

This third edition attempts to outline the field in 1974, with some account of the past and some projections for the future. The effort to come abreast of the newer developments in the field was facilitated by the helpfulness of professional colleagues, authors, editors, and officials.

The Family Service Association of America, publishers of *Social Casework*, gave permission for quotations from that journal. The National Association of Social Workers permitted extensive quotations from *The Encyclopedia of Social Work, 1971*, from *Social Work*, and from others of its publications; and its office staff supplied answers to queries. Publishers and authors were generous in allowing use of copyrighted material, as indicated in footnote references. The Hartley-Salmon Clinic, the Albany Home for Children, and Miss Gertrude L. Sullivan, ACSW, Chief Psychiatric Social Worker of the Schenectady County Child Guidance Center, reviewed and updated material about their operations. New case material was supplied by Frances T. Dover, ACSW, Associate Executive Director, the Jewish Guild for the Blind, and Dorothy H. Alberts, ACSW, Director, Social Work Department, South Florida State Hospital. Floria Antell, Director of Community and Institutional Services, United Cerebral Palsy Association of New York State; Emily A. Gardiner of the Child Welfare League of America; and Elma Phillipson Cole of the former National Assembly for Social Policy and Development made helpful suggestions.

The following officials of the Social Security Administration exerted themselves to provide the most recent figures on payment levels: Mr. Wallace Dooley, former Deputy Press Officer (now retired); Mr. James M. Brown, Assistant Press Officer; and Mr. Robert Normandie, District Manager, Rutland (Vermont) Regional Office.

Separate chapters were discussed with and reviewed by Natalie and Sam Conant, Norma MacRury, and Ruth Chaskel. Judith O. Jordan and Robert L. Patterson, of Castleton State College, and Gale Schricker, copy editor, provided invaluable editorial assistance. The research efforts of Christine Cioffi (Castleton, 1974) and the staff of the Castleton College Library, particularly Mary Costello, Special Services Librarian, and Benjamin Berliner, Acquisitions Librarian, are acknowledged with gratitude.

Appreciation is due Dr. Holman D. Jordan, Jr., Director, Division of Social Sciences, and Dr. Harold Abel, President, Castleton State College, for the released time during which the revision was completed.

Elizabeth A. Ferguson

Castleton State College
Castleton, Vermont
July 1974

introduction

The decade of the 1970s is proving to be a critical one for social work and for prospective social workers. In an action deemed by many to be long overdue, the National Association of Social Workers (the major professional organization of social workers) in early 1970 voted to admit to full membership those holding baccalaureate degrees from undergraduate programs approved by the Council on Social Work Education. Provision was also made to include as associate members those with substantial experience in the field of social work. Thus it was hoped that this professional organization would for the first time represent all those carrying out social work functions. However, there seems to be good reason for feeling that the action by the National Association of Social Workers (NASW) will not achieve the desired effects. By late 1972, of a total of 275,000 people employed in social service positions, only 56,000 belonged to the NASW, and of those, approximately 1,000 were baccalaureate social workers and 1,800 were associate members.[1]

Recent changes in federal policies toward social work are threatening the place of the profession in the delivering of social services. After a period of rapid social change which included the War on Poverty, federal and state encouragement of both graduate and undergraduate social work education, major developments in the area of race relations, and an expanded use of social workers in a wide range of service delivery systems, 1973 witnessed an abrupt

1. *Annual Report of Membership Statistics, 1972* (Washington, D.C.: NASW, March 15, 1973).

reversal of policy on the part of the federal government. Responding to increased conservatism and resistance to social reform, President Nixon ordered sweeping reductions in funds and new federal directives which will have the effect of curtailing social services to large numbers of present and potential clients. At the same time, funding of social work education at all levels is being phased out in fiscal year 1975; positions in the public services are being redefined, requiring lower educational standards, substituting the position requirement of job-oriented in-service training for the requirement of a college degree, and replacing the generalist social worker with a variety of specialized technicians; service delivery staffs are being cut back; and stringent federal requirements for reimbursement will make it difficult for states to expand services. As the National Association of Social Workers puts it: "The present situation involves attempts at both federal and state levels simultaneously to improve social services, reduce their costs, and eliminate services and punish the poor and those who have fought for them."[2] New federal directives mandating the "separation" of social services from money payments have also redefined the position of "public assistance social workers" and stringently limited their activities.

That such profound changes could be effected without consultation with professional social work leaders is a vivid demonstration of the extent to which a field of so much direct concern to so many people is so little understood. Social welfare activities, including both income maintenance and social services programs, consumed in 1972 at least $137,000,000,000 (approximately 12 percent of the Gross National Product) from both public and private funds.[3] In addition to more than 250,000 social services employees, there are the millions of clients whose lives are vitally affected by social welfare activities of all types. Yet misconceptions about what social work is, how it is carried on, and even whether it is necessary are widespread. The average class of college students could frame a reasonably accurate definition of teaching or nursing or the ministry but if asked to define social work, would be likely to invoke a set of outmoded, stereotyped images about "doing good," distributing Thanksgiving baskets, or curbing juvenile delinquency.

2. National Association of Social Workers, "Issues in Social Services," *New Directions for the Seventies* (Washington, D.C.: NASW, 1973), p. 9. Reprinted with the permission of the National Association of Social Workers.

3. U.S. Bureau of the Census, *Statistical Abstract of the United States: 1973* (Washington, D.C., 1973), pp. 286, 314, 235, 238.

The profession of social work is not synonymous with the larger field of social welfare, which has been defined by Smith:

> . . . a related system of social institutions in any society; a system unified by common values, goals, and operational principles; those institutional aspects of social life which express the collective concern of the society for the well-being of its members as individuals and in family and community groups.[4]

Social work as a profession, as a skilled approach to meeting a segment of human needs, has developed within its own historical context, as have other professional specializations (public health nursing or criminology, for example) which meet other segments. But, in its concern for human well-being, social work cooperates with all the other professions engaged in meeting personal and social needs, all within the broad field of social welfare.[5]

It is possible to view the emergence of the professional baccalaureate social worker (BSW) as a focus, around which to organize the current problems and concerns of the profession. Although undergraduate colleges had for years before 1970 offered courses and programs in social work, many in consultation with the Council on Social Work Education (CSWE), these programs were termed "preprofessional," and their graduates were not considered to be prepared for immediate practice. Since May 1, 1970, it has been possible for undergraduates to secure educational preparation, including field experience, which has as its major goal the preparation of beginning-level professional social work practitioners.

This book is designed to introduce students to the field of social work. Some may have already chosen a career in social work. Others may want to consider becoming social workers but are unsure of what is involved in the profession. They "like people" and find that others turn to them with confidences. They are curious about the ways in which people react, especially when these reactions are obviously self-defeating. They may have had an unfortunate experience which has sensitized them to the feelings of others. They may even know personally a practicing social worker and find his or her account of the job appealing. Typically, such

4. Edmund A. Smith, *Social Welfare: Principles and Concepts* (New York: Association Press, 1965), p. 30.

5. For definitions of "social work" and "social welfare," see Ralph Pumphrey, "Social Welfare: History," p. 1446, and Harriet M. Bartlett, "Social Work: Fields of Practice," p. 1480, both in *Encyclopedia of Social Work, 1971* (New York: NASW, 1971).

students know very little about what social work includes, how it differs from philanthropy or social reform, and what the job opportunities and minimum qualifications are. By becoming more familiar with social work, they will be in a better position to come to a reasoned decision about their own suitability for the field. Some may decide that their talents lie in other directions and thereby save themselves (and their prospective clients) some painful experiences. Others may discover that there are opportunities in social work for applying their particular aptitudes and plan to enlarge their understanding and skills through further courses, summer work experience, or planning for professional education.

Some students and other readers of this book may not expect to have any contact with social work. Yet they will be involved to a greater extent than they realize in the operation of social work agencies, even if no more directly than as taxpayers and contributors who will want to know how their money is being spent. They may plan careers in allied fields and thus will be in a position to make use of social work resources in collaborative efforts. Many will find themselves in need of professional assistance at some point in their lives, as they struggle to deal more effectively with problems of job, family, or inner emotions. Many will have the rewarding experience of serving as volunteers, board members, or fund raisers for one of the many social agencies to be found in our communities. Unless the general public is more aware of and sympathetic to the aims of social work, our legislatures cannot be prevented from enacting regressive measures, our United Way campaigns will fall short of their goals, and those welfare programs which depend heavily on lay volunteers will be unable to recruit them.

In the conviction that the human services constitute a major social institution in our industrialized society, this book considers the major programs in which social workers are likely to be involved. Chapters are organized around services to special client groups: families, children, the elderly, correctional clients, the mentally and physically ill, the physically and socially disabled, and minority groups. Social policies and social action and the critical issues confronting the profession are outlined in the final two chapters.

social work in the 1970s

THE PROFESSION OF SOCIAL WORK

Being helpful to others is an ancient human characteristic. Some anthropologists maintain that man, as a relatively weak and defenseless creature, could not have survived in a harsh environment without the ability and the willingness to be of help to his fellow humans. There is ample evidence in ancient writings and folklore that helping friends, and in many cultures even strangers and potential enemies, has always been considered desirable by societies and approved by religions.

Helping others is also emotionally satisfying. Most people have experienced this in informal and personal ways. Relieving someone's anxiety, cheering a discouraged friend, doing something about a misunderstanding, enabling someone to solve problems more effectively—these are warming experiences, and having played a part in resolving such difficulties enhances one's self-esteem and the need to feel needed. Part of anyone's motivations for a career in any of the helping professions is the satisfaction of meeting human needs by skillful use of one's own abilities. Professional social work, as one of the youngest of the helping professions, offers the challenges and rewards of dealing with people who need help in many varied aspects of life, from inadequate financial resources to doubts of their adequacy to perform their social roles, from protection from racism and injustice to understanding their own self-defeating behavior.

While helping people is a very old practice, professional social work, as a disciplined and skillful method of helping people, is less than a century old. Like the other, older helping professions,

5

social work grew out of fumbling, trial-and-error attempts to help people in trouble. As in medicine, teaching, and law, the knowledge gained by learning what proved effective in actual operation became systematized, codified, subjected to scrutiny, and finally conceptualized, to be transmitted to the novice, so that he could be taught ideas and skills more quickly than having to develop them himself, and so that he could be given the relevant material needed to plan his actions, instead of having to sift the relevant from the irrelevant as he progressed.

THE BEGINNINGS OF PROFESSIONAL SOCIAL WORK

Although helping people has always included comforting the unhappy and confused, a historically more prominent component of it has been the relief of poverty. A claim for group support of an individual results in some highly ambivalent responses from the group. Concerns about whether the person in need is "worthy" of help, whether his need is as acute as he pictures it, and whether extending help will undermine his wish to support himself are in conflict with the admonitions of religion, the humanitarian impulses elicited in many people by distress, and the prudent wish to avoid rebellion or violence.

As long as people lived in small, stable groups, ties of kinship and long acquaintance binding them together, there seemed to be little concern about "welfare abuse" or the demoralizing effects of receiving help from the more fortunate. In past ages, noblesse oblige included the responsibility of caring for dependents. Church laws and practices urged the giving of alms as a virtue by which donors could acquire spiritual merit. But with the breakup of feudalism and the rise of trade, free labor, and the work ethic associated with the Protestant Reformation, increasing concern was felt for the "pauperizing" effects of continued relief to the poor. Repressive legislation, the whipping of "sturdy beggars" (as the able-bodied unemployed were called in fifteenth-century England), the "warning out of town" of prospective paupers, the confining of the poor in noisome workhouses, rigorous means tests, and the indenturing of children—all were used in strenuous attempts to prevent permanent dependency. None succeeded, since all operated on the implicit assumption that poverty was a matter of individual choice, not a consequence of social change and cultural lag.

Historically, professional social work emerged from attempts to deal with poverty and not from concern over human happiness. In an effort to correct "welfare abuse," Charity Organization Societies (COS) were established in America in the last quarter of the nineteenth century. These Societies, as the name implies, were formed to "organize" charitable organizations, to prevent duplication and fraud, and to "uplift" clients and restore them to self-support. It was the effort to understand why people fell into poverty or failed to raise themselves out of poverty that gave rise to social casework. Inevitably, therefore, social work has been connected in the public mind with poverty, even though most of the services of professional social workers today are utilized by clients from every socio-economic level. It is indeed ironic that this association of social work and poverty continued in the public mind, in view of the decision of the early COS to exclude from their organizing efforts the tax-supported poor-relief offices and overseers of the poor. This resulted in excluding workers in the public departments from the educational and in-service training efforts sponsored by the COS. It took nearly a century to bring about a reversal of this policy, during which the emerging profession of social work was held responsible for the activities of nonprofessionals, over whom it was unable to exercise any control, and during which the professional techniques being developed grew progressively more and more remote from the poor.

The efforts of the early COS workers centered around securing help from existing sources for their clients. Their activities are well documented in the annual report for 1906 of the Philadelphia Society for Organizing Charity:

> A poor colored woman, a widow, had two children, aged six and three, who had never walked. Before we could get this woman's difficulties straightened out and the legs of the children straightened too, our district superintendent and our volunteer visitor had sought either the advice or the active help of the following agencies: the district doctor, the woman's former physician, the Orthopaedic Hospital, the Philadelphia Research and Protective Association, the Children's Aid Society, the Sunday *Ledger*, St. Christopher's Hospital, the Hahnemann Hospital, the Women's Hospital, a medical inspector of the Bureau of Health, an employment agency, a public school principal, the Octavia Hill Association, the Department of Charities, and the House of St. Michael and All Angels . . . In this particular record, which is by no means the longest, . . . it appears that our district superintendent and her assistant paid 76 visits, wrote 21 letters, and held 41 interviews in the office.[1]

1. Philadelphia Society O.C., *Twenty-Eighth Annual Report* (1906), p. 16, as quoted in Amos G. Warner, *American Charities* (New York: Thomas Y. Crowell, 1930), pp. 440–441. Copyright © 1930 Thomas Y. Crowell Company.

In their eagerness to work out individual plans for each client, the various COS agencies were elaborating techniques which they wished to pass on to new volunteers and also to the paid workers who began slowly to appear, first in district offices and then as visitors to clients' homes. In-service training programs were inaugurated in several of these societies. The New York COS in 1898 established the first training course in America, a six-weeks long Summer School of Philanthropic Workers, which was attended that year by twenty-seven students.[2] After three years, this became the first school of social work, with an academic year of eight months. It is now the Columbia University School of Social Work. By 1919 there were fifteen schools of social work, with their own Association of Training Schools for Professional Social Work. By 1939 all accredited schools of social work were affiliated with universities and offered educational programs at the master's level. The degree became exclusively identified with social work that was deemed "professional."[3]

THE EMERGENCE OF THE BSW AS A PROFESSIONAL

Since the mid 1960s this professional exclusivity has been increasingly questioned. Social needs always grow faster than the supply of trained workers, but even more critical in this period was a growing disenchantment with the profession. This was largely owing to the lack of tangible success which could be demonstrated to occur as a result of professional intervention, proof required by a society increasingly demanding accountability. A number of these pressures, converging upon the National Association of Social Workers (NASW) and the Council on Social Work Education (CSWE), led to that historic decision in the spring of 1970. For the first time, undergraduate social work education programs were recognized as capable of producing professional social workers, and graduates of programs approved by the Council were eligible to join the Association. Instead of continuing as a profession which could be entered only at the master's level, social work was increasingly recognized as a profession which included tasks requiring a range of expertise and training, from the case aide with no educational requirements to the social work educator

2. Stuart A. Queen, *Social Work in the Light of History* (Philadelphia: J. B. Lippincott Company, 1922), pp. 21–22.

3. See Werner W. Boehm, "Education for Social Work," *Encyclopedia of Social Work, 1971* (New York: NASW, 1971), p. 258.

and policy planner with a doctor's degree. The BSW[4] was officially recognized as the beginning-level professional practitioner.

What were the various pressures which resulted in this fundamental shift in policy? Among many, five seem to be critical.

1. Manpower Needs in the
Public Services

As previously mentioned, the original COS movement in the United States excluded employees of public welfare departments, suggesting that these departments limit themselves to providing institutional care, "indoor relief." But ever since the Federal Emergency Relief Administration was created in 1933 and professionals were first hired by every level of government, public welfare departments have increasingly incorporated standards and nomenclature from professional social work. Their employees, originally "investigators," became "social workers." Many departments assigned professional social workers as supervisors. More recently, an addition of services for welfare recipients was mandated in the 1962 Amendments to the Social Security Act, and many Departments of Public Welfare were renamed Departments of Social Services and charged with rehabilitating recipients of public assistance toward increased self-support. For a brief period, it was hoped that all public services could be provided by MSWs (social workers with a Master of Social Work), and staff members were given educational leaves with stipends to attend graduate schools and return to practice in the public sector as MSWs. Social work education more than doubled its output of MSWs between 1950 and 1967 (from 1,747 to 4,606), but social needs increased so much faster that the shortage of MSWs was greater in 1967 than in 1950. In 1965 this goal of employing only MSWs in Departments of Social Services was officially abandoned,[5] and from then until 1972 efforts were concentrated on filling service delivery positions in the public services with baccalaureate-level workers. Under the policies introduced in 1973, even a college degree is not required for many of these positions.

4. The term "BSW," standing for Bachelor of Social Work, is used to describe any graduate of a CSWE-approved baccalaureate program in social work, whether the actual degree awarded is B.A., B.S., B.S. in S.W., or B.S.W.

5. *Closing the Gap in Social Work Manpower* (Washington, D.C.: U.S. Department of Health, Education, and Welfare [HEW], 1965). This report of the Departmental Task Force on Social Work Education and Manpower advocated a diversified staff and a "two-career line" approach, one for baccalaureate degree holders and the other for MSWs.

Partly because the supply of MSWs was never adequate, but even more because legislatures were never willing to make salary levels and working conditions adequate to attract professionals, public departments relied heavily on recent college graduates as beginning-level workers. In the absence of any professional standards for such graduates, public departments developed civil service examinations and in-service training to produce practitioners with the expertise to provide rehabilitation and services. Under this system, baccalaureate degree holders with majors in any field were hired. Lacking the supportive background in the behavioral sciences and the necessary skills in dealing with clients, almost always overworked and inadequately supervised, many of these beginning-level workers found themselves helpless and discouraged and left the field. Others developed self-protective attitudes of cynicism, punitiveness, or sentimentality. Some became disenchanted with "the system" and encouraged clients to take quasi-legal or illegal advantage of it. Increasingly, critics spoke of the "welfare mess," and it became a lively campaign issue in elections at every level of government.

The general public, unaware of differences between these "social workers" and MSWs,[6] as indeed it is unaware of differences between social action and benevolent advice-giving or missionary activities and social work, condemned the profession for failing to solve the social problems of welfare recipients. Social workers found themselves attacked as "parasites sucking the fiscal blood" and told to go out and "find honest labor somewhere else."[7] Professional social work, which had dissociated itself from public welfare through the COS in 1877, was still being held responsible for the performance of anyone terming himself a social worker or so regarded by a public which had an extremely unclear notion of the nature of social work. Such lack of clarity is not found in public understanding of other professions. The American Medical Association is not held responsible for the performance of unqualified practitioners, nor is the American Bar Association blamed for the legal advice given by nonlawyers. Neither of these professions is blamed for the facts that people continue to get sick and plaintiffs do not always win law suits.

In an effort to bring into the profession all employees and potential employees of human services agencies, the 1970 decision

6. The Relf case in Chapter 8 is a recent illustration of this lack of clarity.

7. John Ehrlichman, "If President Wins Again," *Wall Street Journal*, October 18, 1972, p. 1, as cited and rebutted in *NASW NEWS*, Vol. 18, No. 1 (January 1973), p. 2.

opening membership in the professional organization of social workers (NASW) to those employed in human service capacities and those with BSW degrees, the profession hoped to exercise some measure of control over all those calling themselves social workers and induce them to subscribe to the Code of Ethics of the profession.[8] However, it may well be that this action came too late. In view of the financial and credibility crises facing social work in the mid 1970s, the NASW stated in March 1973:

> Perhaps the time has come for the social work profession to clarify its role by declaring that public assistance as such is income maintenance and not a program of social work. Certainly the profession has an interest in the public assistance program and a responsibility to seek its improvement. But where and how the professional social worker relates to it may need to be redefined. Perhaps it will be as planner and administrator, or as an advocate on behalf of clients who have to deal with the public assistance program.[9]

While some of the rationale behind the acceptance of the BSW as a professional social worker may have been negated by the crisis of the 1970s (especially the governmental cutbacks of funds and positions), there are ample grounds for believing that this change is a permanent one.

2. Analysis of the Social Work Task

A second factor in the development of the BSW social worker was the recognition that not all tasks performed by professional social workers demanded graduate preparation. Paper work, transportation services, court attendance, routine interviewing, verification of information, determination of financial eligibility—all these tasks could often be competently executed by other personnel. As a result, in June 1973 the NASW announced a six-level classification for social service manpower: two levels are preprofessional, the Social Service Aide (no specific educational requirements) and the Social Service Technician (a two-year A.A. degree); the other four levels are professional and include the Social Worker (baccalaureate degree from an approved social work program), Graduate Social Worker (graduation from an approved

8. See "Profession of Social Work: Code of Ethics," *Encyclopedia of Social Work, 1971*, pp. 958–959, hereafter cited as "Code of Ethics."

9. National Association of Social Workers, "Issues in Income Maintenance," *New Directions for the Seventies* (Washington, D.C.: NASW, 1973), p. 26, hereafter cited as *New Directions*. Reprinted with the permission of the National Association of Social Workers.

MSW program), Certified Social Worker (certification by the Academy of Certified Social Workers), and Social Work Fellow (doctorate or substantial specialized practice as a Certified Social Worker.)[10]

Increased attention to cost factors as well as the concept of career ladders and upward mobility within the job indicate this kind of hierarchy as the path of the future. No longer is the social work task seen as something for which the MSW is at once the prerequisite and also the terminal degree. Educational programs which prepare workers for each level are being developed. Up to now, the Council on Social Work Education has not set up criteria for program approval of the two lower levels on this ladder, but it has been developing advisory materials.[11]

However, the Council has been active in the field of undergraduate social work education since its inception in 1952, when departments offering such programs were encouraged to enroll as constituent members. Between 1952 and 1970, consultations, publications, and sessions at Annual Program Meetings were devoted to undergraduate education. In 1970 CSWE approved programs which met its criteria, and in 1974 it began to accredit baccalaureate programs as it has always accredited MSW programs. Emphasis has shifted over those years from a preprofessional program, preparing students for admission to graduate schools of social work, toward a program which prepares undergraduate students for professional practice. The Council is also supporting efforts to secure recognition from civil service systems of the B.S.W. degree as distinct and on a different level from the undifferentiated B.A. graduate who has majored in some related or even totally unrelated academic field.

Valuable pioneering work in delineating the skills and competencies essential for beginning-level practice was carried out by a task force of social work educators and practitioners under the sponsorship of the Southern Regional Education Board (SREB). Its publications, particularly *A Core of Competence for Baccalaureate Social Welfare and Curricular Implications*,[12] outline a variety of

10. "Professional Standards Division Announces Classification Plan," *NASW NEWS*, Vol. 18, No. 6 (June 1973), p. 7.

11. See Donald Feldstein, *Community Colleges and Other Associate Degree Programs for Social Welfare Aides* (New York: CSWE, 1968), and *Community Services Technician, Guidelines for Associate Degree Programs for Social Welfare Areas* (New York: CSWE, 1970).

12. Harold L. McPheeters and Robert M. Ryan, *A Core of Competence for Baccalaureate Social Welfare and Curricular Implications* (Atlanta: SREB, 1971), hereafter cited as *Core of Competence*. See also the other publications of the Southern Regional Education Board. See as well Robert L. Barker and Thomas L. Briggs, *Differential Use of Social Work Manpower* (New York: NASW, 1968).

objectives for intervention in social systems and a set of roles which workers might play in meeting these objectives. Since the concern of the social worker is the person or family in need, his training and orientation should make him a generalist—one who plays whatever roles and utilizes whatever activities seem best to meet the client's needs. The Task Force considered four levels of competence: Level 1, the social work aide, can be expected to carry responsibility for small numbers of cases with rather simple, common problems either in the clients' homes or in institutional settings such as old-age homes, children's institutions, and mental hospitals, and carry information to and secure consultation from workers at higher levels; Level 2, the social work technician, can be expected to carry somewhat more responsibility, deal with somewhat more complicated problems for a somewhat larger number of cases, using more complex skills; Level 3, the BSW, serves as consultant on unusual problems, carries some cases requiring complex skills and knowledge, and carries administrative responsibilities including program development and evaluation; Level 4, the MSW and the DSW (social worker with a Doctor of Social Work), operate at a high level of skill with very difficult multiproblem families and serve as the chief administrators of agencies, responsible for program development, public relations, and legislative activities.[13] It can be predicted that the bulk of the service delivery personnel in the human services will be Level 3 social workers.

3. Social Work's Estrangement from the Poor

A third factor in the emergence of the BSW social worker has been what critics of traditional social work have called the "disengagement" or the "alienation" of the social work establishment from an extremely large segment of its potential clientele. Casework, long the primary method used by the MSW, has been singled out as the greatest offender. The recent criticism of casework concepts, with their emphasis on diagnosis and treatment and their insistence on the crucial importance of the client-worker relationship, is summed up by Scott Briar:

> The casework method, the very method that caseworkers worked so hard and long to perfect, *systematically* excludes many of the persons most in need of attention from case-

13. This classification is summarized from pp. 38–40 of McPheeters and Ryan, *Core of Competence*. Frequent reference will be made in subsequent chapters to this report's excellent summary of the knowledge, skills, and attitudes and values essential for the Level 3 social worker.

workers. For those persons not disposed to see a prolonged and often indefinite series of interviews as a solution to their problems, the casework method has little to offer, and such persons have been referred elsewhere or simply have not returned. And the proportion of such persons is greatest among the poor and disadvantaged, groups to whom the profession has an historic commitment. The second new element is the charge that the casework method is not effective even when properly applied to persons disposed to use it.[14]

Richard Cloward, of the Columbia University School of Social Work, has been one of the severest critics of traditional social work's estrangement from the poor. As early as 1963, he called attention to the extent to which private agencies were dealing with middle-class citizens and ignoring lower-class clients as "unmotivated."[15] This "disengagement from the poor" Cloward attributes to social work's search for the prestige which follows from upgrading the socio-economic character of its clientele. There is a culture conflict between the middle-class value systems of social workers and the poverty-adaptive value systems of clients from the "culture of poverty." This problem is not peculiar to social work. The well-known studies of Hollingshead and Redlich[16] underline the difficulties of communicating personal feelings across class lines. Law, education, and medicine have encountered similar difficulties.

Preoccupation with psychoanalytic techniques, narrowly specialized education and fields of practice, and the constraints of bureaucratic organization have been cited as causes of the unsatisfactory performance of current casework. Caseworkers are seen as aloof, uninvolved, more dedicated to maintaining agency policies than to meeting the needs of clients. In order to be truly effective in improving the lives and living conditions of many

14. Scott Briar, "The Casework Predicament," Social Work, Vol. 13, No. 1 (January 1968), pp. 5–11. Reprinted from p. 6 with the permission of the National Association of Social Workers.

15. Richard A. Cloward has written prolifically on the subject; one of the earliest articles is "Social Class and Private Social Agencies," Education for Social Work, Proceedings of the Eleventh Annual Program Meeting (New York: CSWE, 1963), pp. 123–144. One of the most widely anthologized statements is Richard A. Cloward and Irwin Epstein, "Private Social Welfare's Disengagement from the Poor: The Case of Family Adjustment Agencies," in Mayer N. Zald, ed., Social Welfare Institutions (New York: John Wiley & Sons, 1965), pp. 623–644.

16. August B. Hollingshead and Frederick C. Redlich, Social Class and Mental Illness (New York: Wiley, 1958).

clients, social workers must become "client advocates,"[17] although this may well jeopardize their right to employment when such advocacy is against agency policy.

Efforts to become easier to reach, such as in the establishment of neighborhood welfare centers, will not solve the problem if the sponsoring agency is regarded with distrust by its potential clientele. If graduate education is an obstacle to rapport with clients, then one possible solution is the deployment of less narrowly trained generalists, who can function with greater ease and less social distance from their clients. The use of "indigenous personnel" (those from the same socio-economic level as their clients) as Level 1 workers, the development of two-year and four-year programs for those who cannot afford or do not want graduate education, and the delineation of function which reserves MSWs for areas requiring the highest level of skill—all serve to make social work less remote and estranged.

4. The War on Poverty

When the War on Poverty was declared in 1964, it mandated the "maximum feasible participation of the poor" in programs set up by the Office of Economic Opportunity (OEO). This was a conscious effort to involve those in the culture of poverty, who ordinarily feel powerless and unable to control their own situations, in the power structure. It was expected that, having experienced poverty and discrimination, they would be able to work more effectively against them. In the perspective of the intervening decade, we can now see that this expectation was somewhat naive. Not only was there difficulty in identifying participants from the target population, but the planners did not foresee the problem created by the role conflicts these participants encountered.[18] When members of the target population identified themselves and were identified by their constituents as part of the power establishment, they lost much of their effectiveness. In addition, their unfamiliarity with parliamentary procedure and

17. For one suggestion as to how this might be done, see Irving Piliavin, "Restructuring the Social Services," *Social Work*, Vol. 13, No. 1 (January 1968), pp. 34–41.

18. This point has been discussed and documented by Louis Zurcher in his description of the anti-poverty program in Topeka, Ks., *Poverty Warriors: The Human Experience of Planned Social Intervention* (Austin: University of Texas Press, 1970). Note his extensive bibliography. See also Peter Kunkel and Sara Sue Kennard, *Spout Spring* (New York: Holt, Rinehart and Winston, 1971), an account of role conflict in a southern black community.

bureaucratic machinery caused them to be outmaneuvered by others, even when they overcame their uneasiness and advocated specific actions.

Methods of dealing with these obstacles can be evolved, and successful Community Action Programs (CAPs) have developed ways to organize the poor in their own behalf. Professional social workers, accustomed to dealing directly with clients, need to learn these organizational and supportive skills to enable clients to help themselves and each other. Such self-help programs have been demonstrably successful in areas where more orthodox treatment methods have been singularly unproductive. Repeated experience with such self-help groups as Alcoholics Anonymous and Gamblers Anonymous and with groups of ex-convicts, ex-drug addicts, and ex-mental hospital patients indicates that there are assets in programs incorporating those who have experienced self-defeating behavior and have been able to change it.

The traditional professional role of social worker has been to treat the client as a troubled or malfunctioning individual, which tacitly assumes the "fault" lies within himself. It is apparent that many of the problems which poor clients bring to social agencies have their roots in social conditions (racism, continued unemployment, inadequate housing, chronic ill health, inferior schools) which demand collective action and social change rather than clinical treatment. Client advocacy, outreach, mobilization of resources, and planning, as part of the generalist role, should replace narrow concentration on a clinical model of treatment. The clinician needs the additional specialized training of the master's level program, but the BSW, particularly with ready consultation available, can function effectively as client mobilizer and change agent. Programs preparing BSWs must provide the knowledge, background, and opportunity for acquiring skills in these areas of service.

5. The Role of Social Work Educators

A fifth and final factor in our analysis is the experience and convictions of social work educators at both the graduate and undergraduate levels, but particularly at the latter, concerning the feasibility of the BSW position. Many years of experience in teaching undergraduate students have made it apparent that much of what had been reserved for the graduate curriculum was applicable to undergraduate education. Students coming better prepared from high schools, often with substantial experience in community programs and greater sophistication in social action, were unwilling to postpone until a hypothetical graduate career the opportunity for personal involvement in social work experience. It was increasingly impossible to confine undergraduate courses to teaching "about social work" rather than "teaching social work"[19] or to maintain semantic distinctions between "field observation" and "field experience."

Undergraduate social work educators, who had been attending CSWE Annual Program Meetings almost as guests rather than as genuine participants, found themselves at the 1966 meeting in New York City being accorded a new respectability. Consultation to undergraduate programs was expanded, federal training grants included baccalaureate-level programs, and the stage of program approval by CSWE was reached in 1970 with accreditation mandated in 1974.

Such a move was heartily endorsed by those students who had been frustrated by the repetition of material in their first year of graduate school. Just as the undergraduate colleges were slow to adjust to the improved high school curricula of their entering freshmen, resulting in much duplication and wasted time in the freshman year, so MSW programs have been slow to take account of the increasingly better prepared students that come to them. Need for continuity and linkages between BSW and MSW programs is now stressed in every curriculum study. Many graduate schools are admitting BSWs to the second year or offering them special twelve-month programs. Nor is the lack of continuity limited to the BSW-MSW linkage, according to the SREB Task Force:

> A major area of inconsistency in the field is the continuum between the baccalaureate programs and the master's degree programs. Most master's level professionals are aware of the marked increase in quantity and quality of BSW programs, yet MSW programs continue to produce graduates to be primary service delivery agents. These programs have ignored student experiences and have resisted curriculum adjustments to allow for the individual differences between students coming from undergraduate social welfare programs and those coming from more general undergraduate curricula. The BSW programs are, unfortunately, becoming guilty of the same rigidity as graduates of associate of arts programs in social welfare are moving into four year programs.

19. The first edition of this book (1963), for example, stated in the Preface: "It is a book *about* social work rather than a manual of instruction in social work techniques. The teaching of techniques properly belongs in the curriculum of the professional schools."

At present the graduate schools are preparing a fairly good clinician, but the number of graduates employed in direct clinical work within two years of graduation is so small that their educational experience becomes virtually irrelevant. Furthermore, the junior colleges and baccalaureate degree programs are preparing practitioners to do the traditional clinical work. To become a relevant profession, social work will have to deal with these issues.

In many respects, these same issues are relevant to other human service professions. Psychology continues to see the Ph.D. as the only legitimate professional, while more and more MA's are being employed to provide psychological services. Like social work, psychology is losing many of its traditional functions to other workers in the public sector. The nurse and physician's assistants are making much the same kind of inroads into medicine. In short, as the professions have become more concerned with enhancing their own status than with meeting needs of people, the public has found alternatives which are serving to force these professions back into relevancy.[20]

THE ATTRIBUTES OF A PROFESSION

By now it should be clear that pressures from the public, from official governmental agencies, and from the social work profession have moved the definition of "professional social worker" away from attribution solely to the MSW and have broadened it to include at least three levels of responsibility and preparation. What then do we mean by "professional"?

We have referred to the BSW as the beginning-level professional practitioner, with the implication that there is something distinctive about the value orientation of practitioners in the profession and their sanctions from the community which differentiate them from lower levels of training or from those without professional social work training. Definitions of "profession" abound. The *Encyclopedia of Social Work, 1971* contains articles on "Professions, Human Services" and "Profession of Social Work" which utilize concepts from sociology, law, and philosophy. Many years ago, the great social work philosopher Eduard C. Lindeman, in answering affirmatively the question of whether or not social work constituted a profession, stated his criteria in these words:

> Social work may be said to be traveling towards maturity as a profession when it is capable of assimilating knowledge and skill from many sources without loss of identity; it is able to adapt itself to a variety of managerial auspices and controls

20. McPheeters and Ryan, *Core of Competence*, pp. 139–140.

without loss of integrity; it is capable of merging its methods with those of other professions dealing with related situations; it is capable of and prepared to translate its technical conceptions into language comprehensible to the layman; it has achieved consistency between its goals and its methods and is willing to subject itself to self-imposed standards of conduct; it recognizes its sphere of social responsibility; it is able to adapt itself to the dynamics of the society in which it operates; it evolves methods for merging its empirical and theoretical knowledge; and it is able to recruit its candidates from the higher levels of intelligence.[21]

Subsequent statements of the Hollis-Taylor Report in 1951,[22] of Greenwood in 1957,[23] and of Hall in 1968[24] have not substantially improved upon Lindeman's criteria. Kermit Wiltse utilizes the sociological concept of role in defining social work as a profession. To him, the professional role includes the notion of professional responsibility, and the essence of the professional relationship is:

Responsibility is accepted both for the *giving* of information, service, or treatment and for the patient's or client's *use* of it . . . Verifying financial destitution and passing out relief checks . . . is not professional social work activity. Accepting responsibility for understanding the effect of the aid upon the client and the implications of his need for aid and for helping him to make effective use of the assistance marks the activity as a professional one.[25]

Wilbert E. Moore in 1970 suggested that we should view occupations as distributed along a continuum, with professionalism regarded as a scale and with professions differing from nonprofessional occupations quantitatively rather than qualitatively.[26]

21. Eduard C. Lindeman, "Social Case Work Matures in a Confused World," paper given at the annual meeting of the New York State Conference on Social Work, 1946 (Albany, 1947), p. 51.

22. Ernest V. Hollis and Alice L. Taylor, *Social Work Education in the United States* (New York: Columbia University Press, 1951).

23. Ernest Greenwood, "Attributes of a Profession," *Social Work*, Vol. 2, No. 3 (July 1957), pp. 45–55.

24. Richard N. Hall, "Professionalization and Bureaucratization," *American Sociological Review*, Vol. 33, No. 1 (February 1968), pp. 92–104. Hall lists five essential characteristics of a profession: 1) use of the professional organization as a major reference; 2) a belief in service to the public; 3) self-regulation; 4) a sense of calling to the field; 5) professional autonomy.

25. Kermit Wiltse, "Social Casework and Public Assistance," *Social Service Review*, Vol. 36, No. 1 (Chicago: The University of Chicago Press, March 1958), pp. 43, 44. Copyright © 1950 by The University of Chicago.

26. Wilbert E. Moore, *The Professions: Roles and Rules* (New York: Russell Sage Foundation, 1970).

Membership in the NASW

Membership in the National Association of Social Workers designates one as a social work professional, conforming to the professional Code of Ethics. The Code of Ethics, adopted by the NASW in 1960 and amended in 1967, carries the following preliminary note.

> Social work is based on humanitarian and democratic ideals. Professional social workers are dedicated to service for the welfare of mankind, to the disciplined use of a recognized body of knowledge about human beings and their interactions, and to the marshaling of community resources to promote the well-being of all without descrimination.
>
> Social work practice is a public trust that requires of its practitioners integrity, compassion, belief in the dignity and worth of human beings, respect for individual differences, a commitment to service, and a dedication to truth. It requires mastery of a body of knowledge and skill gained through professional education ane experience. It requires also recognition of the limitations of present knowledge and skill and of the services we are now equipped to give. The end sought is the performance of a service with integrity and competence.
>
> Each member of the profession carries responsibility to maintain and improve social work service; constantly to examine, use and increase the knowledge upon which practice and social policy are based; and to develop further the philosophy and skills of the profession.
>
> This Code of Ethics embodies certain standards of behavior for the social worker in his professional relationships with those he serves, with his colleagues, with his employing agency, with other professions, and with the community. In abiding by it, the social worker views his obligations in as wide a context as the situation requires, takes all the principles into consideration, and chooses a course of action consistent with the code's spirit and intent.[27]

One of the problems in discussing the professional status of social work is that so many of those employed in what the Bureau of Labor Statistics terms "social welfare positions" do not meet NASW membership criteria and are not therefore in a position to subscribe to the professional Code of Ethics. For at least two decades, the proportion of professional social workers in "social

27. "Code of Ethics," p. 958. Reprinted with the permission of the National Association of Social Workers.

welfare positions" has been about 20 percent, which means that the bulk of social welfare activity is carried out by those who do not meet professional educational levels.

The Core of Competence Approach

A radically different approach to the definition of a professional by educational preparation was utilized by the SREB Task Force in establishing its "Core of Competence" for BSWs as professional workers. In analyzing the tasks being performed by the existing professionals and factoring out those tasks which could be assigned to other levels of preparation and skill, the Task Force chose a "developmental" approach which reexamined the basic human needs which first brought the profession into existence. This approach recognizes:

> . . . that the professions, in the process of becoming professions, have probably ignored some of the basic needs, and also that the basic needs of society change over time. For example, the need of society for social welfare services some years ago was believed to be only for case work services for the poor and disabled; now society feels the need for more social prevention and the development of social competence in addition to case services for the disabled. After identifying society's needs, the developmental approach determines what must be done to meet the needs and what constraints there are on the way jobs are put together by grouping the various tasks. It then develops a rationale for assigning the work to various levels of workers. This is a more difficult procedure than job factoring; the new jobs are not so likely to fit the existing agencies and professions, and they are likely to require more independence of action and judgment. But they are likely to be more sensitive to the needs of society than to the needs of the professions.[28]

Out of this developmental approach to human needs came four major goals of intervention designed to help individuals, families, and communities move to higher levels of social functioning: 1) the promotion of positive social functioning; 2) the prevention of stresses and problems; 3) assistance to individuals, families, and communities in the resolving of their problems; and 4) supportive and maintenance services to those who are unable to solve their problems.[29] These goals, in turn, led to the delineation of twelve major objectives to which social welfare activities should

28. McPheeters and Ryan, *Core of Competence*, p. 11.
29. *Ibid.*, p. 16.

be directed and to the corresponding roles which workers might play in meeting these objectives. These objectives and roles are:

1) Detection. The identification of individuals or groups at crisis or at risk, and the environmental conditions responsible. Role—Outreach Worker.

2) Linkage of the service system to those who can benefit and to link elements of the system to each other. Role—Broker.

3) Advocacy or fighting for services to individuals or for changes in laws or regulations which prevent people from exercising their rights or receiving the benefits they need. Role—Advocate.

4) Evaluation of alternatives and priorities for action after securing adequate information and analyzing it. Role—Evaluator.

5) Mobilization of existing resources or the creation of new resources to bear on existing problems, or to prevent potential problems from developing. Role—Mobilizer.

6) Instruction. The conveying of information and techniques for improved social functioning. Role—Teacher.

7) Behavior Change. The modification of behavior patterns or attitudes which are hampering individual or group effectiveness. Role—Behavior Changer.

8) Consultation with other workers or agencies around improving services to their clients. Role—Consultant.

9) Community planning by participation in neighborhood, community, or larger groups, private and public, toward better meeting of the human service needs of the community. Role—Community Planner.

10) Information Processing by collecting and analyzing data generated in the area of human services. Role—Data Manager.

11) Administration or the effective management of a program or agency. Role—Administrator.

12) Continuing Care for those who need ongoing support or care on an extended basis. Role—Care Giver.[30]

The SREB Task Force feels that workers at every level of skill will find themselves playing any of these roles, although some will be more likely to be associated with certain levels of skills than others. The roles of Administrator and Community Planner may be more likely associated with Level 4 and Care Giver with Level 1 (see page 13), but all human services workers, as gen-

---

30. *Ibid.*, pp. 18–20. This description of objectives and goals is summarized from these pages. Chapter II is recommended in its entirety.

eralists, should be prepared to carry out whatever role is indicated by client needs and agency goals.[31]

Manpower Deployment

An essential element of professionalism is taking responsibility
for one's actions and the potential effect those actions may have
on clients and others. As long ago as 1962, the NASW outlined
two criteria by which a decision could be made as to whether a
task should be assigned to a professional or a nonprofessional,
although at that date the nonprofessional included what we would
recognize today as the beginning-level professional—the BSW.
These criteria are: 1) client vulnerability (How liable is the client
to harm from the educational limits of the worker serving him?);
and 2) worker autonomy (To what extent is the worker called upon
to exercise independent judgment in the absence of specified
directives?).[32]

Teare and McPheeters of the SREB Task Force deplore the classification of jobs by educational degrees, preferring that demonstrated competence rather than academic standing determine the
level at which any individual can work effectively. They believe
that assignment of workers to jobs should be based on three
factors:

> 1) Complexity of the problem—We have generally assumed
> that working with a single person is generally simpler than
> dealing with groups, that working with neighborhoods is less
> complex than working with cities or states, that working with
> single problem families is less complex than working with
> multi-problem families. The more complex problems are more
> appropriate to the higher levels.
> 2) Risks of doing a bad job—Some situations involve consid-
> erable risk (suicide, serious disability, etc.) if done poorly.
> Others involve only minor inconvenience or nuisance if done
> poorly. Higher risk problems call for higher levels of workers.
> 3) Parameters within which work must be carried out (dif-
> ficulty)—Tasks which have very narrow parameters, within
> which the work to be carried out requires high levels of knowl-
> edge or skill are assigned to higher levels of workers.[33]

31. See Robert J. Teare, Ph.D. and Harold M. McPheeters, M.D., *Manpower
Utilization in Social Welfare Services* (Atlanta: SREB, 1970), hereafter cited as *Manpower Utilization*, especially Chapter 3.

32. *Utilization of Personnel in Social Work: Those with Full Professional Education
and Those Without* (New York: NASW, 1962), pp. 10–17.

33. Teare and McPheeters, *Manpower Utilization*, p. 39.

This model obviously poses problems for agency administrators in assigning cases, since it demands not only an extremely careful diagnosis of the client and his situation but also an accurate evaluation of the skills and competencies of all staff members. It demands, in addition, the provision of adequate back-up staff for consultation and transfer if the assigned worker should encounter difficulties. However, too often in the past, case assignments have been made for agency convenience rather than for client service, and this model would help change that situation. Also, use of this model would enable those at the lower levels, now prevented by the imposition of an educational ceiling from moving to a different level of responsibility, to be assigned to tasks of increasing complexity as they become more competent.

This situation, however desirable, is not likely to be universally found in social welfare agencies in the foreseeable future. Whatever unreality exists in educational requirements, they are likely to continue because of their relative convenience. By requiring A.A. or B.S.W. degrees for employment, human services agencies benefit from the preliminary screening done by educational institutions, which counsel out of their programs those manifestly unsuitable or inadequately motivated. There is a further potential advantage of educational requirements, especially as curricula become more and more relevant to the types of practice situations in which graduates will find themselves in the 1970s and 1980s: while it is impossible to teach skills except in a practice situation, educational institutions are in a strategic position to give the background knowledge demanded of professionals and to examine and compel students to scrutinize their own attitudes and those of the society in which they plan to practice. To be truly professional, competence must be based on knowledge, skills, and attitudes. Of these three, attitudes, including values, constitute the element most likely to differentiate professionalism from non-professionalism.

THE VALUE SYSTEM OF SOCIAL WORK

Values are socially acquired and widely held assumptions about what is desirable and worth striving for. The social work practitioner, to be truly professional, must recognize societal and subcultural values and the extent to which his or her own internalized value system reflects or differs from those that are institutionalized in the human services. The goal of social work education is not to produce a skilled manipulator of people with a superior theoretical knowledge of human behavior and social institutions, if the manipulator will operate for self-aggrandizement, socially disapproved purposes, or the client's ultimate destruction. Only if skills and knowledge are harnessed to further positive, produc- ' tive, integrative purposes, and if the worker has the self-aware-ness to recognize his own involvement in his activities and the willingness to accept responsibility for the consequences of his actions can his activity be fully professional. Instead of the dichot-omy between the "trained" and "untrained" worker, between the professional and the nonprofessional, which has been the traditional attitude toward personnel in social work, the applica-tion of the objective-role model, with assignments made accord-ing to levels of competence, seems more compatible with the no-tion of professionalism as an attitude distributed on a continuum and with the goal that workers at every level of skill develop and maintain a fully professional attitude toward their work.

THE BASIC WORTH OF THE INDIVIDUAL

The central premise on which all social work intervention is based is that each individual is worth helping. This notion is strongly supported by our Judeo-Christian ethic as well as by the political philosophy of democracy. The extent to which this pre-mise pervades all social work thought can be demonstrated by visualizing the form of human services in a caste society or in a totalitarian one. The belief that the individual is worthy of the social worker's concern and best efforts stands in marked contrast to working assumptions in other fields, where differential treat-ment is given individuals according to their intelligence, their moral "goodness," or their socio-economic status. The responsi-bility which this principle places on the social worker is that he must consider every individual, however ignorant or dirty or de-viant, worthy of respect. Many of us have no trouble accepting the young widow struggling to bring up her fatherless children but find it difficult to accord the same respect to the drug addict, the abusive parent, the sex pervert. And yet, if the social worker does not feel that each of these is worth salvaging, he adds his sense of failure and defeat to that which each of these unhappy clients is already bearing. For some people, the first hopeful sign in their lives in many years is the knowledge that a social worker feels that they are valuable enough to help.

THE RIGHT OF SELF-DETERMINATION

Inherent in the conviction of the worth of any individual is respect for his opinions and decisions. Within the limits of ac-cepted social standards and serious harm to others or the self (which apply to all citizens in a society), the client has the right to make his or her own decisions. This position is in sharp contrast to a layman's view of social workers as people who remold the lives of clients into some approved pattern of the social workers' devising. In actuality, social work philosophy is based on the conviction that people can be helped to make wiser decisions, to become more self-sufficient and more adequate. When people have difficulty in learning to live within the law and the mores, social work tries to help them with whatever is interfering with their meeting their obligations to society. If this seems at the moment impossible and actual or potential harm seems likely, the resources of courts and other authorities may have to be invoked, as in the case of children whose physical or emotional health is put in jeopardy by parents' actions.

A problem arises when it is the social worker's or the profession's conviction that the laws to which a client is being asked to conform are obsolete or unjust. Racism, inadequate public assistance allowances, and inadequate facilities demand that social workers become change agents, working through their professional organizations toward improved social policy and supporting their clients in social action. Although many public assistance clients consider social workers their adversaries, it was social workers who sponsored the Welfare Rights Organization. If, as Turner said in 1968,[34] social work is at a crossroad, it must choose between becoming a highly professionalized and delimited area, far removed from the political sphere, and supporting whatever social action is necessary to produce a human services system which truly meets the needs of its clients. This latter course would involve new roles (broker, advocate, mobilizer) and new political expertise and techniques of action, some of which (strikes, protest marches, boycotts, and full cooperation with indigenous personnel) may run counter to social workers' typically middle-class value orientations. Social work has given lip service to the principle that the client has the right of self-determination, but the harsh realities of discrimination, chronic unemployment, and disability make this right meaningless for many of the clients of the largest social agencies.

In addition to the limitations on self-determination placed by inequities and rapid social change, there are the more subtle constraints which the value orientation of the social worker may place on the client's actions. Awareness of the social worker's own fixed notions about what constitutes "right" behavior is essential; un-

34. John B. Turner, "In Response to Change: Social Work at the Crossroad," *Social Work*, Vol. 13, No. 3 (July 1968), pp. 7–15.

less the worker has learned to be aware of them, he may not recognize the indirect as well as the direct ways he may be imposing his own standards on clients and thereby infringing on their rights to make decisions for themselves.

For example, we all have strong feelings about what constitutes a "good" mother, feelings that stem from our own childhood experiences. It is difficult to feel comfortable with a mother who deviates too much from these concepts, but disapproval, often expressed unconsciously, will be felt as rejection and lack of sympathy by a mother who has already met with rejection from her children and who probably has no sympathy for herself. To tell (verbally or nonverbally) a mother, who is not quite sure herself whether she loves her children enough and whether she is a good mother, that she should love her children more hardly solves the problem she has brought to the social worker. Another area in which care must be taken that the social worker's own standards are not imposed on the client is housekeeping. There was a time when cleanliness and order were considered by some rigid homefinders as more important in a potential foster home than warmth and flexibility. In some communities, threats to cut off relief or remove children are used by public welfare workers who have not really accepted the basic principle of the clients' right to self-determination.

This is not to imply that social work condones law-breaking, cruelty to children, or slovenly housekeeping. When it is apparent that community standards in any regard are being flagrantly violated, the decision-making may have to be done for the client. The aim of social work, ultimately, is that the client develop his own capacity to meet standards and not have them imposed on him without his understanding or acceptance. Cleaning up the house because the social worker is coming is a less satisfactory long-range solution to the problem of dirt and disorder than acquiring a preference for cleanliness.

THE NECESSITY FOR CLIENT PARTICIPATION

This respect for the client's ability to make his own decisions is related to the concept that social work is a cooperative endeavor between client and worker, not something imposed on the client by the worker. Another basic assumption on which social work is based, this concept is summed up in the phrase, "Social work is done *with* and *for* the client, not *to* the client." It assumes that the client is capable of taking some part in the social work process. He may not be able, because of age, illness, mental deficiency, or confusion, to play a large part at the beginning, but he should be involved in the discussion of what is happening. Just because children are young, it should not be supposed that they can be transferred from one foster home to another without warning or explanation. Just because people are ill, it should not be supposed that plans for their medical care need not be discussed with them and that they need not be given an opportunity to choose among alternatives. Plans imposed on people without their active involvement have a way of not turning out well. For this reason, if for no other, it behooves social workers to be sure that their clients have an active investment in whatever treatment is going on.

Often the key difficulty in a problem presented to a social worker is that the client cannot become involved in any plan because of ambivalent and conflicting feelings. Consider Mrs. Adams, who comes to a social agency to ask for help in separating from her husband. If the social worker assumes that this is what Mrs. Adams really wants and provides a flood of advice about Legal Aid, court orders, financial assistance, and custody of the children, he is likely to find that Mrs. Adams has not been listening. If, instead, the social worker listens to Mrs. Adams explain how she has come to the decision to leave her husband, he is likely to learn that Mrs. Adams is not at all sure that a separation is what she really wants. What she is really asking the social worker to do is, "Help me to make up my mind." By using the social worker as a detached yet interested listener, Mrs. Adams can sort out the pros and cons of leaving her husband and possibly be helped to reach a clearer assessment of the situation. Whatever action she then takes will be her decision, not one made for her. Incidentally, one hopes that Mr. Adams also becomes involved, at some point, in the decision-making process. What the social worker can do is help both Mr. and Mrs. Adams to see what is involved in their remaining together and what would probably be involved in separation. The ultimate decision must be theirs. And, it is hoped, the social worker expects that eventually Mr. and Mrs. Adams will come to some decision. When social workers make all the decisions for people, they become dependent on the workers and postpone the time when they can move effectively for themselves.

CONFIDENTIALITY

For many years, the confidentiality of information conveyed to social workers by clients has been a basic principle of social work and has been one of the advantages of talking to a professional listener rather than blurting out confidences to friends. Unhappily, this assurance of trust can no longer be extended so readily to clients as was the norm a decade ago. New federal regulations in early 1973 made it possible for determination of eligibility for public services to include verification of information without the client's permission, including unannounced home visits. Also, the necessity for extremely strict cost accounting is an impetus toward computerization, which gives no guarantee that access to computerized material can be restricted to professional staff. The general public is well aware of the potential hazards of data banks, particularly when individuals are not permitted to know what data about themselves are contained in them. There is less public concern about the computerization and storage of information about recipients of social services—just one more indication of the second-class citizenship so often assigned to the economically and culturally deprived.

Attempts have been made to secure for social work information the status of "privileged communication" which protects lawyers, priests, and doctors from being compelled to repeat information told them in confidence. Yet confidential records have been subpoenaed in courts and social workers interrogated. The need for clarification and protection of clients' rights has assumed new urgency with the increasing availability of electronic surveillance methods.[35] Until these issues have been more clearly resolved by legal protection, many social workers are excluding from their written records material which could be damaging to clients, although strict quality control measures by auditors will put extreme pressure on such workers in the public services.

Wherever it can be assured, however, social workers do protect their clients' privacy. Whenever cases are discussed outside the agency—at interagency case conferences, for example, or in teaching seminars—identifying information is carefully altered. Similarly, whenever case illustrations are used in published articles in social work journals, the locale, names, jobs, and similar identifying data are carefully changed. A good example of this type of precaution is the "Hundred Neediest Cases" published each December by the *New York Times* as a Christmas appeal. While the need is attested to by the participating agencies, the precise cir-

35. See "Confidential and Privileged Communications: Guidelines for Lawyers and Social Workers," *Family Law Quarterly*, Vol. 3, No. 1 (March 1969), pp. 53–56, for a statement issued by the National Conference of Lawyers and Social Workers. See also John H. Noble, Jr., "Protecting the Public's Privacy in Computerized Health and Welfare Information Systems," *Social Work*, Vol. 16, No. 1 (January 1971), pp. 35–41.

cumstances are modified, and initials are used instead of names. This is a principle which should be stressed with nonprofessionals and students, as well as with clerical staff. Because the worker in the public services cannot totally protect clients' privacy, he should assume the responsibility of warning clients that statements have to be checked and that inquiries about their circumstances may well be made without their permission.

THE ART OF LISTENING

Social workers operate on the belief that people can be helped to function more effectively and with a higher degree of satisfaction to themselves. Social workers assume that, as helping persons, they have the obligation to be as skillful, sensitive, and compassionate as they can train and discipline themselves to become. In order to learn what people want for themselves, social workers must develop the art of listening. This is a professional technique quite different from and much more difficult than what is generally recognized about it. There are few misconceptions about social work that are so hard to correct as the one that social work is synonymous with well-meaning advice from any interested friend and that being a sympathetic listener automatically qualifies one for doing social work. The art of selective, nonjudgmental, interested but not personally involved listening looks easy to the novice who is quite sure that he knows what to do and can be ready with a set of the appropriate exhortations for any situation. Until he has had some experience, either as client or as worker, the beginner will have difficulty in appreciating the skills involved in "just listening."

A unique attribute of the professional "listening" of a social caseworker is his freedom from preconceived goals for the client. Parents, deans, teachers, doctors may listen attentively, but they are likely to know in advance what kind of behavior they wish to encourage—changed attitudes, better academic work, more attention to medical directives, for example. They are less likely than the social worker to want to learn what the child or student or patient wants for himself and more likely to tell him what he ought to do. Usually they are less able to seem accepting of the person as he is, conveying more or less directly their wish that he change and the implication that their acceptance of him is somewhat conditional on that change. A cardinal principle of social work, fundamentally negated by the premature proffering of advice, is acceptance of the individual as he is before he changes, with the offer of assistance to help him change if he wishes and when his goals are more clearly understood.

College students have experienced firsthand the futility of mere advice-giving. They have been exposed to quantities of good advice from parents, advisers, deans, and roommates. They know that recipients of advice "hear" it selectively and in any case are likely to use only that advice which agrees with their own opinions. "Just listening" is infinitely more difficult than advice-giving.

Most of us recognize that it is easier to talk to some people than to others; less apparent is the fact that there are skills in listening and that these skills can be developed and enlarged with instruction and supervision. The recorded interviews released by Redlich[36] illustrate clearly that interviewing is an art. On one record, a client fumbles for the words to describe his situation, only to be interrupted by an inexperienced interviewer, who is anxious to fill in all the blanks on a schedule. On the other records, the client's attempts at explanation are facilitated by the interviewer's perceptive questions, comments, or expectant silences.

If social workers are to respect the right of individuals to make their own decisions and participate in making their own plans, then each worker must learn how his clients view their situations and what their plans are. This demands the time and patience to wait for some inarticulate clients to think out and express inchoate thoughts and feelings. Effective interviewing is based on skill in listening. What Reik calls "listening with the third ear"[37]—the grasping of oblique references, of significant pauses, of slips of the tongue, of what the client does not say as well as what he is willing to talk about—can be learned only with experience and effort, although it does seem to come more easily to some people than to others.

Most people have experienced the clarification and release that result from unburdening themselves. What they may not have realized is that through their efforts to describe the situation clearly, they are sorting out in their own minds the various factors which are involved in the problem and in the decision to seek help with it. Mrs. Perlman puts it very well:

> In order for a person to become "self-possessed," that is, in order to be able to know, understand, consciously take hold, and manage what one experiences, there must be words.

36. See Merton Gill, M.D., Richard Newman, M.D., and Frederick C. Redlich, M.D., *The Initial Interview in Psychiatric Practice* (New York: International Universities Press, 1954), with phonograph records.

37. Theodor Reik, *Listening with the Third Ear* (New York: Grove Press, 1948). Reik acknowledges that he borrowed the phrase from Nietzsche.

Words identify parts of experience; they name differences. But, more than this, the groping to give something a word-name represents the forging of a link between sensing and thinking. To be able to put something felt or experienced into words means that some inner communication system exists between the heart and the mind. Until a human being's experience is transferable to his mind, it is unavailable to his conscious management. In the last analysis, this is why talking, using words to give names to amorphous masses of feeling, is the major tool of psychotherapeutic methods. Social relationships depend heavily on one's ability consciously to appraise and manage one's self in relation to others. This, in turn, depends upon the ability to communicate accurately what one senses, feels, thinks, and does. And this is why social intelligence may in part be gauged by the client's ability to convey meanings in words and why, too, the case-worker attempts to reinforce this capacity in clients by encouraging the verbal expression of feeling and thought.[38]

There are undoubtedly innumerable cases of clients who were not listened to and not involved in plans which agencies made for them. The Baer case is a classic illustration of poor listening, in which an agency, many years later, learned to its chagrin just how poorly its caseworkers actually listened.

The Baers first became known to social agencies when a community nurse made a routine postpartum call on Mrs. Baer and her new baby. The baby was a fine healthy boy, but the mother was a frail, timid, little woman who was reluctantly made to tell that her black eye was caused by a beating from her husband the night before. She explained that he seldom drank and was abusive only when he did. In addition to the baby, there were three other children in the Baer family, a girl of six and boys of eight and ten.

Against Mrs. Baer's protests, the nurse reported the incident to Miss Bridges, a worker in an agency for the protection of mothers and children. The husband, trained in Germany as a maker of precision instruments, told his wife that if she continued to take the advice of the agency, it could take over the family. Miss Bridges withdrew, and for a year nothing more was heard from the Baer family. Then one morning a frightened voice on the telephone asked Miss Bridges to come to the Baer home as soon as possible. When she found Mrs. Baer in the same deplorable state as before, Miss Bridges assuaged

---

38. Helen Harris Perlman, *Social Casework: A Problem-Solving Process* (Chicago: The University of Chicago Press, 1957), p. 194. Copyright © 1957 by The University of Chicago Press.

her own indignation by persuading Mrs. Baer to swear out an assault and battery charge against her husband. Before it could be served, the irate Mr. Baer telephoned the agency that he was leaving his family to their supervision, which he did, literally, by leaving town. The agency perforce took over. Mrs. Baer is still recalled by the various agency workers who became responsible for the family as one of their most cooperative clients.

During the following years, the father wrote his wife and children an occasional taunting letter from Mexico. From this safe distance he reminded them he could not be brought back by extradition. However, he conceded that he would be willing to have his family come to him in Mexico.

In the meantime, supported from both public and private funds, the children were the pride of their sponsors. Herman, the oldest boy, who finished grade school at the head of his class when he was thirteen years old, wanted to go on to high school and then to college. The welfare workers, in solemn conference, deliberated on the factors in the problem. The boy's tested finger dexterity slanted their decision that he should go to a trade school, which he did. When Fritz, the second boy, not too apt in school, finished the eighth grade at the age of fourteen, the welfare workers decided that since he had average ability and no special talents, he should go through high school. When the daughter, Louise, eventually reached high school level, she was advised to enter a vocational school, as her only talent was a flair for clothes.

All during this period, the one flaw in the smooth functioning between the family and its professional helpers was that all efforts to move the family to better quarters provided by the agency had proved fruitless. The Baers gave no reason for remaining in a ramshackle building on a rear lot in a good residential neighborhood, but there they stayed.

By the time Louise entered Vocational High, the financial contribution of the brothers with the proceeds from the mother's home baking sales was sufficient income to make the family independent of any social agency.

Sometime later, in New York City, a national agency was making a spot study of successful casework around the country. The worker in charge wrote to a former colleague who had also known the Baer family, asking that a professional visit be made to the Baers in order to evaluate the help given by the agencies.

Mrs. Baer recognized the interviewer as a former caseworker and graciously invited her in. The Baer home, now across the street from their former abode, was modern and attractive. With quiet pride, Mrs. Baer explained that the children had taken a great deal of satisfaction in buying the house. She revealed for the first time that they had remained in the former hovel because it was the only cheap housing in the district and because the children did not wish to leave their associates in church and school.

Mrs. Baer brought the family history up to date for the worker. She told how Herman had gone to the trade school; she had been afraid to tell the agency that he also had attended high school at night and from 4 to 7 P.M. had scrubbed floors in an office building, and then had finished college through extension courses while working at various odd jobs. With calm pride, Mrs. Baer explained that he was now working in a prominent law firm and had excellent prospects. His engagement to a girl in the neighborhood had just been announced.

"Fritz, the next boy? Oh, he's working now for the B. Instrument Company, making precision tools." He had run away from home after his second year in high school, where his grades were mediocre, and had found a job in a neighboring city. Being unmarried, he was now able to send home $250 per month of his $450 salary—one portion for his mother and the rest for his savings account.

Mrs. Baer's pride in Louise was also apparent. Louise, she explained, had always been crazy about clothes. She had left the vocational school as soon as the family was no longer answerable to the agency and had secured her own job as a stock girl in a well-known women's ready-to-wear shop, where she is now a buyer. Although also happily married, she is definitely a "career girl."

Mr. Baer had kept in touch with his family. He now occasionally sends gifts and writes that he is lonely. Fritz has visited him. Mrs. Baer explained for the first time that their basic quarrel had been over religion. She was a Lutheran; he was an agnostic. Whenever she refused to take birth control measures, they would quarrel and he would generally climax the quarrel with a drunken spree.

Her explanation of this success story, which had run at variance to the advice of the counselors, was quite simple. She said that everyone in the family had always known what they wanted but couldn't seem to make the people in the agencies understand.[39]

THE PURPOSEFULNESS OF HUMAN BEHAVIOR

A vital assumption which social work shares with other helping professions is that human behavior is never purposeless. When it seems without purpose, social workers can assume only that the

39. Adapted from *The Baer Case*, two mimeographed pages, source unknown.

motivations behind it have not been deciphered. It is perhaps this assumption that distinguishes social work most crucially from sympathetic listening. Dismissing people as "lazy" or "uncooperative" or "dishonest" does not tell us why they are reacting to the situations in which they find themselves with behavior we classify in these terms. These are descriptive, not diagnostic terms, and nothing is solved by merely describing a client's behavior. What social workers are really interested in knowing is the hidden purpose behind misleading behavior.

Asking the client is not likely to be helpful, since it implies that he knows and is doing whatever he is doing "deliberately." It takes skill and experience to piece together, from what the client says or from his silences, the clues which explain ostensibly inexplicable behavior. We already know, and social work research is adding to this knowledge, some of the many ways in which people utilize their social settings to work out, often very deviously, the conflicts and anxieties they are feeling. What is often hard to appreciate is that the inner conflict is often so painful that the tangled social situation is preferable to mentally acknowledging the conflict.

Suppose that Johnny repeatedly truants from school, in spite of warnings from the school and thrashings from his father. This behavior is, on the surface, illogical, and yet there must be a logic to it: Is school that much worse than thrashings? Does his father ignore him unless Johnny compels attention by such flagrant misbehavior? Is it easier to truant than to be put in the "special room"? Does being punished for truanting help relieve a guilty conscience which bears something much more serious? The social worker cannot solve the problem without finding out first what the underlying motives are.

We may liken the behavior of a person which draws attention to himself to a cry for help. It is a sign that something is wrong. Some people express emotional conflicts and anxieties through physical symptoms: they cannot sleep, or they lose their appetites, or they have headaches or indigestion. Usually they only come to realize that these symptoms have their origins in emotional problems after every test for physical causes has proved negative. Other people, and probably most people in some ways, express these conflicts in terms of their relationships with others. They have their "bad days," when it is unwise to ask a favor of them; they become argumentative, or overtalkative, or seem highstrung. These phenomena have been observed by all of us in our friends and sometimes have been forcefully called to our attention in ourselves. Usually they are fairly temporary. In some people, however, such disruptive behavior can run to extremes and become frightening or even dangerous.

Less obvious are the people who "work off" their emotions through their usual behavior. For example, Mrs. Bennett is full of good works. She takes extremely good care of her family and her home and participates very conscientiously in neighborhood activities. It might seem that this would make her happy, but she constantly feels unappreciated. She tells how she sits up late at night sewing for her daughter, and she sighs as she tells that her daughter does not appreciate her efforts. She takes custards to a neighbor who is sick and worries that she has never been adequately thanked for it. Her husband takes her for granted. Her children expect her to do everything for them and are unwilling to give her help. She is a "professional martyr." We may ask ourselves: Why does she feel the need to be so useful and so appreciated? Why does she overdo everything to the point that she infuriates and antagonizes the people she serves? Why does she need constant reassurance, repeated thanks, and daily acknowledgement of how kind she is? Her behavior cannot be understood unless the unconscious purposes it is serving are known. Mrs. Bennett cannot be made happier by being told to do less for people; nor will taking her husband and children aside and urging them to be more appreciative solve the problem, except perhaps temporarily.

Efforts to help individuals who are using their social relationships as indirect ways of achieving obscure purposes demand that the social worker develop an ability to see beneath surface behavior to the underlying motivations. Such ability is not developed easily or quickly, and it demands extensive and intensive contact with clients, enough to allow observation and analysis by the caseworker, and the development, on the part of the client, of some awareness of how he is using unsatisfactory methods to achieve his purposes. The traditional method of casework, the one-to-one helping relationship, is based on this kind of approach and process. Similarly, social workers who deal with small groups, neighborhoods, or communities will encounter those whose behavior is impeding the forward movement of the group or the program. The bully, the "teacher's pet," the self-appointed scapegoat, the lone wolf—all impede the smooth integration of effort summed up in the group process. The individuals who are acting out their feelings about themselves in these ways can be helped only if we can see how their particular, troublesome behaviors serve useful purposes for them. In the field of community organization, the "prima donna" who cannot work unless she is chairman, the apathetic "wet blanket," the self-made man who wants to "get tough" with welfare recipients, or the rigid moralist who wants to impose his views on others—all are people whose behaviors demonstrate ways in which they, too, are expressing inner needs. If their energies and talents are to be put to the best possible use, the community organization worker, playing the roles of mobilizer, enabler, and change agent, must deal with these people in terms of underlying motivation rather than surface manifestation.

By reacting to the underlying feelings and attitudes rather than the behavior, the social worker avoids being trapped in the client's distorted picture of his situation. By recognizing that the belligerence of a client is an attempt to deny to himself the helplessness and fear he feels, the worker will not be trapped into responding with hostility, thereby only intensifying the client's fear. The small boy whistling in the dark and the angry applicant threatening the public welfare worker with his powerful "connections" are exhibiting the same kinds of behavior. Each is afraid underneath, and each one needs reassurance, not a glib, patronizing kind of reassurance, but one which acknowledges that the fear is real even though the situation need not produce fear.

As Mrs. Perlman observed (pages 31–32), the process of putting emotions and experiences into words is a way of controlling them. Social work is essentially a verbal profession; clients are helped to talk about their feelings and situations in such a way that they can translate them into more appropriate behavior. Even when the services rendered are material ones, as in public assistance, the feelings of the client about asking for and receiving help need to be dealt with verbally. "Blowing off steam" makes it less necessary to act upon angry impulses. When troubled adolescents find someone they really trust, who can help them express their chaotic and aggressive feelings, they have less need to express these feelings in random destructiveness. *Talking it out* is much safer and less socially destructive than *acting out*.

THE NEED TO INCREASE KNOWLEDGE AND SKILL

The social worker must be convinced that the knowledge base on which social work rests needs constant broadening and deepening, that he has a responsibility both to contribute to and profit from ongoing research which enlarges the knowledge base, and that he must be open to change and committed to continuing self-development.

Much social work teaching and learning is done from case records. It is much easier to see patterns of behavior if one can study them at leisure, can look ahead and then look back to see where hints were first dropped of feelings which turned out to be critical. Beginners at case analysis should experiment to sharpen their alertness to these hints. Instead of reading a case through, it can be illuminating for students to divide it into sections and study only one section at a time, trying to predict future client and worker activity before reading the next section. Another useful technique is the "what if?" approach: How might the situation have been altered if the client had known something he did not know, if the worker had said something different, if the child had not been removed, if the adolescent had been allowed to make his own decisions? Such speculation makes the student more aware of other possibilities and less likely to assume that there is only one method of attack or one consequence from a particular kind of behavior.

On the other hand, generalizing has its uses as well. That no two people are just alike is a truism; yet it is also true that human behavior conforms to certain general patterns and that it is possible and profitable to find similarities in the ways people confront problems. The "case study" approach, for so long characteristic of the medical, nursing, and social work professions, is being increasingly applied to other fields—to law, business administration, and higher education, to name just three. The expectation is that the minute scrutiny of one case will reveal points at which it resembles other somewhat similar cases and at which it may be unique. Probably no other field has so carefully developed its recording methods as has social work.

In using a case record for study purposes, it is not enough to know what the client said or did; the record should also include what the social worker said. "Process recording," or the nearly verbatim reporting of the dialogue between client and worker, makes it possible not only to know something of what the client is like but also to learn a good deal of what the worker is like. Does the worker listen or interrupt and change the subject, and if he does interrupt, in what connection? Does the worker make judgmental comments instead of accepting the client as he is? Does the worker convey unrealistic promises of improvement, or at the opposite extreme, does the worker's attitude as conveyed in his comments indicate hopelessness or pessimism?

It is difficult to keep one's personal feelings out of the interview situation. In order to work effectively, social workers must be aware in themselves of a wide range of attitudes and feelings about various kinds of people. Such awareness does not come easily and seldom comes alone; our own defenses make it impossible for us to "see ourselves as others see us." To make this insight possible, as well as to achieve other vital objectives, social work has developed a highly useful technique—supervision. No other discipline provides for quite the intensive and sustained type of supervision that social work does. It is under supervision that professional attitudes can be learned and put into practice and that the dismay of suddenly seeing how one's own feelings and prejudices have been operating to defeat one's expressed intentions can be softened. Supervision of student social workers is frequent and detailed; their case records are reviewed word by word. After graduation, the amount of work which is supervised is reduced, but even experienced social workers are likely to welcome some supervision as a way of keeping alert to their own possibilities for error. It is often reassuring to beginning students to learn that the client will not be at their untrained mercy. It is probably safe to say that no important decision involving a client need ever be based on one person's unsupported judgment.

THE RELATIONSHIP OF SOCIAL WORK TO OTHER DISCIPLINES

Assisting people to be more effective is a skill which requires instruction, practice, and supervision. Above all, it requires that the social worker be able to see, beneath the seemingly random or harmful behavior of an individual, the self-protective purpose of the behavior, which makes the social worker's condemnation actively harmful, his sympathy useless, and his treatment of surface manifestations of behavior only a self-perpetuating technique which keeps clients dependent and ineffective. Social work is thus both a profession and a science and has alliances with other disciplines and professions, as well.

TO THE SOCIAL SCIENCES

Social work is related to the social sciences in a reciprocal way,[40] although many social scientists are reluctant to acknowledge that social work can make a contribution to their particular discipline.

40. See, for example, Brian J. Heraud, *Sociology and Social Work: Perspectives and Problems* (Oxford: Pergamon Press, 1970).

Of the social sciences, sociology and psychology seem to be most closely allied with social work.

A knowledge of the psychological mechanisms involved in human functioning and in the processes of learning and adjustment derives from psychology. In addition, the development by psychologists of ingenious testing devices for the assessment of psychological attributes of all sorts is an invaluable contribution to the social work profession. From the familiar I.Q. tests to the most subtle and discriminating evaluation made possible by projective tests, these testing devices enable all the helping professions to know with a high degree of certainty what strengths and what weaknesses a client presents. Recent developments in the field of ego psychology have been particularly useful.

Since we view the whole field of human services as institutionalized ways of meeting human needs in a complex, interdependent, postindustrial society, we can understand the field only as we understand the social situation which calls it into being. The necessity for a broad range of programs under both public and private auspices is clear when we recognize that dysfunctioning in contemporary society occurs in every social class and that social work is not concerned only with the problems of the poor or the disadvantaged. The study of sociology clarifies both the social situation and the classes of people within it.

Changing social conditions also greatly affect the operation of social work. Sociology studies such phenomena as mobility, urbanization, secularization, the formation and typology of groups, and the processes of social interaction. The sociological concept of "cultural lag" is well illustrated in the repeated attempts by taxpayers and legislatures to impose residence requirements as qualifications for receipt of public welfare. In a country and at a time when most people were born, lived, and died in the same small town, local responsibility for public welfare was logical and relatively efficient. In a period when people can cross a continent in a few hours and when one of every five people changes his residence every year, local responsibility is a manifest impossibility. For a social agency to insist on fitting clients into its concept of the "appropriate" client or to cling to outmoded agency policies is no less illustrative of cultural lag.

No other field has so carefully studied the area of race relations and prejudice as has sociology, and no social worker can ignore the impact of racism on all the human services: income maintenance, education, health care, and the administration of justice.[41]

41. The literature of the social sciences is full of references to race and racism. An excellent brief summary is Roger Daniels and Harry H. L. Kitano, *American Racism: Exploration of the Meaning of Prejudice* (Englewood Cliffs, N.J.: Prentice-

Learning about the differing value orientations of ethnic groups is of special relevance to social workers in locales where ethnic groups form a substantial part of the clientele.[42]

Theories of social interaction, particularly those of conflict and assimilation; of stratification and awareness of different value systems and child-rearing practices in different socio-economic levels; of family and kinship systems; of anomie; of social disorganization and social control; and of role theory comprise some of the specialized areas of sociological knowledge essential for social workers. An understanding of bureaucracy is also demanded, since all social work activity is increasingly large-scale and bureaucratic.

The fields of government and economics add to our knowledge of the larger social setting in which social work is carried on. The intricacies of our city-county-state-federal government, however cumbersome, seem unalterable at present and require some knowledge of background and mechanics. Problems created by the urban-rural balance in state legislatures, by the urban tax base, and by the competing needs of schools and hospitals for available funds require clarification from economists and political scientists, as do the procedures for inaugurating and carrying out social legislation. Such sensitive issues as family planning, dependency of blacks, and civil disorders in urban areas, as well as such basic policies as the extent of federal control over municipal relief programs involve complex political issues. The operations of the business cycle, the role of labor unions, and the influence upon business conditions of federal fiscal policies are all highly relevant to the field of social work, as well.[43]

Hall, 1970). See also Ira E. Robinson, Donna K. Darden, and William R. Darden, *Cases in Crises: Racial and Minority Conflicts* (Austin, Ts.: Austin Press, 1972), a compilation of forty-four cases of prejudice, discrimination, and violence, involving blacks, Puerto Ricans, Indians, and Spanish-Americans in conflict with the dominant white society. Some cases were successfully resolved and some not.

42. For an extremely good analysis of many of these concepts, still valid for the 1970s, see Sister Frances Jerome Woods, *Cultural Values of American Ethnic Groups* (New York: Harper & Brothers, 1956). The Council on Social Work Education has published valuable material on Chicano, American Indian, and Puerto Rican minorities. See also, Miguel Montiel, "The Chicano Family: A Review of Research," *Social Work*, Vol. 18, No. 2 (March 1973), pp. 22–32.

43. The classic study is Wayne Vasey, *Government and Social Welfare* (New York: Holt Rinehart & Winston, 1958). See also Eveline M. Burns, "Social Security in Evolution: Toward What?" *American Behavioral Scientist*, Vol. 15, No. 5 (May 1972), pp. 713–731. See as well the annual reviews of the federal budget by the Brookings Institution, as cited on p. 59. Harland Padfield and Roy Williams, in *Stay Where You Were* (Philadelphia: J. B. Lippincott Company, 1973) examine a program of job creation for hard-core unemployed men. The role of state government in social welfare is discussed in Samuel H. Beer and Richard E. Barringer, eds., *The State and the Poor* (Cambridge, Mass.: Winthrop Publishers, 1973).

A knowledge of history and anthropology provides some comprehension of the historical background of social work and makes possible some prediction of its future developments. A recognition that the rural, frontier life of America is idealized in our mores clarifies some of the problems faced by public welfare departments. Some understanding of the European, Asian, or African background of various ethnic groups is necessary to deal with clients who derive from those traditions. Facilitating the adjustment of refugees necessitates knowing what world conditions rendered them homeless. International social work and the establishment of the profession in other countries require that methods developed in this country be modified in accordance with other histories and traditions, which must be learned. Aid programs for underdeveloped areas may in the future involve social workers to a greater extent than at present—hence the need for becoming familiar with yet other histories and heritages.

Less obvious, perhaps, than the effect the social sciences have on social work is the contribution that social work can make to the basic social sciences. In the latter half of the nineteenth century, the relationship between social science and "philanthropy" was much more apparent than it is now. Such pioneer social workers as Octavia Hill in England and Jane Addams in the United States were recognized as fact-finders as well as social activists. Later, social work became more closely identified with psychiatry and psychology and drifted away from the other social sciences somewhat, but social work in the 1960s again saw vigorous involvement in social action, increasing use of sociological and political concepts, and growing confidence in the potential contribution social work can make to all the helping professions.

The field of social work possesses a wealth of case material, carefully compiled, critically and analytically discussed, from which useful generalizations may be drawn for all the social sciences. Such basic concepts as the essential purposefulness of all behavior, the dynamics of the helping relationship, and the client's rights in a democracy to self-determination and to claim minimum physical essentials from his society have been more clearly defined by social work than by any of the other fields in which they may be highly relevant. Social work research, much of it of a high order, is available in social work journals and in the summaries of theses published by many of the graduate schools of social work. It is unfortunate that this resource is not more widely utilized by researchers in other disciplines, since much of it would tend to counteract the prevailing stereotyped views of social workers as ineffective, overidentified with clients, or wild-eyed visionaries.[44]

TO THE BIOLOGICAL AND PHYSICAL SCIENCES

The biological and physical sciences offer indispensable information for social work's understanding of human growth and development. The adjustment problems of childhood, adolescence, and aging are all complicated by biological changes in the organism. Since it is recognized that many people express emotional discomfort through some physiological mechanism, social workers need to know something of how human physiology operates to deal intelligently with these symptoms. The role of biological factors in the development of culture and personality has engaged the attention of social science and psychiatry as well as biology.[45] Current interest in physical rehabilitation, in so-called "psychosomatic" disorders, and in the possible physical bases of some mental illness—all demand of social workers some comprehension of biological and physical concepts.

The new field of genetic counseling, stimulated by new discoveries on chromosomal functioning and diagnostic procedures, provides opportunities for social workers with above-average interest and knowledge in biology and genetics. Social workers attached to genetic counseling units participate in a team effort. The actual discussion of genetic risk based on knowledge of the parents' genetic pedigrees is a medical responsibility, but social history-taking, interpretation, and follow-up services; coordination of community resources; and direct casework services to troubled families are carried out by social workers. This is a relatively new field, correlated in many cases with family planning agencies, where expansion of social work services can be anticipated.[46] Whether or not students plan to work in such agencies, it is apparent that as such services become more widespread, all social workers will need to know more about the biological sciences.

While no one would contend that social workers must be competent in nuclear physics, as educated members of a profession

44. See Heraud, *Sociology and Social Work*, pp. 271–289.

45. See Clyde Kluckhohn, Henry A. Murray, and David M. Schneider, *Personality in Nature, Society, and Culture* (New York: Alfred A. Knopf, 1953), especially Part II. See also Anthony F. C. Wallace, *Culture and Personality* (New York: Random House, 1961), which attempts to integrate findings from a variety of disciplines.

46. See Sylvia Schild, "The Challenging Opportunity for Social Workers in Genetics," *Social Work*, Vol. 11, No. 2 (April 1966), pp. 22–28.

they should possess enough scientific information to appreciate the complexities of physics and chemistry in the atomic age. If they expect to deal effectively with many adolescent boys, social workers must be able to read "space comics" and science fiction. It is no longer safe to take for granted that college students are proficient in arithmetic, and yet all public welfare bureaucracies involve the computation of budgets. Day sheets, monthly reports, mileage accounts, and similar routine processes demand accuracy and ease in simple arithmetic procedures. As social work is becoming more research-oriented, social workers need to develop some sophistication about statistics and computers, as well. They may never be asked to carry out the technical procedures involved, but they should be able to present accurate data for statistical analysis and be able to read research reports critically and with understanding.

TO THE HUMANITIES

Study and enjoyment of literature and the arts both enrich the social worker's understanding of the infinite ways in which people respond to inner and outer stimuli and enlarge the possible avenues of communication between social workers and their clients. Whether it is the finger painting of a troubled child or the brilliant "flight of ideas" of a manic patient,[47] the arts are ways of expressing inner feelings. Creative artists in all fields are often peculiarly sensitive to the world about them and illuminate, for the less articulate, feelings that are widely known. Psychoanalysts have found infinite riches for their study in Shakespeare; it has been said that Hamlet has been analyzed more carefully than any living man has ever been. While it is obviously impossible to expect all social workers to be expert critics and performers in every field, the more sensitive they are to any of these fields, the more likely they will be to pick up allusions, to grasp what clients are struggling to say, and to appreciate the depths and the subtleties of their clients' expressions.

One extremely withdrawn, borderline schizophrenic woman was totally unable to tell her social worker any of her anxieties and apprehensions about her situation. In her almost random attempts to find any area of discussion in which this woman could feel comfortable, the social worker asked if Mrs. Cutler ever listened to the radio. In talking about her favorite kinds of music and musicians, Mrs. Cutler was able, most indirectly, to give the

47. For such a literary effort, see John Custance, *Wisdom, Madness and Folly* (New York: Pellegrini & Cudahy, 1952).

worker some idea of the terrors which surrounded her and which she was entirely unable to articulate. For many weeks, music was the avenue of communication between Mrs. Cutler and her social worker, and it helped to establish a supportive relationship between them and give Mrs. Cutler some stability.

TO PHILOSOPHY

Philosophy challenges social work to examine critically its goals and methods. Such questions as the extent to which clients can or should be compelled to conform to social norms involve philosophical and ethical as well as political values. Should contraceptive advice be urged on unmarried mothers? Should welfare departments compel mothers to leave young children in order to work? Is it justifiable to compel unwilling clients, through "aggressive casework," to accept social services for which they have not asked? How far should social workers go to protect the rights of parents when the rights in question conflict with the emotional adjustment of a child? It has been said that behavior which compels attention is a devious request for service. This assumption is not usually shared by the client, however, and he may be threatened with court action, withdrawal of relief, or some other pressure unless he allows some sort of token involvement with a representative of a social agency. These are all questions of values and are illuminated by philosophy.[48]

TO THE APPLIED ARTS

The various applied arts (homemaking, clerical skills, and the like) offer practical avenues of assistance to social work. Nutritionists, budget specialists, and homemaker services are provided by many social agencies. In addition, these fields may suggest how social work, itself largely an applied art, may improve its teaching methods and its functioning.

TO THE OTHER HELPING PROFESSIONS

There is need for reciprocal understanding among the various helping professions, which include psychiatry, medicine, teaching, nursing, law, the church, clinical psychology, vocational rehabilitation, and recreation. A failure to understand the peculiar contribution to human welfare which each of these professions can make will result in a failure to make maximum use of community resources for those in need. Some of the helping profes-

48. See John J. Stretch, "Existentialism: A Proposed Philosophical Orientation for Social Work," *Social Work*, Vol. 12, No. 4 (October 1967), pp. 97–102.

sions are less secure in their status, and their members may occasionally resent what seems to them encroachment on territory they consider their own. But when students from any one of these professions have encountered the others during their training, they are more likely to make wise referrals and work harmoniously. For example, medical students whose hospital work has included helpful cooperation from a medical social service department will make better use of social work agencies. Clergymen whose pastoral courses have included field experience in a mental health facility make better use in their ministry of the mental health services in their community.

Social work also has a vital role to play in relation to such comparatively new fields as housing and urban renewal, work with transients and migrant labor, and personnel social work.[49] The field of genetic counseling has been mentioned as opening up to social workers, and there are needs for social workers in abortion counseling and planned parenthood agencies. Yet another opportunity for social workers is in consumer education and credit counseling.[50]

Imaginative social workers will devise new roles in other fields of service, in cooperation with experts from the other professions. Even as social work expects other professions to recognize the contribution it can make, it should not assume that it has all the answers to every problem. Among the marks of security in any profession is a recognition of its own limitations and a confidence born of knowing what it can do skillfully and well. Social work should not attempt to tell other professions how to carry on their work and will not be tempted to do so if it is secure in the knowledge of its own particular competences.

THE SOCIAL MATRIX IN WHICH
SOCIAL WORK OPERATES

This chapter has outlined the value systems of social work and the knowledge base for social work practice. However, in examining public attitudes toward social work, we can see that the values

49. Personnel social work, or industrial social work, has been more extensively developed in Europe than America; see Council of Europe, Social Committee, *Social Workers: Role, Training and Status* (Strasbourg, France: Council of Europe, 1967), especially pp. 16, 17. In India, it is known as "labour welfare"; see Hans Nagpaul, "The Diffusion of American Social Work Education to India: Problems and Issues," *International Social Work*, Vol. 15, No. 1 (1972), pp. 9–10.

50. See Malinda Orlin, "A Role for Social Workers in the Consumer Movement," *Social Work*, Vol. 18, No. 1 (January 1973), pp. 660–665.

held by professionals are often at considerable variance with those of the larger society, which has highly ambivalent ideas about the helping process. For example, public acceptance of the institutional view of public welfare, as developed by students of industrial society, has been very slow.

THE INSTITUTIONAL VIEW OF WELFARE SERVICES

The traditional view of the welfare institution was to regard it as "residual," that is, as dealing with those who, for one reason or another, could not meet their needs through the regularly established social institutions. This view saw child welfare and family services as helping those whose family structure was inadequate or dysfunctional for them. Public assistance served those who could not support themselves via the economic institution. School social work was intended to "take up the slack" where the standard educational institution and the needs of the child did not mesh. Except in periods of extreme depression, such as during the 1930s or in an area of severe temporary unemployment, it was assumed that the fault was the individual's, because he was unambitious, was without skills, or lacked foresight.

As Wilensky and Lebeaux[51] use the term, "residual" welfare functions in situations where there has been a breakdown, while "institutional" welfare is regarded as normal and a social necessity in a technological society. Just as we acknowledge that an industrial society cannot afford mass illiteracy and therefore maintain free, public education, it is the view of most social planners that adequate housing, income maintenance, health care, and the promotion of good mental health are "first-line" functions, to be provided to all members of the society, in the best interests of the society. Romanyshyn prefers the term "developmental" to "institutional" welfare and contrasts developmental and residual views as follows.

> Historically our response to this question ["Am I my brother's keeper?"] has embodied two antithetical concepts of community responsibility for the well-being of others. First, welfare may be seen as a *residual* function, that of policing deviants and dependents and/or alleviating their distress in some minimal way as an act of public or private charity. Traditionally, this is the way we have tended to think of efforts to assist the "needy." Society intervenes through public or voluntary means to assure some a minimum level of personal

51. Harold L. Wilensky and Charles N. Lebeaux, *Industrial Society and Social Welfare* (New York: Free Press, 1965).

well-being and social functioning . . . Charity, philanthropy, relief, and help to the disabled, deviant, and disadvantaged constitute part of our traditional welfare vocabulary—a vocabulary associated with the residual view that assumes that welfare programs exist to meet the emergency needs of individuals when they are incapable of providing for themselves through the normal institutions of the family and the market. In this view welfare ameliorates the problems of the "unfortunate classes" through middle- and upper-class benevolence. It tends to be a depreciatory term. Stigma is associated with client roles in those social agencies that provide services for "them" ("those poor devils"—or "ne'er-do-wells"), not for "us" (the "self-reliant" and "normal" ones). Illustrations of such services are public assistance, foster care of children, corrections, and state mental hospitals.

The change in views is shown in a new vocabulary using such terms as *social planning, social utilities, community action.* These terms are associated with the *developmental* concept, which may be illustrated by social insurance and Medicare provisions under the Social Security Act and such supportive resources as day care and homemaker services. This is a positive concept that extends beyond services to the needy to the recognition that all citizens in an industrial society may require a variety of social services to develop their capacity to perform productive roles and to achieve and maintain a desirable standard of well-being. Since problems are rooted in the social structure as well as in individuals, emphasis is on planned social change, the provision of essential resources that support and enhance social functioning, as well as on such adjustment services as counseling and therapy.[52]

THE WORK ETHIC

This is a deeply held value for most Americans. It embraces the concepts of self-help, self-improvement, success through one's own efforts, and independence and self-reliance. Humanitarian values, while prized, are usually subordinated to the work ethic, so Americans demand that people who cannot support themselves have a clear and unambiguous reason for that state of being. The disabled, the aged, and small children, especially if orphaned, are considered to be worthy of help, while special resentment is aroused by the able-bodied unemployed man, no matter how willing he would be to work if a job were available. Those who fail at self-support are treated as total failures, whether the treatment is a semi-benevolent campaign to "rehabilitate" them or a vindictive hostility which denies them assistance in any form.

52. John Romanyshyn, *Social Welfare: Charity to Justice* (New York: © Random House, Inc., 1971), p. 4.

Although the insistence on self-help shows most clearly in the field of income maintenance and public assistance, asking for help with any problem carries with it a loss of self-esteem.[53] People are embarrassed at being referred for psychotherapy, feeling they should be able to solve their own problems. Students will often fail to consult instructors for suggestions, because they want to "get it on their own." International programs, such as the Peace Corps and CARE, stress that they are providing not charity but a chance. The urge to help or seek help conflicts with the feeling that help is somehow degrading. In whatever field in which social workers practice, they encounter, in their own prejudices and in the social attitudes of the community, these conflicting values.

The extent to which glorification of the work ethic has affected our feelings about how public monies are to be used is shown strikingly in our willingness to provide forms of subsidy other than public assistance in our industrial society. We are eager to provide for farmers and small businesses, crop payments, student loans, and a host of other tax-supported programs for purposes acknowledged as necessary under contemporary economic conditions. Only public assistance is stigmatized and those who apply for it regarded as inferior. Rising welfare costs are blamed for unbalanced budgets and are often the subject of political protests. An article in the *Washington Post* portrayed one such hypothetical protester.

> A young man lived . . . in Hamilton County. He attended public school, rode the free school bus, enjoyed the free lunch program.
>
> Following graduation from high school, he entered the Army and upon discharge kept his National Service Life Insurance. He then enrolled in an Ohio University, receiving regularly his GI check. Upon graduation, he married a Public Health nurse, bought a farm in southern Ohio with an FHA loan.
>
> Later going into the feed and hardware business in addition to farming he secured help from the Small Business Administration when his business faltered. His first baby was born in the county hospital. This was built in part with Hill-Burton federal funds.
>
> Then he put part of his land under the Eisenhower Soil Bank Program and used the payments for not growing crops to help pay his debts. His parents, elderly by now, were living comfortably in the smaller of his two farm houses, using their Social Security and the Old Age Assistance checks. Med-

---

53. See Donald S. Howard, *Social Welfare: Values, Means, and Ends* (New York: Random House, 1969) for a fine discussion on self-help.

icare covered most of their doctor and hospital bills. Lacking electricity at first, he got the Rural Electrification Administration to supply the lines. A loan from the Farmers Home Administration helped clear the land and secure the best from it. That agency suggested building a pond, and the government stocked it with fish.

The government guaranteed him a sale for his farm products. The county public library delivered books to his farm door. He, of course, banked his money in an institution which a federal agency had insured up to $15,000 for every depositor. As the community grew, he signed a petition to help the economy of his area. About that time, he purchased a business and real estate at the county seat, aided by an FHA loan. His children in college received financial assistance from the Federal Government, his son under the National Defense Student Loan Program and his daughter under the Nurse Training Act. Both lived in dormitories and studied in classrooms paid for with federal funds. He was elected to office in the local Chamber of Commerce. A little later it was rumored he joined a cell of the John Birch Society and also the Liberty Lobby, both right-wing extremist groups.

He wrote his Senators and congressmen denouncing excessive government spending, Medicare, big government, the United Nations, high taxes, etc. and enclosed John Birch propaganda pamphlets, some containing outlandishly false statements. He wrote:

"I believe in rugged individualism. People should stand on their own two feet. I oppose all those socialistic trends you have been voting for and demand return to the free enterprise system of our forefathers.

"I and my neighbors intend to vote against you this year."[54]

THE STIGMA OF PUBLIC ASSISTANCE

The importance placed on the self-help theme in American society is shown indirectly by what happens to those who are in a position of being unable to help themselves. Welfare recipients, alone among the beneficiaries of tax-supported programs, are systematically classified as second-class citizens. When they are already disadvantaged by minority group status, this added disability is profound. In order to establish eligibility for assistance, applicants must deal with income maintenance personnel whose training and experience are in financial calculations, not in human relations. Under the new separation regulations, these workers are

54. © *The Washington Post*, July 15, 1968, p. B–1.

forbidden to encourage clients to talk about their feelings or to counsel them. The process is an adversary, confrontation encounter, rather than a cooperative effort on the part of the client and his representative to determine the facts. While humane supervisors and in-service training may mitigate some of the abrasiveness of the system, consideration of clients' sensitivities is not built into the process in any way. Applicants may have to wait for hours in uncomfortable waiting rooms, where there is no opportunity for privacy or for care of little children or those who feel ill. In many communities, welfare offices are located inconveniently, necessitating expensive transportation costs. Arrangements are for the convenience of the staff rather than the clients.

In a society in which underreporting of income to the Internal Revenue Service is socially acceptable, welfare recipients are supposed to be scrupulously honest in reporting all income and resources. Humiliating inquiries may be made of landlords, employers, creditors, and relatives. Welfare applicants share with all low-income groups disadvantages vis-a-vis the police and the courts. They have less access to good legal advice; they must go to jail instead of paying fines. At the time the United States Supreme Court declared the death penalty unconstitutional, there were some 608 individuals on Death Row awaiting execution; the one characteristic they had in common was poverty.[55]

Welfare recipients share with other poverty groups their exploitation by merchants. It has been repeatedly asserted that food prices go up the day that welfare checks arrive at clients' homes. Utility companies may demand exorbitant deposits before installing services. The rent ceiling, whether fixed by rent control or by departmental policy, is almost universally inadequate for decent housing. Many landlords demand a surreptitious supplement from welfare recipients, who then have to divert desperately needed funds from the assistance grant for the "bonus" to the landlord. In such situations as the "welfare hotel" scandals in New York City, the welfare department has participated in the exploitation.

In a society containing widespread and increasingly acceptable sexual permissiveness, the birth of illegitimate children to welfare recipients is deemed scandalous. Efforts to control the sexual and social lives of clients range from warnings of future consequences to removal from the welfare rolls. Although "midnight raids" to determine if a mother receiving Aid to Families with Dependent

55. See James Q. Wilson, "The Death Penalty," *The New York Times Magazine,* October 28, 1972, pp. 27 ff.

Children (AFDC) funds has a "boyfriend" living with her have been outlawed, surveillance by neighbors and even by hired detectives is often directed against welfare recipients. The sexual habits of their neighbors who are economically self-sufficient are, of course, ignored.

The issue of providing family planning services to welfare recipients encounters mixed reactions. The myth that welfare mothers deliberately have additional children in order to increase the size of their grants is cited as a reason why clients will not use services if provided. Actually, the evidence shows that most welfare families prefer fewer children and will avail themselves of family planning when it is provided. Some black militants view contraception as a type of genocide and resist provision of birth control information and materials to blacks. Welfare departments have been reluctant to sponsor family planning services, although the Office of Economic Opportunity and Medicaid have provided contraceptive services for many welfare recipients. In 1971, however, only 25 percent of AFDC families had received family planning services through the U.S. Department of Health, Education, and Welfare (HEW),[56] and experts estimate that between 3,500,000 and 5,000,000 poor and near-poor families need free or near-free contraceptive assistance if they are to avoid unwanted pregnancies.[57] After New York State adopted a liberalized abortion law, there were attempts to deny Medicaid funds for abortions to welfare recipients, which demonstrates hostility to welfare clients rather than logic.

Welfare recipients have their individual rights violated in numerous petty ways. Housekeeping standards and methods of child rearing are considered to be open to public scrutiny. Store customers and personnel scrutinize critically the contents of welfare recipients' grocery carts at the checkout stands. Complaints are received if welfare recipients go on trips, have parties, or go to movies. Conversely, welfare parents are criticized for not sending children to school in better clothes or for having children who are badly behaved. Criticism of welfare recipients as overweight ignores the necessity of the heavy starch component in the low-cost diet. Second-hand clothes are "good enough" for AFDC mothers requesting additional money for their children's school clothes.

It is in the employment area that these invidious distinctions are most obvious. Welfare recipients are supposed to take any job, no

56. U.S. Department of Health, Education, and Welfare, *Trend Report, 1971* (Washington, D.C.: HEW, October 1972), p. 29.

57. See Gitta Meier, "Family and Population Planning," *Encyclopedia of Social Work, 1971*, pp. 373–385.

matter how repellent or poorly paid, as an alternative to continuing on assistance. The Work Incentive Program (WIN), now mandatory for unemployed fathers or for mothers with school-age
children, while originally designed as a job-training program to
enable the unemployed to move onto a career ladder, is now, owing to the Talmadge Amendments, more a device for filling dead-
end, dirty jobs. While in recent years it has become possible to
ignore a certain proportion of an employee's pay (in contrast to the
former practice of deducting any earnings dollar for dollar from
the assistance grant), real work incentives are lacking when participation in the program is involuntary. Those who complain that
welfare recipients would rather remain on relief are often unwilling to hire people without references or good work experience, or
else they propose to exploit what they regard as a source of cheap
help. Recent agitation against "hippies" seems to be stimulated
by anger against those who deny the work ethic and has led to
stringent limitations on the eligibility of young unemployed men,
both for assistance and for federal food stamps. The latter is particularly ironic, since the whole Food Stamp program is sponsored
by the U.S. Department of Agriculture as a way of subsidizing
farmers.

Over and beyond all the discrimination outlined above are the
additional obligations imposed by the general public on the welfare recipient to be grateful for being helped and to refrain from
agitating about his rights or protesting his invidious treatment.

THE PROFESSION AND ITS CLIENTELE

The social prestige of any professional is affected by the status
of his usual clientele. The surgeon with wealthy, upper-class patients is ranked above the doctor operating in a free clinic, the
college professor outranks the elementary school teacher, the corporation lawyer overshadows the public defender. Because social
work has traditionally dealt with the poor, the disadvantaged,
the less successful, it has not been ranked high in the hierarchy of
professions. Those within the social work profession who engage
in private practice with upper-income clients consider their work
more prestigious than that of the public assistance worker. Some
professionals have tried to avoid the use of traditional social work
nomenclature; the Family Service Association of America recommends the use of the term "family counselor" for those employed
by its member agencies. Otto Pollak, a sociologist with wide experience in collaborating with social workers, regrets the use of
the term "worker," pointing out that we do not talk of "legal
workers" or "medical workers." In American terminology,

"work" carries a connotation of unskilled or semi-skilled labor rather than of a profession.[58] Pollak also points out that, unlike other professions which impinge on the lives of all segments of the population, social work is relatively unknown to large groups of people, so that stereotyped misconceptions of what social workers are usually do not become corrected by personal experience.

The chairman of the Commission on Public Attitudes Toward the Social Work Profession of the NASW outlined, some years ago, several descriptions of the social worker, each representing a view held by a substantial number of people:

> 1. The social worker is a kind, warm, generous, helpful person who makes it possible for people to live richer, more satisfying lives.
> 2. The social worker is a frustrated maiden lady who meddles in other people's business.
> 3. The social worker is a knowledgeable, dedicated crusader for the needs of all people, particularly the underprivileged.
> 4. The social worker is a radical whose real underlying motive is to bring about a change in the social order.
> 5. The social worker is a hard-hearted, denying administrator of rules and regulations who checks on people to see that they don't cheat the agency.
> 6. The social worker is a professional whose training and experience enable him to help with a wide range of problems people have in everyday living.[59]

The discomfort of professional social work in its relationship to public assistance is of long standing. Over the past century, the profession and the public welfare departments have vacillated between separation and rapprochement. The NASW sums up the experience of the profession during that time:

> The federal mandate for separation is the most recent episode in a controversy that goes back at least to the early days of the Charity Organization Movement. Out of that movement came a definition of the social worker's job, which included assistance payment activities involved in determining eligibility and the level of financial need and the social service

---

58. Otto Pollak, "Image of the Social Worker in the Community and the Profession," *Social Work*, Vol. 6, No. 2 (April 1961), pp. 106–111.

59. Melvin A. Glasser, "Public Attitudes Toward the Profession: What Shall They Be?" *NASW NEWS*, Vol. 3, No. 4 (August 1958), p. 7. Reprinted with the permission of the National Association of Social Workers. See also "Clarifying the Public Images of the Social Worker," *NASW NEWS*, Vol. 5, No. 4 (August 1960), pp. 23–28.

functions related to social-psychological diagnosis, casework counseling, referral, and mobilization of community resources. During the 1930's, a de facto separation took place because assistance payment functions were transferred from voluntary charity agencies to state and local public welfare agencies. Between the 1940's and early 1960's a campaign was carried out to recombine the administration of social services and assistance payments, this time under public auspices with federal funding for additional personnel costs. Although some social workers strongly objected to this policy, it was widely endorsed by most social welfare spokesmen. The 1962 Social Security Amendments reestablished this principle of combining social services and assistance payments in the AFDC program and provided 75 percent matching federal funds for additional costs of services.

By the end of the 1960's, however, there were recommendations from many sources for the separation of these two functions. Questions about the social services–assistance payment combination took many different forms.

Social workers were more heavily involved in determining eligibility and enforcing punitive or restrictive regulations on AFDC families than in providing social services. They also found themselves caught between professional expectations that they should be nonjudgmental casework counselors and personal and [client] community expectations that they should be militant advocates for the needs of their clients.[60]

Whether or not the profession advocated separation of income maintenance from social services for professional reasons is clearly beside the point, since the profession was not consulted when separation was mandated by HEW in 1970. In addition to the personal and professional expectations which frustrated social workers in public assistance was the growing resentment on the part of voters and taxpayers that social workers were not being punitive enough, were encouraging clients to utilize little-known provisions of the law to get added benefits, and were encouraging clients to protest. Separation is being used not only to streamline administration and cut costs, as its proponents anticipate, but as a device to punish social workers and reduce their voice in this sensitive sphere of operations.[61] It would be tragic if in endorsing separation, the profession should give any suggestion that it is

60. NASW, *New Directions*, pp. 9, 10. Reprinted with the permission of the National Association of Social Workers.

61. See Harry Wasserman, "The Professional Social Worker in a Bureaucracy," *Social Work*, Vol. 16, No. 1 (January 1971), pp. 89–95.

content to be excluded from public assistance programs because they stigmatize both the recipient and the providers of services.

PROSPECTS FOR THE FUTURE

For the immediate future, all indications point to a period of difficulty for the social work profession. Job opportunities in public welfare for professional social workers are severely limited, now that eligibility determination has been transferred to paraprofessionals and services are limited to actual and potential assistance recipients. Supervisory and administrative positions will be going to budget and management experts rather than to social workers.

Private agencies, too, will be facing increased demands for service and more difficulty in securing funds. Many private agencies have been receiving public funds either as subsidies or on a contract basis for service, and these are being curtailed. Among the assets of private agencies has been their relative freedom from political decisions and their independence from government control. Their traditional sources of support (fees, endowments, and allocations from United Way campaigns) are unlikely to expand to cover the loss of public funds. Theoretically, there is money available in federal revenue sharing, but there will be intense competition for these funds among state and local services.

The stigma attached to the receipt of assistance is not limited to those services provided by Departments of Public Welfare and may well be one of the factors behind the increasing financial difficulties of voluntary agencies. To some extent, all those who demonstrate impairment in self-sufficiency are stigmatized. Applicants are embarrassed to apply to mental health agencies. Past, apparently successful treatment for mental illness was a critical factor in the rejection of a candidate for national office in the 1972 presidential campaign. Parents are often reluctant to acknowledge to a school social worker or to child guidance center personnel that they cannot manage the child unaided. The elderly may respond with anger or denial to the inevitable disabilities associated with the aging process. Unmarried mothers cling unrealistically to children they cannot hope to care for, because they cannot bear to be thought of or think of themselves as "bad mothers." Childless couples apply apologetically to adoption agencies. Students with poor grades avoid their advisors. The list of those feeling ashamed because they are not completely self-sufficient is long. Public aid to dependent people is, however, not a popular project. The needs are great, but unless the community is willing to fund helping services more adequately, needed staff expansion will be postponed, and there will be more applicants than openings in many parts of the country.

The NASW recommends that the profession participate in a coalition of groups with common interests in the human services to press for congressional review of current administrative and budgetary policies, with a goal of establishing some basic principles, including stable and adequate funding for human services programs and clear delineation of the lines of responsibility for control over determination of service priorities and staffing patterns.[62]

The NASW also points to the present lack of coherent planning in all fields of human services, including housing, health, and mental health. In the absence of a master plan, not only are services ineffectively used, unevenly distributed, and poorly coordinated, but they are vulnerable to policy decisions that are politically motivated, and they are not subjected to review by those with expertise in service delivery.

From the perspective of American experience in the past century and of the experience of other industrial and postindustrial societies, social needs cannot go unmet forever; eventually the pressure to meet them becomes overwhelming. The passage of Medicare legislation is a case in point. Put into operation over the organized opposition of the medical profession, it represented a national response to a universally recognized need. That there will be future extensions of social service programs is axiomatic. It is very possible that in the immediate future they will be directed at target groups which appear most dangerous to society—criminals, drug abusers, possibly alcoholics—and that they will be oriented to punishment and deterrence rather than to rehabilitation.

Given the value orientations of self-help and the work ethic, which linger inappropriately in American society, the profession of social work is left with the task of interpreting the nature of human need and the capability of the profession to deal with it. Confrontation with legislative bodies is only part of the program before the profession. The widespread lack of public understanding of professional social work efforts is what makes arbitrary decisions like the 1973 budget cuts possible. Not until the human services are recognized as "front-line" services in a postindustrial democracy (a goal which will require a carefully planned public program of clarification and interpretation of the human services),

---

62. NASW, *New Directions*, pp. 17, 18.

will the profession receive funding adequate and predictable to enable it to meet human needs.

In spite of the efforts of the War on Poverty to increase public awareness of the multiple causes of poverty, the man in the street still regards poverty as the "fault" of the victim. In spite of efforts to demonstrate that emotional disturbances and maladjustments in relationships grow out of the nature of an increasingly complex, impersonal, and anxious time and society, the individual is still urged by many to "snap out of it," to "stop feeling sorry for himself." Recommendations for early detection of potential difficulties in children are answered with the platitude that "he will grow out of it," in spite of repeated evidence that many do not.

This book is designed not only for those students who are interested in becoming professional social workers but also for those students who will be influential in other professions, who will be voters and taxpayers and United Way contributors. By learning more about what social workers do, by seeing ways in which troubled people can be helped to be more self-sufficient and better able to cope with and find satisfaction in their lives, students will be better able to accept themselves and to transmit to others the long-overdue view of social welfare as an "institutional" and "developmental" response to a more sophisticated awareness of human needs in contemporary America.

ADDITIONAL REFERENCES

Chapin, Rosemary and Waldman, Nancy, *The Helping Process* (Minneapolis: Minnesota Resource Center for Social Work Education, 1972). A manual which stresses the development of a generic skills base and includes a section on "Communications" with a listing of available tapes, simulation games, and exercises.

Klein, Philip, *From Philanthropy to Social Welfare* (San Francisco: Jossey-Bass, Publishers, 1968). A readable and inclusive history of the field.

Lowenberg, Frank M. and Dolgoff, Ralph, *The Practice of Social Intervention: Goals, Roles and Strategies, A Book of Readings in Social Work Practice* (Itasca, Ill.: F. E. Peacock, 1972). A valuable collection of readings representing a wide range of authorities and sources.

Pins, Arnulf M., "Changes in Social Work Education and Their Implications for Practice," *Social Work*, Vol. 16, No. 2 (April 1971), pp. 5–15. A review of trends in both graduate and baccalaureate education for social work, with projections for the future.

Purvine, Margaret, *Manpower and Employment: A Source Book for Social Workers* (New York: Council on Social Work Education, 1972). Provides a wealth of information on work and the labor force and suggests a new field of practice—"manpower social work."

Schultze, Charles L.; Fried, Edward R.; Rivlin, Alice M.; and Teeters, Nancy H., *Setting National Priorities: The 1973 Budget* (Washington, D.C.: The Brookings Institution, 1973). A review of the disappointing success of the social programs of the 1960s in the light of the 1973 budget cuts.

Specht, Harry, "The Deprofessionalization of Social Work," *Social Work,* Vol. 17, No. 2 (March 1972), pp. 3–15. A provocative analysis of some ideological currents which are undermining professionalism in social work.

Toren, Nina, *Social Work: The Case of a Semi-Profession* (Beverly Hills, Ca.: Sage Publications, 1972). A sociologist analyzes the profession and recommends replacing casework with group work as more realistic in view of the social milieu of clients. See also the review of this book in *Social Casework,* Vol. 54, No. 6 (June 1973), p. 375.

Whittaker, James K., *Social Treatment: An Approach to Interpersonal Helping* (Chicago: Aldine Publishing Company, 1974). The helping process from the point of view of consumer as well as provider, especially useful for its evaluation of twenty-one different approaches to social treatment.

programs of income maintenance

HISTORICAL BACKGROUND

The way any society cares for its needy members reflects its values. In the "folk society,"[1] where the social structure was tightly integrated, the larger family or tribe took over the support of those whose needs could not be met in customary ways. Children deprived of parental support were taken into the homes of relatives or adopted by childless couples. Food resources were shared at least among relatives, if not among neighbors. The elderly were honored by their descendants or, at the opposite extreme, might be dealt with in ways which seem inhumane to us, like the Eskimo practice of abandoning the old to freeze. Such measures are deemed necessary (and have therefore become institutionalized) in cultures having no meaningful role for the economically unproductive. When the group is tightly knit and survival depends largely on solidarity, any break in the intricate pattern of interrelationships and mutual responsibilities is seen as a threat to the whole group. It is therefore to the group's interests to see that unfulfilled responsibilities are somehow fulfilled. This has been true not only for isolated and preliterate cultures, but also for rural and frontier communities in America.

1. Robert Redfield, "The Folk Society," *American Journal of Sociology*, Vol. 52, No. 4 (January 1947), pp. 293–308. The best illustration of a folk society is the primitive agricultural society—informal, tradition-bound, homogeneous, and relatively unchanging.

The Judeo-Christian tradition has always stressed charity as a virtue and urged believers to care for the "widowed and the fatherless." In the early days, poverty and distress were viewed as spiritual discipline or as evidence of sinfulness. (Job's plaintive inquiries, it will be remembered, centered on the question of why he should suffer misfortune when he was free from sin.) The self-sufficient could acquire merit by being generous to the less fortunate and at the same time feel assured that they were less sinful than those they helped. The alms collected by the church were also distributed by the church in a community small and homogeneous enough to recognize the importance of group solidarity in the face of persecution.

During the feudal period, the serfs could call upon the lord of the manor for assistance, which was granted because the lord needed their labor. To acquire merit, gain prestige, and prevent revolt and dissension, many lords undoubtedly also cared for the maimed and the infirm in spite of their unproductivity. For those not attached to the land, the only recourse was begging. Providing relief through monasteries or foundations was a religious obligation for the faithful, but the emphasis was on the obligation of the donor to be generous, not on the right of the poor to subsistence.

As the feudal system began to give way to a wage economy, emphasis shifted to the relationship between relief and the labor force, and legislation was enacted to compel the poor to work. At no time in the history of social work was the social distinction between the poor and the self-sufficient so marked as during the centuries when relief was seen as a deterrent to industry. At this time, relief was deliberately made so odious to the recipient that the most menial employment at the most meagre wages would necessarily be preferred to "charity." Begging was punished by whipping, imprisonment, and even death. The rights of the needy were almost completely eclipsed, although the claim to the barest of necessities was recognized by law.

The growth of democratic and humanitarian ideas eventually affected even the field of relief, and questions about the adequacy and effectiveness of various ways of assisting people were raised in England and America throughout the nineteenth century. The right of each person to claim help from his fellow citizens had been implicit in humanitarianism for many years, but it took the Great Depression of the 1930s to crystallize these rights into legislation. The failure of industry and thrift to protect citizens from want during the Depression led to a new view of the relief applicant as someone not essentially different from other people but caught up in circumstances beyond his control. It became evident that in the urban society, as distinct from the folk society, the isolation of the small family unit and the shifts to renting instead of owning a home and to weekly wages instead of proprietorship meant that the individual was infinitely more vulnerable to economic changes. The enactment of the Social Security Act in 1935 firmly established the right of those found eligible to call upon the society as a whole for the essentials of life.

The Depression years have faded from national memory, and resentment has mounted over increasingly long relief rolls and continued high taxes. Welfare expenditures have been a convenient excuse for larger budgets at every level of government, and curbing welfare abuse has been a politically effective campaign issue. The movement of the 1970s has been away from a liberalized extension of the philosophy of public responsibility for the well-being of all citizens and back toward the age-old distinction between the "deserving" and the "undeserving" poor. The legislation enacted in 1972 (specifically, the Social Security Amendments of 1972, the Revenue Sharing Act, and the Talmadge Amendments, which were passed in late December 1971 but went into effect July 1, 1972), as well as the budget for fiscal 1974, smacks of medieval efforts to force assistance recipients into the labor market. We need to remind ourselves of some of the lessons learned during the Depression, as well as from most of the other industrialized societies of the world, of the interdependence of all segments of the society and the disruptive effects of allowing a large segment of the population to be systematically excluded from benefits enjoyed by the majority. Tensions and breakdown of consensus and social control in our urban ghettos indicate a need for adequate and effective social services as well as "law and order."[2] At the same time, a disproportionately small share of the manpower and talents of some socio-economic groups is available to industry and defense. The relationship of group solidarity to survival may be less obvious than in the folk society, but it is no less real in the atomic age.

THE SHIFT TO STATE RESPONSIBILITY

During the early years of the Christian era, the folk tradition of caring for one's neighbors was still operative, and up until the end of the sixteenth century, relief of the poor was considered a church rather than a state responsibility. The beginning of the shift of

2. See *Report of the National Advisory Committee on Civil Disorders* (New York: Bantam Books, March 1968), especially pp. 457 ff.

responsibility from church to state is seen first in the restrictive legislation forbidding begging and vagrancy. In England between 1350 and 1530, a series of laws known as the "Statutes of Laborers" attempted to force the poor to work. Whether or not these statutes were effective during the labor shortage immediately following the Black Death, they ceased to have any usefulness by the middle of the sixteenth century. The beginnings of manufacture, the eviction of tenants by landlords who turned to raising sheep for the wool trade, and the changing agricultural methods made it totally unrealistic to forbid begging. The decreasing authority of the church and the increasing tendency to shift responsibility to governmental authorities gave rise in England to a series of measures which culminated in the famous Elizabethan Poor Law of 1601. The revolutionary character of the Poor Law is summed up by Karl de Schweinitz:

> After two centuries of attempts to control poverty by repressive measures, government slowly and reluctantly came to accept positive obligations for the help of people who could not provide for themselves. The experience of the years between 1349 and 1601 had convinced the rulers of England of the presence of a destitution among the poor that punishment could not abolish and that could be relieved only by the application of public resources to individual need.[3]

A number of somewhat similar reform plans had also been advocated in Europe. The reforms of St. Vincent de Paul in the sixteenth century and Martin Luther's Ordinance for a Common Chest in 1523 were both concerned with correcting evils in the ecclesiastical administration of relief. The plan of Juan Luis Vives (1492–1540), drawn up for the city of Bruges in Belgium, provided for the investigation of all cases and the creation of work for the able-bodied unemployed. But it was the English system, specifically the Poor Law of 1601, sometimes known as "43 Elizabeth," which was most influential in the development of public welfare and social work in America. The English colonists who came to America in the early and mid seventeenth century were familiar with this statute, which was then working relatively well in the home country.

---

3. Karl de Schweinitz, *England's Road to Social Security* (Philadelphia: University of Pennsylvania Press, 1943), p. 29. For a detailed account of legislation prior to 1601, see Beatrice and Sidney Webb, *English Poor Law History* (London: Longman's, Green, 1927), Chapters 1 and 2.

Influence of the Elizabethan Poor Law

There are several important principles in the Elizabethan Poor Law which continue to have a dominating influence on welfare legislation three and a half centuries later. The shifting of responsibility from the church to the state for raising the necessary revenue for poor relief had begun at least a century before but was made unmistakably explicit in the Law of 1601. Overseers of the poor were to be appointed in every parish to collect and disburse funds. This principle of the state's responsibility for relief was universally adopted in the American colonies and has never been seriously questioned in this country. Indeed, it is in fundamental accord with the democratic philosophy, as well as with the principle of the separation of church and state.

Another influential principle enunciated in the Poor Law also antedates 1601. The idea of local responsibility for welfare goes back at least to 1388 and a series of acts, designed to discourage vagrancy, which ordered "sturdy beggars" to return to their birthplaces and there seek relief. The term "settlement," still a matter for discussion among legislators today, means that responsibility for supporting an individual rests on the locality where he is "settled." Settlement is a relic of a time when people were born, lived all their lives, and died in the same village, and enormous legal tangles have arisen from attempts to define and interpret laws of settlement in a more mobile society. In 1549, a corollary principle, that of "removal," was clearly laid down when provisions were made for the forcible return of a vagrant to his home parish or place of settlement. This provision was not specifically included in the Law of 1601 but was reaffirmed in the Law of Settlement of 1662 and also adopted by many of the colonies; it empowered justices of the peace to return to his home parish any person who seemed in danger of becoming a public charge.

A third principle in the Poor Law stipulated differential treatment of individuals according to categories, e.g., the deserving poor, children, the aged, the sick. This principle was based on the theory that certain types of unfortunate people have a more legitimate claim for support from the community than other types. It survives in our Social Security categories and in the general assistance programs of the states and localities. The Elizabethan statute provided for the apprenticing of poor children, for the building of workhouses for the able-bodied, and for relief at home ("outdoor") or in institutions ("indoor") for the infirm, defective, or handicapped.

The Poor Law also delineated family responsibilities for aiding dependents. Children, grandchildren, parents, and grandparents were designated as "legally liable" relatives. This designation of responsibility is included in the legislation of most of our states, although it is unrealistic in a mobile, industrial society to insist on such laws too literally, and many public welfare departments exercise a good deal of latitude in enforcing them.

This Elizabethan Poor Law was noteworthy and progressive when it was enacted. It has served as the basis for both English and American public welfare. Unfortunately, the marked changes in all our social institutions brought about by the Industrial Revolution have rendered most of the Law's provisions obsolete, and cultural lag is apparent in those laws and mores of today which still cling to some of the Poor Law's outmoded principles.

THE AMERICAN EXPERIENCE TO 1929

Following the English pattern, responsibility for poor relief during the colonial period and the early years of statehood was placed on the town and only slowly and partially shifted to the states. The poor were "auctioned off" to the lowest bidder, who would board them in his home, or they were sent to "poor farms." Dependent children were "bound out" to work or, somewhat later, gathered into mass "orphanages."[4] The "pauper's oath" (swearing to a condition of absolute destitution) was in widespread use, and relief was granted only to those whose behavior was considered suitable. The spirit of the laws was that of deterrence and repression. In all fairness, however, it should be pointed out that the rigors of repressive legislation were undoubtedly often mitigated by the kindliness of neighbors in a nation that was still semi-rural.

During the nineteenth century responsibility for certain types of dependents was completely shifted to the states. Institutional care for the insane, the feebleminded, and the delinquent was provided by the states, because no one locality had enough such individuals to warrant setting up an institution for them and ad-

---

4. Note the picture given in James Whitcomb Riley's famous poem "Little Orphant Annie":

Little Orphant Annie's come to our house to stay,
An' wash the cups and saucers up, an' brush the crumbs away,
An' shoo the chickens off the porch, an' dust the hearth an' sweep,
An' make the fire, an' bake the bread, an' earn her board-an'-keep.

From *Joyful Poems for Children* by James Whitcomb Riley, copyright ©1941, 1946, and 1960 by Lesley Payne, Elizabeth Eitel Miesse, and Edmund H. Eitel, reprinted by permission of the publisher, The Bobbs-Merrill Company, Inc.

mitting them to almshouses had proved unsatisfactory. The pioneering work of Dorothea Lynde Dix, which brought about the establishment of institutions for the mentally ill (whom she found confined in cellars, stables, and cages), led to the passage of federal legislation by both houses of Congress in 1854 to assist the states in financing care of the insane and in supporting training institutions for deaf-mutes. The bill was vetoed by President Franklin Pierce, on the grounds that welfare programs were not a federal responsibility but a state and local one. This philosophy was dominant until the Depression in the 1930s forced its reversal.[5]

Countless "orphan asylums," under both voluntary and public auspices, also date from the early and mid nineteenth century. The need to care for disabled veterans of the Civil War and their dependents led to the establishment of soldiers' homes, children's institutions, and the beginnings of a pension system. These were usually under state rather than local auspices. Beginning with Massachusetts in 1863, the states organized state boards of charities; by 1897, sixteen states had such boards, which were responsible for supervising both public and private programs and institutions for the delinquent, dependent, and defective individuals within the state. Their concern with poor relief was often confined to those applicants with no town settlement, but to a limited extent they attempted to supervise local welfare departments and overseers and set some standards for them.

Between 1900 and World War I, a vigorous movement of social reform led to the enactment of legislative measures designed to curb child labor, protect women in the labor force, and ease the hardships of workingmen. The growing problems of the slums led to the enactment of housing legislation. Health facilities were increased, and boards of health were empowered to enforce legislation. Industrial hazards were identified and protective measures ordered. Attempts were made to ban child labor entirely but were not successful. Juvenile courts were set up, social workers were added to public hospital staffs, and rehabilitation programs began to develop. Attempts to make local responses to welfare needs more adequate and uniform were not successful, however, and little progress was made in this phase of social welfare until after 1929.

Although the Elizabethan Poor Law made the state legally re-

5. See Arthur P. Miles, *An Introduction to Public Welfare* (Boston: D. C. Heath, 1949) for a detailed discussion of the welfare legislation of the various colonies and states.

sponsible for the poor, private efforts to relieve distress, by the church and by private individuals, foundations, and benevolent societies, continued. Private services were largely uncoordinated and often restricted to particular denominations or groups of citizens. The Charity Organization Society movement has already been described, as well as the landmark decision which isolated poor relief from the professional developments within the COS (see pages 6, 7). The settlement house movement, beginning in the late 1800s, was also a significant development in social reform and in professional efforts to assist one's neighbors.

The growing body of understanding and methodology which was built up in the first third of the twentieth century will be discussed in Chapter 3. It is safe to summarize, however, that by 1929 America had made two parallel efforts to deal with the underprivileged and the troubled: public and private agencies. Excluded from the COS movement, which did so much to bring professional standards to the private agencies, the public welfare departments were operating with inadequate, untrained staffs. Few, if any, professional attitudes had been accepted by these tax-supported departments. Funds provided were inadequate, often not based on any real study of family needs and granted without recognition of the emotional factors involved or the possibilities for rehabilitation presented. Much of the relief in the larger cities was granted by the private agencies; in small towns and villages, local overseers of the poor or county welfare commissioners doled out grocery orders or provided institutional care at the county farm. Cash relief was almost unknown; relief was provided "in kind"—distribution of the actual commodities themselves, purchased in wholesale lots—or by means of orders to grocers, landlords, clothing dealers, and the like. In most states in the nineteenth and early twentieth centuries, the principles of the Elizabethan Poor Law of 1601 were still dominant in the public welfare departments. This, then, was the situation at the beginning of the Depression, which was to change, radically and permanently, the organization of all social welfare in the United States.

THE NEW DEAL

The period from 1929 to early spring 1933 marked the greatest economic change that America had ever undergone. The national income was cut in half; unemployment increased to include approximately a quarter of the civilian labor force. Prevailing attitudes toward economic want were profoundly challenged. It was apparent that a lifetime of industry and thrift did not guarantee independence and security. Life savings could be wiped out in bank failures; the most faithful and reliable employee could be laid off; energy and willingness to work would be of little use if no jobs were available. It was no longer possible to distinguish accurately between the "deserving" and the "undeserving" poor, if by the latter one meant the able-bodied unemployed. Relief rolls increased while tax revenues dwindled.

The voluntary agencies found themselves in a critical position. In some communities, they had been carrying the bulk of the relief load, and in every community their appeals for funds were based on their functions in meeting economic distress. At the very time when calls for help were increasing, the contributions of wealthy and middle-class donors were being sharply reduced. However unhappy they may have felt about it, private agencies were forced to curtail or even suspend the granting of relief and refer their clients to the local welfare departments.

The local welfare departments were inundated, and local funds were soon exhausted. The localities turned to the states for additional funds. Many states set up emergency relief programs, but their resources were not infinite, and by 1932 there was increasing pressure on the federal government for funds to meet relief commitments. The reluctance with which the states relinquished any control to the federal government was matched only by the reluctance of Congress and the President to permit federal involvement in what had been for so many centuries recognized as a state and local responsibility. But with the election of Franklin D. Roosevelt and a Democratic Congress in 1932, the country indicated an eagerness for definite action.

The legislation that accumulated over the next few years to constitute what was termed the New Deal represented long overdue changes in the role of the national government. Under the stress of the national emergency, some measures were enacted which proved ineffective, unwieldy, or unconstitutional, but a residue of effective measures survived. The New Deal was more a continuation of the reform movement which had been interrupted by World War I than a subversive ideology imposed on a defeated people by a group of radicals, as some of its more outspoken opponents have claimed. In the years since, such measures as Social Security, public housing, the TVA, and the Securities and Exchange Commission have been accepted by both political parties, and it is unthinkable to any serious student of government that any of these measures should be repealed or abandoned.

The change in national mores produced by the emergency of the

Depression was drastic, particularly in respect to the responsibilities of the federal government. True, the role of government had been changing for three quarters of a century. The Interstate Commerce Act dates from 1887 and the Sherman Anti-Trust Act from 1890. During World War I, the federal government had assumed powers in areas formerly considered outside its responsibility. But legislation had lagged far behind the needs of a rapidly growing industrial society. How far American views concerning the scope of federal governmental responsibility have changed since the early days of the New Deal is well summed up by Henry Steele Commager:

> It is instructive . . . to put down the things we now take for granted, but did not take for granted even a generation ago: the responsibility of government to regulate the economy, to support agriculture, to provide for job security and social security; the right of workingmen to organize in unions of their own choosing; the prohibition of child labor; the development of hydroelectric power under government auspices; the guarantee of bank deposits; the regulation of securities; slum clearance; Federal aid to public health and education. These and many other things are now the common sense of the matter. But they were not the common sense of the matter in March, 1933; to a great many Americans, then, they were alien and pernicious and they spelled ruin and death.[6]

When Roosevelt took office in March 1933, he found the most prosperous nation in the world so lagging in the field of social legislation that he could proclaim that one third of the nation was ill-fed, ill-clothed, and ill-housed. As a former governor of the highly populated New York State, Mr. Roosevelt already had experience with the problems of relief at the state level. The New York Temporary Emergency Relief Administration (TERA) had been a pioneer effort to set up adequate relief provisions on a large scale. The director of the TERA, Harry Hopkins, was a social worker with experience at Christodora House on the lower east side of New York City. He felt strongly that trained social workers were best equipped to handle applications for relief, and in the TERA and later as head of the Federal Emergency Relief Administration (FERA), he ordered that, insofar as possible, trained social workers act as supervisors in the social services divisions.

It is interesting to speculate on what the development of public

6. Henry Steele Commager, review of *The Coming of the New Deal*, Vol. 2, by Arthur M. Schlesinger, Jr., in *New York Times Book Review*, January 4, 1959, p. 1. ©1959 by the New York Times Company. Reprinted by permission.

welfare might have been had Mr. Roosevelt appointed someone else as administrator of the FERA. A banker, whose interests would undoubtedly have centered much more on the fiscal aspects of the program; an engineer, whose concern might well have been for the construction and efficient renovation of public works; or a politician, whose chief concern might have been party obligations and vote-getting—any of these would have shaped an administration for the FERA which would have been vastly different from that of Mr. Hopkins.[7]

The FERA

In May 1933, in a precedent-shattering act, the Federal Emergency Relief Administration was set up with $500,000,000 appropriated by Congress. Some of this money was granted to the states on a matching basis (states were given federal money to match the amount of state money they reserved for relief), but some was in the form of outright grants to those states whose resources were already depleted. Although the program lasted only two years, its effect on American public welfare was incalculable. The act stipulated that relief be granted to all those in need and that it be sufficient in amount to prevent suffering and insure minimum physical needs. In order to qualify for federal funds, the states and localities had to have at least one trained social worker in a supervisory capacity. Eligible relief applicants were given direct relief and/or work relief on projects devised by the local authorities. Efforts were made to provide in-service training for agency staff; short-term institutes were offered by many schools of social work, and federal funds were provided to send 1,000 workers to accredited schools for graduate training.

There are several far-reaching principles in this act. First is the policy of encouraging state action by the granting of federal funds, provided that state programs meet certain minimum standards. The delicate balance between federal and state prerogatives insures that federal authorities cannot compel any state to set up a welfare system. But federal funds can be made available in an amount which will prove so attractive that the state will be willing to meet standards for the sake of the "free" money. (It is one of the ironies of the United States local-state-federal system of govern-

7. For a vivid and readable account of the pressures of the Depression and the role of Harry Hopkins in the FERA, see Robert E. Sherwood, *Roosevelt and Hopkins* (New York: Harper and Company, 1950), Vol. 1, Part 1: "Before 1941," pp. 1–270. For a lucid and thorough account of the development of social work during the Depression years, see Nathan E. Cohen, *Social Work in the American Tradition* (New York: Dryden Press, 1958), Chapter 6.

ment that the more remote the source of funds from the agency, the more likely they are to seem "free.") In many states, only the federal standards could persuade state legislators to abandon the time-hallowed principle of town settlement for certain classes of relief recipients. By the use of this method of federal funding, a greater degree of uniformity and a closer approach to minimum standards were achieved long before taxpayers and legislators in the various states were ready to establish them out of conviction. This method has proved highly valuable in other fields of social welfare, such as health legislation, housing, and school construction.

A second important principle established by the FERA is the clear-cut enunciation of governmental responsibility for the relief of economic distress. So long as poverty was believed to be the individual's "fault," relief grants were kept purposely low to deter others from applying, and public welfare employees and social workers felt a degree of social distance from their clients. With the sudden reverses of fortune brought about by the Depression, people from the same socio-economic levels as the social workers were in the applicants' line. In some communities, FERA recipients with clerical skills found themselves hired as employees by the welfare department; in moving "to the other side of the desk," many did not lose their sense of identity with the clients.

However distressing it may have been to workers and clients, the emergency was a democratizing experience. Out of it came the basis for the establishment of a professional worker-client relationship instead of a sentimental, authoritarian, or mechanical one. If the law specified that all persons meeting certain eligibility requirements were to receive relief, without regard to their race, citizenship, religion, or moral character, then each client had every right to expect his claim to be treated with respect and to receive adequate service from a civil servant. Yet this expectation, so clearly provided for in the policies of the FERA, never received universal acceptance. Kermit Wiltse, writing in 1958, found that Old Age Assistance had been widely accepted as a "right" but not Aid to Dependent Children.[8] Even the 1972 Amendments to the Social Security Act provide for very different treatment of the aged, blind, and disabled versus treatment of families with dependent children.

A third significant trend in the FERA was the hiring of trained workers. The infusion of professional attitudes and techniques

8. Kermit T. Wiltse, "Social Casework and Public Assistance," *Social Service Review*, Vol. 36, No. 1 (March 1958), pp. 41–50.

altered the local welfare picture almost beyond recognition. Confidential case histories replaced financial ledgers; standard budgets were introduced; political influence was minimized if not eliminated. The earlier "investigators," equipped with flashlights for inspecting cellars, were succeeded by "workers"; "departments of charities and corrections" became "departments of public welfare" (and have now become "departments of social services"); workers who met civil service standards were hired rather than political hacks or the marginally employable who were "good enough to do welfare work."

In addition to direct relief and some work relief, the FERA offered other forms of aid to those in distress. Since large numbers of people had left home in search of employment and were stranded in towns unwilling to assume responsibility for them, transient bureaus were set up to provide for their relief and transportation. Medical services were made available to them. Surplus commodities of various sorts, particularly food and clothing, were purchased by the federal government as a spur to business and agriculture and distributed to relief families. Within two years, the FERA program involved 20,000,000 people.

The WPA

As the name implies, the FERA was never designed to be more than an emergency measure. During the two years it was in operation, study was being made of some permanent provisions for relief of economic distress. In his message to Congress on January 6, 1935, President Roosevelt announced that the federal government would return the operation of direct relief to the states, but would assist the states with federal funds for relief purposes and would create a work-relief program for the able-bodied unemployed. The WPA (first known as the Works Progress Administration and later as the Work Projects Administration) was set up by executive order and began operations in the summer of 1935, replacing the work-relief program of the FERA. At the same time, hearings on a proposed social security bill were being held before congressional committees. The bill was designed to provide the promised assistance to state relief programs and, at the same time, to set up insurance programs which would make unemployment, retirement, and death of the breadwinner insurable risks and thus lessen sharply the need for assistance programs. The bill was eventually passed, becoming the Social Security Act in 1935.

The WPA was a large-scale work relief program, in which projects initiated by state and local authorities could be granted federal funds on a proportional basis. There were stipulations that the work be done on public property, so that WPA labor would not be used to undercut private labor. All but a few supervisory personnel had to meet an eligibility test before being hired, and they had to be either on relief or eligible for relief. Approximately 2,000,000 persons a month were employed, at wages ranging from $21 to $94.90 a month. Most of the projects undertaken involved the construction or maintenance of parks, streets, water supply systems, sewage disposal systems, and public buildings. More than 250,000 projects were undertaken before the WPA was allowed to expire in 1943 because of the shortage of labor caused by the war.

The WPA met with opposition from many sources. Labor and private business were fearful of the competition; certain taxpayers' groups pointed to poorly planned projects and cited the expense involved; some of the special projects set up to maintain skills, such as the WPA Theater and various WPA art projects, were rediculed and regarded as refuges for the maladjusted and subversive. There were jokes and cartoons about "shovel leaners" and tales of sidewalks that were built out into the country, of leaf-raking, and of driveways and swimming pools built for officials. Undoubtedly, there were some instances of political influence, of inefficiency, of unimaginative and unproductive projects. What should be remembered, however, is that in work relief it is the worker who is the primary consideration and not the project. It is unrealistic to expect efficiently operated engineering projects from a work force made up of unemployed bookkeepers, sales clerks, and inexperienced high school graduates. The belief that people should be allowed to work for what they receive rather than remain in idleness means that the utmost in careful and imaginative planning is necessary to utilize the workers available. With all the limitations imposed by business and labor interests, it is amazing that there was not more "shovel leaning" and that so many valuable additions to local and state facilities were made. In addition to the parks, libraries, schools, and other construction projects, many clerical and educational activities were undertaken by the WPA to utilize the "white collar division." A number of enterprises proved so valuable that when the WPA was discontinued they were taken over by other public or voluntary agencies; among these may be mentioned homemaker services and nursery schools.

With the WPA and the Social Security Act, the role of the federal government in the field of social welfare was clearly established. There has been no need since 1943 of work-relief projects on such a massive scale as the WPA, although special made-work projects have been developed in some areas, receiving federal funds. The federal role in relief was made more explicit by the creation of the Department of Health, Education, and Welfare (HEW) in 1953. Federal leadership in raising relief standards and providing relief services continued via the cumbersome network of delicate local-state-federal relationships. In January 1974, assistance payments to blind, disabled, and aged recipients became payable directly from the Social Security Administration. Since the role of Social Security in all aspects of income maintenance is paramount, some account of the origin and subsequent amendments to the Social Security Act is in order.

The Social Security Act

The Social Security Act had its beginning in June 1934, when President Roosevelt appointed a Committee on Economic Security to recommend provisions for "greater economic security." The Committee's deliberations centered on provisions for insurance against unemployment and old age and on assistance for those over sixty-five. Only at the insistence of the Children's Bureau was a provision included for aid to dependent children. Other categories of relief recipients, the Committee recommended, should be cared for by states and localities. In this recommendation, the Committee was at variance with the views of most leading social workers, who were in favor of federal assistance to all relief programs. The report of the Committee was sent to Congress in January 1935, with a request for speedy action. For the next seven months, the Social Security Bill underwent protracted hearings and many modifications. Between January and August, representatives of business, nonprofit corporations, education, and government at all levels appeared at committee hearings in both houses of Congress. Apprehension was expressed over both the fiscal and ideological aspects of the program. The resulting Social Security Act was a compromise, with defects and omissions, only some of which have been subsequently corrected. Fortunately, the Act provided that the Social Security Administration make yearly recommendations to Congress for modification. There have been amendments nearly every year since the original Act was made into law on August 14, 1935.

The Social Security Act reflected in many ways its Depression origin. It aimed at encouraging the retirement of those over sixty-five from the labor force in a period of job scarcity; hence it set up restrictions on the earnings of the retired which have proved inequitable. Monthly benefits were geared to Depression prices and have had to be revised upward periodically since 1937. Insurance coverage was at first limited to employees in commerce and industry and has been gradually expanded to include most employees and the majority of the self-employed. At first, the Act provided insurance benefits only for the wage earner, but the 1939 Amendments included his dependents or his survivors. The original Act was concerned largely with direct income maintenance, although provisions for maternal and child health services were included; subsequent amendments reflect a broadened concept of "social security" as including a wide range of services to citizens.

The provisions of the Act may be divided into insurance programs, assistance programs, and service programs. The Act also included taxing provisions and administrative requirements of various sorts. The aim of the insurance programs was the maintenance of income which had been interrupted or stopped by events beyond the control of the individual. The enactment of such a program was a legislative acknowledgment of the interdependence of the members of a complex industrial society and a formal recognition of the responsibility of government to provide some form of social insurance against economic hazards. Since it would take time for all wage earners to become covered under the insurance programs, and since there were people who could not become covered because they were already retired or otherwise unable to work, the Act also established a program to aid the states in granting assistance to various categories of needy persons. The expectation was that within a generation everyone would be covered by insurance and that the assistance programs would therefore be sharply reduced. As we shall see, this expectation proved false.[9] The Act provided monies to the states for maternal and child health services, child welfare services, vocational rehabilitation, and the development of a nationwide employment service. Although the amount of money involved in the services program was small compared to that in either the insurance or assistance programs, the grants to the states enabled them to expand their staffs and extend their services to a highly significant degree.

With the passage of the Social Security Act, provision of some sort was made for most of the hazards of economic life for the individual. For the first time in the United States, old age, the pre-

9. See Gilbert Y. Steiner, *Social Insecurity: The Politics of Welfare* (Chicago: © Rand McNally, 1966), Chapter II: "The Withering-Away Fallacy." Mr. Steiner is bitterly critical of the social work establishment.

mature death of the breadwinner, and temporary unemployment because of lack of work were viewed as insurable phenomena. Dependency because of inadequate income was included for the blind, for the aged, for dependent children, and, since 1950, for the disabled. Dependency because of temporary disability or overwhelming medical expenses was not included in any federally aided program until 1960; recipients of Old Age Assistance (OAA) have been eligible for medical payments since 1950, but the so-called "medically indigent," those whose income is adequate for routine expenses but not for large medical bills, have been far behind in receiving consideration. A special program for those over sixty-five, Medical Assistance to the Aged (MAA), was set up in 1960, but it was not until the 1965 Amendments that Medicare (insurance against medical costs for those over sixty-five) and Medicaid (an assistance program to pay medical costs for the medically indigent) were provided. Temporary disability still does not qualify one for any federally aided program, nor is public insurance against medical costs available for those under sixty-five; however, the 1972 Amendments to the Social Security Act did extend Medicare coverage to those receiving disability benefits and included in the definition of persons with a disability those who require kidney transplants. This suggests a possible means of expansion of health insurance; if sufficient pressure for national health insurance does not develop in the next few years for general coverage, some progress may be made by extending Medicare coverage to specific categories of recipients and/or to specific illnesses which are catastrophically expensive. The next group to be included would logically be recipients of retirement benefits who are under age sixty-five.

With the establishment and expansion of a social security system, the federal government was at last deeply involved in the welfare picture. Its involvement was finally acknowledged when in 1953 the Department of Health, Education, and Welfare was established and its Secretary given Cabinet status. The Department brought together agencies, boards, and bureaus from other departments, as well as independent agencies. The Department's structure is complex. It includes the United States Public Health Service, the Office of Education, and the Social and Rehabilitation Service (SRS), which brings together the former Welfare Administration, the Vocational Rehabilitation Administration, the Administration on Aging, and the Children's Bureau. HEW attempts to separate payment programs from those providing services and to stress rehabilitation service. There are also welfare-related services in the Labor Department (which administers unemployment insurance, wages and hours laws, the Bureau of Labor Standards, and similar services); in the Veterans Administration; in the Justice Department (which includes the Federal Bureau of Prisons); in the Agriculture Department; and in the Department of the Interior (particularly the Bureau of Indian Affairs).

INCOME MAINTENANCE PROGRAMS

As Eveline Burns has analyzed the question of income maintenance,[10] there are four major types of programs by which an industrial society can attempt to insure economic security for its citizens. The first type of program aims to reduce and prevent loss of income by measures which protect public health, facilitate rehabilitation, and promote full employment and economic stability. These measures help insure job opportunities, the stable value of money, and a productive labor force. A second type of program is designed to insure an adequate return for the labor of those employed by measures such as laws governing wages and hours, protective tariffs, subsidies, crop insurance for agriculture, and laws protecting the rights of unions and collective bargaining. A third type of program comprises measures designed to encourage individuals to protect themselves against possible loss of income by means of savings and insurance; such measures include insurance of bank deposits, encouragement of credit unions, and tax concessions for both individuals and groups. The fourth program of measures provides alternative income to those who have suffered loss or diminution of earnings or provides, at public cost, services which certain segments of the population cannot afford. It is in this fourth program of economic security measures that relief, compulsory insurance against retirement or unemployment, veterans' benefits, and work-relief programs fall. Publicly provided services are exemplified by public education and subsidized housing.

Using Dr. Burns's frame of reference, let us examine the programs of income maintenance in contemporary America, as they relate to the field of social work. In the first category, public health and rehabilitation facilities are provided at various levels of government, but there are great gaps in coverage, both geographically and in services available. The burden of medical costs from disability and illness, much of it preventable, is one of the gravest

10. Eveline M. Burns, *Social Security and Public Policy* (New York: McGraw-Hill, 1956), especially pp. 1–15.

threats to economic security. The role of the national government in maintaining full employment and combating either inflation or deflation seems more accepted in theory than in practice; there is no general agreement as to how these responsibilities can best be carried out.

The second group of measures encompasses a battery of federal and state laws governing and benefiting the employed. Unfortunately, these laws are of little help to the chronically unemployed and the unemployable. Those in seriously depressed areas like Appalachia, minorities who face discrimination in getting and holding jobs, migrant workers, seasonal or occasional workers, and small farmers on marginal land do not benefit from job-related legislation, including minimum wage laws and Social Security. That these laws have benefited regularly employed workers is true; the average per capita disposable income has risen steadily since 1935, in both real and adjusted dollars,[11] but averages are misleading and obscure the fact that the percentage of the population receiving the lowest 20 percent of aggregate income has hardly changed in the past twenty-five years. The existence of "permanent poverty" was one of the discoveries of the 1960s.

The third type of measure is more likely to benefit middle- and upper-income families, who have some reserve for savings. Indirectly, it may benefit social work in that it makes contributions for charitable purposes tax deductible. But, with the steady rise in the cost of living, it has been almost impossible for most American families to save enough to maintain themselves without income for any prolonged period.

Social work is primarily concerned with the fourth type of program described by Dr. Burns. The Social Security Act, the various state and local welfare programs, and the development of public facilities to provide essential health, protective, and morale-building services are included here. Let us now analyze these measures in some detail. Because of the complicated local-state-federal division of responsibility, some programs will be found at every level, some limited to one or another. It is apparent, after threading one's way through the intricacies of these relationships, that they are time-consuming, extravagant, and overlapping. The federal programs were the last to emerge and are, in general, better organized and freer from unfair limitations than those at lower levels. We will discuss the federal programs, then the federally aided state programs, then state programs, and finally the local public welfare activities.

11. "Statistics on Demographic and Social Welfare Trends," *Supplement to the Encyclopedia of Social Work* (Washington, D.C.: NASW, 1973), p. 13.

FEDERAL PROGRAMS
OASDHI

The major federal program for income maintenance is that of Old Age, Survivors, Disability, and Health Insurance (OASDHI), which is administered by the Social Security Administration through its regional offices. This is the only Social Security program which is federally administered. Benefits are provided to fully insured workers age sixty-five or over (age sixty-two if somewhat smaller benefits are taken). Dependent wives or husbands over sixty-two and dependent children under eighteen (no age limitation on disabled children who became disabled before eighteen) are also covered under the retirement benefits. Monthly survivors benefits are paid to the dependent children of an insured worker who dies, and the widowed parent may receive benefits until the youngest child reaches eighteen (twenty-one if still in school). Widowed spouses of insured workers may receive reduced benefits at age sixty. Disability benefits may be paid to insured workers who become disabled at any age. A lump-sum death benefit is paid on behalf of all insured workers.

Participation in the insurance program is compulsory, with a few exceptions. The program is financed by a payroll tax assessed equally to employer and employee. The rate has gone up gradually and is scheduled to reach 6.05 percent in 1978. The self-employed pay approximately one and one half times the employee's rate, filing these returns with their federal income tax returns. Eligibility for benefits is dependent upon the number of quarter-years in which social security taxes have been paid into the employee's account, and the benefits are geared to be more liberal to lower-paid and older workers. Originally, the amount of income taxed was only $3,000, and the rate was only one percent. In recent years both the rate and the tax base have been increased; in 1974 it was 5.85 percent on the first $13,200 of earnings. Since there are no exemptions from this tax because of dependents, no deductions because of business expenses, and since the tax cannot be taken as a deduction from one's income, it is becoming much more of a burden to lower- and even middle-income wage earners than was originally anticipated. Even welfare recipients, whose earnings are such that they pay no income tax, have social security taxes withheld from their pay. While the return received in benefits will ultimately compensate low-paid wage earners, it is increasingly doubtful that upper-income taxpayers are similarly or proportionately benefited. Increasing resistance to Social Security taxes from this group may be anticipated.

Benefits are related to the average monthly wage (up to the tax ceiling for the years worked), but Congress has revised the formula upward several times in line with increases in the cost of living. The last such increase was a flat 20 percent across the board, which went into effect October 1, 1972. At the same time, Congress enacted a built-in "escalator clause," making increases automatic when the cost of living has gone up 3 percent in a calendar year. A wife who is fully insured may receive retirement benefits on her own account or her husband's, but not both. In July 1974, the minimum payment for an individual was $93.80, and the maximum was $304.90; the minimum family benefit was $144, and the maximum was $557. In July of 1974, the average retired worker with no dependents received $181 per month, an aged couple averaged $310 per month, and a widow with two children under eighteen collected $433 per month. The average disability payment was $199. (See footnote 17, page 86.)

One of the controversial features of the retirement provisions has been the limitation on earnings. It must be remembered that the original intent of the Social Security Act was to encourage older workers to retire from the labor force in a period of job scarcity. The original provisions therefore included a strict limitation on the amount that could be earned without disqualifying the recipient from receiving benefits as "retired." The inadequacy of the benefits, the usefulness of some older workers, and widespread recognition of the psychological advantages of continuing some sort of gainful employment after retirement have led to periodic liberalization of these restrictions. It should be noted that the restrictions apply to paid employment in a job covered by Social Security; there is no means test for receiving Old Age Insurance (OAI), eligibility for which depends only on quarters of coverage and the attainment of the specified age. Much of the criticism of Social Security, particularly the common objection that some people who receive it do not need it, stems from the failure of the critics to distinguish between the Old Age Insurance benefits of Social Security (OAI), for which all covered workers are eligible, and the Old Age Assistance payments (OAA), also provided for by Social Security, which depend on financial need.

In order to provide greater protection to the family of the younger breadwinner, eligibility for survivors benefits is attained after only six quarters of coverage within the three and a half years preceding the worker's death. Coverage includes the widow with dependent children, until the youngest child reaches eighteen. Benefits to the widow then cease until she reaches sixty, when she may be eligible for retirement benefits. The supposition is that in the intervening years she will have the opportunity for gainful employment which would qualify her for retirement benefits on her own account.

The occupations covered by Social Security have been steadily extended so that by 1968 virtually all employees and self-employed persons were covered. These include civil servants, railroad workers, members of the Armed Forces, employees of nonprofit organizations (since 1950), clergymen at their option, and doctors (since 1965).

As of January 1, 1973, there were 6,667 Social Security beneficiaries at least 100 years old.[12] The dean of these was Mr. Charlie Smith, who was captured by slave traders off the coast of Liberia and sold at the slave market at New Orleans in 1855. His birth date of July 4, 1842, was celebrated as usual in 1974.

In 1974 benefits totaling $4,300,000,000 were paid to approximately 29,966,000 beneficiaries. The effects of this mass program of income maintenance have been impressive, both in supporting the purchasing power of a large segment of the population and in preventing dependency. Unfortunately, however, older beneficiaries whose earnings records qualify them only for minimal benefits and who have no other income find Social Security benefits insufficient. In February 1972, 1,275,847 individuals were receiving both OAA and OAI.

Medicare

In 1965 Congress enacted Title XVIII as an amendment to the Social Security Act, providing two coordinated programs of health insurance for those over sixty-five. Plan A, which is financed on a self-supporting basis by an additional surcharge on the Social Security tax, provides for hospitalization and extended care as well as some home health care related to hospitalization. There are some deductible costs and some restrictions. All recipients of retirement benefits are covered. Plan B is a voluntary insurance plan for medical services, especially physicians' charges, which covers costs by monthly payments from enrollees with matching payments from general government revenues. More than 90 percent of those over sixty-five participate in Plan B, and the total expended for Medicare in 1973 was $9,584,000,000. Proposed increases in the amount charged to patients proved politically unpopular in 1973 and were not implemented, although increases

12. Figures supplied by Wallace S. Dooley, Deputy Press Officer, Social Security Administration, July 2, 1973. See fn. 17 concerning benefit figures this page.

since 1965 have doubled the cost of premiums to the recipient. Medicare is a federally administered program, but actual administration is carried out by fiscal intermediaries such as Blue Cross/ Blue Shield or a private insurance company.

SSI

Although the Social Security Administration was originally designed to administer payments only to those who had earned benefits through covered employment, its functions now cover some recipients not so qualified. In 1965, the so-called Prouty Amendment to the Social Security Act added to Old Age Insurance rolls those over seventy-two who were not receiving OAA, regardless of their work records. On October 30, 1972, President Nixon signed into law P.L. 92–603, which established a new Title XVI of the Social Security Act. This in effect replaced, as of January 1, 1974, the federally aided, state-administered program of Aid to the Aged, Blind, and Disabled (AABD) with a Federal Supplemental Security Income Program (SSI), to be administered by the Social Security Administration rather than by the various state departments of welfare. It provides a basic floor of $146 a month for a single person and $219 a month for a married couple which meets strict eligibility requirements (footnote 17, page 86).

Although, in theory, the introduction of SSI replaces the assistance programs for recipients, in actuality many states will be forced to supplement SSI with state funds. Additional requirements, such as the ineligibility of SSI beneficiaries for the Food Stamp program, will result in a decrease in benefits for recipients in those states now granting assistance at levels above the national average. Those benefiting will chiefly be recipients of monthly AABD grants below $100, mostly in southern and rural states. Any indication that this represents progress toward a demogrant approach to income maintenance (page 104) is negated by the limitation of eligibility for SSI to those categories of recipients considered by the general public as the "deserving" poor. Introduction of SSI was coupled with stricter quality control measures directed against the "undeserving" poor, needy families with children, and unemployed adults and with new limits on the amount of federal funds available to the states for the Aid to Families with Dependent Children (AFDC) program.

Other Federal Programs

There are other federal programs which employ social workers and carry on social welfare activities. The largest operation is that of the Veterans Administration (VA), which provides a range of programs for veterans and their dependents: pensions, allowances for education and vocational training or retraining, life insurance, inpatient and outpatient care in hospitals and other institutions, guarantees for housing and business purposes. The VA has, since World War II, been largely responsible for the increasing proportion of men in the profession of social work. There also are social welfare programs in the Bureau of Prisons, the Bureau of Indian Affairs, and the Office of Education, and there were social welfare programs in the now dismantled Office of Economic Opportunity.

FEDERALLY AIDED STATE PROGRAMS

Experience has shown that the most effective way for the federal government to operate in the welfare field is to provide money to the states on the condition that they meet minimum standards in their programs. A degree of consistency and adequacy is thus achieved without raising the sensitive issue of states' rights. This is the method used by the Assistance Payments Administration, which carries out the assistance provisions of the Social Security Act. While theoretically it is possible for a state not to participate in federally aided programs or to withdraw from such programs if it chooses, the substantial grants of federal money make the refusal most unlikely. The case of Newburgh, New York, in 1961 (where a local administration attempted to put into effect welfare restrictions not permitted by federal regulations), showed this clearly. The Newburgh plan was opposed by the New York State Board of Social Welfare, partly because it jeopardized about $200,-000,000 in federal payments to New York State.

The original Social Security Act covered three categories of recipients for public assistance: the aged, the needy blind, and dependent children. Assistance for those "permanently and totally disabled" was added in 1950. These assistance programs were carried out by the Assistance Payments Administration of the federal Department of Health, Education, and Welfare by means of grants-in-aid to states. As of January 1, 1974, no federal money is allotted to the AABD program, although there can be some federal financial support of services to adults. The figures in the following descriptions of federally aided state programs reflect the eligibility requirements and payment levels of 1973.

Old Age Assistance (OAA)

OAA is granted to persons sixty-five or over without sufficient income or other assets. States vary in other requirements; some require American citizenship, residence within the state for a specified number of years, and limitations on real estate holdings. In many states, older people may continue to live in their owned homes up to a certain valuation, on condition that the state take a lien on the property which will reimburse the state for funds expended when the recipient's estate is settled. It was originally thought that OAA would be a relatively temporary program and that OASDI[13] would eventually cover all older people. Such did not prove to be the case. Until 1950, benefits under OASDI were so low that OAA was needed to supplement them. Since then, as Social Security retirement benefits have increased, a smaller proportion of aged people have needed both programs.

A 1970 study of the OAA population[14] revealed that the typical OAA recipient was a white woman in her mid seventies, either widowed or unmarried, with less than a high school education, living in her own home (which is more likely to be rented than owned), despite some health problems. As compared with 1965, OAA recipients in 1970 were somewhat more likely to have worked, most often in some service capacity, and a significantly smaller number received financial support from children. At least 70 percent had lived in the same state for at least twenty years and had been receiving OAA for between five and six years. Circulatory diseases and/or arthritis were the most common physical ailments. In December of 1973, the average OAA payment was $76.15. The average is misleading, however; a state-by-state analysis shows thirty-three states with average payments under $75, while in Massachusetts the average was $112.71. There were 1,820,000 persons receiving OAA.[15]

Aid to the Needy Blind (AB)

Provision was made in the original Social Security Act for aid to the blind (AB) who were in financial need. Eligibility is dependent upon the states' definition of blindness, which may include severely impaired vision. Financial eligibility has been somewhat more liberal in this program than others, since the first $85 of earned monthly income was not figured in the determination of need, and special items for housekeeping service and other expenses have been allowed. The effect of the transfer of federal aid

13. The complete title of this program is OASDHI, but when referring to Social Security beneficiaries, the "H" is seldom included, for it refers to Medicare, which is paid on an "as-needed" basis.

14. *Findings of the 1970 OAA Study* (Washington, D.C.: Social and Rehabilitation Service [SRS], September 1972).

15. *Social Security Bulletin*, Vol. 37, No. 5 (May 1974), p. 56.

to the blind to SSI is to eliminate these special considerations, although states may, at their option, continue to supplement SSI payments to the blind at a higher level. Other requirements have included refraining from begging or selling pencils and the obligation to undergo medical or surgical treatment for blindness if recommended. Some states require vocational retraining if available.

The 1970 AB study reported that the average recipient was a white male, sixty years old, widowed or unmarried, with less than high school education, who lived in his own home or with a relative and had been receiving AB for at least six years. Only 8 percent were employed, and one third received OASDI benefits. There had been an increase over previous studies in the percentage of recipients blind from birth. The percentage confined to home or institution had dropped; 80 percent could get out of the home with the aid of a guide, device, or guide dog or unaided (25 percent).[16] In December 1973, there were 178,000 recipients, receiving an average monthly grant of $112.[17]

Aid to the Permanently and
Totally Disabled (APTD)

A program for the permanently disabled, along lines similar to that for the needy blind, was added to the Social Security program in 1950. The somewhat unfortunate title of this program should not be taken to imply that recipients are beyond hope. Rehabilitation is encouraged and is mandatory in some states. Beginning with 68,916 recipients in December of 1950, the program had grown to include 1,275,000 by December of 1973, when it was replaced by SSI. Average monthly payments had increased from $45.41 to $109.92. Like OAA and AB, APTD was a program for the individual recipient; if the breadwinner were disabled and receiving APTD, his family had to meet the eligibility requirements of other relief programs. For example, his disability qualified his dependent children for AFDC. Since many persons have had some work history before the onset of disability, many are eligible for disability benefits under OASDI. A typical situation would be a disabled worker whose disability benefits for himself and his dependents were inadequate to meet their needs; the family would then be eligible for AFDC, rather than for APTD. The average APTD recipient in 1970 was approximately fifty-five years old,

16. *Findings of the 1970 AB Study* (Washington, D.C.: SRS, September 1972).

17. Unless otherwise noted, benefit figures on pp. 81, 82, 83, 86, 90, 101 are supplied by James M. Brown, Asst. Press Officer, Social Security Administration, June 17, 1974.

female, white, widowed, separated or never married, living in her own home, having a disease of the circulatory system or some mental impairment.[18]

Eligibility for APTD excludes those with temporary or partial disabilities, and yet many such clients and their families could benefit greatly from inclusion and would often be better candidates for rehabilitation and services than most APTD recipients. The area of partial disability remains one of the gaps in our present income maintenance system. In most states, those having partial disabilities are eligible only for General Assistance (page 97), which is universally less adequate than one of the federally aided categories.

Combined Programs: AABD

It is apparent that the three categories of assistance described above have many characteristics in common: all recipients have relatively permanent conditions which account for their dependent status; all are long-time residents; most are in stable and predictable financial circumstances; and all belong to that group of welfare recipients who are considered "worthy," i.e., dependent "through no fault of their own." There is relatively little stigma attached to receiving assistance under one of these categories, and administratively they are not difficult to handle. In 1962 it became possible for states to combine these three categories into a single category, Assistance to the Aged, Blind, and Disabled (AABD). While services to all three categories have been combined, statistics have been reported separately. It is the combined category which was discontinued on January 1, 1974. Without federal grants-in-aid to maintain these assistance programs, it will be left up to the separate states to determine what, if anything, will be made available to supplement SSI payments to approach the minimum needs of blind, elderly, or disabled individuals.

Medicaid

Concern for medical services for those who cannot afford them has been slower to make itself felt in legislation than concern for other necessities. The traditional methods of providing essential services included individual arrangements with physicians and hospitals and general acceptance of the idea that well-to-do patients should pay more than the actual costs of services to cover the unpaid doctor and hospital bills of the indigent. Every physi-

18. *Findings of the 1970 APTD Study* (Washington, D.C.: SRS, September 1972).

cian carried a certain number of unpaid and unpayable bills on his books. The American Medical Association stoutly defended fee-for-service as the only acceptable model and protested any type of medical insurance or medical payments not based on fee-for-service. In actuality, the poor postponed indefinitely any dental and medical service which was not critical, and unless they were fortunate enough to live near a large teaching hospital with a range of outpatient clinics, there were no preventive services available to them.

Agitation for some type of universal health service dates back at least to the 1930s, when it was stimulated by the first national study of health costs, 1929–1931.[19] After World War II, specific bills were introduced into Congress, but the first assistance program on a national scale was not created until 1960, when Medical Assistance to the Aged (MAA) was inaugurated. In 1965, amendments to the Social Security Act set up Title XIX, commonly known as Medicaid, designed to replace all other programs of supplying medical services for assistance recipients, as well as for the "medically indigent," i.e., those whose incomes are considered adequate for everyday living costs but not adequate for medical costs. The program was optional for the states, but every state except Alaska and Arizona had joined it by the end of 1971. Costs have gone up much faster than predicted, indicating a great extent of unmet medical needs prior to the program, as well as the mushrooming costs of medical services. In 1971, costs exceeded $6,000,-000,000; this figure includes federal contributions to state programs on a sliding scale from 50 percent to 83 percent, depending on each state's per capita income.

In addition to the problems inherent in the present service delivery system for health care (to be discussed in Chapter 6), there are great difficulties in establishing a realistic eligibility level for receipt of Medicaid. Setting too high a standard results in runaway costs; setting too low a standard (which is much more likely) deprives of any assistance with medical costs those just above the cut-off point whose incomes obviously cannot cover their medical costs. In October 1972, the Social Security Administration reported letters from beneficiaries requesting that they not receive the 20 percent increase in benefits authorized by Congress, because this would put them over the Medicaid ceiling and make them worse off instead of better.

19. See I. S. Falk, C. Rufus Rorem, and Martha D. Ring, *The Costs of Medical Care* (Chicago: University of Chicago Press, 1933).

Aid to Families with Dependent Children (AFDC)

If age, disability, and illness represent acceptable causes for dependency, the trends of the 1970s indicate that being a child does not. Expenditures for the support of families with children are the largest and most resented items in the welfare budget, and charges of welfare abuse are largely leveled at parents receiving this support. There are a number of factors contributing to this resentment. Among these are: the inclusion of illegitimate children in the definition of "dependent," the increasing proportion of black families on the rolls, and the lack of support for families from absent or unemployed fathers.

Widows with young children have for centuries been considered worthy of aid; the early "mothers' pensions" were designed for them. Such programs were in effect in forty-six states before 1935, but, usually operating on a county basis, they were seldom adequate and often hedged with rigid requirements concerning moral and housekeeping conduct. The inclusion of dependent children under the assistance titles of the Social Security Act came at the urgent recommendation of the Children's Bureau, which had been concerned since its inception in 1912 about the customary practice of removing children from their own homes because of poverty. In 1909, at the invitation of President Theodore Roosevelt, a group of leading experts on child welfare was invited to the White House for the first White House Conference on Children. A conference has been called every ten years since, and they represent an invaluable source of information and planning in the interests of children. The first Conference was instrumental in bringing about the creation of the Children's Bureau; the third Conference, in 1930, adopted the famous Children's Charter, which included in its provisions the right of every child to a secure home, to health care, to schooling, and to the "guarding of his personality as his most precious right."[20]

The Social Security Act provided for federal grants-in-aid to those states setting up Aid to Dependent Children (ADC) programs on a basis similar to that of OAA. Originally, the age limit was set at sixteen unless the child remained in school; since 1957, the age limit has been eighteen. Dependency is defined as being "deprived of parental support or care by reason of the death, con-

20. See U.S. Children's Bureau, *The Story of the White House Conferences* (Washington, D.C., 1967).

tinued absence from the home, or physical or mental incapacity of a parent." The child must be living in the home of a reasonably close relative (carefully defined in the various state laws), and since 1950 the "caretaker" may also receive a monthly grant if financially eligible. In 1962 the title was changed to Aid to Families with Dependent Children (AFDC), and provision was made for the inclusion of children whose parents were chronically unemployed, under a program known as AFDC-UP. In 1972 only twenty-two states were granting AFDC-UP, and it was numerically significant in only seven of them. The program began in June 1936, with 521,716 recipients, and covered by November 1973 some 3,150,065 families, including 7,816,296 dependent children. (Re benefit figures here and below, see footnote 17, page 86.)

As was seen in the case of old age, there is theoretically a reciprocal relationship between insurance and assistance programs. As more and more children become covered by survivors' benefits, the number needing AFDC should decline. Instead, the number has risen dramatically: while the number of children receiving survivors' benefits under OASDI has increased sharply, from one per 1,000 of those under eighteen in 1940 to 56 per 1,000 in 1974, the comparable figures for AFDC are 20 and 118, and only 6 percent of AFDC families are also OASDI beneficiaries.

The increase in AFDC caseloads is largely comprised of families headed by an unemployed father and by fatherless homes often headed by an unmarried black mother. As Steiner puts it: "The popular image of the chief beneficiaries of public assistance has changed from that of old, respectable white people to that of young, immoral Negro men and women."[21] The typical AFDC family in 1971 was described in the Third Annual Report of the Department of HEW to the Congress as follows:

> The AFDC program is designed for families in trouble. While the eligibility factor of need is universal in all income maintenance programs, there are additional eligibility factors for AFDC that reflect the difficulties in which the families coming to the program find themselves. The children, to be eligible, must be deprived of parental support or care because of a parent's death, physical or mental incapacity, or continued absence from the home. Absence of a parent may be because of desertion, divorce, or separation or because the father and mother were never married. States may, if they wish, aid the children of unemployed fathers. Families receiving AFDC are not likely to have a father living in the home; if they do, they

21. Steiner, *Social Insecurity*, p. 7. © 1966 by Rand McNally and Company. Reprinted by permission of Rand McNally College Publishing Company.

face the pressure on family life of unemployment or parental physical or mental incapacity. In fact, only about 19 per cent of the families had a father in the home in 1971; the rest were eligible on the basis of the father's or mother's absence or death.

Although orphanhood presents a problem of some magnitude in the United States as a whole, it is currently a relatively minor problem in AFDC. Since the AFDC program began in 1935, there has been a gradual decline in the number of paternal orphans. In 1971, death of the father accounted for only 4.3 per cent of the caseload. Over the years, since the program began, the decrease in the number of orphans on AFDC has reflected the rise of other Federal programs, especially old-age and survivors insurance, to help care for fatherless children and the decline in the mortality rate among men at the age when they would be supporting dependent children. . . .

About 80 per cent of the families are headed by a single parent, usually the mother and usually because of the father's absence from the home . . . Almost half of the AFDC families now require assistance because of marital breakup, including desertion, separation, and divorce. More than a fourth of the families in 1971 were on AFDC because the mother and father were not married . . . Nearly half—48 percent—of the AFDC recipients were white. Blacks make up about 43 per cent of the recipients, and 8 per cent were of other races. The proportion of recipients living in metropolitan areas is growing, up 2 per cent since 1969. Almost 75 per cent now live in the metropolitan areas, usually the central city. The concentration in the cities continues a long-term trend that started at least as early as 1950; it reflects the national problem of urban poverty, brought about by a variety of causes, including the movement of poor rural people to the cities as the nature of the agricultural economy changed.

The program includes more young families than before, and the number of child recipients per family has declined . . . The percentage of children under age 6, the age group for whom it is most difficult to plan child care arrangements, rose slightly from 32.5 per cent in 1969 to 34.3 per cent. Families with only one or two children now represent 54 per cent of all families receiving aid . . . AFDC parents have a higher level of education now than before . . . Other studies, however, show that although the educational level of AFDC recipients is improving, it is also rising for the population generally and at a faster rate.

There is a small but encouraging decrease in the rate of illegitimacy. The length of time families remain in the AFDC

program is dropping . . . and the number receiving AFDC
for the first time increased from 59.7 to 65.8 per cent . . . A little more than 25 per cent of the mothers were either working,
seeking work, enrolled in a work or training program, or
awaiting enrollment . . . Overall, it is clear that many AFDC
families still face formidable barriers to self-sufficiency.[22]

The rising costs of the AFDC program have led to efforts on the
parts of both federal and state welfare officials to limit the size of
the caseload. The long-range solution would be to encourage
smaller families among the poor, since many families are driven
into poverty and dependence by having more children than the
wage-earner's income can support. However, it was not until 1966
that federal support for family planning services to welfare recipients was made available, and in 1971 such services were provided for only one fourth of AFDC mothers. The HEW guidelines
insist that no pressure be used, but indications are that pressure
is not needed, since most welfare recipients would be glad to have
smaller families. This is contrary to the prevailing myth that welfare recipients have more children deliberately, in order to receive
a larger grant. Study of the typical increase in the budget for an
additional child does not support such reasoning. The experience
of Mecklenburg County, North Carolina[23] is illuminating and
should dispel some myths. The number of children on AFDC in
that county decreased with the availability of family planning
services, at a time when the national caseload increased. A follow-
up study of adults from that county who had received AFDC as
children showed that 90 percent were self-supporting and that the
great majority were better educated and had better jobs than their
parents.[24] Such success stories should be better known.

Opponents of the AFDC program are unwilling to wait for family planning to reduce the burden. They would impose strict limitations on the caseload by setting up moral requirements against
illegitimacy and would deny welfare benefits to mothers who bear
out-of-wedlock children, especially more than one. In Louisiana,
22,000 children were suddenly denied AFDC benefits on the basis

22. *Services to AFDC Families* (Washington, D.C.: SRS, October 1972), pp. 20–27.

23. See *Family Planning: One Local Public Welfare Agency's Approach* (Washington, D.C.: Bureau of Family Services, n.d.).

24. John O. Lowery, Jr., *Study of the Current Status of Children Who Received
Public Assistance in Mecklenburg County, North Carolina in January, 1955* (Char-
lotte, N.C., 1967), mimeograph. See also *Facts, Fallacies and Failures* (New York:
Greenleigh Associates, 1960) for a careful study of the AFDC program in Cook
County, Ill.; and Joel Handler and Ellen J. Hollingsworth, *The Deserving Poor*
(Chicago: Markham Publishing Company, 1971) for a Wisconsin study.

that their homes were "unsuitable."[25] The "unsuitability" cri-
terion was applied almost exclusively to black homes. In April
1972, the California Social Welfare Board proposed that a mother
who bears a third illegitimate child should be deemed "morally
depraved" and be required to relinquish the child; unmarried
mothers who refused to name the father of the child within six
months were also to relinquish the child.[26] The illogic of reducing
the AFDC rolls by expanding the number of children in foster
care apparently eluded the Board. In some states, welfare officials
ordered visits at unexpected times, and "midnight raids" were
conducted to learn if there were men living with or visiting AFDC
mothers. The "man in the house" rule, which states that any man
found living in an AFDC home is presumed to be the father of the
children and therefore liable for their support, served as a device
for denying funds to unmarried mothers. Threats were made to
exclude from the budget second and third illegitimate children. As
MacIntyre says: "This would save welfare money, but the implicit
assumption that children going hungry will induce mothers never
to bear other out-of-wedlock babies to starve with them not only
is cruel but involves some questionable assumptions about human behavior."[27]

In an effort to lower costs by securing support from absent fathers, many departments require that unmarried mothers name
the fathers of their children so that court action may be taken to
secure support. On September 9, 1973, the *New York Times* reported that a three-judge federal court had upheld a Connecticut
law requiring unwed mothers to name the fathers of their children
in order to qualify for welfare payments. It is also routine to refer
to the "support unit" the names of mothers applying for AFDC
because of absent fathers and to require that those mothers sign
complaints against their husbands for nonsupport. How arresting
and jailing absent fathers results in lowered costs is hard to see.
Regulations requiring that "boyfriends" or stepfathers contribute
to the support of children in the home have been successfully attacked by Legal Aid in some states but continue in others.

25. See Winifred Bell, *Aid to Dependent Children* (New York: Columbia University Press, 1965) for discussion of the "suitable home" concept. See also Ronald
Chilton, "The Consequences of Florida's Suitable Home Law: A Study of Ineffective Intervention," *Welfare in Review*, Vol. 7, No. 5 (September–October 1969),
pp. 17–22.

26. *Time*, Vol. 99, No. 15 (April 10, 1972), p. 12.

27. Duncan P. MacIntyre, *Public Assistance: Too Much or Too Little?* (Ithaca, N.Y.:
New York State School of Industrial and Labor Relations, Cornell University,
1964), p. 75.

Since efforts to trace missing husbands do not always succeed, and since many AFDC fathers are in prison, in hospitals, or unemployable, recent efforts have been directed toward compelling AFDC mothers to work. The WIN (Work Incentive) Program requires that mothers of school-age children register for employment and participation in training or rehabilitation services as a condition of eligibility for assistance. This represents a reversal of the trend begun in 1935 to permit mothers to remain at home with their children to provide adequate child care. In order to compel mothers to work, adequate day care facilities must be provided, and they are inadequate or unavailable in many areas. The economy of forcing a mother of several small children to work in a low-paid job while her children receive day care at an average cost of more than $2,000 per child is questionable. There may well be benefits to small children in good day care programs, but economy in public funds is not one of them.

Contrary to the stereotype of the "welfare mother" as lazy, shiftless, and unwilling to take a job when one is offered, a recent study[28] indicates that even long-term welfare mothers continue to have a strong work ethic but are insecure about their ability to achieve job success. Their lack of skills and lack of confidence practically guarantee failure in a competitive job market. The Talmadge Amendments (1972), which compel AFDC mothers to work, will force them into the lowest paying, dirtiest jobs, which cannot be filled any other way. This will also result in large numbers of children being placed in inadequate day care facilities (often with other AFDC mothers as baby-sitters) and in school-age children being unsupervised for varying amounts of out-of-school time.

In addition to these methods of reducing costs, federal regulations have limited the federal funds available for services to this highly vulnerable group of clients. The Revenue Sharing Act placed a ceiling on federal financial participation in state welfare programs. Extremely strict cost accounting procedures have been adopted, and states which exceed the allowed margin of error will jeopardize their federal funds. States will be less likely to give applicants the benefit of any doubts under such stringent controls.

Assistance grants to AFDC families are often significantly lower than those to AABD recipients. In December of 1973, the average AFDC family of four received $227 a month. This is shockingly

28. Leonard Goodwin, *Do the Poor Want to Work?* (Washington, D.C.: Brookings Institution, 1972). See also Leonard Goodwin, "Welfare Mothers and the Work Ethic," *Monthly Labor Review*, Vol. 91, No. 8 (August 1972), pp. 35–37.

below the poverty level, and even by state standards, many of which are acknowledged to be inadequate, it represents an unmet need of at least $30 per month.

Other Federally Aided Programs

We have described the federally aided public assistance programs in some detail. The same principle (federal grants-in-aid to states which set up acceptable plans) applies also to the work of the Children's Bureau, which is part of the Social and Rehabilitation Service (SRS). This Bureau is responsible for the child welfare services, maternal and child health programs, and crippled children programs which were included in the Social Security Act. Some of these services antedate the Act. The Children's Bureau has been especially noted for its research activities on the needs of and the resources available for children and for its many excellent monographs. Its consultant service to states and localities and its fact-finding functions have made the Bureau a highly important factor in improving services to all children. The Children's Bureau allots funds to the states on a matching basis, in proportion to the child population of the state and in greater amounts for states with lower per capita incomes. Grants made to welfare and health departments which carry out approved programs are used for staff salaries and also for administrative costs. No money payments are made to clients.

Federal grants are also available to states from the United States Public Health Service and under the Mental Health Act of 1946. Some of these are specifically reserved for professional education; others may be used to provide clinical facilities. The activities of the federal government in the fields of housing and urban renewal also constitute an indirect method of income maintenance, since low-income families are often forced to make use of a disproportionate share of their income for housing.

The Rehabilitation Services Administration, one of the major divisions in the Social and Rehabilitation Service of the Department of HEW, operates on a policy of grants-in-aid to approved state plans for rehabilitation. All states operate rehabilitation programs, some in departments of education or health and many in "umbrella" human services agencies, as advocated in the Allied Services Bill introduced into Congress in 1972. State eligibility requirements differ. In some states, the applicant must meet the requirement of financial need, as well as the general requirement of having a disability which interferes with his earning a living but will not prevent him from being restored eventually to self-support. The largest group of those rehabilitated has orthopedic conditions, and the next largest has visual impairments. There is clear evidence of a loss of valuable time between the onset of the disability and the beginning of rehabilitation, and efforts should be directed toward earlier referral.

Unemployment Insurance (UI)

The unemployment insurance provisions of the Social Security Act, technically speaking, belong in the state-federal class, but in actuality the federal requirements are so broad and general as to exert no control over the state systems. No two state laws are alike; benefits range from $36 to $114 a week and the maximum duration of benefits from sixteen to thirty weeks. Federal participation in UI relates to the financing. The Social Security Act authorized a federal payroll tax, originally 3.1 percent of the first $3,000 earned by an employee, but it was raised in 1972 to 3.2 percent of the first $4,200 of taxable wages.

Since the hazards of unemployment were considered the employer's liability, no provisions were made for contributions by the employee. This is in contrast to the OASDI program, in which both employee and employer pay equal amounts. Since 1935, three states (Alabama, Alaska, and New Jersey) have added a provision to collect from employees also. Employers are allowed to pay 90 percent of the due tax to authorized state agencies, which must expend the funds solely for compensation payments. The 10 percent which is collected by the federal government is used to pay all administrative costs, and any balance remaining goes into a special fund from which states may borrow. Payments to applicants are made at employment offices, where the applicant simultaneously registers for work.

UI was designed to protect employees from unemployment owing to lack of work, not for voluntary resignation, discharge for misconduct, or going out on strike. State laws have been modified since 1935; now many states provide UI restricted by penalties, in the form of longer waiting periods for compensation for unemployment resulting from such personal causes. Since businesses bear widely differing rates of unemployment, those with a relatively stable labor force may take advantage of an experience-rating plan which reduces their tax obligation. However, there is some feeling that this latter plan leads to lower costs to the employer in periods of prosperity and to increased taxes in periods of recession.

It is apparent that greater uniformity and equity in the various state programs could be achieved by the federal government, since it pays the total cost of administration. The recessions of 1958 and 1960 demonstrated the inadequacy of benefit amounts and benefit periods in many states, and emergency appropriations were made to enable states to extend benefits beyond the stipulated time. Many authorities have recommended that the Bureau of Employment Security be more active in establishing optimum standards for state UI programs. The burden of unemployment falls more heavily on some states, particularly if the economic base of the state is narrow—the present plan allows for little spreading of the risk. At the same time, UI has been of substantial benefit to many industrial workers, and UI benefits have helped maintain purchasing power in periods of recession. UI is more effective for seasonal and short-term unemployment and relatively ineffective in areas of chronic depression and unemployment.

STATE AND LOCAL PROGRAMS

Some measure of uniformity in state programs is secured by federal reimbursement for assistance plans under the Social Security Act, although since January 1, 1974 and the inauguration of the Federal Supplemental Security Income Program (SSI), federal funding for the categories of assistance to the aged, blind, and disabled has ceased. Many states are continuing their own programs of supplementary assistance to these categories, using state and local funds only. It is still too soon to assess the operations of such state programs, though it is already apparent that they are diverse. States will continue to receive federal funds for a portion of the costs of AFDC and child welfare programs. In addition, some states support the entire cost of General Assistance (GA)—welfare programs for those who do not meet the eligibility criteria for categorical relief, chiefly the able-bodied unemployed or underemployed.

This "wastebasket category" of GA demonstrates the widest range of standards and administrative structures. There may be some state budgetary standard, but not necessarily. Professional staff may be used, or the first selectman or township supervisor may act as overseer of the poor. Relief may be provided in cash or "in kind"; the latter limits the independence and initiative of recipients by giving them no freedom to choose what they will eat or wear. Sometimes "vendor payment slips" are given the clients, made out to grocers, landlords, or fuel dealers. If they are able, men on General Assistance may be required to do maintenance work for municipal departments of public works. They may be required to prove that they have looked for work for a given number of hours per week. Regulations may militate against persons whose race, beliefs, or life style (e.g., long-haired hippies) displease conservative officials. Since local welfare personnel are not necessarily appointed on a merit system basis, their positions may in some cases depend on political influence. Residence qualifications may be drawn by localities to bar "invasions" by minority groups at a precarious economic level. Rehabilitation efforts are limited or nonexistent. When states participate in the funding of GA, there is more uniformity throughout the state than occurs when GA is entirely local.

The trend in most social services is away from local control, toward state control. Where there is increased interest in community-centered facilities (as in corrections and mental health, for example), such programs are usually state-supervised and state-financed. Other functions of the various state welfare departments may include: licensing of foster homes and of voluntary social agencies; supervision of adoptions; treatment programs for alcohol and drug abusers; rehabilitation programs for deaf, deaf-blind, or mentally retarded persons; services to the blind (which may include vocational rehabilitation, concessions for vending stands, and talking books service); registration of professional fund raisers; institutions for juvenile delinquents; legal services for the poor; provision of day care facilities; special services to veterans; services to Indians; and in-service training to state and local welfare personnel.

At least one third of the fifty states have established human services conglomerates, which bring together under a single administrator former departments of welfare, health, mental health, corrections, rehabilitation, child care, and others. These "umbrella agencies" are still too new for their impact to be measured. Many of the programs receive some federal funds, under a variety of legislative directives; many involve state and local funds only. It is evident that less and less initiative is being left to the localities for administration of social welfare programs, which is a move in the direction of more uniformity of standards and more adequate financing of these programs.

One of the most serious problems for state and local welfare departments is the presence in some communities of large numbers of low-paying jobs which do not enable even a full-time worker to support a family. Even with a minimum wage of $2.00 an hour, a forty-hour workweek does not yield take-home pay adequate to support most urban families struggling to meet the present cost of living. As middle- and upper-income families have moved to the suburbs, the central cities have been left with shrinking tax revenues and an increasing concentration of social problems in the low-income population which remains. Insisting that both parents work may mean that children will be improperly supervised. Insisting that teen-age children help support the family as soon as they are old enough may interrupt the education of those capable of continuing in high school and college. Yet the alternative is indefinite supplementation of inadequate wages, which has undesirable social and economic implications. Only extensive vocational education, retraining of unskilled and semi-skilled workers displaced by automation, and intensive preventive and rehabilitative efforts will be effective. The people caught in this economic bind comprise the group which tends to look on AFDC (for which the real or technical "desertion" of the father makes the mother and dependent children eligible) as a desirable alternative.

Because of the generally salutary effect of federal grants-in-aid on other relief programs, authorities have been suggesting for years that federal reimbursement be extended to GA. As it is currently being operated in most states, GA is less adequate, hedged about with more humiliating eligibility requirements, and less predictable than any of the categorical assistance programs. Federal support of all welfare programs, which could be achieved by abolishing categories and basing eligibility for all assistance simply on need, would result in economies of administration and accounting. However, the 1972 Amendments to the Social Security Act move in the opposite direction. The federal floor provided by SSI and the end of federal support for AABD leave states free to discontinue such categorical programs. With AFDC the only program for which federal reimbursement exists, GA will, in most states, become even less adequate and more regressive. The recent federal mandate of separation of income maintenance from services also effectively isolates GA recipients from receipt of services, unless the state system plan includes them.

VOLUNTARY AGENCIES

Our focus on the public programs of income maintenance should not minimize the indirect contributions of the voluntary (or private) agencies, which have as their ultimate goal the improved social functioning of individuals in our industrial, urban, mobile society. Child guidance and mental health clinics help troubled individuals to achieve a more stable and rewarding economic future. Marital counseling strengthens family unity and guards against the social and financial costs of disrupted homes. Preventive medical care is an economy in the long run. Because about nintey-five cents of every welfare dollar is used for direct income maintenance, it is easy to overlook the crucial importance of the five cents that maintains the service agencies. The money value of preventive work in health has been convincingly demonstrated; no less real, if less adequately documented, is the money value of preventive social work services.

Separation of services from income maintenance in the public welfare programs may be expected to increase the work of the voluntary agencies, since there is now a strict financial limitation on the extent to which services can be provided by public agencies to those not already on assistance payments. Thus, public agencies will be referring more clients to private agencies, but what effect, if any, separation will have on the payment for these services is still not clear. The boundaries between voluntary and public agencies have been blurred in recent years, both by the public agencies' purchase of services from the voluntary agencies and by direct subsidies in public funds to voluntary agencies. It seems apparent that such joint financing will be subjected to closer cost accountability in the immediate future. Under the 1974 budget cuts, all federal support for mental health centers, for example, is scheduled to be phased out completely by 1980. Whether or not communities and states will make up the lost funds is a serious question.

DEFICIENCIES IN THE PRESENT SYSTEM OF INCOME MAINTENANCE

Present programs of income maintenance in the United States are inadequate in both amount and coverage to keep a substantial portion of the population above the poverty level. Assuming the poverty level at a figure of $3,600 income a year for an urban family of four (certainly below the minimum level in a period of inflation), at least one eighth of the population in 1971 was living in poverty; the figures are substantially higher for black people, the elderly, and the poorly educated. Almost all recipients of public assistance are kept in poverty by inadequate assistance grants, which average well below the poverty level. In 1971, for example, the average budgeted need for a family of four on AFDC was $261 a month ($3,132 a year), and the recognized unmet need was

$29.72 a month.[29] Corresponding amounts of unmet need per month for other programs in 1971 were: OAA, $3.86; APTD, $5.30; AB, $8.45.[30]

Current budgeted amounts in the SSI program are $146 monthly for single individuals and $219 for aged couples, with a maximum $20 "disregard" (other income which may be excluded from eligibility determination), which is significantly below the welfare grants of many states. It is obvious that assistance payments and/or SSI are inadequate to raise families above poverty.

Social insurance schemes are somewhat more adequate for those who have worked steadily at the maximum tax base or above it, although it is necessary for such wage earners to have supplemental retirement plans or private insurance to avoid a drastic decrease in the standard of living. A wage earner whose average yearly earnings were $2,660, for example, can expect a retirement income at sixty-five of $181, or $270 if a dependent spouse is also covered.[31] However, since all social insurance is work-related, it does little good for those with no work history or with sporadic or casual work records. Young people growing up in urban ghettos or in areas of chronic unemployment, such as Appalachia, have little hope of acquiring Social Security coverage.

Such indirect income maintenance programs as subsidized housing, school lunch programs, Medicaid, and Food Stamps are not universally available or have upper eligibility limits far below the poverty line, so that large numbers of the poor are excluded from participation. On May 6, 1973, the *New York Times* reported that the number of persons eligible for "food assistance" is estimated to be 25,000,000 to 30,000,000 but that only 15,000,000 participate in any food assistance program.[32]

Unemployment during 1973 averaged 5 percent; among Viet Nam war veterans, blacks, and teen-agers it ran much higher. In addition, the incomes of the working poor, many of whom are ineligible for any type of assistance, continued to fall below any realistic poverty figure. In 1972, the Bureau of Labor Statistics set a figure of $7,183 annual income, as a realistic minimum level of living in New York City and $6,960 as a national urban average.

29. *Findings of the 1971 AFDC Study* (Washington, D.C.: SRS, 1972), Part II.
30. *Trend Report* (Washington, D.C.: SRS, October 1972), pp. 20–25.
31. For source of benefit figures, see fn. 17, p. 86.
32. See "Twelve Million Still Hungry," *New York Times*, May 6, 1973, which summarizes a report issued by the staff of the Senate Select Committee on Nutrition and Human Needs.

These figures would put almost two thirds of inner city families below the poverty level.[33] Yet the maximum budgeted requirement for an urban family of four in New York City in 1971 was $312.89 a month ($3,755 a year),[34] only a little more than half the Bureau's figure. In other words, those working but earning over $3,755 a year would be ineligible for assistance except for extraordinary circumstances, such as a catastrophe. For those who surpass a $5,000 annual income in New York State, eligibility for Medicaid ceases. Most other state levels for cut-off of Medicaid are much lower.

Even though assistance payments do not serve to keep the unemployable, the unemployed, and the underemployed out of poverty, the stigma attached to the receipt of welfare keeps many eligible people from applying for even that minimal income. While farmers accept a variety of government subsidies, homeowners utilize FHA assistance with mortgages, students apply for loans and grants, and Small Business Administration aid is considered respectable, only public assistance carries with it so negative a connotation that people will remain in distress rather than go through the often humiliating application process.[35] Many public welfare departments make information about eligibility for various public programs hard to obtain and deny assistance on technicalities unrelated to current need. Restrictions on suitability of homes, on the social lives of recipients, on work requirements, and on owning property or a car undoubtedly keep off the welfare rolls many whose incomes are below the eligibility level in their states. We cannot delude ourselves into believing that either the social insurance or the public assistance payments in the current income maintenance system solve the problems of poverty.

ALTERNATIVES TO THE PRESENT SYSTEM OF INCOME MAINTENANCE

Inadequate assistance grants and continuing high rates of unemployment indicate that present systems of income maintenance are inadequate to solve the problem of poverty. To attempt to solve so perennial and severe a problem will obviously involve a

33. William Spring, Bennett Harrison, and Thomas Vietorisz, "Crisis of the *Under*employed—In Much of the Inner City 60% Don't Earn Enough for a Decent Standard of Living," *New York Times Magazine*, November 5, 1972, pp. 42 ff.

34. *Findings of the 1971 AFDC Study* (Washington, D.C.: SRS, 1972), tables 52, 53.

35. See David J. Kallen and Dorothy Miller, "Public Attitudes Toward Welfare," *Social Work*, Vol. 16, No. 3, (July 1971), pp. 83–90.

twofold approach: 1) provision of jobs for those capable and desirous of working; and 2) provision of transfer payments, from those whose capacity for self-support is adequate to their responsibilities to those whose capacity for self-support is inadequate. Let us consider suggested approaches to both of these.

EMPLOYMENT PROGRAMS

The provision of jobs or job training for the unemployed presents many difficulties. There is inherent in the economy of the United States a percentage of unemployment owing to frictional or structural changes; much of this is short-term and is caused by seasonal factors, such as retooling in factories, shortages of raw materials, mobility of plants and personnel. During the course of any year, according to the Bureau of Labor Statistics, some 11,-000,000 persons have at least one period of unemployment. The great majority of them return to the labor force within the year. The "hard-core" unemployed, many of whom have given up looking for work, fall outside of this group. It is obvious that they have little chance of competing with the much larger group of people who have the skills and mobility to be called back to their old jobs or hired in new ones.

The alternatives are training or retraining the hard-core unemployed to make them and their skills more competitive. Whether such training is done under public or private auspices, it will obviously be a public cost. Small-scale attempts to do this (such as in Detroit auto plants after the riots) have had mixed results. An intensive nationwide program would be considered prohibitively costly by a tax-conscious public. An additional difficulty is that many of the poor are already employed at low-paying jobs. Upgrading their skills would involve subsidizing them and their families during the training period with little guarantee of offering them better jobs when their training was finished. Opposition from labor unions and the effects of racism would be contributing obstacles.

A more fundamental problem is that many of those who are not physically disabled carry social disabilities which make them difficult to place in jobs. They are likely to have poor health, poor education, indebtedness, and attitudes of defeatism and self-depreciation. Many have prison records or have been in trouble with the police. Many have never been regularly employed or have been unemployed for so long that they would have difficulty in adhering to regular work schedules.

Those who would like to solve runaway welfare costs by making welfare recipients work overlook how few welfare recipients not already working are employable. HEW reports that as of October 1971, less than one percent of welfare recipients were unemployed males. Of mothers on welfare, 40 percent were needed at home to care for small children; 22 percent were employed or involved in work-training programs; 4 percent would need extensive medical or rehabilitative services to become employable; and 34 percent might become employable if transportation, day care, job training, and other supportive services were available. As a whole, children, the aged, and the disabled comprise more than 85 percent on welfare rolls.[36]

There are serious manpower shortages in many of the social services, and it has been suggested that one approach to greater employment would be to prepare welfare clients for jobs in hospitals, child care centers, home health services, and other service organizations.[37] However, it is doubtful if these agencies, already hard pressed for funds, could absorb all those who need work or that the people so hired would be psychologically suited to service careers. Other types of made-work would be highly expensive and would consist of dead-end jobs with few built-in incentives toward careers. No employment program, however well planned, deals adequately with those who cannot leave home.

GUARANTEED INCOME PROGRAMS

Basically, guaranteed income programs may be designed in one of two ways: those which would make a certain amount available to everyone, but would tax it back from upper-income individuals; and those supplementing other income and therefore dependent on some type of eligibility or means test. The first type (also called the "social dividend") would distribute to all families, rich or poor, an amount sufficient to raise them out of poverty (or up to some designated level). Such programs are currently more often designated for certain groups in the population (children under eighteen or those over sixty-five) and are known then as "demogrants," since receipt is dependent on some demographic characteristic. Many countries have such plans. If these stipends are considered taxable income, they will be taxed back from the nonpoor. Even so, the costs would be enormous. The short-lived Family Assistance Plan (FAP), which was proposed by President Nixon in 1969 but failed to pass the Senate in 1971, would have

36. *Welfare Myths vs Facts* (Washington, D.C.: SRS, n.d.).

37. See Frank Riessman and Hermine L. Popper, *Up From Poverty: New Career Ladders for Nonprofessionals* (New York: Harper & Row, 1968).

been a first step in this direction. It has been succeeded by the Federal Supplemental Security Income Program (SSI), which will freeze recipients below the poverty level, owing to its rigorous means tests. There seems little likelihood that any social dividend program will be enacted in the foreseeable future.

Of means-related programs, Robert Harris describes and analyzes two types: income supplement programs and a negative income tax.[38] The first involves stipends to make up the difference between a family's income and some socially defined level of minimum family income. Depending on where that level was set, such a program could eliminate or greatly decrease poverty and could remove many of the present disadvantages of categorical relief, particularly for the family in which the father is in the home but underemployed, not now eligible for AFDC. The difficulty is with the work incentive issue. Such a plan would make it unprofitable to work at earnings lower than the guarantee and could therefore discourage work efforts. By "disregarding" a sliding percentage of earnings, some work incentive can be built in, but this would involve paying subsidies to earners significantly above the poverty level. Costs would be very high.

The negative income tax proposes that families with unused tax exemptions receive a refund from the Treasury Department, rather than apply for welfare and be stigmatized. At present exemption levels, such a program would not meet minimum needs and would not solve the problems of poverty. In some respects, the new SSI program is similar to a negative income tax. None of the plans suggested takes into account the in-kind benefits of Medicaid, housing assistance, and food stamps, which usually are received automatically by welfare recipients and which do supplement the present admittedly inadequate cash assistance grant.[39]

The fear of "pauperizing" welfare recipients—causing them to prefer receiving welfare to working—goes back to medieval times and has been dealt with historically by making the receipt of welfare repellent and the eligibility requirements stringent. Opponents of welfare reform are much concerned lest programs reward nonworkers more than workers. In an effort to test just how fam-

38. Robert Harris, "Selecting a System of Income Maintenance for the Nation," *Social Work*, Vol. 14, No. 4 (October 1969), pp. 5–13.

39. See Henry J. Aaron, *Why Is Welfare So Hard to Reform?* (Washington, D.C.: The Brookings Institution, 1973) for a detailed explanation of these proposals, in-kind benefits, and work incentive issues. See also U.S. Congress, Joint Economics Committee, *Income Transfer Programs: How They Tax the Poor*, Paper No. 4, 1972, and *Issues in Welfare Administration*, Paper No. 5, 1973, both in the series *Studies in Public Welfare* (Washington, D.C.: Government Printing Office).

ilies would react to receiving income supplements, the Office of Economic Opportunity and HEW sponsored a number of programs of supplementing income at various levels of guarantee and break-even points (the level of earnings where benefits stop).[40] The oldest of these experiments, begun in 1968, took place in New Jersey and Pennsylvania. Preliminary findings indicate that the 650 families involved spent the supplemental money on necessities and did not lose the incentive to work.[41] The cost of the program was approximately $5,000,000, not an excessive amount in view of the hidden costs of maintaining poverty.

While many of the costs of poverty are paid directly by the poor, poverty ultimately is costly for society. Children who are inadequately fed and housed are more likely to suffer irreversible brain damage,[42] to have less adequate education and an impoverished family life. In a culture which values materialism and success, the poor are blocked from achievement, and their self-esteem is irreparably damaged. When the handicaps of poverty are compounded by racism, the costs to society are still higher. In addition to direct costs for public services such as welfare, health, police, and housing, society loses the potential contribution of those living in poverty.[43] Attempts to "save money" by decreasing welfare expenditures shifts some of the burden to recipients but leaves a larger burden in indirect costs or in direct costs to other public services. In a society in which all other government handouts are looked upon as a right and are justified in view of their stimulus to productivity, income maintenance subsidies are stigmatized and their recipients degraded.

THE ROLE OF SOCIAL WORK IN INCOME MAINTENANCE PROGRAMS

The budget cuts for fiscal year 1974 and the new federal regulations mandating separation of services from income maintenance both project a greatly reduced role for professional social work in income maintenance programs for the immediate future. Educational requirements for staff have been lowered, and the assump-

40. See Arnold J. Katz, "Four Income Maintenance Experiments, *Social Work*, Vol. 18, No. 2 (March 1973), pp. 4, 111–113.

41. "Negative Income Tax Paid to Poor; Cassandra's Wrong, Experiment Shows," *Rutland Herald*, March 26, 1973, p. 1.

42. See Roger Hurley, *Poverty and Mental Retardation* (New York: Random House, 1969).

43. See Dorothy B. James, *Poverty, Politics, and Change* (Englewood Cliffs, N.J.: Prentice-Hall, 1972), especially Chapter 6, "The Cost of American Poverty," which contains brief case histories of representative poor individuals.

tion that casework counseling was the treatment of choice for the problems associated with dependency (as indicated in the 1962 Amendments to the Social Security Act and in SRS support of social work training until 1973) is no longer held. The function of "income maintenance specialist" is not seen as a social work task but as an essentially clerical and accounting one. The new role of "social services worker" primarily includes being a case manager, providing information about resources and directive counseling around some specific goal. Instead of viewing the services worker as a professional specialist, the new separated system sees the services worker as accountable to quality control auditors in the bureaucracy. Emphasis will inevitably be laid on provision of those services which have visible, especially financial, pay-off, which may well mean that under pressure, services workers will be limited to working with the most promising clients, rather than those most in need.

Training for those who will be filling positions on both sides of the separated system of income maintenance and services should be geared toward the present realities of the system. Returning to the social worker roles outlined in Chapter 1 (see pages 22–23), it seems apparent that the roles of broker, mobilizer, teacher, and behavior changer will be paramount. Emphasis will be laid on client change rather than on client comfort. Advocacy and outreach roles will be discouraged or even forbidden to workers inside the system and will have to be taken over by other individuals or groups. With computerized data and stricter accountability procedures, information processing will assume increasing importance and will offer job opportunities for some students, but not for those whose interests lie in direct service to clients.

Although these changes were not made in consultation with the social work profession and may seem, at first glance, to rule out social techniques altogether, closer scrutiny will demonstrate that the basic premises of social work can be applied in these newer roles. Respect for the individual, protection of his rights, support in his difficulties, sincere interest in seeing him operate more effectively and feel better about himself, skillful listening to his account of his situation, self-awareness and self-discipline in the interests of serving the client—all these skills and attitudes will continue to be highly relevant and useful.

Social work's understanding of the dynamics of human behavior, of how people meet their own needs through their relationships with each other, of self-defeating behavior and the motivations behind it can be applied in the separated services, and those workers with skill and knowledge will be more effective in their dealings with clients and with fellow workers. It will take ingenuity and new skills to apply social work techniques to enlarged caseloads and decreased time, but these problems are not insoluble. The tragic move would be for professional social work to abandon income maintenance and public services programs, as the COS did in the 1890s, rather than take whatever advantages it can find in the separated system to serve clients, enlarge public understanding, and promote justice.

ADDITIONAL REFERENCES

Conkin, Paul R., *FDR and the Origins of the Welfare State* (New York: Thomas Y. Crowell Company, 1967). The personality of Franklin D. Roosevelt and how it shaped his legislative proposals, with a vivid photograph-essay on the Depression.

Howell, Joseph T., *Hard Living on Clay Street* (New York: Doubleday, Anchor, 1973). A portrait of the drab world of blue-collar families in Washington, D.C. by a participant-observer.

Marmor, Theodore K., *The Politics of Medicare* (Chicago: Aldine Publishing Company, 1973). The history of the evolution, the political strategies, and the enactment of Title XVIII of the Social Security Amendments of 1965.

Okum, Arthur M., ed., *The Battle Against Unemployment* (New York: W. W. Norton, 1972). A collection of articles by leading economists on fiscal policies and the experience of the nation under the Employment Act of 1946. The essay by Elliott Liebow, "The Human Costs of Unemployment," is particularly relevant to social workers.

Owings, W. A., *Provision for the Many: Perspectives on American Poverty* (Hinsdale, Ill.: The Dryden Press, 1973). Contemporary poverty viewed in a historical perspective, together with a critique of proposals for anti-poverty programs.

Towle, Charlotte, *Common Human Needs* (Washington, D.C.: National Association of Social Workers, 1965). A reissue by the NASW of a monograph first issued in 1945 by the Federal Security Agency for public assistance staff, which was withdrawn from circulation because of congressional fears of possible subversive intent during the McCarthy period.

Trattner, Walter I., *From Poor Law to Welfare State: A History of Social Welfare in America* (Riverside, N.J.: The Free Press, 1974). A review of the tradition behind modern social work which provides a base for planning future social action.

Wadel, Cato, *Now Whose Fault Is That?* (St. John's, Newfoundland: The Institute of Social and Economic Research, 1973). An analysis by a social anthropologist of the implications of welfare policy in a rural Newfoundland community.

services to families

FAMILY FUNCTIONS AND FORMS

The family is the central institution in American culture. Popular impressions that the American family is in a state of rapid disintegration are not borne out by the facts. Divorce statistics and illegitimacy rates are the most frequently cited indications of family instability. While the divorce rate is somewhat higher today than it was a decade ago, it is substantially lower than in 1946 when ill-advised war marriages were being terminated. Comparing the number of divorces granted in a given year with the number of marriages occurring in the same year is misleading, since the divorces dissolved marriages which had been contracted in many preceding years. A more accurate statistic is obtained by comparing the number of divorces granted in any year with the total number of married couples, since that is the population at risk. In 1971, for example, there were 768,000 divorces and 2,196,000 marriages, a ratio of approximately 1:3. These divorces, however, were from a total of 45,443,000 married couples, a ratio of 1:64.[1] The publicity given to alternatives to marriage gives them undue importance. The great majority of adults live in families, and most children are born and raised in a family setting. Even when families have been broken by divorce, subsequent remarriage usually reestablishes a family situation for the children. Accurate figures on illegitimacy are difficult to se-

---

1. U.S. Bureau of the Census, *Statistical Abstract of the United States: 1972* (Washington, D.C., 1972), pp. 39, 50.

cure, but there is good evidence that it is increasing. Up from an estimated rate of 37.9 per 1,000 population in 1940, illegitimate live births were estimated at 96.9 per 1,000 population in 1968.[2] The increased availability of oral contraceptives and liberalized abortion laws in many states may be expected to decrease both divorce and illegitimacy rates considerably, adding to their un- reliability as indicators of family disorganization.

Where, in former years, illegitimate children were frequently released for legal adoption, thereby becoming part of unbroken families, increasingly, today, unmarried mothers keep their chil- dren and raise them alone or with the help of other relatives. There has been growing concern about the one-parent family, both as to its weakness and vulnerability and to its functional aspects in some cultures of poverty.[3] Most of the one-parent families avail- able for study are in poverty or exhibit some form of social pa- thology, so little is known of the one-parent family as a form of family life among the affluent or those not known to welfare, corrections, or child guidance agencies.

One persistent difficulty encountered in services to families is the assumption that the traditional middle-class version of the nuclear family is the "normal" family form and that deviations from it are pathological. The evidence shows that deviations are increasingly common and that the traditional view of the husband as chief supporter and the wife as full-time homemaker is no longer tenable. In 1973, more than half the married women in the U.S. were working; three fourths of working women have either no husband or a husband whose income is under $7,000 a year.[4] This movement of women into the labor force is primarily owing to economic factors and only secondarily a consequence of the "women's liberation" movement. Equality of employment is still

2. *Supplement to the Encyclopedia of Social Work* (Washington, D.C.: National Association of Social Workers [NASW], 1973), p. 9. Illegitimate live births are reported by the Census and by the Division of Vital Statistics of the U.S. Department of Health, Education, and Welfare as "per 1,000 unmarried female population aged 15 to 44 years."

3. See, for example, the widely criticized "Moynihan Report": Daniel P. Moy- nihan, *The Negro Family: The Case for National Action* (Washington, D.C.: U.S. Department of Labor, 1965), describing the matri-centric black family in urban ghettos. See also John H. Bracey, Jr., August Meier, and Elliott Rudwick, eds., *Black Matriarchy: Myth or Reality?* (Belmont, Ca.: Wadsworth Publishing Com- pany, 1971). For a review of thinking and a bibliography on one-parent families, see Andrew Billingsley and Jeanne M. Giovannoni, "Family, One-Parent," *Ency- clopedia of Social Work, 1971* (New York: NASW, 1971), pp. 362–373.

4. *New York Times*, July 29, 1973, p. IV–4; see also Irene Cox, "The Employment of Mothers as a Means of Family Support," *Welfare in Review*, Vol. 8, No. 6 (November–December 1970), pp. 9–17.

far from being realized, in spite of official bans on discrimination because of sex.

Equalization of opportunity and greater ability to control reproduction have altered the traditional relationship between the sexes, and this has resulted in a variety of modifications of the traditional family form (the childless family, the second-career family, the dual-work family, the remarried family) and in variant forms (the single-parent family, the unmarried couple with a child, the commune). At the same time, forms which once were the norm for all of society persist in some ethnic traditions (the extended family and the three-generation family, for example).[5]

Obviously, the traditional, middle-class family form does not automatically guarantee a stable and secure family life for all members. There is ample evidence of the many stresses placed on the small, conjugal family in a mobile urban society. Programs of all types are greatly needed to strengthen and improve family life. The point is that, in spite of all its inadequacies and even though institutionalized patterns of family living have changed and will continue to change in response to changing social conditions, there is no possibility that the family will be abandoned as the institution which carries basic responsibility for some socially essential functions which cannot be carried out under any other auspices.

The functions of family life are less subject to change than the forms. These functions include the provision of love and protection, the meeting of emotional needs, the opening of opportunities for development of the potentialities of family members, and the mediating between family members and the pressures of the larger society.[6] Basic personality formation of children is carried out by the family, and marriage partners utilize each other and often their children to work out their own unresolved personality problems.

Studies of shifting family functions emphasize the decreased role of the family as an economic unit. This emphasis refers to the economic functions of production only and ignores the continuing vital importance of the family as a consumption unit. Other functions which once were mainly carried out by the family include protection, education, religious observance, recreation,

5. See Marvin B. Sussman, "Family," *Encyclopedia of Social Work, 1971,* pp. 329–340. See also Sheila K. Johnson, "Three Generations, One Household," *New York Times Magazine,* August 19, 1973, pp. 24–31.

6. See Patricia O'Connell, "Developmental Tasks of the Family," *Smith College Studies in Social Work,* Vol. 42, No. 3 (June 1972), pp. 203–210.

vocational preparation, and the preservation of health, most of which are now performed by outside agencies, often governmental. Yet the effect of family influences remains a critical one even in these areas of life; the attitudes of the parents toward education, career choice, religion, and health have a pronounced effect on their children.

The two main societal functions which the family retains in our culture are procreation and early socialization. No acceptable substitute for carrying out these vital responsibilities can be imagined. While the presence of the father in the home may not be essential for the physical process of birth and early child care, his presence is needed if children are to grow up with a realistic view of a world peopled by both men and women. The effeminizing of boys in some suburban communities where men are absent most of the time and boys have little experience with adult males in school is of concern to many child care experts. The continued absence of a father figure is equally, if not so obviously, difficult for female children.[7]

It is precisely in these less tangible aspects of family life that personality factors loom so large. If the family is held together by economic production, with its shared responsibilities and mutual obligations, interpersonal frictions and clashes do not drastically undermine its solidarity. In the contemporary American family, however, which is held together by desire for personality fulfillment, gratification of affectional needs, and emotional security, friction between members is a serious threat to family solidarity. Because of our increased mobility, friends and relatives are less available to help compensate for failures within the family to meet the emotional needs of its members. This relative isolation places a greater strain on the bonds which unite the family. The need to lessen tensions—marital, parental, and sibling—is correspondingly greater.[8]

Child rearing is of critical importance in a democracy. We know that no unit of society can function effectively unless the individuals who compose it are responsible, disciplined, and well socialized. Socialization, by its very nature, demands that the individual be willing and able to subordinate his personal wishes to the values of his society. In a police state, a surface conformity to law

7. See E. Mavis Hetherington, "Girls Without Fathers," *Psychology Today*, Vol. 6, No. 9 (February 1973), pp. 47–52.

8. For an excellent discussion of family functioning, see Nathan W. Ackerman, M.D., *The Psychodynamics of Family Life* (New York: Basic Books, 1958). See also Ross Speck and Carolyn Attneave, *Family Networks* (New York: Random House, 1973), for a novel approach to strengthening support for families in crisis.

may be imposed on the unwilling by force and fear; in a democracy, conformity depends on the effective internalizing of social values in the character structure of the individual in the formative years. Since renouncing or postponing personal gratification in favor of social acceptability is a painful process for the child, it can be learned only in a warmly accepting situation, in which the deprivation is offset for the child by parental approval. The child who conforms out of fear of parental anger is not internalizing the mores but setting up a perpetual conflict between self-interest and fear of being caught. No democratic society can continue if too large a proportion of its members is primarily motivated by self-interest.

FAMILY CASEWORK

It follows, therefore, that today's family is a somewhat less stable institution attempting to carry out increasingly vital functions and that society has a stake in every effort to strengthen the family for its tasks. Family casework is primarily dedicated to this purpose, although social group work and community organization have as part of their basic goals the improvement of family relationships, and all social welfare programs are directly or indirectly involved in making it possible for parents to rear children in better, more stable, and safer surroundings. We are coming to see that communities cannot afford "the high cost of unhappy living."[9] By impairing the effectiveness of all the family members in all their social roles, family disruption not only costs the community in the short run but also tends to be self-perpetuating. Children from unhappy and strife-torn families find it more difficult to establish satisfying marriages and homes for their own children. Family casework is a preventive service, in the fullest sense of that term.

Family casework has traditionally been carried out in family service agencies, the direct descendants of the Charity Organization Societies (COS) of the late nineteenth century and the original source of the method of social work known as social casework. Much of what we now understand about how people behave and how people can learn to behave in more satisfying ways was learned by caseworkers in family service agencies, and intensive work with individuals and families still remains a primary focus of such agencies.[10]

9. See footnote 67, page 160, and the case study on pages 160–161.

10. The May 1973 issue of *Social Casework* presents a series of papers celebrating the fiftieth anniversary of the publication of Mary Richmond's *What Is Social Casework?*, which discusses many of the issues confronting family agencies.

However, it would be a mistake to think that family casework is limited to such voluntary agencies. Promotion of better family life is a goal of public social services, of mental health centers, of school social work, of protective services, and often of corrections. There is increasing interest in moving beyond the traditional boundaries of agency function, toward interdisciplinary and co-operative efforts which will utilize a variety of personnel and develop innovative approaches to meeting family needs. The classic fifty-minute office interview with a graduate social worker has given way both to a range of techniques (from family therapy for which the therapist may move into the family home for a weekend marathon therapy session to encounter sessions with no profes-sional present) and to a range of therapists (including volunteers, paraprofessionals, and professionals at every level of training and preparation). The Office of Economic Opportunity has used sub-professionals as Family Development Aides in the Head Start pro-gram. Family counseling may be carried on in a family service agency, a sectarian agency, a mental health clinic, a public wel-fare department, or by a private social work practitioner. Rather than describe the functions of a family service agency, therefore, it is more realistic to consider some of the problems confronting families in the 1970s and what the objectives and goals are that the family and the social worker, whatever his base of operations, should develop together.

THE EFFECTS OF POVERTY ON FAMILIES

All family functions are hindered and family problems compli-cated by the disadvantages associated with poverty. In the ab-sence of the social supports of adequate income, housing, health care, and recreation, lower-class families are more prone to all types of disorganization. The corrosive effects of poverty include also the damage done to self-esteem, the stigma attached to being poor or to membership in a minority group, and the relative in-accessibility of such status symbols as success in school, recogni-tion of talent, and rewarding social participation. Repeated studies indicate a higher rate of mental breakdown in lower-class families,[11] as well as the relative inaccessibility of lower-class patients to psychotherapy and out-patient treatment. The relative inability of poor families to conceal deviant behavior, particularly

11. The classic study is August B. Hollingshead and Frederick C. Redlich, *Social Class and Mental Illness* (New York: Wiley, 1958). See also, Leo Srole et al., *Mental Health in the Metropolis* (New York: McGraw-Hill, 1962); and Frank Riessman, Jerome Cohen, and Arthur Pearl, eds., *Mental Health of the Poor* (New York: Free Press of Glencoe, 1964).

if they are welfare recipients, produces startlingly higher rates of delinquency, drug abuse, neglect, desertion, and other statistical indices of family disorganization. While deviant behavior occurs in all socio-economic groups, the family in poverty has fewer resources, financial and emotional, to deal with it and is more likely to be forced to use official channels.

Special Services to Families in Poverty

The original family service agencies were much concerned with assisting the poor, and this continued to be one of the family agencies' major functions until the FERA transferred income maintenance to public agencies in 1933. The traditional methods of social work intervention (casework or services to clients on a one-to-one basis, group work or facilitating client participation in small groups, and community organization or developing adequate social resources to meet community needs) all had their origins in attempts to help clients improve their social functioning and escape from poverty. It was not until the 1920s, when social work became absorbed in psychological and psychiatric theories, that family agencies developed a clientele from the middle and upper classes. But in this preoccupation with intrapsychic factors, some family agencies lost interest in and appeal to clients living in poverty. In 1963, private agencies were accused of having become "estranged" from the poor (see pages 13–15) and of devoting their efforts to middle-class clients whose problems and value systems were more congenial to middle-class social workers.

With increased study of variant family forms, it becomes clear that the problems faced by families in poverty differ in degree rather than in kind from those faced by all families. While the poor clients' relative lack of resources may make it necessary for social workers to do more advocacy for their poor clients and to deal with more defensiveness and resistance to involvement in the helping process from them, it would be incorrect to regard family social work with the poor as a different kind of social work, involving different methods. Solutions to the problems of poverty are long-range, necessitating changes in social attitudes and legislation. Whenever social workers can foster such changes, through individual action, through encouraging positive client action, or through professional associations, they are contributing to the ultimate solution. Unhappily, those in poverty cannot wait while archaic prejudices and attitudes are modified, and social work intervention aimed at mitigating the worst evils of the present system must be undertaken. These can be divided into the three types which follow.

1. Those in poverty should have access to accurate information as to the resources open to them and the swiftest methods of securing such resources. Social workers, under whatever auspices they are employed, should be familiar with the local availability of income maintenance resources and have a working knowledge of general eligibility requirements, appeals and fair-hearing procedures, Legal Aid services, and Welfare Rights Organization groups and any other agencies interested in protecting individual rights. These would include NAACP and other civil rights organizations for blacks and other minority group advocacy organizations for Chicanos, American Indians, Puerto Ricans, and Jews. If outreach services (advertising eligibility requirements to potential recipients of benefits) are not permitted in official welfare agencies, they should be carried out by voluntary groups. Such activities are a logical and useful service for student social work organizations.

2. Recognizing that no income maintenance program is adequate to lift clients out of poverty, social workers should be prepared to teach money management. Consumer education information can be secured from government publications, from state extension services, from Better Business Bureaus, and often from manufacturers and large grocery chains. Buying cooperatives formed by welfare recipients can provide food and other necessities at lower costs. Tenant self-help groups can improve housing. Instruction can be secured in sewing, repairing and renovating furniture, and setting up clothing exchanges, transportation pools, and other self-help programs which not only help stretch the inadequate income but build client morale and reduce feelings of helplessness and dependency. Often, families mired in poverty, who are present- rather than future-oriented, have overlooked such methods of conserving money. All too often, they have been victimized by unscrupulous dealers and have been induced to buy extravagant appliances and furniture on installment payments which stretch on indefinitely, with maximum interest charges and a high rate of repossession. Because so many of the poor feel helpless and powerless, efforts to mobilize them in their own behalf must be strenuous and are most effective when they can be directed from within the neighborhood or client population and not imposed from the outside. Subprofessionals, with professional consultation available, may be the most effective mobilizers. It should be remembered, however, that all such efforts to stretch admittedly inadequate incomes are palliative only and do not attack the basic problem, which is the unwillingness of society to tax itself sufficiently to eliminate poverty.

3. Becoming familiar with the attitudes of defeatism, power-lessness, and impaired self-esteem so often correlated with pov-erty and racism, which exacerbate and complicate other family problems, social workers must use whatever skills and techniques can be developed to counteract such attitudes, both in order to increase client motivation to change and to illuminate which family problems are poverty-caused and which are relationship-oriented. The experience of a Pittsburgh family service agency is relevant here. This agency became aware of the extent to which it was selecting as clients those who found useful what services it was providing, instead of analyzing the needs of all potential cli-ents and devising programs to help them. They "chose" as clients a group of badly disorganized families in a black ghetto with a long record of dependency, criminal offenses, and mistrust of social agencies. Initial requests were for tangible help with hous-ing, furniture, or clothing. Only as workers demonstrated their willingness and ability to help did clients request and use help in other areas of their lives. As some of the agency workers in-volved put it:

> Our object in being "helping agents" is to develop a helping relationship in which we and the client will work together. We hope that eventually he will be able to do more for himself and for others. We aim to modify overwhelming environ-mental stresses, to modify behavior patterns, and finally to change attitudes, thereby enabling the individual to take more steps on his own behalf. It is necessary to give much support and nourishment. The adults with whom we are working have suffered deprivation all of their lives, and they need to be nourished tangibly and intangibly before they can be expected to take responsibility and to give to others. Work-ers may at times help clean house, set hair, repair or make clothing. Teaching is less involved in these activities than being in the situation with the client and working along with him.[12]

Tangible help given included homemaker service, day care, big brother/sister programs for elementary school children, broker service with city departments, housing repair, and provision of insecticides. Supportive services ranged from individual counsel-ing, group therapy, and family therapy to encouraging client

12. Henry Freeman, Mary Ellen Hoffman, Winifred Smith, and Howard Prunty, "Can a Family Agency Be Relevant to the Inner Urban Scene," *Social Casework*, Vol. 51, No. 1 (January 1970), p. 16. See also Rosalind I. Edelstein, "Early Inter-vention in the Poverty Cycle," *Social Casework*, Vol. 53, No. 7 (July 1972), pp. 418–424.

efforts at community organization and involved altering many preconceptions of agency workers and developing new methods and approaches. Workers in the Pittsburgh agency sum up the first four years as follows:

> Most of the families are still with us and still need our help, but they have made some distinct gains. They have a somewhat more optimistic outlook on life. They can and do assume more initiative in helping themselves. The self-help is uneven, depending more on their mood and circumstances than on the nature of the task. We have moments when we are proud of almost all of them, and some consistently demonstrate behavior directed toward expanding goals for themselves. With some clients, agreement on focus and goals is easy. With others it is difficult to discover where we and the client can meet in a working relationship. Is it in creating something new, such as a dress or something to eat? Is it in moving toward employment? Is it in fixing up the client's house? Or is it in controlling his behavior in order to keep him out of trouble? . . . We are convinced that within the wealth of experience of the family service field there are a number of resources to help a family agency make sense to segments of the community that are most caught up in the "inner city" catastrophe. However, it has been our experience that to be able to make use of this accumulated experience, it is necessary to depart from established methodology and to use freely our knowledge and skills of observation to develop methods that relate specifically to the group we are choosing to help.[13]

Differentiation of Income-Related Needs

Such projects as those mentioned above may be used by families who need only brief service, when provision of either tangible or intangible services enables the family to function independently. The assumption that there must be "something wrong" with those in poverty (implicit in the residual view of public welfare services, see pages 47–48) is belied by the many competent and adequate people whose only problems are financial and by those who need only income-related services. Competent analysis of the situation will enable family social workers to differentiate the latter group of families, mobilize community resources to meet the needs of its members as adequately as permitted, and strengthen the positives in each family to sustain a more satisfying level of living. These may well be the families that have fallen into poverty suddenly, as a result of sudden un-

13. Freeman et al., "Can a Family Agency," pp. 18, 20, 21.

employment, forced retirement, illness, or catastrophe. They are less likely to demonstrate the deeply held attitudes of mistrust and defeatism which result from long periods of deprivation and hopelessness. Intensive service to such families is, in essence, preventive of further disorganization.

The extent to which poverty tends to distort and confuse other family problems is illuminated by the first of three cases which follow. These cases were originally reported in 1947 but are still highly relevant. Taken as a series, these cases show three levels of complexity of problems and the different social work approaches demanded by each level. Although inadequate income is apparently not a problem in the latter two cases, a little imagination will show how the situations of the A family and the B family would have been complicated if financial pressure had been added to the other difficulties faced by these families.

Consideration of this series of cases anticipates somewhat our analysis of family problems which are not income-related, but comparison among these three families provides a useful introduction to such an analysis. The first case, the G family, demonstrates the pressures of inadequate income on a basically healthy family. By contrast, the A and B cases indicate problems involving relationships, unrealistic attitudes, and the recreating of inappropriate childhood behavior patterns in later life and demand "clarification" rather than "supportive" treatment or environmental manipulation.[14] Clarification involves helping the client to recognize his own self-defeating patterns of behavior and modify them, while support or sustainment attempts to strengthen the client to face his current reality situation more adequately and to modify the external pressures which impede his adjustment.[15]

> "My husband has stopped loving me," was Mrs. G's statement of her marriage problem. She was unhappy, cried frequently in the interview, and seemed completely bewildered

14. The terms "clarification" and "supportive treatment" have been developed by Florence Hollis. See her "Analysis of Casework Treatment Methods and Their Relationship to Personality Change," *Smith College Studies in Social Work*, Vol. 32, No. 2 (February 1962), pp. 97–117. In subsequent analysis, Hollis has developed a classification of six levels of intervention and retermed "supportive treatment" as "sustainment." See her *Casework: A Psychosocial Therapy*, second edition (New York: Random House, 1972), especially chapters 4 and 5. See also Richard M. Grinnell, Jr., "Environmental Modification: Casework's Concern or Casework's Neglect?" *Social Service Review*, Vol. 47, No. 2, (June 1973) pp. 208–220.

15. The three case illustrations which follow are from Elsie M. Waelder, "Casework with Marital Problems," *Social Casework*, Vol. 27, No. 5 (May 1947), pp. 168–174. Used with permission.

by Mr. G's attitude because the first few years of their marriage had been so happy. In response to the worker's questions about the change, this story developed.

Mr. G had no particular industrial skill and so had been employed on low-paid jobs. The family had managed well while she worked, and by careful planning had gotten by after the birth of the first child. Then a second pregnancy had produced twins. The income, barely adequate for three, suddenly had to be stretched to cover five.

Mrs. G was in very poor health. She needed an operation following confinement but had not returned for this because she had no money for hospital and doctor bills, and no one to care for the three children while she was hospitalized. She was continually tired and had frequent pain. She no longer could keep up with the laundry, house cleaning, and cooking as she had been accustomed to. And on top of this her husband had stopped loving her![16]

It is not necessary to probe into Mrs. G's unconscious to find ample reason for her discouragement. Whether her husband was impatient with her because of her lack of time for him or felt guilty because of his inadequate earnings, Mrs. G felt that he was unsympathetic and unloving. In planning for this family, the caseworker had evidence of satisfactory management of both personal and financial affairs for many years. The probability was that if some of the new pressures could be relieved, the family could once again function adequately. Homemaker service, hospitalization, and clinic referral for Mrs. G relieved part of the pressure. Vocational guidance and retraining for Mr. G resulted in increased family income. Casework was directed at reality problems and planning for them. No attempt was made, nor needed to be made apparently, at uncovering buried material or at giving either Mr. or Mrs. G greater self-awareness.

FAMILY NEEDS NOT RELATED TO INCOME

Contrast the case of Mrs. G with the case of Mrs. A.

Mrs. A brought her confusion to a worker when her husband wrote from overseas that he was being discharged, but would not return to her mother's home where the couple had lived since marriage. Mrs. A was an only child whose father had died during her infancy. Her mother, a capable business woman, had centered her emotional life around her daughter. Before marriage, all Mrs. A's social life was with her mother. The mother was jealous of Mr. A, first tried to prevent the

16. *Ibid.*, p. 169.

marriage and later made it almost impossible for the couple to have any privacy.

There was no question in Mrs. A's mind about her husband. She loved him and wanted him to return to her. She sympathized with his feeling about her mother, and agreed that Jeanette, the 3-year-old daughter, was becoming a problem because her mother interfered with her care of Jeanette. The child was learning to play her mother against her grandmother.

However, Mrs. A thought her husband was unreasonable to make such an ultimatum when he knew she could not leave her mother. What would relatives and neighbors say? Her mother had devoted her life to her—was it fair to desert her now? With the housing situation almost impossible, where would they go? He shouldn't have forced this on her so suddenly.[17]

Here is no emergency which can be resolved by provision of concrete services, as in the case of Mr. and Mrs. G. Mrs. A's abnormal submission to her dominating mother is a pattern established in childhood. Her guilt at the thought of leaving her mother (reflected in her concern about what the neighbors would say) and her resentment of her mother's domination are apparent to the worker (and to the reader), but should Mrs. A be made aware of them? She is not hopelessly dominated; at least she did carry through her marriage in the face of all her mother's attempts to break it up, and she is able to see something of Mr. A's point of view. What might be most helpful to Mrs. A would not be to make her confront her ambivalent feelings about her mother but to help her see the advantages of becoming more independent and the reality of her mother's situation, which is not that of a hopeless dependent who needs her daughter in the home to care for her. Supporting Mrs. A in her wish to be with her husband may make it possible for her to contrive other living arrangements and withstand her mother's attempts to interfere.

The following case of Mrs. B shows a complex network of problems touching every area of her life. Sustained improvement in such a case could not be expected until Mrs. B came to have more awareness of her own self-defeating patterns.

Confusion over loyalty to husband and parents had Mrs. B so upset that she thought she would give up and return with her children to be a child again in her parents' home. "If Ed isn't man enough to stand up against my parents for me he's a dope, and why should I stay with him?"

17. *Ibid.*, pp. 170–171.

Married at 20, and now the mother of two children, Mrs. B was still, for all her eight years of marriage, looking to her parents for her standards. She lived next door to them; they interfered with her discipline of the children, and controlled her by their disapproval. "I can't even wear silk stockings in the house because my mother thinks that is extravagant." Throughout her complaints, it was her parents who seemed to cause the difficulty, but she blamed her husband because he took it quietly, didn't fight her battles. She wanted him to move her away from her family but wasn't agreeable to his suggestion that they buy an old house. "No one takes my opinions seriously."

Mrs. B stuttered and stammered when excited, said she had always done this. Now her young daughter had a similar speech defect. She wondered if Ellen was imitating her, or whether Ellen's stammering also was caused by her "personality." Eddie did not stammer. Mrs. B described him as an outgoing, lively youngster.

But not only were the children affected. Mrs. B said "deeper things" were wrong—the sexual adjustment was quite poor. Perhaps this was because she and her husband both had inadequate sex information and the early marriage was difficult because they were "so ignorant."[18]

Here is a situation involving every aspect of the family life, with no real satisfaction for Mrs. B in any area. No change could be made in the unsatisfactory living situation until Mrs. B expressed some of her resentment and frustration. Then her unrealistic expectations of her husband became clearer to her; she was able to see that he had many good qualities and that she had some responsibility for emancipating herself from parental control. There was general improvement in the situation, but Mrs. B still felt dissatisfied, and a further period of treatment was directed at helping Mrs. B see that she had carried over to adult life feelings of rivalry with her brother and resentment that he had been favored over her. She began to see that she was repeating this favoritism in her handling of her children. With the continuing help of the worker's warm acceptance of Mrs. B as a valuable and useful person, Mrs. B showed increased self-esteem, less need to depreciate herself, and a more relaxed and confident attitude toward herself and her family. Five years after her last contact with the agency, Mrs. B was sustaining the improvement she had made. If Mrs. B were being treated in the 1970s, family therapy might well have shortened the treatment process, since it would

18. *Ibid.*, p. 171.

have illuminated earlier the family interactions and involved both Mr. B and the children in altering their responses to Mrs. B's behavioral cues.

THE FAMILY LIFE CYCLE AND POINTS OF STRESS

With this introduction to differing family needs, let us now consider the sorts of problems faced by all families, whether complicated and exacerbated by financial pressure and/or minority group status or not.

FAMILY FORMATION

Family service agencies traditionally have offered premarital counseling to couples contemplating marriage, but evidence indicates that this is less and less utilized.[19] Couples who wish consultation over choice of mate have already indicated some doubt in their own minds. Current emphasis on romantic love as the most important factor in mate selection leads couples to disregard other factors, and questions about the wisdom of their choices are more likely to be discussed with the clergy, particularly in those denominations where some consultation is built into the marriage ceremony. Some premarital counseling may be done in family life education programs under the auspices of school or church organizations. It is evident that there is a great deal of informal discussion about mate selection in the popular press and in nonprofessional settings.

As a result of biological advances, however, two new fields of premarital counseling are emerging which can utilize social work expertise. The field of genetic counseling has already been mentioned (see page 43). Couples who are advised not to marry or to remain childless because of the strong possibility of transmitting genetic defects may well need social work help in accepting the decision and reformulating their plans. It is encouraging to note that the medical experts heading up genetic counseling centers do include social workers on their staffs.

The other area which may be considered a type of premarital counseling is in relation to contraception and abortion. Many Planned Parenthood programs and college health services offer contraceptive information to both married and unmarried indi-

19. See Susan E. Flendening and A. John Wilson, III, "Experiments in Group Premarital Counseling," *Social Casework*, Vol. 53, No. 9 (November 1972), pp. 551–562.

viduals in an effort to insure that unwanted children will not be born and recognizing that sexual activity in all strata of society is no longer limited to the married. Many of these programs are operated by medical personnel and on a tacit assumption that fertility control is always a rational procedure. Social workers are aware of the extent to which people do not always operate rationally and, in addition, are more likely to be familiar with clients at greater than average risk—those in poverty, those with severe emotional problems, and those with demonstrated inadequate parenting, for example—and are therefore in a strategic position to assist clients to come to wise decisions about contraception. More and more family planning services are using social workers, either professionals or subprofessionals with in-service training. There are obviously expanding opportunities for BSWs, especially in the outreach programs which involve teen-agers in working through their conflicts about sexual activity and its potential consequences.[20]

Liberalized abortion laws were enacted in several states prior to the Supreme Court decision on January 22, 1973, which outlawed many restrictive state laws as unconstitutional. Abortion remains a controversial issue to many people, including, as it does, such questions as the right to life of the fetus, the age at which the fetus can be considered a person, the mother's right to control over her body, and state interference with a physician's right to practice medicine as his professional judgment dictates. The decision to seek an abortion may be a difficult one. Once the decision is made, abortion counseling before and after the actual procedure is essential and should be available in any reputable abortion facility.[21]

A comprehensive study of several hundred patients who sought abortions in New York City at the Mount Sinai Medical Center found that the average age was twenty-five; that three fourths were single, separated, divorced, or widowed; that 53 percent requested the abortion for emotional reasons (a feeling of inability to cope with a child at the time); and that two thirds of the patients were distressed about abortion, with the percentage of

20. See Gitta Meier, "Family and Population Planning," *Encyclopedia of Social Work, 1971*, pp. 373–385.

21. See Elizabeth M. Smith, "Counseling for Women Who Seek Abortion," *Social Work*, Vol. 17, No. 2 (March 1972), pp. 62–68. See also Ruth K. Heineman, "The Evolution of an Abortion Counseling Service in an Adoption Agency," *Child Welfare*, Vol. 52, No. 4 (April 1973), pp. 253–260.

distressed patients higher in those under twenty-one and over thirty-five years of age.[22]

In spite of the contention of abortion supporters that the procedure is a simple medical one causing less pain than a tonsillectomy, the majority of patients requesting an abortion have very mixed feelings, including guilt, apprehension, anger, and isolation. While many patients lack factual information on birth control and abortion, which can be provided effectively by physicians and nurses, there is some reason to believe that the termination of life is a difficult subject for medical personnel to deal with because of the conflict with their professional orientation toward saving lives. In light of this, patients may find it easier to express their own conflicts and feelings to nonmedical personnel. Social workers are in a strategic position to render much needed service to these patients.

In a determined attempt to provide some alternatives to abortion for women with unwanted pregnancies, a number of programs offering services and providing twenty-four hour "hot line" telephone referral have been developed to combat what many see as the immorality of abortion. Operating under such titles as "Birthright" and advertising in newspapers and over radio stations, such programs offer counseling, placement during pregnancy, help with hospitalization at time of delivery, and adoption services for the baby. They serve to supplement and make more widely known the already established programs of services to unmarried mothers of the family and children's service agencies. The National Council on Illegitimacy is open to all agencies and organizations concerned with illegitimacy and is dedicated to working for constructive social policy toward it. Services to unmarried parents will be discussed later in this chapter under "One-Parent Families," and adoption and foster care for illegitimate children will be discussed in Chapter 4.

BEGINNING FAMILIES

Young newlyweds, beginning their lives together, inevitably face a series of profound readjustments in establishing new roles with relation to each other and to their respective parents. In

22. Alma T. Young, Barbara Berkman, and Helen Rehr, "Women Who Seek Abortions: A Study," *Social Work*, Vol. 18, No. 3 (May 1973), pp. 60–65. See also Alice Ullmann, "Social Work Services to Abortion Patients," *Social Casework*, Vol. 53, No. 8 (October 1972), pp. 481–487, for a similar study, detailing the emotional conflicts of abortion patients and providing a useful bibliography.

contemporary American society, the "normal" behavior for newly married couples is to emancipate themselves from either set of parents and operate independently. While this may avoid some dissension, it also leaves the couple without the supportive help which exists in the extended family. When "emancipation" also includes, as it often does, a move to a new community, the couple loses the security of familiar surroundings and friends.

Role incompatibility—as when an independent and self-sufficient working woman is suddenly expected to become dependent and content to stay at home, or when a wife's expectations of a husband's role (likely to be largely based on her perception of her father's role in his household) are widely at variance from her husband's perceptions of his own role—can lead to friction and impaired communication. Rather than assuming that any role perceptions are "right" or inevitable, the social worker dealing with such a young couple should help them consider whether their perceptions are compatible with each other. Rigidity in clinging to some fixed roles may lead to difficulty at later stages of the family life cycle. The extent to which cultural assumptions about the "proper" role for women have pervaded our educational systems and our therapeutic endeavors is becoming increasingly clear as more and more advocates of women's liberation analyze reading primers, Freudian psychology, employment patterns, and legislation. Supporting young couples in their efforts to find mutually satisfying role expectations and the willingness to modify them as circumstances may demand is ultimately more productive than trying to "adjust" all wives into a pattern of wifely submission and all husbands into masculine dominance.

A critical area for treatment is likely to be communication, both verbal and nonverbal, and marriage counselors should know a good deal about communications theory. The extent to which verbal messages can be contradicted by such nonverbal methods of communication as facial expression, eye movement, tone of voice, and body movement can be illuminated in joint interviews or with use of video-tapes. Difficulties in communication may also be clarified in group sessions. Many recently married couples feel guilty about expressing hostility to someone they have just promised publicly to love and cherish, and their inability to express negative feelings may also block expressions of warmth as well. A good marital relationship—indeed any good relationship, whether it is parent-child, husband-wife, friend-friend, or therapist-client—should permit acknowledgment of negative feelings without excessive guilt about feeling them.

In addition to the classic casework techniques of sustainment, clarification, and interpretation, family counselors have found two newer methodologies useful. Transactional analysis provides concepts which illuminate the transactions occurring between and among individuals. In diagramming his transactions with another person, the individual becomes aware of the extent to which self-judgments during childhood as "OK" or "not-OK" and resulting behavior patterns interfere with adult decisions and behavior. Transactional therapists, of which Eric Berne[23] is a leading figure, discuss the "games people play" to control others or avoid involvement. Once analyzed by the participants as games, these maneuvers become less effective and hence less utilized. An advantage of transactional analysis is its use of nontechnical language (games, OK-parent, non-OK parent, "I'm OK—you're OK") which does not require involved interpretation and is in itself reassuring.

A second newer method in marital counseling with certain couples is the rapidly expanding area of behavior modification. While its proponents advocate it as an alternative to those therapies which develop self-awareness in order to bring about modification of behavior, behavior modification need not exclude the goals of developing self-awareness and more rational control of one's behavior. Behavior modification has the advantages of being fast and demonstrably effective. In essence, specific items of behavior which are constructive in relation to the short-term goals as defined by the married couple and the therapist are positively reinforced, and destructive behavior is ignored. Ultimately, more successful adjustment becomes a reinforcer. Insight-oriented therapists are concerned about possible dangers of removing a symptom which may be serving some useful psychic purpose, although these fears may be exaggerated. Behavior modification may work best with couples who want tangible results and specific directives. Since it is obviously highly effective with children, it will be described more fully and illustrated in Chapter 4.[24]

The special area of sexual counseling has developed since the

23. See Eric Berne, *Games People Play* (New York: Grove Press, 1964). See also Thomas A. Harris, M.D., *I'm OK–You're OK: A Practical Guide to Transactional Analysis* (New York: Harper & Row, 1969); and Kenneth Lamott, "The Four Possible Life Positions," *New York Times Magazine*, November 19, 1972, pp. 42 ff.

24. For an illuminating article on behavior modification in marital counseling, see Robert Lieberman, "Behavioral Approaches to Family and Couple Therapy," *American Journal of Orthopsychiatry*, Vol. 40, No. 1 (January 1970), pp. 106–120.

pioneering work of Masters and Johnson,[25] who believe that ignorance and fears are more likely to cause sexual maladjustments
than physiological factors. This approach stresses difficulties in
communications between the partners, and specific exercises are
used to improve communication. The Masters and Johnson technique of "conjoint marital-unity therapy" is an expensive and
complicated one, but their approach can be utilized by social work
practitioners in direct discussion of sexual difficulties. Group
counseling of couples has proved to be an effective way of confronting individuals and couples with ways in which they distort
reality or close avenues of communication.[26]

Newly married couples may also be in need of help in reaching
decisions about such reality factors as housing, money management, changing jobs, the wife's continued employment, and loneliness in a new community. Family service agencies can provide
such help or direct clients to special resources within the community. In many ways, social work can compensate for the isolation and vulnerability of the emancipated couple, who feel they
must maintain independence from their parents.

THE FAMILY WITH YOUNG CHILDREN

With the birth of the first child comes a host of new adjustments and the necessity for shifting of roles. Expenses increase,
and often income decreases if a working wife must stop work.
When preceded by careful planning, a couple with good communication and the beginnings of a stable relationship will find
that the satisfactions of becoming parents more than compensate
for any sacrifices entailed. If the first child was unplanned or if
the husband-wife relationship was based on gratification of neurotic needs, tension and discord may result. If, for example, the
husband needs the reassurance conveyed by a wife's absorption
in meeting his needs, he may resent the inevitable diversion of
her attention to the infant. Conversely, the wife who has not felt
adequately needed by her husband may become overabsorbed in
the child and exclude her husband. Grandparents may be a source
of help and support, or they may utilize the new situation to exert

25. William H. Masters and Virginia E. Johnson, *Human Sexual Response* (Boston: Little, Brown & Company, 1966), and *Human Sexual Inadequacy* (Boston: Little, Brown & Company, 1970).

26. See Harry Lawrence and Martin Sundel, "Behavior Modification in Adult
Groups," *Social Work*, Vol. 17, No. 2 (March 1972), pp. 34–43.

undue influence, to recreate old parent-child struggles, or to belittle the new parents' abilities to cope.

Helping the marriage partners to adapt to their new parenting roles involves the same types of service as described above, with the additional component of concern over the adequacy of parental care for the child. Parents who are themselves little more than children in their emotional development may be expected to have difficulty in making the sacrifices entailed in caring on a twenty-four hour basis for a child who may well interfere with their sleep, their spending patterns, and their leisure. A typical illustration of such a childlike mother is one who loves to dress up and show off a pretty, smiling baby but who is impatient or abusive to a crying, sick, or unappealing child. Instead of viewing the child as a person in his own right, this type of mother sees her child as a plaything, a device for securing admiration to her, or a method of securing the attention of a somewhat unreliable husband. Parents who are not deeply committed to each other may find the bond between them threatened by the added responsibility and expense of a child, with separation or desertion offering a possible way out.

With the births of subsequent children, especially if they are closely spaced, family relationships become more complex. Responsibilities are increased, with additional expenses and demands on time and energy. Parents may find themselves reacting differently to different children, intensifying the sibling rivalry normally present as the oldest child finds himself dethroned from his original position as sole child. Housing may become more crowded, and at the same time, parents may be forced to spend more time in the home, since going out is more difficult and involves babysitters or taking small children with them. As Frances Scherz[27] points out, the need for open communication, which exists at all times, is particularly critical at transitional points in the family life cycle. She explores some universal psychological tasks which the family confronts at the various transition points in family life; these include achieving the proper balance between these conflicting attitudes: 1) emotional separation vs. interdependence, 2) intimacy vs. distance, and 3) autonomy vs. responsibility to others. Each addition to the family multiplies the complexities of the family's tasks. A family which can cope adequately with one child may be less and less able to cope with the addition of a second or third child.

27. Frances H. Scherz, "Maturational Crises and Parent-Child Interaction," *Social Casework*, Vol. 52, No. 6 (June 1971), pp. 326–329.

Protective Services

Until the oldest child goes to school, no outside agency is necessarily aware of how well the young family is functioning. Unless laws are broken publicly, so that neighbors complain, or children are physically abused, the tendency is to refrain from interfering in the relationship between the parents or in their child-rearing practices. The public image of protective services is the Society for the Prevention of Cruelty to Children, which advocates a concept from the 1870s that stressed removal of children from homes where they were being mistreated. Newer concepts in protective services stress prevention and rehabilitation, but they are still likely to be regarded by clients as punitive and interfering with their rights.

Referrals to child protective services may be made by visiting nurses or medical personnel who become aware of serious inadequacies in the quality of care of small children, by the police department if they are summoned by neighbors who hear children crying, by clergy, or by preschool or school personnel. Under the separated income maintenance system, welfare recipients may be referred to the services division as a condition for continuing on AFDC grants if the income maintenance worker is aware of the family's need for service. In most states, the responsibility for providing protective services has been delegated to the public welfare departments, although the American Humane Association and the Child Welfare League are national voluntary agencies concerned with services to children. The issue of children's rights, including under what conditions children should be removed from the home, will be considered in Chapter 4. Here we are concerned with protective services to the family, services which will meet the needs of parents and insure that they provide adequate care and protection to the children. Rehabilitating an inadequate home to permit children to remain there is infinitely better for the child than removal and placement with strangers, however carefully selected and willing.

The chief modality for protective services has been direct casework with the parents, recognizing that they have needs and rights but also stressing their responsibilities and their basic desire to do a good job of parenting.[28] The approach has been to offer help with the obstacles that impede their providing better

28. See Matilda T. Bellacci, "Group Treatment of Mothers in Child Protective Cases," *Child Welfare*, Vol. 51, No. 2 (February 1972), pp. 110–116, for a group work approach.

care, which usually involves helping them satisfy their own needs. When too large a proportion of a parent's energy must be directed toward self-satisfaction, too little is left for adequate carrying out of parental responsibilities. Many of the parents who need protective services were themselves neglected as children. They do not have positive maternal and parternal models to follow and are perpetuating with their own children the kinds of behavior which will produce immature and unsatisfied adults. In addition, many have had negative experiences with social agencies and authority figures and therefore have defensive and hostile reactions toward what they regard as unwarranted interference with their lives.

Although serious child abuse requiring hospitalization indicates that neglect and cruelty to children are not limited to those living in or near poverty, families with adequate incomes are much more likely to be able to conceal neglect or delegate child care to hired help.[29] Families referred to service agencies because of neglect are very likely to be those already known to social agencies, whose emotional and relationship difficulties are compounded by inadequate income. As in the Pittsburgh project described earlier in this chapter, provision of tangible services— transportation, homemaking, recreation, child care equipment— serves the double purpose of meeting client needs and demonstrating the agency's wish to help. Protective services workers must play advocacy, brokerage, and enabling roles and should be backed up by adequate community resources. It is difficult, for example, to help parents take more adequate care of children in inadequate housing, but in many communities no better housing is available for low-income families. Good health care is difficult in the absence of clinics, visiting nurses, or funds for health supplies. The overtaxed mother of several small children can be helped more easily if suitable day care could be provided to relieve her for part of the day. Protective services workers are well aware of community deficiencies and should be active in informing the public and supporting pressure groups to improve community facilities.

The Adams Case

Working with people who cannot or will not recognize the need for change or who are so defeatist and discouraged that they are convinced change is impossible is a difficult undertaking. The

29. See Ray E. Helfer and C. Henry Kempe, *The Battered Child* (Chicago: University of Chicago Press, 1968). See also *Speaking Out for Children Protection* (Denver: The American Humane Association, 1973).

experience of the Children's Services of Connecticut in adding protective services to its program of foster care, adoption, day care, and residential treatment is illuminating.[30]

> Until the addition of this newest function the agency's services had been completely voluntary, available to parents who chose to utilize them and to public welfare departments which purchased them. The request to add Protective Services was made to the agency in 1955 by the Family and Child Care Division of the Greater Hartford Community Council, which had been working for three years on the problem of those children whose needs were all too apparent to the schools, the courts and to social agencies and whom the existing resources were not adequately serving. They were the children whose parents were frequently referred to family agencies, child guidance clinics or child placement agencies but who lacked the motivation or the conviction about themselves and their capacity to function differently to follow through. Their case records were characteristically closed with a facsimile of the familiar "client uncooperative." They were also some of the children who came before the Juvenile Court as neglected and, despite the parents' protests, were committed to the Department of Public Welfare as the only way the Court could be assured of their safe and adequate supervision.
>
> The outcome of the work done on this by the Hartford Committee and the agencies involved with it was the decision that an additional facility was needed which would carry the authority to hold parents to the community's minimum of adequate care or to take the appropriate action in relation to court. The need in the Hartford area was focused on the area of protective casework which involves sustained work with parents rather than on some of the other functions frequently associated with Protective Services. The City Department of Welfare already had developed foster care facilities for children who needed to be removed from their homes in an emergency and was giving around-the-clock service to meet this need in the metropolitan area. The City Police Department had developed a staff of Policewomen to whom cases of criminal neglect were referred and who worked cooperatively with the Department of Welfare. The Division of Child Wel-

30. The following material is condensed from Elizabeth R. Nichols, *A Voluntary Agency Adds Child Protective Services* (Denver: The American Humane Association, 1960), pp. 1–12. Used with permission. As of January 1, 1967, these services, having proved their value, were transferred from the voluntary agency (now known as the Family and Child Service of Connecticut, Inc.) to the public welfare department.

fare of the State Welfare Department was carrying by law the responsibility for making social studies on all families for whom neglect petitions had been filed. The Council's focus, therefore, was not on meeting emergency needs but was on providing skilled casework help from an authoritative base to help families, insofar as possible, before the crisis might occur which would precipitate complete family breakdown.

In its simplest and most obvious terms, the ingredient which the Unit has added to the casework services available to the families of the community is the ingredient of authority. To those parents who are neglecting, is given the unique kind of help that is based upon the judgment that the care they are giving is not good enough, that certain changes must be made or suitable action in relation to Juvenile Court will be taken which may abridge their legal rights as parents. The difference for a family in working with a voluntary agency on their own application and working with a protective agency with limits and expectations clearly established was dramatically demonstrated by the Adams family.

Mrs. Adams is an obese, lethargic woman of 26. She comes from a severely deprived background; an alcoholic father and unsympathetic step-mother. At sixteen, she became pregnant and her marriage to Mr. Adams is described by both as something forced on them by Mrs. Adams' father. Mrs. Adams was too frightened to let her father know that she really did not believe that Mr. Adams was the father of her expected baby, and it was not until after the marriage that she acknowledged this to her husband. She carried deep guilt and he entered into the marriage feeling that he had been trapped.

Mr. Adams is a dapper young man whose wide-belted polo coat and second hand Cadillac are cherished possessions. He and his carelessly groomed wife make a somewhat incongruous pair. He is a hard worker with a good job history in low paying positions. He wanted some fun out of life and felt he was earning it. There was little to be had at home where Mrs. Adams was doing a sloppy housekeeping job and where the family increased faster than either parent really wanted, with four children in five years.

Mrs. Adams applied to the Family agency when she complained about her husband. After four months the worker concluded that both Mr. and Mrs. Adams were using the service only to air their grievances. Both were so engrossed in their own difficulties and frustrations that the children's needs were largely overlooked. After an inter-agency conference it was decided to file neglect petitions. Mrs. Adams did not want to give up her children and was inclined to feel that the only way she could care for them adequately was if her

husband left home and she could have the security of support from ADC.

At the court hearing the Judge listened to Mrs. Adams'
hesitating request to have her husband ordered out of her
home and Mr. Adams' complete incredulity that his wife
could be saying such a thing. One was impressed by the complete lack of communication between these two people as well
as their inability to face the fact that the time of crisis had
arrived and that an outside authority was holding them to
substantial change. The Judge pointed out the many areas in
which their care of the children did not meet the community's
expectations and continued the petitions for three months
under the supervision of the Protective Services Unit.

The worker set up the structure within which the agency
and parents would be working together. She let them know
that there would need to be substantial change on the part of
both if she were to recommend that the children remain with
them, and that she had serious question as to whether they
were capable of achieving it. If they really wanted to keep
their family together, however, she stood ready to help them.

Faced with the worker's clear identification with the court's
ultimatum, Mrs. Adams was no longer able to project all of the
shortcomings of her home on her husband. The worker was
ready to acknowledge with her that she might be too discouraged, too physically dehabilitated to do an adequate job. If
this were not true, as Mrs. Adams somewhat lamely maintained, then she would need to demonstrate it by more adequate physical care of the children, regular meals, thoughtful
attention to clothing, responsibility in relation to clinic appointments. Having her own job defined in terms of specific
expectations, Mrs. Adams could begin to move from her absorption in self and direct some of her energies into testing
out her capacity to produce an adequate job.

Mr. Adams responded very differently. According to him
the situation had never been as bad as the social worker portrayed it. Meeting our expectations would hold no problems
for him. We would soon see for ourselves what a devoted
father and adequate provider he was. It was only in response
to specific expectations that he could express his resistance.
If he had to account for his income and the way in which he
used it, he might just as well be in jail. His activities outside
the home were his own business and the right of any man
who worked as hard as he did.

The worker agreed that the choices were still his but
limited now to the choice between giving enough personal
and financial support to his family to insure a secure home or
leaving the home to let his wife see if she could do the job
alone. It was not until the court hearing three months later

that Mr. Adams could verbalize how shocked he had been by this ultimatum, or acknowledge his own awareness of his shortcomings.

Movement of these two people in the following months was faltering, sometimes forward with real purposefulness and then backwards as it tested out how much was really being expected and how much the worker really cared about them and the outcome of their family. By the end of the three-month period, the Adams' could go back to court with a clear conviction that their marriage was worth saving and the worker could report clearly identifiable improvement in the way these parents were operating as parents.

The dynamic which the Adams family used so positively is the authority which intervened to say that their children were the focus of the agency's concerns and that the children could no longer wait. We could understand the almost unsurmountable handicap under which the marriage was initiated. We could accept that the parents' needs as individuals were so great and so unfulfilled that focusing their concern on their children might be impossible. But we valued them as people and were ready to stand by to help them test out the degree to which they could do the job they both thought they wanted to do.

It can hardly be expected that Mr. and Mrs. Adams could, in three months, bring their standards of parenting and housekeeping up to an ideal level. They may need continued recognition for what they have accomplished and encouragement to continue. But if the Adams children can remain in familiar surroundings under even minimally acceptable conditions, their adjustment will not be imperiled by separation and apparent rejection, and Mr. and Mrs. Adams will not be forced to think of themselves as failures. Seriously deprived parents probably need the one-to-one relationship with a caseworker, since it helps to gratify the unmet needs derived from their own inadequate parenting. As they gain more self-assurance in their parental roles, however, they may benefit from group meetings with other parents, and such parent education meetings may offer valuable preventive services before children can become really neglected.[31] A project in Little Rock, Arkansas demonstrated that such group meetings were useful to parents from all socio-economic backgrounds.[32]

31. See Aline B. Auerbach, *Parents Learn Through Discussion: Principles and Practices of Parent Group Education* (New York: John Wiley & Sons, 1968).

32. See Joan Haley Carder, "New Dimensions to Family Agency from Family Life Education," *Social Casework*, Vol. 53, No. 6 (June 1972), pp. 355–360.

In a systematic review of studies attempting to assess various types of social work intervention on the functioning of inadequate or problematic families, Geismar[33] isolated some hypotheses, which he tested in the Rutgers Family Life Improvement Project (FLIP). These findings challenge some of the more traditional assumptions of family casework; Geismar concludes that casework is no substitute for adequate material resources, that baccalaureate-level social workers can handle the service delivery if supervised properly, and that multiservice projects, including help with such specific areas as child rearing, health care, and homemaking, are more effective than interpersonal counseling. He concludes:

> The preventive approach, the special subject of investigation in the Rutgers Family Life Improvement Project, appears to be more than a hope or vision. Early intervention does make a measurable difference, but that difference was found to be significant in only a few specified areas. The need to focus intervention, even preventive intervention, on areas of vulnerability in social functioning clearly applies . . . Some types of instrumental intervention fell short of desirable goals because of the absence of means to effect any fundamental change in unemployment, lack of material resources, and poor housing of many families. Effective service in preventive as well as remedial intervention cannot evade the cardinal issue posed by social programs in this country. Helping efforts must be aimed directly at the target of change. There are neither substitute means nor substitute goals in coping with the problems of man and society, regardless of the program cost and the deep-rooted Protestant ethic.[34]

THE CHILDREN GROW OLDER

As the children grow older and begin to go to school, new strains are put on the family. The parents must relinquish some control over their children, which may create difficulties if there are hostile-dependent relationships, immature clinging to the child by the parent, excessive timidity on the part of the child, or an unwillingness to expose child and parent to outside scrutiny and criticism. Parents may also fear criticism from children who learn different values from teachers or peers. The Amish objection to secondary education, for example, stems directly from such fears and a reluctance to expose Amish children to "the world"

33. Ludwig L. Geismar, "Implication of a Family Life Improvement Project," *Social Casework*, Vol. 52, No. 7 (July 1971), pp. 455–467.

34. *Ibid.*, p. 465.

lest it prove too alluring.[35] Emphasis on community control of schools reflects fear that children will be taught material and given ideas which are at best irrelevant and at worst destructive of their home and cultural situation. Parental attitudes toward education, toward career choices, and toward authority figures are all important in their children's school adjustment. Unfortunately, the very parents whose attitudes may hinder their children are the ones least likely to be involved in PTA or other parent groups, in which they might learn to modify their opposition.

It is not only school which challenges children's conformity to parental norms. The child's play group becomes an important frame of reference for him, and parents will be told by their children how differently other children are being brought up. Parents who are not secure in their own relationships and confident in their child-rearing methods may be threatened by learning of other possibilities and by knowing that their own family life is being scrutinized by outsiders. Mrs. Scherz's psychological tasks of achieving the appropriate mix of intimacy and distance, separation and interdependence, and autonomy and responsibility will be carried on under these added strains. As children develop more and more and wish to test their ability to operate independently, insecure parents will see this as a threat of rejection and be tempted to retaliate.

School may offer the child his first possibility of rewards for achievement from outsiders; conversely, the low achiever may meet his first failures in the school. If not skillfully handled by the parents, low school grades can initiate a cycle of discouragement, low performance, and eventual surrender. There is more and more evidence of the catastrophic effects in later school years of failure to develop reading skills in the early grades. The child falls farther and farther behind as more and more of his school work demands that he be able to read well. Remedial programs are available in many school systems, or parents can learn how to help their children to read at home. Community agencies offer tutorial programs using volunteers, often high school or college students. When parents are threatened by their children's school performance, feeling that it casts reflections on their adequacy as parents, they may battle the school instead of enlisting in a cooperative effort with it. School social workers, now considered an essential part of pupil personnel teams, can help by interpreting referrals for

35. See John A. Hostetler and Gertrude Enders Huntington, *Children in Amish Society* (New York: Holt, Rinehart and Winston, 1971).

remedial work and helping parents see that their child needs to be accepted for what he is, not for the adequacy of his school work.

It is during the school years that many parents, often unconsciously, use their children to work out their own frustrated ambitions and aspirations. The child who must take music lessons because his parent always wanted to and never could, the little boy who must be in the Little League because of his father's enthusiasm for baseball, and the child who is pushed into superior school grades by a parent who was forced to leave school early and could never get ahead because he lacked a good education are all familiar illustrations at the elementary school level. The basic difficulty with such an approach to children is that it conveys clearly to the child a conditional acceptance rather than total acceptance of himself as a person. If he feels he can be accepted only if his performance in some way casts credit on his family, he will tend to devaluate himself unduly and think he can be valued only in terms of his activity and not for his personal qualities. This is a shaky foundation on which to build one's self-esteem and may lead to compulsive over-activity and over-achievement in later life.

The clarity with which some parents repeat the patterns of their own unhappy childhood in the ways they bring up children is such that it is difficult to realize they are not aware of it. Obviously, apprehensions of their own must keep them from recognizing what is so clear to the social worker in a child guidance clinic or a school personnel department.

> A mother came to the clinic complaining of her two girls, who were impudent, thoughtless, and resentful of her authority. In talking of her own childhood, as she frequently did, the mother stressed how differently she was bringing up her daughters from the way she had been brought up, and how perplexing it was that they were not happy as a result. The mother had early showed musical talent and had been exploited by her mother in radio and TV "talent" shows. She bitterly resented the hours of practicing and the pressure from her mother to compete and to excel. She told how she resolved not to make her children take music lessons until they asked to do so, and how she would never nag at them to practice. At the same time she told of the local and regional scholarship competitions she was grooming her daughters for, the amount of time she expected them to spend on homework, and the importance of superior school grades. Until she came to recognize the similarity, with the help of the caseworker who accepted her as a "good" mother who wanted the

best for her children, this mother was sincere in thinking she
was avoiding her own mother's errors.

Parents who push their children to fulfill their own ambitions
and who thus repeat the mistakes they resented from their own
childhood have often not experienced adequate parenting themselves. The acceptance and warmth of the social worker help to
make up for some of the deficiency. It is implicit in our mores that
parents should be good parents and want the best for their children. Parents who are so preoccupied with their own emotional
needs that they cannot comprehend their children's, still feel
guilty and inadequate, and may feel that referral to a social agency
is still another proof of their failure. They are already worried that
they may not love their children enough and that the children's
behavior is an indication of insufficient love. Telling such parents
to love their children more is as useless as telling a person with
pneumonia to be more healthy. If they do not seem to love their
children, it may well be that they do not know how, since they
themselves never experienced uncritical, loving acceptance. "You
cannot give me what you never got" is an old casework jingle
which applies to many of the parents who come to the attention of
the school social worker, the child guidance clinician, the protective services worker, and the family therapist.

Family Therapy

Essential to helping parents who feel inadequate and defensive
is the therapist's warmth and acceptance of them as people who
care and who want to do better for themselves and their children.
As family therapy moves more and more into treatment of the entire family in the home, the therapist has been able to move away
from objective detachment to more personal involvement and include more of himself in the process.[36] Thus the therapist is able
to provide a model of good parenting, both to the parents and the
children, as well as on-the-spot examination of interaction between parents and children. If children can develop more appreciation of their parents' unfulfilled needs, they will be less threatened by what appears to them to be parental hostility.

A well-known family therapist, Dr. Ross Speck, insists on visiting the family home before undertaking family therapy. He views
even family pets as extensions of the family personality and finds

---

36. See Nathan W. Ackerman, *Family Therapy in Transition* (Boston: Little,
Brown & Company, 1970), for an account of these and other trends in family
therapy.

that sleeping arrangements and seating arrangements tell a great deal about family interaction. In his dialogue with Adelaide Bry,[37] Dr. Speck tells of setting out a variety of chairs—overstuffed, straight-backed, easy—and observing who takes which chair. If the youngest child takes the most comfortable chair and leaves one corner of a couch for the father, the therapist has some idea of who is doing the parenting in that family. It is then the joint task of family and therapist to develop more appropriate role definitions.

Where parents have had trouble in differentiating their children as individuals rather than as extensions of the parental selves, the struggle for independence of adolescent children is especially painful. In our culture, as anthropologists have demonstrated, adolescents suffer because we have no clearly defined expectations of behavior for teen-agers; and they suffer from "role discontinuity," which necessitates rapid transition from childhood to maturity. This is compounded in many families by the prolongation of the period of financial dependence upon parents necessitated by higher education. In families where there has been a good mix of separation, autonomy, and distance, the emancipation process can go fairly smoothly. Where the family has been too interdependent and overly intimate, the child cannot break away without feeling guilt and provoking rejection.

Just as childhood has had its essential tasks—gaining mastery over the body, learning language and other communication skills, learning the socially accepted norms of behavior, and learning how to relate to family members and those outside the home—so too does adolescence carry the need for the completion of certain major developmental tasks. Before he can become an adult, the teen-ager must become independent of his parents, make his career choice, and establish his sexual identification. He needs the support and help of his parents in these critical decisions, yet at the same time, he is resisting his own dependency needs. Parents who do not see their roles clearly and do not feel reasonably confident in them will not be able to preserve a serene and tolerant acceptance of the adolescent's uneven progress toward his goals. An adolescent has been defined, with some truth, as "a teen-ager who acts like a baby if you don't treat him like an adult," and this inconsistency can be very trying to live with.

37. Adelaide Bry, a psychotherapist, interviewed nine clinicians representing nine different therapeutic approaches and has presented the edited, taped interviews in *Inside Psychotherapy* (New York: Basic Books, 1972). The interview with Dr. Speck is Chapter 6, pp. 87–102.

While younger children are usually viewed by therapists as expressing troubled family relationships and therefore usually treated concurrently with at least one parent, an adolescent may seek treatment on a one-to-one basis. If this represents his need for help in establishing his own identity, his request should be honored. Thus school social workers and psychiatric social workers may see teen-agers without ever seeing other family members and sometimes without the parents' knowledge. The importance of confidentiality in such contacts should be scrupulously observed, since the young client may see any sharing of information about him as belittling him and undermining his attempts to free himself from parental clinging.[38]

There is good evidence that adolescents today confront many serious problems which were unknown to their parents. Irene Josselyn, the noted child psychiatrist, has commented on how different she finds her adolescent patients today from a generation ago.[39] They seem more demanding, less thoughtful of others, and quite unrealistic, particularly about money. They are also more sophisticated and more sensitive to the views of their contemporaries than accepting of parental views. The youth culture, including the drug scene and early sexual activity, opens many new value judgments for young people. The effects of the peer group in delinquency have been well documented,[40] as has the estrangement of many young persons from their parents and their elders in general. The "generation gap" may widen as education and recreation move away from the home and as children reject their parents' values as meaningless and their behavior as hypocritical. Ackerman refers to a form of "family anomie," in which parents abdicate responsibility, and sees this as a reflection of the disorders of contemporary society.[41]

For adolescents who reject and distrust anyone older, group therapy and self-help programs may be acceptable. Many group work agencies cater to specific age groups and adapt programs to the special interests and needs of adolescents of both sexes. In an

38. See Elizabeth Kerns, "Planned Short-term Treatment, A New Service to Adolescents," *Social Casework*, Vol. 51, No. 6 (June 1970) pp. 340–346.

39. Irene Josselyn, "The Adolescent Today," *Smith College Studies in Social Work*, Vol. 38, No. 1 (November 1967), pp. 1–15.

40. A pioneering study of the "delinquent subculture" is Richard A. Cloward and Lloyd E. Ohlin, *Delinquency and Opportunity* (Glencoe: The Free Press, 1960). See also Kenneth Polk and Walter E. Schaefer, eds., *Schools and Delinquency* (Englewood Cliffs, N.J.: Prentice-Hall, 1972).

41. Nathan W. Ackerman, "Family Healing in a Troubled World," *Social Casework*, Vol. 52, No. 4 (April 1971), pp. 200–205.

experiment with group therapy for adolescents,[42] Epstein reports good results from mixed groups of boys and girls, which met for a six-week period, during which the adolescents were "pushed, cajoled, and exhorted to examine the usual adolescent hangups with parents, school, and community . . . It has been found that reinterpretation of adults' motives and questioning the adolescents' perceptions is a valuable technique."[43] Community mental health centers use group sessions for drug abusers, delinquents, and other young people acting out their difficulties in socially disapproved ways.

The recent phenomenon of drop-in centers for young people has succeeded in enlisting some young people in helping themselves by way of helping their peers. Unfortunately, these centers are not usually stable, are likely to be involved in funding crises, and attempt to serve several mutually exclusive functions. Drug-users, particularly the alienated young, do not wish to become involved with anything suggesting acceptance of "establishment" values but welcome a place in which to find food, warmth, and freedom from "hassling." Those sponsoring such drop-in centers view them as avenues for rehabilitation and favor group therapy, lectures and classes, and organized activities. The staff, usually composed of social activists, prefers projects leading to social change. The incompatibility of these objectives, in the opinion of the Canadian sociologist Kenneth Westhues,[44] makes for instability of operation. The centers meet a need, however, in serving young people who will not involve themselves in any regularly organized social agency.

That leaving home does not resolve the emancipation struggle is evident in the extent to which conflicts over responsibility to parents is a concern in college mental health programs,[45] in military social work, and in correctional facilities. Long after their adolescence, adults must still be viewed in the perspectives of their continuing relationships with the people they grew up with, the effects on their personalities of their early family experiences, and their need to create new family ties in the pattern of or as correctives to their original ones.

42. Norman Epstein, "Brief Group Therapy in a Child Guidance Clinic," *Social Work*, Vol. 15, No. 3 (July 1970), pp. 33–38.

43. *Ibid.*, p. 38. Reprinted with the permission of the National Association of Social Workers.

44. Kenneth Westhues, "The Drop-In Center: A Study in Conflicting Realities," *Social Casework*, Vol. 53, No. 6 (June 1972), pp. 361–368.

45. Gerald Amada and Jacqueline Swartz, "Social Work in a College Mental Health Program," *Social Casework*, Vol. 53, No. 9 (November 1972), pp. 528–533.

THE EMPTY NEST

After the last child has left home (which, in the contemporary pattern of earlier marriage and fewer children, is now likely to occur when parents are in their early forties), comes the readjustment to living as a couple once again. Mothers may resume interrupted careers or, conversely, may be able to afford to give up work, now that the expenses of educating their children are past. Where financial resources are adequate, this can be a time of recovery and increased social participation. Expenses have decreased, earnings are at their maximum, and more options are open to the couple than before. Where problems arise, it is likely to be because one or both parents had been receiving their chief satisfaction from their parental rather than their marital roles. Mental health centers are familiar with the depressed mother whose justification for her existence has left the home with the last child. It is as if she is afraid to face her husband without the buffer of children between him and herself. Such a mother may make protracted visits to her married children to avoid isolating herself with her husband. Husbands may bury themselves in their occupations, as a defense against spending too much time in a lonely house, with a depressed or complaining wife. Efforts to help such a couple should focus on increased social participation, the development or reactivation of outside interests together, and sound retirement planning. The physical changes of menopause require health services for both. Parents who have been ignoring each other to concentrate on the children can be helped to confront each other and develop new ways of relating, which will provide some of the self-esteem formerly derived from parenting their children. A sound relationship between them established during the early years will prevent disorganization now. Some family experts prefer the term "second honeymoon" to "empty nest" as indicating a more positive approach to this stage in the family life cycle.

Where the couple never had or seems to have lost permanently a mutually satisfactory adjustment, the two may continue to maintain the home but involve themselves with other people as a source of self-esteem. Careers, social activities, experimental liaisons with other mates, or absorption in political or volunteer activity to the exclusion of the mate represent substitutes for some or most of the emotional support each should be providing the other. Often, such couples are not consciously aware that they have made a choice. Masters and Johnson report that middle-aged or elderly couples can continue to have satisfying sex lives, but many are unaware that this is possible.[46] Fear of seeming ridiculous may prevent couples from experimenting with new approaches to many aspects of their lives together. The helping process will encourage them to feel secure enough to devise new views of themselves and each other.

Realistic planning for retirement is a relatively new area of family service. In addition to consideration of financial resources, there is the decision of where the retired couple should live. Housing developments for the elderly are being provided for middle- and upper-income couples, and a limited number of subsidized housing projects for senior citizens have been built by public housing authorities. Revised relationships with children may be indicated; parents may become dependent upon their children for financial and/or emotional support, which is an illustration of role reversal and may make for problems when neither parents or children can readjust.[47] The Social Security Administration welcomes inquiries from those approaching retirement age and will calculate Social Security benefits and advise when to apply for them. The field of services to the aging is relatively new and expanding rapidly. In addition to the provision of transportation, Meals on Wheels, home health care, and social activities, the need for protective services for the elderly is increasingly recognized. These and other services for the aging will be discussed in some detail in Chapter 5.

WIDOWHOOD

Although divorce, legal separation, and desertion play a significant role in dissolving marriages, the largest number of couples is eventually separated by the death of one mate. Owing to the greater life expectancy of women (74.6 years in 1970 as opposed to 67.1 for men) and to the fact that men tend to marry women younger than themselves, the husband's death will almost always come first. Where the wife dies first, chances are very great that the widower will remarry. The problems of the aged are much more likely to be faced by the widow. Among these problems are financial support, loss of status, and the breaking of long-established behavior patterns. The fears of disabling illness and a lonely death haunt many solitary elderly persons and make the supportive services of social workers, health care facilities,

---

46. Masters and Johnson, *Human Sexual Response*, Chapters 15, 16.

47. See Robert Anderson, *I Never Sang for My Father* (New York: New American Library, 1970), for an interesting play exploring this topic.

friendly visiting by volunteers, and protective housing essential community needs.[48]

Those widows who have had the most satisfactory relationships with their husbands are more likely to adjust to their solitary status. They have developed enough self-esteem and feelings of adequacy to be able to carry through the necessary readjustments. It is those wives who have lived in a hostile-dependent relationship or have submerged their own identities in those of their husbands who are more likely to develop prolonged grief reactions and transfer their dependency needs to their children. Modifying behavior patterns of such long standing is difficult; often the only useful solution is in supporting those who have to live near and react with the difficult older person, although behavioral modification techniques may be used to eliminate specific irritating items of behavior.

ONE-PARENT FAMILIES

For the typical family, adjustments at each point in the family life cycle are inevitable. Families who find themselves unable to move on in the life cycle may seek help from or be referred to family service agencies, school social workers, mental health or child guidance clinics, or other all-purpose agencies. One-parent families, however, do not go through the "ideal" or modal family life cycle and may well be in need of special services, as yet not well developed.

One-parent families exist for a number of reasons. The "uncompleted" family is the one in which the mother of one or more children has never married. The "broken" family occurs when married couples have been separated, permanently or for temporary periods, by death, divorce, or separation, either voluntary, through desertion by one parent, or involuntary, as in military service or imprisonment. The many possible combinations of these variables force the conclusion that there is no such entity as the "one-parent family"; thus discussions of such families as pathological, poverty-related, or productive of inevitably maladjusted children are simplistic and not useful. It may well be that the divorce, separation, or refusal to marry represent better solutions to the individual situation than the couple's remaining together.

More recent thinking minimizes the pathological and psycho-

---

48. A Widows Consultation Center has recently been established in New York City. See Jo Ann Levine, "Solving the Problems of Widowhood," *Christian Science Monitor*, September 28, 1973, p. 14.

dynamic elements adduced by theorists and focuses instead on the structural problems faced by a family with only one adult.[49] The major functions of the family in our culture are the procreation and socialization of children; while two parents are involved in conception, from that point on the mother can operate alone to fulfill the two family functions. For obvious biological reasons, the one-parent family is likely to be mother and one or more children, although a widower or divorced father may find himself trying to serve as sole parent. It is interesting that our culture puts so many obstacles in the way of this, however; courts are most unlikely to award custody of small children to fathers, and it is doubtful if many fathers would give up their jobs to stay home with the children on Aid to Families with Dependent Children (AFDC), although they would be eligible under the law. We virtually compel all but the wealthiest of such fathers to remarry in order to secure adequate mothering for their children. When mothers have died or deserted their families, except in upper-income levels where mother-substitutes can be hired, the children are almost invariably placed in foster care. It is illuminating to realize the extent to which we consider desertion by the mother as more pathological than desertion by the father. The literature on one-parent families is almost always concerned with mother-headed units.

The extent of illegitimacy has already been cited. Statistics on illegitimacy refer only to illegitimate births, not to children conceived outside of marriage. Since the pressures on a pregnant girl to marry vary in differing subcultures, the rate of births is already skewed toward overrepresentation of those in poverty. The extent to which nonwhite illegitimacy is related to such cultural factors as racism, poverty, and traditional family forms is controversial. The famous Moynihan Report (see footnote 3, page 110) cites the experience of blacks under slavery as a causative factor for the large number of mother-headed black families. Other authorities cite the greater difficulty of nonwhite girls in placing their babies for adoption. The ability of women to secure employment as domestics in an economy which offers no comparable work for males has been offered as an explanation for the greater incidence of mother-headed families in urban ghettos. It will be interesting to see, as contraception and legalized abortion make illegiti-

49. For a careful analysis of this approach, see Paul Glasser and Elizabeth Navarre, "Structural Problems of the One-Parent Family," *Journal of Social Issues*, Vol. 21, No. 1 (January 1965), pp. 98–109. See also Benjamin Schlesinger, *The One-Parent Family* (Toronto: University of Toronto Press, 1969).

macy more avoidable, whether the incidence of uncompleted families declines.

Much less is known about the mothers of illegitimate children in middle- and upper-level one-parent families. Studies carried out in 1966 (before "the pill" was in widespread use) showed that 13 percent of unwed mothers known to social agencies planned to keep their children; these mothers were disproportionately non-white.[50] However, it is very probable that nonwhite mothers were more likely to be known to social agencies. Those who released their babies for adoption reported higher family incomes and were better educated than those who kept them. Much more careful research is needed before accurate knowledge of the relationships among ethnicity, family income, illegitimacy, and mother-headed families can be secured.

The statistics from AFDC rolls are also skewed, since the program is designed primarily for one-parent families. The Social and Rehabilitation Service (SRS) reports that fewer than one third of children on welfare are illegitimate[51]; this does not always mean, however, that they are growing up in fatherless homes. Consensual unions are more common in poverty, and the role of the "boyfriend," as Romanyshyn points out,[52] is a little-studied but frequent phenomenon in lower-class life. Assuming that all AFDC mothers are promiscuous, and ignoring their vulnerability to exploitation and their need for security and gratification, is a reflection of the punitive and conflicting attitudes toward sex in our society.

Figures on the numbers of children living in one-parent homes are difficult to secure. An estimate of 10 percent of all children in the United States is made by Billingsley and Giovannoni,[53] who state that the most common type of one-parent family is that with a divorced parent at the head, and the least common type is that with a widowed or unmarried family head.

Whatever the incidence, it is apparent that a single parent is bearing a heavy burden in attempting to carry out fuctions usually shared by two adults. This is complicated further by the fact that the sole parent is also the only one mediating between the chil-

50. See Lillian J. Grow, "The Unwed Mother Who Keeps Her Child," *The Double Jeopardy—The Triple Crisis* (New York: National Council on Illegitimacy, 1969), pp. 115–125.

51. *Welfare Myths vs. Facts* (Washington, D.C.: SRS, n.d.)

52. John Romanyshyn, *Social Welfare: Charity to Justice* (New York: Random House, 1971), p. 225.

53. Billingsley and Giovannoni, "Family, One-Parent," p. 369.

dren and the outside world. The child is therefore exposed to only one method of interaction with outside figures. Because of the multiple demands put on the single parent, there may be less time and energy for the children. Since the single parent also serves simultaneously as source of love and as authority figure, tensions may result, hindering the carrying out of one or the other of these parental roles. Some authorities have been concerned over the effects on male children of the absence of an adult male, but there is no conclusive evidence of lasting damage. The presence of other males in the household or the extended family or continued contact with the divorced husband may lessen the effects.

Although the absent parent may have left the home, the child continues to be affected by him, either in reality or in fantasy, and it is wise to include him in planning with the single parent for the child. Arthur Leader, for example, points out that the divorced father continues to carry responsibility for the growth of his children.[54] If the divorce was preceded by family conflict or has resulted in hostility, the child will have a distorted impression of his parents and possible guilt about what he conceives of as his failure to keep them together. When immature parents try to force children to take sides or use them as pawns in their own competitive maneuvers, the children's development will be impeded.

A large number of divorced people remarry. While this solves some problems, it raises others. The relation of subsequent children of this marriage to those of either partner's former marriage, the attitudes of grandparents, the reluctance of children to establish ties with a stepparent when these threaten ties to their own parent—all these can complicate the family task.

Essentially, the basic tasks of these variant family forms are the same as those of the modal family. The child must be helped to mature, to find his identity as a worthwhile person, to emancipate himself and achieve independence, and to leave the home for his adult career. The parent, with a new partner or alone, must socialize the child, relinquish him when the time comes without undue clinging, maintain suitable participation in activities outside the home, and prepare realistically for retirement and old age. Some of these tasks are more difficult alone; on the other hand, some may be simpler alone. We have been handicapped in studying one-parent families objectively by a preoccupation with considering the one-parent family as pathological, forgetting that

54. Arthur L. Leader, "Family Therapy for Divorced Fathers and Others Out of Home," *Social Casework*, Vol. 54, No. 1 (January 1973), pp. 13–19.

many of the problems attributed to one-parent families are prevalent in all families.

SERVICES TO FAMILIES

Those who are concerned with helping families carry out their tasks more competently and with more ease should be aware of the developmental nature of the family tasks and the points at which special stress may necessitate intervention. We have talked throughout this chapter of the helping process and the needs of parents and children and have mentioned briefly several methods and schools of thought (clarification, behavioral modification, transactional analysis) without analyzing what the helping person does or should not do.

THE HELPING PROCESS

As with all applied arts, reading about the helping process oversimplifies what is involved and makes it look easy. Skills can be learned only in action, and some people learn certain skills more easily than others. In her excellent book *Working with People*,[55] Naomi Brill reassures the beginning worker that he should know and utilize his own life style and not feel forced into some stereotyped mold of a helping person. She analyzes the helping process as the using of skills, techniques, and tools.

Mrs. Brill specifies six basic skills which the helping person must master. The first, *differential diagnosis*, refers to the worker's understanding of the client-in-the-situation without allowing his own emotions to interfere. *Timing* means both the pace at which client and worker characteristically operate, as well as the strategic moment in contact with the client or in his situation for a precise bit of intervention. *Partialization* refers to the differentiation of an unmanageable constellation of problems into manageable units and helping the client decide where to start. *Focus*, or keeping to the contract,[56] means not becoming sidetracked on peripheral issues and may be particularly needed when clients are so overwhelmed by stress as to become distracted easily. The fifth

55. Naomi Brill, *Working with People: The Helping Process* (Philadelphia: J. B. Lippincott Company, 1973). Reprinted by permission of the publisher, J. B. Lippincott Company. Copyright © 1973. The following analysis draws heavily on Chapter 8.

56. Although Brill uses the term "contract" as meaning an agreement on the goals of the work together, the concept was introduced and elaborated by Margaret Schubert in *Interviewing in Social Work Practice: An Introduction* (New York: Council on Social Work Education [CSWE], 1971), q.v.

skill, which Brill calls *establishing partnership*, is implicit in the notion of contract and involves the mutual understanding of the roles and tasks client and worker will engage in; the roles are complementary and should reflect the expertise which the worker brings to the client's situation as well as the maximum participation of the client. *Structure* refers to the setting and boundaries for the work together. Where, how often, and for how long client and worker should meet, agreement about what resources will be utilized, and a realistic appraisal of what can be achieved together are all included in this skill, with which the worker organizes the helping process.

Mrs. Brill goes on to discuss, in specific terms and with practical illustrations, some of the useful techniques by means of which the worker implements his skills. These include *ventilation* (allowing the client to express bottled-up feelings), *support* (see page 119), *reassurance, confrontation, manipulation* (skillful management of resources, not insidious or devious exploitation of weakness), *universalization* (recognizing that others have developed methods of coping with similar difficulties), *advice-giving* (to be used sparingly and with discrimination), *logical discussion, reward and punishment* (see behavior modification, pages 200–204), *role rehearsal and demonstration,* and the use of *audio-visual devices* to illuminate client interaction.

Mrs. Brill's tools include the *interview, group discussion,* and *referral.* The worker carries the major responsibility for establishing communication through his own questions, comments, or accepting silences. Attempting to phrase the client's feelings in ways which will help him recognize and face them and asking questions which will encourage the client to understand his situation and think of possible solutions are to be recommended rather than criticism, worker's personal reactions, or exhortations. Discussions permit the expression of a variety of opinions and reactions, opening up possible alternatives that had not occurred to the client, and often providing support from others with similar or equally great difficulties. Mrs. Brill's book is a primer, well worth study by any beginner, and will prove valuable to experienced therapists for its freshness and practicality in theory and method.

The basic values underlying social work, discussed in Chapter 1, are implicit in the helping process. The client's rights to be helped, to be accepted for what he is and not for his adequacy in measuring up to other peoples' expectations, to be involved in his own destiny, and to be protected from injustice must be part of the helping person's value system. They involve self-discipline and self-awareness on the part of the worker and a willingness to subordinate his own comfort and anxiety to those of his client. The helping interview may be relaxed and friendly, but the essential difference between an interview and a friendly conversation is that the adaptations are one-sided. The worker cannot ask the client, as he might a friend, to stop talking because what he is saying is too upsetting or cap the client's recital of wrongs with an even greater list of his own injuries. It has been said that it is the worker's obligation to bear the anxiety, not to demand that the client alter his behavior in order to reduce the worker's anxiety.

SPECIALIZED FAMILY SERVICES

The helping process, as sketched above, is carried on wherever client and social worker meet. However, in the interests of efficiency, specialized agencies for dealing with similar types of problems have arisen. Family service agencies, the descendants of the Charity Organization Societies of the nineteenth century, have been described earlier in this chapter. Their function is to assist families to achieve more harmonious functioning at every stage of the family life cycle. Specialized problems, not part of the modal family life cycle, may be dealt with by social workers from specialized agencies or programs.

Travelers Aid–International Social Service of America

America is a highly mobile society. One family in six moves every year, sometimes around the corner and sometimes across the continent. While families of all income levels migrate, those in poverty move oftener, in search of a job or a better job. Migration rates of the poor are largely from rural to urban areas and include whites from Appalachia and southern farm areas, blacks from the South, Puerto Ricans from Puerto Rico, Chicano farm workers from the Southwest, and American Indians from the reservations. Many of these migrants are young, semi-skilled, and only semi-literate. They tend to move into northern and north-central cities and to the West Coast. They tend to choose their destination on the basis of relatives or friends already there, leading to heavy concentrations of individuals from the same area in certain cities. The migration of Puerto Ricans into New York City (a poor place for unskilled labor to select) is an illustration. The migration of these minority group members is not well planned, and often they do not have adequate resources to complete the journey to their destination.[57]

The resources available to these migrants in transit are largely limited to voluntary efforts of churches, filling stations, and the police. Public welfare residence restrictions (imposed by state legislatures as a way to cut welfare costs) have been systematically struck down by higher courts but survive in the "intent to remain" clause which excludes migratory workers and transients, although states may offer emergency aid under General Assistance. Some improvement in the plight of new arrivals in some communities has resulted from the Community Action Programs sponsored by the Office of Economic Opportunity and Legal Aid, but their future is uncertain.

The only agency designed especially for people on the move is Travelers Aid–International Social Service of America (TAISSA), an intercity casework service. Its intensive short-contact assistance to travelers was originally based in railroad stations but now has been extended to bus and air terminals. Some TAISSA offices are located near major interstate highway exchanges, as a substantial number of referrals come from toll booth operators who report families stranded on the throughway, unable to pay the exit toll. Services include providing information, making arrangements for lost or runaway children and for emotionally upset or confused people in transportation facilities, and assistance to travelers who have lost money or arrive without adequate funds or a place to stay. Through their nationwide networks of branches and representatives, TAISSA can arrange for children or disabled persons to be met on arrival or at transfer points and help people return home if there is someone at home to take responsibility for them. Increasingly, TAISSA is attempting to reach prospective migrants with help in planning before they take off to travel planlessly. Unfortunately, these services are not known or not available in many of the rural areas from which these migrants come, and TAISSA encounters them only after they are on the road. One problem with which TAISSA is familiar is that of the family or person who is using flight as a method of escaping his problems and who does not dare settle lest they pursue him there.

The emergency nature of most TAISSA contacts puts a premium on the TAISSA worker's ability to size up situations and people quickly, to know and use community resources available, to press

---

57. See Norma V. Lourie, "The Migration Mess," *Social Work*, Vol. 17, No. 1 (January 1972), pp. 77–86, which recommends a national mobility program; and Joseph W. Eaton, ed., *Migration and Social Welfare* (New York: NASW, 1971).

for more adequate resources where deficiencies exist, and to establish an atmosphere of reassurance and stability in a minimum of time. Since the stranded travelers are faced with critical decisions about going on, staying, or going back, the TAISSA worker must be skilled in his approach, able to use his techniques effectively under pressure of time, both in face-to-face encounters and over the phone, since much of the communication with social agencies and resources in the local community and in the travelers' home town are by telephone, with letters as follow-ups.[58]

Red Cross Service to Military Families

The American National Red Cross, a voluntary agency which is chartered by the United States Congress, provides casework services for members of the armed forces and their families and veterans and their families, in addition to its somewhat better-known programs of disaster relief, first aid, and blood procurement.

In discharging its responsibilities under the charter granted by Congress, this national agency is concerned with helping servicemen and servicewomen and their families adjust to the requirements of a different kind of life. Field Directors at military installations and at military hospitals work with Service to Military Families (SMF) workers in the community, helping service families to understand military regulations and to deal with anxieties resulting from the separation that is inherent in military service. If a husband's or son's entry into the armed forces results in reduced income, the wife or parents may have real trouble adjusting to the situation. Wives may anticipate or have problems with rearing the children in their father's absence or need help in answering the children's questions about their father's continued absence, possible injury, prisoner status, or reported death. With direct communication to Red Cross Field Directors at military installations, SMF workers can learn and transmit vital information, can facilitate emergency leave, and can assist dependents in applying for hardship discharges of servicemen or servicewomen urgently needed at home.

Veterans of all wars come to Red Cross for help in establishing eligibility for state and federal government benefits or help with problems resulting from military service. Families of veterans may ask for help with anxieties about returned Viet Nam veterans, who are bearing an undue share of the onus of an unpopular war.

58. The Travelers Aid Association publishes case material illustrating the variety of problems encountered and the use of community resources. These are valuable teaching records. Write for units currently available to the Association at 33 E. 23rd St., New York, N.Y. 10010.

Those who returned as drug abusers or from prisoner of war camps may feel or create in others special tensions and need professional help. SMF also may be called upon to help in the adjustment of war brides from other countries who are having difficulties in adapting to a strange culture and a language barrier.

SMF workers use the same skills and techniques as other social workers in helping clients analyze their problems objectively and seek constructive solutions. Some people need only specific information about military regulations or community resources; others need more extended casework or referral to a community agency for intensive therapy. SMF workers need to know a good deal about military regulations and procedures, such as those covering emergency leave and hardship discharge, allotment of pay, and provision of medical care and other services for dependents. They must also know something about the benefits available through the Veterans Administration as well as through community resources.

The alleviation of human suffering and distress caused by disaster is another of the responsibilities delegated to the Red Cross by its congressional charter. Red Cross workers counsel on personal or family problems created or aggravated by the disaster— whether it be tornado, flood, fire, or earthquake—and give financial assistance to meet the needs arising from the disaster when these cannot be met by the families' own resources or other funds.

Homemaker Service

Homemaker service originated with the family service agency, although it is now increasingly being carried out by public departments of welfare or health and has been expanded to cover home health aides. The use of visiting homemakers dates from 1904, when the Community Service Society of New York used "visiting cleaners." The program received impetus under the WPA, when it was used to employ women in financial need as well as to provide the service. Homemaker service furnishes help with household tasks to enable a family to maintain itself at home in the face of illness or acute stress.[59] Typical examples would be the illness of the mother of small children, an elderly couple with insufficient strength to maintain themselves who do not want to admit defeat and go into an institution or nursing home, and the sudden death of the mother of young children until the husband can make adequate plans for their care.

59. See Paul Schreiber, "The Community Service Aspect of a Homemaker Program," *Social Casework*, Vol. 52, No. 7 (July 1971), pp. 438–443.

Homemakers are employees of the agency and should be assigned and supervised by a qualified member of the professional staff of the agency. They should be carefully selected for both personal qualities and homemaking skills and be given in-service training to enable them to avoid being manipulated by family members. Homemakers can provide not only a respite from daily tasks for an overburdened parent but can serve a valuable educational function for mothers who need instruction in money management, marketing, and care of the household. Fees on a sliding scale are paid by the family; homemakers are not economically utilized to permit mothers to go to work. Where simple health care needs can be met by the homemaker–home health aide, it can avoid costly hospitalization, and enabling the children to remain at home during a mother's illness or absence is much more economical than placing the children temporarily. In spite of these obvious cost advantages, homemaker service does not receive the support it warrants from either public or private funds. Although the movement has grown from four services in 1904 to an estimated 20,000 in 1970, service is concentrated in urban areas and even there is never adequate for the need.

The National Council for Homemaker Services, under the sponsorship of the National Assembly for Social Policy and Development, was established in 1962 and publishes a directory of public and private services. There is also an International Council, in which England is a leading member. Many European countries have developed homemaker services to a far greater extent than the United States.

The professional social worker or nurse who is making an assignment of a homemaker to a family should share the treatment goals with the homemaker and help her plan how to foster them. Special methods of handling a child, encouraging an overly timid client to assume more responsibility, or helping a frustrated client become more accepting of a disability are goals which a homemaker can plan for in very specific ways. The agency supervisor should be available for conferences and should visit the home to see the homemaker in operation. If the homemaker has not been able to resist becoming involved in family "games" and is being manipulated by one or more family members, it may be necessary to reassign her. Since she is serving a mothering function in the home, she may find herself trapped in excessive demands by deprived family members and unable to resist. Some homemaker services operate as independent agencies, taking cases on referral from community agencies or direct applications from individuals.

However, these agencies need to have substantial financial backing, as the service is a costly one. Professional consultation and direction should be provided by the agency, for the homemakers. Standards for operation are established by the Council for Homemaker Services, and important work in standard setting and interpretation of service has been done by federal agencies in the Department of Health, Education, and Welfare.[60]

OTHER SERVICES OF FAMILY AGENCIES

In many small communities the family service agency, as the all-purpose private agency, may be asked to offer casework services or consultation in "outpost" settings, such as an industrial plant, a summer camp, a housing project, or a suburb. Many full-time services begin in this way. Experimental programs may be developed to demonstrate a method of meeting a need; these may become part of the regular family agency services or may develop into specialized services under other auspices. Debt counseling,[61] camp application service,[62] and family advocacy[63] are illustrative of such innovative programs.

In the 1960s, family agencies became more conscious of the need to adapt their traditionally middle class–oriented methods to deal with the poor and the nonwhite. Funded by the Office of Economic Opportunity and sponsored jointly by the Child Study Association, the National Urban League, and the Family Service Association of America (FSAA), Project ENABLE (Education and Neighborhood Action for Better Living Environment) was designed to develop new methods and utilize new personnel to learn what kinds of services poor families need and can use. Caseworkers and community organizers learned to adapt their techniques to the unaccustomed clientele and to mobilize the efforts of poor clients in their own behalf. Although the funding for ENABLE

60. See *The Homemaker–Home Health Aide in Health Services* (Washington, D.C.: U.S. Public Health Service, 1968); and *Recommendations for Homemaker–Home Health Aide Training and Services* (Washington, D.C.: U.S. Public Health Service, 1969). See also Maud Morlock, *Homemaker Services: History and Bibliography*, Publication No. 410 (U.S. Children's Bureau, 1964).

61. See John L. Laughlin and Robert Bressler, "A Family Agency Program for Heavily Indebted Families," *Social Casework*, Vol. 52, No. 10 (December 1971), pp. 617–626.

62. See Mildred G. Edwards and Edith R. Schmidt, " 'Downtown' Is the Office," *Social Casework*, Vol. 52, No. 10 (December 1971), pp. 634–642.

63. See Earl J. Beatt, "Family Services: Family Service Agencies," *Encyclopedia of Social Work, 1971*, especially pp. 395, 396.

ceased after only one year, it sparked off changes in program emphasis and methods which continue in effect.[64]

The developmental approach to family life (as indicated in our account of the family life cycle and its stress points) emphasizes the importance of the family life education program which family service agencies have traditionally carried on. Members of agency staff serve as consultants or panelists for educational programs under a variety of auspices for group educational purposes, not primarily groups of clients. Information is disseminated about family relationships, personality development, and awareness of potential periods of stress. In addition, the agency carries on public relations functions, which include radio and television interviews, newspaper articles, and pamphlets for general distribution, both for campaign purposes and to make citizens aware of services offered. About half the clients coming to a family service agency hear of the services through the mass media or friends. The balance are referred from other social agencies, the clergy, courts, schools, physicians, or employers. An effective public relations tool has been the provision to interested parties of plays portraying a wide variety of problems and social services. Suitable for acting by amateur groups and open-ended to create discussion (for which a discussion guide is provided), *Plays for Living* includes half-hour dramas dealing with family counseling, school integration, teen-age stresses, drugs, and rehabilitation. The FSAA also makes available filmstrips with accompanying sound for education and public relations.[65]

Voluntary family service agencies may be operated under non-sectarian or sectarian auspices. The sectarian agencies are largely Roman Catholic or Jewish, although other denominations may provide family counseling as part of their overall program. Both Roman Catholic and Jewish agencies are concerned with the family, including the provision of special institutions for children and the elderly. Most sectarian agencies belong to a national sectarian body, the National Conference of Catholic Charities or the Council of Jewish Federations and Welfare Funds; most also belong to the Family Service Association of America, the major standard-setting organization in the field. The FSAA dates from 1911 and

64. See *Social Casework*, Vol. 48, No. 10 (December 1967). This entire issue of *Social Casework* is based on Project ENABLE. See also Ellen P. Manser, *Project ENABLE: What Happened?* (New York: FSAA 1968).

65. Concerning *Plays for Living*, write Family Service Association of America, 44 E. 23rd St., New York, N.Y. 10010, for titles available. There are restrictions on use for profit and on reproduction; a modest royalty may be charged.

accredits more than 350 member agencies, which must meet specified standards for program, staffing, board responsibility, and
financing. The national organization provides consultation to
member agencies and to communities which are considering the
establishment of a family service agency. Its Publications Service
publishes *Social Casework,* the leading periodical in the casework
field, first issued in 1920 as *The Family.* It carries on research in
all aspects of social work, from the education of board members
to the statistical analysis of the work of member agencies. It conducts a Public Relations Service and publishes useful teaching
materials for social work educators.

In line with their feeling of responsibility for recruitment and
professional training of social workers, many family agencies
serve as field sites for baccalaureate- and graduate-level social
work education. Such placements may be for two or three days
a week, with students at school the other days (concurrent field
work), or the student may be on duty full-time in the agency for
a specified number of weeks (block placement). Students participate in agency activities under close supervision, gradually assuming more responsibility as they develop more skill and self-
awareness. These educational experiences are given under the
joint responsibility of the agency and the school: some schools
place field instruction units including a faculty member from the
school in the agency setting; in many instances, regular supervision is provided by agency staff, with a school faculty member
making periodic visits. This type of closely supervised practice is
one of the essentials of social work training and is comparable to
the work of senior medical students and interns in providing real
experience under adequate safeguards to clients.

Most family service agencies have a variety of specialists from
other fields, either as staff members or as consultants. The larger
agencies all have psychiatric consultation, either routinely or at
the worker's request. Agencies may have psychologists on the
staff or may use other community resources for psychological testing and assessment of clients. Most agencies have medical consultants, and some have medical social workers whose training
has familiarized them with some of the emotional concomitants of
physical illness. An agency should also have a legal consultant,
less for service to clients than for policy decisions of the agency.
For example, the question of the admission of social work records
in court or the subpoenaing of a social worker would necessitate
expert legal advice.

To increase public understanding of and support for the work of the family service agency, use should be made of volunteers and advisory committees. Allowing volunteers to play a creative and satisfying part in the work of the agency will not only extend possible agency services but is the best possible kind of public relations. For example, one family service agency used a college student volunteer to enrich the lives of two small girls, both of whose parents were deaf; the parents communicated with each other in sign language, and although the girls were of normal intelligence, they were much retarded in language skills. The volunteer took them on excursions, told them the names of what they saw, and encouraged them to talk. In another case, a volunteer spent two hours regularly each week with an extremely withdrawn child, to see whether the child's behavior outside the home was as bizarre as the mother maintained it was. The volunteer's detailed observations were of great help in arriving at a decision about removing the child from the home.

The provision of services to families is not restricted to agencies with "family service" in their titles. Community mental health centers are serving families through their varied programs, and the distinction between which clients are logical candidates for treatment at a mental health clinic and which at a family service agency is largely a matter of convenience to the client and available agency time. The apprehensions felt in some family agencies about handling seriously disturbed clients have proven unwarranted, particularly if psychiatric consultation is readily available. What was a matter of some concern a decade ago[66] is today taken for granted. A review of the contents of the leading practice journals today will show that many family service agencies deal with treating clients who might equally well be patients at a mental health center. Where emergency consultation and "walk-in clinics" are available, the family therapist can be more confident in accepting for treatment clients who might once have been considered "too sick."

Whatever may be the problem bringing an individual in trouble to a social worker—unhappiness, delinquency, neglect, disability —the family position of the troubled person will be an important aspect of his problems, and attempts to improve his relationships

66. See, for example, David Crystal, "The Family Service Agency as a Mental Health Resource," *Social Casework*, Vol. 47, No. 6 (June 1966), pp. 351–356; Richard Stuart, "Supportive Casework with Borderline Patients," *Social Work*, Vol. 9, No. 1 (January 1964); and William G. Hill and Stanley C. Silber, "Reciprocal Aspects of Mental Health and Family Service," *Social Casework*, Vol. 53, No. 10 (December 1972), pp. 623–630.

with significant family members (or even with his distorted memories of dead family members, since they continue to influence him) will be one objective of treatment. Thus, agencies in the fields of child welfare, corrections, the aging, and rehabilitation are all serving families as a part of providing service to individuals in trouble.

PRIVATE PRACTICE

It is also incorrect to assume that all services to families are carried on under agency auspices. Private practice is a relatively new field for social workers, but private practitioners use casework and family treatment in essentially the same way that agency workers do. A group of private practitioners, sharing offices as the Park East Counseling Group in New York City, states that it serves "individuals, couples and families seeking help for problems of everyday living. These may be problems of growth and development, parents and children, husbands and wives, couples contemplating marriage, and problems deriving from physical or mental illness."[67] These private practitioners, all MSWs and all with a minimum of ten years' experience after graduation, term themselves "counselors." Their fees in 1973 were $25 for an interview with one person and $35 for an interview with two or more persons. It is apparent that such services are designed for upper-income families, but to assume that family problems exist only in slums or in those on public welfare is naive. Delinquency, drug abuse, marital discord, and personal unhappiness exist at every socio-economic level.

The cost to a community, both financial and social, of allowing family disorganization to continue unchecked is tabulated by the FSAA in a hypothetical case.[68] After seven years of increasing friction, the Todds secured a divorce:

> The marriage ended but not the family story. From earliest childhood, Tommy had been a "difficult" boy. As he grew up he was in continual hot water. He was expelled from two schools and was asked to leave college in the middle of his freshman year. A succession of escapades was abruptly halted when Tommy went to the penitentiary for one to three years.

67. "The Park East Counseling Group," brochure (New York, 1973).
68. The following case study is taken from Family Service Association of America, *The High Cost of Unhappy Living* (New York, FSAA 1953), an unpaged pamphlet describing the work of family agencies. Note that the cost figures are out of date and would need to be multiplied many times to be relevant today. See also Beulah Parker, *A Mingled Yarn* (New Haven: Yale University Press, 1972), for a fascinating study of one family's unhappy living.

While drunk he ran down a workman returning from a late shift, and in panic fled the scene. The workman did not recover from his injuries. After his death, his family "went on relief." Tommy's sister Irene was the quiet one, on the edge of every group. She was a shy mouse in class, and walked home by herself. Later she surprised the community when she married a very presentable man. In the third year of her marriage, she too filed for divorce. She was given custody of their only child, Jon. The failure of the Todd marriage reached to a third generation.

How high has been the cost of the Todds' unhappy living? Family experts would agree that Tommy's difficulties in growing up were rooted in the parents' unhappiness and their inability to create a stable and loving home. While it is not possible to itemize accurately all the costs to the community, we can estimate the immediate losses and list the continuing hidden costs. For example, the first year's expenses after Tommy's escapade might be: Tommy's trial and prison maintenance, $1,500; hospital and funeral expenses of workman, $650; public support of workman's family, $1,500. Estimated direct costs to taxpayers for 1st year, $3650. Such money costs can be added up and written down so that we all can know how much we pay for others' troubles. But how do you measure worry and grief? How can we add up the human costs of loneliness, pain and shattered dreams? Severe problems and the suffering they bring can break the human spirit. These are costs of unhappy living that cannot be paid out-of-pocket. It is a debt that cannot be fully repaid in the lifetimes of those who have been deeply affected by personal disasters.

For the Todds' community, the financial burden has just begun. Though the marriage is gone, taxpayers may continue to pay for its failure in years to come. Public expenditures might include: Tommy's imprisonment and parole, public support of workman's family, Tommy's future escapades, possible costs resulting from breakup of Irene's marriage.

We have already discussed the continuing importance of group solidarity in a democracy. Both in impaired efficiency and in decreased social responsibility, unhappy, restless, troubled people lower group solidarity. Not only for humane considerations but for their own self-interest, communities should support and extend the preventive work of family agencies.

Although much family casework is in the interest of children, there are also specialized services for them, both in their own homes and, when circumstances demand, in foster care. Whereas most family casework is carried on under voluntary auspices, services for children are maintained by both governmental and voluntary. agencies. The next chapter will explore a range of these services.

ADDITIONAL REFERENCES

Andrews, Ernest E., *The Emotionally Disturbed Family* (New York: Jason Aronson, 1974). The family as an interlocking, emotional survival system, by a distinguished social work professional and educator.

Barten, H. H. and Barten, S. S., *Children and Their Parents in Brief Therapy* (New York: Behavioral Publications, 1972). Innovative strategies and approaches to children and their families, including therapy, preventive intervention, and behavior modification.

Ferber, Andrew et al., eds., *The Book of Family Therapy* (Boston: Houghton Mifflin Company, 1973). A description of family therapy by a number of leaders in the field, enlivened by reports by trainees and by families in therapy.

Geismar, Ludwig L., *555 Families: A Social-Psychological Study of Young Families in Transition* (New Brunswick, N.J.: Transaction, 1973). A well-written report of a sociological study of young families, which includes a section on the unmarried mother.

Jordan, William, *Client-Worker Transactions* (London: Routledge & Kegan Paul, 1970). Written in nontechnical language with emphasis on worker-client interaction, includes useful case illustrations.

Kelley, Robert K., *Courtship, Marriage, and the Family* (New York: Harcourt Brace Jovanovich, 1974). A standard textbook on the contemporary American family in a changing society.

Minuchin, Salvador, *Families and Family Therapy* (Cambridge: Harvard University Press, 1974). The effectively functioning family, together with families which seek therapy, including transcripts of actual family sessions.

Schulz, David A., *The Changing Family: Its Function and Future* (Englewood Cliffs, N.J.: Prentice-Hall, 1972). Describes the variety of life styles and coping strategies of the contemporary family unit.

Spiegel, John, *Transactions: The Interplay Between Individual, Family and Society* (New York: Science House, 1972). The transactional approach to a wide range of social problems, which draws upon insights from all the humane services professions, including social work.

chapter 4
services to
children

It is a deep-seated belief in our culture, both implied in the mores and backed by the law, that children should be brought up by their parents in a family setting. In the past agrarian society, where the labor of children was an important asset to the family, the rights of children were subordinate to the welfare of the larger family group. With the shift to an urban, industrial society, the older common law (brought to this country by the colonists) has been modified by an ever-increasing body of enacted law that reflects the changed roles of family members.

At common law, both wife and children were almost completely under the control of the husband-father. With the growing economic independence of women and their improved status, the legal rights of the wife have been increased, but at the same time her duties to husband and children have been more extensively defined by law. The rights and responsibilities of both parents have been affected by the passage of legislation making education compulsory, setting up restrictions on child labor, removing some of the stigma on illegitimacy, and granting greater control to government in matters of adoption and guardianship.

The older view of the law, which stressed the obligations of children, has been modified by a new emphasis on children's rights. In an industrial society, where children are a potential more than an immediate economic asset, it is increasingly recognized that government has a responsibility to insure at least a minimum of care and protection to young citizens, its future participants. When this newer view conflicts with the older common law, courts are being asked to rule on the extent to which the state has the right to intervene on behalf of the child.[1]

The rights of the child to "necessaries," that is, to adequate food, clothing, and protection, have been expanded in recent years as knowledge of the consequences of inadequate parenting has become more widely recognized. The quality of interfamilial relationships is now seen as crucial, and "neglect" may include emotional neglect and psychological mistreatment. As the Joint Commission on Mental Health of Children (Joint Commission) stated in its first report:

> The early parent-child, particularly mother-child, relationships constitute the matrix within which are to be found not only those life-damaging factors which may endanger the child's mental health, but also those life-enhancing factors which safeguard and advance it. The parent figures, as principal caretakers, subsume a host of functions of critical significance for the physical, intellectual, and emotional development of their children. The most important place to begin to improve our population is by helping parents do a better job of caring for our children . . . In our complex, demanding, and fragmented society, it has become more and more difficult to be an effective parent, whatever the family's socio-economic status. Many parents experience difficulty in effectively fulfilling their roles as providers, protectors, nurturers, tutors, disciplinarians, and interpreters of the cultural heritage . . . Comprehensive services oriented toward the needs of families and children must be provided if we would seek to avoid imposing on our children the disorganization of our society.[2]

The famous Children's Charter emanating from the 1930 White House Conference on Children includes among the rights of all children in America "understanding and the guarding of his personality as his most precious right." The General Assembly of the United Nations adopted on November 20, 1951, a "Declaration of the Rights of the Child." This declaration stresses the right of each child to a home which will fill his needs, although the right of the state to intervene and remove the child from the custody of

1. For an extremely comprehensive compilation of family law with relevant case citations, see Joseph Goldstein and Jay Katz, *The Family and the Law* (New York: Free Press, 1965). See also Morris Plascowe et al., *Family Law: Cases and Materials* (Boston: Little, Brown & Company, 1972).

2. Joint Commission on Mental Health of Children, *Mental Health: From Infancy Through Adolescence* (New York: Harper & Row, 1973), pp. 10, 11, hereafter cited as *Mental Health*.

his parents when his needs are not being met is still a source of litigation.

HISTORICAL DEVELOPMENT OF SERVICES TO CHILDREN

Historically, children who could not be cared for by their own parents or by relatives were indentured or placed in orphan asylums. Indenturing a dependent child presumably enabled him to learn a trade and thus become self-supporting; in actual practice, indenture was often a form of slavery. Indenture appealed to many because of its emphasis on self-support and industry, characteristics which, it was thought, dependent children should cultivate. The emotional and social concomitants of separation from families, deprivation, and lack of education were not recognized.

The Elizabethan Poor Law did include some provision for "outdoor relief" to children in their own homes, but more frequently young children were admitted, together with one or both parents, to almshouses. These practices were generally followed in the colonies, and the nineteenth century was marked by the continued efforts of social reformers to withdraw groups of children from these mixed institutions and place them in specialized institutions, usually under state or private auspices. Training schools for the blind, the deaf, the delinquent, and the feeble-minded were developed in the middle third of the century. Soldiers' orphans' homes were set up following the Civil War, and their services were extended to other dependent children. Sectarian groups sponsored children's homes limited to a particular denomination, and philanthropists set up endowments for the provision of "orphan asylums," sometimes with eligibility requirements so limited as to make it impossible to keep them in operation.

The life of children in many of these institutions must have been bleak indeed. Dickens has left us vivid portrayals of the inhumane conditions in some of the children's homes of Victorian England. Even where physical conditions were acceptable, there was an almost total disregard for the emotional needs of children. The economies made possible by mass housing, clothing, and feeding and the belief that submission to discipline "built character" led to public support of the usefulness of institutional care, even though its damaging effects on children could be amply documented. There is still evidence that in many parts of America today expense-conscious welfare officials would prefer to keep institutions full rather than develop more costly and time-consuming plans for the individual placement of dependent children.

Although home relief was legally possible both under the Elizabethan Poor Law and its various American counterparts, it was often felt that children of "paupers" were better off separated from their parents. In addition, the removal of the children from the home enabled the parents to leave the home and work. It was not until the first White House Conference on Children in 1909 that the principle was laid down that children should not be removed from their own homes solely for financial reasons. The development of widows' and mothers' pensions to enable children to remain at home with at least one parent dates only from 1911.

In an article which vividly illuminates the shift in philosophy reflected by this principle,[3] Florence Waite has compared casework in the 1940s with that of the 1890s. The two most striking contrasts, she reports, were those in health and in child care. The newspapers of the 1890s were full of advertisements placed by young widows who had to surrender their children, either for adoption or for institutional placement, in order to go out to work. Lest we feel too complacent about the increased acceptance of the understanding that the emotional needs of children may make it preferable for their mothers to stay home and care for them, let us remember the increasing pressure today on AFDC mothers to work and contribute to the family support. The WIN program (see pages 53, 94) is designed to force mothers with no preschool children out of the home and into the labor force. Day care regulations give first priority to employed AFDC mothers, which results in a hardship for the working poor who are not receiving Aid to Families with Dependent Children.

Long before sociological and psychological research had demonstrated it scientifically, child welfare workers had known the value to children of a home environment. In an effort to provide this environment, the foster home movement began in the latter part of the nineteenth century. The work of Charles Loring Brace in the New York Children's Aid Society inaugurated a program of foster home care for homeless children and those whose own home conditions were unsuitable. Children were gathered up from city streets and slums, placed on trains, and taken to midwestern towns and cities, where those interested could meet the trains and select children to care for. We can imagine the feelings

3. Florence Waite, "Casework Today and Fifty Years Ago," *The Family*, Vol. 21, No. 10 (February 1941), pp. 315–322.

of those children who rode to the end of the trip before finding someone who chose them, and we are shocked at what seems like callous disregard of their emotional problems, their bewilderment and homesickness. It is amazing that these placements worked as well as they did, but even unsatisfactory ones were surely better than indenturing or almshouse care and probably better than the majority of the children's institutions available. This plan was still in operation, although somewhat modified and with some safeguards added, as late as 1920.

These were free homes, and the children helped with household chores in return for their room and board. While many of the citizens who opened their homes to these children were undoubtedly motivated by the highest purposes, the Society could not exercise sufficient control over the selection of the homes and the treatment that the children received. Such control became possible when agencies, beginning with the Massachusetts State Board of Charities in 1868, began to pay board to citizens who opened their homes to some of the children removed from almshouses. From this practice developed the program of foster home care now available in all states.

As understanding grew of the psychological and social factors involved in the growth and development of children, greater attention was paid to making plans for children which met their needs. Since the most satisfactory arrangement for most children is to remain in their parents' home, efforts to protect the family from separation because of poverty alone led to the introduction of the first mothers' pension laws in Missouri and Illinois in 1911 and the inclusion of a program of aid to dependent children in the Social Security Act in 1935. While lip service is still being paid to this principle, the growing number of AFDC families headed by an unmarried mother, particularly if she is black, has aroused resentment and charges that the AFDC program is encouraging immorality. Grants have been kept low, often seriously below minimum adequacy, in an effort to compel AFDC mothers to work. "Man in the house" rules have been applied to cut off AFDC. These policies, of course, injure the children more than the "immoral" mothers.

In addition to programs of financial support to children in their own homes, a variety of other services has been developed at the local, state, and national levels of government. These include foster care for children, either in institutions or in boarding homes, together with adoption, day nursery care, clinical and recreational services, and a range of legislative provisions insuring education and health care and protecting children from exploitation in the labor market. That these services are largely unavailable to the children of migrant families is a national disgrace. Also, the protection of legal safeguards is less thorough for some minority groups. Many of these programs are publicly sponsored and carried out by governmental agencies, while some are under voluntary auspices. Ideally, every child should receive the service most closely related to his needs; in actuality, as we shall see, many obstacles make this ideal difficult to achieve.

CHILDREN IN THEIR OWN HOMES

How adequately does society insure the rights of children who are living with their parents, and at what point are these rights so badly infringed that the state is justified in removing children from parental custody?

THE CHILD'S RIGHT TO FINANCIAL SECURITY

By whatever measures used, it is clear that an appallingly large number of children living with their parents do not enjoy financial support at a level which will guarantee them adequate food, housing, health care, and clothing. Orshansky estimated in 1965 that more than one child in five lived in poverty.[4] Schorr found the figure to be somewhat higher.[5] Families with several children are more likely to be poor than smaller families, as are families headed by a woman or nonwhite families.

Financial security to families is underwritten by the Social Security Act. The various titles of the Act, particularly the survivors benefits under OASDI and the AFDC program, are theoretically aimed specifically at the support of minor children. In November 1973, there were just under 8,000,000 children receiving AFDC; at current grant levels, these children are certainly living in poverty. The average survivors benefits for a wife and two children in July 1974 was $433 a month; however, there is a maximum family payment which can amount to no more than that due a wife and two children, so that a larger family is proportionately less well off. The number of child beneficiaries in July 1974 was 3,702,000.[6] It is apparent that the existing programs do not guarantee the rights of many children to adequate physical subsistence.

---

4. Mollie Orshansky, "Counting the Poor: Another Look at the Poverty Profile," *Social Security Bulletin*, Vol. 28, No. 1 (January 1965), pp. 3–29.

5. Alvin Schorr, *Poor Kids* (New York: Basic Books, 1966).

6. Figures supplied by James M. Brown, Assistant Press Officer, Social Security Administration, June 17, 1974.

The effects of being born and growing up in poverty include a greater chance of mental retardation, less good health and mental health, less adequate socialization and preparation for entering school, and attitudes of defeatism, passivity, fatalism, and alienation, which impair chances for success in school and in later life.[7] Obviously, the continuation of so large a proportion of our children in poverty is a denial of their fundamental right to adequate care.

The extent to which poverty can be eliminated in a nation so dedicated to the work ethic is questionable. Schorr estimated in 1966 that a children's allowance of $50 per month per child would raise three out of four children now in poverty out of poverty.[8] His figures on cost have been challenged as too low, but the consequences of increased future expenditures for those raised in poverty might make such preventive costs an economy in the long run. After all, other industrial societies have managed to reduce poverty to a much smaller incidence than the United States.

THE CHILD'S RIGHT TO ADEQUATE PARENTING

The question of the extent to which parental rights may be set aside in the interest of the child's welfare inevitably arises when there is indication of inadequate parenting in the form of serious neglect or mistreatment. When children were viewed as adjuncts of the family, obligated as children to contribute to the support of the family and as adults to provide security for their parents' old age, emphasis was laid on parental rights and justified on the basis that each generation is repaid by the succeeding generation for what it has done for the preceding generation. When children are viewed as future citizens, particularly as future participants in a democracy, there is more interest in protecting their rights to enable them to become responsible adults, even if this means protecting them against their parents. This latter view is still new enough that legislation has lagged behind social thought. Many courts are still more interested in protecting the rights of parents, even at the expense of the best interests of the child.[9] Thus we see that in some courts the fact of blood relationship is considered the vital concern in awarding custody of a child, even at the cost of

7. See Catherine S. Chilman, *Growing Up Poor* (Washington, D.C.: SRS, May 1966); Schorr, *Poor Kids*; and Joint Commission, *Mental Health*, pp. 40–43.

8. Alvin L. Schorr, "Alternatives in Income Maintenance," *Social Work*, Vol. 11, No. 3 (July 1966), pp. 22–29.

9. See Joseph Goldstein, Anna Freud, and Albert Solnit, *Beyond the Best Interests of the Child* (New York: Free Press, 1973), which recommends placing the rights of the child to continuous parenting above all parental claims and blood ties.

disrupting the only secure home a child may have had. The American Humane Association calls attention to the confusion over the conflict between parental and children's rights by citing two cases in which contradictory court rulings over the issue of the best interests of the children were rendered in Iowa and Missouri in 1972. In one case, the Iowa Supreme Court placed the best interests of the children as more important than the parental rights; the Missouri Court of Appeals, however, stated its belief that the Juvenile Court lacks the authority to terminate parental rights because it thinks the children would be better off with someone else.[10]

The Role of Children's Courts

The question of which courts have responsibility for safeguarding the rights and enforcing the duties of both children and parents is a complex one. There is urgent need for the creation of family courts which will centralize all legal processes relating to families and family problems. Questions of jurisdiction and court structure, the ambiguous legal status of many juvenile courts, and the question of how best to apply constitutional safeguards to children have prompted a growing interest in the establishments of special family divisions within the highest court of jurisdiction. The present situation distributes responsibility for family matters among a variety of courts of both inferior and superior jurisdiction. Probate courts, domestic relations courts, and juvenile courts, in addition to some other specialized courts, may be handling related problems in separate and contradictory ways; thus the Children's Bureau can cite a situation in which an adoption was granted in one court to parents who were charged in another court with neglect of the child in question.[11] The Standard Family Court Act[12] recommends integrating the functions of juvenile courts and domestic relations courts in a special division which would also have jurisdiction over adoptions, commitment of mentally ill or defective persons, and certain criminal offenses by one member of a family against another. Instead of setting up

10. "Termination of Parental Rights—Two Opposing Views," *National Child Protective Services Newsletter*, Vol. 2, No. 1 (March–April 1973), pp. 4–5.

11. U.S. Children's Bureau, *Juvenile Delinquency: Facts, Facets*, No. 6 (1960), p. 1. See also Monroe L. Inker, "Expanding the Rights of Children in Custody and Adoption Cases," *Child Welfare*, Vol. 51, No. 6 (June 1972) pp. 355–360.

12. The Standard Family Court Act is a model act prepared by the National Probation and Parole Association (now the National Council on Crime and Delinquency) in cooperation with the National Council of Juvenile Court Judges and the U.S. Children's Bureau, published by the National Probation and Parole Association in 1959.

another specialized court, the Act would establish a family court division in the existing highest court of general trial jurisdiction, which would in most states be the circuit or district court.

In the Children's Bureau publication *Standards for Juvenile and Family Courts,* the following statement of principles is made, to insure that courts operate within their area of competence in limiting the rights of both parents and children.

1. The conditions under which the State is empowered to intervene in the upbringing of a child should be specifically and clearly delineated in the statutes. Whenever the State seeks to intervene, it should be required to show that those conditions do in fact exist with respect to a child and that its intervention is necessary to protect the child or the community, or both. The State should not be able to interfere with the rights of the parents with respect to their child and assume jurisdiction over such child on the generalized assumption that the child is in need of the care or protection of the State merely because it disagrees with the parent as to the "best course to pursue in rearing a child." . . .

2. Both the child and his parents are entitled to know the bases on which the State seeks to intervene and on which it predicates its plan for the care and treatment of the child. They are equally entitled to rebut these bases either directly by questioning witnesses, or indirectly by presenting facts to the contrary. This means that rules of evidence calculated to assure proceedings in accordance with due process of law are applicable to children's cases. There should be an orderly presentation of credible facts in a manner calculated to protect the rights of all concerned. This principle also entails written findings of fact, some form of record of the hearing, the right to counsel and the right to appeal. The court should give clear reasons for its decision as to the finding with respect to allegations made and any order affecting the rights of the parents or the rights and status of the child. Any order for treatment, care or protection does, in fact, affect these rights.

3. The statute should limit the court as to the type of disposition it may make depending on the nature of the case, i.e., delinquency or neglect, rather than allow it unlimited discretion to make any disposition, or to order any treatment that it may think advisable. It should, however, have complete discretion within the range of specific dispositions authorized.

4. Certain procedural safeguards must be established for the protection of the rights of parents and children. Although parties in these proceedings may seldom make use of such safeguards, their existence is none the less important. They are required by due process of law and are important not only

for the protection of rights but also to help insure that the decisions affecting the social planning for children are based on sound legal procedure and will not be disturbed at a later date on the basis that rights were denied.[13]

The laws of most states are relatively clear with respect to the abridgment of parental rights if obvious and severe neglect, delinquency (which is regarded as *prima facie* evidence of neglect), and severe physical abuse can be proven. Parents are responsible, in common law and statute law, for failure to provide "necessaries" to their children or for seriously endangering their children's health. However, the burden of proof is on the complainant, which may be the police, a social agency, or a protective services agency such as the American Humane Association, since a strong presumption exists that parents are the proper guardians of their children.

Child Abuse

Laws against cruelty to children are more likely to be phrased in terms of what they will not permit than in terms defining the right of children to adequate care. However, punishment so severe as to result in injury to children will in any court be construed as a breach of the child's rights. Such child abuse is much more widespread than most people are willing to admit. The Joint Commission on Mental Health of Children estimates that severe child abuse is to be counted in the thousands or ten thousands and severe neglect in the hundred thousands. It may well be that if the factors of neglect and abuse could be adequately measured, such maltreatment would be the leading cause of death in children.[14]

The "battered child" was first called to national attention in 1962. Public reluctance to admit that not all parents are loving and cherishing had kept the problem from scrutiny until a report in the *Journal of the American Medical Association*[15] coined the term "battered child" to describe injuries which could not be rationally explained. Reluctance to report suspected abuse has centered

13. U.S. Children's Bureau, *Standards for Juvenile and Family Courts*, Publication No. 347 (Washington, D.C., 1966), pp. 7, 8.

14. Joint Commission, *Mental Health*, p. 36.

15. C. Henry Kempe et al., "The Battered Child Syndrome," *Journal of the American Medical Association*, Vol. 181, No. 2 (July 7, 1962), pp. 17–24; this article reports on 302 cases, of which thirty-three children died and eighty-five suffered permanent brain damage. See also the Editorial on p. 41 of the same issue. The same authors' *Helping the Battered Child and His Family* (Philadelphia: J. B. Lippincott Company, 1972) reviews the medical approach to the problem.

around liability for slander and libel. But laws in many states now require that doctors and hospitals report to protective agencies all young children with healed multiple bone injuries and provide them with immunity from liability.[16] The American Humane Association, Children's Division, has been the leading agency in the fight against child abuse. It conducts symposia and workshops on the legal rights of children and publishes a series of pamphlets and reports on all aspects of protective services.

The "battered child" has been "battered" by some abusive person. Injuries include bruises, burns, and fractures of the skull, ribs, or long bones, as well as internal injuries such as ruptured spleens. X-rays often show old healed fractures, suggesting repetitive abuse. Since battering is usually inflicted on children too young or too frightened to speak, and since the abusive parents usually deny any responsibility, the situation is a difficult one to handle. The protective services worker must assess the degree to which the child is rejected, the potential danger to his remaining in the home, and the treatability of the parents. Abused children may be rejected with such hostility that it expresses itself directly, as sometimes happens with illegitimate children resented by their stepfathers or with children whose conception forced an unwelcome marriage on the parents and are then blamed for the parents' unhappiness. In what is called "overflow abuse" or "misplaced abuse," the child is not so much rejected as a victim of parental frustration, chronic anger, irresponsibility, or conflict. In parents whose anger smoulders continually, the normal tensions of child rearing may be sufficient to stimulate violent overreaction.[17]

While casework or psychotherapy for abusive parents may be occasionally effective,[18] in most cases the pathology in the situation is so severe that the child must be removed to guard against

16. See Vincent DeFrancis, *Child Abuse Legislation in the 1970's* (Denver: The American Humane Association, 1973).

17. See Serapio Richard Zalba, "The Abused Child," *Social Work*, Vol. 11, No. 4 (October 1966), pp. 3–16, and Vol. 12, No. 1 (January 1967), pp. 70–79, for an extensive bibliography and a typology for intervention. See also Maurice J. Boisvert, "The Battered-Child Syndrome," *Social Casework*, Vol. 53, No. 8 (October 1972), pp. 475–480. An extensive follow-up study is reported in Elizabeth Elmer, "Studies of Child Abuse and Infant Accidents," *Mental Health Program Reports—5* (Washington, D.C.: National Institute of Mental Health, 1971), pp. 58–89.

18. See, for example, Shirley L. Bean, "The Parents' Care Project: A Multiservice Approach to the Prevention of Child Abuse," *Child Welfare*, Vol. 50, No. 5 (May 1971), pp. 277–282; and Roy E. Helfer, M.D., "A Plan for Protection: The Child Abuse Center," *Child Welfare*, Vol. 49, No. 9 (November 1970), pp. 486–494.

subsequent abuse. Often, abusive parents take out their anger at what they regard as outside interference on the child who was the source of the report.

It would be comforting to many middle-class parents to let themselves be convinced that child abuse occurred only in lower-class, slum homes. This represents a refusal to face the facts. While upper-income families may be able to conceal it more successfully, all indications are that child abuse is distributed across the entire socio-economic spectrum. There is no correlation with educational level, ethnic or racial background, or residence. According to the Joint Commission, 90 percent of abusive parents have serious social problems, notably immaturity, instability, and emotional deprivation in their own infancy.[19] They do not welcome help, show little remorse or concern over the injured child, and seem to blame the child for the annoying behavior which precipitated the abuse. Older children may be reluctant to report abuse to authorities because they have internalized the parents' attitude and blame themselves for being "so bad" as to deserve punishment.

Since abused children have spent their early years in troubled family settings, which in themselves impair good psychosocial development, it is difficult to isolate and assess the effects of severe abuse on the children's later lives. A study reported in 1967 to the American Academy of Pediatrics indicated that only about 10 percent of severely abused children fully recovered from the physical effects of the abuse, since so many (70 percent) received head injuries.[20] The emotional scars are harder to assess but must be major. The extent of possible damage is touchingly documented in Dr. Richard D'Ambrosio's story of his ten-year treatment of Laura, a child whose parents had tried to kill her by frying her on the kitchen stove and who had reacted by complete mutism and total withdrawal.[21]

Neglect

Where neglect is less apparent and more subtle, termination or abridgment of parental rights is less clearly stipulated. Authorities

19. Joint Commission, *Mental Health*, p. 37. See also Howard D. Criswell, Jr., "Why Do They Beat Their Children?" *Human Needs*, Vol. 1, No. 9 (March 1972), pp. 5–7; and Peter DeCourcy and Judith DeCourcy, *A Silent Tragedy* (Port Washington, N.Y.: Allen Publishing Company, 1973).

20. See Grace S. Gregg and Elizabeth Elmer, "Battered Child's Trauma Found to Be Lasting," *RN*, Vol. 30, No. 4 (April 1967), p. 28.

21. Richard D'Ambrosio, *No Language But a Cry* (New York: Doubleday and Company, 1970).

were once more willing to remove children from their parents. Largely owing to the work of Anna Freud (daughter of Sigmund Freud, the founder of psychoanalysis) with English children during World War II, the separation of children, particularly very young children, from their parents is being questioned. Miss Freud's studies showed that more emotional damage was done to young children by evacuating them from London and other target areas to areas of safety, when this involved separating them from their mothers, than by allowing them to remain and share the tensions of bombardment with their mothers.[22] The serious emotional damage resulting from maternal deprivation has been summarized in a monograph published by the World Health Organization in connection with United Nations programs for homeless children.[23] The evidence in this and other studies supports the position that the removal of children is so damaging that it should be a last resort, after heroic attempts to improve the situation have failed.[24]

Removal of children because housekeeping standards are unacceptable or because they are exposed to immorality, alcoholism, or inadequate nutrition may not succeed in teaching children more acceptable standards for themselves if they are so emotionally upset by the removal that they are not able to absorb the new standards. Child welfare workers have observed in case after case that children who return to their parents' home after placement in an institution or boarding home may slip back into the parental way of life. If there is a close tie between parents and children, the children will resist the imposition of new standards, as this implies disloyalty to their parents. In the long run, some improvement in the living conditions of the home may prove a wiser investment of social work resources than removal. The emotional, not so much the physical, atmosphere of the home is the vital factor to be considered if removal seems indicated. When the development of the child is being stunted because his emotional needs are neglected by parents who are too immature, too trou-

---

22. See especially Anna Freud and Dorothy Burlingham, *Infants Without Families* (New York: International Universities Press, 1944).

23. John Bowlby, *Maternal Care and Mental Health* (Geneva: World Health Organization, 1962); and *Maternal Care and Mental Health; Deprivation of Maternal Care: A Reassessment of Its Effects,* second edition (New York: Schocken Books, 1966).

24. See Christoph M. Heiniche and Ilse J. Westheimer, *Brief Separations* (New York: International Universities Press, 1965), which is a continuation of Bowlby's work. This work cites two critical periods in which separation is most damaging: the second six months and ages four to six in the life of the child.

bled, or too ill to meet them and who are unresponsive to efforts to help themselves improve, removal of the children to some type of foster care may be warranted. The efforts of protective services to help families remain together has been described (see pages 130–136), and since the high costs of separation to the child have been better understood, the importance of rehabilitation of the home is increasingly recognized.

When children are removed from the custody of parents and committed to some authority (the state, an institution, a social agency, a juvenile court), not all parental rights are terminated. Parents continue to be liable for the support of children, to the extent of their financial ability, and they retain legal guardianship. Commitment cannot be longer than the minority of the children, and the evidence is that children who outgrow commitment return to their families. Parents may appeal the decision of the juvenile court and ask that the home situation be reexamined with a view to revoking the commitment and returning the children to their home.

Less clear is the situation in which neglect is not obvious and cruelty is not physical. Is there, for example, such a thing as "moral neglect?" Does hostile, critical, and rejecting treatment constitute cruelty within the definition of the law? In modern times, what constitutes "necessaries"? Should a child be removed from parental custody because his parents fail to follow the recommendations of the school that he be examined for glasses?

The courts have handed down some precedent-making decisions in regard to the provision of medical care for children when this care has been refused by the parents on religious grounds. The case of an Illinois couple who refused permission for a blood transfusion for an infant was taken to the Illinois Supreme Court[25]; a lower court had appointed a guardian for the child, whose life was endangered by the parents' refusal to allow a blood transfusion, and the guardian ordered the transfusion given. Subsequently the parents appealed, claiming that their freedom of religion under the Fourteenth Amendment had been infringed. The Illinois Supreme Court upheld the lower court, finding that its jurisdiction was based on the duty of the court to protect children from abuse, neglect, and fraud. The court ruled that the freedom of religion guaranteed by the Constitution was not unlimited and cited as precedent a federal case involving a Mormon convicted of polygamy.

25. *Illinois* vs. *Darrell*, 30 American Law Reports 2nd (1952), p. 1132.

The lack of consensus among courts is revealed by a subsequent case in New Jersey where a county judge stated that he lacked the authority to order the transfusion which the Atlantic City Hospital said was critically needed by a child injured in an automobile accident but which the parents refused to permit on religious grounds; the six-year-old girl died.[26]

It might be thought that when parents voluntarily relinquish their rights to a child, his legal status would be clarified. Unfortunately, this is not the case. Courts have overruled relinquishment documents signed by parents; states differ in the legislation which covers the legal status of foundlings and abandoned children. In some states, child care agencies are considered to have guardianship over children in their care; in other states, the courts have ruled that only a judicial body can retain such guardianship. There is real need for clarification and uniformity in guardianship legislation. It is increasingly felt that all terminations of parent-child relationships should be accomplished by judicial process, in order to protect the rights of all concerned.

Even the voluntary release of children for adoption may not hold up in a court of law. Parents who later change their minds may claim that they did not know what they were signing or that they signed under duress. Divorced parents may both need to sign the release, even if custody of the child has been awarded to one parent. The thorny issue of religion has been brought up in a number of states; in Massachusetts, particularly, there has been confusion in the courts over whether a mother's release is valid if the child is to be adopted by parents of a different religion, since the state law specifies that children must be placed in homes of the same religious belief "where practicable" and the courts vary in their interpretation of the statute.

Similarly, the question of what constitutes "desertion" has posed a problem. Some states define desertion clearly, usually in terms of a period of years during which a parent has maintained no contact with the child and made no contribution to his support. New York passed such a law in 1959.[27] If the agency or relative concerned petitions the court, the child can be declared "per-

---

26. *New York Times*, October 23, 1959. In another New Jersey case, a juvenile court judge overruled the parents and ordered a transfusion for a two-year-old boy critically ill with anemia; *New York Times*, March 6, 1962.

27. Chapters 448, 449, and 450 of the Laws of 1959. See Shad Polier, "Amendments to New York's Adoption Law," *Child Welfare*, Vol. 37, No. 7 (July 1959), pp. 1–4.

manently neglected" and parental rights terminated by judicial process, thus freeing the child for adoption.

One of the tragedies in the child welfare field is the thousands of children in foster care who would have been suitable candidates for adoption if their status had been clarified when they were younger. Many of them are children of unmarried mothers who had no real plans to care for them but could not bring themselves to release them legally. Others are children of parents who have deserted, are permanently institutionalized, or have otherwise indicated that they have no further interest in the children. In a culture which glorifies the "good parent," it is difficult for many inadequate parents to take the final step which crowns their failure. Immature and guilt-ridden parents may cling to unrealistic hopes of reestablishing a home and taking the children back. In many such cases, children continue for years in "temporary" placements until they are too old to be readily adoptable.

Keeping Children in Their Own Homes

Services which enable children to remain with their parents include those already described in Chapter 3 (protective services, family therapy, casework with individuals), which are usually provided by public welfare departments and family service agencies. In addition, the efforts of child guidance clinics to modify parent-child relationships and the work of probation and youth corrections agencies to prevent delinquency and to deal with delinquents by supervising them in their own homes will be described in subsequent chapters. There is a growing trend to keep troubled children if not in their own homes at least in community-based programs to avoid the isolation and reintegration necessitated by commitment to a correctional school.

There is little doubt that foster care of children has been too widely used in the past. Children were removed from their own homes for reasons which would not seem to warrant it today. More accurate evaluation of family situations should make it possible for foster care to be used with more discrimination. Protective services will enable more children to remain in their own homes. More careful use of legal termination of parental rights will free other children to establish new parental ties with adopting parents. Better family planning may reduce the number of unwanted children. Foster care can then be used as the treatment of choice in situations where temporary placement for study or treatment seems indicated. It should not be a "dumping ground" for the thousands of forgotten children who are deprived of all family ties and who, if they are lucky, live in a single foster home, but who are more likely to move from foster home to foster home and eventually to an institution, growing more unhappy and bewildered with each uprooting.

THE CHILD'S RIGHT TO EDUCATION

The child's right to education is mandated by compulsory education laws in all states. School social work has grown as part of the auxiliary services found to be necessary if pupils are to be able to take advantage of the education programs of our schools. Not only have school curricula been expanded to include areas once considered completely outside their sphere of competence, but more and more we have come to recognize that unhappy, disturbed, or deprived children cannot take advantage of the best planned and integrated curriculum. The responsibility of "pupil personnel services," which in large school systems include social workers, psychologists, guidance counselors, attendance specialists, school nurses, and medical and psychiatric consultants, is to help pupils with problems which are interfering with their learning. "Goals should center upon helping pupils acquire a sense of competence, a readiness for continued learning, and a capacity to adapt to change."[28] This represents a marked shift from the functions of the original school social workers or "visiting teachers," as they were called in the early years of this century.

School Social Work

The early visiting teachers found themselves involved in the problems of second-generation immigrant children, with children who came to school hungry or could not come because of lack of school clothing, or with children who were not capable of keeping up with the work. As schools became more prepared to diversify the curriculum and introduced special classes for the mentally retarded and slow learners, school social workers found themselves providing background information to the schools and interpreting to parents their children's placements in "special rooms." As understanding of the dynamics of behavior came more to permeate social work thinking, school social workers concentrated on individual casework with troubled children. This is an expensive use of professional time, and authorities in the field are now urging that the school social worker turn away from concentration

28. Lela B. Costin, "Adaptations in the Delivery of School Social Work Services," *Social Casework*, Vol. 53, No. 6 (June 1972), p. 350.

on the individual child to work as pupil advocate and consultant to teachers and school administrators.[29] In addition, the social worker must be familiar with other resources in the community which can be mobilized for help with specific children or groups.

An authority has described two models for school social work practice:

> The most traditional and most written-about model in school social work practice is the *direct service* model. This is the school social worker who plies his practitioner trade as an individual helping, problem-solving person. Most of the time this has been in casework. That is, he works in a one-to-one relationship with children and with parents in an attempt to help them resolve the problems that are impeding the child's progress in school. He works collaboratively with everybody else—with the teachers, the principals, the other pupil personnel specialists, etc. This is a relatively limited delivery system. That is, the service population is more restricted under the direct service model than under other models. The worker, if he is spending a substantial amount of time with individual cases, is not going to have as much time for affecting, indirectly, other students and parents . . . The broadest of all delivery systems is the *community organization* model.
>
> C. O. really refers to the process of helping the social system, rather than the client, through the identification of social needs, the planning to meet them, and the implementation of these plans . . . Potential C. O. use is great in respect to the development of schools as community centers.[30]

An additional dimension is added by Lawrence Merl, who states:

> Prevention, community organization, and social action are to be considered along with and in addition to what have been called the traditional functions and responsibilities of school social work . . . The visiting teacher or social worker, if he is to be engaged in prevention, community organization, and social action, cannot move only from school building to school building or from one hall or desk or telephone to another. He needs to go where the problems, needs, people, and possible

29. See Lela B. Costin, "An Analysis of the Tasks in School Social Work," *Social Service Review*, Vol. 43, No. 3 (September 1969), pp. 274–285.

30. Jerry L. Kelley, ACSW, "Factors Which Affect a Model for School Social Work Practice," *The School as a Setting for Social Work Services* (Des Moines, Iowa: Pupil Personnel Division, State Department of Public Instruction, 1967), hereafter cited as *School as a Setting*, pp. 27–31. These two models represent the two extremes of a series which includes the team leader and the consultation model. Note the use of systems theory in this analysis.

solutions are or might be found. He must reach out—and not wait to be sought out.[31]

For illustrative purposes, let us consider the direct service model and the community organization model.

Direct Service Model

Robert Miller has written persuasively of direct service with parents and/or children.[32] The following case illustrates what Mr. Miller calls concurrent casework with parents and child.

> Mrs. L and her husband requested an appointment with the school social worker because of their concern over their son Dick, a student in the fourth grade. The second of seven children, he had always had a rather precarious social adjustment. Within the past two months, he had become almost intolerable. There were constant fights with his siblings. His demands for attention had become even greater. His school work had fallen off; he constantly daydreamed. Two recent incidents involving pseudo-runaways had climaxed the parents' concern.
>
> Mrs. L had noticed an unusual feature of these incidents, Dick had left home on two dark, winter evenings. Once he was piqued because bedtime denied him the opportunity to watch a television program. The reasons for the second incident were unknown. He had not gone far but had remained in close proximity to the home. To Mrs. L it was almost as if he wished to find out if his parents loved him enough to come looking for him. These two occurrences, temper tantrums, and the oft-repeated complaint, "You do not love me" were intensely frightening to Mr. and Mrs. L.
>
> In discussing the situation, they were able to bring out the precipitating factors. His behavior had worsened after his only friend had moved from town. It had not seemed to the parents that this relationship could have been such an important one, but, as they explored somewhat further, they recognized its seriousness to the boy. He had lost his only social outlet. He was not welcome in his older brother's circle of friends, had never actually functioned well in groups. They could then equate his demands for attention as wishes for fun, recognition, and love from his parents since the first two were pretty definitely missing from his life at that time.

31. Lawrence F. Merl, ACSW, "The School Social Worker as a Link Between School, Home, and Community," *School as a Setting*, pp. 37, 39. See also the well-known article by John Nebo, "The School Social Worker as Community Organizer," *Social Work*, Vol. 8, No. 1 (January 1963), pp. 99–105.

32. Robert Miller, "A Differential Approach to School Social Work," *Social Work*, Vol. 4, No. 2 (April 1959), pp. 79–85.

If these were what he needed to help him through this difficult time, the parents felt they could provide them, as ways were considered to alleviate the situation more permanently. They could permit him to stay up later with the older brother. They could call upon their ingenuity to stimulate and intrigue his interest in craftswork during the short winter days. The social worker would see Dick to evaluate his strengths and the depths of his disturbance for future planning. The parents were to tell Dick of their contact with this school person, his interest in seeing Dick, and the reasons for the appointment.

Dick, at his appointment, showed few of the signs of a seriously disturbed youngster. He was cheerful, related quickly to the purpose of the interview, and speedily showed that he had the capacity to make his own plans. He had been pretty lonely without his friend, no fun, not much to do. There was a new boy in the neighborhood with whom he had had no contact as yet. He was not certain that this boy would want him as a friend, but supposed that this boy might be lonely also and might welcome a call. He left the first appointment determined to call the other boy.

This contact was very successful for Dick and, emboldened, he branched out a little to test out possible school contacts. While this was going on, it was possible to examine his attitudes toward friends, group participation and its problem for him, and the sibling rivalry. It was significant that in his appointments Dick reported both good and bad news. In the latter category was a black eye which he had received after starting a fight with older brother. He decided to discontinue this behavior. Discussing the nature of group relationships made such an impression upon this boy that he repeated it with his mother and explained what he saw as some of his difficulties in this area. His social adjustment began to show steady gains.

With this progress on Dick's part, the nature of the contact with the parents changed. As Mr. L, a railroad worker, was frequently out of town, the contact was mostly with Mrs. L. Her need for help resolved itself into more general areas: how to handle situations between the two boys, understanding some aspects of Dick's behavior at home, and how to continue his gains. She corroborated fully the material which the boy presented and indicated the greater success which he was achieving. He had made friends, his school work improved, and the daydreaming had disappeared. When Dick came in for his seventh interview, reported that all was well with the world, and looked at the clock, it appeared that the time for termination was at hand. Another appointment with Mrs. L, her eighth, supported this conclusion.

> Some four months after the termination of treatment, Dick
> sought out the school social worker to indicate that all con-
> tinued well and that his circle of friends was steadily in-
> creasing. A phone call to Mrs. L revealed that her biggest
> problem now was to get Dick into the house. As soon as
> school was out, he was off with his friends.[33]

There are a number of intriguing features about this case. For
one thing, the concern of the parents over Dick's "precarious social adjustment" is not borne out by his reactions and appearance
in the casework interview. Is their concern exaggerated? In the
beginning, we get an impression of a seriously disturbed youngster; after six interviews, he is watching the clock, a pretty good
indication that he has other plans on his mind. It might seem that
all the caseworker did for him was to suggest that he call up the
new boy in the neighborhood, but obviously much more than
that went on.

Why is there no mention of the other siblings—presumably
five younger ones, since we are told that Dick is the second of
seven? All his conflict is focused on the older brother, and we are
not told anything about the five other children. How deep-seated
must his problems be if sibling rivalry and the loss of his friend
seem to precipitate them with such speed?

Notice also the skill with which the parents are led to discuss
precipitating events. We need not take it for granted that Mrs. L
had noticed the unusual features of his pseudo-runaways herself;
here is undoubtedly another illustration of the skill of the worker
in getting the parents to see Dick's inexplicable behavior in the
context in which it had changed so suddenly. These are not "bad"
parents; with some assistance, they are able to see this annoying
behavior as a cry for reassurance and support. With a father who
is out of town a good deal, a mother preoccupied by the care of her
large family, and an older brother who seems to have lorded it
over him, Dick was left out.

It is fortunate in some ways that children react to inner tensions with enough vehemence to demand that something be done.
We might speculate on what would have happened in Dick's situation had he withdrawn, isolated himself, and become outwardly
conforming but inwardly removed. Because of the other pressures
upon them, teachers and parents are likely to overlook the non-
troublesome child. Aggressive, attention-compelling behavior
may even be considered a sign of health; such behavior is an
excellent illustration of the point we have repeatedly stressed,

33. *Ibid.*, pp. 81–83. Reprinted with the permission of the National Association
of Social Workers.

that behavior is never purposeless and that, when it seems so to the outside world, there is need for careful scrutiny to see what inner purposes are being satisfied in these apparently devious ways. We can assume that Dick's life has not been permanently blighted by the combination of unhappy circumstances that seemed to converge on him and that an investment of a relatively small number of hours on the part of the school social worker may have given him an important new area of success and achievement from which to move forward.

The next case illustrates what Mr. Miller calls "exploration with parents, casework with child":

> Bob K, a 9-year-old third-grader, was initially referred at the end of the second grade. Restless and excitable, he had poor concentration and he avoided written work. He roamed around the classroom, teased the other children, and sought attention by making funny faces. Discipline did not reach him and talks with the teacher only seemed to make him worse. The achievement tests indicated a good potential but it was little utilized.
>
> Initial contacts with Mrs. K produced a fair amount of history material although she was little concerned. Both her husband and her oldest son, a college freshman, had behaved the same way in school. Bob was a highstrung youngster, constantly on the go. While Mrs. K acknowledged no problems currently, they had existed in the past. Extremely curious, Bob had delighted in turning on the gas, and had once drunk Clorox. He had resisted toilet training, taking naps, and discipline in general. He had often been sent to his room in punishment, and had once screamed all day in fury.
>
> Bob had been ill from pneumonia no less than three times. There was a history of vertebratal damage suffered from a bad fall while attempting to climb the fireplace mantel. As a result, one leg was shorter and beginning to turn inward. Braces had caused such discomfort that they had been discarded. Surgery was not indicated at present but might be in the future. A further injury could have serious consequences. Bob had heard this report some two years previously from the family doctor but had never indicated his feelings.
>
> There seemed to be considerable difficulty with a younger sibling, manifested mostly by much competitiveness, but no physical violence. Mrs. K, who was apparently not too concerned, viewed this relationship as a usual one.
>
> A real involvement of Mrs. K seemed doubtful at this point, but there could be a connection between the school difficulties and the sibling rivalry. The boy's feelings about his health could easily enter into the situation. When the worker

mentioned his interest in seeing Bob, Mrs. K did give her consent.

Bob, somewhat pallid, attended his first appointment with considerable poise. The approach to this boy was a careful one. The worker indicated that he did not know whether help was required, although there had been some school difficulties in the past. Bob agreed that there might be some value in looking at the situation for a while to see whether the worker could be of any assistance.

He started slowly with an almost verbatim parroting of parental ideas and the news that he was changing. As he began to feel more at ease, the material became less stilted and more spontaneous. He was fascinated by science fiction and horror films. His mother felt that he was sorry for the monsters in the films. He supposed that this was so. In his fantasies, he was a member of the group that killed them, not the leader, just one of the group. He always felt pretty helpless.

There was no point in touching upon the unconscious meanings of these fantasies. The feeling of helplessness was both real and conscious. To the comment that he must often feel that way, Bob began to delineate the extent of this feeling.

Then the picture of the youngest sister, and his negative feelings toward her, began to emerge with swiftness. She had not always been a threat. At first she slept all the time and he felt superior to her. However, as she grew older, she began to receive increased attention, and no one seemed to have much time for him. At the height of her cuteness, when she was walking and talking, he had started kindergarten. He spoke with vividness of his wish for attention and the techniques which he had used to seek it. To compete with a younger sister, he had acted younger himself, both at home and in the school.

As he discussed this behavior, he concluded that he did have a choice. He preferred to "grow up rather than down." He decided that there were more mature ways to secure attention, through his parents, school and social outlets.

From this point on, his feelings about his sister began to diminish and the school conflict rapidly disappeared. He used his intellectual potential and won recognition both from the school and his classmates as a gifted child. Further contact with Mrs. K was used as a means of evaluating the dynamics of the situation and of considering ways to promote further growth along the lines that Bob himself had delineated. Mrs. K went along with these plans very well, indicating that these were areas she had considered and seeing a real value in the help which she and Mr. K could provide.

Bob's case was terminated after ten appointments. It may
be noted that the area of his health was not touched. He did
not bring up health as a problem. He did not appear hampered in his playground activity, and he participated en-
thusiastically in after-school games. There is a real possibility
that this may be a problem at some future date but if his gains
are maintained, a stronger ego will face future difficulties.[34]

This is, unhappily, a type of situation all too frequently encountered in working with children. A seriously disturbed child,
whose inner tensions have led to dangerously self-destructive
activities, is regarded calmly by a mother who feels that there is
nothing to be alarmed about. Notice that Bob had overheard innumerable comments about himself; it is undoubtedly true that
he has heard how like his older brother and father he is. A troubled, helpless child, with an actual physical deformity necessitating a brace, he has never been encouraged to express any of
the resentment or apprehensions he must feel.

His problems in the area of aggression have been apparent from
an early age, antedating his baby sister's birth, since they go back
to toilet-training and she is apparently four years younger than he
(she is walking and talking when he enters kindergarten). He has
determinedly resisted all efforts to impose behavior on him, from
toilet-training to sitting still in school. The worker's skill is apparent here, as he directs the mother's attention to factors which
she can accept and does not enter the highly charged area of her
rejection of the boy and the latent hostility in the situation. Let
us speculate for a moment on the lack of imagination shown by a
mother who allows an even partially "deformed" child to watch
horror and science-fiction movies with the naïve rationalization
that he "feels sorry for the monsters." The wisdom with which the
worker avoids these areas is rewarded when Mrs. K found herself
able to go along with Bob's efforts to grow up; had the worker
been more interested in the areas of her inadequacies, her guilt
and defensiveness might effectively have prevented her from
helping.

One also gets the feeling of a very gratifying unspoken communication between the worker and Bob, for they both sense that
the sibling rivalry is a convenient handle on which to hang past
troubles, and both are aware of this lad's need for acceptance as he
is and for recognition of his value and of his capacity for self-
direction. Often people assume that the right of self-direction
belongs to adults and overlook the possibilities of making young-

34. *Ibid.*, pp. 83, 84. Used with permission of the National Association of
Social Workers.

sters aware of their growing ability to rise above circumstances that threaten to overwhelm them.

Parenthetically, one wonders if the worker ever suggested to Mrs. K that she limit Bob's television watching. With as adequate a basis as he already has for fantasies of violence and destruction, it seems unnecessary to add further stimuli. We must not overlook, also, the fact that here is a case in which no mention is ever made of financial need; we can assume that this is a family in comfortable circumstances. It should remind us effectively of how far social work has moved from the days of "doing good to the poor."

No assumption is made that Bob has been transformed into a well-adjusted child; but this area of success gives him reassurance and enables him to move forward more confidently. Since the caseworker has not been critical or threatening to Mrs. K, she may be more willing to seek professional help for Bob if there are renewed danger signals in later years.

These case illustrations show pupils whose problems were largely in the area of parental relationships, who could not make appropriate progress in school because they were taking to school too much of what we might call "unfinished homework." In every case, the family was intact and the parents showed enough concern for the child to be willing to modify their handling; in each case, the child had enough potential to respond quickly and positively to these modifications. We are not always this lucky.

Many children who are unable to function effectively in school come from fragmented families, in which the parents are too preoccupied with their own unmet needs to be aware of the children's. Many children lack the potential to respond to minor shifts in school programs, and for them some major remaking of the school situation may be necessary. Fortunately, most modern school systems are flexible enough to permit transferring children to other teachers or other schools, to adapt curricula to special needs, and to deal imaginatively with situations in which a particular child cannot operate. Where school social work has been fully integrated into the educational structure, the recommendation of the school social worker about such shifts can be extremely valuable.

Community Organization Model

The school social worker as community organizer is well illustrated in the following case.[35]

35. Adapted from material supplied by the Pupil Personnel Services of the Schenectady, New York schools. Used with permission.

The school social worker became concerned about the social adjustment of a number of obese boys in one elementary school. These boys were being teased by the other children and were retaliating in various troublesome ways. One boy was stealing money to buy candy for himself and to try to buy friends. In addition these boys refused to participate in physical education classes because they would not shower or use the pool when the "skinny kids" were there to laugh at them. The school social worker took the problem to the Community Welfare Council. A preliminary survey showed that there was a larger number of overweight children in the schools than anyone had suspected, and that many of them were showing adjustment problems. The Council set up a committee with representatives from the YMCA and YWCA, the child guidance clinic, the family agency, the public child welfare department, the school physician, the physical education and home and family living departments of the schools, and the County Home Demonstration agent.

A pilot project was begun in one school. Individual conferences with each of five much overweight boys and their parents were held by the school social worker. Some of the parents were uninterested at first, and one was openly resentful because of repeated calls from the school nurse urging her to "put Joe on a diet." Each child was given a thorough physical examination by the school physician. A volunteer was secured to drive the boys each week to the Y gym and pool, and the boys were released from school so they could be at the pool when no one else was there. They became much more active, learned to swim, and developed more self-confidence about their appearance and their athletic ability.

Following their activity, the boys met with the school social worker for weekly discussions centering on their feelings about themselves and their relationships with other children. They admitted how much they had been hurt by teasing. During the discussion they also talked about foods, about calorie counting and prepared low-calorie refreshments under the supervision of the County Home Demonstration agent. Each boy "weighed in" with the school nurse every week and she kept weight charts for each one.

All the boys lost some weight. One boy was willing to transfer back to his regular gym class although he continued in the discussion group. The grades and school behavior of all the boys improved. The parents were enthusiastic. The entire family of one of the boys joined Weight Watchers and lost a total of thirty-four pounds in the first three weeks. The resentful mother offered to contribute toward taxi fare if that should ever be needed. Another family whose ethnic background led the mother to prepare meals with heavy starch content was urged by their son to learn to "eat American" and the entire family developed new dietary habits. The pilot program was judged a great success and will be extended to other schools and hopefully to overweight girls as well.

Nonattendance and School Drop-Outs

Problems of attendance are also of concern to social workers in schools. A child's persistent absence always indicates that something is wrong. It may be that the school is a repellent and unrewarding place in the child's eyes; that outside activities, almost inevitably predelinquent or delinquent, seem more desirable; that unusual parental demands are keeping the child at home (perhaps household responsibilities he should not be asked to assume, perhaps exaggerated precautions about his health); or that there is no one at home to make sure that the child is ready in time to make the school bus. In urban ghettos or rural pockets of poverty, children may have to stay home because of inadequate clothing or no shoes. Whatever the reason, recurring absences call for inquiry and some attempt to help the family meet its legal obligation to send the child to school. This may seem to the parents like unwarranted intrusion into their affairs, but since all parents are aware, intellectually at least, of the laws of compulsory attendance, to the social worker the child's absences may represent an indirect appeal for help with a situation the parents feel unable to control. It may be less damaging to a parent's self-esteem to have the school learn of his troubled marital situation or his inability to manage his child than to apply to a family agency or a mental health center. Social workers must use "reaching-out" methods[36] rather than passively wait for such parents to take the initiative in asking for help.

Another area of concern to the school social worker is that of drop-outs from school. In the average public school system, the attrition rate approaches 50 percent, largely comprised of sixteen-year-olds in the ninth and tenth grades. By no means are all of them doing failing work, although many of them have failed subjects or repeated grades in earlier years. Many have reading disabilities which have prevented achievement in high school. Many are eager to have spending money or be financially independent or think that work will be "more fun" than school.[37] This suggests that potential early leavers can be detected while there is still time

36. See Robert Sunley, "New Dimensions in Reaching-out Casework," *Social Work*, Vol. 13, No. 2 (April 1968), pp. 64–74.

37. See U.S. Department of Agriculture, Federal Extension Service, *From School to Work: Federal Services to Help Communities Plan with Youth* (Washington, D.C., 1967).

to give them the benefits of personnel services within the schools. More realistic vocational preparation, better occupational advising, the provision of needed remedial work early in their school careers, and enlisting the cooperation of parents are all ways in which such pupils can be retained, with benefit, in the educational system. The alternative is to release undereducated youngsters into a labor market that has no real place for them. Social work is an essential part of the schools' efforts to retain early leavers.

It is a question whether the school-leaving age, now in most states sixteen, is realistic. In conjunction with local industries, some of our school systems have been able to develop vocational training programs which combine formal schooling and apprenticeships. These programs should be more widely available. For some children, the entire school experience has been one of such total frustration that forcing them to stay in school may be worse for them than allowing them to work under carefully controlled conditions at age fourteen. Unfortunately, the very child labor laws which social work was instrumental in bringing about may be an obstacle. The opposition of organized labor to the work of minors, as well as the reluctance of some employers to modify working conditions suitably are both areas about which the social worker as change agent should be concerned.[38]

The Culturally Deprived Child

Racism, as a major flaw in the American society, will be dealt with in some detail in Chapter 10, but its effect on schooling should be mentioned here. Segregated schools were officially recognized as inherently inferior and therefore infringing on the child's right to education in the *Brown* vs. *Topeka Board of Education* Supreme Court ruling in 1954. The massive resistance to integrating schools in both South and North since that date is one measure of the extent of prejudice and confusion of genetic inferiority with cultural deprivation. All comparative studies of the achievement levels of white and black school children are skewed by the impossibility of weighting such intangible factors as aspirations fostered in the home and the persistent erosion of self-esteem induced by prejudice. The social work profession has made the elimination of racism a major priority for the 1970s. Improvement of schools, theoretically a goal accepted by all citizens,

---

38. See Lela B. Costin, *Child Welfare Policies and Practices* (New York: McGraw-Hill, 1972), hereafter cited as *Child Welfare*, especially Chapter 3, "School and Employment."

runs into formidable barriers of vested real estate interests, fear on the part of teachers' unions of community control, lack of expertise of minority group parents, reluctance of public bodies to appropriate funds, and attitudes of prejudice which are seen to be infinitely more pervasive and persistent than was recognized in 1954.

Social workers have a dual responsibility for the education of culturally disadvantaged children. While as advocates, brokers, and change agents, they should support efforts to change the system and alter prejudiced attitudes and discriminatory regulations, social workers can also be of direct service to the victims of prejudice and discrimination. Efforts to adapt schools to the special needs of the culturally deprived, interpretation to school personnel of the disruptive or withdrawn behavior of minority group children, and involvement of parents in their children's education and in school activities are social work activities which constitute a kind of "holding action" in the face of persistent discrimination. More and more authorities feel that such compensatory preschool programs as Head Start will turn out to have no lasting benefits if the children moving into elementary school do not meet a similarly enriched program there.[39]

As educational consultants, school social workers can press for curriculum change and modification, not only to mitigate for the victims of discrimination some of its most blighting effects but also to alter stereotyped prejudices in all students.[40] As Romanyshyn so cogently expresses it:

Education, which is often appealed to as the solution to our social problems, has in fact prepared Americans to see the economic and political world through the myopic lens of an economic individualism that protectively conceals a hierarchical social order and a maldistribution of economic and political power. Most of our public schools do not equip citizens with the capacity for critical social inquiry. Since man is a social man, with his very nature dependent on the kind of society in which he lives, his very freedom to actualize himself requires a critical awareness of his social environment, its constraints and opportunities for action. American education

39. There has been a wealth of material in journals and books on the failure of our educational system to deal adequately with children of lower-class backgrounds, since the pioneering study in 1962: Frank Riessman, *The Culturally Deprived Child* (New York: Harper & Brothers, 1962). Consult the Public Affairs Information Service Index for recent material.

40. See Benjamin H. Gottlieb and Lois J. Gottlieb, "An Expanded Role for the School Social Worker," *Social Work*, . Vol. 16, No. 4 (October 1971), pp. 12–21.

> has fostered the mythology of individualism out of its timid
> compliance with the need of society to restrict social aware-
> ness for its own protection. The fear of "un-American" ideas
> and the uncritical celebration of the American Dream has sub-
> stituted ideology for inquiry in most of our public schools.
> The myth of individualism conceals the structure of oppor-
> tunity, power, and privilege that functions to allocate social
> resources and social rewards.[41]

Until schools succeed in teaching all students the kind of critical
social inquiry Romanyshyn describes, the eradication of prejudice will be well nigh impossible.

THE CHILD'S RIGHT TO HEALTH
AND MENTAL HEALTH

The child's right to health and mental health is, like that
against abuse, defined negatively rather than positively. Parents
are responsible for protecting their children from physical harm,
but the rights of children to dental care, psychiatric treatment, or
even blood transfusions are not clearly defined. Most of the services for health and mental health available to children are used at
the option of parents, unless the child is considered actively dangerous to the community (suffering from an infectious disease or
seriously delinquent, for example). The Children's Charter
adopted at the 1930 White House Conference on Children included as one of its nineteen aims for all children, "full preparation for his birth, his mother receiving prenatal, natal and postnatal care; and the establishment of such protective measures as
will make childbearing safer." The Social Security Act in 1935 set
up a national program for maternal and child health, administered
through state and local health departments. Programs for children
with special needs, such as retarded children, premature infants,
and crippled children may also be administered by health departments or may be under voluntary auspices, such as the agencies
supported by the Easter Seal campaign. The 1971 figures indicate
that these services are not universally available. The Social and
Rehabilitation Service reported that only 1,500,000 children received well-child conference services and 3,300,000 received nursing services through public health departments, while 498,000
children received physicians' care under crippled children's services. Our infant mortality rate is a national disgrace, being thir-
teenth among the nations of the world. This is in large part owing

41. John Romanyshyn, *Social Welfare: Charity to Justice* (New York: © Random
House, Inc., 1971), pp. 202, 203.

to the nonwhite infant mortality rate, which is approximately twice as high as the white.[42]

The introduction of Medicaid (see pages 87–88) has made it possible for low-income families to have medical bills paid for them, but it does not guarantee the availability of health facilities or motivation to seek health care on the part of those not used to it. In November of 1971, the National Center for Social Statistics reported some 3,500,000 AFDC children receiving medical vendor payments. The mushrooming costs of Medicaid have led to setting lower limits on eligibility, which makes health care for children in upper poverty and just above the poverty line largely unavailable. The right of the child to adequate health care is also affected by his residence, since under our present delivery system, health services are maldistributed and are especially lacking in rural areas.

The same maldistribution is also true of mental health facilities for children and is further complicated by the reluctance of many parents to seek help with emotional or behavioral problems of children until they are well established and serious. The all-too-common tendency is to dismiss signs of incipient trouble as something the child will "grow out of" rather than intervene with preventive attention early. A somewhat oversimplified illustration follows:

> Six-year-old Joey, who has been doing well in school, does less well after an upsetting situation at home, say the birth of a sibling or the illness of a parent. He feels less loved and welcome because less attention is being paid to him. In their efforts to stimulate him to do better work in school, his parents nag and scold him. This does not work, so they offer him bribes. Joey is surer than ever that they love him only for his successes and grows more discouraged. His parents, in discussing the problem with the social worker from the pupil personnel services or the child guidance clinic, become more sensitive to the situation as it looks to Joey. They put less pressure on him, find areas of success which they can acknowledge, and try to show by their actions that their love for him is not conditioned on success. As the pressure on him lessens, Joey can relax and has more energy to use in learning. As he achieves success, his morale improves and he is able to achieve more success. The cycle is reversed and now spirals upward instead of downward.

42. See *1972 United Nations Demographic Year Book* (New York: United Nations, 1973), pp. 667–673; and U.S. Bureau of the Census, *Statistical Abstract of the United States: 1973* (Washington, D.C., 1973), p. 51.

While this example is simplistic, some, if not most, serious problems were once this simple. Just as problems develop slowly over a period of months or years, so they may be reversed slowly, and the change which sets the reverse into motion may be relatively slight. Not all parents are sensitive enough to their children's feelings to appeal for help on their own initiative, and social workers from any agency in contact with the family should understand the multitude of ways in which children tell us without words that they are troubled and should help parents to accept their child's way as a sign of trouble and not merely a troublesome stage the child is going through.

Some parents are able to derive a therapeutic effect from even one or two interviews with a noncritical and accepting listener who recognizes them as wanting to do their best for their child. When parents wait until serious difficulty drives them into a mental health center or a juvenile court, they will inevitably see this as an admission of failure on their part. Their conscious or unconscious expectation is that they will be scolded for their failure. To find that their difficulties are recognized and their attempts to deal with them given credit is a salutary experience. Parents need approval and encouragement as well as their children, and parents who are living with extremely difficult children seldom receive adequate recognition, from themselves, each other, or the community, for the efforts they are making. Campaigns to "punish the parents" for juvenile misbehavior overlook the fact that many parents have already been severely punished and need positive help rather than further condemnation.[43]

If the social worker who recognizes the child's need for specialized mental health services is successful in getting the parents to see the need and undertake to apply for social services, it may well be that there is no agency in the area which the family can conveniently reach or that the agency has a waiting list. Some of the problems of inadequate mental health facilities will be dealt with in Chapter 6.

We can conclude that the child's right to health and mental health care is less well recognized and infinitely less well supported than some of his other rights. Inadequate facilities are compounded by stereotyped attitudes about children and by a failure of society to recognize the ultimate high costs of neglected preventive work or remedial work at early stages. The Joint Com-

43. For an interesting discussion of parents who blame themselves defensively, see Anneliese E. Korner, "The Parent Takes the Blame," *Social Casework*, Vol. 42, No. 7 (July 1961), pp. 339–342.

mission calls attention to the "cost benefit" approach to child welfare services and urges that more agencies use this approach and
make the public which resists supporting preventive services
more aware of cost benefits.[44]

Play Therapy

Children, especially young children, are unlikely to be able to
put what is bothering them into words, so that the standard
method of dealing with adults—talking it over—is not useful with
most children. Asking them what is bothering them is futile; the
worker must learn to interpret behavior to get clues to what is
going on in the child's mind and to use the variety of symbolic
language available. Finger painting, play, modeling, and story-
telling will show what is troubling the child much better than
cross-questioning. Dr. Richard A. Gardner has developed a "Mutual Story-telling Technique" which utilizes children's familiarity
with television to induce children to make up and record stories
and to tell at the end what the moral is.[45] Such stories provide
the child with an opportunity to present his worries, fears of inadequacies, and aspirations indirectly. Finger painting allows the
child with aggressive wishes to paint the blood, guns, fights, and
vengeful wishes which express his frustration and anger.

The use of doll houses with family figures gives younger children a chance to show family interaction and feelings toward
family members. Putting the new baby down the toilet, locking
mother in the cellar, or "accidentally" forgetting to let daddy in
the front door for supper not only tell us a good deal about the
child's feelings but provide an opening to talk about the differences between play and reality and the distinction between
imagined feelings and real ones.

Selma Fraiberg, a leading authority on casework treatment of
children, writes entertainingly about the equipment needed for
play therapy.

> We shall see the child, particularly the young child, in a room
> which is inviting to children but which can be equipped at
> modest cost. There will be paper and crayons and Plasticine,
> a few dolls or puppets from the dime store, some toy cars for
> the little boys, perhaps a small fire engine. A doll house and

---

44. Joint Commission, *Mental Health*, p. 183. See also Robert Elkin, *Analyzing
Time, Costs, and Operations in a Voluntary Children's Institution and Agency* (Washington, D.C.: U.S. Children's Bureau, 1965).

45. Richard A. Gardner, *Therapeutic Communication with Children* (New York:
Science House, 1971).

other such equipment can be used but are not necessary. The space under my desk has served at various times as a house, a garage, a fire station, a prison, a burial place for treasure, a secret hide-out for robbers, and a refuge for a sulking client. It is practical and economical. Dart games, guns, and other such weapons are found to be quite unnecessary, and besides they are hard on the caseworker. The aggressive urges in children rarely require these accessories. It is also noticeable that nowadays every little boy comes equipped with a built-in sound track for machine guns and bazookas; there is no need to strain the agency budget for lethal weapons that are only a poor imitation of a little boy imitating a lethal weapon.[46]

The playing of competitive games with the worker as an opponent who does not insist on winning may be a corrective experience for a child who lacks confidence and will help to build up a relationship of trust between child and worker. The provision of a warm, noncritical relationship may help a child correct his view of the world as a totally hostile place. The aggressively competitive child, the poor loser, the cheater, the defeatist will show these characteristics in playing games, often in a way that permits discussion of other situations in which the child reacts similarly.

A high degree of flexibility is possible in choosing activities suitable to working with children. The use of food, especially candy, and a more open expression of affection are appropriate with many younger children. Man-to-man approaches may work well with adolescents who are ambivalent about independence. A placid acceptance of disorder and noise or of long hair or vulgar language in older children may be corrective experiences for children who are hushed, made to pick up after themselves, or threatened with the barber or having their mouths washed out with soap.

In addition to any direct results of the contact between the social worker and the child, there is also the advantage that the worker may be in a strategic position to modify some of the pressures on the child, through discussion with the child's parents or teachers. Often parent groups are useful ways to modify parental feelings about children who represent problems to them. Parents of children with special handicaps (mental retardation, blindness, ortho-

46. Selma Fraiberg, "Some Aspects of Casework with Children," *Social Casework*, Vol. 33, Nos. 9 and 10 (November and December 1952), p. 376; the entire article is highly recommended as giving a picture of what goes on in casework interviews with children.

pedic defects, for example) are reassured to find that the guilt they almost inevitably feel is shared by other parents. Many child guidance clinics regularly involve parents in group programs which combine education about child development and children's handicaps and discussion of parents' feelings about themselves.

Group Work

The use of group treatment of troubled children depends on a careful assessment of the child's need for a one-to-one relationship; some children have been so deprived that casework is the only way to help compensate for the deprivation. Other children can benefit from learning how to relate better to other children and can overcome excessive timidity and develop leadership skills in a group setting. Often the two can be provided concurrently. With younger children, group work is successfully combined with activities—camping, excursions, cook-outs, crafts. The group members' interest in the activity will help to control disruptive behavior on the part of one or two.

Some authorities feel that group programs are the ideal modality for dealing with adolescents. As Gisela Konopka, a leading social group practitioner and teacher says:

> The importance of group life is probably strongest in adolescence. This is closely related to the physical maturation process and the movement away from adult protection. To become adult himself the adolescent must find his way toward independence from those who have sheltered, protected, and taught him. At this period of his life he cannot yet give these up completely. Family ties actually mean a great deal to the adolescent if he feels that they are not interfering with his attempts at independence. The insecurity at this age is almost pervasive . . . This pervasive insecurity needs some balance, and it is found usually in identification with and relation to the contemporary group; other adolescents are not only "co-sufferers," they are also mirrors that help one to learn about one's own image. They are people with whom one can share everything, even feelings of degradation, guilt or shame, without losing one's self-respect because they, too, are living through these same emotions . . . Association with other adolescents also permits actual "trying out" of unexplored territory and fulfillment of the consuming thirst for adventure. Sometimes this appears in forms tolerable to society and sometimes, in forms dangerous to it. Yet, adolescents must be provided with this "trying-out period," which Erik Erikson calls the necessary "moratorium." The society which does not provide for it invites the development of a youth population

that is not only docile, unimaginative, and conforming but also hostile and seriously delinquent.[47]

All people need satisfying group participation, not just adolescents. There are basic psychological needs which can be satisfied only in a social situation. The socialization process, which makes the individual into a conscious participant in his culture, occurs in the family group, and the range of any person's interests and values is likely to be coordinated with the extent to which he is involved in a variety of groups. Isolation from meaningful contact with other people in infancy produces the "feral" child, who is not recognizably human. Isolation in later life produces inhibited and constricted personalities. Withdrawal from other people is considered a warning signal of emotional abnormality, and the most severe punishment for recalcitrant prisoners is solitary confinement.

The development of a sense of self, the famous "looking-glass self" of the sociologist, presupposes a group of people from whom the individual sees himself reflected and against whose reactions he tests himself. There is more than humor in the joke about the two psychiatrists who meet on the street; one says to the other, "You're fine. How am I?" Studies of isolation from other people show that the reality testing of the isolate is impaired or disappears. When Richard Byrd was alone for months at the South Pole, he spent much of his time, according to his diary from the period, worrying about his mental health.

Human relations from infancy onward involve group participation, and an individual who cannot tolerate or benefit from group contacts will be at a disadvantage in every phase of his life. Konopka, in an earlier statement, spoke of the needs which are satisfied only in groups: "acceptance, a feeling of worth, the need to be independent and yet to be fully capable of accepting dependence and of being part of the whole," the need for achievement, the capacity to cooperate, to make decisions, and "to overcome frustration in a healthy and constructive way."[48] In an older way of life, these capacities were developed and these needs met largely through family, neighborhood, and church activities. In the present-day urban, secular society, groups must be provided. These

47. Gisela Konopka, *Social Group Work: A Helping Process*, second edition (Englewood Cliffs, N.J.: Prentice-Hall, © 1972), pp. 33, 34, hereafter cited as *Social Group Work*. By permission of Prentice-Hall, Inc.
48. Gisela Konopka, "The Method of Social Group Work," *Concepts and Methods of Social Work*, Walter A. Friedlander, ed. (Englewood Cliffs, N.J.: Prentice-Hall, © 1958), p. 126. By permission of Prentice-Hall, Inc.

are done under a variety of auspices, voluntary and public, with paid staff or volunteers, and involve individuals of any age and from every socio-economic class.

Groups for adolescents may be set up to fulfill one or more of the needs felt by all members of the society but heightened by the crises of the adolescent years: to learn to participate effectively in group activities; to fulfill and increase potential for self-expression and self-enhancement; for backing and ego support in the search for identity; to prevent social breakdown and impaired personal functioning under stress; for corrective experiences where breakdown has occurred.[49] These purposes may be served through recreational activities, joint social action, community improvement projects, educational excursions, planned discussions, or unstructured "rap sessions." Group leaders will typically be involved in the selection of members: Is the group to be homogeneous as to age and sex or mixed? What will be the primary function (recognizing that other functions will be served also)? Under whose auspices is the group to be organized, and what possible constraints may the auspices put on its activities? What will be the attitude of the sponsoring agency toward drug use or sexual activity on the part of members? Once the group is organized, the leader will serve as resource person, limit-setter, enabler, interpreter, evaluator, and planner.[50]

Skillful and unobtrusive leadership of groups demands just as much in the ways of background knowledge of the dynamics of human behavior and the same disciplined use of self as does social casework, although this is not always recognized, and many groups are led by untrained people. Just because one has lived in group situations all one's life does not automatically qualify him or her for group leadership. The same concern for the person, the same acceptance of differences, the willingness to let people move at a pace they can feel comfortable with, the involvement of the members in the goal-setting or achievement process—all are as basic for the social group worker as for any other professional social worker.

Especially likely to be honored in the breach is the tenet that the group should be as much as possible self-determining and self-governing. The phrase "de-emphasis of the product" has been

49. See Irving H. Berkovitz, M.D., ed., *Adolescents Grow in Groups* (New York: Brunner/Mazel, 1972), which describes a variety of adolescent group experiences.

50. See Konopka, *Social Group Work*, especially Chapter 8, "Principles of Social Group Work in Practice," for a clear exposition of the role of the group worker with helpful illustrative case examples.

coined to describe the need, for group leaders especially, to place less stress on the finished product whether it be a dramatic production, handicraft, or skill, and more stress on the satisfactions derived from the activity itself. There are all too many groups in which tiresomely repeated rehearsals for a play or program have killed all the pleasure of the group members in the activity. Emphasis on a well-made pot or basket or airplane model leads inevitably to rewarding the more highly skilled members, whereas the less skilled ones may be deriving the greater personal benefit from the activity. Thus, when a number of college students were assisting a cub scout pack to plan and put on a spaghetti dinner for the boys' mothers, the students' greatest problems were to control their own anxiety that the dinner be properly cooked and to keep from taking over the kitchen duty themselves. The pride and pleasure of both boys and mothers was in the long run much more valuable than the culinary shortcomings revealed by undercooked spaghetti and slightly scorched sauce.

The skill of the leader is needed to assess the individuals in the group and to insure that its activities are consciously harnessed in such a way as to meet the needs of each member. This means that groups should not be too large. The issue of relationship, between leader and group members and among members, is viewed as critical for the achievement of the purposes of the group and will suffer if the group is too large. Wilson and Ryland, authors of the first definitive book on social group work, summed up the role of the good group leader in the first line of a jingle composed by their students: "Love them and limit them and help them to achieve."[51]

Behavior Modification

While the type of group work described above is relatively unstructured and group-determined, groups may provide the matrix in which changed behavior is produced through behavior modification. This approach was alluded to briefly in Chapter 3 (see page 127). The techniques of respondent and operant conditioning are receiving major emphasis in psychology, and their applicability to all areas of social work practice is expanding rapidly. While they can be widely applicable to clients of all ages, their special usefulness in altering behavior which might otherwise result in family breakdown and the removal of children from the home leads us to include it for consideration here.

51. Gertrude Wilson and Gladys Ryland, *Social Group Work Practice* (Boston: Houghton Mifflin Company, 1949), p. 85.

Instead of focusing on such global objectives as "improving adjustment" or "making for less unhappiness" or "helping clients to lead more satisfying lives," behavior modification concentrates on specific items of behavior. Morton Arkava has summed up the assumptions on which behavior modification is based and indicated how these differ from some of those underlying orthodox casework theory.[52]

> 1. Most behavior—both desirable and undesirable—is is learned. (Genetically determined behavior, of course, is excluded.)
> 2. Most learning results from a process known as reinforcement. Put simply, people learn those behaviors which are rewarded, even undesirable behaviors.
> 3. Undesirable behavior is the real problem that needs elimination, it is not merely a symptom of some underlying disease, but a problem in itself. Seeking out its historical causes, then, is irrelevant because neither the client's intellectual nor emotional understanding ("insight") of the problem will result in or guarantee changed behavior.
> 4. To change behavior—either to eliminate undesirable or to develop desirable behavior—necessitates precisely identifying and systematically controlling those factors which reinforce it.
> 5. Behavior can be changed in any setting which can consistently control reinforcement, including both natural environment of home, school, or work; and the controlled environment of laboratories, hospitals, or therapists' offices.
> 6. Both operational definitions and the specific objectives sought can be precisely defined and openly revealed to the client, thereby ensuring accountability.
> 7. Necessary and careful pre- and post-intervention measurements objectively validate the approach and facilitate detection of those methods responsible for success or failure.[53]

When behavior modification focuses on the stimulus which precedes a given response, it is known as "respondent conditioning" and is most useful in dealing with physiologic responses such as sweating, anxiety, avoidance reactions, and phobias. The subject is trained to associate a given stimulus with a specific new response, as in Pavlov's classic experiment with dogs conditioned to salivate at the sound of a bell. This type of conditioning is less applicable to the situations encountered by social workers than

52. Morton L. Arkava, *Behavior Modification: A Procedural Guide for Social Workers* (Missoula, Mt.: University of Montana, 1973).

53. *Ibid.*, pp. 11, 12.

"operant conditioning," also known as "reinforcement theory." This focuses on the events immediately following the behavior in question.

The basic assumption of operant conditioning is that any item of behavior can be strengthened or weakened by controlling the events that immediately follow it. Positive reinforcers are those things (smiles, praise, money, lollipops, tokens) which strengthen the behavior; negative reinforcers (scolding, punishment, deprivation) weaken it. The reinforcement should follow the item of behavior immediately to make the connection completely clear. It is not necessary that the client understand the theory or even cooperate; the consequences, according to the proponents of this method, are automatic.

Arkava outlines the procedure which a social worker should follow in using behavior modification. The first, and often most difficult, step is to select the target behavior, which must be some specific item of behavior, such as bed wetting, refusal to go to bed on time, not making one's bed, interrupting conversation, or some annoying mannerism. It is wise not to attempt some complex set of behaviors, at least not at first. Often the behavior to be modified or eliminated is indicated to social workers by the nature of the referral of the client—truancy, specific acts of delinquency, some bizarre reaction such as a hallucination. When the behavior to be modified is more diffuse—neglect, for example, or inability to control children—a list of specific items to be encouraged or discouraged should be compiled with family and some agreement reached as to the order in which the items are to be dealt with.

Next, the social worker (and the client, if possible) should consider to what extent the target behavior should be modified in its dimensions of frequency (how often?), duration (how long?), and quality (how well?) of the desired consequences. This involves a period of preliminary observation and study and the establishment of some criteria for quality. Next the worker must find the reinforcers which are effective with the client in question, since what pleases one subject may displease another. A schedule is then drawn up indicating precisely when the reinforcement is to be administered, remembering to keep it as close as possible to the behavior being reinforced but not necessarily each time the behavior occurs. The person most in contact with the client—parent, teacher, ward attendant, or sibling—will actually be the one to administer the reinforcements, the "mediator." This is known as the "triadic model" and is the one most frequently used outside of controlled settings like institutions.

There are various schools of thought within the behavior therapy movement about the use of negative sanctions. Some theorists ignore behavior which is disapproved and reward only positively. Others favor use of negative reinforcement (punishment), provided it is clearly related to the behavior and not so delayed as to become associated with some other behavior. Arkava uses the illustration of children being threatened with spanking "when Daddy gets home," which associates spanking with Daddy's arrival rather than with undesirable behavior. Clients may be shown new, more desirable types of behavior as alternatives, using role playing, prompting, or modeling.[54]

While our discussion has focused on work with individuals, techniques of behavior modification are also adaptable to groups and communities. All such adaptations depend upon very clear delineation of the specific goals to be attained[55] by the group or the community. The late Saul Alinsky, one of the most effective community organizers of our time, used negative reinforcers in the form of boycotts and selective picketing to change the behavior of landlords and supermarkets. The Annual Review of Behavior Therapy for 1973[56] describes token programs in the classroom, behavioral group treatment of hysteria, and the development of anti-littering behavior in a forest campground, among many other behavior modification projects.

Behavior modification owes its beginnings to the work of B. F. Skinner,[57] who was one of the pioneers in adapting findings of behavioral psychology to humans. The ethics of manipulating human reactions have led critics to talk of brainwashing and such destructive obedience as was evident in Nazi extermination camps during World War II. Skinner stresses the importance of programming altruistic behavior and surrendering individual

54. The foregoing summary draws heavily on Arkava's highly useful monograph, *Behavior Modification*.

55. See Edwin J. Thomas, ed., *Socio-behavioral Approach and Applications to Social Work* (New York: Council on Social Work Education [CSWE], 1967), especially Chapter 2; Sheldon D. Rose, "A Behavioral Approach to the Group Treatment of Parents," *Social Work*, Vol. 14, No. 3 (July 1969) pp. 21–30; and Judy Kopp Green and William R. Morrow, "Precision Social Work: General Model and Illustrative Student Projects with Clients," *Journal of Education for Social Work*, Vol. 8, No. 3 (Fall 1972), pp. 19–29.

56. Cyril M. Franks and G. Terence Wilson, eds., *Behavior Therapy: Theory and Practice*, (New York: Brunner/Mazel, 1973).

57. B. F. Skinner, *Beyond Freedom and Dignity* (New York: Alfred A. Knopf, 1971); there are many earlier writings by this leading behaviorist, of which one of the best known is *Walden Two* (New York: Macmillan Company, 1948).

choice in the interests of group welfare.[58] Obviously, the issue is far from settled.

While at present, proponents of behavior modification see it as an alternative to "insight" therapy and "clarification" casework, it seems very likely that with further experience, social workers will be able to develop an eclectic approach, selecting from behavior modification techniques applicable in certain situations and combining the automatic reduction of undesirable behavior with the conscious understanding of why it occurs.[59]

OTHER SERVICES TO CHILDREN IN THEIR OWN HOMES

In addition to the services already described which deal with the quality of care provided to children by parents, welfare departments, schools, and health or mental health facilities, there are some indirect services which may enable children to remain with their parents and avoid the trauma of separation.

Homemaker service (see pages 154–156) may make it possible to keep children in the home during the illness or absence of a parent and avoid temporary placement. It is an economical service in comparison to the costs of placing several children in foster care, and it helps strengthen family solidarity. Homemakers can also be used in protective services with highly inadequate parents, to serve as teachers of homemaking and parenting skills or even to supplement some of the goals of family therapy.

The provision of free legal service to low-income families may result in improving inadequate homes, protecting families from eviction, and supporting families in securing their individual rights vis-a-vis the public schools, housing authorities, welfare departments, merchants, or health agencies. As such, legal service strengthens the possibility that children may remain with their parents without undue suffering.

In a society which demands that many mothers of small children work, the provision of adequate day care facilities may also be viewed as an enabling service to keep children in their own homes. Many of these working mothers are widowed, separated, divorced, or unmarried, so that the children have already been deprived of part of the normal family structure. Removing them

58. See Elton B. McNeil, *Being Human: The Psychological Experience* (New York: Harper & Row, 1973), Chapter 18, "Behavior Control," pp. 298–313.

59. Such an integration is suggested in Stanley I. Greenspan, "Joining Aspects of Psychodynamic and Operant Learning Theories," *International Journal of Psychoanalytic Psychotherapy*, Vol. 1, No. 4 (November 1972), pp. 26–49. See also Phyllis K. Fisher, "Traditional and Behavior Therapy—Competition or Collaboration?" *Social Casework*, Vol. 54, No. 9 (November 1973), pp. 533–536.

because of the mother's necessary employment results in inferior care and is costly in money and effects on the child. Evidence shows that so few approved day care facilities exist that the great majority of the children of working mothers are cared for under substandard conditions during working hours. The Joint Commission estimates that half of the children of working mothers are cared for at home by some kind of babysitter, an additional 30 percent are cared for in someone else's home, and approximately 15 percent accompany the mother to work.[60] These arrangements are often haphazard, easily upset by illness of child or caretaker, and seldom offer the child a constructive experience. Federal support to day care centers, under the budget restrictions of fiscal 1974, stress the provision of day care to welfare mothers working under the WIN program, at the expense of other low-income mothers. Under all auspices, including Head Start, nursery schools, family day care homes, group day centers, and before- and after-school programs, adequate day care services reach only a small fraction of the children who would benefit from them. Estimates are that at least 6 percent of the children of working mothers are left unsupervised.

With the possible exception of Head Start, which has been designed as a compensatory program for culturally deprived children from low-income families, day care facilities have been advocated as an economic measure, freeing mothers to work. Cost accounting will show this to be an erroneous assumption. It costs a minimum of $2,600 per child per year for adequate day care; few unskilled or semi-skilled mothers will earn enough to make placing more than one child in day care a financial benefit. Those responsible for mobilizing community support for day care should stress its other advantages to support their pleas for more adequate funding. Children from low-income homes will benefit from the meals, health services, and educational programs of day care centers, and employers find that mothers who are not worrying over their children make better employees. Some mothers feel overwhelmed by twenty-four–hour care of several children and will actually do a better job of mothering if they are relieved of it for the working day and can spend it in a job which gives them satisfaction in a different role. There are many good arguments in favor of the community's underwriting of good day care facilities, but saving money is not one of them. If cost factors are to be the single most important criterion, as they seem to be for some people, then paying mothers enough to stay at home and

60. Joint Commission, *Mental Health*, p. 43.

take care of children adequately (the original purpose of AFDC and family services) is by far cheaper than any kind of day care or foster care.

FOSTER CARE

Where careful study has indicated that it is in the best interests of the child to be cared for outside his own home,[61] the alternatives are foster care, either in a boarding home or institution, or adoption. Institutional placement is the older form of foster care and will be considered first.

INSTITUTIONS

The middle of the nineteenth century saw the foundation of a large number of "orphan asylums" for the congregate care of abandoned, destitute, or unwanted children. In many communities today, such institutions struggle to carry on adequate programs in antiquated buildings, some of which have been able to construct smaller units more closely adapted to the needs of children.[62] Because it is more economical to run such an institution when all beds are filled and because placement is easier than locating, approving, and supervising a foster home, institutions are likely to be used too much for children needing boarding care.

Institutional placement should be used when it is the best possible plan to meet the needs of the child, not because of administrative economy or convenience. For some older children, adjustment in a foster home is difficult, and the relatively less personal character of an institution makes fewer demands on them. This circumstance holds true for the child who has had no good experience with parental figures or, at the other extreme, for the child whose relationship with his parents is intense enough to make the development of a close relationship with foster parents threatening. For older children, the quasi-"boarding school" may offer attractive recreational opportunities and seem to carry less stigma.

61. See Harriet Goldstein, "A Parenting Scale and Separation Decisions," *Child Welfare*, Vol. 50, No. 5 (May 1971), pp. 271–276, which describes a method of scaling factors involved in evaluating parental capacity and other support systems. See also James K. Whittaker, "Group Care for Children: Guidelines for Planning," *Social Work*, Vol. 17, No. 1 (January 1972), pp. 51–61, which reviews the institution versus foster home controversy.

62. For an appealingly written story of the rebuilding of a children's home, see Eva E. Burmeister, *Roofs for the Family* (New York: Columbia University Press, 1954).

It used to be maintained that when there were too many children in a family to be placed in a foster home together, institutional placement would keep siblings together. This does not happen in most institutions, however, since children are usually grouped by age and sex, and siblings may see relatively little of each other. The effect of a group of peers in teaching more acceptable social behavior is also cited and may in some cases be considerable, although most institutions would have to admit that a great deal of undesirable behavior is also learned in these groups.

Institutions can provide more specialized services for children than can most foster homes; classes in remedial reading, health programs, supervised play activities, and closer control of potential runaways, fire-setters, or bullies may be possible with a twenty-four–hour staff. In spite of the trend away from rigid routine in most institutions, daily activities are scheduled, and this routine comes as a relief to some disorganized children who have never experienced the security that comes from predictability of routine.

Many modern institutions feel that the positive contribution of an institutional placement is such that they should limit their intake to children who need an institutional program and not admit children who need custodial care only. The development of such an institutional program is likely to involve some profound changes in the size and staffing of the institutions. The Albany Home for Children moved in 1961 to new buildings, offering new programs. The following description of the changes and the philosophy behind them is particularly interesting in view of the well-known program of the older institution, described in Hopkirk's classic book on children's institutions.[63]

The Albany Home for Children

The Albany Home for Children was founded in 1829 and is a nonprofit, nonsectarian organization. The original incorporation was as "The Society for the Relief of Orphans and Destitute Children in the City of Albany," and one of its central purposes was the prevention of pauperism. It provided institutional care and also placed children in indenture. The evolution of its program is in part indicated by the changes in its name, to the Albany Orphan Asylum in 1893 and to its current name in 1934. By the turn of the century, the Home had well over 400 children under care

---

63. Howard W. Hopkirk, *Institutions Serving Children* (New York: Russell Sage, 1944).

in one large barracks-type building. In 1907, it pioneered in the introduction of "cottages" for groups of children, which contained dormitories for sleeping, kitchens, dining rooms, and living rooms, as well as quarters for the "house parents." The buildings were considered adequate for 140 children according to the standards of 1907; by 1959, the capacity was considered to be no more than 80 children in the same facilities.

Studies done in 1953 and 1956 by the Child Welfare League of America at the request of the Home and a continuing self-study by the Board and staff led to a wholesale reorganization of the policies and facilities of the Home. Children's institutions were reporting that a growing proportion of the children referred to them were showing disturbed behavior. After a careful study of the trends in referrals and a thorough review of the experiences of similar agencies, in 1961 the Home opened its new buildings and since then it has continuously modified its program to become a multi-service treatment center for socially maladjusted and emotionally disturbed children. The opportunity to sell its old plant advantageously provided the funds for construction of several small one-story buildings specifically designed for the four services operated by the Home. These services are described by the Home:

> *The Residential Center* offers a 24 hour a day individual and milieu therapy program for those children for whom family living is currently unavailable or emotionally detrimental. The routines of living, learning and playing in small groups (usually 7 children) are carefully planned in order to achieve sufficient social and emotional growth to enable adequate coping in the community as rapidly as possible. The team approach is used in the residential program, combining the professional skills of the clinical worker, child care worker and teacher under the direction of a team coordinator. When parents are available, they may join staff and their child as active participants in the team process. Different combinations of treatment modalities are used to meet specific needs of individual children and their families. These modalities include family therapy, parent education and cottage involvement, individual verbal, play and art therapy, and activity and socialization groups.
>
> *Group Homes and Agency Owned Boarding Homes.* Children referred here must have enough strength to manage in the community without serious acting out problems. An essential factor to placement in the Group Home is the child's interest and readiness to participate actively in the Group Home program. As with the other programs, children may be referred

directly, or the program may be used as a transitional step back to the community and family after a period of institutional care. Four homes in residential areas provide a family like setting in the community with Group Parents employed, trained and supervised by the Agency. Clinical and educational services are available for the child and his family.

Specialized and Professional Foster Care and Adoption. Most placements in the specialized foster care program involve only one child per family and tend to be long term (two year minimum). Several placements have led to adoption. The professional foster care program is for a more disturbed youngster who needs intensive care offered by a specially trained foster parent. Many children are referred here as an alternative to placement in a treatment center and the special educational program of the Agency is available for the child who needs it.

Day Treatment. This program offers a combined school-recreational-clinical treatment program for the child who is unable to benefit from community school and who does not need to be separated from his family. Essential to the day treatment program is the involvement of the child's family.

The Albany Home maintains a central intake service, since its programs are highly individualized and can accommodate a limited number of children. All children referred are evaluated by an intake team, consisting of a psychiatrist, psychologist, the intake coordinator who is a social worker, and representatives of the staff of the program to which the child is being referred. In addition to clinical specialists, the staff includes specially trained teachers, child care workers and supervisors, medical and nursing services, an art therapist, social work students, and volunteers. The school program operates on a twelve-month year and aims to return children to community schools as soon as possible. The school is designed for children with at least normal intellectual potential. The average stay in the residential program is sixteen months, and the goal is to shorten the stay and return children to family life as soon as possible.[64]

Residential Treatment Centers

The evolution of the Albany Home for Children from the Albany Orphan Asylum indicates the way in which institutions can adapt to meet the needs of troubled youngsters. There are too few residential treatment centers to begin to meet the need, according to

64. The preceding description has been abstracted from the brochure and the June 1973 *Newsletter of the Albany Home for Children.* Used with permission.

the Joint Commission on Mental Health of Children, and many of them are inadequate.[65] Too many disturbed children are placed in inappropriate settings, such as mental hospitals, poorly selected foster homes, or institutions designed for the delinquent or mentally retarded. The Joint Commission reports that in 1966 there were just over 8,000 in residential treatment centers and an estimated 1,400,000 seriously ill children, many of whom were receiving no treatment at all, particularly if they were from low-income or minority-group families.

The need for a large, highly qualified staff makes the operation of such a treatment center extremely costly. One of the pioneer institutions, the Sonia Shankman Orthogenic School in Chicago, which was made famous by the writings of its former director Bruno Bettelheim,[66] lists charges of $11,200 yearly per child and $12,200 per adolescent in late 1973. The School's enrollment is limited to fifty children, who live in family-sized groups of six or seven, with a professional staff of twenty-nine full-time and ten part-time staff members and a nonprofessional staff of twenty-two janitors, cooks, maids, laundresses, seamstress, and office staff. The average length of stay at the School is a little over four years, although some have stayed eight years or more. Most of the children who have been at the Orthogenic School continue to college and several have completed their Ph.Ds. The School is affiliated with the University of Chicago and is a training and research center as well as a treatment center.[67]

Such well-equipped and superbly staffed institutions are the exception rather than the rule. The majority of institutions do not pay well enough to attract cottage parents or child care workers with professional training, and few have professional social work-

65. Joint Commission, *Crisis in Child Mental Health: Challenge for the 1970s* (New York: Harper & Row, 1969), pp. 271–275. The well-known Hawthorne Cedar Knolls School, a division of the New York Jewish Board of Guardians, is described on pp. 304–306.

66. For a general description of the institution, see Bruno Bettelheim, *Love Is Not Enough* (Glencoe, Ill.: The Free Press, 1950); for four detailed case histories showing its methods and results, see the same author's *Truants from Life* (1955); the case history of "Joey, A Mechanical Boy" has been anthologized in Eric Josephson and Mary Josephson, eds., *Man Alone* (New York: Dell Publishing Company, 1962), pp. 437–446.

67. *The Sonia Shankman Orthogenic School*, a brochure distributed by the School, 1365 E. 60th St., Chicago, Ill. 60637, n.d. See also George H. Weber and Bernard J. Haberlein, *Residential Treatment of Emotionally Disturbed Children* (New York: Behavioral Publications, 1972); and James K. Whittaker and Albert E. Trieschman, eds., *Children Away from Home* (Chicago: Aldine Publishing Company, 1972), for descriptions of other programs.

ers in adequate numbers to treat the children who are placed there.[68]

Child-Caring Institutions

The referral to a child-caring institution may come from the parents, from voluntary or health agencies, from a public welfare department or a court. There may have been a fairly complete diagnostic evaluation of the situation by some other agency, or the institution may make it, in which case the social worker is likely to be involved in the intake process. During the evaluation, the parents should be seen and their views considered. The child also should be consulted, as well as studied, so that he will feel that he is involved in the planning. The decision to accept the child should be based on the conviction that institutional placement provides the best possible solution for the problem presented; the institution should not be used as a last resort.

In many cases, the decision will be that institutional placement is not the most desirable solution; referral should then be made to a family agency or to a children's agency with a foster home program. It is particularly important that very young children not be institutionalized, since they need the affection and individual attention possible only in a home setting. Parents should understand fully, whatever the decision may be, and should come to accept and agree with it as in the children's best interests. To convey the decision to the parents requires casework skill and security of the worker as to the proper function of the institution. Interpretation of the institution's function to other agencies and to the community will minimize unsuitable referrals.

The social worker, who has already seen the child at least once, is usually the person who introduces him to his new environment. He will present him to the house parent or cottage counselor, show him to his room, and arrange for further contact in the office on a regular schedule or an "as needed" basis. Even if there is no continuing casework with the child (and there should be if the child has been admitted because of emotional or behavior problems), the social worker should receive reports of his adjustment and progress. Frequent staff conferences, often involving the psychiatric consultant, should be held to make sure that all the staff workers of the institution have the same plans for the child and that he is not being pulled in too many different directions.

68. See John Matushima, "Child Welfare: Institutions for Children," *Encyclopedia of Social Work, 1971* (New York: National Association of Social Workers [NASW], 1971), pp. 120–128.

Continuing contact with the parents is also the responsibility of the social worker. Financial arrangements will have been made before admission; if parents cannot pay the full fee, the public agency may make up the difference. Endowments and United Way allotments help to cover the administrative and professional expenses. If the child is to return to his own home, casework with one or both parents may be desirable to enable the family to sustain the improvement achieved by placement. Arrangements for visiting, for weekends and vactions at home, and ultimately for discharge are made with the social worker. If all efforts fail at modifying the home situation enough to make it suitable for the child's return, then alternative possibilities for foster home placement should be explored. Children should not remain "forgotten" in institutions for years, as had Jerry.

> Jerry's parents separated before he was born, and his mother rejected him from his birth; he went straight from the newborn nursery into a foster home. Looking back now, we can see that strenuous efforts to find the father and secure an adoption release for Jerry would have been well worth it, but because both parents were not available, the possibility of adoption was not pursued. After a year in the first foster home, where he adjusted normally, Jerry was moved, since this home cared for infants only. A series of unfortunate accidents made it necessary to re-place Jerry several times in the next few years, each move leaving him more and more bewildered and, finally, angry. By the time he was six, Jerry was a fighter, a persistent bed-wetter, a troublemaker in school, and a fluent and convincing liar. The agency recognized the problems he presented and tried hard to find a foster home which could understand Jerry and give him some security. This was not an easy job, for his reputation as a "holy terror" was known in the small community. Two successive foster mothers did their best; one was a widow whose patience lasted for over a year; the next was an unmarried retired school teacher, who was determined to succeed where everyone before her had failed. By the time Jerry was expelled from school permanently, the agency felt that he could not tolerate another foster home even if they could find one and therefore placed him in a small child-caring institution.
>
> Jerry made a good surface adjustment to the routine and the group living. He preferred playing with girls or with younger boys and acted much younger than his nine years. His behavior was girlish and ingratiating, especially with older members of the staff and older teachers in school. It was recognized that he had had almost no meaningful contact

with adult males, and efforts were made to provide this by a college-student volunteer, but Jerry's lack of skill at games and his poor sportsmanship were obstacles. What he most enjoyed was dressing up in women's clothes. The psychiatric consultant recommended strongly that he be removed and that strenuous attempts be made to find, if not a foster home, at least an institution with men on the staff, but the over-worked children's agency, relieved at finding a safe spot for Jerry, ignored the recommendation. Three years later, Jerry is still at the home, his effeminacy more pronounced, his smile more vacant and silly, his school work deteriorating, and his confusion about his sexual identifications more obvious. He has been "forgotten."[69]

Careful planning for the discharge of children when it is apparent that their needs will be better met in some other setting will prevent the development of "forgotten" children like Jerry. Periodic staff conferences should be utilized to assess the child's progress in the institution and determine when he should leave. He may return to his own home, be placed in a foster home or a group home, or perhaps begin to live independently. If he is to continue under the care of a child-placing or child service agency, his history and a summary of his special needs should be prepared by the social worker. If he is not being carried by some other agency, the institution should have some provision for after-care.

Occasionally still, and more frequently in the past, children remained in institutions until they reached the age limit (usually eighteen or graduation from high school) and then had to move out into the community on their own. Being thrown on one's own resources is a frightening experience at best, and for a child coming from the unrealistic environment of an institution, where he has had no experience in the management of the essentials of living, it can be overwhelming. Assistance in getting a job, locating a place to live, establishing friendships, and planning for health care are all ways in which the social worker can be of help. A list of other agencies in the community to which the young person can turn if he feels the need should also be provided, along with help with application to these agencies if needed.

It sometimes happens that families who have manifested no interest in a child during his placement will show a sudden interest when he is a prospective jobholder and a possible financial asset.

69. Unpublished case material from the files of the Hawley Home, Saratoga Springs, N.Y. Used with permission.

Young people in such a situation should be encouraged to make the decision themselves whether or not to return home, with due recognition of all the feelings of guilt, resentment, or obligation such a situation poses. Veteran child welfare workers are continually surprised at the extent to which such apparently rejected children do return to families they may not have lived with in many years, showing their need to "belong."

AGENCY GROUP HOMES

Midway between institutional care and foster family care falls what is known as the group home.[70] This is typically a one-family house or large apartment, owned or rented by the agency in a residential area, and used in caring for five or six to ten or twelve children. It is directed by houseparents or counselors, who are agency staff, and the agency provides psychiatric, psychological, and social work services. Administration is controlled by the agency, although the small size of the group makes for a fair amount of autonomy. The group home is less visible in the community, and the children placed there go to school and make friends in the community, facilitating their readiness to move into foster family care or back to their own families.

Agency group homes can be used for children too troubled to adjust well in a regular foster home but not disturbed enough to require institutionalization. Many agency group homes serve as halfway houses between institutional care and regular family care. There are also independent group homes, which arise when a particularly successful foster home asks permission to enlarge and take more than the maximum number of children permitted by the licensing regulations. These homes are not controlled by the agency, and although they may be highly useful adjuncts to regular boarding home care, the home is controlled by the foster parents, rather than by the agency.

Adolescents may find group homes a more tolerable alternative to the relative strictness of an institutional setting or the closer relationship of a foster home when their own unresolved conflicts with parents make such relationships difficult. The socializing influence of the peer group in such a group home may be more

70. See Paul A. Guerard, ed., *Group Homes for Children and Youth* (New York: Federation of Protestant Welfare Agencies, 1973); and Arthur Greenberg and Morris F. Mayer, "Group Home Care as an Adjunct to Residential Treatment," *Child Welfare*, Vol. 51, No. 7 (July 1972), pp. 423–436. See also the October 1972 issue of *Child Welfare*, Vol. 51, No. 8, which was concerned with groups and group methods. The standard description is Martin Gula, *Agency Operated Group Homes* (Washington, D.C.: U.S. Children's Bureau, 1965).

beneficial than the customary parent-child relationship expected of foster children.

BOARDING HOMES

When a child has to be separated from his parents, unless there are positive indications for an institutional placement, the established child welfare practice is to find a foster home which will re-create a family situation for the child and enable socialization to proceed.[71] In the past, the shock of separation from what seemed to outside observers highly unsatisfactory living conditions was minimized. It was assumed that children would recognize quickly how much "better off" they were. Closer attention to what children actually experience shows that many of them undergo a genuine grief reaction at being separated suddenly from all that is familiar. Approved child placement policies now stress the need for preparation, including a preplacement visit or two if possible and an explanation, couched in terms which the child can comprehend, of why the placement is being made. Without such preparation, the child feels unduly rejected and guilty, imagining that it must somehow be his fault that his life has been disrupted.

Children tell us, by their behavior if not in words, how they are feeling about what is going on in their lives. The cases of Tommy and Bobby illustrate ways in which children react to separation and placement.

> Tommy was taken at the age of three by court order from his irresponsible and immature mother who had been neglecting him. Without warning or preparation he was placed in a temporary foster home. His mother was not permitted to see him. At first he was dazed and his reactions were those of any person suffering from severe shock. This first foster mother was a very warm, sensitive person who understood what was happening and mothered Tommy with tenderness and patience. Gradually he began to show some spontaneity, to smile and laugh occasionally, and to give a little response to affection. His eyes were still sad and he was fearful of many things, particularly new people and places.
>
> Then, after several months, a permanent foster home was found for him, and he was again moved abruptly. This time he screamed and wept, refused to have his coat removed and when he reached the new home, wild with terror, sat in the middle of the floor refusing to let anyone touch him. The

71. See U.S. Children's Bureau, *A Child Is Waiting*, Publication No. 454 (Children's Bureau, 1967), for a clearly written description of foster family care.

worker left, feeling that when he was alone with the new foster mother he would more quickly settle down. The new placement was not a success. This foster mother, lacking the warmth and understanding of the first, grew angry when Tommy soiled and wet, became sullen and resistant, and refused to respond to gestures of affection. And so again Tommy was moved. This time he went with the worker without protest and fell asleep on the way to the new home. When he awoke he was alone with strangers. Truly a lost child, now Tommy withdrew into himself almost completely, his only sign of continuing rebellion the persistence of his soiling and wetting. He did not smile or laugh now and his movements were controlled and secretive, without vitality or spontaneity. His foster mother could not understand this strange unnatural child and so Tommy was placed again.

He now had a new worker who realized what had happened. She had little time to prepare Tommy, because his foster mother wanted him moved quickly, and she was caught between two perils, the damage of another abrupt move and the rejection of the foster home. She spent a great deal of time with Tommy over the short span of a couple of weeks explaining to him what the new home was like. She brought his mother to see him and took them out together in her car to visit the new foster home. And when Tommy was moved, she and his mother placed him together. In short, she sought to reforge those links with the past, the known from which he had been so cruelly and completely uprooted. It would be pleasant to record that she succeeded, but she did not. She came too late.

A year later, Tommy, who has remained in this foster home, has "adjusted" beautifully on the surface. He is conforming, obedient, easy to handle. Of course he is very quiet, never laughs, rarely smiles. With other children in the home, he plays mostly by himself—quiet, mysterious games that are shared with no one. If you ask him about the past, he tells you matter-of-factly that he came directly from his own home to this. Tommy has gone to live in a land where no one can follow him, and for peace he has paid dearly. Over and over again Tommy tried in his actions to tell us what was happening, but no one listened until too late.[72]

It comes as a shock to the reader to realize that it is really "too late" for Tommy. And yet almost everyone who has been hurt repeatedly resolves "never again." Tommy has found that putting

72. Case material abridged from Leontine Young, "Placement from the Child's Viewpoint," *Social Casework*, Vol. 31, No. 6 (June 1950), pp. 252–254. Used with permission.

down roots does not pay; it hurts too much when they are pulled out. We may speculate on what will happen to Tommy if by some lucky chance he is able to adjust in school. What will be his incentive to learn, if new experience is always dangerous? Will he ever dare relax and allow himself to make friends, or is this too hazardous? The community will pay in many ways for its earlier failure. Responsible, self-supporting, and participating citizens must be able to take risks and become involved in relationships. The self-absorbed, schizoid personality foreshadowed in Tommy at the age of four or five does not make him a good social risk.

The same thing might have happened to Bobby, but he was lucky. He found adults who listened and understood. An out-of-wedlock child, he had been placed by his mother in several private boarding homes. When he was 4, she surrendered him for adoption and he came for the first time under an agency's care. Since the private boarding home wanted him removed immediately, he was placed with little preparation. However, the worker took Bobby's own mother with him, talked and played with him in the car, and explained very simply where he was going. He was quiet until they reached the foster home and then he screamed and cried. Almost immediately after his mother and the worker left, he became very quiet, submissive and docile. His new foster parents were warm and intelligent people who understood something of Bobby's terror, and the worker helped them to understand the kind of help that Bobby needed. He had a speech defect, confused the meaning of "yes" and "no," often saying "no" when he wished to say "yes" and vice versa, indicating the extent of his confusion and deep anger and fear. He was too eager to please the foster parents and was very conforming. With other children he readily gave up his toys and quickly withdrew if there was any fighting or quarreling. He was afraid to put on his hat and coat and did not want to leave the house even for short trips to the store. The foster parents made few demands upon him and followed his pace. They did not take him out of the yard until he indicated he was willing to take that chance and go with the foster mother to the store. After that the family made many short trips and visits so that he could have the experience of going out and returning with them. They set up definite schedules for eating and bed and bath since regularity of routine gives some fragment of certainty and security to a fearful child.

The worker came to visit often. Always she brought a gift for Bobby and the foster parents' little girl. At first Bobby greeted the worker with a prompt "goodby" and refused even to enter the room. She took her cue from Bobby, always greeted him but made no effort to break through his reserve. If he did approach closer, she immediately included him in the conversation but did not approach him. In short, during the first weeks she showed him she liked him and was interested in him, but she respected the fact that he had to decide how far it was safe to trust her. After all she had moved him once and what guarantee did Bobby have that she would not snatch him up again and take him away?

With time, love, consistent protection, Bobby began to lose many of his fears, became a more active, spontaneous, normal little boy who could affort to have a personality of his own. Then the worker was able to start more direct preparation for placement in an adoptive home. She did not discuss this directly with him at first. Instead they went to lunch together and for short trips. Several times when she was making short visits to other foster homes, Bobby went with her. He saw other children who were placed in foster homes and could then begin to discuss with the worker some of the questions about why he was placed and what had happened to him. She answered his questions simply and honestly, explaining that his mother had become very sick and wanted him to have a mother and father who could take good care of him. She began to talk to him a little about finding this mother and father who would be wholly his own. Bobby seemed interested but not very concerned.

One day she took Bobby to lunch and the adoptive parents came by the table and spoke to her. She introduced them as friends of hers and asked if he minded their joining the party. Bobby enjoyed them and was pleased when they invited him and the worker to lunch. Later he visited alone. The adoptive parents visited Bobby in the foster home also. Eventually he accepted an invitation to spend the night with the adoptive parents, and the next day he returned to the foster home, saying that he was going to live for a short time with the adoptive parents. He took his clothes but carefully left his piggy bank in the boarding home. For a time both worker and the boarding parents continued to visit Bobby and he returned once or twice to visit the boarding home. But as he put down roots in the adoptive home, his interest in both the boarding parents and the worker waned until it was only that of any normal little boy in adult visitors coming to see him and his family. Bobby had been placed without shock or fear or suffering. He had some anxious moments, but real trauma had been avoided.

Two factors had made the great difference. One, Bobby had been placed slowly at his own pace, as he was able without great anxiety and tension to accept the change from one known experience to another known situation. Throughout, the worker was a constant and steady support, a friend who shared change with him. He never faced strangers alone and he knew from their many shared experiences that the worker never let him down, never deserted him, never betrayed his trust in her. For a child who has been disappointed bitterly by adults, this consistent, continuous relationship is indispensable. There is no other way that a child can learn to trust the new except through his experience in the past that someone important and close is trustworthy. Second, Bobby participated in this placement. He did not choose his permanent home but he was given an honest chance to accept it of his own volition. No child is capable of selecting a foster home, but only the child can make the decision of whether or not he will genuinely accept it. We have the power to place him physically even against his will and desire, but there our power ends—sometimes disastrously. We cannot make him accept that placement and use it for his own happiness.[73]

Selection of Foster Homes

Facilities for the care of children out of their own homes are regulated by statute in order to control the conditions under which children are cared for and to insure minimum protection necessary for children.[74] The licensing agency is responsible for periodic reevaluations of the homes and for supervision and consultation to maintain or improve the quality of care given children. Licensing applies to supplemental care, such as day care centers, family day care, and day camps, as well as to foster homes, children's institutions, and resident children's camps, whether these facilities are maintained by public or voluntary social agencies or under commercial auspices. Slightly more than half of children in foster care are in boarding homes; the bulk of institutionalized children are in special facilities for mental disabilities or in training schools for delinquents, since the trend in recent years has been to place dependent and neglected children in foster families rather than in child-caring institutions.

There are many reasons why couples may apply for approval as foster parents. They may want a larger family but feel they cannot afford to have more children of their own. Their children may be growing up, and they may like to have younger children in the house. In some cases, they may be unable to have children, al-

73. *Ibid.* Used with permission.
74. See Costin, *Child Welfare*, Chapter 10, "The Regulation of Children's Out-of-Home Care," for a detailed discussion of the purposes and nature of licensing.

though in that case the question of adoption should be considered. A genuine love of children, some understanding of them, and either experience with children or flexibility enough to surmount adjustment problems created by placement are essential. Although the free home is seldom used and most agencies pay board, the amount paid seldom covers the out-of-pocket costs, and foster care of children is not a money-making proposition unless the home is overcrowded. Where serious physical or emotional problems exist (bed wetting, destructiveness, hyperactivity), the board rate may be higher, but there are less demanding ways of making money.

Not all those who apply to take children into their homes are approved. The home must meet certain health and safety requirements, as well as provide desirable relationships and acceptance for the child. The health of the foster parents, both physical and emotional, should warrant the extra work involved. The child should be wanted because of what the family has to offer him, not to patch up a failing marriage, to punish a spoiled only child, or to provide a "toy" for the foster parents to play with. Older children should not be requested to exploit as babysitters or farmhands.

The "home-finder" from the agency, or the licensing supervisor if the family is operating independently, will need to visit the home, inspect the physical set-up, talk with the family doctor and often the clergyman, and consult friends or grown children of the couple to learn about the atmosphere in the home and the type of living experience a child placed there might have. Homes which can be approved for certain ages or types of children might be considered unsuitable for infants, adolescents, or those with specific problems. The community where the home is located may need to be considered; a child with health problems should not be placed too far from good medical facilities, or a child with a reading disability should not be placed in a community with no special facilities in its schools.

If it is felt that the home cannot be approved for any type of child, the family should be told so directly, not by avoiding the issue by placing the parents on a waiting list until a "suitable" child should appear. The shortage of foster homes is well known, and this deception fools no one. Sometimes it is difficult to explain why the application is being rejected without betraying confidential material, such as health or mental health factors. The family will be hurt and angered at the rejection, no matter how sugar-coated it may be, and the worker conveying the decision must be secure in himself and in his agency's policies to be able to transmit the agency decision.

Child-caring agencies are reconsidering carefully their requirements for foster parents in light of the increasing body of evidence on the harm done to children by prolonged institutionalization. Is a mediocre or even a poor foster home better than an institution if that is the only alternative? What about a family on public welfare? If the grant were increased to include the child and the home were otherwise acceptable, would not this represent a better solution than an indefinite stay in an institution? In some cities, for example, there are many black and Puerto Rican children needing foster homes, but relatively few middle-income black and Puerto Rican families with room for even one extra child.

State laws insist, in many states, that children be placed in homes of the same racial and religious affiliation, which presents difficulties in some communities and when children of mixed racial background or unusual religious affiliation need foster homes. Foundlings often have some religious identification on them, but if not, they are usually assigned alternately as Roman Catholic, Protestant, or Jewish. Some states insist that parents have some religious affiliation, no matter how nominal, and will not accept atheists or nonbelievers as foster parents.

The child care worker (who may or may not be the home-finder) will be given the information on approved and available homes and will consider, together with his supervisor, whether the child in need of placement should be with children his own age, whether his particular kinds of behavior would be acceptable in the home, whether the standards of the home will be within his reach comfortably, and what the neighborhood has to offer in the way of promise or temptation.

Preparing the Foster Parents

Children entering into foster care have come from homes which are inadequate or tragic and will reflect their prior difficulties in their behavior. A study done by the Child Welfare League of America (CWLA) found that deviant parent behavior, psychosocial stress, parent incapacity, and unacceptable behavior of the child are the leading reasons for seeking foster care.[75] It is obvious that in such cases preventive social services to families have been lacking or inadequate. Few children require foster care because of

75. *The Need for Foster Care: An Incidence of Requests for Foster Care and Agency Response in Seven Metropolitan Areas* (New York: CWLA, 1969), p. 22.

unavoidable catastrophe. The effects of being uprooted from familiar surroundings, no matter how unsatisfactory, will be expressed directly or indirectly by a child entering a foster home, and the foster parents should be warned. Whenever possible, the child should be allowed to visit the home first and feel he has had some voice in choosing it. Foster parents should be prepared for repercussions resulting from the child's guilt or anger at being placed. Will he be withdrawn and conforming at first and then, as he becomes more secure, start to misbehave? Foster parents should be helped by the child care worker to realize that far from representing a failure, this reversal represents the child's growing security and that it is all right for them as foster parents to set appropriate limits and demand that the child stay within them. Will the child react by regressing to more childish behavior—wetting the bed, sucking his thumb, using babyish speech? Foster parents will not be alarmed if they are forewarned. Will the child brag about past glories? The child care worker can help foster parents see this as his defense against the helplessness which is overwhelming him.

Many foster parents find the placement experience so rewarding that they take additional children. As each one moves on to a more permanent living arrangement, they take in another. Every child-caring agency has some of these "old reliables," who can accept, love, and help each child who is placed in their home and, when the time comes, can relinquish him lovingly because it is in his own best interest to move on.

Foster parents must understand that the children they take into their homes remain wards of the agency (or of the natural parents if it is a voluntary placement). Children use their own names, not the foster parents'. No matter how attached foster parents may become to them, the time may arrive when the children have to be re-placed. Although foster parents have prepared themselves, intellectually, for this time, many find it a severe emotional wrench. It is easier for them if the children are to return to their own homes, but it is a blow if the children are being re-placed because the agency is not satisfied with the way they are being handled.

More frequently, the decision to remove the child is the foster parents'. We have already seen, in the cases of Jerry and Tommy, that foster mothers may "give up" and ask to have the child removed. Sometimes this request is an indication that the home should not have been approved in the beginning; sometimes it is owing to circumstances beyond anyone's control; sometimes it means that this particular child should not have been placed in that particular home. If the situation is irremediable, the child should be re-placed, but knowing the dangers to the child of frequent changes of home, the worker should be sure that it really is irremediable and not merely the result of this foster mother's need for greater help in understanding how the child's behavior represents his "cry for help." It is tragic to think in how many cases a few more days or weeks of patience might have enabled a child to relax to the point of accepting and trusting these new adults.

There are never enough good foster homes available to child care agencies, who thus are often forced to place children in homes they have reluctantly approved. The situation is particularly critical for adolescents. Children who have been in a home for many years may have built up a good enough relationship with the foster family to weather the storms of adolescence together, although it may also happen that foster parents who have tolerated disruptive behavior from younger children may find it intolerable in teen-agers. When adolescents need foster care for the first time, it is extremely difficult to find foster parents willing to undertake the task. Fears of sexual activity, drug abuse, and delinquency, as well as the problems of everyday adjustment to the often volatile, moody, and unhappy youngster deter all but the most experienced or courageous foster parents. Child-caring agencies should be prepared to extend extra support and encouragement to both foster children and foster parents at this critical stage in the youngster's life cycle. It may well be that the agency group homes mentioned above (pages 214–215) will be a better solution for the teen-ager than wearing out his welcome in a series of foster homes, each removal compounding his feeling of failure and lowering his self-esteem.

The Child's Own Family

In former times, foster children were not permitted to see or continue contact with their own parents, as this was thought to interfere with their adjustment in the foster home. Parental visits were discouraged or forbidden. With greater sympathy for the feelings of the rejected parents, we can understand some of their unrealistic promises to children and hostility to foster parents. It is hard to be told officially that one is an inadequate parent, unfit to take care of his own children; it is doubly hard to see someone else doing a good job with those same children, taking one's place in the children's affections and teaching them new standards which constitute an implied criticism of one's own. It is no wonder that parents react to this threat in childish ways, promising to take children home "next week," to send expensive presents, to take them on exciting trips. The children wait with impatience and express their disappointment by lashing out at foster parents, who feel with some justification that they do not deserve this. Efforts on the part of the child care worker to interpret the natural parents' behavior to the foster parents and to provide some understanding and support of the natural parents in their difficulties offer more promise than forbidding contact, especially since we know that most children in foster care will at some point return home.

In a provocative article on the continued effect of parents on their children,[76] Almeda Jolowicz points out that memories or fantasies of what their parents were like will color the child's personality. We do not "protect" children by cutting them off from their parents; rather, we leave them at the mercy of their uncorrected imagination of what their parents must have been like. Since they retain the family name, they should be allowed to know something of the family from which they came, to celebrate family anniversaries and keep family pictures. In the long run, attempting to minimize the destructive effects of parental visits offers more to the child than forbidding them altogether.

Never Enough Time

One of the serious problems in the child welfare field is that so much must be done on a semi-emergency basis. Many situations which require placing children cannot be anticipated. Most child care workers are carrying caseloads so large that there is never time for long-range planning. To locate suitable foster homes, to arrange placements which meet needs, to do remedial work with parents to enable them either to take the children home or relinquish them takes time. And time is the one thing an overburdened staff does not have.

> Billy, now fourteen, was born out of wedlock during the war. He came to us [a county department of public welfare] at the age of four when his mother married and his stepfather did not want him. Since he had never had any security, he was already disturbed when he began his life in a series of boarding homes. An appealing child, he was always readily accepted by new boarding parents. But when he would begin

76. Almeda Jolowicz, *The Hidden Parent* (Albany: New York State Conference on Social Work, 1946), pp. 13–27.

to rebel it was always in a way that was difficult to accept—usually setting fire to house or barn—by even the most understanding boarding parents, and he was on his way to another home or institution. Contacts with his mother who was having a new family, decreased and finally ceased. In our early contacts the mother unrealistically clung to the hope that she could eventually persuade her husband to accept him. Although we felt certain the stepfather would never do so, we felt unable to help the mother with her decision as we lacked both the skills and the time. She had left the community, and although it would have been difficult to locate her it would not have been impossible. But it took time and there were always more urgent things pressing—the seven Jones children had to be placed immediately, or Johnny had run away again. As any one of us could have predicted, Billy is now in a state school, and when he comes out he will still have no family. We certainly failed him.[77]

Even the best foster home is less satisfactory for any child than his own home. If a suitable home cannot be provided by his natural parents, the possibility of freeing him to make permanent ties to adoptive parents should be explored.

ADOPTION

Adoption is a legal process, in which a court orders the old parental ties dissolved and substitutes a new relationship between the child so freed and the adoptive parents. An adopted child acquires the same legal rights and responsibilities as natural children of the parents, takes their name, and becomes a permanent part of the new family. Because of the finality of this procedure, particular care should be taken to guard against foreseeable dangers in the new parent-child relationships. Increasingly, legislation is now being sought which requires that adoptive homes be investigated by some social agency, public or voluntary. There is a notable lack of uniformity in the extent to which preliminary investigation is required, and an adoption which would not be legalized in one state may be permitted in the next.

CURRENT DEVELOPMENTS IN THE FIELD OF ADOPTION

The field of adoption is changing rapidly. After increasing steadily since the end of World War II, the number of children

77. Elma Kullman, "An Agency's Use of Administrative Supervision," *Child Welfare*, Vol. 35, No. 7 (July 1956), p. 17. By permission of Child Welfare League of America.

being adopted has dropped markedly, since contraception and abortion offer new alternatives to the unmarried woman and some of the stigma against illegitimacy has gone, permitting mothers who wish to keep their children to do so more easily. In 1970 about 175,000 children were adopted, more than half by nonrelatives. Three fourths of the nonrelative adoptions were arranged by social agencies. An estimated 65 percent of the children adopted in 1970 were born out of wedlock; 21,000 were nonwhite; the median age at placement was 1.9 months.[78] By 1971 the figure had dropped to 169,000, only 83,000 by nonrelatives.[79]

The current scarcity of white adoptable infants has spurred several new developments. First, the number of "independent" placements is growing. These are divided into "black market" (where the adopting parents literally buy the baby) and "gray market" (where the arrangements are made through a third party, usually a doctor or lawyer). While it is true that many independent adoptions turn out successfully, there are hazards to a non–agency placement. These include no impartial check on the family background of the child, no preplacement evaluation of the home, and most critical of all, no clear guarantee that the parents' legal rights to the child have been permanently terminated. If the confidentiality of the transaction is not properly protected, the threat to reclaim the child may be used as a device to extort money from the adoptive parents. Courts have traditionally been protective of blood relationships and have been known to set aside adoptions of many years' duration on the claim of a natural parent that he wished his child returned or that the adoption release was fraudulently obtained.

A second development has been the increased interest in adopting biracial or nonwhite children by white parents. At first hailed as an indication of increased liberalism and diminished racial prejudice on the part of white parents, the practice has been increasingly condemned, by black social workers particularly, as creating an artificial situation for black children.[80] The critical issues of identification and the development of coping mecha-

---

78. *Adoptions in 1970* (Washington, D.C.: National Center for Social Statistics, 1972.)

79. U.S. Bureau of the Census, *Statistical Abstract of the United States: 1973*, p. 313.

80. See, for example, Leon W. Chestang, "The Dilemma of Biracial Adoption," *Social Work*, Vol. 17, No. 3 (May 1972), pp. 100–105, in which he concludes that only black families can assure optimal opportunity for black children. The same point of view is expressed by Edmund D. Jones, "On Transracial Adoption of Black Children," *Child Welfare*, Vol. 51, No. 3 (March 1972) pp. 156–164.

nisms for life in a racist society will be impeded for a black child growing up in a white family. More adequate support systems for enabling black families to adopt black children may provide a better immediate solution,[81] while the long-range goals of eliminating racism are so slowly being achieved. The question of responsibility of American society for the thousands of half-American babies in Asia and Europe demands action on a national scale, since immigration and emigration laws pose obstacles.[82] That adoption is an international issue was indicated by the First World Conference on Adoption in Milan, Italy in September 1971, which concerned itself with the legal impediments to international adoptions and voted to request the United Nations to sponsor an international conference on adoption law.

A third development has been the increasing attention to the hard-to-place child, including those with handicaps, and the older child.[83] Orthopedic and visual handicaps can often be corrected, and parents who are of average intelligence may prove accepting of a child whose intellectual potential is somewhat below average. Parents whose age makes them unsuited for placement of an infant may be of an appropriate age for an older child. The position of the Child Welfare League is that any child who can profit from family life should be considered adoptable, and parents who can meet his needs should be searched out. With an increasing scarcity of babies, adopting agencies are stressing flexibility and warmth as desirable attributes in adoptive parents, pointing out that even natural parents cannot demand a child to specification and yet are able to accept and love the child who arrives. The nationwide Adoption Resource Exchange of North America (ARENA), set up in 1967, is stressing adoptions of hard-to-place children. Since minority group children are considered in this category, some agencies are permitting adoption by single parents. Couples whose financial resources do not permit taking full responsibility for another child may be subsidized by some agencies, thus enlarging the pool of potential adoptive parents.

81. See Elizabeth Herzog et al., *Families for Black Children: The Search for Adoptive Parents* (Washington, D.C.: U.S. Children's Bureau, 1971); and Annie Lee Sandusky et. al., *Families for Black Children II: Programs and Policies* (Washington, D.C.: U.S. Children's Bureau, 1972). See also Frederick W. Seidl, "Transracial Adoptions: Agency Responses to Applicant Calls," *Social Work*, Vol. 17, No. 3 (May 1972), pp. 119–120.

82. See "Adopting Vietnam's Orphans: Efforts Grow to Make It Easier," *New York Times*, August 21, 1973, p. 24.

83. See Joan Shireman and Kenneth W. Watson, "Adoption of Real Children," *Social Work*, Vol. 17, No. 4 (July 1972), pp. 29–38, for an innovative approach to placing older children.

A fourth development is an intensified effort to secure adoption releases promptly for children who are unlikely ever to be able to live with their own parents. It has long been known that the child who remains in foster care for more than eighteen months is likely to remain there indefinitely.[84] Thus, a device intended as a stop-gap turns for too many children into a dead end. A recent article by Chestang and Heymann[85] advocates introducing the discussion of adoption routinely with parents of all children accepted for foster care; their view is that foster care is a temporary arrangement and that extended foster care is damaging to children. Parents should be encouraged to reestablish a home for their children if this is realistically feasible in a reasonable time or else relinquish the children without guilt, supported by the recognition that they are acting in the children's best interests. The authors claim that present child welfare policies allow parents to flounder in indecision and that it is the social worker's responsibility to help them act decisively. With support for their wish to do their best for their children, the strain of placement and replacement, if the family later decides to release the child, may be avoided and the child placed into his adoptive home immediately.

ADOPTION STANDARDS

The process of evaluating an adoptive home is similar to that of approving a foster home. References are secured and enough visits made to the home to enable the social worker to see its informal atmosphere. Childless couples may be required to undergo sterility tests. That adoption by a childless couple is so often followed by the birth of a baby indicates that emotional rather than physical problems may be the cause of their childlessness. Couples who have children of their own are not necessarily barred from adopting a child, especially if they are willing to consider one with special needs. Since, in most cases, the agency will withdraw from the situation once the adoption is made final, care should be taken to assure stability, although more and more it is being felt that the adopted child can take his chances with the other children in the family. Also, there are many children of average potential who need average homes. Insisting on above-

84. Henry S. Maas and Richard E. Engler, *Children in Need of Parents* (New York: Columbia University Press, 1959), p. 421.

85. Leon W. Chestang and Irmgard Heymann, "Reducing the Length of Foster Care," *Social Work*, Vol. 18, No. 1 (January 1973), pp. 88–92. See also Irving W. Fellner and Charles Solomon, "Achieving Permanent Solutions for Children in Foster Care," *Child Welfare*, Vol. 52, No. 3 (March 1973), pp. 178–187.

average financial and educational standards in adopting parents is unrealistic.

The extremely rigid position taken in some states that a child can be adopted only by couples who share his religious affiliation should also be modified, since in many areas the religious affiliation of the children most needing adoption does not correspond with that of the couples most eager to adopt. The position of adoption authorities is that children have the right to learn some religious teachings and that parents should agree to expose them to some formal religion, but insisting on perfect matching may work hardship on the child.[86]

Until a decade or two ago, it was considered essential to wait until an infant was old enough to undergo some psychological evaluation before making an adoptive placement. Recognition of the damaging effects of separation on even tiny infants has led to earlier placement. Obviously, the child who has never known any other home will be in a better position than the one who remembers being moved. This underscores the necessity of careful planning with natural parents to secure earlier release of children for adoption.

The most careful evaluation and matching of child and adoptive home will not guarantee that all will be serene. Agency adoptions are never made final until a waiting period, usually six months or a year, has shown that the placement has stability. It is only natural that during that period the parents wonder if the struggle is worth it. Such misgivings occur to natural parents, too! But the great majority of adoptions succeed. The days when it was a disgrace for children to be adopted, when parents did not tell them (although someone else always managed to), and when pity was felt for childless parents who "had to" adopt or did so "out of the goodness of their hearts" have passed. Adoption announcements are sent out, and adoptions are reported in alumni news magazines. In one adoptive family, there are two annual celebrations—the child's birthday and his "adoption day," one feature of which is to re-hear the tape recording of the child's arrival in the home.

In most states, the judicial process by which the adoption is made final is confidential. The original birth certificate is replaced or amended to indicate the new name. Once permanent guardianship has been transferred to the parents, the agency withdraws from the case. Agency files are confidential, although present pol-

86. See Bernard J. Coughlin, "Religious Values and Child Welfare," *Social Casework*, Vol. 51, No. 2 (February 1970), pp. 82–90.

icy is to tell the child or have the parents tell the child in terms appropriate to his age enough of the circumstances of his surrender to satisfy his anxiety. The current sentimental interest in the adopted child's locating his own parents, stimulated by the 1973 success of the book *The Search for Anna Fisher*,[87] is based entirely on sympathy with the child and ignores the mother's right to have that chapter of her life permanently closed by the contract which forms the adoption release. Not every mother of children released for adoption twenty-one years earlier will welcome the intrusion of that child, now grown, into whatever new life she has constructed for herself.

Indications are that the great majority of adoptions turn out well.[88] Both the Children's Bureau and the Child Welfare League have issued numerous studies and manuals of standard procedure, and there are numerous books, both hard-cover and paperback, written for the general public.[89] With current emphasis on Zero Population Growth, many young couples are planning on two natural children and the addition of adopted children to their families. Some of them will accept hard-to-place children. The importance of good social work services to unmarried mothers and to seriously neglectful or abusive parents will result in earlier decisions to release some children and save their painful shifting around until permanent neglect laws release them. There will be no dearth of couples eager to adopt, particularly if release can be achieved before the children have been damaged by their unsatisfactory living conditions.

SERVICES TO UNMARRIED PARENTS

More than two thirds of the children adopted in 1970 were illegitimate. Social attitudes toward illegitimate pregnancies have changed over the years and vary widely among social classes and ethnic groups. The older rigid attitude which forced the parents to marry, however reluctantly, has been modified, although many such marriages still occur. However, the stigma of illegitimate

87. Florence Fisher, *The Search for Anna Fisher* (New York: Arthur Fields Books, 1973).

88. One of the earliest evaluations is that of Sophie Theis, *How Foster Children Turn Out* (New York: State Charities Aid Association, 1924). See also Elizabeth Lawder et al., *A Follow-up Study of Adoption* (New York: CWLA, 1969); and Alfred Kadushin and Frederic W. Seidl, "Adoption Failure: A Social Work Post-Mortem," *Social Work*, Vol. 16, No. 3 (July 1971), pp. 32–38.

89. See, for example, Colette T. Dywasuk, *Adoption—Is It for You?* (New York: Harper & Row, 1973); and Alan A. Jacka, *Adoption in Brief* (New York: Fernhill Publishing Company, 1973).

pregnancy is still directed almost entirely against the mother, especially if she is receiving public assistance. Social services and health care should be provided for the pregnant woman, and the father, when his identity is known, should be involved in the planning. Unfortunately, many public agencies are more interested in securing financial support from the father than in helping him with his own problems. Unless the father is given the opportunity to acknowledge paternity and does so, the child is in the exclusive custody of the mother, and her signature on the adoption release is the only one needed. Much less is known about unmarried fathers than unmarried mothers, though it is apparent that their sexual activity has special meaning for them and that if it results in pregnancy, it creates problems.[90]

The dynamics underlying illegitimate pregnancy have been more extensively studied since the pioneering work of Leontine Young,[91] who felt that women's unsatisfactory relationships with their mothers were correlated with illegitimate pregnancies. While this may be true for some women, ignorance and chance seem more likely causative factors for most unmarried mothers, especially adolescents.

It is the women who do not find the social services which will help them in their critical need who become involved in bargaining about their babies. Doctors or lawyers, perhaps well-meaning, may enter into an agreement with a couple who want a child, that the couple pay for a pregnant woman's expenses in return for the baby. Such "gray market" placements have been discussed. In addition to the possible leakage of confidential material, the release signed by the mother may be open to doubt. Agreements entered into by a panicky girl relieved to have her hospital costs underwritten may seem less desirable to the new mother once she has seen her attractive baby. If she has not been given an opportunity to think through her decision, she may become embittered, feel defrauded, and attempt to get her baby back on the plea that she did not know what she was signing.

Adequate services for unmarried mothers will include residen-

90. One of the few studies of these "forgotten men" is Weston LaBarre, "The Triple Crisis: Adolescence, Early Marriage, and Parenthood, Part II—Fatherhood," *The Double Jeopardy, The Triple Crisis* (New York: National Council on Illegitimacy 1969), hereafter cited as *Double Jeopardy*, pp. 23–24.

91. Leontine Young, *Out of Wedlock* (New York: McGraw-Hill, 1954). For critiques of her position and an extensive review of the literature, see Jerome D. Pauker, "Girls Pregnant Out of Wedlock: Are They Pregnant Because They Are Different or Are They Different Because They Are Pregnant?" *Double Jeopardy*, pp. 47–68.

tial arrangements for those unable or unwilling to remain at home, schooling for those under sixteen, proper health care, financial planning, hospitalization for delivery, and sympathetic working through with the unmarried mother the decision of whether to give up or keep her baby. When she is very young (and increasingly she is), it is especially difficult to make constructive plans for keeping the baby. The teen-age mother, whose education and progress toward adulthood have been interrupted, is well advised to relinquish her infant, to enable him to have the advantages that come with two adult parents.

Unfortunately, the very immaturity which contributed to the predicament is likely to make it difficult for the unmarried mother to come to a mature decision. If she is a minor, her parents must approve her release. Many of the children who are shifted from one unsatisfactory boarding home to another, only to be relinquished when they are too old to be readily adoptable, have been born to just such young mothers, whose unsatisfied emotional needs incline them to cling to their children out of possessiveness. Adequate social service to such mothers will be directed toward helping them see what their own emotional needs really are and helping them find constructive and socially acceptable ways of satisfying those needs.

The foregoing applies particularly to white, middle-class girls. Minority groups may have less punitive attitudes and the possibilities for finding good adoptive homes may be fewer; remaining with the mother may be the wiser decision for the child in these situations. The rights of the child to the best possible parental situation with people to whom he belongs either by blood ties or adoption should be the paramount concern of the social worker and the parents. Whatever the disapproval of the parents' conduct, it is surely a social concern when children suffer from inadequate parenting and lack of social services.

OUTLOOK FOR THE FUTURE IN CHILD WELFARE

One of the questions which concern child care experts relates to the quality of parenting in contemporary society. Are parent-child relationships less positive than they once were? Are modern "moms" rearing a generation of overprotected Portnoys? Are children left too much to their own devices, with too much exposure to violence and temptation? Certainly there is evidence that socialization is more difficult in the mobile, urban society. The decline of the primary group, with its critical importance for maintaining social conformity, puts added burdens on the school and the community. Economic pressures on mothers to work and fathers to "moonlight" create a demand for better day care facilities. There is urgent need for improvement in all agencies serving children and their parents. The benefits of sound programs to forestall delinquency, promote mental health, and develop productive citizenship for all children are obviously vital for our society.

There will be expanding opportunities for social workers at every level of competence and training in the child care, protective, family treatment, school social work, foster care, and adoption services described in this chapter. There is also critical need for interpretation to a cost-conscious public of the cost benefits of adequate services to children. This task should engage the interest and attention of those not directly engaged in providing service but no less concerned about the future of the nation's children.

ADDITIONAL REFERENCES

Adoption Services: A Bibliography of CWLA Publications, 1960 through 1972 (New York: Child Welfare League of America, February 1973). A compilation of articles, books, and book reviews on all aspects of adoption.

Denzin, Norman K., ed., *Children and Their Caretakers* (New Brunswick, N.J.: Transaction, 1973). An examination of the politically determined age-graded phases through which America's children are forced, with proposals for changes in the institutions which train children.

Engel, Mary, *Psychopathology in Childhood: Social, Diagnostic and Therapeutic Aspects* (New York: Harcourt Brace Jovanovich, 1972). An overview of the field of diagnosis and treatment, including a fascinating study of Lee Harvey Oswald as a disturbed child.

Franks, Cyril M. and Wilson, G. Terence, eds., *Annual Review of Behavior Therapy and Practice, 1973* (New York: Brunner/Mazel Publishers, 1973). A compilation of papers covering theory and practice, with analysis and illuminating comments on each paper by the editors.

Group for the Advancement of Psychiatry, *Diagnosis and Treatment in Child Psychiatry* (New York: Jason Aronson, 1974). A publication by the prestigious GAP designed for all the professions working with disturbed children.

Kline, Draza and Overstreet, Helen-Mary, *Foster Care of Children: Nurture and Treatment* (New York: Columbia University Press, 1972). Stresses the need for diagnostic study to assess parental capacity for rehabilitation, in order to predict the duration of foster care.

National Institute of Mental Health, *Selected References on the Abused and Battered Child*, DHEW Publication No. (HSM) 73–9034 (Rockville, Md.: National Institute of Mental Health, 1972). A selected bibliography from American and foreign sources, covering 1968 through 1972.

Pappenfort, Donnell M.; Kilpatrick, Dee Morgan; and Roberts, Robert W., *Child Caring: Social Policy and the Institution* (Chicago: Aldine Publishing Company, 1973). A discussion of the programs and resources of agencies providing extra-familial care of children, together with recommendations for sweeping changes.

Roby, Pamela, *Child Care—Who Cares?* (New York: Basic Books, 1972). A review of foreign and American infant and early childhood development policies by experts from eight nations.

Sarri, Rosemary C. and Maple, Frank F., eds., *The School in the Community* (Washington, D.C.: National Association of Social Workers, 1973). The report of a three-year project sponsored jointly by the National Association of Social Workers and the National Institute of Mental Health, which includes major papers by many leading school social workers.

Sarvis, M. A. and Pennekamp, M., *Collaboration in School Guidance* (New York: Brunner/Mazel, 1970). Reports the collaborative efforts of a team consisting of psychiatrists, social workers, and educators in an urban school system.

Zukerman, Jacob T., "Support and Custody of Children—International and Comparative Aspects," *International Social Work*, Vol. 12, No. 2 (1969), pp. 18–26. A review of laws and policies in twenty-two countries, presented at the International Bar Association Conference in Dublin in 1968.

5

chapter

services to
the aging

A NEW FIELD OF SERVICE

Attention to the physical and social needs of the aging is a relatively new field of service in the United States and indeed in the world. While the biblical description of the life span of man as "three score years and ten" is still remarkably accurate, the success of modern medicine in lowering the toll of contagious and preventable disease in early life has led to a larger and larger proportion of the population reaching the Psalmist's estimate of the "days of a man." Life expectancy at birth has increased dramatically since the turn of the century—up from 47.3 years in 1900 to 71.1 years in 1971. However, this increase has been accomplished by reducing the number of premature deaths; since 1900, the further life expectancy of those aged sixty-five has gone up by only two years. As medical science turns from the preventable diseases to the degenerative diseases, breakthroughs come slowly, if indeed they come at all. Further marked increases in the life expectancy of adults are unlikely, although the statistics from other countries of the world indicate that some additional months could be added with improved support services.

Clark Tibbitts was one of the first authorities on aging to describe the increased proportion of elderly in our population in positive terms, as a modern social achievement.

America's aging citizenry, then, is in large part the product of population growth, immigration, medical progress, and improved environmental conditions. Since all the causes, except

235

large-scale immigration, will continue to operate, it may be predicted that around the year 2000 the population will have increased to 275 to 300 millions, with from eighty to eighty-five million persons aged forty-five years and over, of whom perhaps twenty-five million will be over three score and ten.[1]

Tibbitts was using figures now more than fifteen years old, but the *1972 Current Population Reports* already bear out his projections: in 1970, just over 20,000,000 people over sixty-five constituted 9.8 percent of the population; the projection for 1980 is 23,600,000 (10.0 percent), and for 2000, 28,900,000 (9 percent). If the recent decline in the birthrate continues, the percentage may be even larger.

While there is no arbitrary age at which one becomes "old," the figure of sixty-five has been accepted by industry, Social Security, and most writers on the subject. At the same time that the life expectancy of both men and women has been extended past sixty-five, we have moved in the direction of earlier retirement, a shorter workweek, and greater mobility of the working population. The emotional and financial problems resulting from forced retirement and inactivity may be accentuated by the physiological changes associated with aging and by inadequate financial reserves in a time of rising taxes and inflation. To live past sixty-five may indeed represent a social achievement, but only if society also makes available adequate resources for dealing with the accompanying difficulties.

There are a number of reasons for the tardy development of services to the aging. In the first place, this is a new phenomenon in history. Anthropological studies of the elderly[2] indicate that relatively few persons survived to advanced ages and that in most cultures they had some meaningful role to perform, as repositories of the accumulated wisdom of the tribe, as arbitrators and advisers, or as performers of tasks within their capabilities. In a few cultures, where pressure on resources was extreme, they were put to death or put themselves to death. Death from "natural causes" was a relative rarity in most preliterate cultures.

In the folk society (see page 61), life expectancy was short, and the proportion of elderly dependents was smaller. People were expected to continue to work as long as they were physically able,

1. Clark Tibbitts and Wilma Donahue, eds., *Aging in Today's Society* (Englewood Cliffs, N.J.: Prentice-Hall, © 1960), p. 6. By permission of Prentice-Hall, Inc.

2. See Leo Simmons, *Role of the Aged in Primitive Society* (New Haven: Yale University Press, 1945).

and for those without families to care for them, there were "poor-houses" and county homes. Industrial society and medical technology combined to make the older worker redundant; they compelled his retirement and prolonged his years in retirement without simultaneously developing mechanisms to provide a meaningful role and adequate income for him. Our ignorance of how to deal with our elderly population is a maladjustment stemming from the speed of industrialization and the failure to plan adequately for its consequences. Such failures to plan ahead have also resulted in mounting problems of pollution, exhaustion of natural resources, and a runaway population explosion in parts of the world.

SOCIAL ATTITUDES TOWARD THE AGING

There are numerous social attitudes toward the aging which have hampered our efforts to provide proper and adequate support services. In a youth-oriented culture, aging and signs of aging are unpalatable. The mass media urge people to stay youthful, to tint graying hair, to wear hair pieces, to use cosmetics, to prevent "tired blood," and to conceal hearing aids. Many people fear that working with the aged will be depressing. Advancing years bring death closer, and the society which will go to any extreme to avoid facing the facts of death[3] avoids confronting those who inevitably remind them of their own mortality. Only the growing political "clout" of the voters over sixty-five has forced attention, first at the federal level, to the extent to which we systematically ignore and deprive our senior citizens. As they become more adept in the use of the political process, groups of the aging can be expected to receive more equitable treatment.[4]

Industrial societies stress productivity and the work ethic, and the great bulk of those over sixty-five are out of the labor force, although a substantial number remain at work, many of them undoubtedly to supplement inadequate Social Security benefits. The upper limit on earnings permitted to Social Security recipients illustrates the extent to which social policy, as embodied in the Social Security Act, compels older people to retire. If self-esteem and social worth are keyed to work and productivity, forced retirement strips the aging of these means of maintaining status and

3. See Jessica Mitford, *The American Way of Death* (Greenwich, Ct.: Fawcett Publications, 1969), for documentation of this aspect of our society.
4. See "Right On, Gray Panthers!" *Christian Science Monitor*, September 12, 1973, p. 18.

relegates them to the status of nonpersons described by Erving Goffman.[5]

Stereotyped notions about aging and the elderly exist in all segments of the population. Many of them are myths, but they are held tenaciously, and sound data to rebut them are scarce. The aging are generally thought to be less intelligent, less able to learn, more rigid, riskier as employees, less ambitious and therefore more easily satisfied, less able to adapt and cope. How often these stereotypes turn into self-fulfilling prophecies is not known, but the existence of those who refute all the myths should be more widely publicized. Aging is an individual process, which occurs at differing rates in different people, and social-psychological factors may accelerate or retard the physiological changes.[6] The stereotypes militate against the provision of adequate economic and social support systems for the over–sixty-five segment of the population.

One further obstacle may be noted. Developmental psychology has been preoccupied until very recently with infancy, childhood, and adolescence, at the expense of later phases of the life cycle. The contemporary view, still not adequately reflected in the literature and in research, is to regard aging as a normal developmental phase, with its own tasks. Most of the helping professions, in which this has not been the accepted view, tend to regard the degenerative processes as abnormal and death as an event to be postponed at all costs. Recent interest in "patients' rights," including the right to refuse further treatment, has raised ethical and philosophical questions which are far from answered. When does life cease? For many years, cessation of heart action and breathing have been considered death. Now that heart-lung machines can keep the organism going well nigh indefinitely, newer criteria must be developed. Do patients' rights include the right to die in dignity? Must all possible surgical, medical, and electronic procedures be utilized over the patient's protests or those of his family? The developmental approach views death as the normal clos-

5. Erving Goffman, *Asylums* (Chicago: Aldine Press, 1961); see also Goffman's *Presentation of Self in Everyday Life* (New York: Doubleday & Company, 1959), for additional discussion of the "nonperson."

6. See Thomas A. Rich and Alden S. Gilmore, *Basic Concepts of Aging–A Programmed Manual* (Washington, D.C.: Administration on Aging [AoA], 1971), especially pp. 13–47. See also George L. Maddox and Marvin J. Taves, "What Social and Behavioral Sciences Say About Aging," *Welfare in Review*, Vol. 10, No. 1 (January–February 1972), pp. 8–12.

ing of the cycle, but doctors, nurses, clergymen, and families may see it far differently.[7]

Social work educators should be concerned about preparing practitioners to deal with elderly clients. As Elaine Brody puts it:

> From the point of view of the social work practitioner, disparities exist between what is known and what is being taught, between knowledge and its utilization in meeting human needs, and between the accumulated fragments of knowledge and their meaningful synthesis. In general attitudes and approaches to the aged are those that developed in relation to other groups of people, for other purposes, and during the earlier phase in history. They are not consonant with current realistics. In the main, social work education has participated with other helping professions in reflecting rather than challenging these attitudes and approaches.[8]

WHO ARE THE AGED?

To speak about "the aged" is an oversimplification. Authorities distinguish several subgroups under the general heading: those from sixty-five to perhaps seventy-five constitute the "young" aged; those seventy-five to eighty-five form the middle group; and those above eighty-five are the very old. In 1970 there were 13,000 Americans over 100 years of age. It is the third group (the very old) which will be increasing fastest in the next decade, and since disability goes up sharply with age, strain on already maldistributed health services and institutions will increase. Most of the available statistics, however, lump all those over sixty-five together, although their needs may be quite different.

In 1973 there were 20,949,000 people in the United States over sixty-five. There are more women than men, and the proportion of men to 100 women drops steadily as age increases, with an average for all those over sixty-five of 71.6 males per 100 females. Nonwhites are underrepresented, reflecting less good health care in earlier years. The great majority of the elderly live in family settings, though often alone; only 4 percent are institutionalized.

7. There has been a spurt of interest in "thanatology" and "terminality" and some attempt to prepare medical personnel to deal with the emotional needs of the dying. See Orville G. Brim, Jr., Howard E. Freeman, Sol Levine, and Norman A. Scotch, eds., *The Dying Patient* (New York: Russell Sage Foundation, 1970); and Avery D. Weisman, *On Dying and Denying: A Psychiatric Study of Terminality* (New York: Behavioral Publications, 1972).

8. Elaine Brody, "Serving the Aged: Educational Needs as Viewed by Practice," *Social Work*, Vol. 15, No. 4 (October 1970), p. 42. Reprinted with the permission of the National Association of Social Workers.

The number of those widowed increases with age: there were in 1971, 542,000 widowers between sixty-five and seventy-four and 2,093,000 widows; of those over seventy-five, 906,000 were widowers and 3,347,000 widows.[9] This reflects not only the longer life expectancy of women but the fact that widowers are more likely to remarry. Almost all of the aging widowed have relatives, surviving children or grandchildren. As income and health make it possible, more of the aging live alone; poverty and poor health may force them to take a nonrelative into the home or to move in with relatives. Their low educational level reflects the generally lower attainments in the early years of this century.

The aged are very much overrepresented in the ranks of the poor. In 1971, at least one fourth of all Americans over sixty-five fell below the poverty level. When nonwhite status is added to age, the percent in poverty goes up to nearly one half. In 1970, the median family income was nearly $10,000, but the median family income for those over sixty-five was $5,053. Inflation is particularly hard on the elderly, since most of them must live on fixed incomes and the escalator clause in Social Security payments provides for price increases a year after they occur. As a result of the increased Consumer Price Index in the spring of 1973, for example, increased Social Security benefits were originally to be deferred until July 1, 1974, until special legislation by Congress in late 1973 mandated the increase on January 1, 1974.

At least one third of the aging outside of institutions have disabling chronic health problems, of which arthritis and heart disease, including high blood pressure, are the most frequent. Close to 80 percent of those over sixty-five have at least one chronic ailment, and 50 percent have two or more. Disabilities increase with age. The health problems of the aged tend to be interrelated, and their physical condition is also closely related to their mental health. The aged are hospitalized oftener, and their stays are longer. Such sensory deficits as partial or total loss of vision and hearing, impairments of motor abilities including speech, and organic mental disorders associated with senile brain disease also occur with increasing frequency as age rises. While rates of hospital admissions for senile psychosis rise rapidly with age, the diagnosis is suspect in many cases, since mental hospitals in many states become "dumping grounds" for troublesome old people, where they fill up the back wards and receive custodial

9. U.S. Bureau of the Census, *Statistical Abstract of the United States: 1973* (Washington, D.C., 1973), p. 37; and *New Facts About Older Americans* (Washington, D.C.: AoA, June 1973).

care rather than treatment. In spite of the large amount of medical service given to those over sixty-five, the area of unmet need is very great. In a survey conducted for the Vermont Council on Aging in 1970, more than half the elderly respondents cited readily accessible low-cost health facilities as their most pressing need.[10]

Closely allied to health needs and compounding them is the chronic malnutrition of the elderly. According to Senator George McGovern, Chairman of the Select Committee on Nutrition and Human Needs, "The elderly are the most uniformly undernourished segment of our population." Difficulties in getting to grocery stores, absence of delivery services, ignorance about proper nutrition, as well as income inadequate to purchase a well-balanced diet are all factors. In July 1973, the Associated Press reported, under the headline "Old Peoples' Solution to Inflation: Go Hungry," that many of the retirees in the Miami area were cutting back to two meals a day and that shoplifting by the elderly in food stores is increasing.

In addition, the elderly face several special problems. Many of them have poor teeth and lack good dentures. Dental care and dentures are not covered under Medicare, and inability to chew greatly limits the diet. The lack of incentive to prepare an appetizing meal to eat by oneself is also a factor, especially to someone recently widowed. Cooking and storage facilities are inadequate in the living arrangements of many solitary aged people. The diversion of money which should be spent for food to other needs is more characteristic of the elderly poor than of families with children; shelter and medical care often swallow up a large part of the food dollar. The exclusion of those receiving SSI (see page 83) from the Food Stamp program is regrettable on this score; purchase of food stamps at least guaranteed that a portion of the income was being used for food. One of the most promising targets for development of services to the elderly is improved nutrition, by such programs as Meals on Wheels, cooperative food purchases, and central kitchen dining clubs. Not only do these make life more pleasurable, but they constitute preventive health care and are a long-range economy for a cost-conscious public.

The stereotype fostered by the mass media portrays the retired as free of money worries, in good health, able to travel and play golf, and for a substantial number of the "young aging" this is true. Retirement villages, interesting social activities, and freedom

---

10. *What Vermont Can Do About It,* a report by the Bread and Law Task Force, Burlington, Vt., 1971.

from responsibility make an attractive picture. The retirement industry is a profitable field for investment in services catering to upper-income groups.[11] Nonprofit retirement communities and institutions under church sponsorship provide for middle-income groups with many of the same advantages. But for the great majority of the aging, idleness is a pervasive problem. Lacking funds for transportation to recreational facilities or equipment, with failing vision limiting the amount of reading or TV viewing they can do, with old friends dead or moved away, loneliness and isolation are the experience of all too many of those over sixty-five. Many of those physically able to go out are too depressed to make the effort and need outreach service from senior citizens centers. Others would profit from sustained friendly visiting, a program which can easily be adapted to college students, assigned to paraprofessionals from social agencies, or performed by volunteers from the aged themselves.

The independence that is valued in the young and mature adult is likely to be considered a nuisance or even pathological in the very old. Insistence on living alone, refusal to be institutionalized, fighting against sedation and restraint represent lifelong patterns in many people. Recognition that a substantial number of elderly recipients of Old Age Assistance were living under unsafe conditions led to the inauguration in the spring of 1967 of a three-year demonstration project in rural Colorado and urban Washington, D.C.[12] Among its findings, to be described later, was the lack of awareness in both urban and rural areas of the difficulties of elderly citizens struggling to maintain their accustomed life style under the pressures of inadequate income, failing strength, and increasing isolation. The restriction of the study to recipients of public assistance meant that all those studied had inadequate income, but indications are that protective services are also needed by people unknown to the welfare department. The Social Security Administration already deals with the legal needs involved in the appointment of a trustee for Social Security beneficiaries deemed incompetent to handle their own benefit checks. As the Social Security Administration becomes more familiar

11. See Thomas Meehan, "Letting the Rest of the World Go by at Heritage Village," *Horizon*, Vol. 15, No. 4 (Autumn 1973), pp. 16–25. See also Sheila K. Johnson, "Growing Old Alone Together," *New York Times Magazine*, November 11, 1973, pp. 40 ff., for a description of two California and one Arizona retirement communities.

12. *Report of the National Protective Services Project for Older Adults*, HEW publication no. (SRS) 72–23008 (Washington, D.C.: Community Services Administration, 1971).

with the problems of those on SSI, the provision of direct services or of referral to the welfare department for services will undoubtedly increase.

THE AGING PROCESS

As has been indicated, less attention has been paid to the later phases of the life cycle than to the early ones, yet the developmental approach sees old age as the completion of a normal process and not as an illness or disease process. Erik Erikson, who is perhaps best known for his work on the development of identity in youth,[13] sees the life cycle as involving eight stages. The seventh is middle age, in which the conflict is between "generativity" (or the guidance of the next generation) and stagnation; in the eighth stage the conflict is between integration of one's previous life and despair. Integration represents the lifelong effort to achieve ego integration, to bring a sense of order and meaning into the individual's life cycle. Despair focuses on the lost opportunity and the inability in the short time remaining to start over. Erikson's approach sees the attainment of ego integrity as the teleological goal of human development and relates it to the first stage, that of infantile trust, when he says, "Healthy children will not fear life if their elders have integrity enough not to fear death."[14] Implicit in not fearing death is the acknowledgment of having been useful and having had a constructive influence on those who survive, and the task to be mastered in the last days is to achieve the most constructive effect possible on the survivors.

Allen Pincus was one of the first social workers to stress the developmental approach to aging and its usefulness for social work. Pointing out that most social work services to the aged see only the unsuccessful or distressed, Pincus cites evidence of what may be innate mechanisms, which have been observed as early as the mid forties in successful and busy individuals.[15] Just as the small child experiences drives outward to explore and master his environment, people in middle age experience some introversion, some shift from active to passive mastery, and less marked mood changes.

In the past, these changes have been considered losses and re-

13. Erik H. Erikson, *Identity: Youth and Crisis* (New York: W. W. Norton & Company, 1968).

14. Erik H. Erikson, *Childhood and Society,* second edition (New York: W. W. Norton & Company, 1963), p. 269.

15. Allen Pincus, "Toward a Developmental View of Aging for Social Work," *Social Work,* Vol. 12. No. 3 (July 1967), pp. 33–41.

ferred to as "disintegration" and "regression," yet we do not refer to the child who moves from the security of total care as an infant into the potentially hazardous world of childhood as "losing" anything. Viewing the socio-adaptional changes of later life as part of the developmental process provides some positive goals toward which social worker and elderly client can move together, remembering that lifelong personality trends and life styles will continue to determine the individual's adaptation to aging. Those who have all their lives blamed others for lack of success will continue to look outside themselves for something to blame; those who have blamed themselves for everything will become depressed or, in Erikson's term, "despair." Those who have achieved their sense of self-worth in physical prowess or business success will find aging more difficult to adapt to than those who have lifelong patterns of satisfaction from activities which can continue past sixty-five.

Part of the integration process of Erikson's eighth stage involves a review of one's life; reminiscence serves a therapeutic and adaptational function for many elderly people. All too often, however, reminiscence by the aging on their past lives is regarded as aimless wandering of the mind, as boringly repetitive, or as implying criticism of the present. Pincus finds that reminiscing may be one of the ways in which the elderly cope with the stresses of the aging process, may serve as an alternative to depression, may facilitate the resolution of grief, and may serve to review and integrate life for those sensing imminent death.[16] Bringing back into the mind experiences which give satisfaction, enhance self-esteem, and recall pleasant associations increases the feeling of identity.

Excessive absorption in the past may, of course, reflect the barren nature of the present, but careful listening will enable the social worker or the family to assess the importance and value it has for the elderly person. Instead of regarding recollections from the past as boring or aimless, young people should be helped to see them as authentic items of local history, some of which will be gone forever unless preserved.[17]

A recurrent problem in delineating the developmental view of the life cycle is the absence of reliable research on normal aging.

16. Allen Pincus, "Reminiscence in Aging," *Social Work*, Vol. 15, No. 3 (July 1970), pp. 47–53.
17. For a fascinating compilation by school children of fast-vanishing skills and folklore, see Eliot Wigginton, ed., *The Foxfire Book* (Garden City, N.Y.: Doubleday & Company, 1972).

Most of the experience of social work and medical personnel has been with those who were not aging successfully, and there are few longitudinal studies of individuals from birth to old age which would illuminate the extent to which earlier life experiences determine behavior in the later stages of the life cycle. Our interest in the aging is too recent to have completed such studies, although some have been begun at middle age and are continuing until the subjects' deaths. Marie Blank[18] reports that these studies indicate the overwhelming importance of physical health, not only for the individual's ability to function but also to prevent loss of self-esteem and consequent depression. Blank feels that depression is an important component of the feelings of the normal aged who experience or confront increasing disability.

THE SPECIAL CONCERNS OF THE AGING

INCOME

While an adequate income is a serious matter to most adults, there are several reasons why it becomes an item of pervasive concern for those over sixty-five. Their working lives, during which their Social Security taxes and other retirement funds were accumulated, saw much lower wage levels and lower prices. Social Security earnings ceilings have been raised rapidly in recent years but too late to benefit workers who had already retired. In February of 1972, of nearly 18,000,000 recipients of retirement benefits, 1,276,000 needed Old Age Assistance in addition. Since the median full monthly standard for basic needs was $130 monthly ($1,560 annually), all these individuals fell markedly below the poverty level. It is unknown how large a segment of the population over sixty-five were eligible for OAA and unwilling to apply or ignorant of their eligibility. Residence laws, restrictions on owning property in some states, or requirements that recipients must assign life insurance policies or place liens on their homes further restricted the use of OAA.

Those who have worked at low wages during their working lives have not had reserves to accumulate savings or purchase private annuities and have not belonged to unions with private pension schemes. There have always been restrictions on the earnings permitted Social Security beneficiaries before their benefits are reduced. While the ceiling has been increased from an

18. Marie Latz Blank, "Recent Research Findings on Practice with the Aging," *Social Casework*, Vol. 52, No. 6 (June 1971), pp. 382–389.

original $600 a year to $2,100 in 1973, it still limits the ability of beneficiaries to improve their level of living. It should be noted that this is a work-related restriction, not an income restriction, and does not apply to the affluent retired who receive income from investments. Inability to live on Social Security benefits is one of the factors that keeps 4.2 percent of the men and 3.8 percent of the women over sixty-five in the labor force.[19]

The 1972 Amendments to the Social Security Act did make provision for a special increase to benefit long-time low-wage earners, and it raised the minimum payment for those with a thirty-year work record to $170 per month, still short of the poverty level and of diminishing benefit to those with less good wage records. As more currently employed workers reach retirement age, they will be proportionately better off; they will have worked for higher wages under a higher tax ceiling, so that their benefits will be higher. In addition, an increasing proportion of them will have a private or a second public pension to supplement Social Security benefits.[20]

Averages are misleading, since a relatively small number of very high incomes can raise a large number of low incomes to an unrepresentative level. In 1970, the median (half fall above and half below) income of families with heads sixty-five or over was half that of families with a head younger than sixty-five, while older persons living alone had a median income of $1,951 as compared with $4,616 for those under 65.[21] This disparity becomes accentuated with inflation, since younger family heads and individuals are more likely to receive cost-of-living increases in earnings or profit from appreciated assets than the aging who live on relatively fixed incomes but still must meet rising prices for essentials. In 1971, 4,700,000 of those over sixty-five lived below the poverty level. This is 18.5 percent of those in poverty, although the aging comprise only 10 percent of the population.[22] Aging nearly doubles one's chances of being poor. The decrease

19. *Middle-Aged and Older Workers in Industry* (Washington, D.C.: National Council on the Aging, May 1973), p. 17.

20. See Lenore E. Bixby and Virginia Reno, "Second Pensions Among Newly Entitled Workers: Survey of the New Beneficiaries," *Social Security Bulletin*, Vol. 34, No. 11 (November 1971), pp. 3–7.

21. *Facts and Figures on Older Americans: Income and Poverty in 1970* (Washington, D.C.: AoA, 1972), p. 1.

22. U.S. Bureau of the Census, *Statistical Abstract of the United States: 1972* (Washington, D.C., 1972), p. 332.

in income poses particular problems for those accustomed to a higher standard of living.[23]

That anxiety over income is widespread among those over sixty-five was demonstrated in a study conducted in senior citizens' centers in southeast Michigan. Retirees considered their incomes inadequate, largely because of financial inability during their working years to assure retirement income and because of high medical costs. The single, widowed, and divorced were more likely to find their incomes inadequate, particularly women and blacks. In general, the respondents felt that two thirds of preretirement income is needed for adequacy.[24] Obviously, few retirees achieve that level.

Certain groups of older Americans bear additional burdens because of their ethnicity or their residence. Older black Americans have had less favorable employment conditions during their working life, which is then reflected in their lower Social Security benefits. Their health care has been less good, which is reflected in lowered life expectancy and higher rates of disability. In addition, segregated housing, ghetto neighborhoods with high crime rates, and fewer opportunities for good recreation make adaptation to aging more difficult. Aged Mexican-Americans have experienced culture shock, job discrimination, language barriers, and alteration of the traditional extended family structure. The intense emphasis on personal dignity makes accepting help from anyone but a family member humiliating. Older American Indians recall with bitterness the suppression of their cultural behavior by government officials, the separation from families, and the heritage of distrust of government agencies carried over from decades of broken promises. Few have employment histories which qualify them for Social Security benefits; most accept government checks resentfully or apathetically. All share with many white elderly persons all the disadvantages of inadequate income but with added psychological burdens.[25]

The rural poor find isolation from the facilities they need an added complication to inadequate income. Transportation is a perennial problem, as public transportation fades away, as village

23. See Thomas Tissue, "Downward Mobility in Old Age," Social Problems, Vol. 18, No. 1 (Summer 1970), pp. 67–77.

24. David A. Peterson, The Crisis in Retirement Finance: The Views of Older Americans, "Occasional Papers in Gerontology No. 9" (The University of Michigan–Wayne State University, 1972).

25. 1971 White House Conference on Aging, The Elderly Indian and The Spanish Speaking Elderly (Washington, D.C.: U.S. Government Printing Office, 1972).

general stores give way to large shopping centers at a distance, and as small-town general practitioners retire or die and are not replaced. In those rural areas where employment opportunities have decreased, the young people have moved away, farms are abandoned, the tax base shrinks, and growth ceases. The proportion of rural, aged persons has increased in some states, particularly those where industrial growth has slowed. While nationally, one in four aged persons is living in poverty, the proportion in rural states is double that. In Vermont, a 1970 survey found the average income of the elderly to be $1,605 and the median for a couple $2,295. In that year, a Bureau of Labor Statistics estimate of a minimum budget for a retired couple was $3,151.[26]

According to the 1971 White House Conference on Aging, there are nearly 9,000,000 Americans (41 percent of those over sixty-five) living in rural areas, over one third of them living in poverty. A third of the rural men and 70 percent of the rural women have incomes under $2,000, and there are fewer opportunities for paid employment, even though many of the rural poor are accustomed to work and would like to do so.[27]

Another financial anxiety for the elderly is rising taxes. Many retirees own their own homes, some of them well-built, comfortable, and in good repair, but all too often old, in poor condition, lacking amenities, and expensive to maintain and heat. Rising property taxes mean that more than the "normal" 25 percent of income must be allotted to housing. Some states have begun programs of tax reduction or tax abatement for senior citizens, but more needs to be done in more realistic ways—rebating taxes means they must first be paid in full; allowing tax credit on next year's income tax still means paying the taxes this year. State income taxes can be withheld from the earnings of those working but must be paid, often in advance, out of savings or Social Security benefits for those not working; exemptions are seldom large enough to be realistic. Sales taxes must be paid on an increasing number of necessities, including utilities, meals, clothing, and even in some states, food. They bear particularly heavily on those living on fixed incomes.

HOUSING

Two thirds of all older people own their own homes, but all too often this is a growing burden and not a resource. There is a

26. *What Vermont Can Do About It.*

27. 1971 White House Conference on Aging, *The Rural and Poor Elderly* (Washgon, D.C.: U.S. Government Printing Office, 1972).

national shortage of adequate housing; with limited buying power, the elderly get the less desirable quarters. The U.S. Senate Committee on Aging estimates that at least 30 percent of older Americans live in substandard housing, with inadequate or absent plumbing and heating, rundown and unsafe construction, no safe fire escape, and poor maintenance. Many elderly people are living in houses too large for their needs, to which they cling, partly out of sentiment and partly because of the prohibitive cost of more suitable alternatives. In many cases, neighborhoods have changed, leaving elderly residents stranded in rural isolation or in hostile, sometimes dangerous, blighted areas.

Unless the elderly are affluent, they have difficulty finding housing designed for older people, with ramps instead of steps, doors wide enough to admit wheelchairs, nonslip bathtubs with grab-bars, low shelves, and doors that open and close easily. The federal government, between 1960 and 1970, produced more than 336,000 housing units, half of them designed specifically for the elderly, under the National Housing Act. This far from meets the need and does little for the rural aging. Many elderly people dislike the isolation of living only with other older people. Many dislike the impersonality of separate apartments in what seems like a beehive or a rabbit warren. The varying needs of senior citizens demand more flexibility in living arrangements.

The 1970 Housing Act permitted some modification in public housing which offers promise for developing the continuum of living arrangements already provided in many upper-income–level retirement communities. Housing developments should include, perhaps in the same building, separate apartments for those who wish and are capable of complete independence, central dining facilities and housekeeping services for those who cannot cope with housekeeping or cooking, supervised dormitory arrangements for those who are not able to be alone at night, and nursing-care areas for those requiring twenty-four–hour care. An important factor in providing housing for the elderly is offering some choice, so that privacy and companionship, activity and rest, homogeneity and variety may be at the elderly resident's option and not dictated by bureaucrats.

Two encouraging illustrations of imagination in planning public housing come from Syracuse, New York and from California. The former is the Toomey Abbott Towers, where two high-rise university student dormitories and a high-rise senior citizen apartment building share a common restaurant-library-shopping plaza. Senior citizens find university facilities open to them; college students have built-in foster grandparents from whom they get home-cooked meals and sewing, and for whom they run errands and do shopping.[28] The other is in Pleasanton, California, where an imaginative architectural firm interviewed prospective tenants in order to incorporate their wishes into the design of a low-income housing project to be located in a suburban, middle-income neighborhood which was somewhat reluctant to accept what they were afraid might prove an eyesore. The firm found that the following considerations, rather than the architectural style or building material, were paramount to tenants: a sense of privacy and personal ownership; safety and easy maintenance; a garden space; ample storage space; a living room large enough to entertain grandchildren; drying space for clothes in the bathroom; a porch large enough for sitting and chatting with passersby; a separate bedroom, not a sleeping alcove in an efficiency apartment; a functional kitchen and no dining room. They did not want: winding paths; slippery floors; cabinets that jut out and have doors that swing low; low fences, walls, or steps to stumble over; dim lighting; and kitchen fixtures too high to reach comfortably. The suggested features did not limit the architect's esthetic expressions and could all be achieved within the stringent cost limitations of public housing.[29]

One critic of urban redevelopment believes that housing planners have failed to recognize that the primary function of urban building is social and that structure should follow function, instead of determining it. Planning for housing for the aging should center around their "life space" and offer them an opportunity to express their individual needs and desires more fully. Decreasing mobility makes ready accessibility of services and social contacts more essential, yet urban renewal frequently replaces the older neighborhood, with its small shops and narrow streets, with new facilities too expensive for the poor who have been displaced. The new broad streets are hard to cross, the new parks are too far to walk to, the cleaner halls and automatic elevators do not replace the front steps as a social center. Social planners who take into account and apply such interdisciplinary efforts should be involved in city planning, along with the engineers and architects.[30]

28. Marjorie B. Tiven, *Older Americans: Special Handling Required* (Washington, D.C.: National Council on Aging, June 1971), p. 77.

29. Ronald Najman, "Architecture for the Aged," *Saturday Review of the Arts*, Vol. 54, No. 49 (January 1973), pp. 59–60.

30. James E. Birren, "The Abuse of the Urban Aged," *Change: Readings in Society and Human Behavior* (Delmar, Ca.: Communications and Research Machines, 1972), pp. 94–96.

HEALTH CARE

Most of those over sixty-five are not in poor health, but keeping well is a preoccupation for many older people, since poor health is the largest obstacle to independence. Much of the chronic ill health of those over sixty-five began years earlier, a fact which underlines the importance of preventive medical care in middle life or before. The physical processes of aging, which occur in the absence of disease in most people, include: less elastic and more fragile skin, leading to wrinkles and easy bruising; some stiffening and bending of the joints and loss of muscle strength; sensory losses in hearing, vision, touch, taste, and smell; slower reflexes and less sharp attention; some digestive difficulties and constipation; urinary frequency, especially at night; less ability to maintain body temperature, resulting in more sensitivity to both cold and heat.[31] In addition to these physiological changes, most of which require some adjustment but are not insurmountable, increased susceptibility to various diseases and disabilities makes periodic screening tests (for diabetes, glaucoma, heart disease, tuberculosis, and cancer) and immunization against tetanus, flu, and polio highly desirable. Unfortunately, many elderly people are not aware of the desirability of such health measures, they are not uniformly available, and many elderly people lack the initiative and mobility to get the preventive care they need. The importance of outreach services by social workers, public health nurses, the Social Security Administration, and senior citizens centers to make the aging aware both of the value and availability of these services cannot be overemphasized.

Although Medicare has improved the service provided the ill elderly, it does not cover preventive services to the well elderly, whose incomes are simply inadequate to pay for medical service which could be postponed. Medical costs rose twice as fast and hospital costs five times as fast as the cost of living between 1960 and 1970, making the gaps in Medicare coverage and the portion of expense for which the patient is responsible a heavy burden on most elderly people. In 1969, Medicare covered only 45 percent of older peoples' health care, and the fees and deductibles have increased since then. Those below certain income levels may be eligible for Medicaid, but coverage is uneven and has the stigma of welfare associated with it, rendering it unacceptable to some. Eligibility limits are unrealistically low, creating problems

---

31. Tiven, *Older Americans*, pp. 20, 21.

for those just above the limit but still living in poverty. The maldistribution of medical services is particularly hard on the rural elderly.

The problem of nutrition has already been mentioned. It is compounded by low income, poor teeth, inability to go shopping, and lack of interest in planning and eating meals alone. Surplus commodities and Food Stamp programs may help some, but the type of food distributed and the size of the packages make surplus commodities less useful to older people, and the transportation and waiting involved in some food stamp centers offsets the added purchasing power provided. A better solution is the development of group meals, with transportation available to them. Public schools, housing projects, church basements, and senior citizens centers can provide suitable meals at low cost for those able to come. There is the added advantage of the social setting, with opportunities for greeting old friends and meeting new ones. Some centers provide a substantial hot meal at noon and a box supper to take out, thereby assuring two well-balanced meals a day. Outreach services are often needed to encourage lonely people to come to the center; once there, they become involved participants, but simple advertising of the facility is not enough to overcome apathy and shyness. Here is an opportunity for social workers, paraprofessionals, and volunteers to be involved in organizing group meals, supportive services such as transportation and education, and outreach.

For those who live too far from such a center or who are unable to get out of the house, Meals on Wheels programs bring well-balanced dinners to the home. These programs are more expensive than group meals and do not serve the widely scattered rural areas but can be a useful supplement to other nutrition programs. The meals are usually contracted for and packed in some central facility, often a hospital, and distributed through volunteer groups or paid drivers. The younger elderly are a good source of manpower for such projects.

Since many of the health problems of the aging are complicated by poor nutrition, any programs which result in improving the diet of the elderly can be considered preventive medicine. The public is often more sympathetic to the idea of providing meals than to supporting higher welfare budgets. The meals are only part of the basic problem, however. Education on nutritional needs, modification of recipes and menus for less active retirees, consumer education on buying (including cooperative food purchasing), and information on new products should be included in any nutrition program for the aging. Since a large number spend time watching television, more programming should be directed to the needs of this segment of the population. Even though their incomes are limited, they constitute a significant consumer group.

MENTAL HEALTH

Mental health is closely correlated with physical health, but the mental health of the elderly tends to be neglected because of the assumptions that senility and mental illness are inevitable and untreatable. They are seldom referred for psychotherapy, on the grounds that they are too old to change. This is not borne out by the facts. Robert Butler reports that older patients respond well, on the whole, to both individual and group psychotherapy,[32] perhaps because they are aware that they have so little time left. The most common problem in old age is depression, which, if it worsens, can lead to suicide; the suicide rate of white men in their eighties is four times that of men in general. Assuming that depression is normal and untreatable leads to ignoring early warning signs, such as poor appetite, loss of interest in activities formerly carried on, and personal neglect. These symptoms are not "natural," and depression is not untreatable. Involvement in useful activities, new social contacts, attention to untreated physical conditions like anemia or some mild chronic infection, can cause depression to lift and the individual to resume a more satisfying level of functioning.

Those who had emotional problems in earlier life will carry them into old age, often intensified. Suspicious, irritable, or demanding young people will continue to present these difficulties in intensified forms as they experience the added stress of aging. It may be difficult to modify long-held attitudes, but with sympathetic understanding, many such people can be managed in the community rather than shunted off to mental hospitals.

Studies on personality patterns identify four lifelong adjustment patterns which become more apparent in older adults: the mature-integrated person, the armored-active person (who fights against growing old and protects himself by overactivity), the rocking-chair personality, and the unintegrated person. The Kansas City Study of Adult Life found in a group of active and healthy seventy-to-eighty-year-olds, the following percentages of each type: 32, 27, 22, and 19, respectively. Only the 19 percent of uninte-

---

32. Robert N. Butler, "Myths and Realities of Aging," address presented at the Governor's Conference on Aging, Columbia, Maryland, May 28, 1970.

grated personalities were unable to maintain adequate levels of life satisfaction in accepting and supporting social environments.[33]

Depression and discouragement may also retard the physical rehabilitation of patients who have had bone fractures, surgery, or cerebro-vascular accidents resulting in loss of speech or motion. Although they may be physically ready for learning crutch-walking, speech therapy, or physiotherapy, they may be fearful or apathetic. Psychiatric evaluation and supportive services should be utilized to help the patient return in so far as possible to his former level of activity, particularly when this will avoid prolonged institutionalization.

Community psychiatry has done almost nothing for the aging, focusing its efforts instead on children and young adults with many years ahead of them. If they are truly to serve the community, however, mental health centers should adapt their services to the special needs of the aging, including home visits, day care programs geared to their pace and interests, and supportive programs to the relatives who are caring for them. Contrary to the myth that families abandon their aged,[34] evidence is that more disabled and even bedridden people are cared for by their families than by all institutions combined. However, families often do this at great costs to themselves, and "respite services" are needed; these include day care, social admissions to hospitals to give the family a vacation, and home health aides. Family agencies can provide counseling services when intergenerational conflicts, often of many years standing, interfere with home care of the aging.[35]

Because of the reluctance of many families to institutionalize aged relatives, placement in a nursing home or hospital is usually postponed as long as possible and then regarded as a final disposition rather than a treatment period with a subsequent return home. State mental hospitals are still the major "treatment" resource for the aged, many of whom are senile rather than mentally ill. In the past, mental hospitals were filled with geriatric patients, most of whom had no other place to go. With the increase in nursing home beds, especially since the advent of Medicare, mental hospitals have shifted large numbers of their aged

33. "Personality Patterns Influence Life of Aging," *Geriatric Care*, Vol. 5, No. 7 (July 1973), p. 1.

34. Brody, "Serving the Aged," pp. 45–47.

35. See, for example, Bertha G. Simos, "Adult Children and Their Aging Parents," *Social Work*, Vol. 18, No. 3 (May 1973), pp. 78–85.

patients to nursing homes, often with no regard for their wishes and with inadequate explanations. Such uprooting from accustomed conditions leads to a significant increase in the death rate,[36] particularly for bed patients, and raises serious questions about the "advantages" to the community of such wholesale closing of mental hospital facilities, antiquated and inadequate though some may be. The loss of familiar surroundings is a significant loss to the very old, who are already feeling helpless and threatened and who do not understand fiscal policy or other theoretical issues. Community pressures might perhaps be used better to develop community-based facilities, aimed at preventing commitment to state hospitals and to improving the conditions for older people already in hospitals, to allow them to remain there.

TRANSPORTATION

All the other difficulties which beset the aging are complicated by increasing limitations on mobility, whether it is to the corner store, to the nearest medical center, or to keep up with friends and family. Only 14 percent of older people have drivers' licenses, sometimes because of vision impairment, arbitrary age limits, or inability to get insurance, but more often because they cannot afford the cost of owning a car. As funds are diverted from public transportation to superhighways, passenger trains and local bus services disappear, or the costs become prohibitive for those with low incomes.

Even where public transportation still exists, facilities seldom take into account the special needs of the aging. Bus steps are high, long flights of steep stairs are involved in subway stations, bus schedules are hard to read, drivers do not wait when the light changes, bus stops and subway stations are not clearly identified. Noise, crowds, dirt, lack of benches to rest on, lack of public toilet facilities, inability to use automatic ticket sellers, turnstiles, or change machines—all make it simpler for many elderly people to stay home. Shopping plazas and supermarkets involve miles of walking, even if one has a ride to the parking area.

Few of the stores and services patronized by low-income people have delivery services, and the increased cost of parcel post has diminished the cost advantages of mail-order purchase for many

36. See Eldon C. Killian, "Effect of Geriatric Transfers on Mortality Rates," *Social Work*, Vol. 15, No. 1 (January 1970), pp. 19–26, which reports on a study conducted on 600 geriatric patients moved to other state hospitals or community-based facilities. See also Margaret Blenkner, "Environmental Change and the Aging Individual," *The Gerontologist*, Vol. 7, No. 2 (June 1967) pp. 101–105.

items. In Project FIND, an outreach program in greater New York, the National Council on Aging reports that at least one third of the respondents, and more of the poor respondents, reported transportation as one of their chief problems. A Vermont survey in 1971 indicated the increased difficulty of winter driving for the rural elderly; fully one half of those over sixty-five who own cars put them up for the winter and are then dependent for transportation on relatives or neighbors.

Experiments have been attempted to increase the mobility of older people who would otherwise be home-bound or limited to activities within easy walking distance. Some communities have buses or vans to transport older people on regularly scheduled runs or less frequently on demand. These services are expensive, but with good organization and publicized schedules, they can be used to take people to senior citizens centers, churches, medical centers, shops, and banks.[37]

In New York City, a reduced fare between 10 A.M. and 4 P.M. permits elderly passengers to use buses, but the hours allowed may not be most convenient. In rural areas, suggestions to use school buses on return runs have run into jurisdictional disputes, although the waste involved in running buses empty for half their trips is apparent. In this connection, one of the recommendations coming out of the White House Conference on Aging in 1971 was:

> To assure maximum use of vehicles and coordination, all passenger vehicles (such as school buses, vans, and other vehicles) in use by Federal, State, county and city programs, shall be made available interchangeably among agencies for the provision of transportation to senior citizens for their respective programs. The use of these vehicles shall be available without prejudice to serve all disadvantaged elderly. An area clearinghouse should be established so that all local transportation resources are used efficiently to meet the transportation needs of the elderly.[38]

In the absence of adequate and affordable transportation, elderly people walk. This presents traffic hazards on rural highways and urban streets and increases vulnerability to crime. *The Village Voice*, a journal more often associated with the youth cul-

---

37. See Edmund J. Cantilli, ed., *Transportation and Aging: Selected Issues* (Washington, D.C.: AoA, 1971), especially pp. 135–168. See also *Connections*, Vol. 1, No. 1 (November 1972), for a description of a Travelers Aid Transportation Service in Florida.

38. 1971 White House Conference on Aging, *Transportation* (Washington, D.C.: U.S. Government Printing Office, 1972), p. 4.

ture than the aging, has reported on the daily schedule of an older citizen in New York City:

> If you are old and live in New York, your neighborhood has a special geography. On the West side, for example, you learn that there are fewer stairs to climb from the subway at 96th Street than at 93rd Street. You learn where police call boxes are, and you worry as you walk down Columbus Avenue in the 90's because all the stores have taken their pay phones out as a precaution against hold-ups. You know it is hard to catch the bus at 99th and Columbus because the double parkers there cause the bus to stop way out in the middle of the avenue. You also learn which buildings kids usually play in front of, and you cross the street to avoid being knocked down.
>
> You know on which bench in the middle of Broadway you're likely to meet a friend, and which bench a wino may frighten you from. If you're cold and lonely, you know that the waiting rooms at Port Authority Terminal and Penn Station are warm and interesting places to find a seat.
>
> Your day also has a special schedule. You're most likely to be robbed after school gets out and kids know which days the checks are delivered, so you go early to the bank. Toll takers and bus drivers are likely to get mad if you try to get onto public transportation with your half-fare card a minute before 10 or a minute after 4, so you time your trips carefully. To be sure of getting to talk to someone at the Medicaid office you have to be down at 34th Street and Ninth Avenue by 7:30, but you must dress warmly as the line on the sidewalk is long. Most of all, you try to be home before dark, because you're an easy target for muggers.[39]

LEISURE TIME

Older people may not have enough money, enough food, or enough medical care, but they have more than enough time. The maintenance of meaningful relationships and satisfying roles is essential if the leisure they have worked hard for is not to be empty and burdensome. In a society which glorifies work, retirement from work brings inevitable loss of status, as well as a loss of opportunities for regular contact with others. Women whose self-esteem has been derived from their roles as mother and homemaker may suffer when they lose all or part of their activities in these spheres. The limitations of income, mobility, and energy

39. Rachel Cowan, "The New Minority: Senior Citizens as Victims of Geronticide," *The Village Voice,* January 21, 1971. Reprinted by permission of The Village Voice. Copyrighted by The Village Voice, Inc., 1971.

make it harder to initiate new contacts or even to maintain old ones.

Many people continue to work past sixty-five, for economic or personal reasons, but retirement is mandatory in most private industry and civil service systems. Opportunities for new employment in the private sector are severely limited for those considered "old," which in many cases is forty-five.[40] The development of paid and volunteer service activities in the public sector is one of the more promising approaches to those who have time, talent, and energy to invest. The Administration on Aging lists some of these:

> The Foster Grandparent Program assigns low income older people to give love and individual attention to institutionalized children. They work a twenty-hour week and are paid the federal minimum wage. Uniforms and at least one meal are often included.
>
> Green Thumb and Green Light are programs sponsored by the Labor Department; Green Thumb employs retired farmers to work on conservation projects, and operates in 17 states. Green Light employees serve as community service aides in outreach programs to elderly, handicapped and shut-ins. The wages paid are planned to be below the ceiling for earnings permitted Social Security beneficiaries.
>
> The Department of Labor also funds two programs for community service aides in OEO Community Action Programs, public housing and food stamp programs, and in Social Security Offices. [These may well be jeopardized by the 1974 budget cuts.]
>
> SCORE (Service Corps of Retired Executives) was launched in 1964 by the Small Business Administration and uses former executives to provide management counseling to small businesses.
>
> VISTA (Volunteers in Service to America) allows individuals of all ages to utilize particular talents in the fight against poverty in both urban and rural areas. Enrollees enlist for a minimum of a year, and receive travel, maintenance and medical care, plus an allowance of $50 a month toward a separation payment.
>
> The Peace Corps has no upper age limit and has sent volunteers of all ages for work in developing countries. [Both VISTA and the Peace Corps, now combined in ACTION, are threatened by budget cuts.]
>
> The Office of Education sponsors the Teacher Corps, which

40. See *Industrial Gerontology—Studies on Problems of Work and Age* (Washington, D.C.: National Council on Aging, Fall 1972).

places experienced teachers, many of them retirees, in schools in urban slums and rural poverty areas, where they are paid by the local school system. Similar programs in many states are sponsored by state education departments.

The Census Bureau employs part-time interviewers on its regular payroll, and those over sixty-five who can qualify are eligible.

RSVP, the Retired Senior Volunteer Program, developed by the Administration on Aging, enables people aged sixty and over to serve in a variety of needed community services. States receive some federal support for these programs.[41]

However potentially useful these opportunities may seem, they offer few openings relative to the numbers of senior citizens, their funding is currently insecure, and they do not appeal to many retirees, particularly those with less energy and no transportation. Preretirement planning may help; cultivation of hobbies, use of leisure to make new friends, continuation of gardening and home maintenance make retirement less of a shock.

Since most people have spent their lives in a series of group situations, the need for social interaction with other people continues. Project FIND reported that church-sponsored activities were of most service to the older poor. Senior citizens centers offer opportunities for recreation, education, involvement in social projects, and excursions. Dining clubs provide social participation as well as good nutrition. Loneliness accelerates the aging process and leads to the disengagement of the individual from meaningful relationships and consequent depression. The Senior Advisory Service, a project sponsored by the Community Service Society of New York in four housing projects in South Bronx, found that loneliness was a way of life for many. More than half the elderly lived alone; most reported few friends; and one third reported no visits with friends either inside or outside the project during the preceding year.[42]

The aged are also, in Harvey Gochros's words, "sexually oppressed." The prevailing cultural attitude is that sex is for the young. Recognition of the sexual needs of older persons is lacking, and their sexual activity is considered shameful or pathetic. The aged themselves share this feeling, in many cases, and need

---

41. *FACT SHEET: Employment and Volunteer Opportunities for Older People* (Washington, D.C.: AoA, March 1973), bracketed comments added.

42. Jean Wallace Carey and Jeannette Katz Friedman, "Nonprofessionals Serve Aged Public Housing Tenants," in Julius Segal, ed., *Mental Health Program Reports–5*, DHEW publication no. (HSM) 72–9042 (Rockville, Md.: National Institute of Mental Health, 1971), pp. 188–203.

sex education, as well as provisions for romance, privacy, and dating.[43]

The problems of loneliness increase as the individual grows older. Losses multiply, widowhood occurs, contemporaries die, and physical disability restricts activities. The return of "friendly visiting" from the nineteenth century, when the English housing reformer Octavia Hill introduced the term, is badly needed, as is the extension of home health aides. In addition to performing household tasks no longer possible for the aging person, the home health aide provides some companionship and can estimate the ability of the individual to continue to live independently. Telephone reassurance services, which telephone at a specified time each day and insure that a visit is made immediately if the person fails to answer, may be sponsored by any group in the community and make use of other older persons as volunteers. Begun in 1957 by Mrs. Grace McClure, when an elderly friend lay helpless for eight days after a stroke, these services are found nationwide.[44] In addition to prompt identification of medical crises, the daily calls provide an opportunity for friendly conversation, information on weather, and sending of messages. Some telephone companies have responded with special low rates for subscribers to such reassurance services.

The White House Conference Section on Retirement Roles and Activities points out the extent to which society's perception of the aged should be modified. There is no "one ideal role" which all older people should adopt and feel inadequate if they cannot measure up to. Instead, society should recognize the different life styles and different personalities of the aging and encourage acceptance of the legitimacy of noneconomic activity rather than glorification of the work ethic into retirement.[45]

The gifted French writer Simone de Beauvoir has written eloquently of the degradation of the old by a society which cares about people of all ages only insofar as they are profitable and which buries the topic of aging in a "conspiracy of silence."[46] This has been dubbed "ageism" and is analogous to racism and

43. Harvey L. Gochros, "The Sexually Oppressed," *Social Work*, Vol. 17, No. 2 (March 1972), pp. 16–23. The other categories considered are homosexuals, the hospitalized mentally ill, and the imprisoned.

44. See Virginia Rogers, *Guidelines for a Telephone Reassurance Service* (Washington, D.C.: AoA, 1972).

45. 1971 White House Conference on Aging, *Retirement Roles and Activities* (Washington, D.C.: U.S. Government Printing Office, 1972).

46. Simone de Beauvoir, *The Coming of Age*, Andre Deutsch, trans. (New York: G. P. Putnam's Sons, 1972).

sexism in stereotyping and discriminating against persons solely on the basis of age. Unlike blacks and women, who have organized power groups to support them, there is no corresponding group for "senior power," even though the political power of the over–sixty-five vote is real. Elderly women are neglected by women's liberation[47] in a society which stereotypes them as old maids if unmarried or as family nuisances when they are widowed. Their chances of remarriage are inferior to older men's, their sex needs are regarded as disgusting, and their economic position is inferior to that of men. The 11,000,000 women over sixty-five are more likely to live alone, to be vulnerable to exploitation and crime, and to fear and experience loneliness.

DEATH

The ultimate in loneliness is a lonely death, and preoccupation with dying, particularly the circumstances surrounding it, is an ever-increasing concern with the very old. This is complicated by the current reluctance to allow death to occur in the home and the transfer of the terminally ill person to a medical facility. The great majority of older people, in a survey of attitudes and fears about death, expressed their wish to die at home, painlessly in their sleep.[48]

Not only are older people concerned about possible pain and suffering and about the trouble and annoyance they may cause others by the manner of their death, they also worry over the potential costs of their final illness and whether their resources will permit a dignified funeral. The fear of a pauper's death is a very real one to those who grew up when it was a more frequent occurrence. While Medicare, supplemented for the aged poor by Medicaid, underwrites the major part of the costs of terminal care, the exhaustion of Medicare benefits and the increasing costs of deductibles and co-insurance may realistically cause anxiety that one's own resources and those of one's family will be inadequate for a long-term expensive hospitalization.

The extension of Medicare to cover post-hospital care in an extended care facility has proved a mixed blessing. While the number of beds available for long-term care increased dramatically as payment of patients' charges was underwritten, it encouraged the proliferation of poorly designed and badly run facilities with

47. See Myrna I. Lewis and Dr. Robert N. Butler, "Neglected by Women's Lib," *The National Observer*, July 29, 1972, p. 20.

48. See Herman J. Loether, *Problems of Aging* (Belmont, Ca.: Dickenson Publishing Company, 1967), especially Chapter 8, "Death."

inadequate and poorly prepared staffs. The level of care provided the elderly in nursing homes is largely a function of the standards set by federal and state legislation and the strictness with which regulatory agencies hold to these standards. In the past, emphasis has been laid on physical equipment and safety: fire escapes, adequate space per bed, number of staff on duty, sanitary condition of the kitchens, and the like. While no one would deny the importance of these features, the atmosphere of the nursing home is harder to regulate, and this is a significant factor to the person confined there.

The best nursing homes overprotect and infantilize their patients. Part of this is a sincere wish to protect patients from falls, but restraints on beds and overuse of sedation may also serve to lessen the work of the staff. In some otherwise acceptable nursing homes, patients are put to bed for the night before the day staff goes off duty, dooming them to fourteen hours of inactivity. The worst nursing homes, usually inhabitated entirely by helpless old people receiving Medicaid, treat their patients with an inhumanity which verges on the unbelievable.[49] As Ralph Nader writes in the introduction to a task force report:

> There is a colossal amount of collective callousness that pervades society, from the organization to the individual levels. The most intense focus of what has been wrought for old people is the nursing home. The few homes that are humane, competent, and mindful of their residents' need for activity and meaning in their day highlight the staggering gap between what an affluent society should attain and what is too frequently the reality for most nursing homes. The full scope of nursing home abuses and profiteering has yet to be told. Although the Federal government pours over a billion dollars a year into this two-and-a-half billion dollar industry through Medicare and other subsidy programs, there have been neither the full-fledged Congressional hearings, nor the enforcement of adequate Federal and state standards, nor the administrative inquiries and disclosures that are needed to reduce the institutional violence and cruelty that are rampant. Such moves have not occurred in spite of major fire disasters, fatal food contaminations, corporate manipulations, drug experimentation beyond proper medical discretion, kickbacks

49. See Claire Townsend, *Old Age: The Last Segregation* (New York: Bantam Books, 1971), for an account of a task force composed of young graduates of Miss Porter's School which conducted a survey of nursing home conditions for the Ralph Nader Study Group on Nursing Homes of The Center for Study of Responsive Law in the summer of 1970.

in drug sales for the residents, abysmal lack of medical supervision, and strong evidence that such abuses are more epidemic than episodic.[50]

There is ample evidence, from demonstration projects in this country and from the experiences in other countries, that such appalling betrayal of old people need not occur. Anthony White-head describes the continuum of services developed in Great Britain, which includes adequate support to maintain old people in their own homes; community care (including night sitters, home health aides, provision of sick room aids, day patient care, day care centers, nutrition services, and volunteer visiting); geriatric wards in local hospitals with adequate emergency service; foster home care; and in-patient care in long-term facilities.[51] Every precaution is taken to prevent loss of independence, and return home is encouraged, with subsequent readmission deemed better for the patient than long-term hospitalization. Sweden and Denmark have also developed imaginative and satisfactory provision for the care of the elderly, including enlightened legislation and strict enforcement by institutional inspectors who visit unannounced.

Eleanor Clark reports on the development of a Transfer Office at the Massachusetts General Hospital, which improved both the matching of institution and patient and the general level of after-care facilities in the state.[52] A demonstration project in Michigan and Minnesota indicated that coordinated efforts of the regional federal agencies, state agencies, and public and private agencies at the local level can produce comprehensive plans for meeting the needs of the elderly, and it stressed the necessity for involving senior citizens in both planning and operation.[53] But public indifference to those it "shelves" and competing bureaucracies are continuing obstacles to providing a satisfying continuum of services to the aging.

Hospital and nursing home personnel have seldom had adequate training in caring for the dying, particularly the emotional

50. *Ibid.*, p. x. Copyright 1970, 1971 by The Center for Study of Responsive Law. Reprinted by permission of Grossman Publishers.

51. Anthony Whitehead, *In the Service of Old Age* (Baltimore: Penguin Books, 1970).

52. Eleanor Clark, "Improving Post-Hospital Care for Chronically Ill Elderly Patients," *Social Work*, Vol. 14, No. 1 (January 1969), pp. 62–67.

53. Donald F. Simpson and Frank G. Farrow, "Three Community Systems of Services to the Aging," *Social Casework*, Vol. 54, No. 2 (February 1973), pp. 96–104.

distress of the terminal patient. Anxiety and depression, fear of pain, need for added emotional support, sympathy for the grief of loved ones, resentment that life will go on without them—all these compound the physical condition and often bring on the apathy that hastens death. The experience of concentration camp survivors testifies to the effect of emotional factors on survival and surrender of life, and many doctors report that it is apparent when a mortally ill patient gives up the struggle.

Individuals face imminent death differently, as they have all lived differently, and should not be stereotyped. Some wish to discuss it but are prevented by visitors and staff who are themselves distressed by thoughts of death. Some stubbornly deny it, and their self-protective mechanisms should be supported, unless it is obvious that they are neglecting ordering their affairs under unrealistic expectations of recovery. Some are fearful and may need tranquilizing drugs, as well as the emotional support of family and staff.

Many medical personnel are reluctant to tell patients the truth about their illnesses, especially if the prognosis is poor. John Hinton reports that doctors are less ready to tell patients their illness is mortal than patients are to be told.[54] Less well trained personnel may deal with their own discomfort at death by callousness, forced cheerfulness, or infantilizing patients as if they were babies who needed only to be tended bodily.

The patient's right to die, or at least refuse further treatment, is undoubtedly to be a topic of increasing concern among medical, theological, and lay people in the future. With the very old, there may be doubts as to the clarity of the patient's mind when he asks to be released. The wishes of the family should be considered, although the extent to which they should determine the decision is another question. The most loving relative cannot really know how the situation feels to the person experiencing it. The most shocking situation is the one where further life-prolonging treatment is wanted by patient and family, but the cost is prohibitive. The extension of Medicare to the costs of kidney dialysis is one small indication that society's responsibilities for the provision of medical care are being recognized. The inclusion of coverage for life-sustaining drugs and equipment to patients in their own homes is equally necessary but has not yet been enacted.

Many older people are concerned about the type and cost of the

---

54. John Hinton, *Dying* (Baltimore: Penguin Books, 1967), is an English psychiatrist's discussion of his many years of treating patients with incurable diseases.

funeral they will have. Inflation has rendered any insurance and savings set aside for funeral costs inadequate. There are some pre-paid funeral plans (known to the trade as "pre-need services") which are reputable, but some are frauds. Discussing the funeral and the disposition of belongings is comforting to some elderly people and allows them to retain some control over their environment after death. A more adequate death benefit from Social Security, consumer education on funeral costs before the last illness, and social support of alternatives to costly and elaborate funeral and burial plans would all serve to allay some of the anxiety of the aging. Every social worker knows of lonely old people who would have welcomed attention and little gifts from families who could not afford the time or money while the old people were alive but who borrowed money for an ostentatious display of "respect" after death.

THE PROVISION OF SERVICES TO THE AGING

In the broadest sense, social work services to children and families may well serve to prevent some of the emotional problems of the aging, since an unhappy child or adult is likely to be an unhappy senior citizen. However, many of the needs of the aging can be met only by massive legislative programs. Adequate income, adequate housing, better distribution of health care, better community support services—these require social action on a large scale. The realistic political strength of the elderly, a very large percentage of whom are registered voters who go to the polls, is still largely unorganized. Organization will be most effective if carried on by the aging themselves, although they may well use professional help in planning strategies and utilizing resources.

NATIONAL AGENCIES

Organizations to serve the elderly saw their beginnings in the 1940s. The Gerontological Society, a multidisciplinary professional organization, dates from 1945 and the National Retired Teachers Association (NRTA) from 1947. The American Association of Retired Persons (AARP), open to those over fifty-five whether retired or not, was organized in 1958. In March 1973, the two Associations had a combined membership of over 5,000,000 persons. These organizations provide low-cost insurance and drugs, sponsor conferences, arrange tours, and publish newsletters and monthly magazines. In February 1973, the Ethel Percy Andrus Gerontology Center was opened in Los Angeles, as a tribute to the founder of both Associations, with a substantial portion of the funding coming from Association members. The Associations maintain an active legislative program, testify before congressional committees, and publicize legislative changes to their membership.

Concern over the empty days of unemployed older people during the Depression resulted in the organization of centers, the first being the Hodson Day Center in New York City (1943). By the time of the 1971 White House Conference on Aging, there were more than 1,300 senior centers serving 5,000,000 persons. About one fourth of their funding comes from federal subsidy, with the remainder from state and local taxes and United Ways. The centers do not attract the very poor, racial minorities, or the emotionally disturbed but do provide activities and a place for informal meeting, as well as serve as a convenient center for nutrition and educational programs in many communities. There are numerous local and special interest groups which may or may not be affiliated with any national organizations. The National Council on Aging, affiliated with the National Assembly for Social Policy and Development, was set up in 1961 as a national clearinghouse for all activities related to the aging.

WHITE HOUSE CONFERENCES

Growing interest in the aging led the Congress in 1958 to authorize the first White House Conference on Aging, held in 1961, and to set up a Special Subcommittee on Aging in 1959 which became the Senate Special Committee on Aging. The chief concerns of the 1961 White House Conference were the inadequacy of Social Security benefits and the problems of health care. In 1963, President Kennedy created the President's Council on Aging, which in 1965 under the Older Americans Act became the Administration on Aging (AoA) in the Department of Health, Education, and Welfare. The Office of Economic Opportunity in 1964 was also charged to consider programs for meeting the needs of the elderly, but the 1974 budget cuts threaten these programs.

Some of the priorities for action coming from the 1961 White House Conference on Aging have been achieved. The liberalization of Social Security in the 1962 and subsequent Amendments lowered the retirement age to sixty-two for both men and women, increased the ceiling on earnings for retirees under seventy-two, raised the benefit levels, and in 1965 enacted Medicare. However, the Administration on Aging has been progressively downgraded in the HEW set-up, and many of the recommendations for action from the 1961 White House Conference were never implemented. In October 1969, President Nixon appointed a Task Force on Aging to review existing programs, both public and private, and to recommend action. Its report, in 1970, recommended a new Executive Office on Aging to make it more effective. The 1971 White House Conference on Aging reiterated many of the concerns of the one a decade earlier, including renewed attention to private pension plans. The absence of vesting (guaranteeing some equity to a worker who leaves or loses his job before he reaches retirement age) and of portability for workers who transfer from one company to another makes it necessary for most employed persons to rely mainly on OASDI benefits. Recommendations for protecting the rights of employees have been made by the President's Task Force, the Senate Special Committee on Aging, and the Senate Subcommittee on Labor, but no action has been taken.

In preparation for the 1971 White House Conference, the NRTA-AARP assessed the progress made toward implementing the recommendations from the 1961 Conference.[55] Although some successes were noted, the inventory indicates that most or all of the problems identified in 1961 persist. Many of the recommendations of the 1971 Conference and the President's Task Force were incorporated in the 1972 Amendments to the Older Americans Act, which strengthened the role of the Administration on Aging, proposed more unified planning of services at state and local levels, and provided $2,200,000,000. This was pocket-vetoed by President Nixon, and a compromise version was passed and signed by the President in May 1973, which cut the funding significantly and abolished certain provisions but did retain coordination of services, upgrading of AoA, volunteer service programs, expanded research and training, and paid community service employment.[56] It remains to be seen whether the decade of the 1970s will improve on the record of the 1960s.

The 1971 Conference Section on Government and Non-Government Organization issued the following statement as an appendix to its twelve broad recommendations:

55. *The 1971 White House Conference on Aging: The End of a Beginning?* (Washington, D.C.: National Retired Teachers Association, American Association of Retired Persons, 1971).
56. See U.S. Senate, Special Committee on Aging, *The Rise and Threatened Fall of Service Programs for the Elderly*, Report No. 93–94, 93rd Congress, 1st Session, 1973.

Advocacy and service are major functions of organizational activity in the field of aging. Under advocacy come all the efforts an organization makes to call attention to the needs of a special group and to create support for programs that will help them. The service an organization performs may include conducting research, demonstration and training programs as well as providing more direct benefits to the group whose interests it represents.

There is now an extensive array of governmental, voluntary, and private organizations whose operations involve the aging directly, if not exclusively. Their number includes service agencies and professional and membership groups most of which were established in the past two decades. Over this period, too, governments have organized aging units, among them an Administration on Aging in the Department of Health, Education, and Welfare, some 55 state and territorial agencies on aging, and numerous local committees or councils on aging. Nevertheless, there remain today critical gaps in awareness of the needs of the elderly, in program coverage, in commitment of resources. Still, without minimizing the record of neglect, one can now speak of a different problem: How to get existing organizations in the aging field to work together effectively to improve conditions for older people.

In the opinion of some observers, the ultimate need in organizational matters related to aging is for the elderly themselves to make some hard decisions about what organizations and policies best serve their interests, and whether or not they are prepared to develop the political power to back their choices.[57]

SOCIAL WORK AND THE AGING

Until recently, few social workers saw services to elderly clients as the chief aim of their work. Elderly clients were supposed to adapt themselves to the existing service delivery systems instead of receiving services delivered with their specific requirements in mind. Long waiting lines, scattered offices, inconvenient locations of facilities, steep stairs, and insistence on office visits pose special hardships for the elderly. Demonstration programs indicate that services are more utilized when they are more accessible.[58] Resistance to increased costs of outreach programs are lessened somewhat when the clients are elderly or disabled.

57. 1971 White House Conference on Aging, *Government and Non-Government Organization* (Washington, D.C.: U.S. Government Printing Office, 1972), pp. 13, 14.

58. Carey and Friedman, "Nonprofessionals Serve Aged." Compare this with the pessimistic conclusions of Stanley J. Brody, Harvey Finkle, and Carl Hirsch,

Social workers have tended to view the aging as clients with little potential for change and have therefore set low priorities on their needs other than for what amounts to custodial care. Increasing evidence of the response of elderly clients to psychotherapy[59] should stimulate increased interest in services to utilize the socio-adaptive abilities of the elderly more constructively.

The Aging in Social Work Curricula

The limited participation of professional social work in programs serving those over sixty-five is reflected in the lack, until very recently, of material on aging in both baccalaureate- and graduate-level programs of social work education. A glance at the index of almost any social work textbook will confirm the scarcity of information on aging and services for aged clients. Now, however, courses in psychology, sociology, and social work incorporate material on aging, and program material is being prepared under a number of auspices. Field placements for students are being developed in both direct services and planning agencies. Research on aging is proliferating, but the demand for knowledge on service needs, techniques for delivering service, and techniques of evaluation is far from being met.

The Council on Social Work Education (CSWE), in 1958 sponsored a week-long seminar at Aspen, Colorado, made possible by a grant from the Ford Foundation, and there issued the first professional publications on social work education for practice with the aging.[60] These have been succeeded by additional materials, including case records, bibliographies, and source books.[61] In its accreditation standards for graduate and undergraduate programs, the Council surveys the extent to which material on aging is integrated into supporting courses and courses in social work.

"Benefit Alert: Outreach Program for the Aged," *Social Work*, Vol. 17, No. 1 (January 1972), pp. 14–23—that public assistance programs are too rigidly bureaucratic to incorporate advocacy and outreach programs.

59. See Robert N. Butler and Myrna I. Lewis, *Aging and Mental Health* (St. Louis: C. V. Mosby Company, 1973). See also Maurice E. Linden, M.D., "You Won't Believe It," an address before the Governor's Conference on Aging, 1967, available from the State of New Jersey, Division on Aging, Trenton, N.J., 18625, mimeographed.

60. Council on Social Work Education, *Toward Better Understanding of the Aging*, and *Social Work Education for Better Services to the Aging*, Seminar on the Aging, Aspen, Colorado, September 8–13, 1958 (New York: CSWE, 1959).

61. Constance E. Kellam, *A Literary Bibliography on Aging* (1969), *Teacher's Source Book on Aging* (1964), audio-tapes and individual teaching records, all available from the Council on Social Work Education, 345 E. 46th St., New York, N.Y. 10017.

The Family Service Association of America (FSAA), the leading national agency in the field, similarly published in a double issue of its journal, *Social Casework,* [62] the proceedings of a seminar on aging held in 1960 at Arden House of Columbia University, where nearly eighty educators, social workers, and resource persons from related fields participated in discussions on the provision of adequate casework services to older people. The interest of the FSAA in this special client group resulted in a casebook demonstrating theories and techniques in casework with the aging. [63] However, an examination of the indices of social work journals and *Abstracts for Social Workers* will indicate that interest, although increasing, is still markedly less in social work practice with the aged than with other client groups.

Social Workers in Agencies
Serving the Elderly

Social workers are not a significant part of the staff of most of the specialized agencies serving the aged. Paraprofessionals, volunteers, and professionals from the health field and from education are more likely to serve in Councils on Aging, Senior Citizens Centers, and OEO-sponsored programs for the aging. As BSW social workers become more available, particularly those with undergraduate field experience in aging, they may be hired for planning and service delivery. The requirement that social work service be provided in extended care facilities under Medicare was eliminated in the 1972 Amendments to the Social Security Act, a regressive move in view of the multiple needs of institutionalized elderly patients.

The extent to which state departments of social welfare will provide services to recipients of Federal Supplemental Security Income who are not receiving Old Age Assistance is not yet known (see pages 83, 242). Some responsibility for protective services will have to be assumed, by the Social Security Administration or the welfare department, and such services must be extended to those on marginal incomes and unknown to any social agency but living under conditions injurious to their welfare. If neglected too long, such individuals eventually become known to the police because of a crisis and more or less routinely committed to a mental hospital. The National Protective Services Project [64] recom-

62. *Social Casework*, Vol. 42, Nos. 5–6 (May–June 1961).
63. See Edna Wasser, *Casebook on Work with the Aging* (New York: FSAA, 1966).
64. See p. 242, especially fn. 12.

mends that a special service unit be established in the state welfare department to supervise and support a protective services unit at the local level. These units, based on Project experience, should consist of one MSW supervisor, three BSW social workers, and six case aides. Homemaker services should be available as needed, and homemakers should be selected and trained for work with the elderly. The Project points out that few social workers have had the requisite training and experience and that higher salaries may be justified because of the special demands of the job.

> [The] usual desirable characteristics of an employee apply to the protective service staff. However, the crucial quality in the protective services worker appears to be an appropriate balance between potentially conflicting characteristics. The worker must be sensitive to the client's wishes, but skillful enough to know when wishes and needs clash. He must be sympathetic and kind, but firm in taking authoritative action when necessary; aware of what makes for quality in living but not thrown by extreme illness, destitution, and filth; aggressive but not bossy; capable of exercising professional authority, but willing to seek out and use opinions of other professionals; willing to work long hours when necessary, but retain proper perspective on work demands and other facets of life; able to take pleasure in the gratitude of a lonely elderly or disabled person without becoming the indispensable factor in the client's life; able to make quick decisions if necessary, but patient in working out a situation which requires time and persuasion; tending toward optimism in resolving problems, but capable of accepting the reality that certain life situations cannot be changed with the skill, facilities, and resources available.[65]

Implicit in our discussion of the concerns of elderly people have been the functions of the social worker who serves as the helping person for the elderly client. Fulfillment of the need for individualization in a society which stereotypes the aged and relegates them to a lower status is perhaps the primary service a social worker can render in any agency with elderly clients. This is particularly true concerning the institutionalized aged, whose helplessness renders them vulnerable to mass treatment and denial of their individuality. The following poem nicely captures the infantilization so often forced upon institutionalized old people who struggle to retain their individuality in the face of well-meaning but patronizing denigration by care-takers.

65. *Report of the National Protective Services Project for Older Adults,* p. 101.

Ninety-two is a silly age
I'm a foolish old man, laughing
To keep from dying.

Busy Work!
I won't do that dizzy work
I didn't live through 70 hard years
To make potholders.

I'm an individual
Don't call me "we".

"We" don't want to go to the bathroom
"We" don't want to eat my nice dinner
"We" won't take my medicine
Even if it is good for "us".

"We've" got you fooled, Nurse.
You think I'm contrary
I would do what you want, Miss
If you would only ask me.[66]

Social workers, trained to be sensitive to clients' feelings, can help individualize clients, and where social workers are consultants to or on the staff of nursing homes and hospitals, they can help busy nurses and aides become more aware of the impact of their manner of service delivery.[67]

Social Work Roles and the Needs of the Aging

To consider how social workers can operate on behalf of elderly clients, let us return to the roles of the social worker as enunciated by the Southern Regional Education Board (see pages 21–22) and correlate them with the special concerns of the aging as discussed in this chapter.

Outreach is a clearly useful role in all areas of concern.[68] Identifying the groups of aging who need income maintenance, housing, and health care services, and identifying conditions in the environment (lack of transportation, lack of companionship, lack of protection against fraud and exploitation) which raise the level of risk are social work objectives in this role.

66. Julia Houy, "Ramblings." Reprinted with permission of *Liguorian*.
67. In September 1973, the NASW announced that it had been selected by the Public Health Services to carry out an eighteen-month training project for staff in long-term care facilities. See *NASW NEWS*, Vol. 18, No. 8 (September 1973), p. 1.
68. See Ruth G. Cohen, "Outreach and Advocacy in the Treatment of the Aged," *Social Casework*, Vol. 55, No. 5 (May 1974), pp. 271–277.

The *broker* role provides linkages which facilitate use of service systems. Clearly, information about how to negotiate the complicated channels of bureaucratized service delivery systems is needed for those who lack energy, who are easily confused, fearful, or victims of outmoded prejudices against seeking assistance. The elderly may need to have services delivered to their homes rather than administered in offices and to have help with transportation, with legal aid, with escort service, or with interpreters. The mere offering of the service does not guarantee that clients will seek it out.

Advocacy aims at removing barriers that interfere with use of resources as needed. The social worker as advocate fights for services for the individual aging client from welfare departments, health care facilities, mental health centers and hospitals, landlords, taxi companies, and any other service provider who does not adapt his delivery to the special needs of his clientele. In addition, the social worker serves as advocate for the elderly as a segment of the citizenry, to secure reform of present injustice and extension of inadequate service to potential clients.

The social worker as *evaluator* is particularly needed when protective services may require a change in living conditions, when elderly persons are assessed in terms of their capacity for independence, when a family's ability to cope with the problems of an elderly relative must be weighed, when the capacity of the aged individual to withstand shock and transition must be assessed. In addition, the social worker as evaluator will be called upon to study community problems involving the aging, to assign priorities to community needs, and to suggest and weigh alternatives to current or proposed actions which affect the elderly.

Mobilizer roles are assumed by social workers who energize existing groups or stimulate the formation of new ones to meet problems which, as experts on the needs of the aging, they recognize more clearly than the rest of the community. The development of a telephone reassurance service, of special transportation facilities, of Meals on Wheels or dining club programs for improving the nutrition of the elderly are all illustrations of the mobilizer in action. Sometime in the future, when more is known about the multiple needs of the aged, the mobilizer may be able to stimulate the development of better preventive services, instead of remedying problems already developed.

The *teacher* role provides new information and skills. Special needs of the elderly suggest that consumer education, nutrition, sex education, and the development of new skills in daily activity to conserve energy, guard against accidents, and protect disabilities will be useful.

The social worker as *behavior changer* can succeed, to a degree formerly believed impossible, in modifying the behavior of elderly people to promote improved functioning. No one has questioned the ability of the aged to modify their behavior in the direction of passivity and acceptance; this is a major objective of most extended care facilities and mental hospitals, since it minimizes management problems for the staff. The social worker has the task of modifying staff attitudes toward elderly clients in the direction of encouraging client change toward improved self-esteem and a more satisfying life. The social worker as behavior changer works not only with the elderly client to facilitate his adjustment and conserve his individuality but also works with his family to help them alter behavior which is unhelpful to their aging relative. Fairly minor changes may make it possible for clients to be less fearful, more active, more outgoing, and more positive. The rehabilitative potential of older clients is not widely acknowledged, and therefore not appropriately encouraged.[69] The continued productivity and zest for life of many very old people indicate that aging need not rule out flexibility and adaptability.

The roles of *consultant, community planner,* and *data manager* clearly apply to the objective of improving our services to the aging. We have repeatedly noted in the course of this chapter the lack of good research, good planning, and adequate data. Any of these roles might well be combined with the advocacy role, since pressing for social reform should be based on accurate information and sound planning.

Social workers, unfortunately, are not often *administrators* of services for the aging. Institutions are likely to be administered by medical and nursing personnel, as are health care and mental health facilities. Profit-oriented proprietors deal with the aging in the fields of housing, transportation, leisure time activity, and funerals. Public income maintenance programs are increasingly administered by budget and management specialists. When social workers are in administrative positions or are in a position to influence administration, they can stress individualization of the aged clientele and the maximum feasible participation of the elderly in decisions which affect them directly.

The *care giver* to the elderly is more likely to be a paraprofes-

69. See Elizabeth A. Hefferin, "Rehabilitation in Nursing Home Situations: A Survey of the Literature," *Journal of the American Geriatrics Society*, Vol. 16, No. 3 (March 1968), pp. 296–315.

sional than a social worker, but the services of nurses' aides, home-health aides, providers of boarding care, eligibility determination specialists, and others who provide ongoing support and care should be supervised by professionals. Care should be given in ways which encourage the participation and activity of the elderly person. He should not be infantilized, patronized, or pushed around because he is helpless or disadvantaged. The lack of social work involvement in extended care facilities is particularly marked. The Ralph Nader Study Group on Nursing Homes comments:

> The nursing home with a full-fledged social services program is generally more attuned to meeting patient needs—whether they be occupational therapy, activities, community involvement, or obtaining a piece of furniture from the patient's former home, or arranging for a volunteer to visit a patient without a family. Nurses and aides can fulfill these needs only in the most haphazard fashion, particularly if they are not trained or have not been taught to recognize them in the first place. [70]

Of all the roles which social workers and the profession of social work can enact in the service of the aging, that of advocate may be the most crucial. Calling attention to the part played by past social workers in social reform, Kosberg says:

> Some time in the not-too-distant future there may well be a thundering outcry against the conditions in which the aged live. Call it an eruption of social conscience. Such a phenomenon has occurred in regard to racial prejudice, poverty, the status of women, pollution, and overpopulation. Social workers have the motivation and responsibility to care for the disadvantaged; this care is the raison d'etre of their profession. If they are not in the vanguard of such a movement on behalf of the aged—making sure that it is a long-range effective effort—they will be denying their commitment to their profession and to society. [71]

70. Townsend, *Old Age*, p. 131. Copyright 1970, 1971 by The Center for Study of Responsive Law. Reprinted by permission of Grossman Publishers.

71. Jordan J. Kosberg, "The Nursing Home: A Social Work Paradox," *Social Work*, Vol. 18, No. 2 (March 1973), p. 109. Reprinted with the permission of the National Association of Social Workers.

ADDITIONAL REFERENCES

"AoA Catalog of Films on Aging" (Washington, D.C.: Administration on Aging, 1973). An annotated, classified list of films on all aspects of aging, including their availability and costs.

Atelsek, Frank et al., *Long-Term Institutional Care and Alternative Solutions*, two volumes (Washington, D.C.: Social and Rehabilitation Service, 1973). An account of a project carried out by staff at American University, which reports on the health needs of the elderly, current patterns of health care, and proposed alternatives.

Blau, Zena Smith, *Old Age in a Changing Society* (New York: Franklin Watts, 1973). The dilemma of the aging in a postindustrial society which does not prepare people to become old.

Cull, John G. and Hardy, Richard E., eds., *The Neglected Older American: Social and Rehabilitation Services* (Springfield, Ill.: Charles C Thomas, Publisher, 1973). The characteristic problems of the older American and the inadequacy of the programs designed to meet these needs.

Curtin, Sharon R., *Nobody Ever Died of Old Age* (Boston: Little, Brown and Company, 1972). A nontechnical survey of the problems of the aging in contemporary society, with vivid illustrative vignettes.

Field, Minna, *The Aged, the Family, and the Community* (New York: Columbia University Press, 1972). Contains a useful chapter on social work practice with the aged.

Group for the Advancement of Psychiatry, *The Right to Die: Decision and Decision-Makers* (New York: Jason Aronson, 1974). The right of an individual to terminate his life, as discussed by psychiatrists and philosophers, with a cross-cultural comparison and selected case material.

Hoffman, Adeline M., ed., *The Daily Needs and Interests of Older People* (Springfield, Ill.: Charles C Thomas, Publisher, 1970). A useful handbook on social, psychological, and biological aspects of aging.

Nicolson, Robert, *The Whisperers* (Baltimore: Penguin Books, 1966). A moving account of an elderly woman trapped in the welfare state.

Sarton, May, *As We Are Now* (New York: W. W. Norton and Company, 1973). The diary of an indomitable old lady confined to a nursing home.

Stotsky, Bernard A., *The Nursing Home and the Aged Psychiatric Patient* (New York: Appleton-Century Crofts, 1970). The role of community-based facilities rather than mental hospitals for the care of the elderly.

Working with Older People: A Guide to Practice, four volumes, DHEW publication no. (HSM) 72–6007 (Rockville, Md.: Division of Health Care Services, issued at various times from March 1969 to May 1972). A highly useful compendium of information on aging. Vol. III, *The Aging Person: Needs and Services*, will be of particular interest to social workers.

6

services for
health and
mental health

HEALTH SERVICES

The impact of poor health on all aspects of human functioning is apparent. Illness interferes with carrying out family responsibilities, with employment, with social life, and with one's perception of himself and the world around him. Ill health is a major cause of dependency, and continued ill health makes it impossible for many in poverty, of all ages, to entertain realistic hopes of ever getting out of poverty. The poor are sick oftener, recover more slowly, have less access to preventive and rehabilitative services, and live under less healthy conditions. But all, even the wealthy, are disadvantaged by an archaic system of health care stubbornly resistant to change.

The profession of social work knows from firsthand experience the staggering social and personal costs of ill health, and since the 1940s its policy statements have called for improved and comprehensive medical care for all Americans. However, social work has played very little part in designing new health delivery systems, and in some cases may have a vested interest in the continuation of the present wasteful and maldistributed delivery methods. Since some form of national health insurance seems inevitable in the 1970s, social workers should involve themselves both in attempts to restore funds for health-related services which were cut in the 1974 federal budget and in legislative activities centering around the issue of national health insurance. As the National

277

Association of Social Workers (NASW) stated in the spring of 1973:

> At no other time is the issue of a broad national health insurance, which includes mental health coverage, likely to be more germane than it is to the current situations. The risk in moving aggressively to support national health insurance is that it may mean continued rise in costs if the delivery system remains unchanged. Restructuring of the delivery system is an integral part of national health insurance lobbying.[1]

Bertram Black suggests that social workers have some definite skills to offer in planning for community health services but that they are ignoring their opportunities.[2] He cites examples of neighborhood health and mental health planning which did not include any social work component and urges that social workers be trained for the development and administration of new social institutions which will operate on a geographic basis with proper attention to the "whole person." The relative lack of influence of social work on medical care is attributed by Hirsch and Lurie to the fact that social work in medical settings has always assumed a subordinate role and that its structure has been modified by following the structure of the medical model.[3] These authors also stress the need for the profession of social work to assume more initiative in health planning, particularly in assuring that health needs can be met by ever more technically specialized means and personnel without undermining the patient's individuality and dignity. With the perennial crisis state of medical care and the increasingly more insistent demand for improved methods of financing and delivering health care, social work must modify its traditional methods to meet health needs as defined by the community rather than, as in the past, by the medical profession.

THE PRESENT HEALTH CARE SYSTEM

To call the unintegrated, overlapping, and unorganized health care services in the United States a "system" is almost a contradiction in terms, since it implies a degree of integration and coordination that is totally lacking in the present hodge-podge of

1. National Association of Social Workers, *New Directions for the Seventies* (Washington, D.C.: NASW, 1973), p. 44. Reprinted with the permission of the National Association of Social Workers.

2. Bertram J. Black, "Social Work in Health and Mental Health Services," *Social Casework*, Vol. 52, No. 4 (April 1971), pp. 211–219.

3. Sidney Hirsch and Abraham Lurie, "Social Work Dimensions in Shaping Medical Care Philosophy and Practice," *Social Work*, Vol. 14, No. 2 (April 1969), pp. 75–79.

proprietary, nonprofit, and tax-supported health care facilities. A number of factors contribute to this "non-system."

The Market Model

First is the insistence on the market model, which theoretically assumes that the most efficient providers of service will be selected by consumers and the inefficient will be eliminated. The applicability of the market model to the field of health care is extremely questionable, since the consumer in all too many cases has no real choice, care is often on an emergency basis, and there is no real price competition among providers of service. By none of the usual criteria for determining national health (life expectancy, infant mortality, maternal death rate, days missed from work because of illness) is the United States a spectacular success. As an examination of the *United Nations Demographic Year Book* shows, from ten to twelve other countries outrank the United States on one or more of these criteria. On every index available, the health of minorities and the poor falls far below that of the white, affluent society.

The market model, particularly fee-for-service, puts a premium on illness rather than rewarding providers of health services for prevention of illness. The shortcomings of this model of medical practice have been documented for many years, beginning with the 1932 report of the Committee on the Cost of Medical Care. While the quality of medical care in the United States can reach great heights of skill and competence for some patients, the general level available to the average patient is depressingly low. Organized medicine has successfully blocked a series of attempts to move away from fee-for-service, and fee-for-service remains the basic financing method for the two massive federal programs in the health field: Medicare (health insurance for those over sixty-five), and Medicaid (payment of medical costs for those declared "medically indigent").

Utilization and Coordination
of Resources

Health care resources have increased faster than the population in recent years, and the growing health industry is an important labor market, employing approximately 4,400,000 people in 1970[4] Medical schools, which resisted enlarging enrollment for many years, have begun producing physicians at a faster rate than the

4. U.S. Bureau of the Census, *Statistical Abstract of the United States, 1972* (Washington, D.C., 1972), p. 71.

population is growing. However, the geographic distribution of physicians is most uneven, ranging from 219 per 100,000 population in New York to 73 per 100,000 in Mississippi and 71 per 100,000 in Alaska.[5] Even within one state, there are disparities between urban and rural regions and between wealthy and poor counties.

Not only are physicians unevenly distributed geographically, but the total number of physicians is misleading, since an increasing percentage is attracted to the better-paying and less demanding types of specialized practice and away from the role of "primary care" as represented by general practitioners, internists, and pediatricians. Between 1931 and 1967, the percentage of doctors providing primary care had declined from 75 to 39 percent, and the number of primary care physicians per 100,000 people declined from 94 to 39.[6] The increased production of physicians has, therefore, done very little to solve the problem of the unavailability of medical care for large segments of the population.

Compounding the maldistribution of facilities for health care is the prevalence of solo practice and the lack of coordination among facilities, both resulting in improper use of the time of skilled health personnel. The reluctance of professionals to use paraprofessionals, trained assistants, or specialized administrators means that professional time is used for tasks which could profitably be delegated. Trained pediatric assistants, according to the Joint Council of National Pediatric Societies, could perform 75 percent of the tasks performed by a physician. Nurse-midwives and dental assistants could immeasurably expand the effectiveness of obstetricians and dentists. The relative economies possible by expanding these ancillary services have been ignored or downplayed by those with vested interests in the present system and are largely unknown to the general public.

A third factor is a lack of organization which leads to inappropriate use of some facilities. Since many insurance plans, including Medicare, will pay only for hospital-related costs, patients are often hospitalized unnecessarily. The prestige attached to certain dramatic procedures, such as open-heart surgery, for example, leads to duplication of facilities and thus underuse. The development of better ambulatory services, including home health

5. *Towards a Comprehensive Health Policy for the 1970's: A White Paper* (Washington, D.C.: U.S. Department of Health, Education, and Welfare, May 1971), p. 12, hereafter cited as the HEW *White Paper*. See also Robert S. Daniels, "The Future of Medical Care Delivery Systems," *Social Service Review*, Vol. 45, No. 3 (September 1971), pp. 259–273.

6. HEW, *White Paper*, p. 9.

care, would release needed hospital and extended care beds and result in lowered costs. It is impossible to prove to what extent apparent "shortages" are actually mismanagement of available resources. As Melvin Glasser of the United Auto Workers Union points out:

> The majority of America's physicians function today in a "cottage-type industry" organization pattern that is a major cause of the present health care crisis and is a roadblock to change. It is widely recognized that the advances in medical-scientific knowledge call for closely integrated functioning teams of medical specialists in conjunction with the allied health professions of nursing, social work, psychology, and other disciplines. Recent developments in technology call for the use of expensive medical equipment manned by specially trained technicians. Yet most Americans continue to receive their medical care by the cumbersome fee-for-service method with individual visits to general practitioners, separate visits to physicians practicing more than thirty medical specialties, and additional trips and bills for X-rays, laboratory tests, surgery, hospital care, nursing home care, and so forth.
>
> The general practitioner attempts to function at the center of this nonsystem, where he is expected to be a trained diagnostician and therapist, wise counselor, psychologist, social worker, laboratory technician, businessman, and committed community worker. Last year he put in an average of fifty-eight hours a week at these tasks. It is small wonder that he has not been able to succeed in most of them. It is less surprising that the isolated way in which he practices medicine, except when he relates to a hospital, is proving to be grossly inefficient, wasteful of highly trained and scarce manpower, and costly to his patients and society.
>
> An essential prerequisite to change in the health care system is the replacement of individual practice with organized health care teams that are linked to other health care providers and facilities. Hospital-based comprehensive programs that provide in- and out-patient care, neighborhood health centers related to the entire range of health facilities, prepaid group practice programs, and regional medical programs are but a few of the newer types of organization that are required to replace today's "piecework medicine."[7]

7. Melvin A. Glasser, "The Approaching Struggle to Provide Adequate Health Care for All Americans," *Social Work*, Vol. 15, No. 4 (October 1970), pp. 7–8. Reprinted with the permission of the National Association of Social Workers. See also John P. Huttman, "Marketing Medical Care: The Health Insurance Plan Alternatives," *American Journal of Orthopsychiatry*, Vol. 42, No. 2 (March 1972), pp. 234–237.

The Cost Factor

Lack of organization of health care delivery is an important cause of the mushrooming costs of medical care, which are increasing at twice the rate of the cost of living. In 1972, the total expenses for health amounted to $83,417,000,000, 7.6 percent of the Gross National Product, of which 64.2 percent was privately paid, about half of it through insurance.[8] In spite of these massive expenditures, certain groups of the population are excluded from insurance coverage, and insurance, whether private or public, fails to provide adequate benefits, particularly for outpatient and preventive care. Eligibility requirements for Medicaid virtually exclude the working poor, the unemployed and lower-income self-employed, and migrants.

One critical element in the costs of medical care is the inability of consumers to introduce any measure of cost control. Medical facilities have resisted the inclusion of consumers on regulatory or administrative bodies and insist on controlling health care as a virtual monopoly. The increased costs of operation are passed on to consumers, either directly in charges or indirectly through proprietary insurance companies or nonprofit schemes like Blue Cross. Under such a system there is no incentive for cutting costs and, indeed, every incentive for keeping them high.[9] Unfortunately, professional insistence on control results in protecting the small but dangerous minority of incompetent and unethical practitioners who charge for services not rendered, perform unnecessary procedures, and inflate their bills for Medicare or insurance claims.

IMPROVING THE HEALTH CARE SYSTEM

The entry of the federal government into the health field, which began in the late 1950s and was greatly expanded in the 1960s, has done nothing to improve the organization of the health care delivery system. In order to have health legislation passed by Congress, provisions to protect the present "market model" have been written into each program, and the programs have been frag-

8. U.S. Bureau of the Census, *Statistical Abstract of the United States, 1973* (Washington, D.C., 1973), p. 68.

9. See Robert R. Alford, "The Political Economy of Health Care: Dynamics Without Change," *Politics and Society*, Vol. 2, No. 2 (Winter 1972), pp. 1–38, for a discussion of the vested interest groups which oppose rational change in the delivery of health care. See also Roger Rapoport, "A Candle for St. Greed's," *Harper's Magazine*, Vol. 245, No. 1471 (December 1972), for an account of the profits earned by proprietary hospitals.

mented and directed at specific targets rather than coordinated and related to broad issues. Thus the Rockefeller Committee found in 1971 that there were sixty-eight different controlling agencies in the health field at federal, state, and local levels; the Department of Health, Education, and Welfare (HEW) alone contains twenty-five major health programs, which overlap, often work at cross purposes, and include some which have outlived their usefulness. [10]

Proposals to improve the distribution of health care must include in their projected services those groups whose health needs are now largely unmet. The prevailing assumption that Americans put health care high on their list of priorities is belied by the extent of unmet health needs, particularly among the poor. Draft rejections for remedial defects document the large number of children who never see a physician. Even in families with incomes over $7,500, only 75 percent of children see a physician; the percentage drops to 53 for families with incomes under $3,000. [11] Inadequate dental care is even more prevalent. Melvin Glasser estimates that 25,000,000 to 34,000,000 Americans are presently denied adequate health care. [12] Thus, it is not enough to plan better delivery of care to people already receiving it; any new comprehensive program must be set up to provide for the whole population, not just those with geographic or financial accessibility.

Health Maintenance Organizations

Social workers are aware of the importance of preventive care to forestall trouble in every potential problem area. The profession should, therefore, support endeavors to set up health maintenance organizations in place of the present largely curative system, which concentrates on illness and injury rather than on preventive services. Most health insurance schemes do not cover periodic health inventories or screening examinations but provide hospital and medical care only when the individual is actually sick or injured. The alternative is some form of Health Maintenance Organization (HMO). The HEW *White Paper* defines HMOs as follows:

> HMOs are organized *systems* of health care, providing comprehensive services for enrolled members, for a fixed, prepaid

10. The Governor's Steering Committee on Social Problems, *Preliminary Report on Health and Hospital Services and Costs* (Albany, N.Y., April 15, 1971), pp. 16, 17.

11. HEW, *White Paper*, p. 8.

12. Glasser, "The Approaching Struggle," p. 13.

annual fee. No matter how each HMO may choose to organize itself (and there are various models), from the consumer's viewpoint they all provide a mix of outpatient and hospital services through a single organization and a single payment mechanism.

Because HMO revenues are fixed, their incentives are to keep patients well, for they benefit from patient well-days, not sickness. Their entire cost structure is geared to preventing illness and, failing that, to promoting prompt recovery through the least costly services consistent with maintaining quality. In contrast with prevailing cost-plus insurance plans, the HMO's financial incentives tend to encourage the least utilization of high cost forms of care, and also tend to limit unnecessary procedures.

HMOs provide settings for innovative teaching programs using the entire team of health professionals and supporting personnel, as well as for continuing education programs for practitioners. They also provide a setting in which new technologies and management tools can be most effectively employed, in which the delegation of tasks from physicians to supporting personnel is encouraged, and in which close and constant professional review of performance will provide quality control among colleagues. . . .

In contrast with more traditional and alternative modes of care, HMOs show lower utilization rates for the most expensive types of care (measured by hospital days in particular); they tend to reduce the consumer's total health-care outlay; and—the ultimate test—they appear to deliver services of high quality. Available research studies show that HMO members are more likely than other population groups to receive such preventive measures as general checkups and prenatal care, and to seek care within one day of the onset of symptoms of illness or injuries.[13]

Such plans are already in operation and serve several million subscribers. Among them are the Kaiser-Permanente, the Health Insurance Plan of New York, and the Group Health Association of Washington, D.C.[14] However, long-standing opposition from the American Medical Association makes consumer-owned and -operated group prepaid plans illegal in seventeen states. The extension of Medicare to such HMOs and the support given them by the HEW *White Paper* cited above may make it easier to in-

13. HEW, *White Paper*, pp. 31, 32. See also Doman Lum, "The Health Maintenance Organization," *Social Work*, Vol. 18, No. 5 (September 1973), pp. 17–25.

14. See W. Palmer Dearing, M.D., "Health Care System: Group Medical Practice," pp. 538–451, and Eveline M. Burns, "Health Care System," pp. 510–523, both in *Encyclopedia of Social Work, 1971* (New York: NASW, 1971).

augurate this new model of service delivery. Vested interests, including the private insurance companies, proprietary hospitals and nursing homes, and private and government bureaucracies may be expected to slow needed progress.

The Interests of the Consumer

The growing demands of health care consumers for a voice in planning and controlling health services is a new phenomenon. With expertise in the areas of community organization and helping people articulate their needs, the social worker in the health services has an added area of service in protecting the patient's interests as a consumer, in addition to his concern about the patient's psychosocial adjustment as it is affected by his condition of health. These new roles for social workers will need to be interpreted and clarified to those health care managers who see social workers only as facilitating services to benefit the system rather than as, in Elizabeth Rice's words, "preventing, lessening, or removing social and emotional hazards that affect health or adequate medical care."[15] Here are opportunities for social workers to become advocates, brokers, and mobilizers in securing improved health services for the community.

HOSPITAL-BASED SOCIAL WORK

Social work grew out of attempts to understand and help people in trouble. In its earliest days, the trouble seemed to be largely economic, although economic problems are almost always intertwined with health problems. The English forerunners of medical social workers, "lady almoners," were appointed to select patients for free and partly free medical services and, although primarily concerned with financial eligibility, also served as referrers for other community resources. Paralleling the work of the Charity Organization Societies, the role of the lady almoner was to insure that the most effective use possible was made of community resources. Little was understood then about the complex interrelationships of social and physical discomfort.

In this country, the earliest medical social workers were employed in 1905 at Massachusetts General Hospital and Bellevue Hospital in New York to secure needed social data and to make appropriate referrals to community agencies, especially for after-

15. Elizabeth P. Rice, "Social Work Practice in Medical Health Services," *Encyclopedia of Social Work, 1965* (New York: NASW, 1965), p. 470. See also Miss Rice's pioneering article on the role of the medical social worker in the community health field, "Social Work in Public Health," *Social Work*, Vol. 4, No. 1 (January 1959), pp. 82–88.

care. Selected patients were referred to medical social services for these purposes, and the social worker was likely to be thought of as "handmaid" to the physician. As it became apparent that the education of doctors and nurses should include some orientation to the social problems of patients and the resources in the community, medical social workers began to be involved in teaching seminars and in field work experience for student nurses and medical students. In the social hierarchy of the hospital (a subculture with stress on status and status symbols), the prestige of the social worker increased.

Although medical social service has been increasingly used by programs outside the hospital, it remains predominantly hospital-oriented and -sponsored. Social service departments are likely to be found in the larger private hospitals and in most federal hospitals but are still largely lacking in smaller hospitals. The original Medicare requirement that social work services be provided in all Medicare-approved nursing homes was removed July 1, 1973, a regressive consequence of the 1974 budget cuts. Social workers preparing to operate in the health field are likely to have field experience in hospital settings. If new programs of comprehensive community health care are to be organized around hospitals, the importance of hospital-based social services will increase.

The profession of social work, sensitized to ways in which people may react to pain and anxiety, is uniquely able to assess the social and emotional concomitants of health difficulties. To be effective, social workers in the health services should have some medical information, including the typical effects on patients of disabling conditions and surgical procedures. Increasingly complex and anxiety-producing medical advances, such as organ transplants, open-heart surgery, and artificial life-sustaining machinery, bring unprecedented strains on patient and family.[16] Psychosocial evaluation of patients, potential donors, and families is a task usually assigned to social work. In addition, the social worker is the member of the hospital team with most expertise in locating and using concrete services—finding funds, helping plan family responsibilities during hospitalization, securing transportation—which meet real needs and are highly supportive.

16. See, for examples, Lillian Pike Cain, "Casework with Kidney Transplant Patients," *Social Work*, Vol. 18, No. 4 (July 1973), pp. 76–83; Lydia W. Whatley, "Social Work with Potential Donors for Renal Transplants," *Social Casework*, Vol. 53, No. 7 (July 1972), pp. 399–403; and Elliot C. Brown, Jr., "Casework with Patients Undergoing Cardiac Surgery," *Social Casework*, Vol. 52, No. 10 (December 1971), pp. 611–616.

Social Work in a "Host" Setting

In the hospital setting, the social worker is a member of an interdisciplinary team. The primary focus is on the patient's health, and social and emotional factors are relevant when they are obviously related to the patient's progress. The patient does not enter the hospital for social service; in fact, he may resent what he regards as an intrusion into personal affairs unrelated to his illness. This is in contrast to other types of social service, brought about when the client approaches the social worker with a request, sometimes admittedly devious, for service. Social service is, in a sense, a guest agency within a setting where control is in the hands of another profession. This may result in a role conflict in the social worker, and it raises questions about the social worker's relation to authority.

The directive approach and chain of command characteristic of the medical profession are unlike social work's traditional insistence on self-determination for clients and lack of status symbols for workers. Some writers have made much of the incompatibility of the authoritarian approach of medicine and the social work approach of freedom for the client. The question of the difficulties in which the social worker is placed in his own dependent relationship to medical authority has also been raised, with the suggestion that the physician will be put into the role of "father figure" by social worker as well as patient and reacted to inappropriately by some.

It is undoubtedly true that "doing what the doctor ordered" without too much protest is accepted by many people, who feel that the special knowledge of the physician qualifies him for authoritative statements. However, health services is not the only field in which social workers practice within the limits of another profession's authority. All correctional services are limited by the authority of judges, wardens, and parole boards. All public assistance is carried on within the framework of legal authority. Those who worry about the comfort of the social worker caught between the commands of the doctor and the protests of the patient must remember that one of the functions of social work is to clarify with clients the reality of the limits within which they are free to operate. The social worker may attempt to interpret the client's special circumstances to a judge but cannot alter a judicial decision or advise a client to ignore it. Similarly, the medical social worker can interpret the patient's resistance to medical orders to the physician but cannot diagnose or prescribe for nor advise the patient not to follow the orders. The social worker's responsibility is to be sure the patient understands clearly the alternatives, referring him back to his physician for explanation of the medical directives.

With newer understanding of the interrelationships of physical and mental health, physicians are more interested in the patient's reasons for refusing to follow medical advice. Compelling an unwilling patient to undergo a dangerous procedure is adding risks. Preoperative evaluation of the patient's suitability for such a procedure should include the social worker's evaluation of the patient's social adjustment and family setting.[17] How well can the family respond to the added needs of a severely disabled member? How willing will it be to support the patient in lengthy, time-consuming, or perhaps unpleasant procedures at home? How realistic are the family members about duration of symptoms, costs (emotional as well as financial), possibility of change? All these are critical factors in decisions about such procedures as renal transplants, open-heart surgery, and orthopedic surgery, and in aftercare planning.

Although medical social workers have been involved in the education of medical students for at least thirty years, not all doctors know how or are willing to use social workers at their maximum level of skill. Some view them as concerned only with hospital bills or with transferring patients to extended care facilities. A 1967 study showed that doctors and social workers defined the expectations of the social work role somewhat differently and that doctors tended to specify the means by which the social worker should deal with the problems presented by the referred patient, instead of fully accepting the social worker as a professional colleague and trusting his judgment.[18]

Without the active support of the medical staff, hospital boards of directors will be unlikely to include a social service department in the budget. The experience of one hospital is illuminating. In this hospital, the so-called medical social service department was staffed by nonprofessionals and spent most of its time dealing with area welfare departments. Relatively unknown to the medical staff, it received no support from them for its budget requests. It became possible to appoint as director an experienced social

17. See Kathleen M. Hickey, "Impact of Kidney Disease on Patient, Family, and Society," *Social Casework*, Vol. 53, No. 7 (July 1972), pp. 391–398.

18. Katherine M. Olsen and Marvin E. Olsen, "Role Expectations and Perceptions for Social Workers in Medical Settings," *Social Work*, Vol. 12, No. 3 (July 1967), pp. 70–78.

worker who was convinced that a demonstration was needed of the contribution of medical social work to the medical program of the hospital. It was decided to offer a casework program to one service, and the pediatric service was chosen. Contacts with the welfare department were delegated to the controller's office. Pediatric residents and attending staff were notified of the readiness of social service to receive referrals. Medical social workers participated in case conferences and teaching seminars. The referrals, at first largely for concrete services and discharge arrangements, were broadened as the staff became convinced of the contribution of medical social service. At the end of six months, the chief of the medical service, formerly indifferent to social work, requested that his staff also be allowed to refer patients. Soon this was extended to other services of the hospital. The chief social worker was appointed to the faculty of the medical school, and a program of field work in a social agency in the community was inaugurated for third-year medical students. This led to improved understanding of the resources outside the hospital and to greater awareness of the ways in which medical social service could serve as liaison.

Where the social worker's contribution to team understanding has been a positive one, anxieties about authority and resentment at what seems like the low status of the social service department in a "host" setting are minimized.

Referral to Hospital Social Service

There are various times in the patient's course in the hospital when the hospital social worker may be brought into the picture—no general standard. Some hospitals screen patients for social services at admission and provide nearly all patients with some social service; in others, cases are referred only when some special problem has become obvious. In many hospitals, the effective use of social services is not equally available to all patients; those from semi-private and ward beds are more likely to be referred than those from private rooms. Where such is the hospital policy (and it may be conscious policy or the result of unconscious screening), it indicates a need of interpretation to the medical staff. As Teague put it:

> Health care managers all too often take for granted that the poor and members of minority groups are the ones in need of social services, rather than focus first and foremost on the need for social services as the essential criterion for referral.[19]

19. Doran Teague, " 'Social Service Enterprises': A New Health Care Model," *Social Work*, Vol. 16, No. 3 (July 1971), p. 70. Reprinted with the permission of

One of social work's potential contributions to the health care team is its understanding of the many possible ways in which people may react to fears and anxieties. Any hospital admission brings with it apprehensions, no matter how convinced the patient may be of the necessity for admission. There is fear of pain, of helplessness and loss of control over one's own activities, of the possibility of a sinister diagnosis or that something may go wrong, of possible disfigurement or disability. There is separation from loved ones and anxiety about how they will manage in one's absence. If they do not manage well, one may feel guilt at having deserted them; if they do manage well, it is proof of one's dispensability. For the great majority of people, there is worry over loss of income and added expenses. Social workers know of the ways in which people express such anxieties. Some take it out in hostility; others become depressed; others may become overexcited and overtalkative; some deny the reality of their physical condition; some demand extra attention; and others want to be left strictly alone.

In addition to fears and anxieties inherent in being hospitalized, a number of things conspire to infantilize the patient. He has been put to bed; his meals are brought to him; his elimination is no longer his private concern; he is awakened in the morning and tucked in at night very much as a baby is. The emotional consequences of this may take the form of regression to a more childish level of behavior, of defiance of medical orders, of depression and apprehensiveness, of whining and attention-getting behavior, or of withdrawal and repression. Medical social service can help interpret to staff and patient his reactions to this stress situation, as well as look for ways in which the patient used these mechanisms in his everyday life outside the hospital. Social workers are familiar with the ways in which people "use" other people and may be able to ease difficult relationships between patient and staff and between patient and family. An understanding of the patient's customary life style can foresee and plan for possible obstacles to his recovery after discharge.

One of the real concerns of the patient in a modern, highly specialized hospital is that he may feel as if he were on an assembly

the National Association of Social Workers. See also Barbara Gordon Berkman and Helen Rehr, "Early Social Service Case Finding for Hospitalized Patients: An Experiment," *Social Service Review*, Vol. 47, No. 2 (June 1973), pp. 256–265, for evidence that the traditional system refers too few patients too late in their hospital stay for maximum benefit from social service.

line. He is seen by a bewildering variety of professional and para-professional specialists; his doctor's visits are brief and hurried; and there is no one to answer his questions. The hospital social worker sees him, not as an assortment of symptoms or specific tasks, but as a personality reacting to the stress situation of disability and hospitalization in specific ways. His reactions can be assessed better by someone who sees him as a "whole person" (which is the aim of the hospital social worker) and who can regard his adjustment as the primary goal.

It is obvious that social service could be helpful to many more patients than are traditionally referred. However, few hospitals have social service staffs adequate to refer all patients or even have social service screen all admissions. Some hospitals routinely refer certain categories of high-risk patients, such as unmarried mothers, mothers of premature babies, patients with deforming diseases, and those whose convalescence will be lengthy. When the prognosis is hopeless or when wholesale reorganization of family living patterns will be needed, medical social service is usually brought into the picture. However, in all too many cases it is brought in late, when its effectiveness is minimized by pressures of time, and in many small hospitals it is unavailable.

Expanding Social Work Roles
in the Hospital Setting

Social casework with individual patients and their families has been the traditional method of hospital social workers. Increasingly, this is being criticized as too time-consuming to be the most effective way to use social work expertise. As Hallowitz puts it: "The hospital social worker, in addition to being a caseworker, needs to be a group therapist, social systems intervenor, educator, consultant, and perhaps most important, a change agent."[20] Group sessions may be carried on with patients but are more likely to be with the relatives, especially with the parents of children with serious and long-term illnesses. These sessions may be used to provide information about the illness and possible treatments, as well as to provide an outlet for the emotional reactions of parents, who feel guilt, anger, anticipatory grief if the prognosis

20. Emanuel Hallowitz, "Innovations in Hospital Social Work," *Social Work*, Vol. 17, No. 4 (July 1972), pp. 89–97. This article describes ways in which the social work staff was able to make the hospital more responsive to human need. The quotation is from p. 97 and is reprinted with the permission of the National Association of Social Workers.

is fatal or who may deny the reality of the patient's condition.[21] Similar group activity may benefit the children of elderly parents who must be transferred to nursing homes, the families of individuals needing renal transplants, or patients whose life styles will have to be drastically modified as a result of heart damage or cerebral accidents.

Mr. Hallowitz asserts that the hospital social worker may function as a change agent and illustrates with cases of modification of attitudes toward racism of which a staff was largely unaware and the inauguration of improved emergency services to victims of rape. The establishment of a free clinic for "street people," who rejected the traditional social and health agencies but who were in desperate need of health services, counseling, and pregnancy verification tests, has been carried out by social workers impatient with the bureaucratic restrictions they found in established agencies.[22] The contribution of social work to research on health and illness is apparent from the table of contents of any of the professional journals or from abstracts of masters theses or doctoral dissertations from schools of social work. The emphasis is likely to be on social and emotional factors precipitating the illness or breakdown or on the socio-adaptive changes in patient's and family's life styles resulting from illness or disability. A study of the acute emotional stress in congestive heart failure, for instance, was carried out by the social worker member of an interdisciplinary team and has obvious implications for hospital care and discharge planning of these patients.[23]

In their roles as patient advocates and brokers, social workers are aware of the obstacles presented by hospital red tape and regulations designed for staff rather than patient convenience. Forcing all clinic patients to arrive when the clinic opens instead of making appointments, failure to have evening or weekend hours, lack of adequate play space for children who must accompany their par-

21. See Chancellor B. Driscoll and A. Harold Lubin, "Conferences with Parents of Children with Cystic Fibrosis," *Social Casework*, Vol. 53, No. 3 (March 1972), pp. 140–146; Vrinda S. Knapp and Howard Hansen, "Helping the Parents of Children with Leukemia," *Social Work*, Vol. 18, No. 4 (July 1973), pp. 70–75; and Louise A. Frey, ed., *Use of Groups in the Health Field* (New York: NASW, 1966).

22. See Ellen Dunbar and Howard Jackson, "Free Clinics for Young People," *Social Work*, Vol. 17, No. 5 (September 1972), pp. 27–34.

23. See Kathleen Holt Bergum, "Social and Psychological Factors in Congestive Heart Failure," *Social Work*, Vol. 14, No. 1 (January 1969), pp. 68–75. See also Ann Murphy and Lois Pounds, "Repeat Evaluations of Retarded Children," *American Journal of Orthopsychiatry*, Vol. 42, No. 1 (January 1972), pp. 103–109, for a collaborative research report involving a social worker and a pediatrician.

ents, uncomfortable chairs in unattractive waiting rooms or corridors—all help dehumanize people. Visiting hours that are difficult for the patient's family, inhumane billing procedures, apprehensions over medical rounds (when the patient will suddenly be confronted by a group of inquiring strangers) are all areas where the social worker as change agent can work toward modification or, if that proves impossible, toward better preparation of the patient to deal with these concerns.

The cases which follow are illustrative of the various situations a social worker encounters in a hospital setting and the roles he plays in them.

Mr. Perry, a forty-five-year-old bachelor who lives with his elderly mother, is hospitalized for diagnostic study of possible ulcers. He is on a carefully regulated diet to which he will not adhere. His mother smuggles in forbidden food which she has cooked herself. Mr. Perry tries to bribe ward personnel to bring him extras from the coffee shop. While protesting his eagerness to improve and his willingness to cooperate, Mr. Perry is sabotaging his own treatment. The medical social service department is asked to interview both Mr. Perry and his mother in an effort to enlist their cooperation.

Mme. St. John, for many years a celebrated operatic coach, was hospitalized two months ago after a stroke which left her paralyzed on one side. Although now over eighty, Madame resists the recommendation that she go to a nursing home, insisting that she is well enough to return to her apartment. Her financial resources are slender, but she refuses to consider exploration of her eligibility for public assistance. She insists that her concert grand piano accompany her if she has to be moved. Medical social service is asked to explore with her the resources available and help her plan more realistically.

Mr. and Mrs. Lee must decide whether or not to give permission for open heart surgery on their year-old daughter. Medical opinion is that chances of success are 50 percent but that death from pneumonia is a greater risk. Friction between the parents makes it impossible for them to agree on permission. Medical social service is asked to work with the parents to help them reach agreement, since whatever happens, under the present circumstances one will always blame the other.

Mrs. West, a young attractive mother of three small children, whose husband is devoted to her, has been informed that she must have surgery for the removal of a malignant tumor. Although she has not yet been told, the prognosis is very poor. Her husband is immobilized by grief and worry. He will need help in planning for the few months of life Mrs. West has remaining, both in terms of homemaker service and in helping the children and Mrs. West face the future.

The parents of children with leukemia attend a series of weekly group sessions with members of the medical social service staff and visiting consultants. Not only do they receive factual information about the condition, its probable progress, and the kinds of treatments, but they are given opportunities to express their anger and grief, to assess the impact on other members of the family of their absorption in their sick child, and they are made aware of facilities in the community for transportation, blood donors, and educational programs for home-bound children.

Mr. Morse, a fifty-year-old civil service employee, was admitted to the hospital following an automobile accident. Physical examination and X-rays indicate no real injury, but Mr. Morse insists that he has been badly hurt, that the doctors are incompetent, the nurses inattentive, and his family unsympathetic. He is unwilling to be discharged, but there is no medical reason for keeping him. He threatens to sue if forced to leave. Medical social service is asked to interview him to see if his hostility can be modified and to learn if this is typical of his life style or reaction to some unexpressed anxiety.

Mr. Doyle, a seventy-five-year-old retired railroad engineer, was hospitalized after breaking his hip. Always active and busy, Mr. Doyle has not accepted his forced immobility well. At first vocal in his complaints, he has become increasingly apathetic and depressed. Now he is ready to learn crutch-walking, but he is afraid of falling again and says, both in words and actions, that his life and usefulness are over. Medical social service is asked to work with him around his feelings of uselessness in an effort to enable him to use rehabilitation services. The social worker also involves volunteers to visit Mr. Doyle and bring him news of his dog, which is being cared for by neighbors.

Patty, eight, is in the pediatric ward to have her severe diabetes regulated. The oldest of three girls whose father deserted several years ago, Patty has reacted to the sudden discovery of her illness by tantrums at home and poor work in school. Her mother works all day to support the family and cannot understand why Patty has become such a problem.

Medical social service is asked to help mother understand Patty's feelings about her illness and the limitations it imposes. Community resources will be discussed with the mother, and an appointment is arranged for the mother to talk with the hospital dietician about substitutes for the forbidden sweets which Patty misses so much.

The Hospital Social Worker and
Community Resources

A major function of hospital social service is to act as liaison between the hospital and community resources. To secure needed data from agencies; to transmit medical information and recommendations to outside agencies; to refer patients for casework help, material assistance, home health aides, nursing home care, rehabilitation, employment, or any other community service, the medical social worker must have a thorough knowledge of the resources available and their potential usefulness and accessibility to the patient. With such supportive services, it is often possible for patients to leave the hospital sooner and take advantage of more normal and less costly health facilities.

With twenty-four–hour observation and a variety of personnel reporting, data of a different type from that received in an office interview are available to assess the patient's capabilities for adjustment. The case of Ruby James, which follows, shows how a medical social worker was able to make a judgment about the quality of care Ruby could give her baby and arrange for protective care of the infant. If Ruby had not been hospitalized for accidental reasons, the situation might have gone on for years before it came to the attention of some protective agency.

Ruby James, an eighteen-year-old unmarried mother, was admitted by ambulance with her three-month-old baby, Lily, following a hotel fire. Ruby had third-degree burns, and both she and the baby were suffering from smoke inhalation. The medical social worker's first interview with Ruby, on the afternoon of admission, was held under difficulties, since Ruby was in an oxygen tent and still highly excited. Her account of the preceding twenty-four hours was pieced together by the worker, Miss Williams, as Ruby was not able to tell a coherent story, interrupting herself to ask about the baby's clothes and to express hatred toward her mother, toward the father of her child, and toward the welfare department.

On the preceding afternoon, Mrs. Barnard, Ruby's mother, had returned home unexpectedly and found her husband, Ruby's stepfather, making advances to Ruby. She quarreled violently with Ruby and threw her and the baby out of the house. Ruby went to the nearest welfare department office,

and as it was so late in the day and she could not be given a
regular intake appointment, she was given money enough for
supper and breakfast and was directed to a cheap hotel which
catered to clients from the welfare department. She had an
appointment for the following morning in the intake department. This was not her first contact with the welfare department. Ruby had applied there for funds following the birth of
her baby but was unable to supply the necessary information
about paternity or secure the cooperation of the alleged father,
so the application was rejected. Since she was able to go to her
mother's home, Ruby was not too upset at her failure to secure public assistance at that time. This time she had no place
to go; her mother meant it when she told her never to come
back. Ruby's anger toward her mother seemed to Miss Williams to be mixed with real fear.

Ruby did not remember anything about the fire, as she and
Lily were both asleep. Her concern seemed to be more about
Lily's clothes than anything else. Throughout this and subsequent interviews, Miss Williams was impressed by Ruby's
attitude toward her baby. She wanted her to be prettily
dressed and look nice but seemed unconcerned about necessities. Miss Williams's concern for the quality of care Lily
would get from Ruby, beginning in this first interview, was
intensified as the contact went on. To Ruby, Lily was a toy, to
be dressed up and played with and then put aside and forgotten.

In her daily interviews with Miss Williams, as well as in her
contacts with ward personnel, Ruby showed an alternation
between highly excitable and withdrawn, trance-like behavior. Arrangements were made for psychiatric evaluation, and
the psychiatrist reported: "Patient appears somewhat silly
and euphoric and gives silly and irrelevant answers at first.
She states she has been unhappy since childhood but has to
be cheerful so as not to lose her child. *Impression*: No psychosis; severe chronic psychoneurosis. Psychological testing
recommended."

In the meantime, Miss Williams had been very busy on the
telephone. The hotel reported that the room had been gutted
and the baby's and Ruby's clothes were ruined. Ruby's account of her contact with the welfare department was verified.
A sister was located, who confirmed that Ruby had always
been hard to get along with, does not appreciate being helped
but gets mad when help is not forthcoming, and advised
that Ruby not return to her mother's home. The sister would
be willing to take Ruby and Lily temporarily but really did not
have room for them.

Ruby's physical condition improved rapidly, and she was
ready for discharge in ten days. However, Lily had suffered

severely from smoke inhalation, and there was a question of brain damage and possible blindness. Further stay in the hospital was indicated. Ruby reacted to this with her customary anger, followed by remorse and tears. In daily interviews, Ruby had begun to form some sort of relationship with Miss Williams, although she continued to present difficulties on the ward, getting into fights with the nurses, misquoting the doctors, and complaining that she was being neglected. Miss Williams's patient acceptance of her feelings seemed to be a new experience for Ruby. At first she felt it necessary to try to provoke Miss Williams into rejecting her—apparently her usual way of relating to people. Her mood changes came frequently: one minute she would cling to Miss Williams' hand begging her not to leave the bedside; and the next minute she would ask what in blazes Miss Williams was doing, asking all these questions and bothering her. In later interviews, when Ruby had become less hostile, she expressed guilt over her anger and seemed genuinely attached to Miss Williams, whose first name she had learned and which she insisted on using.

The psychological tests which were done as soon as Ruby was able to be out of bed showed an immature, inadequate person reacting like a child, with rage. The psychologist's report began: "Ruby was most uncooperative and negativistic, to the point of open hostility toward the examiner. She was verbally assaultive, legalistic, and circumstantial. She approached every task in an impulsive, disorganized way, did only those tasks which she wanted, and sulked aggressively whenever she was requested to do or pushed into doing a task. There was little or no motivation, and her frustration tolerance was very low. There is a narcissistic concern for the self that cannot be pierced. She cannot think or act in any other manner but only as 'personal I,' with little knowledge of others. Her erratic and disorganized functioning renders her incompetent to evaluate reality well, and her perception is defective. She is very immature, childish, and the only feeling she can activate is anger. It is more akin to a very young child's rage reactions—selfish, egocentric, manipulative, and in search of immediate gratification or pleasure."

The first day she was able to be out of bed, Ruby presented herself at the social service department asking for "Valerie." She told Miss Williams something about her childhood, feeling that her mother had always blamed her for everything, that she had been wanting to leave home for a long time and now refused ever to go back. She was scornful about her stepfather, claiming he was "not much" but that her mother was very jealous and possessive.

As the time for Ruby's discharge neared, Miss Williams

tried to help her plan. She had no clothes, since hers were destroyed in the fire, so some were provided for her. Ruby's sister agreed to try to get some of her clothes from Mrs. Barnard's house once Ruby had a place to stay. In an effort to pave the way for her intake appointment at the welfare department, Miss Williams talked with the Intake Supervisor, outlining the situation and preparing them for Ruby's approach, which would undoubtedly be an angry one. Ruby was able to accept the fact that Lily was not well enough to be discharged and would need to remain under care a while longer.

In spite of her protestations of devotion, Rudy did not make any attempt to visit Lily in the month after her discharge. By then electroencephalograms (EEGs) had indicated no permanent brain damage, and it was definitely found that the baby was not blind. Contact with the welfare department indicated that Ruby was living in a furnished room with no facilities for taking care of Lily. An interagency conference, involving the public assistance worker, the child placement worker, Miss Williams, and the Social Service Director, produced an agreement that Lily should be placed in a foster home, since Ruby was in no position to care for her properly and was too immature and disorganized herself to take responsibility for a child.

The public assistance worker interpreted this decision to Ruby and secured her signature to the necessary papers for a temporary placement. In her anger and sorrow, Ruby turned to Miss Williams, coming to the office and demanding to see "Valerie, because she is my worker." Ruby poured out her feelings of rejection and anger that her baby was being taken away from her. She produced a number of impractical alternatives to placement, and in succeeding days several relatives telephoned, apparently at Ruby's urging, to offer to take Lily. They were referred to the child placement worker, who reported, after investigation, that none could offer suitable facilities.

Since there was no further medical need for Lily to remain on the ward, the medical staff urgently recommended discharge, and Miss Williams conferred with the doctor, pointing out the legal and social complications of the situation. The child placement worker made strenuous efforts to locate a foster home for Lily.

Six weeks after her discharge, Ruby appeared asking to see "Valerie," as she had news for her. She was dressed in new, flashy clothes, with a new hairdo, bright red nail polish, and a lot of cheap red jewelry. She looked more attractive than Miss Williams had ever seen her, seemed better organized, and looked and acted bright. She announced that she was leaving town that day with an older man, who was taking her to Florida with him and who treated her "like a princess." She asked Miss Williams to call Mrs. Barnard and give her the news and to "tell her I've got a man of my own now." She seemed to have relinquished Lily with hardly a regret, asking Miss Williams to look out for her and saying that "some day" she'd send for her. Her attitude seemed to be one of triumphant defiance, particularly of her mother. Her mind was made up, and she was not interested in discussing her plans with anyone. She had only stopped to say goodbye, because the worker had been good to her and she was afraid "Valerie might worry about her." She brushed aside any suggestion that she see Lily and fairly ran out of the office. Apparently she followed through on her plans, as Miss Williams got a scrawled postcard from Florida ten days later.

With desertion of Lily so obvious, arrangements were made for her immediate transfer to a foster home. Indications were that Ruby would not make further attempts to keep the baby. If she is not willing to release her for adoption, the "permanent neglect" law of New York State may make it possible for Lily, an attractive and apparently normal youngster, to be freed for permanent ties with two grown-up parents.[24]

While hotel fires and elopements are not frequent events in the experience of medical social service departments, cooperation in planning for suitable discharge arrangements is one of the major social service responsibilities. By enlisting the interest and support of other community agencies, the medical social worker helped provide more adequate care for Lily than her childish and impulsive mother could have done. If little was done to change Ruby's defensive behavior, she at least had the experience of a warmly supportive, helping relationship in her period of crisis. When she finds herself again in difficulties, as we may well expect, the next social worker who deals with her may find it easier. While this may not seem like progress, it is a slight step forward for Ruby.

In addition to the services offered patients and staff, the medical social service department functions as the liaison between the hospital and community agencies. As Miss Williams did in the case of Ruby James, medical social workers relay relevant material to other agencies to help them with their planning. It should go without saying that these contacts are always with the patient's permission, preferably in writing. Information which will be

24. The preceding case illustration was adapted from unpublished records in the files of the Social Service Department of the Beekman-Downtown Hospital. Used with permission.

helpful to the hospital in its total treatment of the patient is secured. Where inquiries are received from other hospitals or out-of-town agencies, they may be referred to medical social service for reply.

Hospital social service departments should be included in interagency conferences and in councils of social agencies. In addition to their direct work with patients, medical social work may also serve to interpret to these other agencies the policies of the hospital. At the same time, it enables the medical social service department to keep abreast of changes in the community's facilities and agency policies.

THE MEDICAL SOCIAL WORKER IN THE COMMUNITY

While medical social work originated in acute-care hospitals and is still largely based there, the growing emphasis on extended care, outpatient clinics, home health services, and prevention indicates that the bulk of social work manpower in the health services may be moving outside the hospital. This will involve the development of new roles and new practice models, although the focus will remain on the social and emotional concomitants of health. A few of the newer areas of practice will be sketched briefly.

Medical social workers may be used to serve certain target groups of patients in community-based programs of detection and care. Such target groups may be those with certain diseases (tuberculosis, cancer, mental illness, for example) or groups distinguished by age (preschool children, the aging), residence (housing projects, neighborhoods, rural areas), or economic level (poverty, public assistance recipients, middle-income prepayment health maintenance organizations). The social worker will be interested in those socio-economic and emotional factors which interfere with securing adequate medical care, such as inaccessibility, stigma, prohibitive cost, apprehension that patients will be experimented upon, fear of publicity, or distrust of professionals. The unwillingness of patients to stay in follow-up treatment,[25] particularly if they do not feel sick, may indicate some social problem. The adaptation of service delivery systems to minority

25. Such programs are worldwide. See, for example, Promila Maitra and V. Subhadra, "Team Approach in Reactivating Drop-Outs in a Tuberculosis Programme: A Case Study," *International Social Work*, Vol. 14, No. 3 (1971), pp. 511–518, for a project in India.

groups may involve outreach tactics and adjustment of hours, the use of interpreters, of paraprofessionals from the neighborhood, or of special educational programs.[26]

The role of social workers in such health facilities as abortion clinics, genetic counseling clinics, and homemaker service has been described in Chapters 1 and 3. Although in most cases social workers are employees of the clinic, it is possible for a social worker in private practice to be hired on a contractual basis. Such a policy is described by Theresa Barkan.[27] A private medical clinic, catering mostly to middle-income families, hired her as "counselor" to see families and patients as referred by the doctors of the clinic. The conclusion, after six months, was that counseling made a valuable contribution to comprehensive health care for the patients attending this medical center and that this pattern of a private practitioner affiliating with a group of professionals from another discipline might be a useful trend. Patients were better able to accept the counseling within the clinic than referral to a social agency in the community.

Medical social workers are often used as consultants to maternal and child health services, crippled children services, industrial health facilities, neighborhood health centers, and regional health planning agencies. Their function is to interpret to the other professionals involved the meaning of illness to families and individuals, how family relationships affect patients, and the meaning of separation when patients are institutionalized. Such insights may result in modifications of existing practices (as in adapting traditional case-finding methods to meet the needs of certain target groups) or in the establishment of new services to meet needs

26. See, for example, Milton Nobel, "Community Organization in Hospital Social Service," *Social Casework,* Vol. 53, No. 8 (October 1972), pp. 494–501, for a project which extended its areas of service into the community; James C. Stewart, Jr., Michael Lauderdale, and Guy E. Shuttlesworth, "The Poor and the Motivation Fallacy," *Social Work,* Vol. 17, No. 6 (November 1972), pp. 34–37, for a description of an immunization program in a black area of Tulsa, Oklahoma; *Medicaid Guidelines: Early and Periodic Screening, Diagnosis, and Treatment for Individuals Under 21* (Washington, D.C.: Medical Services Administration, June 28, 1972), for guidelines for screening programs for such conditions as sickle cell anemia, lead poisoning, vision and hearing testing, developmental assessment, and the provision of treatment and preventive services, with the involvement of social workers indicated.

27. Theresa W. Barkan, "Private Casework Practice in a Medical Clinic," *Social Work,* Vol. 18, No. 4 (July 1973), pp. 5–9. See also, P. H. Wolfe and Genevieve Teed, "A Study of the Work of a Medical Social Worker in a Group Medical Practice," *Canadian Medical Association Journal,* Vol. 96 (May 27, 1969), pp. 1407–1416.

not yet recognized by the community (such as the free clinic for "street people" already described).

As comprehensive family health care facilities and neighborhood or regional comprehensive health care centers are developed, social workers will be functioning in capacities other than direct services to clients. They will be supervising paraprofessionals and neighborhood aides in outreach services and in community organizations to support and insure some measure of community control over health care centers. Their role in research is less well recognized in the health field but is potentially very valuable. If health care is to move away from its present uncoordinated, episodic, treatment-centered, and fragmented character toward family-centered, comprehensive, continuous, and prevention-oriented delivery systems, there will be an increased role for health social workers to become full participants in the multidisciplinary team effort needed. Medical social work can then modify the long-standing conception of its role as "handmaid" to the medical profession and permit the establishment of new models of social service delivery. Teague suggests a new type of agency—Social Service Enterprises—which would be administratively autonomous and serve all community health facilities on a contractual basis. Teague specifies the elements he considers essential to such a model:

1. An areawide health-care-system approach to social service planning in which the organizational arrangements facilitate the articulation and translation of consumer-identified needs and priorities for service into programs.

2. A governing board whose membership is truly representative of the socioeconomic and ethnic characteristics of the area to be served.

3. A structured advisory mechanism that will facilitate governing-board deliberations with the exchange of ideas between social workers, health care administrators, and consumers of health services.

4. A reorientation of social work toward (a) therapeutic intervention, by means of placing more emphasis on strategies that are "physical" rather than "dynamic," (b) the case situation, by adopting the view of team responsibility for providing the needed social services, (c) the professional service role, i.e., program manager, consultant, adviser, and educator to auxiliary social work staff and other health workers with regard to the needed social treatment, (d) an understanding that bureaucratic structures are not fixed or impreg-

nable organizational entities to be endured, but rather are
entities to be adapted to the betterment of social goals.[28]

Such an organization would permit social work to deliver services
of a high quality based on client needs and priorities rather than
on merely facilitating the work of health professionals, as so much
hospital-based social service has been expected to do. It also
makes possible the expansion of preventive work, which should
be a primary goal for all social work.

SERVICES FOR MENTAL HEALTH

The connection between physical and mental health is a close
one, but society approaches them quite differently. While physical illness usually calls forth a sympathetic response, many people
fear and reject the mentally ill, and the development of facilities
for their care reflects the wish of the general public to dissociate
itself from the "insane."

WHAT IS MENTAL ILLNESS?

Historical and anthropological data indicate that the human
group has always felt threatened by behavior which is markedly
at variance with what is expected or usual. The methods by which
the group has attempted to deal with this threat have depended
upon the explanations available in the culture for such behavior.
The individualized treatment of the troubled person characteristic
of modern mental health care could not have occurred until the
understandings of dynamic psychiatry became available to illuminate behavior which seemed bizarre, inappropriate, or "mad."
Because we disapprove of the inhumane ways in which the mentally ill have been treated in other times and cultures, we tend to
overlook how logically these treatments were related to the explanations of the behavior. Given the premise that the "madman"
was possessed of devils, attempts to frighten or drive them out of
his body are just as logical as current attempts to alter his behavior
by the latest refinements of diagnostic techniques and chemo-
therapy.

Until the pioneering work of Freud and his associates, no logical explanation other than some kind of supernatural influence
was available to account for the sudden changes of personality,
the hallucinations, or the delusions of the psychotic person. Such

28. Teague, "Social Service Enterprises," p. 72. Reprinted with permission of
the National Association of Social Workers.

persons were felt to be set apart by influences beyond ordinary comprehension and therefore automatically dangerous. In small primitive groups, in which there was only an occasional individual whom we would call mentally ill, the group could afford to tolerate his oddities; he was often considered to be in some special relationship with the supernatural and therefore treated with awe. The relationship between mental deficiency and mental illness was not understood, and this confusion persists in both medieval and modern use of the word "fool" to indicate a person who is defective or who is the "jester."

Larger groups, which naturally had a greater number of such deviants, could not afford to maintain them all in positions of honor. Depending on the explanation given for each aberration and the severity of the management problem presented, the group might expel, execute, punish, isolate, or treat such individuals. Treatment methods were based on the available explanations for illness and included incantations and prayers; physical manipulations such as rubbing, sucking, scarification, and the sweat bath; and administration of a variety of drugs. Some of the latter had unknown chemical efficacy; rauwolfia (used for centuries in some Asian cultures) has been found to contain tranquilizing substances, and narcotics were used by a number of preliterate tribes. The resilience of the human spirit, rather than the effectiveness of the treatments, probably accounted for most of whatever improvement occurred.

We should not overlook the role of the primitive medicine man, which prefigured that of the psychiatrist and social worker. In a small group which he knew intimately, the medicine man might be able to size up personality and family factors which were disturbing to his patient and suggest ways of modifying them. Those who view the medicine man as a charlatan and imposter have not reviewed the cross-cultural evidence of his dedication to his tasks and his real usefulness in the emotional life of his group.[29]

Many so-called primitive societies were actually a good deal more advanced in their understanding and treatment of the mentally ill than were some of the civilizations in our own tradition. Until the age of enlightenment, in Europe and in colonial America religious explanations for mental disease led to cruel and repres-

29. See Gay Luce, "The Importance of Psychic Medicine: Training Navaho Medicine Men," in Julius Segal, ed., *Mental Health Program Reports–5*, DHEW publication no. (HSM) 72–9042 (Rockville, Md.: National Institute of Mental Health, 1971), for a description of "family therapy" by medicine men.

sive treatment. Victims were believed to be possessed of evil spirits or to be undergoing punishment for sin. Belief in witchcraft, in lycanthropy, and in black magic of all sorts gave rise to practices of torture and death to free the soul of the victim from imprisonment and to protect the innocent (those not possessed) from contamination.

During the nineteenth century, attempts to classify the mixed population of prisons and almshouses led to the establishment of special institutions for the mentally handicapped and disordered. (We have already discussed this trend as it related to the provision of institutions for children in Chapter 4.) There was an increase in the number of these mental hospitals following the work of Dorothea Dix, but until roughly the turn of the century, such institutions were providing custodial care only, under conditions which were at best uninspiring and at worst on a subhuman level.[30]

The Beginnings of a Scientific Approach

Interest in rehabilitation of the mentally ill received its major impetus from the work of Clifford Beers. Written about his own experiences as a mental patient in Connecticut, Mr. Beers's *A Mind That Found Itself* was published at a strategic time for American social thought. The reform movement which had begun in the 1880s, with such pioneers as Jane Addams, Jacob Riis, and Alice Hamilton, was in full swing. Citizen interest in legislation had brought about the inauguration of programs to protect the public and improve social services. The insane, isolated in remote "asylums," came dramatically to public attention when Mr. Beers described his treatment.

The mental hygiene movement, as it was at first called (now generally referred to as mental health), focused attention on both the prevention and treatment of mental illness. The National Committee for Mental Hygiene (now the National Association for Mental Health), to which Clifford Beers devoted the rest of his life, has been primarily a lay organization, dedicated to improving conditions for the mentally ill, promoting optimum mental health in the population, and educating the public. It has been of inestimable benefit in increasing public understanding and support of both public and private agencies and institutions, not only those which serve the psychotic patient, but also those

---

30. For a detailed account of the conditions under which mental patients were kept, see Albert Deutsch, *The Mentally Ill in America* (New York: Columbia University Press, 1949).

which help persons whose maladjustments interfere with their capacity for leading a normal life.

The nineteenth-century antecedent of the professional psychiatrist was the medical superintendent of a mental hospital. As early as 1844, a group of these superintendents formed an association which became, many years later, the American Psychiatric Association. Like the American Correctional Association (formerly the American Prison Association), this organization was concerned less about the causes of social problems than about their management. It is an interesting commentary on American culture that so much of the theoretical basis for understanding human behavior has come from Europe and that so much of the application of these theories has occurred under American auspices.

Not until Sigmund Freud (1856–1939) was there a body of theory which offered both explanation and possibilities of treatment in the field of mental illness.[31] Whether one follows Freudian psychology or some alternative "school," the overwhelming importance of Freud's insights in developing a scientific approach to the study of human behavior cannot be ignored.

In a tribute published at the time of Freud's death, Karl Menninger, a noted psychiatrist in his own right, said of Freud:[32]

> Freud is not a man about whom one can write a few casual words, a few comments of praise, a few notes of criticism, and feel that an appropriate gesture has been made to his passing. For Freud was no ordinary man; he was not an ordinary scientist. He was so nearly unique an individual that it is difficult to find anyone with whom to compare him. No one in the field of psychology ever attained to a fraction of his stature. Among medical scientists almost none can be said to have approached him in brilliancy, originality, or influence upon medical practice. Perhaps no other one individual in the field of science lived to see the thinking of the entire world so profoundly modified by his discoveries within his lifetime as

31. There is a wealth of published material on Freudian psychology. In addition to translations of Freud's own body of writing, see Ernest Jones's monumental *Life of Freud*, three volumes (New York: Basic Books, 1953–1957). For a disarming presentation of many of her father's controversial concepts, see Anna Freud, *Psycho-analysis for Teachers and Parents* (Boston: Beacon Press, 1960). For some understanding of Freud as a person, see Hendrik M. Ruitenbeek, *Freud as We Knew Him* (Detroit: Wayne State University Press, 1972); and Irving Stone, *The Passions of the Mind* (New York: Doubleday, 1972), for a fictionalized biography.

32. The quotation is taken from Karl Menninger, M.D., *A Psychiatrist's World* (New York: Viking Press, 1939), pp. 820, 821. Copyright 1939, Copyright © renewed 1967 by Karl Menninger, M.D. Reprinted by permission of The Viking Press, Inc.

did Freud. Galileo, Dalton, Lavoisier, Darwin, these and others contributed discoveries which greatly modified our thinking and our ways of living, but the effect was more gradual in its permeation. For not only medical science and psychological science and sociological science, but literature, art, anthropology, pedagogy, and even popular speech show the influence of Freud's discoveries and show them in unmistakable terms.

All that Freud did stems from one simple discovery, a discovery based on knowledge which many had possessed before him. This was the knowledge that beneath the surface manifestations of human behavior there are deeper motives and feelings and purposes which the individual conceals not only from others but even from himself. Freud discovered a method for ascertaining and eliciting this hidden material; he called this method psychoanalysis. By means of it he and many others working with him gradually accumulated a considerable body of systematic knowledge about the unconscious processes of the human personality . . . More clearly than anyone else he saw how stalwartly the human mind defends itself against the acceptance of unpleasant truth. This helped him to be tolerant in the face of ridicule, the misrepresentation, the distortion, the bitter and unscientific refutation of his theories which they initially aroused throughout the world. He reminded himself and his students that all scientific discoveries which diminish the feeling of self-importance in mankind stimulate resentment and incredulity.

It was not until the unconscious had been elucidated and its importance as a driving force behind behavior had been demonstrated that what we could call a scientific approach to mental illness became possible. Even those psychiatrists who reject many Freudian theories or who disagree with neo-Freudian approaches do not reject the theory of unconscious determinants to human behavior. Only the recognition of buried impulses makes it possible to decipher the "cry for help" and to unravel the continued patterns of self-defeating behavior which so perplex those who observe them in themselves and others. It is no wonder that social workers grasped eagerly at these new concepts and found them extremely helpful in seeing where continued efforts to redirect a client had been dealing with surface manifestations instead of getting at the underlying causes.

So profoundly have ideas about mental adjustment and maladjustment been altered by the scientific approach that it is hard for us to realize how comparatively recent this approach is. It was less than three centuries ago that witchcraft trials and executions were socially approved; only a little more than one century since Dorothea Dix found the insane chained in cellars and outbuildings; less than eighty years since Clifford Beers groped his way back to sanity; and only about sixty years since Freud's work first became known in America.

The availability of a scientific approach to the causes and treatment of mental illness has not meant, however, that older, unscientific ideas have disappeared. While the mentally ill are no longer chained in cellars, conditions in many of the large state hospitals were, until a few years ago, almost incredibly primitive. Mental illness is still to many people an embarrassing phenomenon, and to have been hospitalized carries a stigma which interferes with employability and social acceptability. The reluctance of patients to consult clinics or psychiatrists until driven to it by the severity of the symptoms is an indication of lingering prejudice. There is a feeling that people ought somehow to be able to handle their own emotional problems without expert assistance, even though they would not be expected to handle a problem in any other area of their lives without counsulting an expert. Combined with this minimizing of the problem on the one hand is the irrational fear of the psychotic person as dangerous and the insistence on his secure custody in an institution. This dissociation from the mentally ill would seem to indicate an underlying fear of recognizing any kinship with them; the general public assumes an unrealistic dichotomy between "normal" and "insane," being unwilling to acknowledge the continuum from mental health to mental illness. This theoretical dichotomy is apparent in the commitment process, in which "insanity" is determined in a court of law on the basis of outmoded evidence.

In spite of our increased scientific knowledge about mental health, there is a lack of consensus as to what constitutes positive mental health and whether mental health means the absence of mental illness or is qualitatively different from it. In its first publication, The Joint Commission on Mental Illness and Mental Health made an extensive review of the literature and found a striking lack of agreement. Dr. Jahoda's analysis of concepts current in the literature stressed six factors: the individual's attitudes toward himself, the degree to which the person realizes his potentials through appropriate action, the integration of his personality, the degree of his autonomy, his perception of reality, and his degree of mastery of his environment.[33] More than a decade later,

---

33. Marie Jahoda, *Current Concepts of Positive Mental Health* (New York: Basic Books, 1958). The six factors mentioned above are outlined on pp. 96–99.

The Joint Commission on Mental Health of Children was hardly able to improve the definition:

> The mentally healthy individual thus becomes one whose private life is evaluated against such somewhat vague but still highly meaningful concepts as integrity, authenticity, and self-determination, and whose relationships with others may be judged in the light of such notions as effective intimacy in love and friendship, contributory participation in the affairs of a community, and the breadth of his sympathy with others whose background of experience differs from his own.[34]

Such stress on the ability of the individual to shape his own destiny and on his relationships with others demonstrates the shift in emphasis from the medical model of mental illness, as defined by symptoms, toward a community mental health model which considers mental disorder as an episode in a person's life in the community, for whom the community is responsible.[35]

THREE APPROACHES TO MENTAL HEALTH

The Medical Model

The medical model stresses the differences between the mentally ill—the "insane"—and the sane. Thus, it favors separating disturbed persons from society in institutions where they receive, in addition to psychotherapy, such somatic treatments as electroconvulsive therapy (ECT), insulin shock, lobotomy, and after 1955, tranquilizing drugs.

The medical model also uses psychotherapy, especially for middle- and upper-class patients who can verbalize their feelings and profit from discussing and trying to understand them. Intensive psychotherapy is virtually impossible in public hospitals, though it may be used in private hospitals and is likely to be the predominant treatment in outpatient facilities and private psychiatric and social work practice.

The Mental Hospital

Mental hospitals were traditionally located in rural areas (where activities would not be upsetting to neighbors), which effectively isolated patients from familiar surroundings and family. Staffing was seldom adequate to permit any but somatic treatment, and the more seriously ill patients drifted toward the back wards

34. Rita Pennington, ed., "Studies of Adolescents and Youth," *Mental Health from Infancy Through Adolescence* (New York: Harper & Row, 1973), p. 234.
35. See Philip M. Margolis and Armando R. Favazza, "Mental Health and Illness," *Encyclopedia of Social Work*, 1971, pp. 773–783.

where custodial care was about all they could expect. Many patients did recover, particularly because of the efforts of dedicated staff and partly because of the recuperative powers of the individual, but their reentry into community life was hampered by the stigma associated with mental illness and the fact that families had, in many cases, closed ranks in their absence and were afraid or reluctant to welcome them back wholeheartedly. The "good" patient in such hospitals was the one who did not give trouble, who was cooperative, did his assignment faithfully, attended activities, and followed orders. In other words, he had become "hospitalized."[36]

Increased attention to the effects of hospitalization has led to some improvement in many state hospitals. In 1957 there were 1,200,000 patients in all mental hospitals, two thirds of them in state hospitals.[37] The widespread use of tranquilizing drugs has resulted in a steady drop in total patient population, until in 1972 it was 286,000, of whom a large number are aged who may not really belong there. The reduction in size of population has enabled hospitals to develop more innovative programs, stressing unlocked wards, patient government, trial visits home, employment outside the hospital, and "milieu therapy" (attention to the effect on the patient of his surroundings) to reduce the artificiality of his surroundings and speed his return home or release to a boarding home or group home.

Drugs are not a panacea. Tranquilizing drugs do not, so far as we know, cure mental illness. The diminishing of anxiety by chemical means, however, permits the person who has been absorbed in his inner conflicts to profit from the therapeutic services around him. The use of tranquilizing drugs has the potential for revolutionizing institutional care for the mentally ill. If patients can be effectively kept from harming themselves or others, there is no need to isolate them in rural hospitals; general hospitals can provide diagnostic and intensive treatment facilities in the patient's own community,[38] as well as a "calming-down" period for

36. See Ken Kesey, *One Flew Over the Cuckoo's Nest* (New York: Viking Press, 1962), for a chilling account of what life can become in such an institution. See also Mary Jane Ward, *The Snake Pit* (New York: Random House, 1940), for a view of what an "enlightened" hospital was like in the 1940s; and for contrast, see Morton M. Hunt, *Mental Hospital* (New York: Pyramid Books, 1962), for an account of the experience of New York State's Pilgrim State Hospital with large-scale use of tranquilizing drugs.

37. Joint Commission on Mental Illness and Mental Health, *Action for Mental Health* (New York: Basic Books, 1961), p. xxvii.

38. For an account of a treatment program in a general hospital in a small community, see Donn M. Brechenser, "Brief Psychotherapy Using Transactional Analysis," *Social Casework*, Vol. 53, No. 3 (March 1972), pp. 173–176.

a patient in acute stress. The pressure for security measures and control in a mental institution comes from a general public whose attitude toward the mentally ill is an illustration of cultural lag. But, paradoxically, the public which favors hospitalizing the mentally ill does not support funding for adequate staff and facilities.[39]

For the foreseeable future, all too many of these hospitals will inevitably be custodial institutions, where long-term stay means regression and development of secondary disabilities which are self-perpetuating. Newer treatment methods should be expanded. Integrating the hospital into the community, converting the institution into a "therapeutic community" in which the patient is individualized and has a voice in the management of his life, the establishment of half-way houses, and foster home placements in the community are all encouraging measures and should be extended. The development of day and night hospitals (patients work in the community and sleep in the hospital or, conversely, live at home but spend their days at the hospital) provides greater flexibility for individual needs. A novel approach at Connecticut Valley State Hospital was the "quarter-way house" for patients who had been hospitalized so long (five to forty-five years) that they were not yet ready to move into the community. This project included college students to create a small-group living situation on the grounds of the hospital to ready patients for moving back into the community.[40] To social workers, individualization of clients and their needs is a familiar concept.

The extent to which mental hospitals fall short of their potential is apparent. State hospitals continue to be understaffed, with inadequate facilities, questionable legal status, and pressure toward apathy and conformity.[41] The rights of patients to treatment instead of custodial care, recently affirmed in the Alabama case of *Wyatt* vs. *Stickney*,[42] may force improved treatment and a wide range of rights for involuntarily committed patients. There are also

39. See Joel Freedman, "One Social Worker's Fight for Mental Patients' Rights," *Social Work*, Vol. 16, No. 4 (October 1971), pp. 92–95.

40. Michael J. Wiernasz, "Quarter-way-house Program for the Hospitalized Mentally Ill," *Social Work*, Vol. 17, No. 6 (November 1972), pp. 72–77.

41. Thomas Szasz has been a particularly outspoken critic of our present system of mental health care. See his *The Myth of Mental Illness*, revised edition (New York: Harper & Row, 1974); see also Seymour Halleck, *The Politics of Therapy* (New York: Science House, 1971), and Ronald Leifer, *In the Name of Mental Health* (New York: Science House, 1969).

42. Jack Drake, "Enforcing the Right to Treatment: *Wyatt v. Stickney*," *American Criminal Law Review*, Vol. 10 (October 1972), pp. 587–609. See also Walter Goodman, "The Constitution and the Snakepit," *New York Times Magazine*, March 17, 1974, pp. 21 ff.

some dangers that patients may be denied certain treatments by overcautious hospital administrators who fear possible litigation. The passage in 1965 of legislation to protect patients' rights by reforming antiquated commitment procedures in California has been studied.[43] This new legislation put a limit on the time patients might be held for evaluation, intensive treatment, or extended treatment and affirmed the right of the person so detained to judicial review. The resulting strain on established facilities for screening, emergency service, and aftercare of large numbers of recently released patients resulted in less good care, although there is potential for improved care ultimately. The vested interests of hospital employees are seldom taken into account in changes mandated by legislative action but are critical in attempts to institute reforms (since hospital employees may resist closing of wards or wings of state hospitals) or in legal modifications of their job descriptions.

The Community Mental Health Model

It is the view taken of the patient, rather than the treatment modality, which distinguishes the community mental health model from the medical model of mental illness.[44] The community mental health model, instead of stressing the dichotomy between the mentally ill and the mentally healthy, operates on the basis of a continuum of mental health ranging from optimal functioning on the one hand to complete disability on the other and stresses the interplay between the individual and his environment. Such an approach raises questions as to what and who is actually sick in a society which tolerates racism, continued poverty, drug abuse, and social isolation. It focuses on the mental health of an entire population and concerns itself with prevention of disability (primary prevention) and treatment to prevent further disability (secondary prevention). It aims to provide care that is continuous and comprehensive for a population, set at 200,000 people by the Community Mental Health Centers Act of 1963.

The Community Mental Health Center

Not just those individuals readily identifiable and accessible for treatment are to be served, but the positive mental health of all those people in the catchment area is the responsibility of a

43. See Doris Seder Jackson, "From Protective Custody to Treatment in a Hurry," *Social Work*, Vol. 18, No. 2 (March 1973), pp. 55–64.

44. For a comprehensive delineation of the medical model, see Thomas P. Detre, M.D. and Henry G. Jarecki, M.D., *Modern Psychiatric Treatment* (Philadelphia: J. B. Lippincott Company, 1971).

Community Mental Health Center. Crisis intervention and prevention are seen as a two-pronged attack on mental illness. To be eligible for federal funds, such centers must offer five services: inpatient, outpatient, day and night hospital, emergency services, and consultation and education. The last named are essential to a community mental health program and help to differentiate it from the program of any enlightened mental hospital. Consultation and education are crucial elements in primary prevention, which is a basic responsibility of the center. Knowledge of the community—not only its resources but also those factors which militate against optimal psychosocial functioning, such as slums, inadequate social services, disadvantaged minorities—is essential. Services are close to the clients, direct, and based on crisis intervention, often by someone not a mental health professional but a policeman, teacher, paraprofessional, or volunteer. Consultation with these providers of service probably takes more professional time than direct service to clients in the average mental health center.

The professionals in a community mental health center come from all the helping professions. The director is a psychiatrist in comprehensive mental health centers, and the staff is comprised of psychologists, social workers, psychiatric nurses, specialized consultants, paraprofessionals, and volunteers.[45] The program will include case-finding; diagnosis; psychotherapy; activity groups; educational programs for staff, patients, and community groups; and aftercare clinics and activities. Most centers serve as a training base for all the mental health professions, at both the baccalaureate and graduate levels. Centers may sponsor halfway houses for former patients to smooth their transition from inpatient care to the community. Day hospital programs may also serve to help patients bridge the gap from institution to independent living and may be located in one section of the general hospital or in rooms in the mental health center itself.

In its responsibility for the mental health of the total population served, community mental health centers are increasingly aware of the adverse social conditions which militate against positive mental health. As Bernard Bandler says:

> Our patients' lives are inextricably involved with education,
> housing, jobs, welfare, church, police, city, county, state, and

---

45. See Charlotte W. Michener and Hank Walzer, "Developing a Community Mental Health Volunteer System" *Social Work*, Vol. 15, No. 4 (October 1970), pp. 60–67.

federal bureaucracies, and the complex shifting structures and substructures of their communities. Here, neither we nor our patients nor the communities themselves have control and power. Here, the citizens and neighbors of the communities, particularly minority communities, the inner-city ghetto communities are incredibly helpless and powerless to effect any control over the organizations which determine their destinies.[46]

Such pioneering studies as the "Midtown Manhattan Study,"[47] *Distress in the City*,[48] and *Social Class and Mental Illness*,[49] done respectively in New York City, Boston, and New Haven, demonstrated not only the extent to which the poor receive less adequate care and the extent of unmet need but also the degree to which diagnosis is slanted by class position and racial affiliation. What is "charming eccentricity" in a wealthy person may be considered occasion for commitment in a working person. Behavior which can be tolerated in a one-family house on a substantial lot is unacceptable in a crowded tenement. The ability of clients to verbalize their feelings, much less characteristic of the lower class, may determine whether the individual is considered suitable for outpatient therapy or inpatient treatment with drugs and other somatic treatments. We are only beginning to recognize the strength and usefulness of some of the adaptations of the culture of poverty and of specific adjustments of minority groups. By defining any behavior which differs from middle-class norms as "deviant," we fail to do justice to what may be positive adjustment to overwhelming stress. As William Mayfield says:

> Although discussions about mental health in the black community usually begin with illustrations of the pathologies found there, one rarely hears explanations about why these pathologies exist. Traditional analyses of the black community would lead one to believe that black people are inherently deficient in some way. But whites have set the standards by which blacks are measured. By placing numerous stumbling blocks and often insurmountable barriers in the path of blacks, whites have made it almost impossible for

46. Bernard Bandler, "Community Mental Health and the Educational Dilemmas of the Mental Health Professions," *Journal of Education for Social Work*, Vol. 8, No. 3 (Fall 1972), pp. 5–18. The quotation is from p. 15.

47. Leo Srole, Thomas Langner, Stanley Michael, Marvin Opler, and Thomas Rennie, *Mental Health in the Metropolis* (New York: McGraw-Hill, 1962).

48. William Ryan, *Distress in the City: A Summary Report of the Boston Mental Health Survey* (Boston: United Community Services, 1966).

49. August B. Hollingshead and Frederick C. Redlich, *Social Class and Mental Illness* (New York: Wiley, 1958).

them to measure up to these standards . . . The black child,
like all children, learns how to function in his own culture.
His language is the legitimate form of communication in his
immediate surroundings. His diet, music, religious expression, and the like are different from those of other ethnic
groups. Furthermore, the behavior patterns he learns enable
him to survive in an environment that is often hostile and
complex.[50]

That much of the behavior of those outside the mainstream of
middle-class culture is adaptive and not pathological is borne out
by the experience of several of the community mental health centers funded by the National Institute of Mental Health. In one
center in Eastern Kentucky, reluctance to talk about personal problems is one indication of the strength of the family system, and
in western San Francisco, an unusually heterogeneous clientele
(ranging from the elite and fashionable to black ghetto dwellers,
Orientals, Spanish Americans, and "street people") makes it possible to study cross-cultural differences in discerning what behaviors constitute mental health and mental disorder.[51]

The development of community mental health centers has been
paralleled by a drop in the total of hospitalized patients and a
threefold increase in the number being seen in outpatient facilities. The extent of unmet need has been mentioned. The Joint
Commission on Mental Health of Children estimates that 1,200,-
000 children and adolescents will receive care by 1975, but there
will be 8,000,000 needing help.[52] The estimate that one in ten
adults is in need of help for some form of mental illness is one
commonly met in the literature, although the definition of "needing help" is admittedly inexact. The statistics on patient care
underrepresent the need, obviously.

The development of community-based facilities for treating
mental patients at home received overoptimistic endorsement by
The Joint Commission on Mental Illness and Health in 1961. In
spite of massive increases in funding, the establishment of comprehensive mental health programs in almost every state, and the

---

50. William G. Mayfield, "Mental Health in the Black Community," *Social Work*,
Vol. 17, No. 3 (May 1972), pp. 106–110. The quotations are from pp. 107 and 109
and are reprinted with the permission of the National Association of Social Work-
ers. See also Barbara Lerner, *Therapy in the Ghetto: Political Impotence and Personal
Disintegration* (Baltimore: Johns Hopkins Press, 1972); and Alvin Poussaint, *Why
Blacks Kill Blacks* (New York: Emerson Hall Publishers, 1972).

51. See "A Community Mental Health Center in Appalachia," pp. 90–139, and
"San Francisco Westside: A Community Mental Health Center Serves the People," pp. 174–187, both in Segal, *Mental Health Program Reports–5*.

52. Pennington, *Mental Health*, p. 296.

expansion of training programs for mental health workers at every level, there is little evidence that the national level of positive mental health has improved. After more than a decade of over-optimism, critics of the community mental health movement are urging renewed attention to intrapsychic factors, away from what they regard as overconcentration on the social.[53]

The Psychodynamic Model

The alternative model of mental illness, and one which under-lies most psychotherapy, is the psychodynamic model, which derives from the pioneering work of Freud and his followers, notably Erik Erikson and Anna Freud.[54] In this view, those help-ing the emotionally disturbed person must have some knowledge of the dynamics of human behavior.

The Dynamics of Human Behavior

As used in psychiatric terminology, "dynamic" refers to ex-planatory and causal concepts rather than to descriptive and classificatory ones. Attention is focused on the mental mech-anisms behind behavior as they operate (dynamic) rather than on constellations of symptoms characteristic of a particular diagnosis. We have already seen how forces within themselves, of which they are unaware, impel individuals to act against their own self-interests. Before such patterns of acting can be modified, the purpose which they serve must be understood. The dynamic approach thus involves determining *why* a person is behaving in a deviant way.

This book has repeatedly stressed that all human behavior is purposeful; where it does not appear so, it is because the purpose is obscure. Sometimes the symptoms of the mental patient seem to the observer to serve no useful purpose. From the dynamic

---

53. See Carl B. Buxbaum, "Second Thoughts on Community Mental Health," *Social Work*, Vol. 18, No. 3 (May 1973), pp. 24–29, which questions the informa-tion base on which community mental health planning was done; see also Joel Fort, M.D., "The Persecution and Assasination of the Inmates of the Asylum of the United States of America as Performed by the Community Mental Health Move-ment," *Psychiatry and Social Science Review*, Vol. 5, No. 7 (June 26, 1971).

54. For a comprehensive view of Freud and the various schools which followed him or grew up in opposition to him, see Dieter Wyss, M.D. *Psychoanalytic Schools from the Beginning to the Present* (New York: Science House, 1973); and Alfred M. Freedman, M.D. and Harold I. Kaplan, M.D., eds., *Interpreting Personality: A Sur-vey of Twentieth-Century Views* (New York: Atheneum, 1972). Still useful and readable is Ruth Munroe, *Schools of Psycho-Analytic Thought* (New York: Dryden Press, 1955). Reuben Fine, *The Healing of the Mind* (New York: David McKay Company, 1971), presents an eclectic approach in nontechnical language.

viewpoint, the symptoms may be analyzed as desperate attempts on the part of the psyche to maintain some kind of equilibrium. Forcible alterations of the symptom will not solve the problem but will give rise to some new set of symptoms as the organism struggles to deal with inner conflicts. However troublesome the symptoms may be, they are some indication of strength and wish to function. The mechanisms by which the individual attempts to deal with both inner and outer pressures result in behavior, some socially approved and some which deviates from social norms. The brief and highly overgeneralized account of dynamic mechanisms which follows may be useful in illuminating just what it is that social workers in psychiatric settings are attempting to discern in their clients.

Some human behavior is consciously directed, and the reasons for it are obvious, understood by the individual. To a far greater extent than most people admit, however, behavior is motivated wholly or in part by impulses of which the individual is unaware (i.e., unconscious). Not everything of which the individual is unconscious is "bad," but we all have a greater reluctance to become aware of impulses within us which we fear or disapprove. We devote energy to keeping such material out of awareness ("repression"). This energy is deducted from the total available energy which the individual has at his command for effort of any sort. A person who has most of his energy tied up in maintaining repressions becomes "immobilized," that is, unable to perform with any degree of effectiveness.

The human organism has many unconscious mechanisms at the physical level. The processes which keep the heart beating, control circulation, maintain a constant body temperature, and the like are below the threshold of awareness. We know of their existence only when something goes wrong, and the signal of this dysfunctioning is pain. The organism has other unconscious mechanisms which it sets into operation to combat dysfunctioning. Fever, the formation of scar tissue, the lowering of blood pressure after a hemorrhage are mechanisms of defense for the physical organism. As such, these are really signs of health rather than pathological symptoms.

Similarly, the psychic structure of the individual involves unconscious mechanisms. When these do not function properly for whatever reason, the psychic equivalent of physical pain is "anxiety." While the term "fear" properly refers to apprehension about external dangers, anxiety refers to less well-defined apprehensions without any logical basis, often related to internal dangers, such as loss of self-esteem, guilt feelings, or feelings of rage and destructiveness. Such psychic pain is acutely uncomfortable, and it may be accompanied by physical symptoms of panic, such as a pounding heart, shortness of breath, or feelings of faintness. Just as the temperature-regulating mechanism swings into action without our awareness of it, so the psychic mechanisms which defend us from feeling anxiety are often set in operation without our realizing it.[55] While repression is a useful mechanism for some unacceptable impulses and is the only one available to the infant, the process of socialization involves learning to control and modify infantile wishes. If they are completely excluded from consciousness, this learning cannot occur. Repression, therefore, is not an adequate defense mechanism.

The infant is born irresponsible and selfish. In the course of his socialization, he learns that some of his impulses are unacceptable, and he learns to feel guilty and ashamed of these. Where conflicts exist between what he wants to do and what he must do or ought to do, tension is created and anxiety results. It is in the characteristic methods which each individual develops to deal with this anxiety that both normal and neurotic personality traits are formed.

When unacceptable impulses cannot be repressed and insist on coming into awareness, the ego (the coordinating and executive aspect of the psychic structure) makes use of a variety of "mechanisms of defense" against anxiety.[56] Some are healthier than others. Sublimation, or the diversion of impulses into socially acceptable channels, is the most favorably regarded one. Rationalization, or the thinking up of acceptable reasons to justify doing what we want, is successful to a limited degree; it usually deceives others less well than ourselves. In both these mechanisms, tension is released through activity and the anxiety is contained, although rationalization may get a person into social difficulties as a consequence of the behavior so sanctioned.

A related, but less healthy, defensive mechanism against forbidden impulses is "reaction formation." This mechanism operates when a person is so afraid of doing what he basically wants

55. For a discussion of the physical and psychological factors in the "general adaptation syndrome," see Hans Selye, *The Stress of Life* (New York: McGraw-Hill, 1956), and *Stress Without Distress* (Philadelphia: J. B. Lippincott, 1974).

56. These various mechanisms, while defined originally by Sigmund Freud, have been systematically analyzed and presented in their clearest form by Anna Freud in *The Ego and the Mechanisms of Defense* (New York: International Universities Press, 1946).

to do that he overdoes behavior in the opposite direction. He sees to it that everyone, including himself, is prevented from doing what he both fears and longs to do. Examples might be the censor who imputes obscene motives to authors and the fanatic crusader against alcohol. To a less extreme degree, the compulsively clean or orderly or polite person may be thought of as having developed habits which protect him from being as dirty or rude as he would really prefer. The danger in overuse of this mechanism is that the defenses are often as annoying to other people as the behavior which they protect against. Instead of insuring social acceptability for their user, they may get him heartily disliked for officiousness or nagging.

There are numerous other mechanisms of defense which are less healthy and result in unacceptable behavior or the formation of neurotic symptoms. These include "projection," the attributing to others of impulses in oneself, and "conversion," the converting of anxiety into physical symptoms or sensory loss. The former, in psychotic patients, shows up in hallucinations and delusions, while the latter may manifest itself in blindness or paralysis, of sudden origin and differing from similar symptoms brought on by disease or injury.

The classification of mechanisms of defense and their correlation with diagnostic categories of neurotic and psychotic behavior is not the responsibility of the social worker. For our purposes, it is more useful to look at the various ways in which people may express their anxieties and conflicts in their social relationships. Let us therefore consider the various avenues of expression of conflict. These will involve several of the mechanisms of defense, sometimes representing a successful defense (in that the individual remains unaware of the anxiety) and sometimes representing the failure of defense mechanisms to deal adequately with the anxiety.

How Tensions May Be Expressed

When people have a strong wish to act in some socially forbidden way, there are a variety of methods with which they may handle the resultant tension. They may, of course, give in to the impulse and carry out the behavior. Some crimes and other major social maladjustments arise from such self-gratifying behavior. Some people have apparently never developed any alternative to direct expression of aggressive impulses. Social workers, particularly in protective and correctional services, frequently encounter people who need to learn to repress, sublimate, and otherwise develop substitute behavior which is less destructive.[57]

The well-socialized person, through a combination of defenses, should be able to modify, control, and compensate for the forbidden impulse in a way which does not use up too much psychic energy or cause unpleasant repercussions in his social life. He is in all probability not aware of the processes going on. Impulses so handled pass through the mind as fleeting thoughts (Wouldn't it be nice if the college burned down before exams?), to be treated in a casual or humorous way.

Another way of dealing with tension-producing conflicts is to turn them against oneself in the form of a physical illness. These "psycho-physiologic reactions," as they are known technically, may be of all degrees of severity and represent feelings expressed through the various organ systems of the body.[58] Some people have "nervous stomachs"; in moments of stress, they react with indigestion, nausea, or loss of appetite. Others may have asthma, skin allergies, certain types of arthritis, or high blood pressure. It is interesting that the connection between high blood pressure and anger was recognized by the ancient Greeks, who used the word "choleric" to describe both the appearance and the temperament of the hot-tempered person.

The precise relationship among predisposing factors in the physical constitution of the individual, conditioning experiences in early life, and precipitating factors in later life has not been clearly defined and probably differs in individuals. Social workers, both in hospital settings and in family and children's agencies, will encounter many persons with illnesses of primarily emotional origin. Continuing ill health interferes with carrying out responsibilities as breadwinner, homemaker, or student. The problem of identifying and treating such persons calls for collaborative efforts of medicine, psychiatry, and social work.

These psycho-physiologic reactions are often called "psychosomatic illnesses," but the term is a misnomer, since all illness involves both a psyche and a soma and the reciprocal effects of morale and physical health are obvious. There is a tendency for

---

57. See Ronald L. Akers, *Deviant Behavior* (Belmont, Ca.: Wadsworth Publishing Company, 1973), especially pp. 253–284; see also Nicholas N. Kittrie, *The Right to Be Different* (Baltimore: The Johns Hopkins Press, 1971). Behavior modification may be used in some cases to develop acceptable substitute behavior.

58. For a readable account of psycho-physiologic reactions, see Howard R. and Martha E. Lewis, *Psychosomatics: How Your Emotions Can Damage Your Health* (New York: Viking Press, 1972).

many people to be unsympathetic toward psychogenic illness and to imply that such patients do not need treatment and should "snap out of it." If emotional tensions are being expressed in physiologic reactions, the discomfort is real and not in the least imaginary. Physical treatment of the symptoms (diet or surgery for ulcers, medication for allergies) is to be used by all means, but for permanent relief the individual must learn to direct his emotional tensions into other channels. Since he is often unaware that he is using physical illness in this way, the process of developing awareness and new patterns of reacting is a lengthy one.

What are technically termed "secondary gains" may also retard progress. Particularly in our culture, illness constitutes a highly acceptable excuse for avoiding unwanted tasks. It is the best possible alibi for the person who needs one. It allows one to relax and be taken care of without loss of self-esteem. The person who is avoiding emotional discomfort by physical symptoms would (unconsciously) much rather have his symptoms, since they bring him extra attention and consideration and explain his inadequate performance. Such people may become known to medical social workers for their refusal to undertake needed medical treatment, to stay on restricted diets, to take corrective exercises, or to observe proper precautions. The medical social worker obviously would not confront them point-blank with a declaration of what they are trying to accomplish by such self-defeating behavior and would never assume the medical management of the case, but he needs to understand the underlying dynamics to be able to help the patient follow medical directions.

Instead of through physiologic reactions, the individual may express tension in emotional reactions. He may experience feelings of depression, hopelessness, worthlessness, or undue exhilaration. In attempts to prevent or deny such feelings, the individual may engage in behavior which antagonizes or harms other people in his life. The person who is compulsively busy, so that he will not have time to let himself realize how unhappy he feels is an illustration of this; less obvious, perhaps, is a person like Mrs. Bennett (see page 36), who is excessively active in good works of all sorts in a desperate effort to combat feelings of uselessness and worthlessness. These people "use" others in an effort to counteract their inner feelings. Since they are often unaware of the relationships between their activity and their inner discomfort, they cannot understand why the activity does not make them happy, popular, or successful.

Many of the clients of social agencies fall under this heading. The unsuccessful parent who is punishing the child for his own childhood deprivations, the child whose school adjustment is impaired by an unhappy relationship with his parents, and the employee who cannot keep a job because he reacts to his employer as he once reacted to his father are illustrations. The patient unraveling of the tangled web of emotions and relationships is the essence of the diagnostic process, and the ability of the client to perceive and modify some of these unsuccessful patterns is the essence of the treatment process.

So far in this discussion, we have been dealing with people whose functioning in the community is impaired but who are still able to maintain themselves. But, for a variety of reasons, the defensive mechanisms in some people are ineffective, and their patterns of thinking and reacting become noticeably different from those of the group. It is the acceptability of the individual's "definition of the situation"[59] which determines whether he should be classed as "psychotic" or not. While the neurotic person recognizes that he is unhappy or dissatisfied, he is in general agreement with the consensus of the group as to who he is and what is expected of him. The various means of "reality testing" in the psychotic person are lacking. Such a person may claim to be a famous character in history, to possess some magic powers of communication or unlimited financial resources.

The cultural norm and the particular social situation of the individual have a great deal to do with his classification as psychotic. Many of those persecuted or isolated for markedly deviant views in the past have turned out to be pioneers who were too far ahead of their contemporaries. How much deviation can be tolerated depends on the flexibility of the culture and the firmness with which the mores and norms are sanctioned. What would be considered psychotic in one subculture, at one time, for one socio-economic class, might not be so considered elsewhere under other circumstances. The question has been raised as to whether a whole society can become psychotic and whether there are universal standards of mental health and normality apart from specific cultural definitions.[60]

Because differing cultural and personal demands operate with

59. The term is usually attributed to William I. Thomas, *The Unadjusted Girl* (Boston: Little, Brown and Co., 1923). It has been widely adopted to describe the way the individual perceives what he may expect and what is expected of him in any social role.

60. See Erich Fromm, *Escape from Freedom* (New York: Holt, Rinehart and Winston, 1941) and Fromm's *The Sane Society* (New York: Holt, Rinehart and Winston, 1955). See also D. L. Rosenhan, "On Being Sane in Insane Places," *Science*, Vol. 179, No. 4070 (January 19, 1973), pp. 1–9.

varying degrees of severity on individuals, there is no clear-cut line between neurotic people who may be maintained in the community and psychotic people who may not. Many delinquents are neurotic; some law-abiding citizens are psychotic. Social agencies have struggled for years with what are called "borderline" clients, whose maladjustments are severe but who can, with supervision and help, continue to live and work in the community. It is an oversimplification to say that the family agency worker and the social worker in a psychiatric outpatient clinic see the less sick persons and the social worker in the hospital setting sees the sicker ones. What differentiates the caseloads many times is a social definition rather than a clinical one.

THE SOCIAL WORKER IN THE MENTAL HEALTH SETTING

An understanding of the dynamics of human behavior is essential for the social worker in any mental health setting. Not only does it illuminate the behavior of the client, but it helps social workers to understand their own motivations and "hang-ups" and makes it possible for them to be of better service as helping persons.[61]

Child Guidance Clinics

Child guidance clinics have as their primary concern the social and emotional adjustments of children. Their origin was in the treatment of delinquents, and emphasis was laid in the early days on antisocial behavior, with its emotional concomitants of unhappiness, rebelliousness, aggressiveness, and destructiveness. The discovery of the importance of early childhood events for later life, stemming from the Freudian approach to mental illness, was impetus to setting up preventive treatment facilities for children. In the 1920s, the Commonwealth Fund sponsored a series of demonstration child guidance clinics, and by 1968 there were 147 members in the American Association of Psychiatric Clinics for Children, organized in 1946.[62]

However, as the number of community mental health centers has increased, the number of independent child guidance clinics has decreased, and more and more have merged into Family and

61. See Norman A. Polansky, *Ego Psychology and Communication: Theory for the Interview* (New York: Atherton Press, 1971), for a useful discussion of dynamic theory.
62. The Joint Commission on Mental Health of Children details the inadequacy of present clinic facilities for children and adolescents in *Crisis in Child Mental Health: Challenge for the 1970's* (New York: Harper & Row, 1969), especially pp. 266–276.

Children's Services or Community Mental Health Agencies. This has been the experience of the well-known Hartley-Salmon Clinic in Hartford, Connecticut:

> The Hartley-Salmon Child Guidance Clinic was established in 1923 through the efforts of Mrs. Helen Hartley Jenkins, who was interested in mental health projects, and Dr. Thomas Salmon, an outstanding psychiatrist acting as consultant. For a number of years, the Clinic was financed through funds of the Hartley Corporation. When these funds were no longer available, partial support came from the Hartford Board of Education and City Board of Finance and private subscription. Finally in 1933, the Clinic became a member of the Greater Hartford Community Chest. In 1962, it became part of the Child and Family Services of Connecticut.
>
> As one part of the clinical services provided children (which include residential treatment, group homes, specialized foster care, day treatment, and emergency inpatient treatment), the Hartley-Salmon Clinic provides diagnosis and treatment for children (all ages up to eighteen) and their families by clinic teams composed of psychiatrists, psychologists, and social workers. Many kinds of treatment are utilized: individual psychotherapy for the child, marital counseling for the parents, whole-family treatment, group therapy for children and/or parents. In most cases, the duration of treatment is short (sixteen weeks or less). A centralized intake service receives the first call and takes basic information. The intake is assigned as quickly as possible to a staff therapist who sees the child and family for diagnosis and treatment. The usual therapist for both child and family is a social worker, although psychiatrists may treat some children. In 1971, 351 families received diagnostic service and 404 received treatment; some of these 404 cases had been opened the previous year. In addition to direct treatment, the Clinic took part in 168 interagency conferences.[63]

The traditional practice in child guidance clinics for many years was to see child and mother in concurrent treatment, with different therapists. This acknowledged the critical importance of the mother in the early development of the child, but it overlooked the influence of the father and other members of the family on the child's life and also failed to take into account the impact on the rest of the family of treatment of only a part of it. Increasingly,

63. Data supplied by the Hartley-Salmon Child Guidance Clinic of the Child and Family Services of Connecticut, Inc., July 17, 1973.

clinics are involving the whole family in one or another of their treatment-oriented activities.

The staff of a child guidance clinic is headed by a psychiatrist; he supervises and consults with other staff members and sees patients for diagnostic study and treatment. All psychiatrists have the M.D. degree and two to four years additional training; child psychiatrists have had further specialized training. There will be one or more psychologists in the clinic; the Ph.D. and five years of supervised clinical practice are required for accreditation by the national association. Most social workers in a child guidance clinic are MSWs, although clinics are beginning to hire BSWs, who will be supervised by an MSW. The clerical staff and the receptionist are essential for proper functioning of the clinic. While they are not trained professionals, they should observe professional standards on confidentiality, dealing with anxious applicants, and securing accurate information by telephone. In addition to the staff, many clinics will have students from one or more disciplines, who may carry cases under supervision, conduct activity groups, tutor school children, help with clerical work, or serve in the agency library.

Referrals to child guidance clinics were originally made largely from juvenile courts but now come more from parents ("self-referrals"), schools, and pediatricians. The kinds of problems referred may be roughly divided into two types. In the first, the child's behavior seems appropriate to his age level but does not meet the expectations of his parents, which are incompatible with the child's ability or personality. Treatment efforts will be directed toward modifying parental attitudes. In the second, the child is reacting to inner and outer pressure by behavior which is inappropriate to his age or situation.

The Schenectady Child Guidance Center

The work of a small, independent clinic may be shown by a description of the Schenectady Child Guidance Center, established in 1957. In addition to diagnostic, treatment, and consultation services, the Center carries on research on diagnosis and treatment of children and serves as a training center for psychiatrists-in-training, psychologists, social workers, nurses, and medical students. In 1972, a staff of two psychiatrists, three social workers, three psychologists, and several trainees conducted 3,187 diagnostic and treatment sessions and was actively involved in the lives of 1,869 families. The Center provided 1,167 consultations to schools, Family Court, Probation, Child Welfare and Community Action agencies.

In addition to concurrent treatment of parents and child, the Center has inaugurated a series of Child Management Classes, which are set up for a specified number of weeks, use a textbook with assigned readings, and are oriented toward behavior modification. The Center has noticed some trends in the referrals coming to them. Children are being referred at a younger age and are more likely to be hyperkinetic, presenting not only behavioral and relationship problems but serious learning difficulties owing to inattentiveness and short attention span.[64] Many of them respond well to medication; they are seen periodically by the psychiatrist and maintain frequent telephone contact with the social work staff. The Center also reports a much larger number of parents and youngsters who are not neurotically disturbed, not introspective or sophisticated, and not interested in lengthy "talking out" sessions. Instead, they are likely to be dependent, deprived, much less well educated people, with a diagnosis of character disorder.[65] Work with these clients is less in the direction of developing awareness of their own unconscious motivations and more directive, of shorter duration, and focused on current functioning.

The usual procedure is for applicants to see the social worker first, and then the psychologist or psychiatrist sees the child. Instead of having parents return for several visits, the diagnostic procedure may be done in a half-day. Diagnostic evaluation is the result of a staff conference; the parents are considered active participants and not passive recipients of the Center's decision. Treatment is recommended for about half the cases evaluated. Alternatives to treatment include referral to other agencies, medication, suggestions for modified handling of the child, recommendations for remedial tutoring (the Center is carrying on an experimental program in training volunteers to tutor children with perceptual handicaps), or reassurance that the parents are handling the problem competently. Treatment, if recommended, may be for child and parents, for parents alone, for child alone, for

64. See W. G. Conrad, Ph.D.; E. S. Dworkin, Ph.D.; A. Shai, Ph.D.; J. E. Tobiessen, Ed.D., "Effects of Amphetamine Therapy and Prescriptive Tutoring on the Behavior and Achievements of Lower Class Hyperactive Children," *Journal of Learning Disabilities*, Vol. 4, No. 9, (November 1971), pp. 509–518.

65. See Rosalind M. Sands and Arthur K. Young, "The Retooling of a Child Guidance Center: Change and Champion for the Tasks of the Seventies," *American Journal of Orthopsychiatry*, Vol. 43, No. 1 (January 1973), pp. 65–71.

any of these in combination with group therapy for other members of the family.

The Center is flexible in arranging which staff members carry a case. Assignments are made partly on the basis of staff schedules and partly on the basis of family needs. If more than one therapist is involved, there will be periodic conferences to assess progress. As with most other clinics, the Center is moving toward limiting the number of treatment sessions. The family is free to return if progress is not maintained, and many patients do keep in touch by telephone. The expansion of consultation services to schools and courts is considered a more productive use of staff time than concentrating exclusively on treatment. This results in improved handling of children by teachers and court workers and also in earlier referral, which is good preventive mental health care.[66]

The Case of Tony Russo

The role of the social worker in a child guidance center is illustrated in the case of Tony Russo. In general, children may be said to have the same avenues for expressing tension as do adults. They may turn them out against the world in the form of angry, acting-out behavior; they may turn them in against themselves in the form of unhappiness and guilt; or they may express them by some psycho-physiologic reactions, as Tony did. "Talking out" their tensions is more difficult for children than for adults. Part of the evaluation process is learning how the child feels about his situation. Asking him directly is of little use, since he cannot put it into words. The use of symbolic language, through play, story-telling, painting, or modeling, will indicate more clearly what is going on in the child's mind than would cross-questioning.[67]

> On 1/5/71, a telephone call was received from Dr. Boyd, local pediatrician, referring eleven-year-old Tony because of symptoms of skin allergies, itching, dizziness, headaches, and extreme fear of illness and death, which made it almost impossible for Tony to leave his mother and go to school. According to Dr. Boyd, mother had always been overprotective of Tony, but the situation had been acute since father's

66. Data on the Center were adapted from material supplied by the Schenectady County Child Guidance Center. Used with permission.

67. For an excellent description of play therapy and other treatment means, see David Maclay, M.D., *Treatment for Children: The Work of a Child Guidance Clinic* (New York: Science House, 1971). See also the discussion in this text, on pages 195–197.

sudden death last summer. The usual request was made that mother call for an appointment, which she did later the same day.

On 1/8/71, Mrs. Russo came for her first appointment with the social worker. She was an attractive well-groomed Italian woman in her early forties, who talked freely and wept as she told of her husband's death and Tony's reaction to it. Mr. Russo had died without any warning. Tony was present, as were a great many paternal relatives, and witnessed the highly dramatic scene in the home and subsequently at the wake and the funeral. Mother felt that Tony had always been easily upset but that his serious skin irritation and inability to go to sleep at night had occurred since father's death. With some helpful questions from the caseworker, mother began to see how extremely upsetting father's death had been to Tony. In addition to the loss of his father, Tony had lost his much-loved dog less than a week later. He had overheard a good deal about the reduced financial circumstances and was worrying about how they would manage on Social Security. Another difficulty arose when Tony's bed, which was a borrowed one, had to be returned. Tony was therefore sleeping in his mother's bed until a new one could be purchased for him. The worker was definite in her advice that this be done immediately.

Mother was able to see that she had pushed Tony aside in her first shock and bewilderment and had not even recognized his needs. Some of his symptoms, she acknowledged now, were related to his need to stay close to her. During the summer vacation they had not been too troublesome, but it was after school started in September that they became so severe. Tony had been seen by dermatologists, who found no physical basis and told him he was a big boy now and should act like one. This had only made him mad. Mother thought one reason it did no good to tell Tony there was nothing wrong with him was that so far as anyone knew, there had been nothing wrong with Mr. Russo.

Mrs. Russo seemed much relieved at unburdening herself to the social worker, who thought that she had had very little opportunity in her family situation for such interested and uninterrupted listening. From what mother said throughout the interview, it seemed that she had been the recipient of much well-intentioned but contradictory advice and criticism from her own relatives as well as her in-laws. Appointments were arranged for her to return with Tony, and some suggestions were made for explaining the procedure to him.

On 1/12/71, Tony was seen by the psychiatrist, who found him quite reluctant to talk about his feelings, preferring the safer ground of his symptoms. They were clearly related to having to leave his mother and go to school and did not occur afternoons or weekends. The psychiatrist reassured Tony very positively that his symptoms would pass and did not indicate any serious organic illness. The psychiatrist concluded his interview notes by saying: "He did describe terrific histrionic and highly dramatic scenes in the household of his family, grandparents, aunts and uncles, and friends in the days following his father's death in a way which gave one an impression that he had shown very little outward manifestation of having been deeply affected by it, so that my impression is very strongly that a good deal of his somatic complaints represents an unresolved grief reaction greatly intensified by his mother's anxiety about herself and about him and his mother's seeming belief in the possibility that he has an organic condition which could take him away as suddenly as one killed her husband."

If psychological tests had seemed indicated, they would have been arranged for Tony at this point. However, there was no question of school adjustment; Tony had not missed enough school to affect his very good academic work. The diagnostic picture did not seem to require the additional information to be derived from projective tests. The psychiatrist felt that two or three further interviews might be enough to relieve some of Tony's symptoms.

In the meantime, Mrs. Russo had been telling the caseworker about Tony's early life. She had been told she could probably never have any children and had had a series of miscarriages before Tony's birth. Her pregnancy was complicated, and she was extremely solicitous about him when he was a baby. His birth and progress were normal, and he walked and talked early. Some of her ambivalence about her late husband was expressed, particularly in relation to his continued dependence on his mother and her interference in their lives. Tony's mother had refused to wear deep mourning for a full year, as paternal grandmother thought she should. She was also beginning to go out socially and take some part in neighborhood activities again but wondered if she should stay at home and devote all her time to Tony, who resented her other interests. The caseworker told her that she had a right to some life of her own and that whatever helped her to be less tense and more satisfied would, in the long run, benefit Tony.

Mrs. Russo came to the Center alone on January 22. She seemed restless and found it hard to stay on one subject. She said Tony had been anxious and upset, and his inability to go to sleep because of his scratching had been particularly trying.

She had been embarrassed and reluctant to talk when he asked for some sexual information. Tony had refused to keep any more appointments at the Center, claiming it would not help him, and the worker pointed out that Mrs. Russo might be feeling the same way but that she really needed to talk about her bottled up feelings, even if she did not want to. In this interview, mother indicated that she was aware of her own overprotectiveness when she asked the worker if she should pay any attention when Tony told her to go away and leave him alone when she was fussing over him.

On the 29th, there was a crisis. Tony flatly refused to go to school, claiming he was too dizzy and was standing by the telephone contradicting everything his mother was saying to the caseworker. The worker pointed out that letting him stay home would not solve anything and told Mrs. Russo she could telephone again after she had got him to school. She did call back later, saying that she had not been able to get him to go, but that his grandmother had been able to persuade him to go. It later developed that his feelings had been hurt, because he had not been selected for an all-star basketball team. Mother had taken him to school and been touched by the warm reception given him by the school nurse and his teacher.

On February 2, both Tony and his mother came to the Center for interviews with the psychiatrist and social worker. Tony came reluctantly and much preferred discussing a museum trip his class had taken to talking of his feelings or the situation at home. He felt some resentment for the Center for backing up his mother in making him go to school. He said he did not want to continue to come and gave the impression that he felt the Center was not on his side. The psychiatrist was able to convey some reassurance by telling him that "usually kids who had this difficulty found it worse on Monday than on any other day in the week and that if they had a week's vacation it was always more difficult going back to school." Tony's response was prompt: "Boy, is that right! If you really want to know when I was terrible, it was right after the summer vacation."

During the same hour, Mrs. Russo told her caseworker of indications of improvement in Tony and of the success she had had when she followed the caseworker's suggestions (although in some cases, mother attributed suggestions to the worker which had not been made by her). The greater part of the hour was taken up with mother's account of her relationship with paternal grandmother, who interfered with the marriage from the very beginning. Mr. Russo had been dominated by his mother, had given in to her requests, and until a few years ago had sided with his mother against his wife. Mr. Russo had also resembled his mother and the rest of his family in being very fearful of injury and pain. Mrs. Russo seemed to be increasingly aware of how much Tony was copying his father in his concern for his health.

The following week, Mrs. Russo was enthusiastic in reporting how well Tony had been all week, going to school without any complaint and going right to sleep at bedtime. She spent part of the hour talking about plans for herself, including the possibility of taking a refresher course in typing or going to a school of hairdressing. At the same time, Tony was resisting the psychiatrist's efforts to involve him in a discussion of his feelings about his father but was indirectly treating him like a father, telling him of his activities and asking if they could make model planes together.

On February 16, mother was continuing to find Tony improved in every way. The social worker told her that Tony would not be seen again, that a conference was being planned to discuss future appointments for her, and that it seemed apparent that she would not need to come in for more than a few more weeks. In spite of the fact that this decision seems warranted by the improvement in the problem, clients who are finding the casework relationship rewarding are likely to regard any talk of terminating as a rebuff. We might expect, therefore, that Mrs. Russo, who had been having a new and satisfying experience in her weekly interviews, would resist having them end.

When she came in on the 23rd, Mrs. Russo was depressed, cried, told of feeling rejected and not helped. Tony had told her the Center had only made him worse. The caseworker let her get rid of a lot of negative feelings without criticizing or arguing with her, and at the end of the hour Mrs. Russo was saying that, unlike the paternal grandmother, the worker always understood her.

On March 1, the psychiatrist and social worker held a diagnostic conference to assess the situation and plan for the future. It was felt that there had been noticeable improvement in Tony. The recommendation was made that mother be continued in supportive casework with the social worker, "to give her the necessary strength to allow her to separate more from Tony and to make plans for an independent life of her own as well as to help her work through her grief reaction. The boy will be placed on the waiting list with the plan to re-evaluate him when his name comes up to be transferred to the treatment list. It is likely by that time that he will have achieved considerable independence and that with this his multiple phobic and somatization reactions will have either largely diminished or disappeared."

On March 3, Mrs. Russo participated in the postdiagnostic

conference and accepted the suggested plan of weekly interviews for herself and reconsideration of Tony when there was
an opening on the treatment list. She was reassured that her
feelings of grief and loneliness were normal and encouraged
to allow Tony more independence and to be more independent herself.

In the next six weeks, Mrs. Russo saw her caseworker four
times. While there were periods of discouragement, especially when Tony lost his temper at her, Mrs. Russo came
increasingly to see her own panicky reaction to his demands
for attention. As she began to be more active socially and to
consider employment possibilities, she used the interview
time more and more for discussion of her own needs and
feelings. She reported Tony's growing independence with a
mixture of pride and sadness that he did not need her so
much. By the middle of April, Mrs. Russo decided she would
not continue to come in regularly but was pleased to know
she could call for an appointment if she wanted to.

Nothing further was heard from Mrs. Russo, and in October the worker telephoned her to say there was an opportunity for Tony to start treatment if it seemed indicated.
Mother reported a good summer but some recurrence of
Tony's itching and temper when school started. He found
junior high quite different from his former school. There
seemed no urgent need for treatment, and it was left that
Mrs. Russo would call the Center after the first of the year to
report on how things were going.

On January 18, 1972, just about a year from her first call,
Mrs. Russo telephoned to say that Tony was doing beautifully in school, active in extra-curricular activities, being
much less demanding and practically free of itching and diz-
ziness. She herself was still often discouraged and found the
future unpromising but was keeping up some social activity,
brushing up on her typing at home, and contemplating a
part-time job.[68]

The case of Tony Russo is atypical in some respects. Few cases
have so dramatic a precipitating factor as the sudden death of the
father. Tony's rebellion might have taken the form of acting out
against the world in delinquency or truancy. He might have been
seriously depressed by his father's death instead of developing
physical symptoms. Most child guidance cases have both parents
available and treatment aims at including both in the modifications and increased understanding which are desired. Not all

---

68. Data on the case of Tony Russo were adapted from material supplied by the
Schenectady County Child Guidance Center. Used with permission.

mothers are as quick to see their own involvement in their children's problems as was Mrs. Russo; many parents deny that there is any need for them to change and insist that all the changing be done by the child.

Tony's case illustrates well the necessity of working with the parent-child relationship in the context of their daily living. It also shows that substantial modification can be achieved relatively quickly in some situations. Tony had three interviews, while his mother had eleven. His rather quick response was undoubtedly due more to the changes in his mother's attitudes than to his own treatment, since he resisted discussing his feelings with the psychiatrist. We should not minimize, however, the importance of the doctor's acceptance of Tony's symptoms as troublesome and his understanding of the panic Tony felt about sudden death. Tony had been scolded, told to act like a man, and given medication which did not help by the various medical doctors to whom his mother had taken him. The psychiatrist accepted his feelings, talked about them indirectly when Tony could not bring himself to discuss them openly, and provided a welcome contrast to the excitement with which Tony's behavior was discussed by his mother and other relatives.

Mrs. Russo also had a new and corrective experience with someone who was calm and accepting, who was interested in her feelings, and who gave her credit for the difficult adjustment she was having to make. In addition, the social worker pointed out ways in which Mrs. Russo was succeeding and times when she was defeating her own purposes. No fundamental changes were made in Mrs. Russo, but the support that she was given enabled her to modify her handling of Tony enough to effect a change in his behavior and relieve his symptoms. We cannot predict that all will go well; it is doubtful that Mrs. Russo will be able to accept with equanimity the emancipation struggles of an adolescent. She shies away from the whole area of sex but cannot postpone much longer the recognition that Tony is maturing. Although Mrs. Russo maintains that her whole life is centered in Tony and that she could never think of another man, the possibility of remarriage cannot be discounted and raises questions about Tony's reaction to being displaced by an outsider.

Too easily, in reading of the dramatically successful cases reported by clinics and social agencies, one gets the impression that problems are often permanently solved and that most clients "live happily ever after." In most cases, as in this one, improvement is neither spectacular nor guaranteed. Tony and his mother understand each other a little better, but she is still overprotective and dependent on him. She still identifies him with his father and feels toward Tony some of the ambivalence that characterized her relationship with her husband. Tony knows that physical symptoms are the most effective way to control his mother and no doubt still harbors deep resentment at having been pushed aside at the time of his father's death. But the physical symptoms have subsided, his school successes are real and rewarding, and Mrs. Russo is learning to take some pride in her ability to allow Tony more independence.

Both Tony and his mother know that they have allies in the Center. Even though Tony protested his unwillingness to keep his appointments, they were gratifying to him. Mrs. Russo, from the very beginning, was able to express the gratitude and relief she felt. She knows that if things get worse she can return to a place where people have confidence in her ability to manage. And since success tends to be self-perpetuating, the measure of success she has already achieved will give her confidence as she goes along.

Community Mental Health Centers

In an effort to utilize the time of their professional staff to best advantage and to extend their services to more people, mental health centers have inaugurated a variety of programs in addition to the more traditional types of psychotherapy found in the literature. Short-term treatment[69] is more likely to be used than extended psychotherapy without a time limit. Emergency services include a twenty-four–hour telephone service, which may result in seeing the caller immediately, referring the caller to the emergency room of a hospital, or alerting a responsible person nearby if the caller is too far away or unable to travel. Such "hot lines" are often referred to as suicide prevention services[70] but may be

69. See Elizabeth Kerns, "Planned Short-Term Treatment, A New Service to Adolescents," *Social Casework*, Vol. 51, No. 6 (June 1970), pp. 340–346. See also Howard J. Parad and Libbie G. Parad, "A Study of Crisis-Oriented and Planned Short-Term Treatment," *Social Casework*, Vol. 49, No. 6 (June 1968), pp. 346–355 and Vol. 49, No. 7 (July 1968), pp. 418–426, for an explanation of PSST (planned short-term treatment). See James Mann, *Time-Limited Psychotherapy* (Cambridge: Harvard University Press, 1973), which suggests a limit of twelve sessions as optimal.

70. See Elaine S. Feiden, "One Year's Experience with a Suicide Prevention Service," *Social Work*, Vol. 15, No. 3 (July 1970), pp. 26–32. The experience of one suicide prevention clinic was shown in the 1965 Paramount production, "A Slender Thread," later adapted by Stirling Silliphant in a book, *The Slender Thread* (New York: New American Library, 1966). See also S. M. Heilig and David J. Klugman, "The Social Worker in a Suicide Prevention Center," *Social Work Practice, 1963* (New York: Columbia University Press, 1963).

used by callers with panic attacks or by families concerned about sudden uncontrollable behavior by a member of the household. Drop-in clinics offer immediate crisis intervention to patients who cannot wait for scheduled appointments. Group treatment may be offered to families or individuals who share emotional problems or who are receiving medication to control symptoms. Activities groups of all sorts may be conducted for former inpatients who are readjusting to community life or in an effort to stabilize persons in the community and avoid hospitalization. These may take place in a day hospital on the premises of the mental health center or in schools, churches, or community meeting rooms. As do child guidance clinics, community mental health center consultation services to other community agencies and schools, clergy, physicians, and law enforcement officers enlarge their knowledge of mental health principles and extend preventive services.

The Staff

The team approach to treatment is generally accepted; all disciplines interview and treat patients, but certain tasks are more likely to be assigned to one discipline than another. In addition to direct treatment, which in many clinics is the social workers' major task, social workers are likely to take social histories, interview relatives, and serve as liaison with community agencies. It is essential that each discipline be secure in its own competence and not feel threatened by the legitimate activities of any other group. The Henry study[71] suggests that in comparison with other mental health professionals, social workers are more interested in helping others, have the most liberal political outlook, are least concerned about professional status, but are also least motivated by intellectual interests. This seems to confirm some of the findings of a 1957 study,[72] which reported that social workers felt relatively secure in their roles. With the concerted aim of the best possible service to patients, there is no room for competitiveness and vested interests.

Time studies of the activity of clinic staffs indicate that social workers are taking increasing responsibility for administrative duties. Since mental health centers serve as training sites for trainees, social work staff time will be needed for supervision and for liaison with programs of social work education at baccalaureate

71. See William E. Henry, *The Fifth Profession* (San Francisco: Jossey-Bass, 1971), for a discussion of the past and future of social work in the mental health team.

72. See Alvin F. Zander, Arthur R. Cohen, and Ezra Stotland, *Role Relations in the Mental Health Professions* (Ann Arbor: University of Michigan Press, 1957).

and graduate levels. Social workers may also be supervising and coordinating the work of volunteers.

Clinics are utilizing a larger number of nonprofessionals to enlarge their service capacities. William Waters suggests that the professional team (psychiatrist, psychologist, and social worker) must assume responsibility for decision-making, consultation, and supervision but that nonprofessionals may serve as professional assistants to and be supervised by each member of the team.[73] Thus, the psychiatrist would supervise psychiatric interviewers and psychodynamic therapists; the psychologist would supervise psychometric specialists and behavior modification specialists; and the social worker would supervise family interviewers and family therapists. The training programs for these assistants should be developed, according to Waters, by the relevant national professional organization.

The Patients

Patients coming to mental health centers range from the mildly unhappy to the seriously disturbed. The initial interview at the center is likely to be with a social worker. In addition to factual data on family, employment, health, education, previous clinical experience, the interviewer will attempt to evaluate the patient's capacity to form a relationship, to see his situation realistically, and to modify his attitudes. How he uses the defense mechanisms described earlier (pages 317–320) will be of interest in showing how long-standing his patterns of behavior may be. If there has been a sudden change in behavior or mood, the worker will ask gently about any changes in the patient's life condition at the same time or just previously. Social workers should be familiar with the major classifications of mental illness and are usually encouraged to write up a diagnostic impression, in which they sum up the patient's social situation, the apparent emotional problems, and an estimate of his capacity to change.

"Transient situational disorders" occur in individuals with no apparent underlying mental illness, as a reaction to overwhelming stress. Such situations can be helped by the methods of crisis intervention and are usually self-limiting. The neuroses are characterized by excessive anxiety and tension without obvious cause. However handicapped neurotics may be by exaggerated fears, compulsions, persistent fatigue, or depression and lack of self-

---

73. William F. Waters, "Non-Professional Manpower in Mental Health: A Paradigm," *Journal of Operational Psychiatry*, Vol. 2, Nos. 2–3 (Spring–Summer 1971), pp. 53–56.

confidence, they are in touch with reality and know that they are disturbed. Most of them continue to function in their jobs and social life, but with a loss of effectiveness and enjoyment. When there are severe distortions of reality, delusions or hallucinations, bizarre behavior, or extreme withdrawal from involvement with others, a diagnosis of psychotic disorder is likely. Affective psychoses are those involving severe disturbances of mood, either wild exhilaration or extreme depression, which so dominate the mental life of the patient that he loses contact with his environment. Schizophrenia includes a group of subtypes of which the common thread is disturbances of thought and impaired reality testing.

There are people whose disturbed mental processes are expressed through deeply ingrained patterns of deviant behavior and who do not show the unhappiness and guilt characteristic of most psychotics and neurotics. They are likely to be involved in antisocial behavior which arouses in them no guilt, and they do not seem to learn from unsuccessful experience. The "sociopath" who poses such management problems in prison, the "paranoid personality" who blames everyone but himself for his misfortunes, and the "schizoid personality" who can never form close relationships with anyone because they are too threatening are all illustrative of "character disorders."[74]

The following vignettes give some idea of the variety of patients which might be seen by a social worker in a mental health clinic.

> Mrs. Stock, a middle-aged, divorced woman, was referred to the clinic by children's court. Neighbors complained about her children, and the Society for the Prevention of Cruelty to Children visited and found the home in an "unbelievable" condition of filth and disorder. Petition was filed to remove the children, and the court was so puzzled by Mrs. Stock's dazed manner that it continued the case and requested psychiatric evaluation. A diagnosis of "inadequate personality" was made, together with a treatment plan of supportive casework to see if she could be helped to function more adequately as a mother. In the course of a year, Mrs. Stock was able to relax a little, discuss her feelings more directly, and form a warm relationship with her social worker. The latter was able to secure an increase in her AFDC grant and help the patient with reality problems about housing and furniture. In spite of her indifferent manner, Mrs. Stock had warm

---

74. For a clearly written classification of mental disorders, see Armando Favazza, B. Favazza, and Philip Margolis, *Guide for Mental Health Workers* (Ann Arbor: University of Michigan Press, 1970).

feelings for the children and they for her. The case was continued on recommendation of the clinic, since it was felt that
removal of the children would jeopardize mother's precarious
adjustment. Psychiatric reevaluation of Mrs. Stock resulted in
a new diagnosis of schizophrenic reaction, chronic undifferentiated.

Mr. Gorman, a promising young executive, was persuaded
by his wife to come to the clinic after he had undergone a
pronounced personality change. He was moody, irritable,
and restless, and this behavior was endangering his career in
a rapidly expanding company. Exploration and planned
short-term treatment illuminated for Mr. Gorman his feeling
that by accepting an offered promotion he would be competing with his father toward whom he had hostility and
many childish fears.

Mr. Ives, a young man with two small children, was referred to the clinic for evaluation and differential diagnosis.
Of extremely limited mentality, Mr. Ives had difficulty in
communicating with the welfare department worker, who
was not clear on how much factual basis there was for his
complaints of persecution and discrimination in employment
and housing. Psychological tests indicated that Mr. Ives was
in the middle moron range and needed protected living and
job arrangements. The social worker, through extensive use of
local and state resources, was able to make suggestions to
Mr. Ives for improving his situation. The welfare department
was reassured that he was not dangerous, and his worker
there assumed responsibility for taking the initiative in securing new housing, an AFDC grant, and other services.

Miss Clark, a college student with a good academic record, was referred to the clinic by one of her professors, who
had become concerned about incompleted work. Miss Clark
was in the grip of a paralyzing indecision which was gradually extending itself to all areas of her life. She would spend
hours deciding which paper to write first or which examination to study for first, to the point where she was unable to
write or study at all. Every occasion, academic or social,
brought on almost endless debates with herself and her exasperated roommates. Her academic work, formerly good,
was suffering, and her graduation was endangered. Her intake interview showed a girl in the midst of unresolved conflicts about her independence from her parents, who had
sacrificed to send her to college and were pressing her to take
a job. As she came to understand mixed feelings about independence and a childish longing to continue as the little

girl whose parents took care of her, she was able to mobilize her good intelligence and plan her work more effectively.

Mr. Quinn, a chronic alcoholic, was referred to the clinic by his employer, who said he would otherwise have to discharge Mr. Quinn, as he missed so much time from work. An ingratiating and attractive man, Mr. Quinn overwhelmed the intake worker with a barrage of intellectual explanations for his alcoholism, gleaned from wide reading in psychiatric literature. In spite of frequent past attempts to stop drinking, Mr. Quinn assured the worker that *"this* time is different." Married to a woman older than himself, who cared for him devotedly but more as a mother than a wife, Mr. Quinn had had numerous shallow affairs with other women, none of which gave him any real satisfaction. He seemed to have no real insight into himself, giving an impression of rueful amusement and almost pride, as he described some of his drunken exploits. Because of his lack of motivation to undertake any real change in his personality, Mr. Quinn was not considered a suitable candidate for treatment. He accepted this decision without any noticeable disappointment.

When a drug education program was inaugurated at Harboro High School, the local mental health center assigned one of its social workers to the program, hoping an "outsider" might seem more approachable to students than academic personnel. After one of Miss North's appearances, Luke, a sixteen-year-old sophomore, dropped into her office for a chat about his drug use, past and current. He was not asking for help, but he seemed to enjoy the contact with Miss North. He described his experimentation with a wide range of drugs and reported that he had never had a "bad trip." Soon after, on his seventeenth birthday, Luke dropped out of school, in which he was not doing well academically, to enlist in the Navy.

The next September, Luke arrived at Miss North's office in a panic. The Navy had turned him down, and he had decided to try returning to school. Three weeks before (five months since his last use of LSD), he had begun to experience terrifying flashbacks. These included visual hallucinations, especially in math class when he tried to concentrate on symbols. Miss North took him at once to the mental health center psychiatrist, who prescribed a fairly powerful tranquilizer. The doctor and Miss North agreed that treatment should focus on Luke's feelings of anxiety about returning to school and seek to reduce the anxiety enough to permit him to continue his studies. Miss North met with Luke twice a week for four weeks, by which time he was able to continue on his own, with a standing invitation to return if he felt the need.

Even before he entered high school, Luke had had a reputation as a troublemaker, long-haired nonconformist, and underachiever. An only child, he could not even remember the father who had deserted years before, and his mother was distracted by her own problems. Returning to school was threatening to Luke; the flashbacks were a learned response to his anxiety and a wish to escape. Though his adjustment to school remained marginal, he managed to continue to graduation. Two and a half years after his last talk with Miss North, they met on the street. Luke had been accepted by the Navy, was no longer using drugs, and had not had further flashbacks.

Mrs. King, described by her husband as usually vivacious and busy, had grown apathetic and depressed following the marriage of her youngest child. She refused to continue managing the household finances but was dissatisfied with her husband's management. She complained of aches and pains, sleep disturbances, and feeling unappreciated. She was seen weekly for four weeks by the psychiatrist, who prescribed antidepressant medication, and seen twice a week for eight months by the social worker. During the acute stage of the depression, casework was supportive and encouraging. Later, treatment focused on her lifelong feelings of being exploited and unloved, and she was able to see how she was precipitating and exaggerating rejection.

It is discouraging but essential to remind ourselves that not all emotional problems are capable of solution. There are some people who cannot be maintained in the community, no matter how extensive the resources for mental health. They need the protected twenty-four–hour environment of the hospital. Even the best therapeutic efforts will not succeed in returning every patient to the community. But a properly staffed mental health center, supported by adequate resources in the community, can enable many emotionally handicapped people to remain at home or to return home after a short hospital stay. One important function of the mental health center is its aftercare program.

Most aftercare programs rely on group activities, typically in a day care center.[75] Patients in aftercare may be receiving medication, for which they will be checked at monthly intervals by a

75. For a good description of an aftercare program in west Philadelphia, see Pascal Scoles and Eric W. Fine, "Aftercare and Rehabilitation in a Community Mental Health Center," *Social Work*, Vol. 16, No. 3 (July 1971), pp. 75–82.

psychiatrist, and may be receiving some psychotherapy as individuals or in groups. In addition to psychotherapy, social workers are likely to be involved with such concrete helping tasks as assistance with locating housing, facilitating contacts with the welfare department, and helping the family with necessary readjustments. In view of the critical importance of the family to the chronic mental patient, the use of family service agencies to work with total families and to view aftercare as a service to "clients" and their families rather than to "patients" is a positive approach.[76]

Unlike a day hospital in a mental health center, family service aftercare includes home visits, recreational activities for whole families, and services to children who are being affected by the mental illness of a parent. Since many discharged hospital patients are unable to work and are carried by public welfare departments under the Aid to the Disabled program, aftercare programs can profitably be sponsored by public assistance departments.[77] Sheltered workshops are also a valuable resource in aftercare,[78] since they provide opportunities for paid employment under protected working conditions for individuals with various handicaps, who would not be able to compete in an open job market.

Inpatient Facilities

The provision of intensive psychiatric care in general hospitals is a relatively new development and a beneficial one in reducing the separation from family and social ties in the community. Many patients are able to go directly home from such an emergency service. Where longer-term treatment is indicated or where such facilities are lacking, admission to a state hospital is usual. Such admissions may be voluntary or may be ordered by a court under a commitment procedure. Mention has already been made of the recent interest in the civil rights of such committed patients and the necessity for legislation to protect them.

Ideally, social work service begins at admission and involves interpretation to the family, assistance with problems arising from

76. See Anne C. David, "Effective Low Cost Aftercare," *Mental Hygiene*, Vol. 55, No. 3, (July 1971), pp. 351–357; see also Thais Fisher, Nathan S. Nackman, and Ashutosh Vyas, "Aftercare Services in a Family Agency," *Social Casework*, Vol. 54, No. 3 (March 1973), pp. 131–141.

77. For an illustration of such a program, see Alice L. O'Connor, "A Creative Living Center for the Mentally Ill," *Social Casework*, Vol. 51, No. 9 (November 1970), pp. 544–550.

78. See Celia Benney et al., "Facilitating Functioning of Mentally Ill Young Adults," *Social Casework*, Vol. 52, No. 7 (July 1971), pp. 420–431, for an account of a program at Altro Health and Rehabilitation Services in New York City.

the patient's admission, explanation to the family of hospital policies and treatment procedures, and the establishment of a relationship with the family which will facilitate the patient's ultimate
return to it. The skills of the social worker in history-taking will
prove to be especially useful, as data on the patient's present and
past social functioning are secured.

The social worker can assist the patient at reception by presenting himself as the link between the patient and family and assisting with some of the personal problems resulting from admission.
The location of the patient's sister and arrangement for storage of
furniture and clothing were critical factors in the help a social
worker was able to give Nettie, in one of the illustrative cases
presented below. Hospitals vary in the amount of participation in treatment which is assigned to the social worker. Some
hospitals involve the social worker directly with the patient; in
others, work is mainly with family[79] and with discharge planning.
The assessment of the readiness of the patient's family to receive
him at home will be an important factor in determining his discharge, and some hospital social workers are finding new value
in an underused task—that of the home visit. Some families are
all too happy to transfer their responsibilities to the hospital and
are reluctant to resume them. They must be helped to realize that
the hospital's responsibility is a temporary one, that of providing
specialized care, not a dumping ground.

Illustrative Cases

The following case summaries illustrate a variety but by no
means all of the ways in which the social service department can
be helpful in furthering the improved adjustment of patients in a
state mental hospital. The therapeutic effect of the social worker's
concern for their well-being was apparent to these patients, even
when the service rendered was a minor one. Understanding the
purposes behind hostile or rejecting behavior made it possible for
the staff to offer patients used to being rejected the new experience of being accepted.

The specific Social Work Department whose functions are illustrated by the case summaries which follow is an integral part
of a modern dynamic state hospital in south Florida. The hospital
is located in a rapidly expanding metropolitan area, where the

---

79. See Helen M. Bergen and Anton O. Kris, "Services to Parents of Adolescent
Mental Patients," *Social Casework*, Vol. 53, No. 2 (February 1972), pp. 85–90, for a
well-written account of involving parents in their adolescent children's treatment,
with case illustrations.

population explosion has far exceeded the growth of social services, both public and private. Because so many individuals are drawn to the "land of sunshine," the hospital's caseload includes an unusual number of disturbed people who have left their family ties behind. Although there has been an increase in psychiatric clinics and community receiving facilities, the community resources are still too few.

The hospital has a population of approximately 1,400 and accepts patients from twelve years up. The total staff numbers 1,050 and besides administrative personnel, includes psychiatrists, nurses and psychiatric aides, psychiatric social workers, clinical psychologists, employment evaluators, recreational, occupational, and industrial therapists, a school faculty, a librarian, and dietary, housekeeping, and maintenance personnel. The hospital offers a complete diagnostic and treatment program for patients and is a training center for students in the various disciplines.

Patient self-government on the wards, a night hospital program, and short passes to the community encourage responsibility and a prompt return to the community. The State Divisions of Family Services and Vocational Rehabilitation have units in the hospital, which facilitates referrals for their services. Efforts are made to enlist civic and service organizations in providing recreational and employment opportunities for patients. Referrals to alcohol and drug abuse programs in the community and to Recovery, Inc. help patients with readjustment to the community. The social work staff is actively involved in all aspects of the patient's treatment, from admission, through hospitalization, to release planning and aftercare. The cases which follow illustrate various phases of the activities of the Social Work Department.[80]

> Nettie Turner was referred to social service by the psychiatrist who admitted her. She was alone, with no family, and refused to give information. She was apparently six months pregnant, hostile, and uncooperative. When she spoke, it was to express her hatred of doctors and her plans for revenge. The admitting diagnosis was schizophrenic reaction, paranoid type with delusional trends.
>
> The social worker's comments follow: "At my first interview with Nettie, a few days after she entered our hospital, her attitude was one of hostility toward all doctors and every-

---

80. The previous description and following case illustrations have been adapted for teaching purposes from material supplied by the Social Work Department of the South Florida State Hospital. All names and identifying information have been altered to preserve confidentiality. Used with permission.

one with authority. She met me with: 'What do *you* want? I don't know why you want to talk to me. I want to know what happened to Jane, the only sister who cares about me. She always helped me out. All the rest of them don't care what happens to me, and I hate them. Where are my things? I'm not sick. I don't need to be here. Why am I here? I only went to the hospital because I wanted medical care because I was pregnant. Then the police came and took me to the County Hospital.' This was only the beginning of an outpouring of hate over the treatment she had had. I listened and finally was able to penetrate this front, assuring her I would try to find some answers for her. I would find out about her things, would try to locate her sister, and assured her we would not take her baby away from her (this accusation had been included in her rush of talk). I told her my interest was in helping her with what needed to be taken care of. Could she give me names and addresses of friends or relatives? I remained calm and accepting in the face of her hostility, trying to bring her back to the reality of her material problems and not becoming involved in her attacks on the doctors. Finally, Nettie was able to accept my offer in a suspicious way. I felt that she was not really sure I would do as I had said."

With the information secured in this first interview, the social worker was able to locate the sister and secure needed background information. The worker also got in touch with Nettie's landlady and learned that Nettie's belongings had been packed up and stored. She wrote two other sisters, asking for return of a family history questionnaire and asking if they would be willing to work with social service if Nettie wished. The worker also wrote the state department of child welfare, outlining the situation and asking what procedures would be necessary to arrange for services for the expected baby, since it could not remain at the hospital with Nettie.

"At the time of my second interview with Nettie, two weeks later, I was able to give her information about her belongings. Nettie was also worried about furniture she had in storage in Memphis. She asked me to write Jane and see if she would pay the charges. She asked for Jane's address and said she would write her. At this interview, Nettie was much calmer, was able to concentrate on arrangements, and did not display the overt hostility previously present. Later, arrangements were made and I personally picked up Nettie's belongings, as Nettie would not permit anyone else to do it. The landlady was presented with the patient's signed authorization for them to be turned over to me. In turn, a list of boxes and general contents was receipted by me. This list was subsequently turned over to the marking room and arrangements made with nursing service that an aide accompany patient to go through her belongings, repacking for storage and keeping out clothes she could wear. The valuable papers would be sent to medical records for safekeeping, and if needed, I would be available for conference with the patient about them. Four weeks later, a much better relationship with the social worker was apparent. Nettie was calm, expressing her gratitude for assistance in securing her personal belongings and the opportunity to go through them. I was able to approach the problem of providing care for her expected baby, which at that time was her only interest. She was happy that she was going to have a child, someone of her own to love and provide for. Her attitude was typical of many unmarried mothers, not wanting the father of the child to know of her pregnancy or have any claim on the child.

"The plan offered by the State Child Welfare Division, to provide care for the baby in a foster home on a temporary basis until she would be able to care for him, was discussed at length. The detailed procedures necessary, the removal of the baby from the hospital soon after birth, and the juvenile court jurisdiction needed were all accepted and understood and fully agreed to as the best plan for her baby. At the end of the interview, her comment, 'I have found out there are good people in the world,' was quite revealing of her change in attitude toward the social worker."

From this point on, Nettie was able to use casework services for following through on plans for the care of her child, and six months later went to Juvenile Court to regain custody of her child before leaving to make her home with a sister in the North. This sister had been in touch with the social worker throughout Nettie's hospitalization and cooperated fully. Both from the medical and social standpoint, Nettie was well enough to take the responsibility of herself and her child. She left in good remission, with the knowledge that should the condition again occur, the services of a social worker might be helpful. While we might worry over the adequacy of the care this mother will give her child, the inclusion of her sister in the planning offers some protection. With so favorable an impression of social workers, Nettie may be able to turn to a social agency for help again.

Mr. Robert Arms was fifty-one when he was admitted, having been a patient at a state hospital in another state for twenty years. During those years, he had little in the way of psychotherapy or drugs and his condition did not change. For the first four years following his transfer, Mr. Arms was treated with drug therapy, psychotherapy, industrial therapy, and occupational therapy and improved to the point where he was referred to the Social Work Department for casework, looking toward his release into the community.

For two years, his social worker and Mr. Arms worked to rebuild his self-esteem. The local employment service found him a job in a car wash, and Mr. Arms worked during the day and returned to the hospital at night. When he was laid off after six weeks (because of his age, not his mental condition), he had made some gains in self-confidence. In fact, he became somewhat unrealistic in the type of job he felt able to locate on his own, and his caseworker had to combine building his confidence and focusing on reality.

Mr. Arms was given day passes to follow up newspaper ads, but he sabotaged his own efforts by stressing his status as a patient in a mental hospital. He did have another brief period of employment as a caretaker and lived away from the hospital, but he was not able to undertake the responsibility required, and it became apparent he would need a closely supervised job and living arrangements. During his period of employment, he had been able to open a small savings account, which was a source of great satisfaction.

During the next two years, Mr. Arms continued to see his social worker, who was in constant touch with the public welfare department and the counselors of the Vocational Rehabilitation Unit in the hospital. Finally, Mr. Arms was able to move into a supervised boarding home, with employment at a sheltered workshop, earning a small salary. He is supervised by a public health nurse and returns regularly to the Follow-Up Clinic at the hospital, where he can maintain contact with his social worker.

Mr. Arms is now able, after many disabling years as a mental patient, to live a marginal existence in the community, be partially self-supporting, and yet feel that the hospital stands behind him.

Mrs. Sarah Allen, a widow in her mid forties, was admitted to the hospital from a community receiving facility as a voluntary patient. The admitting diagnosis was schizophrenia, paranoid type. She was accompanied to the hospital by a friend who had known her only a few months and was not able to give much background information except that Mrs. Allen had been severely depressed for eight months, had threatened suicide on several occasions, and had intermittent outbursts of anger which had interfered with her holding jobs. She worked as a waitress, and when she became upset she threw glasses and dishes, screaming that people did not like her because she was ugly. Mrs. Allen had had outpatient electro-convulsive therapy (ECT), had read a number of books on psychiatry, and had committed herself to the hospital determined to have ECT.

At the receiving conference, where her admitting diagnosis was changed and prognosis considered good, it was suggested that Mrs. Allen be referred to social service, since she appeared never to have had any positive relationships except to her dead husband about whom she talked constantly, although he had died more than three years before. Mrs. Allen also needed help with business arrangements about mortgage payments on her home. At the onset of the casework interviews, it became obvious that Mrs. Allen had not the slightest insight into her problems and that she was unable to relate to other people except in the most superficial way. She was excessively quiet and unobtrusive. As the weeks went on, Mrs. Allen was able to form a relationship and to talk a little, although still superficially, about her anxieties. She continually referred to the fact that she was depressed and that the only thing that would help her was ECT, which she was being denied. The social worker kept in touch with the doctor about her treatment, and when repeated interpretation by the social worker was ineffective, the psychiatrist told her flatly that she did not need ECT. She was finally able to accept medication as the treatment of choice.

Because Mrs. Allen was threatened by any discussion of her past, casework was directed toward helping Mrs. Allen utilize to the maximum the therapeutic environment of the hospital. It took patient encouragement from the worker before Mrs. Allen was willing to participate in social activities. Once she began to participate, however, she found herself enjoying them and, in a complete reversal of personality, became very gregarious and acquired the reputation of "cottage clown." It became apparent to the social worker and the psychiatrist that Mrs. Allen was becoming more comfortable in the hospital setting and needed to be stimulated to make plans for leaving. Interviews then were focused on these plans. Mrs. Allen was encouraged to inquire about waitress jobs in the area and was given a weekend leave to follow up some ads. The doctor feels she is about ready for release, at which time casework services will no longer be needed.

Gerry Morse, age thirteen, was admitted to the hospital on an involuntary order not to exceed six months from a local receiving facility with a diagnosis of "schizophrenia, chronic undifferentiated." His parents had recently moved to Florida, and Gerry's behavior had been radically affected by the move, particularly in school. He lost his temper at the slightest provocation, made threats, and got into fights with other boys, which he always lost. His parents took him first to a pediatrician, then to a neurological consultant, and finally to a psychiatrist, who recommended a brief psychiatric hopitalization. When no change in his behavior resulted, long-term hospitalization was advised, and he was admitted to the receiving facility for evaluation and transfer to the state hospital.

The examining psychiatrist at the state hospital could not find any evidence of a major mental disorder. His impression was "unsocialized aggressive reaction of adolescence associated with a convulsive disorder." Gerry's history, as secured by the social worker, showed a series of illnesses and accidents which had interfered with his growing up normally. He was the seventh of eight children, all of whom were reported as healthy. At the age of five months, Gerry had meningitis, and eighteen months later he began having convulsive seizures. Severe injuries occurred when he was three, when he was run over by a tractor and nearly castrated, and several months later when he ran his trike into a barbed-wire fence, sustaining injuries to his throat. Formation of scar tissue in his throat necessitated a tracheotomy, which remained open until he entered school. His muscular spasms caused falls, and he had sustained several bone fractures. These multiple medical problems had resulted in isolating him from his peer group, in overprotection by his family, and in close supervision, particularly by his mother.

Gerry's school adjustment had been made difficult by his self-consciousness about his appearance, the awkwardness resulting from his muscular spasms, and his lack of experience with strangers. Understanding teachers helped ease his adjustment in elementary school, but when he moved to junior high and more was expected of him, his frustrations grew. He tried to win friends by bribery; when this did not work, he lashed out aggressively against his peers. His convulsions were controlled by medication, but muscle spasms involving the small muscles interfered with writing, and he was unable to complete tests on time. His new instructors did not make the same allowances for his inability to finish tests on time, since they were unaware of his difficulties. To the busy teachers, he was a source of disruption in their classrooms, and they wanted to get rid of him. Parenthetically, had his needs been recognized, the school social worker might have intervened, referred Gerry and his parents to resources in the community, and avoided his hospitalization. As it was, the upheaval resulting from the move to Florida put the finishing touches on his adjustment problem, and the family sought professional help for him outside the school system.

Gerry was cooperative with the admitting physician and gave his inability to form friendships and his acting-out behavior as the reasons for his admission. Since there was no adolescent unit in the hospital at the time, he was assigned to a regular ward and placed on psychotropic medication. Evaluation by the clinical team, of which the social worker who secured his history was an important member, led to the decision to enroll Gerry in the hospital school—the Educational Rehabilitation Program—and the team devised a behavior modification approach to be followed by all therapists. His progress was slow but steady and improved after Mrs. Morse was seen regularly by the social worker. She needed help with the guilt feelings so characteristic of mothers of disturbed children and with specific suggestions for continuing the behavior modification techniques when Gerry was home for weekends and for extended leaves. Good behavior was rewarded and antisocial behavior was not. Mrs. Morse became able to say "No" when appropriate, and to her surprise, Gerry accepted this without becoming violent and angry. Both in the hospital and at home, Gerry responded best to discussion of his behavioral problems on an individual basis rather than in a group setting.

Because Mr. Morse's job involved extended absence from home, Mrs. Morse carried most of the responsibility for Gerry's adjustment, although it was recognized that family counseling would have been preferable. Mr. Morse was fully cooperative when he was at home, and Gerry's relationship with him improved.

Within three months, Gerry began to show marked improvement in his therapeutic program, which allowed the social worker to become more directly involved with him in planning for his release. Although he had made gains in school work, he was not yet ready for a regular classroom. Both Gerry and his parents agreed with this decision, but the family could not afford private schooling. The social worker was able to locate a public school program for emotionally disturbed children, which utilized behavior modification techniques and was not too far away from Gerry's home. Gerry was able to recognize that his altered behavior had real pay-off, particularly in the areas of making friends and doing better school work. He participated fully in the plans for his post-hospital treatment and was able to verbalize his need for continued improvement. His participation was formalized by having him cosign with his mother the form which permitted the hospital to forward confidential information to his new school.

Thus Gerry has been enabled to return to his family, and both he and they have gained some understanding of his problems and have learned more constructive ways of dealing with them. A year after his discharge, Gerry is now achieving in school at a level nearly commensurate with his chronological age, his social adjustment is much improved, and his relationships with his family are satisfactory. The role of medical problems in his escalating self-destructive behavior is acknowledged in his final diagnosis: adjustment reaction of childhood associated with convulsive disorder in remission.

It is difficult to illustrate adequately in a brief summary the concurrent social work treatment carried on with the families of patients. In this hospital, work with relatives is a major part of the service rendered, but all too often there are no relatives or resources, and part of the social work task is readying the patient to take full responsibility for himself. In only one of these cases was there a family available for concurrent treatment. In all the cases, we can see the application of traditional social work principles: clients are accepted without retaliation when they are hostile or rejecting; goals are modified to conform with realistic expectations; a corrective experience is provided in which patients can learn more satisfying ways of relating to others; social work functions as part of an interdisciplinary effort to bring about a better adjustment of the patient to his situation.

It is illuminating to analyze the social work roles demonstrated in these cases in relation to those described by the Southern Regional Educational Board (see page 22). While each case demonstrates a wide range of social work roles, some are more obvious than others in specific cases. The roles of data manager, evaluator, and behavior changer are apparent in all four cases. Particular emphasis on the outreach role is seen in Arms; consultant in Allen; broker in Turner, Morse, and Arms; teacher in Morse and Allen; administrator in Morse and Arms; care giver in Turner; advocate in Arms; and mobilizer in Arms and Turner.

In addition, the case of Gerry Morse indicates the extent to which psychiatric labeling may be misapplied; although emotionally disturbed in the community, Gerry was not considered psychotic by the hospital. The case of Robert Arms also illustrates how a long-term "hopeless" psychiatric patient can be helped to lead a more productive and satisfying life under protected conditions. Both Mr. Arms and Mrs. Allen needed the help of the social worker to move out of the security of the hospital.

In all these cases, the Social Work Department worked closely with the other therapeutic services of the hospital, utilizing the skills of social work to facilitate the patient's acceptance of treatment as well as working with family and community agencies to speed his return to the community.

POSSIBLE FUTURE TRENDS

What may the baccalaureate social worker expect if he wishes a career in health and/or mental health services? A number of trends may be discerned.

First, what was a critical manpower shortage not so long ago no longer exists in most parts of the United States. As funding is cut for many social programs, agencies are increasingly unable to add to staff, no matter how much this is needed. For the first time in the memory of most social workers, there is actual unemployment of MSWs and a dearth of openings for new BSWs. Some agencies will employ BSWs, since their salaries are lower. Thus, baccalaureate-level social work education must prepare students more adequately to acquire the additional skills to deal with the acutely ill or seriously disturbed client. Instead of leaving it to the graduate schools to include courses in medical and psychopathological information, these must be included in undergraduate curricula.

Another trend is to use social workers for indirect service. Patients are being given direct treatment increasingly by members of other professions or by paraprofessionals—the teacher, the clergyman, the policeman, the psychiatric aide, the mental health aide, the volunteer. Social workers will be increasingly functioning as team leaders, as coordinators, as planners, and as consultants. Expertise in community organization, in administration, and in planning will become even more essential in the preparation of BSWs. The role of patient advocate will assume greater importance, lest the patient become overwhelmed by fragmented services.

Individual therapy, while indispensable, will be increasingly supplemented by group therapy, both because of the more economical use of staff and because of the reinforcing effect of the group on behavior change. Social workers must learn group techniques and have educational field experience which prepares them for being group leaders. Where individual therapy is the modality of choice, it will be more and more time-limited, crisis-oriented, and directive. The social worker must be able to assess situations and clients rapidly, to develop relationships quickly, to define objectives clearly, and to make maximum use of community resources.

As we come more and more to recognize that social injustice, inequality of income, inhumane bureaucracies, and inadequate facilities are at the root of much mental and physical illness, social workers must be change agents, working to change systems which dehumanize and harm members of society. Social action to improve living conditions of the disadvantaged is an indispensable part of preventive care. Through their own professional organizations and through affiliations with local, state, and national activist groups, professional social workers have a responsibility for documenting the effects of maldistribution of resources and for stimulating and supporting legislative reform and increased social concern.

Of the twelve roles outlined by the Southern Regional Education Board, several are critical: advocate, behavior changer, and consultant are certainly foremost for the mental health worker, and advocate, broker, mobilizer for the health social worker. Specific assignments may involve the roles of evaluator and teacher as well. Community planner and administrator are roles in which social work expertise could make a real contribution, but as yet social workers are not sufficiently involved in planning and administering services for health and mental health. Once fields traditionally dominated by medicine and psychiatry, health and mental health care are increasingly becoming socially oriented, as awareness grows of social components in cause, treatment, and prevention of illness and disability. Social workers in the 1970s are in a strategic position to contribute their understanding to other health and mental health professionals.

ADDITIONAL REFERENCES

Caplan, Gerald, *Support Systems and Community Mental Health* (New York: Behavioral Publications, 1974). A community psychiatrist considers the roles of the nurse, the social worker, the family physician, and the teacher in preventive psychiatry.

Gerber, Alex, *The Gerber Report* (New York: David McKay Companies, 1971). Subtitled "The Shocking State of American Medical Care and What Must Be Done About It," this study by a California surgeon documents the defects of the present health care delivery system.

Glenn, Michael, ed., *Voices from the Asylum* (New York: Harper & Row, 1974). Details the day-to-day depression, suffering, and degradation of life in American mental hospitals.

Hodgson, Godfrey, "Politics of American Health Care," *The Atlantic Monthly*, Vol. 232 (October 1973), pp. 45–61. Documents the present health care crisis and advocates a national health insurance scheme with a Health Maintenance Organization approach.

Jefferson, Lara, *These Are My Sisters* (Garden City, N.Y.: Doubleday and Company, 1974). A schizophrenic's account of her stay in a midwest mental hospital.

Lewis, Howard and Lewis, Martha, *The Medical Offenders* (New York: Simon and Schuster, 1970). A well-documented and chilling account of the small minority of M.D.'s who engage in swindling, profiteering, unnecessary treatment, and illegal activity, and the reluctance of the profession to discipline its own members.

McGee, Richard K., *Crisis Intervention in the Community* (Baltimore: University Park Press, 1974). A study of crisis intervention delivery systems designed for professionals, paraprofessionals, and volunteers in a comprehensive crisis service.

Mechanic, David, *Politics, Medicine and Social Science* (New York: John Wiley & Sons, 1973). The social and political contexts within which health care and the practice of medicine are provided.

Robinson, David, *The Process of Becoming Ill* (London: Routledge & Kegan Paul, 1971). A British sociologist analyzes the "gamesmanship" aspects of illness.

Sobey, Francine, *The Nonprofessional Revolution in Mental Health* (New York: Columbia University Press, 1970). Report of a survey conducted by the National Institute of Mental Health of more than 10,000 staff in more than 185 mental health programs, which documents the increasing use of paraprofessionals and the blurring of traditional boundary lines between the professions.

Strauss, Anselm L., ed., *Where Medicine Fails* (New York: E. P. Dutton, 1973). A critique of medical practice and health care, including psychiatric labeling, chronicity, dying, and community hospitals.

Titmuss, Richard M., *The Gift Relationship: From Human Blood to Social Policy* (New York: Random House, 1971). A study of the commercialization of blood donation, which places immense social costs on those least able to bear them and exploits the poor as blood yielders.

social work
in corrections

"Crime" and "delinquency" are legal la-
bels for behavior found unacceptable to a given society at a given
time. What is considered a crime in one society may not be so considered in another society or in the same society at another period.
Tampering with the food supply or breaking a solemn taboo are
serious crimes in some cultures. Religious heresy was the most
heinous offense at the time of the Inquisition, while in modern
America (where protecting religion against heresy is not regarded
as the responsibility of the state), the offense which carries the
most severe penalty is treason in time of war. Changes in law may
make forbidden behavior tolerable overnight; underage drinking
by eighteen-year-olds is no longer a delinquent act in many states,
as the age of majority is lowered to eighteen. Dumping raw sewage into running streams—acceptable behavior for centuries—becomes illegal where environmental laws are passed banning it. It
is, in other words, not the specific behavior itself but its current
legal definition which labels the behavior as criminal or not.

The above understanding of crime and delinquency runs counter to many of the theories of causation, which attribute criminal
tendencies to persons with specific physical or psychological characteristics, which discuss "born criminals" and consider them defective people. But, the first approach to crime and delinquency is
congruent with the sociological understanding of the relationship
between social control and innovation. A society which frowns
upon deviation and enforces strict controls may have fewer criminals, but it will also have fewer innovators, creative artists, in-

ventors, and improvements. Part of the price a society has to pay for its creativity and innovation is a higher rate of deviant behavior, some of which will be disapproved of and labeled criminal. One need only consider the "crimes" of poets and musicians in totalitarian countries to see the potential dangers in a society of rigidly enforced "law and order."

ANTISOCIAL BEHAVIOR

Disapproved behavior is always divisive to the group, and historically it has been dealt with in ways believed to protect group solidarity. Punishment of the offender, both to atone to the group for his offenses and to deter others from similar behavior, has been the classic treatment and has included banishment, mutilation, public shaming, deprivation of property, or death, either at the hands of the victim's family or state officials. These ancient punitive attitudes toward offenders, particularly if they are lower-class or of a minority group, unfortunately remain in our present correctional system. At the same time, the tacit acceptance of "white-collar crime,"[1] such as income tax evasion, political corruption, padded medical bills, and other types of fraud, indicates a basic ambivalence in cultural values. Lawbreaking, especially if successful, does not meet with uniform condemnation.

Theories as to the causes of crime are many, varied, and not definitive. Attempts to pinpoint a single cause or even a constellation of causes are more likely to illuminate the bias of the investigator than to illuminate the behavior in question. Crime has been attributed to original sin, to possession by evil spirits, to mental defect, to heredity, to alcohol or nicotine, and to a "racial predisposition." Such physical causes as endocrine imbalance, somatotypes, the double-Y chromosome, and "constitutional defects" are adduced by biological determinists. Sociologists emphasize ecological factors in delinquency areas, the concepts of role and status, the differing value systems of subcultures, and the shifting roles of the family. Psychology and psychiatry have called attention to emotional maladjustment, frustration, anxiety, "superego lacunae" (which postulates that parents subtly encourage children to act out their own forbidden impulses), and imperfectly controlled aggression.

1. The term is attributed to Edwin S. Sutherland. It was first articulated in an article, "White-Collar Criminality," *American Sociological Review*, Vol. 5, No. 1 (February 1940), pp. 1–2, and developed in a book, *White-Collar Crime* (New York: Dryden Press, 1949).

Whatever the theories, it can be stated categorically that they fail to explain behavior deemed criminal by the society, since they are all based on a badly skewed sample—those *detected* in delinquent behavior. These theories may illuminate factors such as poverty, slum residence, membership in a minority group, low intelligence, or poor impulse control, but they cannot adequately take into account those individuals committing identical acts who "get away with it," either because of the protection which money and influence can provide them or because law enforcement officials never apprehended them. Studying those already in the correctional system may be really measuring the effects of the system on the individual rather than revealing the causes of the behavior.

Porterfield's survey of college students in Texas[2] indicated that the only essential difference between the delinquent child and the child considered nondelinquent is that the former was apprehended. The college students in Porterfield's study reported delinquency in high school which differed little in frequency and type from the offenses of high school students known to the Fort Worth Juvenile Court. As Sophia Robison, a leading authority on such "hidden crime," puts it, "The findings of these systematic studies are consistent with the memories which most of us have, although we may repress them."[3] More studies of successful adults whose backgrounds include undetected criminal acts are needed before any definitive statements about "causes" of crime can be made. Such a study, "The Adolescent Behavior of Currently Respectable Males," compares the hidden delinquency rates in two area probability samples from a middle-class Long Island community and the Boston slum area made famous by William F. Whyte in *Street Corner Society.* This study indicates that relatively serious delinquent acts in adolescence are not an insuperable obstacle to successful adult adjustment and reinforces the impression that the stigma associated with being labeled "delinquent" and subsequent experience with the so-called "correctional" system has a self-fulfilling effect. The study also raises provocative questions about the role of the police in determining who will and who will not be labeled a delinquent or a criminal.[4] The racist attitudes of

2. Austin L. Porterfield, *Youth in Trouble* (Austin, Ts.: Potishman Foundation, 1946).

3. Sophia M. Robison, *Juvenile Delinquency: Its Nature and Control* (New York: Holt, Rinehart and Winston, 1960), p. 233.

4. Sophia M. Robison, "Hidden Delinquency: A Challenge to Social Work Concepts and Programs," paper delivered at the National Conference on Social Welfare, May 27, 1965.

many police may well be largely responsible for the often-heard charge that blacks are prone to crime.[5]

The population which enters the correctional system, then, is not typical of all offenders. The 1958 statement of the Council on Social Work Education (CSWE) was an early recognition of this fact; but this fact is still not generally recognized, perhaps because it is too threatening to many people to accept their inherent similarity to "criminals."

> Clients of the correctional agency are a small proportion of all delinquent and criminal offenders. They have been selected for correctional treatment through social processes which are affected by many factors. Among the factors are: lack of social resources on the part of the individual and his family; the special jeopardy resulting from having been previously designated an offender; the practices of local law enforcement; public concern about certain crimes; the inadequacies and rigidities of laws; and many others. . . .
>
> In general the correctional caseload is made up of the least adequate offenders. It includes very few white-collar criminals, professional criminals or members of organized criminal gangs. Persons who are assigned to the correctional caseload tend to be difficulty prone, lacking in social and personal resources, evasive and unskilled in dealing with community services, impulsive and lacking in the basic skills essential to the acceptable performance of the necessary social roles of parent, student, employee, etc. Many of them are failures of previous social agency efforts; they do not voluntarily seek help and may have to be held within a mandatory relationship if they are to be served. They come primarily from lower economic groups and so act and think according to "working class" cultural patterns and values. Because of their repeated classification with others of the same kind many of them are part of the delinquent sub-culture and become part of the correctional sub-culture.[6]

Such a multiplicity of factors necessarily means that attempts to understand antisocial behavior, to modify the social functioning of those offending, to remove the injustices inherent in our present correctional system, and, ultimately, to lower the incidence of criminal acts must be interdisciplinary efforts. Although social

5. For an excellent description of police attitudes toward ghetto blacks, see Robert Conot, *Rivers of Blood, Years of Darkness* (New York: Bantam Books, 1967), a vividly written account of the Watts riots of 1965.

6. Council on Social Work Education, *Description of Practice in the Correctional Field*, #8–34–1, March 14, 1958, p. 5.

work has a potentially important contribution to make, at present it plays a very small part in the correctional field. Efforts to make the skills of social work more available to correctional agencies involve not only interpretation and demonstration of the value of social workers in these agencies but also the development of curricular material in social work education, which will show corrections as one of the public services in which social workers may find rewarding employment.[7] As Elliot Studt puts it:

> In part because social workers have continued to maintain their distance from the "dirty work" of corrections, the profession of social work has only occasionally been in a position either to influence the basic structure of institutional programming from the inside or to help design an alternative model for the correctional process. Today, when there is a widespread demand for a new way of viewing what happens to offenders after they have been convicted, social work is seriously limited in its capacity to contribute to the design of the imminent new correctional models.[8]

THE JUVENILE COURT

Although juvenile courts established by statute are of relatively recent origin, the principles on which they are based have been evolving during several centuries. The Judeo-Christian judicial tradition, epitomized in the biblical precept of "an eye for an eye and a tooth for a tooth," conceived of the criminal as a willful offender who should be punished, the punishment to be determined by the nature of the crime, not the situation of the criminal. The validity of this conception as it applied to young children and the mentally incompetent came to be challenged toward the end of the eighteenth century, when child offenders were segregated in "Houses of Refuge" and attempts were made to reeducate them. The responsibility of the state to protect minors was clarified and extended by English common law. As *parens patriae*, the sovereign had been responsible for protecting the property of minors; this protection was later extended to their persons, as clearly enunci-

7. Elliot Studt, *A Conceptual Approach to Teaching Materials: Illustrations from the Field of Corrections* (New York: CSWE, 1965), contains excellent case material and references. See also Marguerite Wilson, "Strategies of Teaching in Corrections," *Social Casework*, Vol. 51, No. 10 (December 1970), pp. 618–624.

8. Elliot Studt, "Crime and Delinquency: Institutions," *Encyclopedia of Social Work, 1971* (New York: NASW, 1971) p. 188. Reprinted with the permission of the National Association of Social Workers.

ated in 1847.[9] The chancery courts in England had jurisdiction in this area and also pioneered in the use of the informal hearing as opposed to the formal trial procedure for minors.

The jurisdiction of the state over neglected, dependent, and delinquent children is thus defined by law. The innovation of the juvenile court did not so much create new responsibilities as provide a special area of jurisdiction. The first juvenile court in the United States has been traditionally credited to Chicago, where "An Act to Regulate the Treatment and Control of Dependent, Neglected, and Delinquent Children" was passed by the Illinois legislature in 1899, after a decade of agitation led by Jane Addams, other civic-minded citizens, and the Chicago Bar Association. This Act provided for a courtroom and records separate from adult facilities. By 1945, all states and federal territories had enacted juvenile court laws. The philosophical basis for juvenile courts is summed up by Robison:

> Since the juvenile court is not a criminal court, the child within its jurisdiction is not charged with crime but is regarded as a ward of the state subject to its discipline and entitled to its protection . . . In most states the juvenile court act provides: (1) that the care, custody, and discipline of the children brought before the court shall approximate as nearly as possible that which they should receive from their parents; (2) that as far as is practicable, they shall be treated not as criminals but as children in need of aid, encouragement, and guidance; (3) that no child shall be denominated criminal by reason of an adjudication in the children's court, nor should such an adjudication be deemed a conviction.[10]

All juvenile court systems were based on the principles of individualized treatment for children, separation of minors from adults, informal hearings, the use of social investigations as an aid in arriving at a disposition, and an emphasis on protection and rehabilitation rather than punishment and deterrence.

However, for a variety of reasons, the lofty aims of the founders of the juvenile court movement were not realized. Not only did juvenile courts fail to solve the problems of delinquency and not only did many courts fail to meet minimum standards of procedure and staffing, but serious doubts arose about "due process" and the constitutional rights of parents and children. "Instead of

9. For a detailed account of juvenile courts, with extensive annotation, see Helen I. Clarke, *Social Legislation*, second edition (New York: Appleton-Century Crofts, 1957), Chapters 14, 15, 16.

10. Robison, *Juvenile Delinquency*, p. 233.

developing as intended, the juvenile court became a paternalistic and punitive system paralleling the impact of a criminal court . . . Procedural niceties, such as letting the child know why he was being taken away from home, were not essential."[11]

Juvenile courts have jurisdiction over children guilty of acts which would be criminal if committed by an adult and also over children who have not committed any criminal act but are described as "wayward," "unmanageable," or "in need of supervision." The landmark decision of the United States Supreme Court in *In re Gault* on May 15, 1967[12] cast grave doubt on the constitutionality of much of our juvenile court legislation.

> *Gault* revolutionized state juvenile court systems by holding that in proceedings where commitment to a state institution was possible, the following due process guarantees were required: (1) notice to parents and child adequate to afford reasonable opportunity to prepare a defense, including a statement of the charge alleged with particularity; (2) right to counsel; (3) privilege against self-incrimination; and (4) right to confrontation and cross-examination of witnesses. *Gault* recognized the fact that unlimited judicial discretion, no matter how benevolently implemented, was no substitute for procedural safeguards.[13]

The distinction between the fact-finding functions of the court and its latitude in disposition are being more clearly separated:

> Juvenile court law is coming to realize that the factual issues at stake in a contested adjudication are indistinguishable from those at issue in a contested criminal matter, and consequently the fact-finding processes in the two systems are fast becoming identical. However, the rehabilitative and individualized aspects of juvenile court jurisprudence maintain their full validity at the dispositional stage of the juvenile court

11. Jeffrey E. Glen and J. Robert Weber, *The Juvenile Court: A Status Report* (Washington, D.C.: National Institute of Mental Health, 1971), pp. 2, 1.

12. The text of the Supreme Court opinion and commentary on its implications are included in the President's Commission on Law Enforcement and Administration of Justice, *Task Force Report No. 4: Juvenile Delinquency and Youth Crime* (Washington, D.C., 1967), hereafter cited as *Task Force Report*.

13. Robert G. Rose, *Juvenile Statutes and Noncriminal Delinquents: Applying the Void-for-Vagueness Doctrine* (Washington, D.C.: Office of Youth Development, 1972), p. 5. The study cites legal decisions over such vague terms as "in danger of becoming morally depraved," "wayward minor," "stubborn child," and "growing up in idleness or idly roaming the streets at night." See also *Juvenile and Family Courts: A Legal Bibliography* (Washington, D.C.: Youth Development and Delinquency Prevention Administration, 1973), for detailed references to legal decisions affecting administrative justice for juveniles.

process. Here an attorney for the State is rarely present, the rules of evidence are not in effect, and the atmosphere, ideally, is one of cooperation between all parties toward discovering the best treatment pattern for the child . . . Along with procedural formalities, there has been a shift away from viewing the juvenile court as a catchall social agency and toward viewing the court as the governmental agency of last resort in dealing with children. The emphasis now, in many courts, is toward maximum diversion of cases, discouraging the police from arresting children for minor misbehavior, in favor of stationhouse adjustment rather than court referral, in favor of refusing court action at the intake stage, and in favor of dismissing petitions rather than placing children on "paper probation."[14]

THE HEARING

The customary procedure in a juvenile court is the petition alleging the facts, usually filed by the police but sometimes by a social agency or the parents. The child may be held in detention before the hearing if he is a potential runaway or a danger to himself or the community; increased procedural controls have been put on holding children for extended periods, but crowded court calendars may make lengthy detention inevitable. The President's Commission on Law Enforcement and the Administration of Justice estimated in 1967 that 93 percent of juvenile court jurisdictions had no suitable detention facilities; in fact, in 1972 more than 7,800 children were held in adult facilities, usually jails.[15] The conditions under which some of these children are held are unbelievable if one subscribes to the principle of the court as a child advocate.

Even those detention facilities reserved for children awaiting hearings may be a rude shock to young first offenders. They are seldom adequately staffed with house parents, social workers, teachers, medical personnel, and psychological and psychiatric consultation. Seldom are they large enough to segregate first-time offenders from more experienced ones or to provide adequate sleeping, school, recreation, and dining space. More selectivity in the use of detention is recommended; many if not most children can safely be left at home while the social study is being made.

14. Glen and Weber, *The Juvenile Court*, pp. 12, 13.
15. U.S. Bureau of the Census, *Statistical Abstract of the United States, 1973* (Washington, D.C., 1973), p. 165. See also John J. Downey, *Why Children Are in Jail and How to Keep Them Out* (Washington, D.C.: Youth Development and Delinquency Prevention Administration, 1971).

The use of detention facilities as a type of juvenile jail, to "teach children a lesson," is contrary to the purposes for which they were established. Periodic reviews should be conducted by the court or, failing that, by some outside agency, to determine how many children are in detention and how long any child has been held.

The hearing consists of two separate parts, which may occur continuously or may be separate. The first is a fact-finding session, to hear the evidence and make a determination as to the court's jurisdiction and the facts alleged in the petition. The child's right to counsel, his right to remain silent, his rights to have his parents present, to produce witnesses, and to have the testimony of witnesses corroborated are all now required by various state laws and court decisions. Only competent and relevant evidence should be introduced; the social study is not considered relevant to the allegations of fact. While procedures are official, they need not be formal or intimidating.

The second part of the hearing, which may follow immediately, is for the purpose of hearing the social evidence and making a disposition. Contrary to earlier practice, the U.S. Children's Bureau[16] now recommends that the judge not read the social study until this point. All relevant material should be admitted, including the recommendations of the probation staff. All facts presented should be open to rebuttal, and if desired, witness may be introduced for this purpose. The social study remains confidential. "No judicial decision should be based upon an undisclosed fact."[17] A fair hearing does not necessarily mean that child or parents must be present the entire time, but their counsel should be. The judge may hold a private interview with the child, but counsel should again be present.

The judge should have discretion under the law to decide who may be admitted to the courtroom. The press and general public are usually barred, but the judge may allow persons interested in the work of the court, such as lawyers, students, the clergy, or civic leaders, to observe the court in session with the understanding that the identity of the child and his family be kept confidential.

A stenographic or taped record of the hearing should be kept, in case the decision of the court is questioned at some later date. Since the disposition in almost every case involves the rights of both parents and child, care should be taken that the information

16. U.S. Children's Bureau, *Standards for Juvenile and Family Courts* (Washington, D.C., 1966).
17. *Ibid.*, p. 74.

on which the court relies in making the disposition is stated specifically. The essential quality of the hearing should be the court's concern for the child and his future, not an assessment of blame or a taking of sides.

Children's court cases may be appealed to the proper appellate court, and the parents' right to appeal should be made clear to them. In the presentation and trial of these appeals, the same precautions taken by the juvenile court to insure the confidentiality of records should be observed. The appellate court may sustain the judgment of the juvenile court, may authorize the dismissal of the original petition, or may send the case back for reconsideration of the disposition. It may not specify a particular disposition, however. Appeals from juvenile court decisions are relatively rare but are increasing. This may be due, in large measure, to the ignorance of parents as to their legal right of appeal, although in many cases the parents find themselves in agreement, however reluctant it may be, with the findings of the court.

Wherever possible, youthful offenders of federal laws are referred to state authorities, but when state courts are unwilling, the youth is dealt with by federal district courts. He may be placed on probation, committed to the Attorney General, or sent to one of several institutions under the direction of the Federal Youth Correction Division of the Department of Justice. Violations of the National Motor Vehicle Theft Act are the most frequent offenses. The federal government has also been concerned with youthful violators of the Harrison Act, the federal narcotics law, although there are no federal facilities specifically for young drug abusers.

THE DISPOSITION

The disposition of the case is made on the basis of the best solution for the child; the social study and the recommendations of the probation staff which did the study, as well as recommendations of other social agencies involved and the views of the child and the parents are all taken into account. There are several possibilities open to the judge. He may continue the case for further investigation. He may dismiss the case on the basis that no further action is needed. He may, especially in neglect cases, order protective supervision of the child, as in the Adams case cited in Chapter 3. In all these situations, no change has been made in the legal custody of the child, which remains with the parents.

Probation

The child might also be placed on probation, during which the child lives at home but receives casework and supervision provided by the court. This is a period, usually indefinite, during which a member of the probation staff works with parents and child to help them meet the standards of conduct expected by the community. Too often, this normative aspect of probation is overlooked by the child and the public, who are all too prone to interpret probation as tacit permission for the child to continue as he was. If the probation staff is well-trained and the caseloads small enough, extremely valuable help can be provided to the child on probation. Unfortunately, neither condition exists widely, and much probation work revolves around the meaningless ritual of reporting in. Public support for improved probation standards, for adequate salaries to attract competent personnel, and for suitable community facilities has been generally lacking, and it has sometimes taken an epidemic of delinquency and violence to awaken a community to its deficiencies.

Probation may carry with it restrictions on activity, such as a curfew, mandatory school attendance, attendance at a mental health center or supervised recreation program, or other individualized stipulations. Few probation officers have adequate time to be sure probationers are meeting the stipulations. Probation continues until it is felt that the child has received maximum benefits; thus, the period may be terminated when the child achieves a better adjustment or when it becomes evident that probation is not producing any change. Whenever probation is to be terminated, the child should be returned to the court; if the child is to be removed from the home because probation has been unsuccessful, a second hearing should be held.

Commitment

When the situation does not give promise of rehabilitation via probation, the court may vest the legal custody of the child in an authorized agency or institution. Care must be taken that children so committed for delinquency not be placed in the same institution as those committed for neglect. Difficulties have arisen over the vague definition of "unmanageable" children or PINS (Persons in Need of Supervision, as they are known in New York State), who are handled as delinquents in many courts even though they may be only "in danger of becoming" delinquent. In July 1973, the New York State Court of Appeals struck down the practice of placing PINS in reform schools,[18] on the basis that PINS were entitled to supervision and treatment and were not getting it in state "training schools."

18. *New York Times,* July 6, 1973, p. 1.

Children who must be removed from their own homes may be placed in foster homes, child-caring institutions, or correctional schools. A few children should probably be committed to mental hospitals. Those children for whom foster-home care seems desirable are likely to be the younger and less seriously delinquent children, for whom a change of environment and some experience in stable family living may provide a corrective. Foster parents of such children should be specially selected, experienced, and able to convey quickly an impression of warmth and authority. Unfortunately the bulk of children who could benefit from foster care are adolescents, and there is an acute shortage of foster parents who are willing to take older children known to have behavior problems. Some of these adolescents may be accommodated and treated in agency group homes, but the bulk of them will have to be placed in a more closed setting.

Ideally, training schools should be used for children who can profit from their programs. Because there is a general reluctance to use such institutions except as a last resort and because of a greater willingness to let less seriously delinquent children be cared for in the community, training schools tend to fill up with seriously disturbed, confirmed delinquents. This hampers the rehabilitation program, makes maximum security precautions necessary in some buildings, and inevitably brings an aura of imprisonment and punishment to an institution which should be treatment-oriented.

Commitment to a training institution may be for a period of months or for the duration of the child's minority, which in many states is still up to age twenty-one, although there is a trend toward lowering it to eighteen. Unless special legal provisions have been made, the guardianship of these children remains with the parents, who have the right at any time to ask the court to review the situation and alter the child's legal status. The practice of committing children for the duration of their minority for vague offenses may amount to as much as a ten-year "sentence" and has been attacked in superior courts. The U.S. Children's Bureau recommends that no commitment for neglect or delinquency be longer than three years. In actual practice, most children remain in correctional schools for less than one year, although they may be retained on parole status after discharge.

Forestry camps, where the youthful energies of older delinquents can be productively channeled, have received public support in recent years, partly because the idea of hard physical labor in the out-of-doors appeals to middle-class values. The high rate of rehabilitation claimed for these camps is partly owing to the fact that more treatable boys are sent there and partly owing to their small size, which makes individual attention possible. Camps are open, but runaways are few; boys do reforestation, fire prevention, and environmental work under the supervision of foresters and engineers. They are paid for their work, are evaluated frequently, and earn special privileges by accumulating credits. Job skills and remedial education secured at forestry camps are useful in employment after the boy has earned his way out.

While such camps have great usefulness, they do not solve all the problems of retraining juvenile delinquents. They are not appropriate for every youthful offender: some boys are too disturbed to profit from camp experience; some are not physically equal to the work; some demand the greater control possible in an institution. When camps are used selectively, they may be highly effective in teaching good work habits, fostering a sense of responsibility, and giving a sense of accomplishment to young people who may never have been encouraged to perform worthwhile projects.

New Jersey has pioneered in the use of small institutions which use group therapy. At Highfields, the former Charles A. Lindbergh estate, twenty boys, ages sixteen and seventeen, live together informally, doing maintenance work for the state during the day and participating in group therapy sessions five evenings a week. That this program has been successful compared to that of the large congregate training school at Annandale, N.J. is at least partially owing to the selected population sent to Highfields. Emphasis is laid on decision-making and learning new social roles and new self-awareness.[19] The use of self-help groups in resocializing deviants has already been mentioned (page 16). Since the group is such an important frame of reference for adolescents, it can be a valuable resource for forcing the individual to evaluate his behavior and can support him in learning new techniques.

It would seem strikingly obvious that increasing the size of the probation staff and retaining the child in the community would, in the long run, be much less costly to the community than institutionalizing him. The public is not convinced of this, however, and all probation staffs, whether attached to the court or in a sep-

---

19. Lloyd W. McCorkle, Albert Elias, and F. Lovell Bixby, *The Highfields Story* (New York: Holt, Rinehart and Winston, 1958).

arate agency, are inadequately trained and undermanned. An experiment carried out in California should be more widely known; this was an attempt to subsidize probation in direct relation to the reduction of commitments.[20] It was set in operation as a result of two facts: correctional institutions were adjudged only 55 percent successful, while probation reported a 60 percent success rate; the cost per probationer in 1964 was $300, while the cost of maintaining one offender in a Youth Authority institution was $4,500. The experiment involved subsidies to counties in proportion to the number of cases they kept out of an institution and in the community. Counties earned their subsidies by building up their probation staffs. The direct and indirect savings to the communities were impressive, and the program has important implications for other states. As the author puts it:

> The principle of shifting correctional dollars to critical decision points within the justice network where adequate money and resources will have the greatest impact . . . can also be accomplished by other State administered parole and probation systems where improved performance can reduce the necessity for State and local institutional care.[21]

Parole

Theoretically, planning for parole and aftercare should begin at admission; in practice, few institutions have the necessary time. All too often, the best efforts of the institution are handicapped by a lack of community resources for aftercare. The responsibility for supervision of parolees may be in the institution, may be transferred to other agencies in the community, or may be handled by a separate county or state parole agency. Whatever the agency, it is essential that before release the parole worker, who will be supervising the child, have an opportunity to establish a relationship which will make parole a therapeutic experience, not a meaningless, routine "checking-up."

Parole provides an opportunity for a youngster to reestablish himself in the community under guarded conditions. If he cannot return to his home, a foster home or group residence provides opportunity for developing independence and self-support. Many parolees have had unsuccessful school experiences and will be uninterested in staying in school after the legal school-leaving age.

20. See Robert L. Smith, *A Quiet Revolution: Probation Subsidy* (Washington, D.C.: Social and Rehabilitation Service, 1971), which describes the California experiment in detail, with its rationale and implications and case examples.
21. *Ibid.*, pp. 84, 85.

The problem of finding suitable employment for these young semieducated young people is a critical one. Training schools would increase their usefulness to juveniles it they had realistic work-training and work-experience programs, preferably including some form of apprenticeship. Some training schools do provide training in shop work, auto mechanics, or printing, but many use the work time of juveniles in meaningless maintenance chores. The Federal Bureau of Prisons has pioneered in the use of pre-release guidance centers for youthful parolees from federal facilities.

QUALIFICATIONS AND ROLES OF JUVENILE CORRECTIONS PERSONNEL

The Judge

The judge of the juvenile court is the court's key figure, since in addition to his judicial duties he carries major responsibility for the court's administration and public relations. Unfortunately, few states have statutes which adequately specify qualifications for the judge. He or she may be elected or appointed, for life or for as little as two years. It is not even required that he be a lawyer, although the increased emphasis on legal procedure makes this requirement more likely in the future. He may serve only part-time as juvenile court judge, serving on other days of the week as judge in probate, criminal, or domestic relations courts.

An alternative to the present inconsistent system is a state-wide juvenile court system served by a full-time traveling juvenile judge. The local bar association may be asked to recommend a list of nominees to the mayor, governor, or political parties but not necessarily. Religious and ethnic pressures also operate to insure that major faiths and minority groups have their share of juvenile judgeships.

The Children's Bureau recommends appointment of judges, as opposed to election, and salary and prestige sufficient to attract experts of the desired caliber. In addition to being experienced in the practice of law in his state, the children's court judge should be:

1. Deeply concerned about the rights of people.
2. Keenly interested in the problems of children and families.
3. Sufficiently aware of the contribution of modern psychology, psychiatry, and social work that he can give due weight to the findings of these sciences and professions.
4. Able to evaluate evidence and situations objectively, and make dispositions uninfluenced by his own personal concepts of child care.

5. Eager to learn.

6. A good administrator, able to delegate administrative responsibility.

7. Able to conduct hearings in a kindly manner and to talk to
children and adults sympathetically and on their level of
understanding without loss of the essential dignity of the
court.[22]

Such an impressive array of qualifications is seldom found in
one judge. In a study done at the New York School of Social Work
and reported in detail by Dr. Robison,[23] two graduate students observed fifteen New York City children's court judges over a period
of eight months. On the basis of their observations, the students
identified five fairly distinguishable roles into which these fifteen
judges could be classified. The "parent judge" tended to identify
with the parents against the child and stressed obedience and filial
duty. The "counselor judge" individualized the children before
him, utilized the findings of the social study with discrimination,
and was primarily concerned with the needs of the child. The
"chancellor judge" served as the arbitrator between the rights of
the parent and the rights of the child and tended to stress the legal
aspects of the situation. The "lawyer judge" also viewed the process in a predominantly legal light but shared the attitude of the
adult court in that he tended to carry out a legal proceeding against
the child rather than a treatment-oriented proceeding in behalf of
the child. The "antagonist judge" was characterized by the intensity of his own personal reactions to the child and his family,
by severity and hostility, by a refusal to individualize cases, and
by uneasy or even sharply critical relations with the staff and the
police.

The "counselor judge," as described above, comes closest to the
ideal juvenile court judge as described by the Children's
Bureau. Like the social worker, such a judge is aware of his own
feelings and how they operate. Such a judge can utilize the services of the professional workers involved in a case without becoming threatened or defensive. A court structure which allows this
type of judge to remain in the children's court full-time for a long
period of service would be preferable to one which uses him only
part-time or between elections. It also seems obvious that the
skills and sensitivity evidenced by the "counselor judge" can be
developed best in such a full-time structure.

22. Children's Bureau, *Standards for Juvenile and Family Courts*, pp. 103, 104.
23. Robison, *Juvenile Delinquency*, pp. 254–267.

Probation Staff

As the chief administrative officer of the juvenile court, the judge is also responsible for the work of the probation staff. The position of the Children's Bureau that probation workers should be trained social workers has been widely endorsed, but in actuality few courts even approach that standard. The *Task Force Report* cited the following findings: judges were usually elected; most were lawyers with an average of nine years experience in law practice; one third had no probation officers or social workers regularly available to their courts; and 83 percent had no regularly available psychiatrist or psychologist. Although juvenile probation is provided by statute in every state, in more than 100 counties there were no juvenile probation services of any type at the time of this report (1967). The report also indicated that probation may be administered by courts, by correctional agencies, or by welfare departments; only about half the probation officers had civil service status; caseloads were high, averaging seventy-five supervision cases per officer; more than 10 percent of all children on probation were in caseloads of more than 100; and salaries were too low to compete for well-educated staff.[24] In spite of some increase in expenditures for law enforcement, including additional personnel and in-service training, it is doubtful that the picture is much brighter today. The director of The National Information Center on Volunteers in Courts sums up the current situation:

> We've taken children that parents have failed with, that teachers have failed with, that police have failed with, and we've said to the juvenile probation officer: we'll give you 15 minutes a month to work with this kid (because we won't budget enough staff to make more intensive work possible).[25]

The responsibilities of probation personnel are not markedly different from those of any social worker with troubled clients. The roles of client advocate, mobilizer, enabler, teacher, and broker are utilized in helping the client use community resources. The support and warm interest of the helping person is a new and corrective experience for many isolated, angry, and embittered youngsters. The fact that the child on probation has no choice but is ordered to remain in treatment with his probation officer may

24. President's Commission, *Task Force Report*, p. 6.
25. Isolde Chapin Weinberg, *Volunteers Help Youth* (Washington, D.C.: Social and Rehabilitation Service, 1971), p. 31.

make it more difficult to establish a helping relationship, but once established, the relationship need not be impaired by the element of authority. As Robert Smith reports in the California experiment with subsidized probation, "Probation officers with time, skill, opportunity, and resources can demonstrate to probationers that someone does care and that probation means help as well as control."[26] The opportunity for experiences which will enhance the young person's self-respect and show him that he has some voice in plans made for him and that he can find a meaningful place in the community can be done better in a probation setting than by removing him from familiar surroundings and institutionalizing him.

In a study of juvenile probation officers, Brennan and Khinduka[27] find a discrepancy between the way professional social workers view their roles and the demands of the bureaucracy in which juvenile probation work is carried on. They feel that social workers who are sure of their identity as helping persons are able to contribute social work expertise in such areas as diagnosis, rehabilitation planning, and changing behavior and will not be caught in trying to operate as amateur lawyers or policemen. The service and treatment components of the social worker's task in the team effort of the juvenile court demand more attention to corrections in the social work curriculum at both the baccalaureate and the graduate levels.

Institutional Staff

Where children cannot be cared for in the community and must be committed to institutions, the social worker has, in addition to serving as a helping person to the involuntary client, the responsibility of sustaining contact between the child and his family, with a view to facilitating his readjustment to the family when he is released. Since the administrators of correctional institutions are likely to be experts in corrections rather than social workers, the part that the social work staff can play in altering the repressive conditions of institutional life is limited. Wherever possible, social workers should support the youngster's decision-making, his ability to get on better with others, and the improvement of

26. Smith, *A Quiet Revolution*, p. 73. See also Richard E. Hardy and John G. Cull, *Introduction to Correctional Rehabilitation* (Springfield, Ill.: Charles C Thomas, 1973).

27. William C. Brennan and Shanti K. Khinduka, "Role Discrepancies and Professional Socialization: The Case of the Juvenile Probation Officer," *Social Work*, Vol. 15, No. 2 (April 1970), pp. 87–94.

his educational and vocational skills. Smaller institutions, run on a cottage plan, and group homes are more conducive to realistic preparation for reentry into the community than large-scale, regimented, fortress-type structures. Throughout, the emphasis should be on helping the young person develop more socially acceptable ways of dealing with what is troubling him rather than on denying his troubles and punishing him as a "nonperson."[28]

Many institutions assign a social worker to each cottage or residential unit, and he or she meets regularly with the cottage parents to review the progress of the children in that unit. The social worker may be able to make recommendations as to whether the child can go off campus to a community school or must go to the on-campus school facility and may recommend group therapy, individual therapy, or some combination. In consultation with the psychiatrist and with the social work supervisor, modifications in the child's schedule, privileges or their curtailment, weekend or vacation visits home, and relationships with the other staff and residents of the unit will concern the social worker. In some institutions, all children have regularly scheduled conferences with their social workers; in others there may be only an intake conference and further consultation at the child's request or at crisis points. Much depends on the size of the social work staff and the prestige assigned to social work in the hierarchy of the institutional personnel. In all too many institutions, there will be no social work services, few constructive programs, inadequate housing, unappetizing food, and physical abuse. Such "training" schools raise the question of what they are training for; as many as three fourths of the graduates of such schools graduate into adult crime and eventually prison.

Improvement of correctional institutions is not a high-priority item on most legislatures' lists. Adequately staffed, well-equipped rehabilitation centers are expensive and unappealing to a public which still believes in punishment. Institutions are likely to be located in some remote area, where there will be few neighbors to be worried about "contamination" and where the community can send its offenders and not be reminded of them. Intensive efforts to develop community-based facilities will face obstacles but will permit easier reintegration of the children into the community and will mobilize volunteer efforts more effectively. Such programs as

28. See Erving Goffman, *Asylums* (Chicago: Aldine Press, 1961), for the classic statement on ways in which institutions depersonalize their inmates. Gisela Konopka applies this concept and suggests alternatives in "Our Outcast Youth," *Social Work*, Vol. 15, No. 4 (October 1970), pp. 76–86.

Foster Grandparents, college-student tutors, "adoption" of children by civic groups, and group activities through schools and recreational agencies are easier to secure if the children remain in the community.

It should be apparent that the same individualization which characterizes other fields of social work is needed in working with juvenile offenders. Antisocial behavior can be understood and corrected only in the context of relationships which foster and support constructive change. Such relationships cannot be developed in mass detention facilities with punitive and repressive programs. Most of the youngsters who come into training schools have already been deprived and discriminated against, and much of their aggressive behavior is their reaction to what they, often quite rightfully, regard as injustice. Every delinquent knows full well how many young people have carried on activity every bit as "bad" as his own and got off scot-free, because of either luck or influence. To change his attitudes demands that those who attempt to treat him acknowledge that he has ample reason for bitterness and that they assume responsibility for social action on his behalf, as well as help with his feelings.

DELINQUENCY PREVENTION

In the absence of wholesale programs to reduce poverty, racism, inadequate parenting, inappropriate education, and inadequate recreation, delinquency prevention is limited to dealing with those children demonstrating early signs of trouble. There is no dearth of programs labeled "delinquency preventive" but no clear evidence of their effectiveness. Joel Fischer, in a review of research studies on the effectiveness of "delinquency preventive" casework intervention with an experimental group as contrasted with an untreated control group, concludes that there is no evidence of effectiveness in the former, although he points out defects in the research designs of many of the projects, which may make his conclusions unnecessarily pessimistic.[29]

One of the widely known research efforts in the delinquency field is the attempt by Sheldon and Eleanor Glueck to isolate char-

29. Joel Fischer, "Is Casework Effective?" *Social Work*, Vol. 18, No. 1 (January 1973), pp. 5–20. Note the extensive bibliography included. See also Irving A. Spergel, "Community-based Delinquency-Prevention Programs: An Overview," *Social Service Review*, Vol. 47, No. 1 (March 1973), pp. 16–31.

acteristics and factors which are predictive of delinquency.[30] Their predictive tables are based on a comparison of boys committed to a state school and a control group of Boston school boys who had not been adjudged delinquent. The defects in such a research design are at once apparent: what of delinquents brought before the court but not committed to an institution; what of those, possibly some of the control group, who have engaged in antisocial behavior not reported to a court? Other criticisms of the unrepresentativeness of the research group's ethnic and racial composition have been made. In spite of these drawbacks, the predictive tables have been validated, first by a large-scale study in New York City and subsequently elsewhere. The factors weighted in the predictive tables were: (1) discipline of boy by father; (2) supervision of boy by mother; (3) affection of father for boy; (4) affection of mother for boy; (5) cohesiveness of family. It seems clear that a child unloved by either parent, unsupervised by either parent, and lacking a cohesive family would be much more likely to end up in court; whatever their behavior, such children have fewer resources at their disposal to avoid being labeled delinquent.

Whatever one's reservations about the predictive tables, all authorities would acknowledge that nearly all delinquency is preceded by warning signals, which can be recognized but are all too often ignored. Poor school adjustment, academic retardation, inability to accept restrictions, stubborn insistence on immediate gratification of impulses, aggressiveness as a predominant method of interaction, all spell trouble ahead. While it is an oversimplification to equate delinquency with deteriorated and overcrowded neighborhoods, with inadequate incomes, with broken homes, with prejudice and discrimination, and with poor employment prospects for school-leavers, each of these conditions does contribute to increased pressure toward delinquency. In a culture which puts a premium on material success and comfort and accepts, with minimum condemnation, wrongdoing by people of influence and means, young people who find themselves deprived and feel betrayed are more likely to become discontented, resentful, and rebellious against an establishment they regard as "phony" and unconcerned.

30. Sheldon and Eleanor Glueck, *Unraveling Juvenile Delinquency* (New York: The Commonwealth Fund, 1950); *Delinquents in the Making, Paths to Prevention* (New York: Harper Brothers, 1962); and as editors, *Identification of Predelinquents* (New York: Intercontinental Medical Book Corporation, 1973), which includes application of the Glueck Social Prediction Table in a variety of American and European settings.

Programs of prevention may be geared toward improved services for the individual or toward community improvement projects in housing, employment, recreation, and health. Since the police have so much discretion in detaining suspected delinquents, special youth details should be developed with training and empathy for young people. The use of volunteers can supplement inadequately staffed youth service agencies. Involving young people in helping themselves, as in youth hotlines,[31] offers them a chance to develop self-respect as helping persons, as well as refer the callers to community resources.

The *Task Force Report* on *Juvenile Delinquency and Youth Crime* of the President's Commission on Law Enforcement and the Administration of Justice concludes its extended study of the "Prevention of Juvenile Delinquency" thus:

> To prevent juvenile delinquency, one must go far beyond the individual delinquent and his illegal act. What causes a youth to become delinquent is usually a complex network of factors relating to his own personality, his friends, his family, his community . . . We believe, first, that social institutions, especially those in the innercity, need to change and adapt in a flexible manner to the upheavals in the society around them; they need to broaden their services to reach those most in need of them; they need to make these services more accessible and more understandable to the target populations; and most important, they need to involve these populations in planning and implementing programs which will affect them. Second, and a corollary to the above points, the youth population should be given a special share and stake in society by making available to them useful, constructive, creative, and interesting opportunities to find themselves, their role, and their contribution to society . . . The high rate of recidivism attests to the inefficacy of current correctional programs. New ways of handling those youth now sent to court would decrease their further delinquency.[32]

31. See Betty Jo Johnson, *Hotline for Youth* (Washington, D.C.: Social and Rehabilitation Administration, 1972), for a description of how to set up and operate this type of crisis intervention resource.
32. Virginia M. Burns and Leonard W. Stern, "The Prevention of Juvenile Delinquency," Appendix S, *Task Force Report*, pp. 353–408. The quoted material is from the Summary, pp. 407–408. See also the various publications of the Youth Development and Delinquency Prevention Administration in Washington, D.C., which publishes reports of research projects and a monthly *Delinquency Prevention Reporter.*

EVALUATION OF PROGRAMS FOR THE
JUVENILE DELINQUENT

It is difficult to set up reliable criteria for measuring the success of rehabilitation and preventive programs.[33] One of those most frequently used is the rate of recidivism, i.e., subsequent appearances in court or institutions. This yardstick is open to many criticisms: the absence of an official record is not positive proof that no further delinquency has occurred; the arbitrary age limit in many states results in juggling figures to obscure the facts; statistics do not take into account the severity or circumstances of subsequent behavior or measure changed attitudes.

More positive criteria of success, such as the completion of school, acceptable job performance, and improved family life are also subject to error from many sources. The direct and indirect effects of prejudice, as has been indicated, slant all findings. As Vinter points out:

> Persons in certain social categories are differentially handled: persons from minority groups or lower-class families are especially liable to be apprehended, to be charged, to be adjudicated as delinquents, to be placed on probation, and to be committed to institutions.[34]

Juvenile delinquency rates have risen much faster than the youth population. In 1972, 1,125,000 delinquency cases were handled by juvenile courts, a rate of 34.1 per 1,000 children aged ten to seventeen. The number of adult criminals who have been processed through the juvenile correctional system shows how ineffective it has been in altering behavior. The growing sense of disillusionment about current programs has expressed itself in demands that police "crack down" on youthful offenders and that controls be tightened. Many social workers, along with their critics, have expressed doubts that social workers, as presently trained, are any more successful than other professionals or nonprofessionals.[35] Use of "indigenous" personnel, self-help groups,

33. See Allen F. Breed, *National Study of Youth Service Bureaus* (Washington, D.C.: Youth Development and Delinquency Prevention Administration, 1973), especially pp. 3–6.

34. Robert D. Vinter, "The Juvenile Court as an Institution," *Task Force Report,* p. 87.

35. See Edwin M. Lemert, "The Juvenile Court—Quest and Realities," *Task Force Report,* pp. 91–106; Homer W. Sloane, "Relationship of Law and Social

and volunteers is helpful in supplementing the efforts of professionals but cannot replace them. There are very few MSWs in juvenile work, even though professional associations have for years declared that as their goal. The most frequently recommended educational level is a bachelor's degree. Now that baccalaureate programs in social work are officially recognized, new opportunities in juvenile probation and parole, as well as in correctional institutions, should be opening up. The complexity of behavioral problems and the difficulties of changing behavior under the stigma and repressive conditions associated with so much of delinquency treatment, demand that those engaged in the field of juvenile corrections have training in basic social work methods, including a recognition of their own repressed hostility to offenders. This should be supplemented by in-service training specifically related to the legal regulations of the particular department and by refresher courses designed to keep abreast of new developments. As more and more colleges offer concentrations in corrections and criminal justice, collaborative educational programs are increasingly possible, with the development of undergraduate field experience in correctional settings a useful development.

CORRECTIONAL SERVICES FOR ADULTS

Much of what has been said about social attitudes toward delinquency is applicable to adult criminals. Research on adult crime and its causes is equally suspect, since it is carried out on those who were apprehended (and usually imprisoned, since a captive population is easier to study). An additional difficulty is that the conditions of prison life are such that emotional disorders found in prisoners may be the result of imprisonment and not causal to the crime. Historically, Americans have been more interested in practical questions of what to do with criminals than in theoretical and philosophical explorations of the causes of crime. The modern prison system is an American contribution to the world.

THE AMERICAN PRISON SYSTEM

Arising as a humanitarian protest against the brutality with which criminals were treated (torture, maiming, flogging, branding), the first innovation in the housing and treatment of prisoners came as a result of the efforts of a group of Pennsylvania Quakers. Whether or not Thomas Jefferson drew up the design for the first American prison, as has been claimed, the system really began with the pioneer work of Dr. Benjamin Rush, who established the Philadelphia Prison Society in 1787. The members of the Society were united in protest against the prevailing methods of treating offenders, which included public degradation and corporal punishment. They visited the notorious Walnut Street Jail and in a series of horrified memorials to the Pennsylvania legislature succeeded in securing remarkably speedy reforms. By 1790, the first penitentiary (literally, "a place in which to become penitent") had been erected on the grounds of the Walnut Street Jail for solitary confinement of the more serious offenders. The prisoners in the Jail proper were separated by sex, and debtors and witnesses kept apart from criminals. Liquor, formerly sold to the inmates by the jailkeeper, was banned, and work was made available inside the jail yard.

From 1790 to 1800, the Society accomplished a great deal toward its aims of reformation, repentance, and uplift. But it soon became apparent that the facilities at the Jail were inadequate, and the Society began in 1801 to petition the legislature for the erection of a new building where the salutary effects of solitude and hard labor could be properly provided. By 1821, the famous Cherry Hill Penitentiary had been authorized, and it received its first inmates in 1829. This amazing building was designed to make it impossible for prisoners to communicate with each other. Each cell opened into a small, walled exercise yard, and the cell blocks radiated like the spokes of a wheel from a central observation tower. Food and supplies for the various work projects carried on in the prison were taken to each cell; on the few occasions when prisoners left their cells, they had to wear blindfolds to prevent them from seeing each other.

In theory, the Pennsylvania system had much to recommend it. The cells were roomy by modern standards, inmates were allowed to use their exercise yards for gardens or even for pets, and the isolation of solitary confinement was partly mitigated by the efforts of members of the Society. Part of the Society's philosophy of reformation included regular visits to prisoners, discussion of their past misdeeds and their future conduct, and keeping them informed of the welfare of their families. From what we now know of the conditions under which changed attitudes may be fostered, we can surmise that this personal interest and discussion may have been the most valuable feature of the Pennsylvania system.

This institution attracted much attention abroad, and certain of its features were widely adopted, but it never proved wholly successful in America. Overcrowding led to doubling up in the cells, thereby nullifying the effects of solitary confinement; members of the Society were unable to maintain the sustained personal effort of visiting; ingenious methods of communication between prisoners were devised. As industrialization proceeded, the use of machinery in prison workshops was indicated rather than individual hand production in each cell. Its advocates continued for several decades to uphold its advantages, but the rival system, named for Auburn, New York, where it was first tried, proved more appealing to legislators and penologists. The system of solitary confinement for all prisoners was legally abolished in 1913, but it had not been used for many years previously.

The Auburn Prison was erected on a very different principle and philosophy. Prisoners were to work in shops during the day and were confined to very small separate cells at night, observing absolute silence at all times. Discipline was harsh, and efforts to make the prison self-supporting led to exploitation of the prisoners. Reformation was to be secured by punishment and hard labor. One of the most poignant incidents in prison history occurred when groups of Auburn prisoners were taken by boat, in leg irons, to quarry the rock and build the first cell blocks at Sing Sing.

Since the prisoners were to be in their cells only at night, the cells were barely large enough for a man to lie down in. These cubicles were placed back-to-back, four and five layers high, inside the prison walls. Light and air entered, if at all, from skylights or from small windows on outside corridors; to minimize escape attempts, no cells had windows to the outside. This pattern survives in maximum security prisons today, although the cells have been somewhat enlarged and minimum plumbing and lighting have been added.

Because the Auburn system seemed efficient, saved money, and protected society from convicts regarded as dangerous, it was widely adopted by state legislatures. From time to time, various citizen groups became concerned with the widespread brutality and dehumanizing influence of prisons. These groups evolved into the American Prison Association, now called the American Correctional Association. Influenced by the Irish prison system, which made use of the indeterminate sentence and parole, the Association in 1870 adopted a Declaration of Principles. These farsighted and progressive ideals were applied only to young offenders, and then only in part, although some of them have been gradually adopted by prisons.

The reformatory, as its name implies, was designed to reform wrongdoers. The institution at Elmira, New York, was built to incorporate some of the principles laid down in the 1870 Declaration. All men were placed in the middle of three grades; good behavior, based on an elaborate marking scheme, led to promotion to the upper grade; bad behavior led to demotion. Academic and vocational training were provided. Parole was granted when a man had achieved a specified number of good conduct marks.

Hopeful as this sounds, the reformatory movement did not succeed in reforming prisoners any more than the Pennsylvania or Auburn systems. It was never really put into full operation; overcrowding, unsuitable physical quarters, poorly trained guards, and legislation outlawing prison labor, all operated to make "reformatory" a misnomer. Regimentation, emphasis on security measures, and inability to distinguish between true rehabilitation and surface conformity to rules nullified the philosophy behind the movement, though it contributed some of its ideas, particularly the indeterminate sentence and parole, to the general prison system. Only in recent years, with the development of forestry camps and treatment-oriented training schools, are we beginning to approach anything like what was recommended by the Cincinnati Declaration in 1870. For the great majority of youthful offenders and adult prisoners, prisons are still artificial, impersonal, regimented, and all too often inhumane.[36]

According to John B. Martin,[37] the Illinois State Penitentiary at Joliet, called Stateville, is one of the best-run prisons in America. Here is his description:

> A lot of people have the idea that to go to prison means merely to withdraw from free society. They think it might be a rather monkish experience. Nothing could be more mistaken. Going to prison is not merely withdrawing from free society: it is entering caged society. There is no peace in prison.

36. The foregoing summary of the history of the American prison system draws heavily on a textbook in criminology, Harry Elmer Barnes and Negley K. Teeters, *New Horizons in Criminology*, second edition (Englewood Cliffs, N.J.: Prentice-Hall, 1951), especially Chapters 20, 21, and 26.

37. John Bartlow Martin, *Break Down the Walls* (New York: Ballantine Books, 1954). This is a nontechnical account of modern American prisons, prison riots, and needed reforms, written in reportorial style. The following quote is reprinted by permission of Harold Ober Associates Incorporated. Copyright 1951 by The Curtis Publishing Company. Copyright 1954 by John Bartlow Martin.

A prisoner's day at Stateville begins at 6:15 A.M., when he is wakened by a bell in the cellhouse. He cleans his cell, stands at the door to be counted, and, when the door is unlocked at 6:45, steps out into the gallery and lines up with the other men. The line starts moving at once, treading the circular galleries four tiers high and descending the iron stairs and marching through the short tunnel into the big circular dining room. He eats in twenty minutes, is marched back to his cell, and is locked in for a half-hour. At 7:45 he is let out and marched to his job. At 11:15 he is marched to his cell, to the dining room, then back to his cell and counted. He is marched back to his job at 12:15, back to his cell at 3:30. After a half-hour there he is marched to the dining hall and fed his supper. At 4:30 P.M. he is marched back to his cell, counted, and locked in for the night. The lights go off at 9:00 P.M. He is counted twice during the night.

He cannot go anywhere alone without a ticket signed by a guard. Once a week he is marched to the commissary (where he can spend $4 a week), to a movie, to a ball game, to church, to the bathhouse (four minutes under the shower with guards watching); twice a week he is marched to the barber shop for a shave and once a month for a haircut; once every two weeks he may receive a visit from relatives. Once a year, on New Year's Eve, he may yell in his cell.

He may smoke in his cell or at work—anywhere except in the dining room, the chapel, or in line. If he has no money he is issued a sack of free tobacco every week . . . He can listen to the radio in his cell till 11:00 P.M. He has a choice of three stations but a guard monitors the programs, tuning out crime programs. He may receive newspapers, magazines, and books by mail, but only direct from the publishers, never from friends. He may borrow books from the prison library. He may write one letter a week to a relative or an approved correspondent (plus special letters in emergencies).

New inmates do the prison's manual labor. Later they may be assigned to better jobs. Men without money want to work in the shops, where they are paid. (Everybody in a shop receives the same pay. In few places on earth are men so equal as in prison.) Others want to work in the kitchen; they can choose their food and eat it at leisure. On certain jobs, key inmate workers and clerks have more actual authority than the guards in charge. Runners, clerks, and hospital nurses are all, socially, a cut above the other prisoners. They have more freedom. Freedom, even mere freedom of movement inside the wall, is the most precious thing in any prison. . . .

All the cells have toilets and running water. The cells in the roundhouses are 10 feet 8 inches long, 5 feet 9 inches wide, and 8 feet 1 inch high. The cells were designed to hold only one man, but since the prison is about 100 per cent over-crowded, most cells hold two men, and many three . . . It is hard for men to live together in so small a space, if one wants to pace the floor, the other must stay in bed. If one wants to use the tiny top of the chest of drawers—the only furniture—to write a letter, the other cannot. If one wants to move from the cell door to the toilet at the rear, the other has to get into bed to let him pass. There is no privacy in prison. . . .

It is still one of the toughest prisons in the country, say the convicts, because of the discipline. The rule-book lists no fewer than 111 rules, forbidding, among other things, inso-lence, note-writing, swearing, staring at visitors, whistling, running, criticizing the institution. It says that an inmate must address guards respectfully by their proper title, touch-ing his cap or forehead; he must keep two buttons on his coat buttoned.[38]

One of the major difficulties in the American prison system is the inequities which arise from widely differing state and local laws. What may be a capital offense in one state may not be in the next; armed robbery may carry sentences from one year to life. Some judges are more lenient than others; in some states, judges are given little discretion as to the sentence. These inequities deepen the sense of bitterness felt by all prisoners, who know also that many criminal acts go unpunished. The result is an atmos-phere which scarcely augurs well for rehabilitation.

The Federal Prison System

The Federal Prison Bureau, reorganized in 1929 after a series of riots and a congressional investigation, has pioneered in the de-velopment of a classification system, by which violators of federal laws are sent to the institutions best suited to their needs. The fed-eral prison system is made up of six long-term adult institutions (penitentiaries); six intermediate-term adult institutions, includ-ing one with separate facilities and programs for women and another with separate facilities but co-correctional programs for women; six young adult institutions, including two reformatories; thirteen short-term adult institutions, including seven camps; three youth and juvenile institutions, including one with separate

---

38. *Ibid.*, pp. 137–149. Conditions have not changed much since 1950. See, for example, Malcolm Braly, *On the Yard* (Boston: Little, Brown & Company, 1967); Erik Wright, *The Politics of Punishment* (New York: Colophon Books, 1973); and Jessica Mitford, *Kind and Usual Punishment: The Prison Business* (New York: Alfred A. Knopf, 1973).

facilities but co-correctional programs for women; a women's institution (reformatory); a medical center that provides a full range
of diagnostic and treatment services for federal medical and psychiatric patients; and fourteen community treatment centers (halfway houses).[39] The institutions range from maximum-security
prisons to completely "open" camps. Institution employees have
civil service status and receive formal training to develop professional skills needed to help redirect offenders into productive,
law-abiding life styles. Two out of three federal inmates are involved in some kind of education or training activity daily in the
system's twenty-six schools and forty-six skills-training programs.
About 22 percent of the inmate population is employed in the
prison industry program, which produces goods and other services for other federal agencies.

The Bureau of Prisons is engaged in a long-range improvement
program involving construction of new facilities, renovation of
present institutions, and development of innovative treatment
programs, in an effort to provide a model for state and local corrections. The Bureau works in conjunction with the Law Enforcement Assistance Administration (LEAA), giving technical assistance to state and local correctional agencies while LEAA gives
them financial assistance to carry out correctional improvements.[40]

Racism in Prison

We have already mentioned the importance of socio-economic
class in determining who becomes an official convict. The use of a
fine as an alternative to imprisonment discriminates against low-
income groups. Blacks are more likely to be arrested, convicted,
and sentenced than white men guilty of the same behavior.[41] Although blacks made up only about 11 percent of the national
population in 1970, they made up over 40 percent of state and federal prisoners.[42] This heavy percentage of blacks in some prisons

39. For further data on halfway houses, see John M. McCartt and Thomas J.
Mangogna, *Guidelines and Standards for Halfway Houses and Community Treatment
Centers* (Washington, D.C.: U.S. Department of Justice, Law Enforcement As-
sistance Administration, May 1973).

40. All data on the federal prison system supplied by Mr. Larry F. Taylor,
Executive Assistant, Bureau of Prisons, U.S. Department of Justice, July 30, 1973.

41. The *New York Times* of August 26, 1973 reported that although blacks
made up only 20 percent of the population of New York City, they constituted
59 percent of those killed by police and 62 percent of those arrested for crimes
of violence.

42. U.S. Bureau of the Census, *Persons in Institutions and Other Group Quarters, 1970* (Washington, D.C., July 1973), pp. 5, 6.

has contributed substantially to prison unrest. The Attica riots of September 1971 were caused in large part by allegations by black prisoners' groups of racist attitudes on the part of guards and discrimination practices toward black prisoners. Black Muslims have claimed they were not allowed religious freedom in prisons. Black militants have claimed unjust treatment, extra-heavy sentences, and political oppression. The death of George Jackson during a purported escape attempt and the Angela Davis trial in 1972 indicate some of the bitterness engendered in blacks at the discriminatory treatment they suffer under our present correctional system.[43] In spite of promises of no reprisals after the Attica riots were put down, outside observers reported brutal punishment of ringleaders and followers. When charges were brought in July of 1973 as a result of the deaths of thirty-nine prisoners and hostages, none was made against state police and others who led the break-in, in spite of evidence of indiscriminate shooting against groups of prisoners.[44] Blacks claim, with reason, that they are discriminated against both in and out of prison and that they become "politicized" and activist as a result of their prison experiences.

Services for Women Offenders

There are many fewer convicted women criminals than men, a ratio of about one to eight. Police and courts may be more reluctant to arrest and sentence women. Because of family responsibilities, women more often receive suspended sentences or are placed on probation. Women are more likely to be dealt with by unofficial agencies, especially for sex irregularities. In the past, writers attempted to explain the disparity between male and female rates of crime on the basis of some innate qualities. This is hardly borne out by the facts. Women do most of the shoplifting and are very likely to be accomplices in a wide range of illegal activities.

Whatever the reasons, there are many fewer institutions for women, and they are smaller and usually more progressive than institutions for men. There are more likely to be social workers on the staff, less rigid discipline, few if any cell blocks, and more opportunities for group activities and social occasions. Vocational

43. See George Jackson, *Soledad Brother: The Prison Letters of George Jackson* (New York: Coward, McCann and Geoghegan, 1971).
44. See Tom Wicker, "Justice or Revenge," *New York Times,* July 16, 1973; and *Attica: The Official Report of the New York State Special Commission on Attica* (New York: Bantam Books, 1972).

training, once largely for domestic work, has been supplemented by training for clerical and service jobs.

A perennial problem for women's institutions is the number of prisoners who are pregnant when committed, although with contraception and abortion more available, this may decline. Most institutions provide for nursery care of the infant, but depending on the length of sentence and the mother's future plans, the baby should be placed in a foster home or released for adoption. The social worker should help the mother arrive at a decision. Here is another example of a situation (also discussed in Chapter 4) in which careful work with mothers will minimize the number of children left forgotten in foster homes until they are too old to be readily adoptable.

The problems of monotonous routine, institutional food, and loss of freedom exist in the most progressive institutions. In general, federal facilities are superior to those of the various states, yet in a carefully written account of her own experiences in the federal prison for women in Alderson, West Virginia, Helen Bryan described the defeatism and absence of counseling services. Convicted of contempt of Congress for failing to reveal names to the House Un-American Activities Committee, Miss Bryan received a three-months sentence. The physical plant was adequate; discipline was mild; there was no mistreatment of prisoners. But daily prison life was lonely and unhappy. No psychiatric consultation was available, nor were there caseworkers on the staff.[45] For many women there, treatment in the community would have been infinitely more beneficial.

The programs at some state prisons for women seem superior to Alderson, since they include academic programs, counseling, and cottage-type plants. New York State maintains the Westfield Reformatory and State Farm Prison for Women in Westchester County. Westfield meets many of the standards set up as ideal, yet nearly a third of the parolees have to be returned for parole violation. That the parole program, with the individualized attention it entails, can succeed is illustrated in the following case study.

The Case of Ruth Miller
Ruth Miller first came to the attention of the City Magistrates' Court in New York City on February 2, 1956, when she was eighteen years old. A petition was brought by her widowed mother, with whom Ruth was living. Mrs. Miller had gone to

45. Helen Bryan, *Inside* (Boston: Houghton Mifflin, 1953). See also Kathryn W. Burkhart, *Women in Prison* (New York: Doubleday & Company, 1973).

the Legal Aid Bureau for advice about breaking up an intense affair between Ruth and a thirty-five-year-old musician of a different racial background and had been referred to the Court.

The Court Intake Worker's report indicated that Ruth apparently had had a secure and happy childhood. She was the younger of two daughters; her sister was ten years older, and Ruth and she had been quite close until Emily married and moved to California. Emily had graduated from college with honors. Mrs. Miller felt that Ruth's troubles began with Mr. Miller's death in 1947. She had grieved deeply, shut herself into her room, and withdrawn from her mother's attempts to comfort her. She did average work in high school, in spite of better than average ability, but college was out of the question with the family's reduced income. Following graduation in June of 1955, Ruth had secured work as an assistant bookkeeper, earning $45 a week, out of which she paid her mother $15 for board. Her employer considered her capable and wished to keep her in his employ. The probation officer visited the home in Brooklyn and found it small but comfortable and well-kept.

Early in 1955, Mrs. Miller had required a period of prolonged hospitalization, and it was then that Ruth met Ali Huseem. Mr. Huseem had interested Ruth in astrology, the occult, hypnotism, and mental telepathy. His dominance over her was so extreme that Mrs. Miller became alarmed. She had made determined attempts to break up the affair, especially when it became apparent that Ruth was sexually involved with Huseem. She had argued and pleaded with Ruth, had taken her to a psychiatrist, and had threatened Huseem with police action. In desperation, she took her problem to the Court.

Huseem's reputation was well known in the Brooklyn area where the Millers lived. He had been involved with several teen-age girls. The welfare department had a warrant charging him with nonsupport of his wife and children. Ruth maintained that she knew all this but that he had changed and was planning to secure a divorce and marry her.

Ruth was placed on probation, ordered to cease seeing Huseem and to secure psychotherapy, since psychiatric evaluation had recommended this. She was brought back into court in May of 1956, charged with violating the terms of her probation, and new, stricter conditions were laid down. Ruth carefully observed all the restrictions except those involving seeing Huseem. By March of 1957, when she was five months pregnant, Ruth was removed from the home, placed in a maternity home, and following the birth of her daughter in

August, was given an indeterminate sentence to the Westfield State Farm, which she entered on September 19, 1957.

In her initial interview at the Reformatory, Ruth impressed her parole officer as upset and overwhelmed by all that had happened to her, particularly by the separation from her baby. Her only solution was to marry Huseem, and nothing else seemed real to her. She was distressed because she had felt compelled to sign an application for boarding-home placement of the baby.

During her month in the reception cottage, Ruth was seen by the guidance counselor, who recommended an academic program. She was given a complete health examination and found to be in good physical condition. Her cottage report indicated that she was likable, cooperative, and neat about her room and her person. She was seen by the institution's psychiatrist, who found her well motivated for psychotherapy. The impression was of a basically schizophrenic personality.

During her stay in the institution, Ruth took commercial courses and worked as a bookkeeper. Her work was of high quality. She saw the psychiatrist at regular intervals, the discussion centering around her ambivalent feelings toward her mother and her unconscious search for a father substitute. She gained more insight into her behavior and was aware of the benefits she gained. When the time approached for her release, she indicated a desire to continue in psychotherapy. Although always quiet and somewhat shy, Ruth made some friends and always had an excellent cottage report.

It was in her work with the institution parole officer that Ruth showed most concretely her growing maturity and self-sufficiency. Miss Neale's first concern was in helping Ruth work out plans for the baby. At first Ruth would only consider marrying Ali Huseem and keeping the baby. Her attitude about the problems to be encountered in an interracial marriage with a man almost twice her age was unrealistic. Without condemning Ruth, Miss Neale tried to present the realities of the situation and made strenuous efforts to reach Huseem, who was traveling with a jazz band and ignored the efforts of the welfare department to reach him.

After many unsuccessful attempts, Miss Neale finally arranged an interview and found Huseem to be a highly verbal man, who tried to overwhelm her with explanations and rationalizations of his past and current behavior. Although he claimed he had secured a divorce in Illinois, he failed to produce the papers. While protesting his eagerness to marry Ruth, he never followed through on any of the necessary arrangements. Miss Neale helped Ruth to acknowledge her disappointment and growing disillusionment as the weeks passed without any definite action on his part. By the time Ruth's progress was reviewed at a Staff Committee in April of 1958, Ruth was becoming increasingly dubious about the possibility that she could marry Huseem and keep her baby. Miss Neale was careful not to push her, but together they discussed Ruth's relationship with him and the probable meaning of his continued failure to sign paternity papers for the baby and produce his divorce papers.

It was hard for Ruth to give up the hope that Huseem really had changed and would marry her. Her own growing doubts were intensified by the questions she was asked in her interview before the Staff Committee. No doubt she was also receiving pressure from her mother and Emily. Perhaps she was also influenced by the success she was achieving in her school and work placement in the institution and her correspondence courses. Whatever the reasons, one April day she appeared in Miss Neale's office to say, happily, that she had finally made up her mind to give up Ali, release the baby for adoption, and explore the possibilities of nursing training. Miss Neale's interview notes said: "Ruth seemed happier than she has the whole time she has been here. Making this decision seemed to have freed her."

Between April and July, Miss Neale continued to work with Ruth. Having made up her mind to terminate the contact with Huseem, Ruth felt some guilt and was given special permission to write to him and convey her decision. (Permission to write and receive letters is ordinarily given only for relatives.) Miss Neale took the letter and delivered it personally to Huseem, who seemed both angry and relieved, although he complained that he had changed all his plans to no avail now. Miss Neale also arranged for the adoption agency worker to talk with Ruth and helped Ruth fill out the final surrender papers.

Ruth and Miss Neale spent a good deal of time discussing parole plans. Ruth wanted to return to her mother's, and Miss Neale visited the home, approved it as adequate, and discussed with Mrs. Miller ways in which she could help Ruth. Mrs. Miller could hardly believe that Ruth had at last been willing to give up Huseem, and Miss Neale was able to reassure her that Ruth was determined to put that part of her life behind her and start fresh. When Ruth appeared before the Board on August 8, 1958, she was granted her parole. Miss Neale's summary for the Board included the following: "She appears to be a very intelligent girl and has been taking a college correspondence course in journalism which has given her a good deal of satisfaction. She has adjusted very well in the institution and gets along well with officers and girls. She has gained insight into her behavior. She has been willing to discuss her problems and has been able to work out her feelings for the father of her child and to feel satisfied that she has made the right decision in giving him up and planning for adoption of her daughter. She feels that this man could not give her the type of life she would want for herself and her daughter and that she could not by herself give her daughter the things needed and therefore wants her to have a normal home life with an adopted family. This has not been easy for Ruth as she loves this man and her daughter, but she is doing what she thinks is best. Because she has derived benefit from her contacts with the psychiatrist in the institution, it is recommended that she continue in psychotherapy."

On August 8, Ruth signed her release and had her last interview with Miss Neale. While in some states the same parole officer continues to follow a client during the parole period, in New York State, the case is transferred to a member of the field staff assigned to the appropriate district. Although Ruth had grown attached to Miss Neale, she was prepared to find her new parole officer helpful and friendly. She was outfitted with new clothes, provided with $20 and her train ticket, and on the morning of August 12, she was driven to the station and put on the New York train.

In the meantime, a copy of her court and institutional record had been sent to the New York City Parole Office, and her new parole officer, Miss Olson, was expecting her when she made her arrival report shortly after noon. Miss Olson explained the rules and regulations of parole and told Ruth she was to report each week.

Miss Olson's first summary on Ruth covered the period August 13 to November 11. During that time, there were twelve interviews in the office, four visits made by Miss Olson to the home, and a number of telephone calls regarding jobs. Ruth secured a job as an office assistant in a doctor's office. Through the worker at the adoption agency, arrangements were made for her to secure psychotherapy at a reduced rate, which Ruth paid out of her salary. Relations between Ruth and her mother were relatively harmonious. Ruth used some of her earnings to have needed dental work done, paid board to her mother, and purchased a hi-fi set which she enjoyed greatly. She and Miss Olson got on well, although Ruth's discussions were more on everyday matters than on her feelings.

After six months, Ruth was put on a monthly reporting schedule, instead of a weekly one. Between December 1 and March 17, 1959, there were five office interviews, three home visits, and several telephone calls, and Miss Olson's report was "satisfactory adjustment." This continued for the next year. Ruth reported each month to the office, and Miss Olson visited the home about monthly, sometimes talking with Mrs. Miller and sometimes with Ruth. Ruth continued in her job and received two raises in pay but found the work tedious and began to look for another position. She began to make friends her own age, joined a YWCA group, and continued in psychotherapy on a private basis.

In her discussions with Mrs. Miller, Miss Olson learned of the strenuous efforts made by Ali Huseem to renew his relationship with Ruth and of her firmness in resisting becoming involved again. Although Mrs. Miller regretted that Ruth had been sent to the Reformatory and had some guilt about her own part in it, she felt the great change in Ruth's attitude had been worth it.

In April of 1960, Ruth found an apartment with a friend she had made at work. She asked permission to move, and Miss Olson was glad to approve, since in spite of good will on both sides, there was increasing minor friction between Mrs. Miller and Ruth. Her weekly visits to the psychiatrist were spaced out to once a month, as Ruth felt increasingly able to handle her problems. She did not tell Miss Olson much about what went on in her psychotherapy, but from little remarks she dropped from time to time, Miss Olson gathered that her ambivalent feelings toward her mother and her competitiveness with the brighter older sister both figured in her discussions with her psychiatrist. Ruth's growing stability and success, for which Miss Olson gave her recognition and praise, helped her to overcome her childish feelings of resentment toward the sister who had been her mother's favorite.

In the spring of that year, Ruth and Miss Olson spent a good deal of time discussing Ruth's job. The work in the doctor's office had grown routine, with no possibility of advancement. Although Ruth had abandoned her original hope of going into nursing, she still wanted something in an allied field. Through an agency which specialized in medical placements, Ruth secured a job in a medical laboratory as a trainee. Although the salary was lower, the outlook was brighter, and without her weekly psychiatric sessions to pay for, Ruth could manage.

As Ruth's period of parole drew to a close, Miss Olson saw her less often and encouraged her in her belief that she could manage her own life successfully. Although the restrictions must have been irksome, Ruth never complained about them, and carefully observed the regulations. Miss Olson probably knew Ruth less well than Miss Neale had, but she was able to build on the good foundation Ruth and Miss Neale had built together during the year at the Reformatory. Through her

regular contacts with Ruth, Miss Olson supported her readjustment to her mother's home and provided support in her
decision to start a new life for herself.

In August 1960, three years after her commitment, Ruth's
parole period was officially terminated. The bewildered, unhappy adolescent, trapped in an unhealthy relationship, had
become a poised, self-sufficient working girl, with living and
working conditions which gave her adequate opportunities
for social contact and normal relationships. Ruth's assets of
intelligence, ambition, warmth, and ability to accept limitations enabled her to use the resources offered by her institutional placement and her parole supervision.[46]

Not all troubled adolescents become caught up in preoccupation
with the occult. Neither do many make such constructive use of
the help offered them. There are several interesting questions we
may ask ourselves about Ruth Miller. Her grief for her father may
well have influenced her search for a father figure, but what led
her to select one so obviously unsuitable as Huseem? What were
her feelings toward the older sister who had been the mother's
favorite and whose academic success she had no realistic hope of
achieving? In her frantic efforts to break up the affair, what
arguments must Mrs. Miller have used? Why was the probation
officer unable to involve Ruth in any meaningful relationship?

Here is a situation where the element of authority operated in
Ruth's defense. She was unable to terminate the contact herself,
and Huseem refused to abide by any court ruling. Relations between Ruth and Mrs. Miller, apparently basically good, were so
strained that continuing in her mother's home was not helping
Ruth. Only the removal of Ruth from the home and her protection
from contacts with Huseem gave her a chance to withdraw from
the situation enough to see that it was not what she really wanted.
Once she had made her decision, Ruth never looked back but concentrated on building a new life for herself.

Miss Neale's role at this crucial period in Ruth's life was a highly
significant one. By accepting Ruth as she was and not arguing
with her, she replaced, temporarily, the mother who was so desperately eager for Ruth to change. By keeping Ruth's attention
firmly directed to reality and not allowing her to plan unrealistically on marriage with Huseem, she helped Ruth gradually to
recognize how futile her expectations were. By her willingness to
talk to Huseem and to keep him informed of developments, Miss

---

46. This case was adapted from unpublished material in the files of the New
York State Division of Parole. Used with permission.

Neale placed herself on Ruth's side rather than in opposition to her. The role of the psychiatrist as a substitute father figure must not be overlooked, also. We know that Ruth missed her father deeply, and the psychiatrist's supplying part of this need undoubtedly made it easier for Ruth to relinquish her neurotic attachment to Huseem.

We should not minimize the importance of the institutional routine. What has been called the "current life space" of an individual is highly influential in the development and modification of attitudes. The acceptance and approval of cottage staff, teachers, and work supervisors must have been a salutary and welcome change to a girl who had had little but disapproval for many months.

Although Ruth mourned for her baby, she had actually had little contact with her, and the decision to release her for adoption, however hard, was obviously a wise one, as Ruth replanned her life to resume her interrupted adolescence. There was no real place in this situation for a baby.

While the case of Ruth Miller shows the constructive use of authority, of casework relationships and psychotherapy, and of the development of increased maturity, it is doubtful that sentencing this troubled adolescent to an institution represents the most constructive way of helping her. Liaisons with a member of another race today would not constitute a crime for an adult, and the age of majority is now eighteen in many states. More effective probation work, involving psychotherapy, provision of further education, an opportunity to move to a new location, foster care from understanding foster parents or in a group home or in the maternity home, all might have represented less costly means of helping Ruth. Rather than illustrating the constructive use of prison, Ruth's case underlines the essential uselessness of incarcerating young people who have so much capacity to respond to treatment and supports the advocates of community-based treatment facilities as a better alternative to even the most progressive prison.

The Police and the Courts

We have already mentioned that the police have broad latitude in making arrests. The enormous disparities in methods and procedures followed by overlapping and competing jurisdictions point to an urgent need for centralization of police authority and simplification of court procedures, together with enlargement of court facilities for rapid processing. With the presently overcrowded court calendars, those charged may be detained for months before their cases come up in court.

The philosophy of "individualized justice" as seen, at least in principle, in the juvenile court is not characteristic of adult courts. Instead of a mandatory social study and an individualized treatment plan, the criminal court attempts to determine the legal aspects of the cases in terms of complicated technicalities. Individuals are persuaded to plead guilty to lesser offenses,[47] and upper-income defendants hire lawyers to find legal loopholes. Evidence of law-breaking in high places, most recently brought vividly to public attention by the Watergate affair, contributes to a general lack of respect for law and the administration of justice. Sentence may be determined within wide discretion by the judge or be strictly prescribed by law. Obsolete and vague charges (vagrancy, for example) may be made when evidence is lacking for stronger charges.

The 1960s saw increased concern over the civil and human rights of suspects and offenders. The Supreme Court decisions in the cases of *Gideon* vs. *Wainright* (1963, guaranteeing counsel at trial and appeal to all felony defendants) and *Miranda* vs. *Arizona* (1966, prohibiting the questioning of a suspect in custody unless counsel is present) have altered police procedures in many states, but much inequity still prevails. Inmates of prisons have much justification for claiming that they are there only because they were unlucky.

DO PRISONS SUCCEED?

It is all too apparent that prisons do not succeed in their professed aim of reform and rehabilitation. Between 60 and 70 percent of prisoners have been through the correctional system at least once before. Since 99 percent of those in prison will be returned to the community, at least temporarily, more attention should be paid to their ability to adjust in the community rather than, as at present, to socializing them into the prison subculture. Readjustment is made doubly difficult by the stigmatization of prison. The released prisoner faces handicaps in securing employment, restrictions placed on his activities as a condition of his parole, loss of civil rights, and loss of privacy. Labor unions may not admit his prison training as acceptable apprenticeship, and his attempts to form new social relationships and avoid maintaining contacts with criminal friends will be hampered by popular stereotypes of "ex-convicts."

47. George Jackson claimed he had been promised leniency if he "copped a plea." See Abraham S. Blumberg, "The Practice of Law as a Confidence Game," *Law and Society Review*, Vol. 1, No. 2 (Winter 1966), pp. 1–25.

The late Harry Elmer Barnes, one of the most vocal advocates of abolishing prisons in favor of community-based programs, talked of the "convict bogey," the irrational fear of a convicted criminal. The individual who has committed a criminal act is regarded very differently from the convict who has been found guilty, although only a court verdict differentiates the two.

> Until the public ceases to approach the problem of crime and the convict in much the same attitude as primitive man regarded the violator of the taboo, there is little hope for any rapid progress of a rational penology. If and when we can dissolve the convict bogey, we may be able to make some headway in abandoning prisons and institutionalization, and in adopting more rational, more hopeful, and less expensive modes of dealing with convicted criminals. And we shall also then become fearful of *criminals* and insist that more of them be apprehended and convicted.[48]

Public attitudes toward the released prisoner are severely handicapping and often based on myths and half-truths. Daste and Perkins[49] suggest that since stigmatization is such a barrier to readjustment in the community and a pressure toward renewed criminal activity, corrections-oriented workers might profitably devote their attention to the "social audience" of the released prisoner. Employers would be a strategic target for these educational efforts, since employment is so crucial a factor in the readjustment of the offender.

Modifications of the prison system itself are being made experimentally in some states. Regional correctional centers, some of which permit the prisoner to continue to work at his regular job and return to the center for group therapy and other programs in the evenings and weekends, make it possible for selected offenders to remain near their families and continue to support them. Weekend passes home, conjugal visiting,[50] coeducational prisons, more prisoner voice in management, more attention to the legal rights of inmates—all these are at best a patching-up of a system which has little to recommend it. Nor can the reformers agree on what approaches do offer promise. As David Rothman says, in

48. Barnes and Teeters, *New Horizons in Criminology,* © 1951, pp. 819, 820. By permission of Prentice-Hall, Inc.

49. Barry M. Daste and Robert A. Perkins, "Stigma Reduction and the Corrections-Oriented Worker," *Social Casework,* Vol. 54, No. 7 (July 1973), pp. 418–423.

50. See Wolfram Rieger, "A Proposal for a Trial of Family Therapy and Conjugal Visits in Prison," *American Journal of Orthopsychiatry,* Vol. 43, No. 1 (January 1973), pp. 117–122.

his essay-review "The Correction of Practices of Correction," even prison reformers have no grand solutions:

> Today's reformers, having inherited past failures, correctional facilities that do not correct and release procedures that only embitter inmates, can only bemoan the Atticas, point to the community, and state that efforts at amelioration will not make things worse . . . They know they lack the knowledge and skill to rehabilitate deviants, and they cannot even imagine eliminating crime from our society.[51]

Seymour Halleck, a psychiatrist for the Federal Bureau of Prisons and author of *The Politics of Therapy*,[52] a challenging account of the role of psychiatrist as social change agent, feels that appeals to compassion, humanitarianism, and rationality may not be the effective way to persuade a vengefully hostile public to insist upon and fund adequately an adequate correctional system. He suggests an appeal to economy, since the present correctional system is at once extremely costly and largely ineffective.

> It would help if somebody would try to figure out what a correctional system characterized by efficient police work, adequate court facilities, short sentences, less attention to criminals without victims, indeterminate sentences, and real rehabilitation facilities in our prisons would actually cost. I am convinced that it would cost less than our current system . . . An appeal to materialism might bring on reforms that the most eloquent pleas for humanity have thus far failed to achieve![53]

PROBATION AND PAROLE

When social workers are employed in the correctional system, it is likely to be in the probation and parole programs.[54] Probation has many advantages if properly carried out. It enables the indi-

---

51. David J. Rothman, "The Correction of Practices of Correction," *New York Times Book Review*, May 27, 1973, p. 4. © 1973 by the New York Times Company. Reprinted by permission.

52. Seymour Halleck, *The Politics of Therapy* (New York: Science House, 1971).

53. Seymour Halleck, "Crime and the Dilemmas of Psychiatry," *Psychotherapy and Social Science Review*, Vol. 6, No. 3 (March 3, 1972), p. 25.

54. The National Council on Crime and Delinquency publishes case material showing both probation and parole with juveniles and adults. Each case is accompanied by teaching notes and discussion guides. For a list of cases available, write the Council, 44 E. 23rd St., New York, N.Y., 10010. See also Elliot Studt, *A Conceptual Approach to Teaching Materials: Illustrations from the Field of Corrections* (New York: CSWE, 1965), which contains excellent case material and references.

vidual to remain at his job, in his community, relatively unstigmatized, and gives the first offender another chance. It disrupts his family life little and enables him to continue to support his dependents. It avoids the bitterness and feelings of injustice which inevitably result from imprisonment. Probation should be long enough to enable lasting changes to take place, and the probation officer's caseload should be small enough to enable him to provide individualized service. The President's Commission on Law Enforcement recommends a caseload of no more than thirty-five. Where caseloads are in the hundreds, the supervision becomes meaningless, and the public's already low opinion of probation is confirmed. If eighteen months to two years of good supervision does not result in improved adjustment, the offender was not a good risk. The probation officer should supplement individual counseling by serving as a linkage between the probationer and other community resources.

The relative costs of probation and incarceration should be more widely publicized, to encourage funding for more adequate staffs. The President's Commission also recommends more extensive use of volunteers and paraprofessionals to supplement the work of probation officers, as well as in-service training for probation staff.[55]

It is in connection with parole planning and supervision that social workers have been used most extensively. Parole is conditional release under supervision, granted when the behavior of the prisoner warrants taking the risk involved. Under typical state law, parole application may not be made until the expiration of the minimum sentence, less time off for good behavior. Since "good time" is usually ten days per month, the earliest a man with a three to five year sentence could apply would be at the end of two years. Many authorities favor much earlier parole for selected prisoners. If the parole is granted, it is for the remainder of the sentence, and the parolee may be returned if he violates the conditions of his parole, which may be extremely limiting.

Not all prisoners are paroled; some serve the maximum sentence in prison but then must be released unsupervised into the community. Prisons may be forced to release men who are potentially dangerous because they have completed their maximum sentence and there is no legal way to detain them longer. Pre-release centers and day-furlough plans may ease reentry into the community

55. The use of volunteers is well established in Great Britain. See W. R. Weston, "The Use of Volunteers in Probation and After-Care: The First Five Years," *International Social Work*, Vol. 15, No. 2 (1972), pp. 36–43.

and would facilitate employment arrangements when employment is a requirement for leaving the institution.

The parole board visits each prison at scheduled intervals to
review applications. The file on each prisoner is reviewed, including his conviction, background, institutional adjustment, contacts
with chaplain, counseling contacts, parole plans, and the recommendations from the institutional parole officer. But the most
carefully prepared dossier is of little use if the parole board is incompetent. In most states, appointment is made by the governor.
There have been glaring illustrations of political influence, and
few states require any relevant training. There is no uniformity
among states as to leniency; some boards parole a much larger percentage of applications than others.[56]

The paroled prisoner is ordered to report immediately to the
parole office in his district, where he has the rules of parole explained to him. He will have many restraints placed upon him;
he must work regularly, may not associate with undesirable ac-
quaintances, must keep regular hours, must not use alcohol or
narcotics, must not move or change his marital status without
permission, and he may not be allowed to vote. For violation of
these or numerous other regulations, he can be returned to prison
as a parole violator.

All this makes the caseload of a parole officer very different from
that of a worker in a voluntary agency whose clients have chosen
to use his services. Dealing with such handicapped clients puts
special burdens of maintaining patience, understanding, warmth,
and skill on the parole worker who is trying to support the
parolee's efforts to "go straight" in a hostile world. For many
parolees, the notion that they are worthy of respect and worth
helping is a new experience, greeted initially and perhaps for a
long time with skepticism but ultimately as helpful. Acknowledgement of the very real handicaps under which the parolee
operates and attempts to develop with him adequate strategies for
overcoming some of these handicaps are more productive uses of
worker time than exhortations to the parolee to behave himself.

How successful is parole? The evidence is difficult to secure,
since it depends largely on whether the parolee is detected in
illegal behavior. In New York State, a ten-year study completed in
1966 showed a parole violation rate (much of it technical viola-

56. For an account of a parole board meeting, see Robert Wool, "The New
Parole and the Case of Mr. Simms," *New York Times Magazine*, July 29, 1973,
pp. 14 ff., which describes the Federal Parole Board sessions at Lewisburg Penitentiary in Pennsylvania.

tion of parole regulations) of 11.6 percent the first year, gradually rising to 41.7 percent.[57] In the last analysis, even if only half successful in terms of further convictions, parole must be considered valuable. However full of flaws present parole systems may be, the principle of a transition period between institutional confinement and complete freedom is a sound one. Yet even a well-trained, adequately staffed parole agency cannot succeed in a society so committed to its present punitive and unjust correctional system.

THE PLACE OF SOCIAL WORK
IN CORRECTIONS

The number of professional social workers in the correctional field is extremely low; where jobs classified as "social work" exist, they are likely to be filled by people with other types of training. Some authorities are not entirely sure that social workers can work appropriately in corrections; the field of corrections finds social workers largely uninformed about the law. The field of social work questions the possibility of adapting its principles to so authoritarian a setting. Yet there is some evidence of rapprochement between the two fields,[58] and the recognition of baccalaureate training in social work may make it possible for correctional agencies to hire more social workers. In direct work with prisoners and parolees, in maintaining contact with families, in serving as broker between the prisoner and community resources, the correctional social worker views the prisoner or ex-prisoner as a client who needs service rather than as an offender who is being punished.

The effectiveness of self-help programs was referred to in Chapter 1 (page 16). The efforts of such groups as the Seventh Step, in-

57. New York State Division of Parole, *Thirty-sixth Annual Report, 1966,* p. 191.

58. See *Manpower and Training for Corrections* (New York: CSWE, 1966), for a report of a workshop under joint social work–correctional sponsorship; Jack C. Sternback, "Issues in Corrections from Both Sides of the Bars," *Social Casework,* Vol. 54, No. 6 (June 1973), pp. 342–349; Lloyd E. Ohlin, Herman Piven, and Donnell M. Pappenfort, "Major Dilemmas of the Social Worker in Probation and Parole," *The NPPA Journal,* Vol. 2, No. 3 (July 1956), pp. 211–225; Elliot Studt, "Crime and Delinquency: Institutions," *Encyclopedia of Social Work, 1971,* pp. 186–191. McCartt and Mangogna, *Guidelines and Standards for Halfway Houses and Community Treatment Centers,* recommend that directors and assistant directors should be MSWs and that ex-offenders be employed as counselors. For an account of a well-known halfway house, Dismas House, write to 5025 Cote Brillante Ave., St. Louis, Mo., 63113, for their annual report and descriptive brochure.

augurated by Bill Sands,[59] and the Fortune Society[60] in New York City owe much of their success to their ability to mitigate the hostility felt by society toward released prisoners. Social workers should foster the development of these groups and assist as resource persons but not attempt to direct them.

In the long run, social workers can be most effective if they operate as change agents, both from within the system and outside it, to bring about more enlightened attitudes. The criminal is not a different kind of human being who must be caged but a citizen with tremendous social handicaps whose stigmatization reflects our guilt. This is an unpalatable concept for many to accept, but no meaningful reform of the correctional system can occur until its truth is recognized.

ADDITIONAL REFERENCES

"A Helping Hand: Halfway Houses Draw Both Praises, Criticism for Care of Ex-Cons," *Wall Street Journal*, Vol. 179, No. 44 (March 3, 1972), pp. 1, 20. A balanced appraisal of the usefulness and shortcomings of halfway houses for ex-prisoners.

A National Strategy to Reduce Crime (Washington, D.C.: National Advisory Commission on Criminal Justice Standards and Goals, 1973). Outlines a goal of 50 percent reduction in high-fear crimes by 1983, with four areas for priority action: delinquency prevention; improved service delivery; prompt determination of guilt or innocence; increased citizen participation.

An Analysis of Federal Juvenile Delinquency and Related Youth Development Programs for Juvenile Delinquency Planners (Washington, D.C.: Interdepartment Council to Coordinate All Federal Juvenile Delinquency Programs, February 1973). Catalogs and classifies all 197 programs operated in 1972 by thirteen different federal agencies.

Fenton, Norman, *Human Relations in Adult Corrections* (Springfield, Ill.: Charles C Thomas, Publisher, 1973). A cooperative effort by clinical psychologists, psychiatrists, social workers, and others interested in penology, which offers a philosophy of treatment for those working with imprisoned adult offenders.

---

59. See Bill Sands, *My Shadow Ran Fast* (New York: New American Library, 1966) and *The Seventh Step* (New York: New American Library, 1967), for the fascinating story of the author's rehabilitation at San Quentin and subsequent efforts to rehabilitate other ex-convicts.

60. See William C. Kuehn, "The Concept of Self-Help Groups Among Criminals," *Criminologica*, Vol. 7, No. 1 (May 1969), pp. 20–25; and Edward Sagarin, *Odd Man In: Societies of Deviants in America* (Chicago: Quadrangle Books, 1969), especially Chapter 7, "Convicts and Ex-convicts: Using the Skeleton to Open the Closets," pp. 163–195, which includes a description of the Fortune Society and other self-help groups.

Forer, Lois G., *No One Will Lissen* (New York: Grosset and Dunlap, 1970). A municipal judge describes how every normal avenue for obtaining justice is systematically closed to the child whose parents lack money and knowledge.

Glaser, Daniel, *Adult Crime and Social Policy* (Englewood Cliffs, N.J.: Prentice-Hall, 1972). The development of a ten-part typology for adult criminals to provide guidelines for social action and public policy, with the recommendation that the primary emphasis in corrections should be the provision of legitimate alternatives to crime more gratifying than the crime itself.

Hawes, Joseph M., *Children in Urban Society: Juvenile Delinquency in Nineteenth-Century America* (New York: Oxford University Press, 1971). The history of the understanding and treatment of delinquency and of the pioneers in the establishment of the juvenile court.

Jackson, Bruce, *In the Life: Versions of the Criminal Experience* (Bergenfield, N.J.: New American Library, 1972). First-person narratives of chronic criminals in prison and outside.

Palmer, Stuart, *Prevention of Crime* (New York: Behavioral Publications, 1973). Broad strategies for altering the social system to prevent crime, to reorganize the correctional system, and to introduce new, effective methods of rehabilitation.

Radzinowicz, Sir Lionel and Wolfgang, Marvin E., eds., *Crime and Justice* (New York: Basic Books, 1971). A three-volume compendium which brings together articles from experts in the United States and abroad.

Struggle for Justice: A Report on Crime and Punishment in America, prepared for the American Friends Service Committee by a working party of seventeen members (New York: Hill and Wang, 1972). Explores the fallacies of trying to cure people by punishing them.

Taylor, Ian; Walton, Paul; and Young, Jack, *The New Criminology: For a Social Theory of Deviance* (New York: Harper & Row, 1974). A comprehensive critique of European and American studies of crime and deviance.

Warren, Marguerite Q., *Correctional Treatment in Community Settings: A Report of Current Research* (Washington, D.C.: Department of Health, Education, and Welfare, 1972). Juvenile delinquency in the United States and selected other countries.

8 chapter

social work
with selected
disabilities

The Southern Regional Education Board,
in its provocative analysis of the social work task which has
been repeatedly cited in the book, considers the social functioning of individuals as falling along a continuum from "ideal"
through normal, stress, crisis, temporary disability, and finally
permanent disability. When people are blocked from meeting
their basic human needs, stress, crises, and disabilities arise;
and people living under such conditions have traditionally been
the clients of social welfare agencies. The SREB describes four
categories of obstacles to functioning: 1) inadequacies or deficiencies in the individual; 2) environmental deficiencies; 3) rigid laws
and policies; and 4) catastrophes. The efforts of social workers are
directed toward improving the level of functioning, moving away
from the disability end of the continuum toward the ideal level of
social functioning. In these terms, then, the goals of social work
intervention range from promoting positive social functioning
through preventing obstacles from blocking the meeting of basic
needs, through helping individuals resolve their inadequacies and
deficiencies, to supporting and maintaining those persons so disabled that they cannot resolve their problems.[1] Social work services to those with serious disabilities will be considered in this
chapter.

1. Harold L. McPheeters and Robert M. Ryan, *A Core of Competence for Baccalaureate Social Welfare and Curricular Implications* (Atlanta: SREB, 1971), pp. 14–16.

DEFINING DISABILITY

The distinction between disabilities arising from inadequacies within the person and those in the environment, while at first glance readily apparent, turns out on closer scrutiny to be extremely difficult. War-injured veterans, with missing arms or legs, are disabled indeed, but whose was the inadequacy that caused the disability? Mental retardation is an impaired ability of the individual to adapt to his environment, sometimes owing to some obvious physical abnormality, mongolism (Down's syndrome) for example, but more often with no detectable nervous system deficit. The close relationship between poverty and mental retardation[2] raises questions as to the basic source of the problem. Attempts to explain poverty as the consequence of a process of natural selection are efforts to shift the responsibility from the society back to the supposedly genetically inferior poor person.[3] "Blaming the victim" is an attitude widely encountered by those who try to help the delinquent, the mentally ill, or those suffering from discrimination.[4]

Poverty and racism are obvious social conditions which disable their victims. But what of deviants, who may actually be innovators too far ahead of their times for social acceptability? Shifting definitions of acceptability make hard and fast lines impossible to draw. Is homosexuality a disease for which individuals should be treated, forcibly if necessary, or is it a viable alternative to heterosexual behavior, as it was once considered in ancient Greece? Is cigarette smoking a matter of personal taste or a potentially lethal addiction to be "controlled" by banning the sale of cigarettes? Man is a bio-psycho-social organism operating in a complex physical and social environment. Those who yearn for simplistic answers to questions about "cause" and "responsibility" are doomed to disappointment, unless they can conveniently ignore all but one or two of the factors

2. See Roger Hurley, *Poverty and Mental Retardation: A Causal Relationship* (New York: Random House, 1969), especially Chapter 4, "Public Education and Mental Retardation: The Self-Fulfilling Prophecy Fulfilled," pp. 91–127. See also Marjorie H. Kirkland, *Retarded Children of the Poor: A Casebook* (Washington, D.C.: Social and Rehabilitation Service, 1971).

3. Social Darwinism was a commonly held philosophy in the nineteenth century and is still reflected in attitudes about welfare recipients and in recent budget pronouncements. See the discussion on pp. 47–53 of this text.

4. See William Ryan, *Blaming the Victim* (New York: Pantheon Books, 1971), a study of the extent to which the urban poor, particularly blacks, are blamed by white middle-class America for their own difficult situation.

involved. We have already seen how indefinite are any distinctions between the mentally ill and those not so labeled. Similarly, disability must be viewed as a continuum ranging from those with gross physical abnormality which makes it impossible for them to adapt in customary ways to the world around them to those whose functioning at their highest level, their "optimizing ability,"[5] is only slightly impaired. In this chapter, we shall consider mental retardation and blindness as illustrative of disabilities clearly related to handicaps of the individual, and drug abuse, alcoholism, and homosexuality as illustrative of reactions to stress, childhood experience, social attitudes, and other factors beyond those immediately observable in the disabled individual. Our previous discussions of physical illness, delinquency, and crime, as socially defined, and of individuals' reactions to poverty and racism are obviously of relevance also.

THE DISABLED

There are groups of people who have observable and measurable deficiencies which limit their social adaptation. The physically handicapped, the blind, the deaf, the mentally retarded, those with chronic or acute disabling illness, and those enfeebled by advancing age are demonstrably unable to compete in a world where the majority are not similarly disadvantaged. It has been estimated that 2 percent of the population need rehabilitation for some disability and that 500,000 become disabled annually.

Social attitudes toward those with obvious disabilities are ambivalent and changing. Disfiguring disabilities and those which impede interaction with others are more upsetting to us than those which render the individual pathetic or appealing. The Easter Seal campaign features a child with a winsome smile courageously gripping her crutches; campaigns for the mentally retarded do not show us the profoundly retarded sitting in sawdust but a child who looks almost like normal children. Pictures of wounded war heroes are of those whose faces are undamaged. The differences in attitudes elicited by disabilities are illuminating. The blind call forth pity and a desire to help; the deaf arouse impatience. An artificial leg can be concealed more easily than an artificial arm, and both are more acceptable than an artificial nose.

However, all disability is upsetting, and the traditional

5. William A. Spencer and Maurine B. Mitchell, "Disability and Physical Handicap," *Encyclopedia of Social Work, 1971* (New York: NASW, 1971), p. 205.

method of dealing with it has been to segregate the disabled with others like them, often under the guise of special education and rehabilitation programs. Blind or deaf children have been sent to training schools, the mentally retarded institutionalized, the elderly immured in nursing homes. Those living at home were supposed to remain in the house, out of sight. No accurate estimate can be made of the extent to which such isolation from normal life may have solidified the disability. Deaf children, for example, found it easier to learn sign language to communicate with other deaf children, thereby impeding their readjustment into the community, where few hearing people know sign language. The absence of good role models in cottages for the moderately and severely retarded made it difficult for such children to learn better methods of adaptation. The expectations of staff that the disabled would behave in certain "abnormal" ways fostered such adaptations, so that disability became self-perpetuating. Being waited on by parents prevented independence in home-bound children.

There is some indication of changing attitudes. Thanks to some courageous parents who wrote appealing accounts of their experiences with retarded or disturbed children[6] before such subjects were freely discussed and to the openness with which President Kennedy acknowledged that he had a retarded sister, public attitudes are somewhat more accepting. The accomplishments of a handicapped writer like Christy Brown,[7] who learned to type with his toes, and the International Sports Organization for the Disabled, which fields basketball teams operating from wheelchairs, have also modified the older view that associated disability with helplessness. The remarkable success of the Veterans Administration and the Institute of Rehabilitation Medicine, headed by Dr. Howard Rusk, in rehabilitating badly injured people has reinforced efforts to interpret to employers and the general public that disability need not be an insuperable obstacle to effective social participation. Increasingly sophisticated prosthetic devices, electronic pacemakers, and such equipment as electric golf carts for those unable to walk, cassette recorders for the blind, electronically operated doors and

6. See for example, Pearl Buck, *The Child Who Never Grew* (New York: John Day, 1950), an early account by the mother of a retarded child. See also Josh Greenfield, *A Child Called Noah: A Family Journey* (New York: Holt, Rinehart and Winston, 1972), by the father of an autistic child; and Nancy Roberts, *David* (Richmond, Va.: John Knox Press, 1968), by the mother of a mongoloid child.

7. See Christy Brown, *The Story of Christy Brown* (New York: Pocket Books, 1971).

touch telephones for those unable to see or operate a dial make it possible for those who would have been relatively helpless a few decades ago to carry on many normal activities today.

Advances in surgery and medicine have made it possible to repair defects, rebuild lost or missing features, prevent disabling metabolic disorders such as phenylketonuria (PKU), and, via amniocentesis (testing the amniotic fluid in which the fetus is bathed for evidence of chromosomal abnormality in the unborn child), recommend therapeutic abortion if major genetic defects are indicated. These preventive and therapeutic measures are not universally available, however. Adequate prenatal and obstetrical care is less often possible for the poor, the uneducated, and those in rural areas. Lack of knowledge of rehabilitative measures, lack of resources to take advantage of them, and obsolete attitudes of defeatism are complicated by the scarcity and maldistribution of services. Legal obstacles, especially by departments of welfare and education, may place artificial barriers between those needing services and service delivery.[8] The civil rights of many disabled groups are systematically violated by commitment procedures, arbitrary decisions made on their behalf, exploitation by unscrupulous employers, and, for the retarded, involuntary sterilization. Except for veterans, who do maintain a pressure group, most of the disabled have little political power and small appeal to voters who are not personally involved. Custodial care is cheaper and less bothersome, and appropriations for rehabilitation programs have a low priority in most legislatures.

MENTAL RETARDATION:
THE PREVENTABLE DISABILITY

The largest group of the disabled are undoubtedly the mentally retarded. According to the President's Committee on Mental Retardation,[9] 3 percent of the population under 65 suffer some degree of mental retardation. There are conflicting

8. See, for example, *Issues Relating to Rehabilitation of Individuals with Behavioral Disorders* (Washington, D.C.: Rehabilitation Services Administration, Department of Health, Education, and Welfare, 1971), which specifies the conditions under which individuals exhibiting disordered behavior may and may not be eligible for vocational rehabilitation services.

9. President's Committee on Mental Retardation, MR 72: *Islands of Excellence*, pub. no. (OS) 73–7 (Washington, D.C.: Department of Health, Education, and Welfare, 1973), which sets as a goal the moving of at least one third of the institutionalized retarded into the community.

opinions as to basic causes. For many years, mental retardation was attributed almost entirely to genetic defect, as indeed was most socially disapproved behavior, and there is still a tendency to overestimate the biological (and therefore unavoidable) factors in causation. Hurley[10] finds that the 1965 estimate of 15 percent of mental retardation attributed to genetic causes is too high and believes that future research will prove that emphasis on heredity as a major cause of retardation is a distortion. As more and more evidence shows the relationship between poverty, malnutrition, poor schools, and the labeling of a child as mentally retarded,[11] society can no longer afford the comforting alibi of genetic causation.

Many of those termed severely or profoundly retarded do have some kind of brain damage or chromosomal abnormality. These persons are in the I.Q. range of 0–39. (Ranges of retardation are traditionally denoted by I.Q. ratings in spite of the unsuitability of measuring adaptability by tests which stress abstract reasoning and are unfair to the culturally deprived.) In addition to chromosomal abnormality and genetic defect, there are specific but not genetic causes, such as brain damage during birth, German measles in the first trimester of pregnancy, untreated syphilis in the mother, hormonal imbalance in mother or fetus, and malnutrition in the mother, not just during pregnancy but during her own development.[12] Dramatic illustrations of abnormality caused by drugs taken by the mother during pregnancy occurred in Europe and Canada in the late 1960s when "thalidomide babies"[13] were born with undeveloped arms and legs. It may well be that less drastic damage from other drugs or poisons is occurring to children without as yet being suspected.

10. Hurley, *Poverty and Mental Retardation*, p. 10.

11. See Florence Haselkorn, ed., *Mothers-at-Risk: Perspectives in Social Work,* "Adelphi University School of Social Work Publications," Vol. 1, No. 1 (1966), which defines as "social risks" poverty, slum housing, poor diet, poor education, multiple births spaced too closely, and out-of-wedlock pregnancy. See also Robert Perlman and Arnold Gurin, *Community Organization and Social Planning* (New York: John Wiley & Sons, 1972), pp. 188–193, for a description of the resistances to acceptance of a social-structural view of retardation.

12. *How Children Grow* (Bethesda, Md.: National Institute of Health, 1972), a nontechnical account of prenatal, child, and adolescent growth and development. See also *The Child with Central Nervous System Deficit* (Rockville, Md.: Maternal and Child Health Service, 1965).

13. See Ethel Roskies, *Abnormality and Normality: The Mothering of Thalidomide Children* (Ithaca, N.Y.: Cornell University Press, 1972). See also Cynthia P. Deutsch and Florence Schumer, *Brain Damaged Children* (New York: Brunner/Mazel, 1970).

DEGREES OF RETARDATION

The profoundly retarded (I.Q. 0–25) make up less than 20 percent of the total classed as mentally retarded in the United States. For years, it has been thought that little could be done for them except care on a purely custodial basis. However, recent team efforts at the Willowbrook State Hospital in New York showed that with properly directed efforts, even the profoundly retarded can make some progress. Those who had been unable to get out of bed learned to sit in special chairs and even to walk. Participation in activities and staff satisfaction increased, although the staff had earlier resisted efforts to change its usual approach on the grounds that no improvement could be expected.[14] The severely retarded (I.Q. 25–39) have few communication skills but can learn to walk, feed themselves, and accept toilet training. Behavioral modification and repetitive habit training will often enable them to function comfortably in a secure, protected environment.

The profoundly and severely retarded are likely to be distributed across the socio-economic spectrum. The 80 to 90 percent who make up the moderately and mildly retarded, however, are so heavily concentrated in the poor and minority groups as to support Hurley's assertions that poverty is the largest single cause of mental retardation and that the schools are the chief culprit among the influences which bear on the poor. The moderately retarded (I.Q. range 40–55) show delays in speech and motor skills but can learn elementary reading and arithmetic and simple language skills. They need protection, such as a sheltered workshop or boarding home, but are capable of a fair amount of independence if the setting is familiar and the work routine. Many can be kept at home, attending special school programs, with parents trained in rehabilitation techniques.

The mildly retarded are not so recognized by the casual observer and may develop physically at a normal rate. It becomes more and more apparent that mild mental retardation, as demonstrated by poor intellectual performance, is a socio-economic disease, affecting the poor primarily. Poor mothers have less prenatal care and less adequate diets, and their children are much more likely to be born prematurely and to suffer serious illnesses during infancy. In addition, their children are

14. Data supplied by United Cerebral Palsy Association of New York State, Inc.

likely to get less stimulation, particularly in the language skills which are critical for success in school and on I.Q. tests. Hurley cites some significant unpublished data from a study reported in 1966 by the New Jersey Division of Mental Retardation; this study reports a very significant correlation between placement in special education classes and poverty, particularly as indicated by low income, unemployment, below average educational attainment of parents, and nonwhite status.[15]

Inferior, overcrowded schools, irrelevant curricula and reading materials, teachers who demand middle-class standards in dress and speech, a larger proportion of inexperienced and substitute teachers, expectations of poor performance, all lead to the development of children who do not learn, who fall farther and farther behind, and who do less and less well on standardized tests which pose questions and use words unrelated to their experience. After some years of this kind of failure, they may be assigned to a special education program or sent to an institution. Or they may drop out of school and join the 50 percent of retarded children who get no schooling, according to the National Association for Retarded Children. There is evidence that such children *can* learn; demonstration projects under a variety of auspices have shown that with programs geared to meet their special needs, disadvantaged children can learn as well as any other children. A major obstacle is the conviction of teachers, administrators, and taxpayers that poor children have low potential, are genetically inferior, and will not profit from compensatory programs. Hurley quotes Horace Mann Bond as stating that it takes 12,672 fathers who are professional and technical workers to produce one National Merit Scholar but 3,581,370 fathers who are laborers.[16] The responsibility of the school in this disparity is apparent.

A diagnosis of mildly retarded is based on I.Q. tests, with all that such testing implies for the culturally deprived. Such labeling becomes a self-fulfilling prophecy, and the label is incorporated into the child's self-image and the goals developed for him by parents and teachers. According to Segal, mildly retarded adolescents are aware that they have been classed as mentally retarded and resent it.[17] They may refuse to stay in

15. Hurley, *Poverty and Mental Retardation*, p. 47.

16. *Ibid.*, p. 97.

17. Arthur Segal, "Some Observations About Mentally Retarded Adolescents," *Children*, Vol. 14, No. 6 (November–December 1967), pp. 233–237. For a moving and imaginative account of how it feels to be retarded, see Daniel Keyes, *Flowers for Algernon* (New York: Harcourt Brace World, 1966).

special programs if labeled "for retarded." They have the same aspirations as other adolescents, although they may have been overprotected and may have had no opportunity to learn age-appropriate behavior. According to the stereotype, the mildly retarded may be able to learn to do sixth-grade–level academic work. More important, they can learn vocational skills adequate to maintain themselves in the community, although they may well need a special job placement. Both Sweden and Denmark are ahead of the United States in employing mentally retarded in factories and in permitting them to achieve greater degrees of independence in their living arrangements. As Perske points out, overprotection denies the mentally retarded the experience of facing risk, which is an important ingredient in learning and in self-esteem.[18]

FACILITIES FOR THE MENTALLY RETARDED

Proper community services should begin with a diagnostic center where children can be referred and examined early. Complete physical, neurological, and psychological examinations will indicate the extent of the retardation, and the staff and parents together can develop realistic goals, stressing the positive aspects of what the child *can* learn to do instead of a defeatist attitude toward his disabilities. Parents of retarded children tend to blame themselves and feel pity for their plight; they need to be helped to see their retarded child as a human being, with feelings and potentialities. Planning for children should be supported by services to parents, a task often assigned to social workers.

Once the child has been determined to be retarded, there are several possible avenues, and communities should provide alternatives to institutionalization, formerly considered the only way to care for retardates. Supportive services may enable the parents to keep the child at home and should include educational provisions for parents, to teach them how to train their child until he is old enough for a group program. Visiting nurse services, home health aides, group therapy, and informational meetings conducted by a health, welfare, or specialized agency should be available.

When the child cannot be maintained in his own home, it may be possible to place him in a specially selected foster home. The Retarded Infants Services, Inc. of New York City describes

18. Robert Perske, *The Dignity of Risk and the Mentally Retarded* (Arlington, Tx.: National Association for Retarded Children, 1972).

foster home programs for retardates: Foster families are carefully screened and supervised by social workers. Some parents find foster care difficult to accept initially, since it is easier for them to think that if they cannot manage the child at home, he should be institutionalized rather than placed in a foster home. Usually, the natural parents visit their children in foster care. The range of retardates considered for foster care varies; it is easier to find foster homes for the mildly and moderately retarded and extremely difficult to find a family willing to assume care of a severely retarded child.[19]

Children who cannot be cared for in a foster home may be able to adjust in a group residence, and this is often the best arrangement for retarded adults who have received special training in an institution. Such placements should be carefully planned and supervised to be sure that the residents are not being exploited, that staff is adequate to give individual attention, and that the residents are satisfied. To assume, as some people do, that retardates "don't know the difference" is not borne out by repeated observation.

For the profoundly retarded, placement in an institution is virtually unavoidable, but the institution should be well equipped and properly staffed. Instances of brutality, neglect, overuse of drugs, and mechanical routinization are too often encountered in large barracks-type state institutions, starved for funds by an indifferent legislature.[20] The use of foster grandparents (see page 258), college student volunteers, and natural parents to provide individual attention and stimulation should be encouraged. Unfortunately, all too many parents consider that they have solved their problems by placing their retarded child in an institution and maintain little or no contact with him once he has been admitted.

Even if adequate funds were forthcoming, large state institutions are no longer considered a suitable solution, since the atmosphere is at best regressive and abnormal. However, there are few private institutions, and their cost is prohibitive for the majority of parents. For all but the most severely retarded, living at home with ready access to special educational programs is the recommended plan, and foster care the next most desir-

19. Data supplied by Retarded Infants Services, Inc., 386 Park Ave. S., New York, N.Y., 10016, December 10, 1973.
20. See Joel Freedman, "Warehouses of Neglect," Social Work, Vol. 17, No. 5 (September 1972), pp. 94–96, which describes the situation in Massachusetts in 1970 and 1971.

able alternative. This demands the provision of training resources not currently provided in most states. There is a fine network of services in California and encouraging demonstration projects in many large cities nationwide, but adequate resources are largely unavailable in most states, particularly in small towns and rural areas.[21]

Evidence is that many mildly and moderately retarded now in institutions could move into the community and maintain themselves there under minimum supervision, if they could receive rehabilitation services in the institution.[22] Not only would this permit them a more normal life, it would also repay the cost of extra rehabilitation services in one to three years and save the annual $5,000 cost of maintaining a retarded person in an institution.

Education programs, whether under the auspices of the school system, a community mental health center, a university, or a special residential facility, concentrate on building up the adaptive capacity of the retardate. Increasingly sophisticated techniques have made it possible to facilitate the adjustment of the retarded in the community to a degree not believed possible when all the mentally retarded were viewed as "defective." Speech therapy, physical therapy, and special teaching methods for elementary school subjects are being supplemented by applications of behavioral modification techniques[23] to all aspects of daily living and self-care. Positive reinforcement of learning not only makes the retardate more independent but fosters the self-esteem which has been so damaged by the long series of failures he is likely to have experienced. The use of direct reward such as candy or fruit may be extended to tokens, with which the individual can select his choice from a canteen or privilege list, thereby developing options and encouraging the ability to choose.

Court decisions in Pennsylvania and other states have con-

21. See Tadeshi A. Mayeda, *Delivery of Services to Mentally Retarded Children and Adults in Five States* (Washington, D.C.: Department of Health, Education, and Welfare, 1972), a report prepared for the President's Committee on Mental Retardation, describing programs in California, Colorado, Ohio, North Carolina, and Washington State.

22. See Vol. 5, No. 3 (March 15, 1972) of *Research and Demonstration Brief* (Washington, D.C.: Research Utilization Branch, Social and Rehabilitation Service), for a report on the postinstitutional adjustment of sixty-five retarded adults with I.Q.s ranging from 45 to 80, with an average of 75.

23. See William I. Gardner, *Behavior Modification in Mental Retardation* (Chicago: Aldine Press, 1971), for a clearly written explanation of techniques with case illustrations.

firmed the responsibility of the educational system to provide special education for handicapped and retarded children.[24] Even where school systems have set up special classes and training schools have tightened their criteria and returned children to the community, not all communities have proved willing to integrate the retarded into community activities and not all families have been able to accept their own feelings or their neighbors' attitudes about their retarded child. It is in the area of services to families that social workers are most likely to become involved with mental retardates, although direct service to them is being developed as the adaptive ability of those formerly considered hopeless is increasingly recognized.

SOCIAL WORK SERVICES IN MENTAL RETARDATION

The involvement of social work in the field of mental retardation is relatively recent.[25] Up until the report of the President's Panel for a National Plan to Combat Mental Retardation in 1962, few social workers were engaged in direct service, and the subject of mental retardation was not included in the standard social work curriculum. In part, this reflected both the prevailing conception of mental retardation as a hopeless condition and a lack of funding, surfacing in salaries too low to attract skilled manpower. The medical model and the heavy emphasis on hereditary and genetic factors, coupled with a minimizing of the social and environmental aspects of causation and treatment, contributed to social work's lack of involvement. Since 1962, however, social work has been increasingly interested in both prevention and treatment of mental retardation. As evidence mounts of the relationship between deprivation and levels of functioning termed "retarded," social workers are more and more concerned about traditional agency clientele, who represent a population at risk.

Preventive methods include genetic counseling, family planning, good prenatal and obstetrical care, adequate nutrition and health care for infants and children, and parenting which encourages early development of communication skills and intellectual stimulation. These are all areas which demand community support, adequate funds, improved and extended facil-

24. However, the President's Committee on Mental Retardation reported in 1972 that no state provided educational services for more than 60 percent of its mentally retarded children, and in some states the figure was much lower.

25. See Arthur Mandelbaum, "Mental Health and Retardation," *Encyclopedia of Social Work*, 1971, pp. 791–802, especially "Social Work Services," pp. 796–798.

ities, and greater public understanding and which engage the community organization and social action efforts of the social work profession. Maldistributed health care, inadequate welfare payments, prejudices against those different from the majority, and parental feelings of guilt and helplessness are obstacles to preventive services. Since the parents of the moderately and mildly retarded tend to be less well educated and less affluent, they have little real knowledge about retardation, have only limited access to private physicians and diagnostic centers, and may be somewhat slower to recognize behavior which is an early indication of retardation. Social workers in the public services should be knowledgeable about normal growth and development in order to alert parents who may not suspect or are afraid to face possible retardation.

In an interesting study of barriers between the parents of retarded children and their securing of services, Diana Brown[26] surveyed parents and agency personnel and classified two types of obstacles, which she describes as "profession-related" and "client-related." The former include restrictive and rigid agency procedures; a lack of sensitivity to parents' feelings; poor communication among agencies; poor planning, especially for young retarded adults; inadequate financial support for agency programs; and an unwillingness to confront such issues as outmoded reliance on I.Q. tests, inadequate welfare budgets, the legal and civil liberties of the retarded, and racism. These demand professional action on individual, agency, and profession levels.

"Client-related" obstacles suggest a need for corrective actions by professionals at the community level but also include difficulties that can be resolved by social workers who give direct service to families. Parents are upset and confused by overly intellectual and technical explanations which do not answer their questions or tell them what to expect. They resent being thought poorly motivated and the "parent as patient" attitude of many professionals. Long waiting lists may mean that children become too old for preschool programs before their names come up for admission. Some parents cannot accept services that treat children of different racial and socio-economic backgrounds or of different diagnostic or functioning levels. Costs are a major obstacle to many parents, including not only direct costs of diagnostic and training programs but also indirect costs

---

26. Diana L. Brown, "Obstacles to Services for the Mentally Retarded," *Social Work*, Vol. 17, No. 4 (July 1972), pp. 98–101.

of transportation, babysitters, or housing adapted to the retarded child's needs. Medicaid and health insurance coverage of
costs is incomplete or lacking. Communities seldom provide
recreational facilities specially equipped to serve handicapped
children; and prejudiced views of the retarded as dangerous,
prone to sexual misbehavior, or disgusting to look at militate
against including the retarded in many community leisure time
activities. Language problems intensify the difficulties faced by
Spanish-speaking and other linguistic minorities in obtaining
services for their retarded children.

Social workers should be active in pressing for better services
for the mentally retarded, for inclusion of special education in
local schools, for sheltered workshops[27] or protected employment, for the full range of services from diagnostic to total care,
so that parents may be able to make a reasoned decision as to
what services to seek for their retarded child. All too often,
parents flounder in guilt, misunderstanding, and reluctant acceptance of the "only plan available." As it becomes increasingly possible for retardates to remain at home and avoid the
damage of placement in a large barracks-type institution, support services for parents must be strengthened, including the
provision of respite services for parents who need periods of
freedom from the stress of trying to care for their retarded child
at home.

Services to the Family
of the Retarded Child

For parents of a severely or moderately retarded child, the
recognition that all is not well is inevitable, sometimes at birth
but more often when the child fails to develop speech and
motor skills in the first two years. Since parents tend to blame
themselves for producing "defective" children, they may react
to their own feelings and anxieties by denial, panic, depression, or anger.[28] Sooner or later the diagnosis is made, and the

27. See Carl Gersuny and Mark Lefton, "Service and Servitude in the Sheltered Workshop," *Social Work*, Vol. 15, No. 3 (July 1970), pp. 74–81, for a discussion of the benefits and potential dangers of exploitation and overprotection
in sheltered workshops. See also Harold M. Kase's comment on the above article
in *Social Work*, Vol. 15, No. 4 (October 1970), pp. 103–104. See also Robert D.
Shushan, *Coordination of Workshops for the Mentally Retarded in a Metropolitan and
Suburban Area* (Los Angeles: Exceptional Children's Foundation, 1972), which
reports successful employment of retardates with a median I.Q. of 54, and a
range of 23 to 89.

28. See Norman A. Polansky, Donald R. Boone, Christine De Saix, and
Schlomo A. Sharlin, "Pseudostoicism in Mothers of the Retarded," *Social Casework*, Vol. 52, No. 10 (December 1972), pp. 643–650.

parent is confronted with the necessity of planning for a child who is not normal. The social worker who is to help the family with this acute phase will find the techniques of crisis intervention applicable.[29] A careful evaluation of the parents' coping capacity, an assessment of the impact on other children of the program developed for the retarded child, and interpretation of the interdisciplinary evaluation of the child and its meaning for his future adaptation are part of the social worker's task.

Some parents may insist on keeping the child at home, underestimating the burden involved and the effects of the diversion of attention from siblings to the retardate. They may ruthlessly sacrifice the siblings as they overprotect and "smother" the handicapped child. At the other extreme, some parents reject the child as though they had not produced him, insisting on institutionalizing him and refusing to consider alternatives. Overconcern with relatives' and neighbors' opinions may be masked by rationalizations about the child's best interests or the excuse that he is too retarded to mind separation. Evidence shows that retarded children suffer keenly at being removed from familiar surroundings and placed with strangers, even though they cannot verbalize their feelings. A too-easy assumption that placement ends the adjustment problem for family and child is challenged by a study carried out by Hersh,[30] indicating the need for supportive social work services to families after as well as before placement of their retarded children. His study reported a four-step response [1) loss, 2) relief, 3) guilt and ambivalence, 4) fulfillment and well-being] in parents of children successfully placed and recommends that institutions make greater efforts to serve families as well as the admitted children.

During the second stage of adjustment to their retarded child, the social worker offers supportive services through casework or group work.[31] Parents need help with their feelings about the child and themselves. Groups of parents find they have similar concerns and derive strength from sharing them with others

29. See Howard J. Parad, ed., *Crisis Intervention: Selected Readings* (New York: Family Service Association of America, 1965), especially Chapter 4, "A Framework for Studying Families in Crisis," pp. 53–72, and Chapter 24, "Preventive Casework; Problems and Implications," pp. 284–298.

30. Alexander Hersh, "Changes in Family Functioning Following Placement of a Retarded Child," *Social Work*, Vol. 15, No. 4 (October 1970), pp. 99–102.

31. See Ann Murphy, Siegfried M. Pueschel, and Jane Schneider, "Group Work with Parents of Children with Down's Syndrome," *Social Casework*, Vol. 54, No. 2 (February 1973), pp. 114–119; see also Simon Olshansky, "Chronic Sorrow: A Response to Having a Mentally Defective Child," *Social Casework*, Vol. 43, No. 4 (April 1962), pp. 190–193.

who have like experiences.[32] An experienced couple can pass on techniques of handling and suggestions for dealing with relatives and neighbors. Those who have been through diagnostic evaluations can prepare those who have still to go through them. The group can serve as an enthusiastic audience for each new accomplishment reported of any child. Anxiety about the future is a recurrent theme, including doubts about parents' ability to love an older child whose handicap grows more visible.

The impact on siblings is a concern, whether the retarded child is at home or "away." How does the family deal with inquiries? How often should they visit the institutionalized child? Should vacations be encouraged? If the child is at home, what will be the effect on the social life of parents and siblings? If the retarded child is the first child, the parents will have concern about possible future pregnancies. The reactions of relatives may be helpful or upsetting. Parents of retarded children often encounter rejection from friends who do not welcome the retarded child at social occasions or who stay away because of embarrassment.

Whether seeing these families in casework or in group meetings, the social worker is accepting of their feelings, is helpful in suggesting ways of explaining the situation to others, and should be a resource for community programs not known to parents. Knowing the "backlash" of guilt, the social worker should attempt to keep the family from rejecting the child permanently as some parents may be tempted to do. The social worker should also be available to serve as parents' liaison with the staff of whatever specialized facilities are serving the child, remembering that many parents of retarded children are unsophisticated and unused to dealing with professionals. Parents may be resentful, demanding, overcritical, or oversubmissive. They may be afraid to press for simple explanations of technical terms. Professionals who are uneasy at transmitting bad news may be tempted to be vague, leaving parents confused, or they may be overly pessimistic, urging institutionalization too readily. Parents may expect miracles from specialists, or they may go from one to another, hoping for a new diagnosis, exhausting their financial resources, and becoming easy prey for quacks. The family's feelings about those who work with their retarded child in an institution, a boarding home, or special programs in the community are important and thus are of interest to

32. It was the parents of retarded children who were instrumental in founding the organization now known as the National Association for Retarded Children.

the social worker. The parents may expect too much and be disappointed and critical, or they may resent seeing someone do better than they did at the task of raising their child. The child is always viewed as part of the family system and not as an outsider or as if he had died.[33]

Social workers extending such services to families may be attached to institutions for the mentally retarded, to community agencies such as the welfare department or the community mental health center, or to a specialized agency for mental retardation. Professional social work services to parents are largely unavailable to those who need them most—the rural and ghetto poor and the members of minority groups. In 1969 the President's Committee on Mental Retardation estimated that there were 18,000 full-time staff members in public facilities for the mentally retarded, but fewer than 1,000 were social workers. These are not enough to begin to meet the needs of residents and their families, to say nothing of retarded children living at home.

Direct Service to the
Mentally Retarded

For many years, it has been assumed that the mentally retarded were unsuitable candidates for direct casework treatment, but evidence is mounting to show that retarded young people need help with their sense of identity, defeatism, and dependency. Group work seems to be the modality most commonly used.[34] Goals are the provision of opportunities for maturation and a concentration on strengths and individualizing group members, rather than focusing on their deficiencies and stereotyping them.

The stereotyped view of the happy and carefree moron is an incorrect picture. Most retarded, except the severely, are aware of their status, wish to conceal it, and have the same goals as other members of the society. They want jobs, homes of their

33. See Maud Mannoni, *The Backward Child and His Mother*, translated from the French by A. M. Sheridan Smith (New York: Pantheon Books, 1973), for a challenging analysis of the behavior of the retarded child as a response to the expectations and fantasies of his parents. See also Leslie J. Shellhase and Fern E. Shellhase, "Role of the Family in Rehabilitation," *Social Casework*, Vol. 53, No. 9 (November 1972), pp. 544–550.

34. See Meyer Schreiber, "Some Basic Concepts in Social Group Work and Rehabilitation with the Mentally Retarded," *Rehabilitation Literature*, Vol. 26, No. 7 (July 1965), pp. 194–203; see also Larry D. Richards and Kenneth A. Lee, "Group Process in Social Habilitation of the Retarded," *Social Casework*, Vol. 53, No. 1 (January 1972), pp. 30–37.

own, and normal satisfactions. Some are emotionally disturbed and need treatment for their emotional problems. The Joint Commission on Mental Health of Children states that a great many mentally retarded children show symptoms of emotional maladjustment, either as a result of the strains of living as mentally retarded children, from the same cause as the retardation, or coincidentally.[35] The reverse is also true; some mentally disturbed children may not respond to testing and may be labeled mentally retarded and sent to institutions, where they may never achieve their potential because of lack of stimulation and treatment. Psychotherapy would benefit many of the mentally retarded; unhappily, it is seldom available.

The role of advocate is an appropriate one for social workers in relation to the mentally retarded. Not only is prevention of much retardation possible, not only are new treatment and training methods being developed, not only are facilities in the public schools being adapted to provide special education for those unable to progress in the regular curriculum, but the public is becoming more aware of the extent to which the civil liberties of the mentally retarded are abridged. Commitment procedures, originating in a period when mental retardation was believed to be a permanent defect, need modification. Job restrictions militate unfairly against the mildly retarded. Guardianship and inheritance laws do not adequately protect them. Their sexual relationships are a particularly sensitive issue. News stories in July of 1973 of the sterilization of two Negro girls in Alabama, aged 12 and 14, called dramatic attention to the violation of civil rights carried out systematically against blacks by overzealous health workers.[36] Although the news media at first attributed the decision forced on the family to a "social worker," the prompt reaction from Chauncey Alexander, Executive Director of the National Association of Social Workers (NASW), forced a retraction[37] from the former OEO Director who had maligned the profession.

35. Joint Commission on Mental Health of Children, *Mental Health: From Infancy Through Adolescence* (New York: Harper & Row, 1973), p. 13.

36. *Time*, July 23, 1973, p. 5. See also Felix F. de la Cruz and Gerald D. LaVeck, eds., *Human Sexuality and the Mentally Retarded* (New York: Brunner/ Mazel, 1973), for a collection of essays by experts in genetics, medicine, law, education, and social science on this neglected topic. Ed Skarnulis, "Noncitizen: Plight of the Mentally Retarded," *Social Work*, Vol. 19, No. 1 (January 1974), pp. 56–62, points out that professionals as well as the public deny human and civil rights to the mentally retarded.

37. "NASW Rebuts Relf Case Slur," *NASW NEWS*, Vol. 18, No. 8 (September 1973), p. 1.

Social workers should recognize the needs of the mentally retarded and their families in direct service, in advocacy and brokerage roles, and in modifying social attitudes which obstruct the provision of adequate community resources for prevention and rehabilitation. Social work curricula, at both the baccalaureate and graduate levels, should include content on mental retardation and, where possible, provide some field experience, either in a special agency for mental retardation or in a generalized agency which includes families with retarded members in its clientele.

BLINDNESS: THE OVERPROTECTED DISABILITY

Blindness and severe visual impairment are obvious physical handicaps, which demand specialized facilities for housing, education, vocational training, mobility, and psychological adjustment. As with other disabilities, much depends on the cultural expectation of appropriate goals for the blind. In the past, blind people were supposed to resign themselves to a dependent role, refrain from calling attention to themselves (although begging by the blind was reluctantly accepted), and either sit with idle hands or busy themselves with caning chairs or making potholders. As Madeline Shipsey points out,[38] many of society's negative attitudes toward the blind are carried over from times when the leading causes of blindness were dangerous, infectious diseases. The blind were included as permanent dependents under the categorical programs set up under the Social Security Act. Many states made refraining from begging a condition of receiving Aid to the Needy Blind (AB), and little inducement was offered toward greater independence.

Attitudes and social expectations have changed in the last three decades. As the infectious diseases which caused blindness directly were brought under control, the role of pre- and postnatal illness became recognized as an important cause of blindness in children, particularly German measles in the mother early in pregnancy and that caused by the administration of too much oxygen to premature infants, neither condition of a nature to endanger the general population. The success of rehabilitation efforts for blinded veterans of World War II made greater independence for the blind more possible. Substantial

38. Madeline Shipsey, "Disability and Physical Handicap: Visual and Auditory Disorders," *Encyclopedia of Social Work, 1971* pp. 228–236.

federal support for rehabilitation came in mid 1940s. Such re-habilitation aids as guide dogs and Hoover canes and improved methods of teaching blind children have made it possible to provide alternatives to the expectation of lifelong dependency which colored our attitudes toward the blind for so long.

There are some 400,000 legally blind people in the United States; legal blindness is defined as less than 10 percent of normal vision and includes many who have sufficient visual acuity to be fully self-sufficient and mobile. Only 18 percent are totally blind—that is, unable to distinguish light; and the majority of the totally blind are over sixty-five. Between the two falls the range of disability, requiring support services from minimal help to total care.

ACHIEVING INDEPENDENCE

Blindness removes one avenue by which the individual com-municates with his social world, and as such it inevitably has a damaging effect on self-image. Blindness is construed by many as a kind of punishment, and this may be internalized in the blind person as guilt. Instead of using their remaining senses to communicate with the outside world, some blind people retreat into isolation, passivity, and depression.

Much depends on the age at which blindness begins. A well-constructed research study[39] measured the adjustment of the blind along a continuum from dependence to independence in their behavior, including employment, mobility, shopping, eat-ing, and self-grooming. Findings indicated that those whose blindness occurred at birth or in early childhood were more likely to achieve independence than those blinded in later life and that independence was correlated with more pres-tigious social status, as measured by intelligence, education, and socio-economic class. The importance of social expectations in encouraging or limiting what the blind expect of themselves is critical and should be so considered by social workers in-volved with the blind and their families.

Achievement of maximum independence represents a new view of the blind, who need no longer be relegated to institu-tions or their homes. It is underlined by the conviction of those social workers dealing with blind clients that they should not be categorized and singled out for treatment by "one of their

---

39. Irving F. Lukoff and Martin Whiteman, *The Social Sources of Adjustment to Blindness*, "Research Series No. 21" (New York: American Foundation for the Blind, 1970).

own kind," as has so often been the case. They should be served in the same manner as other individuals trying to cope with a serious reality problem, using the same methods of casework and group work intervention and community organization. While some of their problems demand some specialized knowledge and resources to deal directly with their handicap, for personal and family problems they should be referred to general community agencies and not be segregated as a specialized clientele.

Blind from Birth

For the family whose child is born blind, crisis intervention similar to that needed for parents of a mentally or orthopedically handicapped child is appropriate. The early socialization of the blind child is well within the capabilities of the typical parents, but they may be fearful and overprotective, and they will need help in handling their own feelings of guilt and anger. The mother-child relationship will lack the important ingredient of visual response, so taken for granted in the normal family interaction, where smiles of approval, frowns, and gestures are highly important means of socialization.[40] Parents may need to be given information about home care, special services in the community, and help with the impact on other children in the family of the special attention given to the blind sibling.

The case of Tina illustrates some of the ways in which a middle-aged couple reacted to the birth of a blind child and the consequences for the child of their isolation and overprotection of her. Casework treatment of the parents and psychotherapy for Tina resulted in enabling a bright, attractive little girl to utilize her abilities and minimize her disability.

> Tina, aged six, was referred to a specialized agency for the blind by a Community Lighthouse for psychiatric services. The immediate reason for referral was Tina's refusal to talk, except to her parents and to another family which boarded in her home. Her mutism was interfering with her adjustment in kindergarten. The school had been reluctant to admit Tina in the first place and was now urging that she be sent to a school for the blind. Tina's evaluation at the agency psychiatric clinic extended over a three-month period, since it included a complete physical, neurological,

40. See Dorothy Burlingham, *Psychoanalytic Studies of the Sighted and Blind* (New York: International Universities Press, 1972), the famous child analyst's study of how mothers of blind children must compensate for the sensory lack.

psychological, communication, and psychiatric work-up. An extensive family history was secured by the social worker whose report to the school follows: "Tina has been evaluated at our Psychiatric Clinic. Neurological examination revealed no neurological damage, and the EEG tracing was normal for a blind child. The ophthalmological examination showed retrolental fibroplasia, with no light perception. Our speech and hearing specialist reported good receptive language; expressive language, which was studied with the use of tapes brought by parents, was also good.

"The psychiatric examination revealed a basically intact child whose most prominent symptom was selective mutism. This symptom, with some variation, has been evident since Tina started speaking. Tina showed good affect and ability to form object relationships. She was responsive and also showed good ability with nonverbal communication.

"Psychological testing placed Tina in the bright-normal range of intelligence. Her I.Q. is estimated at 115. It was not possible to obtain a more exact I.Q., because standard testing procedures could not be used. This estimate, however, correlates with her ability to conceptualize and with other behavior demonstrated during the period of evaluation.

"Psychotherapy was recommended for Tina, and the prognosis is very favorable. It was the opinion of the Clinic staff that she could manage well in a class with sighted children. There appears to be no intellectual difficulty that would interfere with her academic progress. She will need the help of an itinerant teacher for her Braille work, and her mother is prepared to supplement the work of a teacher."

The social worker had weekly interviews with the parents while Tina was being seen by a battery of specialists for evaluation. The parents were always interviewed together. From the beginning, the social worker was aware of how important speech and the manner of speaking were to these parents. They spoke in very low, controlled tones, apologized for "shouting" when they had become excited, insisted on correct pronunciation and grammar at all times, and were very conscious of other people's speech. Tina had copied them, speaking precisely (as revealed on tapes, since no one at the Clinic had heard her utter a sound) and being amused if she overheard people mispronouncing words.

The overtones of depression in these parents were reflected in the way they described their early lives, which had been filled with tragedy and deprivation. They had married somewhat late in life and had given up all hope of a child when Tina was born three months prematurely. At her birth, her mother was 44, and her father was 57. They were overwhelmed when they learned of Tina's blindness and had never been able to bring themselves to discuss it with her. They asked the worker to tell them how to explain blindness to the child. Throughout the contact with the social worker, both parents asked for specific directives, demonstrating no confidence in their own ability to handle problems except by avoiding mention of them.

As the parents described Tina's infancy and early childhood, it was apparent to the social worker that they had isolated and overprotected Tina and that she had actually had very few contacts other than with her parents. Father was a tailor, and the family lived upstairs over the shop. When the mother helped in the shop, Tina was brought downstairs and placed in a playpen in the back room. Recently, father had given up the shop and taken a job in a clothing store to enable mother to spend more time with Tina.

Tina's motor development was extremely slow. She did not begin walking by herself until she was four-and-a-half and still walked cautiously. She could ride a tricycle, and she used her hands well. Her manual skill was also noted by the psychologist who tested her. In contrast to her motor skills, Tina learned to talk early, putting sentences together before she was eighteen months old. According to her parents, who were the only ones Tina talked to, her vocabularly was good. It was not until she was more than four that her parents noticed that she would not talk to or in the presence of other people. Although they have urged her to do so and have observed her moving her lips, she would not utter a sound except when alone with them.

Tina presented problems with eating from the beginning. She was always very small, and her slow weight gain was a source of anxiety for several years. She continued to have a bottle three times a day until she was five and still had a bottle at night. Her food must be cut into tiny pieces, and her diet was extremely limited. Her mother used to coax her to eat, but on the pediatrician's advice gave up trying to push Tina. Meals at their home were very slow affairs, as the parents considered the dinner table a place where things are talked over.

Like her mother, Tina was fastidious, concerned about being clean, having things neat, and cleaning herself after toileting. She was still sleeping in a crib in the parents' bedroom but had been asking for a bed and a room of her own. The parents were fearful of having her sleep on another floor.

Throughout the evaluation interviews, the parents' words and actions indicated to the social worker that they considered the world a hostile and threatening place and the family unit the only real safety for Tina and themselves.

Although they said that they were coming in for recommendations about Tina's schooling, the parents readily accepted the worker's suggestion that they continue to come for discussions of their handling of Tina and their own feelings. During the twelve weeks they were in treatment, they demonstrated more flexibility than the worker originally expected. At first reluctant to discuss their feelings of guilt, anger, and depression and the extent to which they had overprotected Tina, they became increasingly able to see how they had transmitted to the child their view of the world as a place in which one had to be on one's guard. They made a real effort to get out of the home more, to take Tina out for excursions, meals out, and visits to friends. She got her own room and bed, with an intercom system so she could call them in the night. When she abandoned her crib, her nighttime bottle was abandoned, too. The parents became able to discuss her blindness with Tina, to explain that it was not a punishment, and to feel less guilty about it themselves.

An area of concern they were able to discuss with the social worker was their age relative to Tina's and their apprehension that they would die before she was grown and able to be independent. It was a comfort to them to know that the agency would be there for Tina to turn to if the need arose. They were also able to recognize that by fostering her independence now, instead of overprotecting her, they were preparing her more adequately for the time she would be on her own.

As her parents modified their handling of her, Tina was also profiting from her sessions with the agency psychiatrist. She enjoyed play therapy, entering into games with zest. Since it was the psychiatrist's feeling that Tina used her mutism to control those around her, he was careful not to appear threatened by her silence or to urge her to speak. Her first vocalizations were imitations of airplanes, cars, and animals. From there she moved to nonsense sounds and to rhythm and singing games. When she did, finally, talk to the therapist, it was in spurts; she would talk fairly excitedly for a few minutes, then recollect herself and lapse into stubborn silence. When the therapist remained unmoved by this withdrawal, she was able to relax once more and communicate again.

By the time the parents' twelve weekly sessions had concluded, Tina had made enough progress so her visits to the therapist were reduced in frequency. She continued to come in at monthly intervals for the balance of the school year, during which she made good progress in learning Braille and achieved and maintained a satisfactory, if limited, verbal contact with her teacher and several members of the class.[41]

Not all blind children have as many assets as did Tina, and few have access to evaluation and treatment resources as superb as those available to her and her parents. But social workers in any agency are familiar with guilt, with overprotective parents, and with children who use deviant behavior as a way of controlling a world they perceive as threatening. While the comprehensive evaluation done for Tina might not be available in all communities, casework treatment of her parents and the psychotherapy for her would have been available in many mental health centers, child guidance clinics, or family service agencies.

Many schools systems now incorporate blind children into the regular school program, using specially trained teachers and teaching aids such as cassette recorders. In rural areas or small towns, children who cannot be taught at home may need to be sent to school, but they should not be permanently institutionalized. Few communities have included blind children in their recreational planning, although summer camps have demonstrated that blind children can enjoy many of the same activities as sighted children. Vocational training is increasingly geared toward independence in employment, although the sheltered workshop may be needed for many. "Peripatology" (the art of teaching mobility to the blind) is still not widely enough available.

Emphasis in most state programs for the blind has been concentrated on vocational adjustment, with inadequate attention to the emotional concomitants of blindness. The necessity for social work support of vocational rehabilitation efforts is vividly demonstrated when loss of vision occurs in an adolescent or adult. Here casework intervention is indispensable, as the individual struggles to incorporate blindness into his self-concept and reintegrate himself on a new basis into his social group.

Adjustment to Blindness

Frances T. Dover, Associate Executive Director of the Jewish Guild for the Blind in New York City, describes the adjusting process which the newly blinded person goes through and

41. The preceding case was adapted for teaching purposes from material supplied by the Jewish Guild for the Blind. All identifying information has been altered to preserve confidentiality. Used with permission.

which the social worker should understand.[42] Isolation is the typical response to the shock of becoming blind, with the individual cutting himself off from social activities and outside stimulation. Many of the symptoms of acute depression are present—crying, loss of appetite, lethargy, all representing a reaction to loss. The well-integrated person will be able to emerge from this stage and reorganize his life, but the less well integrated person, suffering already from lowered self-esteem, will demonstrate longer and more severe depression. Treatment during this period should be supportive, with emphasis on the client's ventilating his anger and frustration. Long-range planning should be avoided, as it will overwhelm him, and emphasis should be on practical needs and realizable short-term goals. Work with the client's family is vital at this stage.

Projection and denial are used by the newly blinded person as a defense against his own anxiety; he may deny that the condition is permanent, and he may deny his own part in causing blindness (such as failure to follow medical directions) by putting the blame outside himself, often on his doctor. When these reactions are recognized as part of the adjustment process, they can be dealt with by the social worker directly, as well as indirectly through the client's family. The duration and intensity of these reactions are a measure of the individual's capacity to adapt, to move into what Mrs. Dover calls "integration" and "mobilization." In these stages, the blind person begins to test reality and respond positively to the demands of living as a handicapped person. Each new situation that is conquered strengthens the adaptive capacity to move ahead. "Mobilization" refers to the individual's moving back into the world rather than staying narrowly protected in his family or in a group of blind people.

Not all blinded individuals complete these stages, and each goes through them at his own rate. The social worker who is helping the newly blind person adjust must individualize his client, assess his strengths and capacities and the support he can expect from his family and other social relationships, and together with him plan his own rehabilitation program. This may occur while the client is living at home. However, in many larger communities, the newly blind person is referred to a multi-discipline rehabilitation center for a residential stay of several months. His adjustment to the diffficulties of managing

42. Frances T. Dover, "Use of Casework in Help to Blind People," *The New Outlook,* Vol. 57, No. 8 (October 1963), pp. 287–295.

without vision can be facilitated by the specialized personnel and equipment of such a center. The social work staff will be involved throughout his stay and will be particularly needed when he returns to the community, in mobilizing community support services.

The Elderly Blind

Blindness encountered in old age poses some additional problems. There may be more difficulty in accepting a further insult to the self-image, since the physical changes associated with aging have already impaired it. The fear of rejection and abandonment, all too often a warranted apprehension, is common among the elderly blind. They feel dependent and vulnerable and need reassurance that they will be cared for. Suitable living arrangements are difficult, and many elderly blind are forced to move into institutions, when they would rather remain in the community, because of fear of crime and inability to maintain themselves in run-down housing. Inadequate income leaves the blind elderly person little choice of housing. Mrs. Dover reports[43] that many aged blind clients of her agency depend entirely on their Social Security benefits, even though they are eligible for supplementary public assistance; they find it physically and emotionally impossible to negotiate the complexities of applying for a public assistance grant. The elderly blind are people with individual life styles, each coping in his own way with the double stresses of aging and blindness. In many, the onset of blindness is gradual, which minimizes the shock stage of their adjustment, but they may linger longer in the depression stage and use denial as a major defense against anxiety.

SOCIAL WORK SERVICES TO THE BLIND

The social worker's major contribution to the rehabilitation services offered to the blind is his acceptance of the blind person as an individual with dignity and worth, who faces obstacles but who is not hopelessly impaired or unworthy of salvaging. The social worker therefore plays the roles of enabler and mobilizer for the blind client and the roles of teacher, consultant, evaluator, and planner with the client's family. The worker's activities as advocate and outreach worker on behalf of the blind include support of new legislation, modification of

---

43. Frances T. Dover, "Aging and Blindness: Special Needs," a paper presented at the Midwest Regional Conference on Services to Aging Blind Persons, American Foundation for the Blind, April 27, 1972, Chicago, Ill.

bureaucratic complexities which impede blind clients in receiving services for which they are eligible, and better coordination of existing programs. But the paramount concern of the social worker must be the promotion of the highest possible level of social functioning for the blind client. Recent advances in rehabilitation make it possible for the level to be much higher than most people think.

DRUG ADDICTION:
THE CRIMINAL DISABILITY

Both blind and mentally retarded persons are regarded as victims of conditions beyond their control, whose disabilities are permanent, and for whom cultural requirements must be modified. Less is expected of them; they are exempt from many of the demands placed on other members of society. Quite different attitudes prevail toward those individuals who become addicted to the use of substances considered by society to be illegal. The illegality of substances represents political decisions and alters with time. Narcotics were not forbidden in nineteenth century America. Soothing syrups for babies and headache remedies for adults contained opiates; and addiction to morphine was a white, middle-class, Protestant, rural phenomenon, to be deplored perhaps in the individual, but not regarded as a social menace or a vice.

The Harrison Act of 1914[44] was a revenue act, which is why the Bureau of Narcotics was until 1968 located in the Treasury Department rather than the Justice Department or, more properly, in the Department of Health, Education, and Welfare. The Act made no mention of addicts, and until 1923, public clinics existed which dispensed narcotics at low cost to addicts. The prohibitionist philosophy of the Volstead Act, a neat illustration of political maneuvering by a minority pressure group,[45] was applied by the Treasury Department to violations of the Harrison Act. By 1922 its jurisdiction had grown to include the

44. The Harrison Narcotics Act of 1914 was basically a revenue measure designed to make narcotics transferrals a matter of record. A nominal tax was imposed on the narcotics, and persons authorized to manufacture or handle drugs were required to register, pay a fee for, and keep records of all narcotics in their possession.

45. See Peter H. Odegard, *Pressure Politics: The Story of the Anti-Saloon League* (New York: Columbia University Press, 1928).

area of medical treatment of addiction.[46] What should be dealt with as a public health problem, therefore, is dealt with as a legal problem, with a prison sentence the usual "solution," and with addiction viewed as a vice to be prevented by fear and cured by willpower. Experiments with increasingly severe laws, from the Boggs Act of 1951 and its Amendments in 1956 to the mandatory life-sentence laws in New York State in 1973, have failed to cure addiction. In the view of many, making drugs illegal not only forces the addict into dealing with the underworld in buying his supply but also makes it necessary for him to resort to crime to support the expense of his habit, which contributes heavily to shoplifting, burglary, and robbery. It also encourages illegal activities on the part of law enforcement officers, including techniques of entrapment, infiltration, and no-knock raids. In 1973, several well-publicized raids in Illinois involved innocent people who were terrorized by the intrusion into their homes of agents without search warrants, who threatened them and damaged their property searching for drugs.

The extent to which breaking the law contributes to the thrills sought by discontented young people or represents their gesture of defiance against "the establishment" cannot be accurately measured but is known to be significant. There are many authorities who feel that no real progress can be made in identifying and treating narcotic addicts and in preventing addiction until the legal penalties attached to drug use are removed.[47]

CAUSES OF ADDICTION

Attempts to describe a profile of the "typical" addict have failed, since it is usually impossible to know which characteristics in the known drug abuser antedated his use of drugs and which are a consequence of his negative self-image as a "junkie." The factors seen as predisposing (absence of father,

46. See Troy Duster, *The Legislation of Morality: Law, Drugs, and Moral Judgment* (New York: Free Press of Glencoe, 1970); and Gilbert Geis, *Not the Law's Business: An Examination of Homosexuality, Abortion, Prostitution, Narcotics and Gambling in the United States* (Washington, D.C.: National Institute of Mental Health, 1972).

47. See Irving Weisman, "Narcotics Control by Government Clinics in England," *Social Casework*, Vol. 53, No. 10 (December 1972), pp. 604–612, which finds the British method of providing free clinics a more humane way of dealing with addicts, although admittedly not eliminating the problem of addiction. See also Horace Freeland Judson, "The British and Heroin," *The New Yorker*, Part I, September 24, 1973, pp. 76–113, and Part II, October 1, 1973, pp. 70–112.

slum residence, minority group membership, poor job records) are those correlated with a variety of antisocial and self-destructive behaviors and do not tell us why drug use was the neurosis of choice. Many addicts come from disorganized homes and have hostile feelings toward authority. Most come from groups whose status is ill-defined (the adolescent, the poor, the blacks) and from which success is uncertain. Yet the majority of members of these groups do not become drug abusers.

Little useful research was carried out on addicts so long as addiction was considered a vice limited to slums and ethnic minorities. But in the 1960s drug use began to spread into middle-class suburbs and to younger school children, and research efforts have increased. The existence of "hidden" drug abusers[48] in the middle class, in which drug use has not prevented the meeting of social responsibilities, reinforces the impressions that the addicts who are studied are a skewed sample of unsuccessful users and that there is no one clear-cut drug-prone personality.

Some generalizations can be made, however; there is a cycle through which the addict progresses. Beginners have to learn to experience the effects as pleasurable, and this almost inevitably occurs in a group under pressure. Extended experimentation with various drugs and methods of taking them can lead to use of heroin and socialization into the criminal drug subculture. The new addict's life becomes increasingly preoccupied with drugs, and he breaks off associations with those outside the drug subculture. In time, he becomes a fully acculturated street addict, under an overwhelming compulsion to continue and probably unable to extricate himself until he is arrested or dies from an overdose, from impurities in the adulterated drugs he buys on the street, or from infection from a dirty needle. The addict seldom experiences euphoria from his drug intake; instead he uses it to reduce his depression and fear of withdrawal symptoms. Thus, abstinence to him holds less the possibility of a better future life than the certainty of immediate physical and mental suffering. Those attempting to treat the drug addict should know the point he has reached in the cycle of addiction and gear their intervention accordingly. The ultimate goal is not

48. See Arthur D. Moffett and Carl D. Chambers, "The Hidden Addiction," *Social Work,* Vol. 15, No. 3 (July 1970), pp. 54–59, who apply the term to non-narcotic drug abusers, 90 percent of whom were addicted to barbiturates. The term is more widely applied to undetected users of other drugs, including narcotics.

total abstinence but improved social functioning, a reduction in criminal behavior, and an improved self-image.[49]

TREATMENT PROGRAMS

Because drug possession and drug use are defined as crimes, the life of the narcotic addict is far more complicated than that of the alcohol addict. The profit from selling cut and adulterated smuggled drugs at high prices makes it an attractive field to organized crime. The inflated price leads the addict to criminal activity to purchase his supply. Help from traditional social agencies is avoided, for fear of being reported to police. Public hostility toward the drug user demands punishment and objects to treatment programs. It is a profound criticism of the helping professions that the most successful programs for addicts are not operated by professionals but by former addicts via self-help programs. The earliest of these was Narcotics Anonymous, established at Lexington (the federal drug hospital) and modeled after the mutual assistance program of Alcoholics Anonymous. The Black Muslim movement was able to keep many of its members drug-free by developing their loyalty to a mission and a charismatic leader. One highly publicized and somewhat controversial mutual aid program is Synanon House, a home for ex-addicts in California with branches in other states. Synanon provides a strictly controlled living situation, with small group therapy meetings in which the rationalizations and easy untruths so common to addicts are ruthlessly exposed and dealt with by fellow members.[50] The Synanon approach has been criticized for providing a substitute family and delaying or preventing the ex-addict's integration into the nonaddict society. However, it continues to be one of the few reasonably successful treatment methods available in this discouraging field.

Beginning in 1963, at the Rockefeller Institute in New York, a program of methadone maintenance has been extensively developed and widely praised as a way of keeping chronic, compulsive heroin users free of heroin and available for rehabilitation. Methadone relieves the addict from preoccupation with heroin, keeps him comfortable, can be taken orally, and in essence, substitutes a legal, medically supervised, and controlled addic-

---

49. See Leon Brill, "Addiction: Drug," *Encyclopedia of Social Work, 1971* pp. 24–38.

50. See Lewis Yablonsky, *The Tunnel Back: Synanon* (New York: Macmillan, 1965); see also Daniel Casriel and Grover Amen, *Daytop: Three Addicts and Their Cure* (New York: Hill and Wang, 1971).

tion for an illegal, uncontrolled, and self-destructive one. After being stabilized on methadone, ex-addicts demonstrate greatly reduced illegal behavior, improved vocational adjustment, better social relations, and better response to individual and group therapy. Whether or not they can continue to maintain this level of functioning on reduced doses of methadone or after the drug is withdrawn is still the subject of controversy. There are outspoken critics who deplore methadone maintenance as a substitute addiction and demand a goal of total abstinence for treatment of addicts. There is some possibility of methadone abuse, including illegal sales, but in the absence of any better program, methadone maintenance is serving as a remarkably useful treatment aid.[51]

Because of the legal complications, treatment of drug addiction is a far more difficult and complicated task than treatment of other compulsive, self-defeating patterns of behavior. Social workers are involved in drug treatment programs[52] but are even more widely involved in drug education and abuse prevention programs. To illustrate social work practice in the treatment of addiction, therefore, we will consider alcoholism as a field of growing concern, to which social work has a real contribution to make.

ALCOHOLISM:
THE NEGLECTED DISABILITY

Our attitudes toward drugs and alcohol represent an intriguing contrast. According to Grinspoon,[53] alcohol is culturally accepted because it is associated with the Protestant work ethic, being used by people who follow that ethic. Narcotic use, especially of mari-

51. See Vincent Dole and Marie Nyswander, "A Medical Treatment for Diacetyl-Morphine [Heroin] Addiction," *Journal of the American Medical Association*, Vol. 193 (August 1965), pp. 646–650, for the original presentation by the inaugurators of methadone maintenance; see also Richard R. Lingeman, *Drugs from A to Z: A Dictionary* (New York: McGraw-Hill, 1969), which defines "methadone," "heroin," "addiction," and other drug terms.

52. See, for example, Martha J. McLaney, "Casework with a Troubled Teen-ager and Drug Abuser," *Social Casework*, Vol. 52, No. 9 (November 1971), pp. 553–558, and the subsequent "Discussion" by Leon Wurmser, M.D., pp. 558–561.

53. See Lester Grinspoon, *Marijuana Reconsidered* (Cambridge: Harvard University Press, 1971), who advocates legalizing the sale of marijuana on the grounds that it is nonaddicting and physically harmless. See also Robert Salmon, "An Analysis of Public Marijuana Policy," *Social Casework*, Vol. 53, No. 1 (January 1972), pp. 19–29.

juana, is associated with a non-Western ethic of passivity and indolence and with rebellious youths and blacks representing a counterculture and politically suspect. Whatever the rationale, cultural attitudes do not condemn drinking *per se*, only being drunk in public or breaking laws while under the influence of alcohol. Toasts are drunk, social events celebrated, hospitality epitomized, social tensions eased, and sorrows "drowned" in alcohol by the great majority of Americans without guilt or lowered self-esteem.

At the same time, alcohol is condemned as a wrecker of homes, a menace to health, and the cause of serious loss of life and money. "The demon rum" and "the cup that cheers" demonstrate the ambivalence with which alcohol is used, and alcoholics and nonalcoholics alike try to draw sharp distinctions between those who can "hold their liquor" and those who cannot. There are many "hidden" alcoholics, whose consumption is out of control but who manage somehow to avoid arrest or being fired and who cling desperately to the conviction that they can stop whenever they want.

Measures of the extent of alcoholism in the United States are estimates, since the usual criteria are so inaccurate. Admissions rates to hospitals ignore those being treated privately or on an outpatient basis. Alcoholism is a killing disease, more often indirectly than directly, via road accidents, malnutrition (the alcoholic forgets to eat), and suicide, but alcoholism is seldom listed as the principal cause of death.

THREE VIEWS OF ALCOHOLISM

The Criminal Model

The President's Commission on Law Enforcement and the Administration of Justice reported that drunkenness accounts for one out of every three arrests, which places an enormous burden on law enforcement agencies. Many of those arrested are skid-row alcoholics with long arrest and conviction records. Arrest is usually followed by detoxification in jail ("drunk tank"), appearance in court, sentence to a short jail term, and release back into the community, where the cycle is repeated. This "revolving door" therapy does nothing to help and indeed contributes to the alcoholic's already low self-esteem.[54]

---

54. For a brief summary of the legal aspects of alcoholism, see Nicholas N. Kittrie, *The Right to Be Different: Deviance and Enforced Therapy* (Baltimore: Johns Hopkins Press, 1971), pp. 265–271 and 276–285.

The concept of alcoholism as a disease was slow to be accepted, although Bacon and his associates at the Yale School of Alcohol Studies[55] were advocating it as long ago as 1946. It has been most closely associated with the name of E. M. Jellinek,[56] who viewed alcoholism as a public health rather than purely medical problem. As this view of alcoholism came to be generally accepted, the uselessness of fines and short-term imprisonment became apparent, and a search began for other methods of dealing with the legal, social, and health problems of the chronic alcohol abuser.

More than the half the states now have noncriminal procedures for hospitalizing disturbed alcoholics, via voluntary or involuntary commitment to a mental hospital. However, few state hospitals have adequate treatment facilities. The *Driver* case and the *Easter* case,[57] both in 1966 and involving chronic alcoholics, have affirmed the right of the chronic alcoholic to treatment rather than punishment. The court held that the constitutional prohibition of cruel and unusual punishment prevented a state from punishing a symptom (public drunkenness) of a disease, while holding that excessive drinking by a nonalcoholic is still punishable. The problems of distinguishing between the alcoholic and the excessive drinker, lack of treatment facilities, and the essential lack of differences between the old jails and the new "alcoholism centers," all make these important decisions ineffective. The United States Supreme Court failed in 1968 to extend the principle of the *Driver* and *Easter* cases to the whole of the U.S. The Court was unable to agree on the disposition of *Powell* vs. *Texas*,[58] and hence the substitution of a therapeutic model for the criminal one is dependent on the statutes of the various states not already covered by the *Driver* decision (Virginia, West Virginia, North Carolina, South Carolina, and Maryland).

There is a growing feeling that treating deviants as criminals is a wasteful use of the criminal justice system. The so-called

55. See Seldon D. Bacon, *Sociology and the Problems of Alcoholism* (New Haven: Hillhouse Press, 1946). The Yale School was later transferred to Rutgers University.

56. E. M. Jellinek, *The Disease Concept of Alcoholism* (New Haven: College and University Press, 1960).

57. *Driver* vs. *Hinnant*, Court of Appeals for the Fourth Circuit (356 F. 2d 761); and *Easter* vs. *District of Columbia*, United States Court of Appeals for the District of Columbia (361 F. 2d 50).

58. *Powell* vs. *Texas*, 392 U.S. 514, 549–50 (1968).

"crimes without victims"[59] (gambling, prostitution, homosexuality, adultery, use of liquor or narcotics) are demonstrably uncontrollable by legislation. People engaging in these forbidden behaviors may damage themselves and their families, but the courts are not the logical place to refer them. Punishing people for wasting their money, for addictive behavior they cannot control, or for unusual sex practices between consenting adults is considered by many authorities an unwarranted interference by the state in what should be private concerns.

A therapeutic model of alcoholism does not, of course, relieve an alcoholic of liability for criminal activities other than public intoxication. Driving while intoxicated, breach of the peace, rape, murder, and other offenses committed by an individual under the influence of alcohol are no less criminal than when done by someone sober.

The Disease Model

In spite of some progress in moving away from the criminal model to a therapeutic one, too little is known about alcohol and alcoholism. There was no federal legislation to support research and treatment in alcoholism until 1968. On December 31, 1970, President Nixon signed into law the "comprehensive Alcohol Abuse and Alcoholism Prevention, Treatment, and Rehabilitation Act of 1970." This law called for the establishment of a National Institute on Alcohol Abuse and Alcoholism (NIAAA), to be located in the National Institutes of Health. It mandated the setting up of a National Advisory Council on Alcohol Abuse and Alcoholism to make recommendations and approve program grants. The law also directed the Civil Service Commission to develop a program for federal employees having alcohol problems in cooperation with the NIAAA, to encourage and support similar programs for state and local governments and private industry.

Because of limited knowledge about alcoholism, one of the new Institute's priorities was the sponsorship of research, which is reported yearly in the published "Proceedings" of

---

59. See Edwin F. Schur, *Crimes Without Victims: Deviant Behavior and Public Policy* (Englewood Cliffs, N.J.: Prentice-Hall, 1965). See also Alexander B. Smith and Harriet Pollack, "Crimes Without Victims," *Saturday Review*, Vol. 54, No. 49 (December 4, 1971), pp. 27–29; and Board of Trustees of National Council on Crime and Delinquency, "Crimes Without Victims—A Policy Statement," *Crime and Delinquency*, Vol. 17, No. 2 (April 1971), pp. 129–130.

annual Alcoholism Conferences.[60] Some of the research is carried on in collaboration with the National Highway Traffic Safety Administration, U.S. Department of Transportation, which has an obvious interest in the relationship of accidents and drinking.

The disease model of alcoholism relies heavily on the premise of some physiological differences in the alcoholic which make his reactions to alcohol different from those of the "normal" individual. Nutritional, hormonal, and metabolic factors have been adduced, but no convincing evidence has been produced to show a clear-cut physiological basis, and evidence for a psycho-socio-cultural base for alcoholism is more compelling. However, the physiological model has produced some treatment modalities which may be supplemented by other therapies. Administration of disulfiram (Antabuse) will cause violent illness if alcohol is ingested; it can be useful in reinforcing the alcoholic's desire to refrain from drinking, although the uncooperative patient can stop taking the daily pill. Various aversion techniques which condition strong revulsion to the taste, smell, and even appearance of alcohol use emetics or electric shocks, which the patient learns to associate with alcohol.[61]

Evidence that such conditioning fails to produce long-lasting results in the absence of attention to the patient's social and psychological condition has led to increased interest in behavioral modification techniques.[62] The preliminary analysis of the positively and negatively reinforcing features of his environment may be the first time the confirmed alcoholic, accustomed to evading reality, is forced to confront his situation objectively. The development of social ties with other participants in the program will help reward the alcoholic and lessen his need for specific rewards (privileges, tokens, money, food).

60. The first Institute was held in Washington, D.C., June 25–26, 1972, and the "Proceedings," under the title Research on Alcoholism: Clinical Problems and Special Populations, was published by the NIAAA in 1973. On September 17, 1973, the Alcohol, Drug Abuse and Mental Health Administration (ADAMHA) was created, incorporating the NIAAA, the National Institute of Mental Health, and a new National Institute of Drug Abuse.

61. See Herbert Barry, "Discussion of Research on Therapeutic Drugs," pp. 112–121; and Peter E. Nathan, "Review of Behavioral Techniques," pp. 122–126, both in NIAAA, Research on Alcoholism.

62. See J. D. Keehn, et al., "Interpersonal Behaviorism and Community Treatment of Alcoholics," in NIAAA, Research on Alcoholism, pp. 153–175, which describes Bon Accord, a residential program in Ontario for the rehabilitation of confirmed skid-row alcoholics through techniques of behavior modification.

The Psychodynamic Model

Increased attention to the dynamics of the alcoholic's behavior makes it clear that there is no such thing as the "born alcoholic" or the "alcoholic personality." Very different rates of alcoholism prevail in ethnic subcultures. Both Jews and Italians have low rates, although alcohol, particularly wine, is widely used. Both American Indians and Irish have high rates, believed to be related to the uncertainty of life and to emphasis on hospitality[63] in these groups which have had to adjust to poverty and discrimination.

There are personalities which are vulnerable to addiction; those with insufficient ego strengths to cope in healthy ways are more likely to use neurotic and damaging ways, but it is not yet clear why some individuals use alcohol while others turn to drugs, become depressed and suicidal, or turn their aggressions outward in antisocial behavior. Alcoholics demonstrate low self-esteem, which their continued drinking perpetuates, but so do many troubled people. Alcoholics feel rejected and compel others to pay attention to them, but there are less destructive attention-getting mechanisms. Alcoholics are dependent and may use their addiction to compel those around them to provide care for them, but many very dependent people do not touch alcohol. Alcoholics may set impossibly high goals for themselves and then use alcohol simultaneously to punish and comfort themselves for not reaching them, but many overachievers are demonstrating their questions about their own adequacy without using alcohol. Alcoholics are egocentric, putting their own need to dull their anxieties above the comfort and well-being of those around them, but egocentrism may be demonstrated in countless other ways.

What is characteristic of the alcoholic is the way in which he uses his addiction to control the lives of those around him and to maintain himself in a privileged position, catered to, rescued, excused, and supported.[64] His perception of reality is blurred

63. See Jerrold E. Levy and Stephen J. Kunitz, "Indian Drinking: Problems of Data Collection and Interpretation," pp. 217–236, and Jack Waddell, " 'Drink Friend!' Social Contexts of Convivial Drinking and Drunkenness Among Papago Indians in an Urban Setting," pp. 237–251, both in NIAAA, *Research on Alcoholism.*

64. See David C. McClelland, William N. Davis, Rudolf Kalin, and Eric Wanner, *The Drinking Man* (New York: The Free Press, 1972), which concludes that drinkers use alcohol because of their need for power over others.

by his drinking and further blurred by the efforts of his family, his employers, his friends, even the cab drivers and policemen who cover up for him, listen to his bragging about his drunken exploits, help him home, and accept his unsatisfactory level of functioning. To these unwitting accomplices must often be added the family agency or public welfare worker who provides his troubled family with counseling and assistance and thereby makes it possible for him to continue his unsatisfactory method of coping.[65]

SOCIAL WORK IN ALCOHOLISM

It is estimated that there are between 6,000,000 and 10,000,000 alcoholics in the United States. Alcoholics Anonymous (AA), the highly effective self-help program founded by two ex-alcoholics in 1935 to reinforce their mutual efforts to stay dry, has between 150,000 and 200,000 members. There are perhaps 150 specialized alcohol treatment agencies. It is obvious that the great majority of alcoholics go untreated and that the best avenue for reaching them with treatment is the general community service agencies in which social workers are the front-line therapists. Yet social work has been very slow to recognize alcoholism as a social problem susceptible to social work intervention.

Social workers in every agency know the toll of alcoholism in the families they serve. The extent of human unhappiness, accidents, marital friction, child neglect, dependency, poor job records, and frequent difficulties with law enforcement officials, can be documented in the records of family and children's service agencies, mental health agencies, public welfare departments, and hospital social service departments. And yet in most of these case records, alcoholism will not be the central problem being treated. Traditionally, social workers have rejected the alcoholic and focused on helping the family compensate for the ravages of its alcoholic member. Thomas Plaut attributes this to a conviction on the part of most social workers that alcoholics are difficult to treat, demanding and unrewarding as clients, and prone to spectacular relapses.[66]

An additional factor has been the insistence on alcoholism as an illness. The disease model, while useful in reducing punitive

65. See Claude Steiner, *Games Alcoholics Play: The Analysis of Life Scripts* (New York: Grove Press, 1971), which applies transactional analysis to the understanding and treatment of alcoholics.

66. Thomas F. A. Plaut, "Addiction: Alcohol," *Encyclopedia of Social Work*, 1971, pp. 16–24.

attitudes toward alcoholics, has made it easier for social workers to regard alcoholism as a condition requiring medical treatment rather than social work intervention. Referring alcoholics to specialized treatment facilities and treating their families supportively has been the pattern of social work in the field of alcoholism.

With increased emphasis on alcoholism as a behavior disorder rather than either a vice or an illness, social work can become more involved in treating alcoholics directly, using methods found useful for other clients with self-defeating and maladaptive patterns of living. Recognizing the impact on the family and viewing the family as a system in which the alcoholic is involved and which he is manipulating for his own purposes,[67] the profession of social work can no longer refuse to treat the alcoholic on the grounds that he is not motivated for treatment. Many other types of client are poorly motivated to change; one of the tasks of the social worker is to increase the motivation by providing some hope that change will be possible and profitable.

Recognizing the lack of information on alcoholism and its treatment in the social work literature and curricula, the Council on Social Work Education commissioned an experienced social worker, the administrator of the Cleveland Center on Alcoholism and Drug Abuse, Herman Krimmel, to prepare a source book for social work students, educators, and practitioners.[68] The following discussion draws heavily on this useful volume.

The alcoholic is defined as a person who can no longer control his drinking behavior and who is utilizing his drinking, however painful its consequences, as an adaptive technique to cope with what he perceives as reality. The extent to which his drinking patterns affect his life, rather than the amount or timing of his drinking, is, according to Krimmel, what differentiates the alcoholic from other drinkers, even admittedly heavy, chronic drinkers. Krimmel defines alcoholism as "a pattern of drinking that, on a continuous basis, interferes with

---

67. For an analysis of how systems theory is illustrated in social work practice with an alcoholic and his family, see Allen Pincus and Anne Minahan, *Social Work Practice: Model and Method* (Itasca, Ill.: F. E. Peacock Publishers, 1973), pp. 55–63.

68. Herman Krimmel, *Alcoholism: Challenge for Social Work Education* (New York: CSWE, 1971).

adequate functioning in any significant area of a person's life."[69]

Direct Treatment

Alcoholics demonstrate several characteristics which offer social workers an avenue for intervention. They almost always suffer from feelings of inferiority and lowered self-esteem.[70] It is in order to feel more successful and powerful that they drink. The feelings may seem justifiable; the skid-row alcoholic *is* inferior, and his low self-esteem is paralleled by the low esteem in which he is held by others, but his inferiority feelings are shared by many apparently highly successful business and professional people.

Most alcoholics feel rejected and alienated but are extremely sensitive to any sign of rejection and continually test the therapist, as well as family and friends, trying to provoke them into becoming rejecting persons who can then be blamed for disappointing or failing the alcoholic. Alcoholics overuse the mechanism of projection (see page 319) and may bewilder their wives by accusing them of infidelity, their fellow employees of treachery, or their therapists of being uninterested. The social worker treating alcoholics must not fall into their traps and must provide realistic recognition of their efforts.

Most alcoholics deceive themselves (but not usually other people) by denial, rationalization, and evasion—all attempts to deal with their guilt feelings. They may insist that they are not alcoholics because they do not carry out some bit of behavior that to them defines the "true" alcoholic. The alcoholic will lie about his drinking, hide bottles, sneak drinks. He always has an excuse for drinking, but it's never that he needs it. Trying to discuss his drinking with him is nagging, invasion of privacy, or persecution. He denies that he is inconveniencing or hurting others, though his denials are not convincing even to himself. In order to be helpful, the social worker must not accept the denial nor encourage his family to do so. The first step in getting the alcoholic to enter treat-

69. *Ibid.*, pp. 15, 16. For amplification of this concept, see Sidney Cahn, *The Treatment of Alcoholics: An Evaluative Study* (New York: Oxford University Press, 1970), pp. 36–37.

70. One of the first social workers to concentrate on this aspect of the alcoholic's problems was Perry M. Sessions, "Social Casework Treatment of Alcoholism with the Focus on the Image of Self," in Ruth Fox, ed., *Alcoholism: Behavioral Research, Therapeutic Approaches* (New York: Springer Publishing Company, 1967), pp. 229–306.

ment may be to persuade the spouse, the parents, and the employer[71] whom the alcoholic is exploiting to refuse to cover up for
him any longer and insist that he accept the responsibility for his
own situation and future. His rationalizations must be confronted
with realities.

By puncturing the alibis with which the alcoholic has surrounded himself, the social worker may create the crisis which
will result in the decision to seek help. Or the crisis may come
from the loss of a job, the decision of a spouse to leave, the orders
of a court. Most confirmed alcoholics are so paralyzed in their pattern of narcissistic living that they can move only when acute discomfort has been created. The use of authority in protective services has already been mentioned (see page 135). Like the neglectful
parent who cannot move on his own initiative, the alcoholic may
be unable to take any initiative and needs duress.

Alcoholics have enormous unsatisfied dependency needs. Their
drinking assures them the support and protection they feel unable
to get by their own merits. In our culture, dependency is more
acceptable for females than for males, and some authorities feel
that is why male alcoholics outnumber females, since women can
accept dependency without feeling threatened more easily than
men. Once a relationship with a therapist has been established,
the alcoholic client is well nigh insatiable, demanding service
and attention from the therapist very much like a spoiled child,
and threatening to resume drinking as a way of controlling the
therapist. Only a therapist who is secure in his own competence,
able to withstand hostility and remain supportive, able to meet
the demands of extremely dependent clients without becoming
drained and depressed, and able to find positives in a treatment
whose progress is uneven or painstakingly slow, should undertake to treat alcoholics; and even then he probably should not try
to carry a caseload made up entirely of alcoholics.

The alcoholic desperately needs and wants to be accepted as a
person but finds it difficult to imagine that anyone without an
ulterior motive could so accept him. The acceptance of people
whose self-defeating behavior has antagonized the world is an old
story to social workers. Confidence that people *can* change is es-

71. See Margaret M. Heyman, "Employer-Sponsored Programs for Problem
Drinkers," *Social Casework*, Vol. 52, No. 9 (November 1971), pp. 547–552, which
stresses employment as an important avenue for early identification of alcoholism, together with the need for adequate community resources to meet the
needs of identified alcoholic employees.

sential in any helping relationship and is particularly critical with clients as discouraged and hopeless as most alcoholics.[72]

Indirect Treatment

While direct treatment of the highly motivated alcoholic would promise the most success, in fact social workers seldom see such situations. Most alcoholics who do come into social agencies for treatment come reluctantly, ordered by courts, nagged by families, or threatened by employers with loss of jobs. Many resist being referred to a mental health center as confirming their deep-seated fear of "going crazy." Much of the treatment of alcoholics is done indirectly, chiefly with their wives.[73] Casework treatment of alcoholism involves more than the customary amount of information giving, in addition to discussion of management problems and some attempt to understand the alcoholic husband's feelings as well as those of the client. It has been found that when wives of alcoholics are being treated, it is easier to engage the husbands in treatment. Even where the husband refuses treatment, the wife and children have needs of their own which should be recognized. All too often, the family of the alcoholic feels submerged by the enormity of the problems presented by the alcoholic and needs to be helped to put their own needs in perspective. There are even situations where the wife must be helped to free herself and her children from a highly destructive relationship.[74]

There has been some discussion in the literature about whether the wife of an alcoholic man is herself a disturbed person who "needs" a dependent, inadequate mate whom she can infantilize and dominate. A more generally applicable explanation may be that her husband's incapacity has forced the wife to take over management of the family and that she has found unanticipated satisfaction in playing the dominant role. Her "need" to keep her husband incapacitated may be motivated also by skepticism about the possibility that he will ever recover.

72. See Eileen M. Corrigan, "Linking the Problem Drinker with Treatment," *Social Work*, Vol. 17, No. 2 (March 1972), pp. 54–60. See also Peter M. Miller, Ann G. Stanford, and Diana P. Hemphill, "A Social-Learning Approach to Alcoholism Treatment," *Social Casework*, Vol. 55, No. 5 (May 1974), pp. 279–284.

73. See Cahn, *The Treatment of Alcoholics*, especially "Indirect Therapy," pp. 120–122. A four-year research and demonstration project carried out by the Family Service Association of Cleveland is reported in Pauline C. Cohen and Merton S. Krause, *Casework with Wives of Alcoholics* (New York: Family Service Association of America, 1971).

74. See John F. Mueller, "Casework with the Family of the Alcoholic," *Social Work*, Vol. 17, No. 5 (September 1972), pp. 79–84.

The wife of the alcoholic typically feels guilt that she has contributed to "driving him to drink" and is therefore driven to pacify and cater to him for fear of precipitating a drinking binge. This is one of the many ways in which alcoholics control the lives of their families. She typically also feels anger and self-pity, because she is likely to believe his continued uncontrolled drinking could be controlled by sufficient willpower. Once she has been helped to see that she did not cause his illness and she cannot cure it single-handed, she can be freed of some of her guilt and of her need to compensate for it. Allowing her alcoholic husband to suffer some of the consequences of his drinking from which she has been protecting him may be a useful spur to him to seek treatment. Where marital incompatibility, unacknowledged hostility, or other conflicts have led to a troubled home situation, direct treatment for these with the wife and a consequent improvement in the home atmosphere may support the husband's efforts to stay sober. The goal should be a satisfying family life for all members and not merely sobriety for the alcoholic. When the wife is helped to see her husband's emotional needs for reassurance, appreciation, and recognition as a capable person, she can turn her attention to these and away from nagging or supervising his activities. When he is in treatment, the wife will then be reinforcing the efforts of the social worker; if he is unwilling to enter treatment, his wife can serve in some ways as a surrogate therapist.

The pessimism many social workers feel about treating alcoholics has been mentioned. Plaut[75] feels that an additional obstacle is the social worker's ambivalence about the moral issues in drinking and a conviction, perhaps unconscious, that the alcoholic *could* stop drinking if he really wanted to. The reluctance to deal with alcoholism is also demonstrated, according to Krimmel,[76] in the extent to which social workers persistently ignore warning signals, such as personality changes, increased marital conflict, and even physical symptoms. Sensing the social worker's reluctance to get involved in discussion of the alcoholic member of the family, the client will hesitate to bring it up but will respond to questions which demonstrate interest and willingness to help. When social workers know what warning signals to look for, alcoholism will be recognized as a central problem in many cases in which treatment goals may have been presumed to be quite different.

75. Plaut, "Addiction: Alcohol," p. 18.
76. Krimmel, *Alcoholism*, Chapter 2, "Identifying the Alcoholic," pp. 27–46.

Learning Sobriety

Much has been made in the literature of Alcoholics Anonymous of the alcoholic's need to recognize that he has "hit bottom" and that he is powerless to help himself stop drinking; such a confrontation is considered an indispensable first step in rehabilitation. Social workers have tended to accept this and to wait for alcoholics to be driven into asking for help in desperation or threatened into treatment by exasperated wives or employers. If the motivation seemed inadequate, little effort was made to encourage the alcoholic to become better motivated. Reread the case of Mr. Quinn (page 339) in this light. The social worker's sigh of relief is almost audible. Social workers in protective services are not similarly discouraged by inadequately motivated parents and do not abandon the situation as untreatable.

Krimmel lists the tasks of the social worker as three-part: 1) to help the alcoholic feel like a worthwhile human being, able to cope with his life without the artificial crutch of alcohol; 2) to help him abandon denial and face reality, which may mean confronting him with his lies and evasions or encouraging the significant people in his life to do just that and pointing out the positives in his life when he is sober as opposed to the negatives when he is drunk; 3) to help the alcoholic to learn sobriety, developing substitute behavior which brings immediate as well as long-range satisfactions and developing socially acceptable coping mechanisms.[77]

The goal of the alcoholic in treatment is complete abstinence, but he may not be able to achieve it at once. The alcoholic desperately needs the crutch of drinking, because without it he feels alienated, helpless, inferior, and hopeless. If he can be helped to feel more capable, more valuable, and more useful, he may be better able to abandon his crutch. But to insist on total abstinence as a condition of treatment is unrealistic for many alcoholics. Social workers are used to clients who backslide; the depressed client is not uniformly cheerful overnight but experiences periods of depression at less frequent intervals as treatment proceeds. The overprotective mother relapses into infantilizing behavior occasionally. If improved functioning in some aspects of his life is seen as the goal for the alcoholic, rather than equating a relapse with failure, as many alcohol counselors do, casework help can focus on meeting the problems and tensions of everyday life with alternative techniques and use relapses as an area for discussion.

77. *Ibid.*, Chapter 7, "Social Work Treatment of the Alcoholic," pp. 136–173.

Reducing the frequency and duration of alcoholic binges represents a positive gain, not an admission of defeat.

The AA insists on lifelong total abstinence as the ultimate aim for all its members and declares that the ex-alcoholic can never drink again. Some therapists who conceive of alcoholism as maladaptive functioning believe that once the alcoholic has learned better methods of meeting his needs, he will no longer resort to so destructive a means as alcoholism and can resume social drinking. There are therapists whose goal is to reduce the addict's drinking to acceptable amounts.[78] Some former members of AA have resumed social drinking, but they had to break away from the organization to do so.[79]

PROGRAMS FOR ALCOHOLISM

Comprehensive Community Programs

A comprehensive program for alcoholism would include four components, in each of which social workers may have a useful part to play. The first is the detoxification unit or, as some authorities prefer to call it, "the emergency care" service.[80] "Drying out" is primarily a medical responsibility and provides an opportunity for screening patients for other medical problems, such as hepatitis, anemia, tuberculosis, and other diseases known to be common in chronic alcoholics. Such a service may be located in a general hospital or in a separate center, with hospital back-up as required. The center should also provide psychiatric and psychological screening and a detailed social history, which will require a longer stay than that needed for physical detoxification. The emergency care service should include a diagnostic work-up and treatment plan, in which the social worker's assessment of the patient's family background, the family's readiness to change and to support change in the patient, and linkage to community facilities,

78. See Paul E. Baer, "Aversion and Avoidance Conditioning as a Treatment for Alcoholism: Short Term Effects," in NIAAA, *Research on Alcoholism*, pp. 139–152. See also E. Mansell Pattison, E. B. Headley, G. C. Glaser, and L. A. Gottschalk, "Abstinence and Normal Drinking: An Assessment of Changes in Drinking Patterns in Alcoholics After Treatment," *Quarterly Journal of Studies in Alcohol,* Vol. 29, No. 3 (September 1968), pp. 610–633.

79. See Arthur H. Cain, *The Cured Alcoholic: New Concepts in Alcoholism Treatment and Research* (New York: John Day, 1964), which criticizes AA as a cult on which people become as dependent as they formerly were on alcohol and cites numerous cases of treated alcoholics who were able to resume social drinking.

80. See George G. Pavloff, ed., *Proceedings: Seminar on Alcoholism Emergency Care Services* (Rockville, Md.: NIAAA, 1972), for a complete description of the structure and functions of emergency care centers.

especially for housing, are an integral part. The NIAAA recommends a minimum of five days for this step.

The second component is inpatient facilities in general hospitals or state mental hospitals, for those patients who need the controlled structure of a closed institution to carry them through the initial interruption in the stress-drinking-detoxification-renewed stress-renewed drinking cycle. Such inpatient facilities make extensive use of group therapy and individual counseling, either by social workers or by paraprofessionals who have been given in-service training and consultation from social work staff. Group therapy is especially effective in breaking through the alcoholic's denial of his problem and in exposing his rationalizations on the basis of the experience of other group members.

When patients are ready to move back into the community but are not yet able to function independently, the next move may be to a halfway house, in which some supervision and control are available, together with further group therapy; or the patients may be able to go directly from the emergency service into such a halfway house. Vocational retraining and job placement may well be combined with counseling, adequate nutrition, and work with the family. Skid-row alcoholics, who are alienated from their families and alone, are particularly vulnerable to relapse if they return to their skid-row lodgings, and a halfway house will retain them in treatment and help them locate housing in an area which will not be a constant reminder and temptation to backslide.

The fourth component is outpatient services,[81] either in general multipurpose clinics or in special clinics for alcoholics. The time at which the patient is ready for outpatient service should be determined by an interdisciplinary team, including social workers. Some patients may go straight from emergency care into outpatient care; some may go through all four types of service; and some may be referred to outpatient clinics without even having to go through detoxification.

Treatment of alcoholism is a long-time process. Dr. Bell estimates that it will be at least a year before the ex-alcoholic will stop missing the alcohol which has for so long been in the forefront of his thinking.[82] New friends, physical activity, involvement in community affairs, and time spent with formerly neg-

81. See Jon Weinberg, "Counseling Recovering Alcoholics," *Social Work*, Vol. 18, No. 4 (July 1973), pp. 84–93.

82. R. Gordon Bell, *Escape from Addiction* (New York: McGraw-Hill Book Company, 1970), describes the interdisciplinary three-phase treatment at the Donwood Institute in Toronto. Dr. Bell also describes a hierarchy of three teams: the professional team, the community team, and the patient team.

lected families will help to fill some of the vacuum left in the ex-alcoholic's life, as well as provide opportunities for satisfying experiences which will build his self-esteem. The alcoholic would be well advised to avoid his former drinking companions and the surroundings which were associated with his drinking days. Those who provide social work and counseling support during his months of adjustment—what Krimmel calls "learning sobriety"— must be supportive, patient, concerned, but resist being manipulated by the alcoholic's "games." His family will also need support, as well as specific information about alcoholism, anticipatory guidance about what to expect, and linkage to community resources.

Alcoholics Anonymous

One of the best known and most successful resources is Alcoholics Anonymous, the self-help organization of "arrested" alcoholics. AA is based on the premise that alcoholics cannot be cured but that they can stop drinking. The program is based on a spiritual (not necessarily religious) philosophy which insists that the alcoholic acknowledge that he is powerless over his own drinking and must rely on a power greater than himself for help. He must examine himself and his behavior rigorously, make restitution where he has harmed others, and help other alcoholics in AA. There are no dues and no formal organization. Meetings are social occasions and feature testimony by recovered alcoholics.

There are sound reasons for the success of AA. It provides new friends and new social occasions to fill empty time. By assigning each new member to an older one for individualized help, it reinforces the wish of each to succeed. The older member sees in the newer one what he was and does not wish to be again, and the new member sees what he may become. Spin-off organizations are Al-Anon for mates (mostly wives, since there are relatively few women members of AA) and Alateen, for the children of alcoholics. During the early years of AA, the organization was reluctant to collaborate with professionals, but more mutual respect and cooperation between AA and professionals exist today.

AA is not an approach that is suited to all alcoholics. They must be highly motivated, willing to adopt the AA "Twelve Steps," and aim for permanent abstinence. Its critics accuse AA of substituting the organization for the alcohol and perpetuating dependence rather than fostering independence. Its advocates point to its high success rate. It is essentially a middle-class program and offers relatively little to lower-class alcoholics. Whether or not to refer a patient to AA should be based on an understanding of the patient's needs and judgment as to whether they can be met in an organization which features gregariousness, total involvement, and a high degree of motivation.

Skid Row Programs

Evidence is that most alcoholics in AA or in outpatient programs are middle-class and not from skid row.[83] Emphasis on verbal ability and motivation tends to select out for clinic treatment the better-educated clients with more money, a work history, and family ties. The skid row alcoholics are left for the mission, of which the Salvation Army Harbor Light Program is the prototype. Missions retain the nineteenth-century notion that alcoholics are in need of redemption through religion before they can undertake social rehabilitation. The programs, whether residences or community centers, emphasize formal religious services, revival and prayer meetings, and religious counseling, as well as providing food, shelter, work, and recreation. The Salvation Army Men's Social Service offers a sheltered workshop with live-in facilities for the unattached, unskilled, often mentally disabled derelicts who are unlikely to be cared for in middle-class halfway houses.[84]

The residence program is explained to men coming in off the street for a free meal or referred in by police, courts, or jails, as an opportunity for salvation and redemption. This operates as a screening device which tends to exclude the chronic unmotivated skid row residents, who float from mission to mission securing free meals, an occasional shower or clothing, or a place to sleep in cold weather. For those considered a good risk, after a period of initial adjustment work is provided, together with social activities, group meetings, and in a few large programs, professional therapy by both Salvation Army personnel and other professionals. Some Salvation Army (SA) programs have

83. Cahn, *The Treatment of Alcoholics*, pp. 98, 99. See also Jacqueline P. Wiseman, *Stations of the Lost: The Treatment of Skid Row Alcoholics* (Englewood Cliffs, N.J.: Prentice-Hall, 1970); Sheldon Zimberg, Harry Lipscomb, and Elizabeth B. Davis, "Socio-psychiatric Treatment of Alcoholism in an Urban Ghetto," *American Journal of Psychiatry*, Vol. 127, No. 12 (June 1971), pp. 1670–1674; and Howard M. Bahr, *Skid Row: An Introduction to Disaffiliation* (New York: Oxford University Press, 1973).

84. See Sally L. Perry, George J. Goldin, Bernard A. Stotsky, Reuben J. Margolin, *The Rehabilitation of the Alcoholic Dependent*, "Northeastern University Studies in Rehabilitation," No. 11 (Lexington, Mass.: D. C. Heath and Company, 1970). See also John J. Judge, "Alcoholism Treatment in the Salvation Army: A New Men's Social Service Center Program," *Quarterly Journal of Studies on Alcohol*, Vol. 32, No. 2 (June 1971), pp. 462–467.

developed group residence in the community away from skid row, to encourage return to the community. Total abstinence is demanded, and a relapse results in expulsion from the residence. Salvation Army programs are supported from United Way campaigns, donations, and services offered to the public by residents. Housecleaning, paint removal, second-hand stores, and house-to-house delivery of flyers are such sources of income. The religious dedication of Salvation Army personnel permits an extremely low salary scale and a larger proportion of available funds going into the program. Although some professionals look down on mission efforts as amateurish and moralistic, no other established alcoholism treatment service welcomes the skid row derelict, and missions are meeting a real social need.

Obviously, professional social agencies have not responded adequately to the problem and challenge of alcoholism. The bulk of service to alcoholics and their families must be provided by general community agencies, since there are only 150 specialized alcoholism clinics in the U.S. It is apparent that social workers will be increasingly involved in treating alcoholics and their families, in educating the public about alcohol abuse, and in training and supervising paraprofessionals, who will provide the bulk of service delivery in most agencies.

HOMOSEXUALITY:
THE DUBIOUS DISABILITY

Where there is general agreement that alcoholism is self-destructive behavior and that the alcoholic should be treated and his behavior altered, there is no such consensus when it comes to the question of homosexuality and no clear mandate to social work in treating homosexuals. Historically in Western culture, seeking sexual gratification from a partner of the same sex has been viewed as a crime. State laws forbid such practices as "sins against nature," and police harass homosexuals. They may be unable to secure employment in schools, government agencies, and private industry. Evidence of homosexuality in the armed services leads to a "less than honorable" discharge.[85] For many years, it was assumed that homosexuals had some genetic predisposition to behavior considered a "perversion," which they could only resist and not alter. Such celebrated cases as

85. See Colin J. Williams and Martin S. Weinberg, *Homosexuals and the Military* (New York: Harper & Row, 1971).

that of Oscar Wilde revealed how little tolerance there was in Victorian society for a known homosexual. Homosexuals were dismissed from government service during the McCarthy "witch hunts" in the 1950s.

In the 1960s, the disease model of homosexuality was gradually introduced by psychiatrists, led by Edmund Bergler,[86] who claimed to be one of the first psychiatrists successfully to treat male homosexuals. The disease model conceived of homosexuality as arrested development and attributed it to poor relationships with parents and fixation at an adolescent level of confused sexual identification. Homosexuality was no more "normal" but was considered now to be treatable. This substitution of therapy, often enforced, was regarded by the Mattachine Society and other homophile groups as dubious progress. They maintained the right of the adult homosexual to engage in sexual activity with consulting adults and refused to consider themselves either as criminals or as sick.

The issue of individual rights which came into prominence in the 1960s stressed the extent to which minority groups—blacks, women, prisoners, anti-war protesters, and homosexuals—were oppressed and denied their rights. After operating in anonymity and secrecy for years, some organized homosexuals "surfaced" as the Gay Liberation Front and demanded the right of complete sexual liberation. Increasingly, homosexuals insist that their way of life is an acceptable alternative life style. They demand freedom from entrapment, from raids on gay bars, from discrimination in employment and housing. They want the sanctions of the state in "marriages" and the right for homosexual couples to adopt children, just as childless heterosexual couples may. They see themselves as pioneers and liberals and seek to ally themselves with other liberal movements.[87]

The 1970s have so far witnessed greater recognition of the rights of homosexuals. Several cities are considering or have adopted bills condemning discrimination against homosexuals, especially in the area of equal opportunity in employment. On

86. See Edmund Bergler, *Homosexuality: Disease or Way of Life* (New York: Macmillan 1962). See also Lionel Ovesey, *Homosexuality and Pseudohomosexuality* (New York: Science House, 1964); and Lawrence J. Hatterer, *Changing Homosexuality in the Male* (New York: McGraw-Hill, 1970), for representative discussions of "curing" homosexuals.

87. See Edward Sagarin, "Sex Raises Its Revolutionary Head." *The Realist* (May–June 1970), reprinted in R. Serge Denisoff and Charles H. McCaghy, eds., *Deviance, Conflict, and Criminality* (Chicago: Rand McNally & Company, 1973), pp. 174–190. See also George Weinberg, *Society and the Healthy Homosexual* (New York: St. Martin's Press, 1972).

April 8, 1974, the American Psychiatric Association voted to dis-
avow the disease concept of homosexuality. Homosexuality is
more and more being considered an alternative life style when
chosen by consenting adults.

While public attitudes have been modified, evidence is that
the great bulk of Americans are not ready to accept homosexuality as an acceptable alternative to heterosexuality. Because of
social condemnation of their behavior, many homosexuals suffer
from emotional conflicts and impaired self-image. In an effort to
justify their deviance, some homosexuals have claimed greater
sensitivity and superior artistic ability. Many deny, not always
convincingly, that they suffer any guilt or discomfort. To what
extent the psychological orientation of homosexuals is a reaction
to the discrimination they suffer and what may be characteristic
of homosexuality is not known. Research is clouded by secrecy,
by the preconceptions of the investigators, and by skewed
samples. There has been an upsurge of interest in the subject (a
recent bibliography cites over 3,000 items[88]), but too many
writings on the subject are polemical, impressionistic, or based
on atypical samples.

SOCIAL WORK WITH HOMOSEXUALS

The subject is largely neglected in social work literature. The
extent to which social workers are expected by the public to be
norm-enforcers has troubled the profession for some years,
stimulated by the provocative work of Piven and Cloward,[89]
which stressed the extent to which the public welfare system
supports the status quo and functions as a means of social control. Brian Segal suggests that politicalization of social deviance
is a logical next step for which social workers should be prepared.[90]

> Social work with marginal groups has focused on helping
> marginal man gain entry into society's mainstream. How-
> ever, the target population and the type of intervention

88. William Parker, *Homosexuality: A Selective Bibliography* (Metuchen, N.J.:
Scarecrow Press, 1971). See also Edward R. Sagarin, "The Good Guys, The Bad
Guys, and the Gay Guys," *Contemporary Sociology*, Vol. 2, No. 1 (January 1973),
pp. 3–13.

89. These authors called attention to the regulative functions of social welfare
in a series of articles before the publication of their definitive and troubling
book; see Frances Fox Piven and Richard A. Cloward, *Regulating the Poor: The
Function of Public Welfare* (New York: Pantheon Books, 1971).

90. Brian Segal, "The Politicalization of Deviance," *Social Work*, Vol. 17, No. 4
(July 1972), pp. 40–46.

used depends on how marginality is defined. If it is defined as a social problem, intervention is geared toward changing the individual. If it is defined as a political problem, interventions directed at systems change are popular and efforts to change people have lower priority. For example, poverty, which for many years was considered a social problem, is now regarded as more of a political problem and is debated in the political arena. Thus social work interventions have shifted from therapeutic to advocate roles. However, because social deviance is still considered a social problem, professional role changes have not occurred in this area. Social work with deviant groups . . . maintains a therapeutic rather than a partisan advocacy position.[91]

In the past, social workers who have become involved in treating homosexuals have bent their efforts toward "converting" them to a heterosexual orientation. Whether or not such a change is possible through social work intervention, the attempt represents imposing the worker's own standards on the client whose right to self-determination demands professional respect.[92] In one of the extremely limited number of discussions of social work treatment of homosexuals, Harvey Gochros[93] points out that the vast number of homosexuals keep their sexual orientation secret, and it is this which complicates their lives and which may constitute some of the problems with which social work intervention can be helpful. Gochros suggests that the social worker, to be helpful, must be willing to accept the sexual orientation of the confirmed adult homosexual and focus on the problems which are consequent on that orientation.

> Many of the homosexual's problems are similar to those who bear any other social stigma. This is not a stigma of their own choosing . . . But the homosexual suffers the consequences of these stigmas that can but do not necessarily include self-hatred, guilt, seeking out others with similar stigmas, rejection by family, striking out against an unjust world, alienation, and relative social isolation. It is with the consequences of these stigmas and the problems of living a

91. *Ibid.*, p. 40. Reprinted with the permission of the National Association of Social Workers.

92. See Richard Green, "Homosexuality as a Mental Illness," *International Journal of Psychiatry*, Vol. 10, No. 1 (March 1972), pp. 77–98; and the reviews by Martin Hoffman and Judd Marmor, pp. 105–107, and pp. 114–117, which outline the criticisms of the illness model of homosexuality and raise issues of the abuse of this model to justify aggressive intervention into the lives of homosexuals.

93. Harvey L. Gochros, "The Sexually Opressed," *Social Work*, Vol. 17, No. 2 (March 1972), pp. 16–23.

satisfying, productive life that the social worker can be of most help.

The social worker has a responsibility for helping those homosexuals who are not interested in conversion to achieve as much satisfaction in life as possible and to deal with the legal, vocational, social, and interpersonal problems that result from their orientation. Further, the social worker should work to alter societal attitudes and sanctions and reform laws to help insure that homosexuals' rights as human beings are preserved.[94]

With adolescents whose sexual identifications are not yet confirmed and who may confuse anxiety over heterosexual failures or inadequacies with homosexual tendencies, the social worker should support wishes to adopt a heterosexual orientation by helping resolve distorted ties to parents, discussing fears, providing referrals to group work agencies or community programs which will provide them with opportunities for developing successful social relationships with members of the opposite sex. Fear and hostility to the opposite sex, based on limited or distorted experiences, may confirm the customary ambivalence of the adolescent in a homosexual orientation when it was not really the young person's first choice.

Many basically heterosexual individuals resort to homosexual activity when they are deprived of contact with the opposite sex for long periods of time, in prisons, military service, or mental hospitals. Co-correctional programs (introduced in Massachusetts and the federal prison system in 1972) and conjugal visiting (carried on without publicity in Mississippi since 1918 but only recently publicized and more widely adopted) support heterosexual identifications and diminish the extent of forced homosexuality. "R and R" (rest and recuperation) leaves from military service and relaxation of on-base restrictions in the "new army" help keep marriages intact and reduce management problems. Mental hospitals have been less ready to recognize and support the sexual needs of patients, possibly because of the widespread notion that the mentally ill are sexually disturbed and dangerous. Social workers have a responsibility to intervene on behalf of these groups of sexually oppressed groups, as therapists, advocates, brokers, and teachers.[95]

94. *Ibid.*, pp. 20, 21. Reprinted with the permission of the National Association of Social Workers.

95. See Stuart A. Kirk, "Clients as Outsiders: Theoretical Approaches to Deviance," *Social Work*, Vol. 17, No. 2 (March 1972), pp. 24–32, which discusses the dilemma of social workers as norm-enforcers.

SOCIAL WORK ROLES

The disabilities selected for this chapter represent varying locations on the continuum outlined by the Southern Regional Education Board (see page 403) and illustrate several of the SREB's categories of obstacles to social functioning. The efforts of social workers are directed toward improving functioning, modifying outmoded public attitudes which condemn and stereotype the disabled, and fostering the integration of disabled individuals into normal social functioning instead of excluding and isolating them. In carrying out these tasks, social workers will use most if not all of the SREB roles outlined in Chapter 1, page 22.

All disability, from whatever cause, results in lowered self-esteem. Direct treatment to disabled individuals, therefore, will endeavor to build self-esteem to a more realistic level and encourage the client to make the best use possible of his potentials. Where he is using denial to avoid coming to terms with his disability, he should be confronted with reality, but in a constructive rather than a punitive or negative way.

The disabled individual should not be viewed as an isolated entity but as a handicapped person living in a network of family and social relationships. The social worker can help mobilize these relatives and associates since their deliberate or unconscious rejection, defeatism, or overprotectiveness will tend to consolidate the disability rather then allow the individual to maximize his potential. Supportive services to families will be needed, as they struggle to accept and maintain the disabled person.

Social action, to modify rigid laws and policies, to protect the civil rights of the disabled, and to support community-based facilities for preventing disability and meeting special needs, will involve social workers as change agents, mobilizers, planners, and administrators. Their concern for the individual and his well-being can serve as a counterbalancing force against policies which categorize problems and plan mass treatment programs.

Improving the social functioning of the disabled is invariably a team effort, involving medical, psychiatric, nursing, educational, and legal professionals, as well as social workers. The special goal of the social worker in such multidisciplinary efforts is to see the whole person, with all the forces impinging on him, and make him the focus of social work intervention. It is a challenging task.

ADDITIONAL REFERENCES

Adams, Margaret, *Mental Retardation and Its Social Dimensions* (New York: Columbia University Press, 1971). A comprehensive view of the multiple needs of the mentally retarded and their families and the place of social work in the field.

Alcoholism Treatment and Rehabilitation: Selected Abstracts (Rockville, Md.: National Institute on Alcohol Abuse and Alcoholism, 1972). A review of worldwide literature on the subject through September 1971.

Altman, Dennis, *Homosexual: Oppression and Liberation* (New York: Avon Books, 1973). An analysis of the Gay Liberation Movement.

Blodgett, Harriet E., *Mentally Retarded Children: What Parents and Others Should Know* (Minneapolis: University of Minnesota Press, 1971). Information on all aspects of causes, education, living with and planning for the mentally retarded.

Brill, Leon and Lieberman, Louis, eds., *Major Modalities in the Treatment of Drug Abuse* (New York: Behavioral Publications, 1972). A compilation of writings by behavioral scientists, physicians, social workers, and psychiatrists, demonstrating a range of techniques appropriate for different types of addicts.

Edgerton, Robert B., *The Cloak of Competence: Stigma in the Lives of the Mentally Retarded* (Berkeley: University of California Press, 1971). A sympathetic view of mildly retarded adults struggling to maintain themselves in the community after care in a California institution.

Grinker, Roy R. et al., eds., *Psychiatric Diagnosis, Therapy and Research on the Psychotic Deaf* (Washington, D.C.: Social and Rehabilitation Service, 1971). Describes the neglected deaf abandoned in mental hospitals, without educational services though not retarded, and some successful efforts to return them to the community.

Hewett, Sheila, with John and Elizabeth Newson, *The Family of the Handicapped Child* (Chicago: Aldine Publishing Company, 1970). Report of a study done in England with parents of cerebral-palsied children and their reactions to the professional personnel who served them.

Jacobs, Jerry, *The Search for Help: The Retarded Child in the Community* (New York: Brunner/Mazel, 1970). The problems faced by the family of a retarded child.

National Institute of Mental Health, *Halfway Houses Serving the Mentally Ill and Alcoholics* (Rockville Md.: NIMH, 1971). A survey of facilities, programs, and staffs, which shows that the largest group of professional staff in such facilities is social workers; it includes a useful, extensive bibliography.

New Dimensions in Training Rehabilitation Facility Personnel (Washington,

D.C.: Rehabilitation Services Administration, 1972). Discusses the relationship between universities and rehabilitation facilities for training human services workers.

Quigley, Stephen P., ed., *Vocational Rehabilitation of Deaf People* (Washington, D.C.: U.S. Department of Health, Education, and Welfare, 1972). A discussion of this neglected field, with special emphasis on vocational training and job placement.

Roberts, Alvin, *Psychosocial Rehabilitation of the Blind* (Springfield, Ill.: Charles C Thomas, Publisher, 1973). A compilation of techniques being developed by the helping professions as related to psychosocial development and functioning.

Weinberg, Martin S. and Williams, Colin J., *Male Homosexuals: Their Problems and Adaptations* (New York: Oxford University Press, 1974). An extensive sociological study of homosexuals in the United States, the Netherlands, and Denmark.

chapter **9**

community
organization
and planning

While there is general agreement as to what constitute social casework and social group work, the field of community organization enjoys no such clear definition, either from within the profession or from those outside it. Is it synonymous with social planning? Is it primarily interested in improving service delivery or in changing social systems? Is it a method unique to social work, or is it used by other professional groups? Is it a multidisciplinary approach to the community? Does it include nonprofessional citizen groups which work together to improve their communities?

According to Arnold Gurin, the practice of community organization by social workers involves at least three aspects, each of which presents interfaces with other fields within and outside the profession.[1] These aspects are: 1) community organization as one of the three methods of professional social work; 2) social welfare planning; 3) social action. Let us discuss the practice of community organization (CO) from these three aspects, acknowledging that boundaries are unclear and methodology is not yet clearly formulated.

COMMUNITY ORGANIZATION AS A
SOCIAL WORK METHOD

Attempting to differentiate clearly the method of community organization from the methods of social casework and social group work is difficult and is being increasingly abandoned in

1. Arnold Gurin, "Social Planning and Community Organization," *Encyclopedia of Social Work, 1971* (New York: NASW, 1971), pp. 1324–1337.

social work education. The Southern Regional Education Board's analysis of social work roles (see page 22) does not differentiate roles by whether the target system is an individual, a group, or a community. A social worker may serve as advocate, for example, to any elderly client who needs help in getting Food Stamps, or to a neighborhood which needs a neighborhood center, or to a disadvantaged group which needs legal aid. There are aspects of community organization in the enabling functions of casework and group work to individuals. People who are too troubled to make or are blocked from making use of the facilities available may be enabled, through modification of attitudes and reaction patterns, to utilize facilities more productively. We have already discussed, for example, how reluctant some parents of retarded children are to use special facilities. The stigma attached to mental illness may keep clients from rehabilitative services from which they would profit. School social work, by helping children derive greater benefit from the educational programs of the school is, ultimately, one type of community organization. The knowledgeable use of other agencies by caseworkers or group workers is further illustration. Documentation of the extent to which clients are deprived of access to service by rigid policies, discrimination, or maldistribution of facilities is indispensable to the knowledge base for social planning and is readily provided by group workers and caseworkers. Increased interest in "generic social work method" is indicated in the curricula of some graduate schools, and an increasing number of outpost workers are serving as all-purpose workers, utilizing all three methods.

An illustration of such all-purpose work comes from a small town, where there was only one professional social worker employed by the school district. She began by seeing individual children in treatment, moved from there to setting up several groups, one of children, one of parents, and one of both children and their parents. The groups engaged in handicrafts for a Christmas sale as an avenue for improving social relationships, learning more about child care and parent-child relationships, and expressing a concern and a wish to do something about drug abuse in the town. The social worker mobilized leaders of the groups to approach the school board with a request for a drug education and counseling program in the junior high school. In all these activities the worker was using social work methods flexibly and interchangeably. There is need for more generalists of this type in community-based programs to serve the multiple needs of the community or the neighborhood.[2]

ORIGINS OF COMMUNITY ORGANIZATION

The earliest social and health agencies came into being as a direct result of the urbanization brought on by the Industrial Revolution. The need for laborers to work in newly established factories led to the crowding into cities of young migrants from rural areas. Long hours, low wages, and poor transportation facilities were responsible for the increase in cheap rooming houses and tenements clustered around the industrial areas of the city.[3] The situation in our largest cities became particularly acute in the latter part of the nineteenth century, when hundreds of thousands of immigrants crowded into the low-rent districts.[4]

The first community organization efforts were those of the Charity Organization Societies (COS), originating in London and carried to the United States in 1877. As the name implies, the Societies aimed to organize the efforts of the many small, unrelated agencies which had been set up to deal, in a piecemeal way, with the worst problems of the cities. They maintained a central registration bureau to avoid duplication of services and sought services from private sources in the community. Since the founders distrusted governmental involvement in social services, they excluded the public welfare departments from their efforts, with the far-reaching results described earlier (see pages 6–8). Thus the community organization efforts coming

2. See Edward J. O'Donnell and Otto M. Reid, "The Multiservice Neighborhood Center," *Welfare in Review*, Vol. 10, No. 3 (May-June 1972), pp. 1–18, 52, which takes the position that workers in such centers must be generalists.

3. For the classic statement on urban ecology, see Robert E. Park, Ernest W. Burgess, and Roderick D. McKenzie, eds., *The City* (Chicago: University of Chicago Press, 1925). Critiques by many later urban sociologists do not affect the critical importance of these first theories of city growth. The "Chicago School" studies of spatial distribution of social problems, of the ghetto, of special institutions like the taxi dance hall, the artists' colony, and ethnic distribution in Chicago were significant contributions to the emerging field of urban sociology. For a recent statement, see Jack Tager and Park Dixon Goist, *The Urban Vision: Selected Interpretations of the Modern American City* (Homewood, Ill.: Dorsey Press, 1970).

4. For a vivid account of living conditions in New York City, see Jacob Riis, *How the Other Half Lives* (New York, 1890, reissued by Hill & Wang, 1966). See also James B. Lane, "Jacob A. Riis and Scientific Philanthropy During the Progressive Era," *Social Service Review*, Vol. 47, No. 1 (March 1973), pp. 32–48.

out of the COS movement were essentially aimed at organizing voluntary agencies. These efforts took the form, in the early twentieth century, of councils of social agencies and Community Chests as the principal source of funds.

The Settlement House Movement

The role of the settlement house in community organization must not be overlooked. Just as the COS interest in helping clients become independent led to the development of casework, the settlement house movement was the beginning of social group work. As with the COS, the influence of England is apparent. England's Toynbee Hall, founded in 1884, was the prototype of America's first settlement house, the Neighborhood Guild, established in 1886 in New York City. More widely known were the Hull House in Chicago, which dates from 1889, and the Henry Street Settlement, founded as a nursing center in 1893 by Lillian Wald. Jane Addams of Hull House, the crusading social worker whose interests not only embraced the welfare of immediate neighbors in distress but also included concern for social problems at the local, state, national, and international levels, lived from 1860 to 1935.[5] In her lifetime she saw profound changes in the society in which she lived and was instrumental in bringing about a host of reform measures to relieve and prevent human distress resulting from social change. The active participation in social action which characterized Miss Addams's life makes her unique in the history of social work. Hull House became a center for research and action in the interests of better labor conditions, improvements to slum housing, industrial hygiene, more humane courts and prisons, the adjustment of immigrants, and improved educational facilities. Born a Quaker, Miss Addams was repelled by brutality in any form, from the harsh treatment of juvenile offenders to international war. Although she died before the United Nations was established, she would have been heartily in favor of the political aspects of international cooperation, as well as the social aspects of U.N. relief and development programs.

The settlement house movement took its name from the fact that upper-class volunteers "settled" in the slums to become neighbors with the residents there and help show them a better

5. Both Miss Wald and Miss Addams were prolific writers. For representative works by each, see Lillian Wald, *The House on Henry Street* (New York: Holt, 1915); and Jane Addams, *Twenty Years at Hull House* (New York: Macmillan, 1910). See also Allen F. Davis, *The Life and Legend of Jane Addams* (New York: Oxford University Press, 1973).

life. Hull House, an elaborate Victorian mansion, was designed to be an inspiration to the tenement dwellers who came there for classes and meetings, to look at paintings, or to borrow books. Many of the prominent social reformers of the early twentieth century lived for a time at Hull House, and it had a remarkable influence far beyond Chicago.[6]

The settlement house movement was widely copied in the years following the establishment of Hull House. With immigrants crowding into the slum areas of large cities, the early emphasis in many settlement houses was on Americanization. Classes in civics, reading and writing, child care and homemaking were supplemented by recreational clubs, nurseries for children of working mothers, and provision of low-cost meals.

There were certain differences in outlook between the early COS workers and the residents of settlement houses. The latter were less distrustful of government intervention and bent their efforts to introduce legislation which would improve social conditions. Settlement house workers, like COS staffers, were largely upper-class volunteers but seemed to feel less social distance than the COS workers between themselves and their clients. In their efforts to ease the adjustment burdens of slum dwellers, settlement house workers were also less prone than early COS workers to see dependency as connoting a lack of moral fiber. Their clients were too obviously the victims of profound social changes. Rather than concern themselves with reforming the characters of their clients, settlement house workers concentrated their efforts on education and reforms in living and working conditions, believing that thus their clients would attain more normal and satisfying lives. Much informal counseling and "friendly visiting" was carried on, in addition to the group activities from which social group work, in part, derives. Just as concerned for the well-being of their clients as those in the COS, settlement house workers had a somewhat different approach to community organization—one remarkably like the neighborhood-based programs in the War on Poverty many decades later. Rather than organizing voluntary agencies for most effective service delivery, which in effect supports the status quo, they attempted to change the system, which makes them relevant to the third of Gurin's emphases, that of social action.

The community organization efforts of the settlement house

6. See the biographical sketch, "Jane Addams," *Encyclopedia of Social Work, 1971,* pp. 8–10.

pioneers—which included Grace and Edith Abbott, Alice Hamilton, Sophonisba Breckenridge, as well as June Addams—were concerned with reform in behalf of disadvantaged groups. They were deeply involved in doing things *for* people and derived their support not so much from potential recipients of the services they advocated as from other groups to whose humanitarian feelings they appealed. With all the dedication to democratic principles which was characteristic of these pioneers, early community organization efforts were basically undemocratic. The modern philosophy of community organization emphasizes self-help and "participatory democracy."

The reform movement of the "Great Humanitarian Awakening" came to an abrupt halt with the beginning of the first World War,[7] not to be resumed until the Depression forced the social legislation now referred to as the New Deal.

Community Chest and Community
Council Movements

During the 1920s, the coordination activities of the COS were dominant in the welfare field. The Community Chest movement, with the companion councils of social agencies, began just before World War I, when the advantages of unified fundraising drives led to joint financial efforts in Denver, Cleveland, and Cincinnati, among other cities. The success of War Chest drives for patriotic purposes in the War stimulated the rapid growth of Community Chests. At first local, Chests in the 1940s became United Funds, when they included affiliated chapters of national organizations in their appeals.

By stressing the community-wide services supported by these funds ("everybody gives, everybody benefits"), contributions are secured from virtually all levels of the community, not just from upper-income groups. The door-to-door campaign is much less significant in the totals raised than solicitation through employers. In some industrial cities, the refusal of large companies to permit more than one solicitation in a plant has compelled national organizations to join, although they resist budget review by local United Fund boards. There are some

7. For a discussion of the reform movement and its interruption between World War I and the New Deal, see Russell E. Smith and Dorothy Zietz, *American Social Welfare Institutions* (New York: John Wiley & Sons, 1970), especially Chapters 2 and 3. See also Herman Borenzweig, "Social Work and Psychoanalytic Theory: A Historical Analysis," *Social Work*, Vol. 16, No. 7 (January 1971), pp. 7–16.

national organizations which will not join, feeling they can raise more money by intensive national campaigns; the American Heart Association, the March of Dimes, and some smaller health agencies do not participate, which weakens the once-a-year slogan of the united appeal.

The United Way of America (as the national association of United Funds has been known since 1970), included in 1972 a total of 2,224 campaigns which raised $914,622,000 to support 37,000 health, welfare, and character-building agencies. Approximately 3 percent of the funds raised support Health and Welfare Councils.[8]

The first councils of social agencies grew up in connection with Community Chests, to participate in budget planning and allocation of funds. The coordination of agency activities came about secondarily, in an effort to justify budget allotments. These councils were usually composed of representatives from each of the agencies deriving support from the Chest. If the council was large enough, it might have a paid executive and a clerical staff. Activity would be concentrated in the months just preceding the annual campaign, when each agency would present its request for funds for review by a committee of the Chest. In order to become a Chest member, each agency had to agree not to conduct independent drives without specific Chest sanction.

These councils did not succeed in effective coordination of community resources. For one thing, the connection with the Chest tended to exclude public agencies which did not receive Chest allotments. No efforts at coordination can be effective which ignore the basic social and health services provided through governmental agencies.[9] And not all the voluntary agencies belonged to the council; for some, the allocation from the Chest was a relatively minor item in their income, so Chest policies were less crucial for them than for agencies deriving their total support from the Chest. In other communities, sectarian agencies objected to the policies of other agencies in the council on such touchy issues as contraception and abor-

8. Data supplied by United Way of America, 801 N. Fairfax St., Alexandria, Va., 22314, October 9, 1973.

9. See Edward J. O'Donnell, "Service Integration: The Public Welfare Agency and the Multiservice Neighborhood Center," *Welfare in Review*, Vol. 9, No.4 (July-August 1971), pp. 7–13, which reports a survey of 250 of the 3,385 such centers in the U.S. and stresses the needs for integration and for decentralization of public welfare agencies.

tion and withdrew their participation. Some agencies were reluctant to have final budget decisions made by an outside and perhaps unsympathetic group or were unwilling to abandon door-to-door solicitation.

As the Community Chest concept gave way to the United Fund, with fund raising for national as well as local services, councils moved from their preoccupation with fund raising and allocations toward the development of Welfare Planning Councils deriving support from sources other than United Funds and inaugurating research and development activities. Among the trends which may be seen in community councils are the following: the extension of council programs to a wider area; increasing efforts to coordinate the activities of voluntary agencies and governmental programs, especially in the model cities and community mental health programs; increasing attention to the "consumer" of social services and to his involvement in the planning of services;[10] development of new services to help families break out of the poverty cycle; extension of agency services more intensively to residents of blighted areas; development of new programs to reduce crime, drug abuse, alcoholism; assisting agencies to increase their incomes through fees and other non–United Fund sources.[11]

The impact of the cutback in funding for many social service programs directed in the 1974 budget cannot yet be assessed. It is obvious that voluntary agencies will be meeting increased demands for service as services in departments of public welfare are curtailed. In addition, many United Way agencies have been receiving public funds through subsidies, purchase of service, research, and demonstration grants, many

---

10. See Esther Stanton, *Clients Come Last: Volunteers and Welfare Organizations* (Beverly Hills, Ca.: Sage Publications, 1970), which points out that it is the satisfaction of donors and volunteers rather than clients which determines programs and survival in the voluntary agency.

11. See C. F. McNeil, "Financing Social Welfare: Voluntary Organizations," *Encyclopedia of Social Work, 1971*, pp. 443–450. See also the extensive publications list of the United Way of America (formerly the United Funds and Councils of America), 801 N. Fairfax, Alexandria, Va., 22314. See as well Frank Baker, Anthony Broskowski, and Ruth Brandwein, "System Dilemmas of a Community Health and Welfare Council," *Social Service Review*, Vol. 47, No. 1 (March 1973), pp. 63–80, which reports a three-year study of community funds and councils, noting that the bulk of contributions come from the suburbs and are expended in the city. See also Harold H. Weissman, *Community Councils and Community Control: The Workings of Democratic Mythology* (Pittsburgh: University of Pittsburgh Press, 1970), which includes a good historical account of the development of community councils and the author's skepticism about community control.

of which are jeopardized or discontinued. It will tax all the ingenuity of councils to meet campaign goals and to allocate funds without drastic curtailment of services.[12]

There are an estimated 400 councils in Canada and the United States; almost all cities of over 100,000 population have such an organization as do many smaller communities. The larger councils have paid staff, usually social workers, while many smaller ones make extensive use of volunteers. A typical council is made up of delegates from both public and voluntary agencies in the fields of health, welfare, and recreation. Schools and the clergy are also represented, as are civic and business organizations. A board of directors, with an executive committee, establishes policy and program. Activities of the council are usually organized into service aspects and planning aspects. Planning committees for each division (health, family and child welfare, recreation) should include agency representatives and lay volunteers. Service activities are more likely to be done by the professional staff and include some or all of the following: compilation and publication of a directory of social agencies; recruitment and operation of a volunteer bureau; research efforts for the council, member agencies, and the community as a whole; public relations contacts with press, radio, and television, as well as newsletters and campaign brochures; assessing community needs not currently met by any agency or program.

In former years, many councils sponsored Social Service Exchanges, where any agency contact with a family or an individual was posted on a central file card, to enable inquiring agencies to learn what agencies already knew an applicant. The Exchange dates back to the COS central registry and is of declining usefulness, with all relief-giving centralized in the public agency. From a high of 320 in 1946, the number in operation has steadily declined to well under 40; no community which has closed an Exchange has been moved to reopen it. Some communities are considering establishment of central registries for specialized groups of clients to assure that they are identified and that facilities are used to capacity; such examples are registries of abused children, special categories of illness, and camp registrations.

Special mention should be made of the separate Jewish fund drives, which differ from the usual United Way drives in their

12. See Dwight S. Adams, "Fund Executives and Social Change: A Study," *Social Work*, Vol. 17, No. 1 (January 1972), pp. 68–75.

attention to the needs of overseas Jews. In cities with a large Jewish population, the Jewish Fund appeal will be coordinated with the United Way drive, and allocations to specifically Jewish organizations will be made in consultation with the United Way committees. There may even be a Jewish Federation or Council, parallel to and coordinated with the council of social agencies.[13]

STATE, NATIONAL, AND INTERNATIONAL COORDINATING BODIES

Community organization at the state level is least well developed. While the various State Welfare Conferences could serve in this capacity, in practice few do so. In most states, the departments of health, mental health, corrections, and education have the power to review and approve the policies and activities of local and county agencies. However, little may be done to coordinate the efforts of these departments with each other. The inauguration of large "umbrella" agencies of human services in many states may make coordination easier in the future, although lumping together agencies which compete for legislative appropriations and struggle to maintain their vested interests may make effective coordination no easier.

Coordination on the national level has been, by and large, more effective than on the state level. The earlier national organizations were affiliations of local agencies, established to coordinate, set standards, and provide consultation services to local agencies. The Family Service Association of America, the Florence Crittenton Association of America, and the Child Welfare League of America are examples. In 1974 these three agencies considered a merger.

There are several hundred national voluntary agencies and more than sixty governmental bureaus, departments, and specialized administrations, all of which are active in some field of health or welfare. The National Association of Social Workers (NASW) published in July of 1973 a *Directory of Agencies*,[14] which includes the purpose and activities of, the number and nature of membership of, and the periodicals published by national and international voluntary agencies and foundations. In

13. See William J. Reid, "Sectarian Agencies," *Encyclopedia of Social Work, 1971*, pp. 1154–1163. The American Jewish Committee, 165 E. 56th St. New York, N. Y., 10023, maintains a social work consultant and issues bibliographies and materials relating to Jewish social work activities.

14. *Directory of Agencies*, available for $4.00 from the Publication Sales Office of NASW, 1425 H St. N.W., Washington, D.C., 20005.

addition to the long-established agencies, this *Directory* includes new agencies in such related fields as environmental protection, minority rights, consumer advocacy, drug education, and student organization.

A significant attempt at overall coordination was the establishment in 1945 of The National Social Welfare Assembly, which became in 1967 The National Assembly for Social Policy and Development, and in late 1973 The National Assembly of National Voluntary Health and Social Welfare Organizations. The mission of the reorganized Assembly is described as follows:

> . . . to enable intercommunication and interaction among national voluntary health and social welfare agencies in the interests of increasing the impact of the individual agencies and of voluntarism on human needs . . . The basic purpose of the interagency association is to increase the capacity of the individual organizations to perform their individual jobs, to help them pursue cooperative interests, and to pursue their mutual convictions, opportunities and responsibilities to strengthen voluntarism . . . Membership will be open to national voluntary health and social welfare organizations that meet the following criteria: 1) the organization is national and it is voluntary; 2) the organization involves broad lay citizen participation; 3) its basic support is provided by voluntary contributions; 4) it is non-profit; and 5) its orientation is to improve the delivery of human services.[15]

The various White House Conferences, which have been held every ten years since 1909 on Children and since 1960 on Aging, represent national attempts at community organization. They call attention to unmet needs, assess progress made in the decade since the last Conference, and provide compilations of data on a national scale. The United Nations, through a variety of Commissions, the Economic and Social Council (EcoSoC), the United Nations Childrens Fund (UNICEF), the World Health Organization (WHO), the U.N. Education, Scientific and Cultural Organization (UNESCO), and the Food and Agriculture Organization (FAO), attempts to coordinate welfare and related programs on an international level. In 1968 the first U.N. Conference of Ministers of Social Welfare met to examine the role of social welfare programs in the eighty-seven nations repre-

15. Final report of the Implementation Committee, approved by the Board of Directors of the National Assembly for Social Policy and Development, Inc., October 18, 1973, and reported in *Memo to Members*, p. 2.

sented, to determine priorities for action, and to make recommendations. The conference strongly supported the rights of citizens of all nations to look to their governments for social services and stressed the importance of preventive and developmental social welfare functions. The need for training of top-level personnel in the developing countries was stressed, as well as the value of exchange programs.[16] The great majority of those wishing advanced training have come to the United States, but this may be shifting as developing countries expand their own training facilities. In addition, there is mounting criticism of United States social work education as being incompletely adapted to the needs of some developing countries.[17]

The International Council on Social Welfare and the International Federation of Social Workers are leading international professional organizations, as are the League of Red Cross Societies, the International Union for Child Welfare, and the International Society for Rehabilitation of the Disabled.[18] In addition, there are various regional international bodies, such as the Social Committee of the Council of Europe and its counterpart in the Organization of American States.

THE METHOD OF COMMUNITY ORGANIZATION

Insofar as these various councils, from the local to the international levels, seek to organize services for more effective delivery, determine needs, and mobilize services to meet those needs, they illustrate the social work method of community organization. In spite of many prior years of experience in carrying out the organizing of communities, the topic was not

16. See *The Essential Task: Training Social Welfare Manpower* (New York: Council on Social Work Education [CSWE], 1969), a report of the U.N. Conference of Ministers Responsible for Social Welfare, published by CSWE for the Council for the International Association of Schools of Social Work and the International Council on Social Welfare. See also Stuart Rees, "International Cooperation in Community Work Training," *International Social Work*, Vol. 15, No. 1 (1972), pp. 29–33; and Dorothy Lally, *National Social Service Systems: A Comparative Study and Analysis of Selected Countries* (Washington, D.C.: Social and Rehabilitation Service, 1970).

17. See *New Themes in Social Work Education*, Proceedings of the Sixteenth Congress of the International Association of Schools of Social Work, The Hague, August 8–11, 1972. For some specific criticisms by the dean of the School of Social Administration in Zagreb, Yugoslavia, see Eugen Pusic, "Differentiation of Social Service During Rapid Social Change," *International Social Work*, Vol. 16, No. 1 (1973), pp. 4–12.

18. See Dorothy Lally, "International Social Welfare Services," *Encyclopedia of Social Work, 1971*, pp. 676–686.

considered in the National Conference of Social Work until 1910. Between that date and 1939, efforts were made to define and describe the process. The Lane Report of 1939 represented a landmark definition of the place of community organization in the profession of social work. Lane's description of the aim of community organization as promoting the adjustment between social welfare resources and social welfare needs[19] emphasized the provision of services rather than improving the relationships and capacities of the people within the community, an emphasis which many community organization specialists favored. The thirteen-volume "Curriculum Study" issued by the Council on Social Work Education in 1959, included as Volume 4, *The Community Organization Method in Social Work Education*, although it acknowledged the existence of different approaches to community organization by social workers.

Those who stressed the common elements in all methods of social work included Violet Sieder:

> The common core is found in a disciplined use of self in working with people; a common working philosophy; a continuous emphasis on working with (not for) clients; a problem-centered approach; the use of social diagnosis based on analysis of the articulation of the problem and the facts; formulation of a plan toward solution or action; evaluation; and involvement in varying degrees of each area of specialization with interpersonal, group, and intergroup processes.[20]

A similar position was taken by Genevieve W. Carter, who defined the core elements of the three social work methods as: "(a) social study and diagnosis, (b) the assessing of strengths in the situation, and (c) the utilization of resources, leading to (d) modification, and (e) change and subsequent evaluation."[21]

In 1962 the National Association of Social Workers published a working base of community organization practice which applied the generic base of all social work practice ("a constellation of value, purpose, sanction, knowledge and method") to

19. Robert P. Lane, "The Field of Community Organization," *National Conference of Social Work Proceedings* (New York: National Conference of Social Work, 1939), pp. 495–511.

20. Violet Sieder, "What Is Community Organization Practice in Social Work?" *Community Organization in Social Work* (New York: CSWE, 1956), p. 12.

21. Genevieve W. Carter, "Social Community Organization Methods and Processes," *Concepts and Methods of Social Work*, Walter A. Friedlander, ed. (Englewood Cliffs, N.J.: Prentice-Hall, © 1958), p. 222. By permission of Prentice-Hall, Inc. The concept is elaborated and includes an interesting case illustration, pp. 201–282.

community organization.[22] After more than a decade of study, the Council on Social Work Education in 1962 approved curricula in professional schools of social work which provided concentrations in community organization. In 1972, thirty-three graduate schools (of seventy-eight) offered concentrations in "Community Organization and Planning," and 1,922 students were enrolled in these concentrations. However, a number of schools have dropped the three-fold differentiation (casework, group work, and CO) and are offering courses in "Generic Social Work Method," combined concentrations, and "Macrointervention."[23] Thus the number interested in preparing for work in community organization is considerably larger than those officially registered in the concentration. There are no statistics available for measuring undergraduate interest in careers in community organization but ample indication that involvement in community activities appeals to many young people.

Unlike social casework and social group work, which have built up well-organized bodies of theory and related techniques, community organization is still in the process of identifying and codifying its wealth of accumulated experience.[24] Because so much of the work in the field was done in the past and is still being done by those outside the profession of social work (those from other professions, citizens' groups, governmental agencies, private industry, and volunteers), there is confusion over terminology and activities. The 1962 assertion that community organization was a specifically social work field of expertise has proved untenable. Developments in the 1960s have made it clear that adequate community organization and social planning involve multidisciplinary efforts. While social workers can be helpful in many aspects, more and more of what were once considered social problems are being politicized[25] and demand political action and reform rather than

22. *Defining Community Organization Practice* (New York: NASW, 1962). See also Jack Rothman, "An Analysis of Goals and Roles in Community Organization Practice," *Social Work*, Vol. 9, No. 2 (April 1964), pp. 24–31.

23. Margaret Purvine, ed., *Statistics on Graduate Social Work Education in the United States: 1972* (New York: CSWE, 1973), pp. 6, 7, 25.

24. See Pranab Chatterjee and Raymond A. Koleski, "The Concepts of Community and Community Organization: A Review," *Social Work*, Vol. 15, No. 3 (July 1970), pp. 82–92.

25. See Phyllis Barusch and Harriet Nathan, "The East Palo Alto Municipal Advisory Council: A Black Community's Experiment in Local Self-Government," *Public Affairs Report (Bulletin of the Institute of Governmental Studies)*, Vol. 13, No. 5 (October 1972), pp. 1–7, available as a Warner Modular Publication, Reprint 153.

treatment and amelioration. The student who is interested in entering the field should therefore acquire a good working knowledge of the political process, the sociology of groups, and the power structure, as well as research methods and public relations techniques. All this can be added to the basic understanding of human behavior and how people can be helped to change themselves and their circumstances, which comes from a knowledge of the interventive methods of social work.

For those wishing an idea of the kinds of activity carried on by social workers in the traditional welfare council model of practice, reference should be made to the volume of case illustrations of all phases of community organization work, published by the Council on Social Work Education to be a companion volume to the textbook and curriculum guides on the subject.[26] These volumes resulted from a three-year community organization curriculum study sponsored by the Council and by the Office of Juvenile Delinquency and Youth Development of the Social and Rehabilitation Service. Among the four volumes are covered the theoretical, educational, and practical aspects of community organization as a social work method.

SOCIAL WELFARE PLANNING

Like the coordination aspect of community organization, social planning has a long history in the Charity Organization and settlement house movements, as well as deriving significantly from city planning and theories of planned social change.

In the broadest sense, community organization represents an adaptation to two basic inventions in human history. The first is industrialization, whose impact led to the development of public and private welfare services in the areas of income maintenance, services to children and families, clinical services for

26. Joan Levin Ecklein and Armand A. Lauffer, *Community Organizers and Social Planners* (New York: CSWE and John Wiley & Sons, 1972), Chapter 9, "Welfare Councils—Planning or Coordinating?", pp. 234–271; Robert Perlman and Arnold Gurin, *Community Organization and Social Planning* (New York: CSWE and John Wiley & Sons, 1972); Arnold Gurin et al., *Community Organization Curriculum in Graduate Social Work Education: Report and Recommendations* (New York: CSWE, 1970); and Jack Rothman and Wyatt Jones, *A New Look at Field Instruction: Education for Application of Practice Skills in Community Organization and Social Planning* (New York: CSWE and Association Press, 1971). For a critical view of the practice model, see Ben Lappin, *Community Workers and the Social Work Tradition* (Toronto: University of Toronto Press, 1971).

the ill and the maladjusted and to the need for coordination among these services. The second basic invention is the concept of scientific planning. We are all familiar with the striking social effects of the first, but we think less often of the revolutionary changes in social life made possible by the purposeful direction of human activities to forestall anticipated difficulties or to deal with current ones effectively. Prehistoric or even medieval man would be amazed at a modern city and find its patterns of living totally foreign to him. He would find the philosophy of scientific inquiry and planning just as foreign to his way of thinking. The idea that it is possible to alter social conditions instead of accepting them fatalistically is a Western idea, utterly at variance with the passivity and acceptance so characteristic of peasant societies in other parts of the world[27] and in our own culture until the Age of Discovery. It lingers in the culture of poverty as a feeling of powerlessness and alienation.

COMMUNITY PLANNING

Scientific study of the community was stimulated by the results of in-migration to the cities, resulting in overcrowding and its accompanying strains.[28] Architects became interested in the field after the Chicago World Fair of 1893, which was built around the theme "The City Beautiful." In England the work of Ebenezer Howard and his Garden Cities (which featured ample green spaces, separation of industry from residential areas, and a maximum size above which the population was not allowed to grow) was also an inspiration. The early city planners were interested in esthetics, social relations, economic conditions, living conditions of workers, and provisions for a more healthy life for city residents. The concept of zoning (developed in Germany), which is based on regulating land use, was seen as an instrument by which city planners could regulate growth of

27. For an elaboration of this contrasting view of the world in southern Asia and particularly in Burma, see Robert Sinai, *Challenge of Modernization* (New York: W. W. Norton & Company, 1964). The definitive work on the subject is F. S. C. Northrop, *The Meeting of East and West* (New York: Macmillan, 1946).

28. The classic report of Charles Booth, *Labour and Life of the People in London* (London: Williams and Norgate, 1891), is sometimes considered the first scientific community study. The first American community study was Paul Kellogg, *The Pittsburgh Survey*, six volumes (New York: Russell Sage Foundation, 1909–1914). For a more recent statement, see Roland L. Warren, "Application of Social Science Knowledge to the Community Organization Field," *Education for Social Work*, Vol. 3, No. 1 (Spring 1967), pp. 60–72.

cities in an orderly way and forestall some of the urban problems in the heart of older cities.[29]

The efforts of early city planners and ecologists were based on some premises which were rendered untenable by rapid developments in transportation. The classic Chicago School position posited a steadily expanding central business district which engulfed the residential areas immediately around it. This "zone in transition" contained old mansions which were converted to multi-family occupancy in an effort to make them profitable for a temporary period, after which business would buy the property, demolish the buildings, and erect new business buildings. There was little incentive to keep buildings in repair, since the speculative value of the land was the important factor. The slums around the central business district were inhabited more or less temporarily by different immigrant groups, who moved out as their economic conditions improved (the ecological processes of "invasion" and "succession" in the Burgess analysis). Thus the oldest and worst of the deteriorated housing would be demolished as the central business district expanded and land use in the "zone in transition" shifted from residential to business and industry.

The automobile changed all that. Increasingly after World War II, business followed the population shift to the suburbs. The central business district, instead of expanding, began to contract, as downtown stores lost business to suburban shopping centers. As European immigration slowed to a trickle, the dilapidated housing in the slum was taken over by blacks, Puerto Ricans, and migrants from rural areas of chronic unemployment like Appalachia. Unlike the immigrants who found unskilled jobs available and could "work their way" up and out of the slums, these new urban residents found formidable barriers to upward mobility in a labor market with declining opportunity for the unskilled and prejudice against minorities. The "zone in transition" became the "zone of stagnation." Housing congestion increased, as middle-income families fled to the suburbs and migrants with large families were forced to crowd together to pay high rents. Calls on municipal services multiplied while tax revenues failed to keep pace, and increased tax rates accelerated the departure of property owners and business.

29. See Roy Lubove, *The Progressives and the Slums: Tenement House Reform in New York, 1890–1917* (Pittsburgh: University of Pittsburgh Press, 1962), especially Chapter 8, "Progressivism, Planning and Housing," pp. 217–256.

The problems of the inner city, rather than the development of the metropolitan area as a whole, became the focus of city planning in the 1960s. The War on Poverty allotted large sums to cities, directed primarily at improving the living conditions of deteriorated neighborhoods. Urban renewal (caustically called "Negro removal" by black activists) was replaced, in many cities, by massive efforts to involve the citizens of depressed neighborhoods in decision-making and to shift the power structure to give those previously powerless more control over policies affecting them. In spite of the rosy hopes of the experimenters and planners, the Community Action Programs of the 1960s did not create Utopias. In New Haven, Connecticut, a pioneer in the model city movement, after the expenditure of some $230,000,000 in federal and foundation funds, there were still major lacks in housing, employment opportunities, adequate schools, police-public relations, and effective participation of new citizens groups from underprivileged segments of the community.[30]

Planning for Future Communities

City planning in the 1970s is demonstrating a broadening of interest, forced by several converging forces. The inadequacy of schools in the inner city, as compared with those in wealthy suburbs, is causing pressure for legal means to plan for schools on a larger base than the political boundaries. Beginning as a method of achieving racial integration, such enlargement is moving toward decreasing inequality of school financing between school districts. Reliance on property taxes as the basic school support is being attacked. More equitable financing of schools can be expected, with the need for more widely based planning than now exists.

The transportation problems of urban areas, a badly neglected area of planning for any but automobile users, is receiving increased attention. The diversion of money from the sacrosanct Highway Fund in 1973 toward mass transit facilities in cities is an encouraging step, as is the inauguration of suits by citizens' groups to block the building of superhighways where these will destroy needed housing and recreational facilities. The energy crisis will force increased attention to mass transit. New anti-pollution laws, if enforced, will reduce some of the urban blight of our largest cities. New environmental laws may con-

30. See Fred Powledge, *Model City: One Town's Efforts to Rebuild Itself* (New York: Simon and Schuster, 1970).

trol some of the ravages of open-pit mining, destruction of resources, and the attendant rural blight.

The disappearance of open space, especially along the Northeast Corridor and the Pacific Southwest, is forcing states and communities to face the possibility of regulating land use in undeveloped areas to prevent future blight. Resisted by commercial developers and property owners, the pressure of citizens' groups is forcing state-wide and even regional planning for land use, sanitation, transportation, impact on schools, and location of industry to a degree that would have seemed impossible two decades ago.[31]

Thus, planning in the 1970s will be an important social sphere, offering enormous possibilities for social workers and other professionals to contribute to a multidiscipline effort to create living and working conditions which will humanize instead of dehumanize people. Future social planning aspects of community organization are therefore much broader than the traditional view of examining the needs of a community and determining the most effective mobilization and allocations of resources to meet the needs. It will be increasingly possible to shift attention from remedial to preventive action. Community planning will increasingly approximate "community development" as this term was used for many years to refer to the developing nations of the world.[32]

COMMUNITY DEVELOPMENT

Community development involves the facilitation, direction, and fostering of processes of social change in the direction of greater well-being for the individuals of a community, be it a neighborhood, a city, a rural region, a nation, or a group of people tied together as a community of interest. Since the most rapid and extensive social change is going on in those areas of the world just emerging into industrialism and nationalism, community development has been most visible in such programs as technical aid to underdeveloped countries, the Peace Corps, projects of the Friends Service Committee, and the like.

31. See "The New American Land Rush," *Time*, Vol. 102, No. 4 (October 1, 1973), pp. 80–99.

32. For a clear differentiation, with a review of relevant literature, see Charles E. Hendry, "Implications for Social Work Education in Community Planning, Community Development, and Community Organization," *Education for Social Work*, Proceedings of Ninth Annual Program Meeting, Council on Social Work Education (New York: CSWE, 1961), pp. 49–64. Critical comments on Mr. Hendry's paper subsequently appear on pp. 65–74.

Equally eligible for inclusion under the term, although operating on different philosophical and political principles, are the "five year plans" and "forward leaps" of such totalitarian countries as the U.S.S.R. and the Peoples' Republic of China.[33] In such endeavors, the role of government and technical agencies overshadows the programs more obviously social work in character.

In the United States, community development was widely used during the War on Poverty to foster self-help activities in low-income areas. It stresses collective action by the people involved to improve their lives. By working together for attainment of some specific objective, whether it is a safe water supply for a Mexican village or garbage collection for an inner-city slum, individuals will learn to understand and work together better, will overcome traditional reluctance to participate in joint efforts, and will be more ready for participatory democracy. To succeed, social planning must utilize methods found effective in community development.[34] In other words, along with planning techniques must go ways to increase the problem-solving capacities of the residents of the community so that they will be better prepared for dealing with the unpredicted, and possibly unpredictable, problems of the future.

SOCIAL PLANNING

Social Problems

Planning activities begin with the recognition of a problem. Not all undesirable conditions are defined as social problems, and not all segments of a society will agree on what constitutes a problem. Industry and environmentalists do not define the problem of pollution similarly. Some people may not want a certain social problem solved, since they profit from its continuation. Some people regard the existing problem as less bad than its alternatives; poverty as a national problem is preferred by many people to the overhauling of our economic structure, which would be necessary to eliminate poverty. Some problems are regarded as unsolvable through social efforts, and

33. See Malcolm J. Brown, "Community Development, the Non-Democratic State and the Concept of Open-Endedness," *International Social Work*, Vol. 15, No. 4 (1972), pp. 20–25. See also Ruth Sidel, "Social Services in China," *Social Work*, Vol. 17, No. 6 (November 1972), pp. 5–13.

34. See William W. Biddle and Loureide J. Biddle, *Encouraging Community Development: A Training Guide for Local Workers* (New York: Holt, Rinehart and Winston, 1968), especially Chapter 3, "What Is the Process?", pp. 33–44.

people resist social attempts to alter what they consider inevitable, an "act of God," or part of "human nature." We have encountered such attitudes in earlier discussions of mental illness, criminal behavior, alcoholism, and inadequate parenting.

Horton and Leslie have proposed a sociological definition of a social problem which is of usefulness to social planners. Their definition stresses the social judgments involved in determining what constitutes a social problem. To them, the condition in question must: 1) affect a significant number of people; 2) be considered undesirable; 3) be susceptible to change; and 4) require collective social action to be changed. If these four conditions are met, Horton and Leslie say, a social problem exists.[35] The relative power of special interest groups facilitates or hinders the definition of social problems, and the conflict between what is to be a public issue and how it is to be resolved generates action.[36]

Social planners must make policy decisions in setting goals. Are their efforts to be treatment-oriented or preventive? Should they focus on individuals or on altering the status of whole groups? To what extent should costs be a factor? Is it better to provide inadequate services for a very large population than to provide better services for some and none at all for the rest? The weighing of desirability against feasibility is a constant element in the planning process. All these factors must be evaluated in a series of decisions as to identifying conditions which need to be changed.

The next step is exploring the nature of the problem and alternative strategies for dealing with it. In the past, benevolent planners and reformers often assumed they knew best and made decisions on behalf of those most affected. Increasingly, it is considered essential that those to be most directly affected participate in the identification process and the proposal of strategies of intervention. Urban renewal is a classic example of social change introduced without consulting the residents of the area to be renewed. To their surprise, urban planners have found that many residents preferred the old neighborhood, inconvenient though it was, to high-rise mass-dwelling units with

35. Paul B. Horton and Gerald R. Leslie, *The Sociology of Social Problems*, fifth edition (Englewood Cliffs, N.J.: Prentice-Hall, 1974). This readable text analyzes the major social problems in the U.S., with a wealth of illustrative detail and proposed solutions.

36. See Robert Ross and Graham L. Staines, "The Politics of Analyzing Social Problems," *Social Problems*, Vol. 20, No. 1 (Summer 1972), pp. 18–40.

superior facilities but no individuality.[37] Instead of improving ghetto neighborhoods, as planners assumed they would, some low-income housing projects concentrated problems to a degree unbearable to tenants. The massive Pruitt-Igoe project in St. Louis finally had to be demolished in 1972 as a total failure.[38]

"The Dialectics of Social Planning"

Gilbert, Rosenkranz, and Specht present an interesting notion, that of the "dialectics of social planning," which involves competition among three important social values—participation, leadership, and expertise.[39] Pressures for securing widespread participation in the decision-making process, therefore, are in conflict with those which value skilled leadership and technical expertise. In their view, the 1950s was a period when expertise was dominant, and the master plans of urban renewal exemplified this. In the 1960s, participation became most highly valued,[40] as a result of citizen dissatisfaction with urban renewal schemes. The maximum feasible participation of the poor was mandated in the War on Poverty. Leaders and experts were unhappy about the time-consuming discussions, the postponement of decision-making, and the ineffectiveness of citizen-based community action agencies. Often with good intentions, professionals were able to utilize their experience in parliamentary maneuvering and grantsmanship to dominate the agencies.[41]

With the 1974 budget cuts has come a new shift in emphasis,

37. See Jane Jacobs, *The Death and Life of Great American Cities* (New York: Random House, 1961). For a contrast, see Leif Ahlberg et al., "The Aspudder Project," *International Social Work*, Vol. 15, No. 2 (1972), pp. 17–24, a report of a preventive planning project in a potential slum.

38. "The Tragedy of Pruitt-Igoe," *Time*, December 27, 1971, p. 38.

39. Neil Gilbert, Armin Rosenkranz, and Harry Specht, "Dialectics of Social Planning," *Social Work*, Vol. 18, No. 2 (March 1973), pp. 78–86. See also Martin Rein, *Social Policy: Issues of Choice and Change* (New York: Random House, 1970).

40. See Stanley J. Brody, "Maximum Participation of the Poor; Another Holy Grail?" *Social Work*, Vol. 15, No. 1 (January 1970), pp. 68–75; and Charles S. Levy, "Power Through Participation: The Royal Road to Social Change," *Social Work*, Vol. 15, No. 3 (July 1970), pp. 105–108.

41. See, for example, Edward R. Lowenstein, "Citizen Participation and the Administrative Agency in Urban Development: Some Problems and Proposals," *Social Service Review*, Vol. 45, No. 3 (September 1971), pp. 289–301. See also Eustace D. Theodore and Carol N. Theodore, "Citizen Awareness and Involvement in Poverty Action," *Social Problems*, Vol. 19, No. 4 (Spring 1972), pp. 484–496; and Neil Gilbert, *Clients or Constituents* (San Francisco: Jossey-Bass, 1970), an account of how citizen participation was bypassed in the Pittsburgh Community Action Agency.

back to leadership. The decision to cut federally sponsored programs in favor of revenue-sharing under the direction of state and local governments, to ignore professionals in the welfare and health fields in favor of budget and management executives, and to stress accountability—all point to a devaluing of participation and expertise. If history repeats itself and the cycle of competition continues, planners will be called upon by leaders to improve the effectiveness of projects. There will, therefore, be urgent necessity for planners to work with citizens' groups to avoid the dehumanizing of social change. Insofar as can be achieved, selection among alternative goals should therefore be through participatory democracy.

Since the adoption of a particular strategy to achieve the selected goal involves giving up or exchanging some present asset for some anticipated benefit, whether the asset is money, time, influence, or prestige, the strategies and programs adopted must be those which will minimize the impact on those least able to bear them. The planner's chief task is to match his resources against the resistance he can expect to encounter, which demands thorough knowledge of the community as well as skills in rational persuasion, inducement, control of information, and political influence.[42]

Monitoring and Feedback

During the change process, the social planner must be concerned with evaluating the consequences of earlier steps in planning, as they are carried into operation. Monitoring and feedback mechanisms must be built into the plan.[43] When planning is based on sound research, which includes accurate data collection, careful specification of objectives, and study of the impact on the target population of alternative strategies, the monitoring can be an ongoing process. The newer techniques of cost-benefit analysis, originally developed in the Department of Defense and subsequently applied to the social sector, have proved useful in evaluating programs of social planning. A difficulty arises from defining "benefits." The easiest definition to use—money—is not always applicable to the goals social planners hope to achieve. They often involve value judgments— inadequate parenting, unhappiness, or tension, for example—

42. See Robert Perlman, "Social Planning and Community Organization: Approaches," *Encyclopedia of Social Work, 1971*, pp. 1338–1345.
43. See Perlman and Gurin, "Monitoring and Feedback," *Community Organization and Social Planning*, pp. 226–233.

and are difficult to translate into cost figures or any other terms which will make cross-comparison possible. There is urgent need for accurate research to make more precise and measurable judgments possible, since all large-scale operations are increasingly dependent on computerization. The social workers involved in social planning will be working as data managers, evaluators, advocates, outreach workers, and consultants. For specific illustrations of social workers in these roles, reference should be made to the casebook, *Community Organizers and Social Planners*, already referred to. There are vignettes of a harried grantsman meeting a deadline, of a planning project that failed because vested interests were not adequately considered, of a successful project to stimulate greater understanding by legislators of the AFDC program, and an excellent and disarming explanation of PPBS (Program Planning and Budgeting Systems). Reading these will give the interested student a good idea of opportunities and tasks for him in the field of social planning, as well as a revealing picture of how obstructionist some social workers can be when projected planning impinges on their own vested interests.

SOCIAL ACTION

The more one studies social planning the more apparent it becomes that what is really needed to make communities more adapted to the needs of the residents is basic system change, which is the aim of social action, Gurin's third aspect of community organization. The therapeutic approach, which has been central to so much social work intervention, is basically conservative—patching up a system which perpetuates injustice and inequality. Early social workers realized the limit placed on their efforts by existing legislation and considered it part of their task to modify the social structure by sponsoring reform legislation. Increasingly in the 1960s, social workers rejected their professional neutrality and returned to being social activists. This often involved protest actions against existing agencies and programs.[44]

Social action, according to Perlman and Gurin, is directed toward changes in structural arrangements governing the dis-

44. For a discussion of the relationship between the conservative nature of traditional welfare programs and needed reform efforts, see John M. Romanyshyn, *Social Welfare: Charity to Justice* (New York: Random House and CSWE, 1971), Chapter 9, "Social Welfare as Social Development: The Quest for Community."

tribution of rights, privileges, and resources.[45] Where the other aspects of community organization are principally aimed at improving resources within the system, social action aims to change the system. Target of system change may be specific institutions, such as schools, social agencies, or the economic institution, or may be such social systems as communities or even a whole society. Efforts at bringing change about may be through normative processes (rational discussion, voting, use of the courts) or through norm-violating methods (civil disobedience, disruption, or violence). The use of violence by social workers is ruled out by the ethical principles embodied in the Social Work Code of Ethics. As Thursz puts it:

> The crux of the matter is that a professional worker cannot and must not condone violence. The destruction of human life as well as the destruction of the ordered democratic society cannot receive his support. Violent activities must be regarded as intolerable regardless of the race, creed, or status of the perpetrators or the justice of their objective.[46]

In his arsenal of social action strategies, Thursz includes the following: political activity, including petitions, individual letters, lobbying, and testimony; nonviolent protests, including picket lines, marches, and sit-ins; civil disobedience, with full acceptance of the price to be paid; disruption, to be used sparingly to call public attention to a cause and as prelude to negotiations; and the watchdog role over administrators, since they are not, like legislators, directly answerable to their constituents. Thursz feels that the political process is more susceptible than some social activists will admit to well-informed testimony adequately buttressed by facts. Social workers should learn more about lobbying and the ways in which individual legislators react to public pressure.[47] Social workers should ally themselves with other civic groups in coalitions to undertake the

45. Perlman and Gurin, *Community Organization and Social Planning*, p. 101.

46. Daniel Thursz, "The Arsenal of Social Action Strategies: Options for Social Workers," *Social Work*, Vol. 16, No. 1 (January 1971), p. 31. Reprinted with the permission of the National Association of Social Workers. The entire article is recommended for its clarity of analysis and rational recommendations. For an opposing view, see Anatole Shaffer, "Community Organization and the Oppressed," *Journal of Education for Social Work*, Vol. 8, No. 3 (Fall 1972), pp. 65–75.

47. See Maryann Mahaffey, "Lobbying and Social Work," *Social Work*, Vol. 17, No. 1 (January 1972), pp. 3–11.

educational efforts needed to inform public opinion of legislation considered essential for social welfare goals.

Such coalitions were formed during the War on Poverty, but social workers were not always comfortable in them nor in agreement with their methods. Where traditional social agencies were not flexible enough, splinter groups of more radical social actionists were formed but seldom were long-lived.[48] The impatience of black social workers with a white-dominated profession has led to the formation of a special Association of Black Social Workers, for example; this will be discussed in Chapter 10. The extent to which professional social workers are willing to ally themselves with those whose goals they share but whose methods they question is an unresolved issue in the 1970s.

POLITICAL ACTIVITY

The importance of political activity to achieve social action is obvious. Indeed, all social action may be seen as political at base. Politics is, in the last analysis, the process within any state which determines how resources will be allocated. Social action is aimed at altering these allocations in ways which seem more desirable. As such, they involve political realignments, as well as redistribution of rights and resources. Social action is by no means limited to social work but is carried on by any group which wants to alter the system. The right to change social policy is an inherent right in a democracy; in totalitarian states it may be severely limited.

Social action and reform have been part of social work from its beginnings. However, the ferment of the 1960s (seen by some writers as a revolt against the apathy of the 1950s) provided not only a focus for action—the War on Poverty—but some uneasy alliances with non–social work groups such as black militants, disenchanted and alienated young people, and revolutionary anarchists. According to Thursz,[49] social work learned from the 1960s that all professional social workers must accept action for social change as part of their professional commitment. This means that social action should be taught as a

48. See Herbert Krosney, *Beyond Welfare: Poverty in the Supercity* (New York: Holt, Rinehart and Winston, 1966), a fascinating account of HARYOU-ACT in New York, which is highly critical of established social agencies. See also Thomas Owen Carlton and Marshall Jung, "Adjustment or Change: Attitudes Among Social Workers," *Social Work*, Vol. 17, No. 6 (November 1972), pp. 64–71.

49. Daniel Thursz, "Social Action," *Encyclopedia of Social Work, 1971*, pp. 1189–1195.

specialization within the field in all programs of social work education.

SOCIAL POLICIES

To be effective, social action must be goal-oriented. Change merely for the sake of change is aimless and wasteful of effort. Goal-directed change involves the determination of a social policy which will meet the needs of the members of a society more fully than present policies or a lack of policy. In an illuminating article, originally presented at an International Symposium on Social Welfare, Charles Schottland, president of Brandeis University, suggests six basic goals for the good society: economic justice, economic balance, economic growth, equality of opportunity, access to community and social services, and participation in decision-making.[50] These are society-wide goals, and the means adopted to achieve them constitute a society's social policies. As David Gil develops the concept, social policies regulate the development, allocation, and distribution of roles and statuses and their concomitant rewards, constraints, and rights, thereby shaping the quality of life of the members of the society.[51] Social policy is shaped by the society's view of its right to intervene in the affairs of individuals for the general welfare. Social policy is thus intimately involved with economic planning, with programs of income maintenance, and with social services.[52]

When various New Deal measures were being challenged in the Supreme Court as unconstitutional, it was alleged that they derived constitutionality from the Preamble and Section 8 of Article I of the U.S. Constitution, which states that one aim of the Constitution is to "promote the general Welfare" and which empowers Congress to provide for the "general Welfare of the United States" and to make all laws necessary and proper for carrying its powers into execution. The Social Security Act of 1935, a New Deal measure, illustrates a massive shift in social policy and is considered entirely constitutional.

50. Charles I. Schottland, "Translating Social Needs into Action," *International Social Work*, Vol. 14, No. 4 (1971), pp. 3–15.

51. David G. Gil, "A Systematic Approach to Social Policy Analysis," *Social Service Review*, Vol. 44, No. 4 (December 1970), pp. 411–426.

52. See Howard E. Freeman and Clarence C. Sherwood, *Social Research and Social Policy* (Englewood Cliffs, N.J.: Prentice-Hall, 1970); and Charles S. Levy, "The Social Worker as Agent of Policy Change," *Social Casework*, Vol. 51, No. 2 (February 1970), pp. 102–108.

One difficulty of social planning in the United States is that there is no clear and comprehensive statement of national goals or of the social policies to attain them.[53] Instead, there is an accumulation of uncoordinated policies, often working against each other. In the fall of 1973, for example, the social policy represented by laws regulating air pollution was in conflict with policies of economic growth necessitating increased fuel and power generation. Alvin Schorr[54] finds three definitive traditions in America which have shaped social policy. These are individualism, minimum intervention by the state, and negotiation among diverse interest groups.

The formation of policy is a political process, increasingly centered in the legislative, executive, and judicial branches of the federal government but also in state and local governments. The decision of the federal Department of Health, Education, and Welfare to "separate" income maintenance and services (see pages 106–107), for example, is an important policy decision which was not submitted to either legislative or professional review. Whether or not to supplement the Federal Supplemental Security Income Program for aged, blind, and disabled recipients is a policy decision made at the state level. The allocation of revenue sharing funds to cities and towns is a policy decision made at the local level. Both the latter are dependent on the preceding federal policy decisions to federalize the AABD assistance program and to share federal revenues with states and localities.[55] These programs illustrate the piece-meal nature of policy planning in the United States. (See Chapter 2 for a more thorough discussion of these programs.)

SOCIAL INDICATORS

The term "social indicators" was coined in 1966 by the social psychologist Raymond Bauer[56] and refers to attempts to measure quantitatively the "social health" of a society, as

53. The Brookings Institution each year since 1970 has prepared an analysis of national priority-setting, primarily through the allocation of federal funds. See Charles L. Schultze, Edward R. Fried, Alice M. Rivlin, and Nancy H. Teeters, *Setting National Priorities: The 1974 Budget* (Washington, D.C.: The Brookings Institution, 1974). See also Daniel P. Moynihan, ed., *Toward a National Urban Policy* (New York: Basic Books, 1970).

54. Alvin L. Schorr, *Explorations in Social Policy* (New York: Basic Books, 1968), pp. 144–147.

55. See Melvin B. Mogulof, "Special Revenue Sharing and the Social Services," *Social Work*, Vol. 18, No. 5 (September 1973), pp. 9–15.

56. See Raymond E. Bauer, ed., *Social Indicators* (Cambridge: The Massachusetts Institute of Technology Press, 1966). See also Howard E. Freeman and Eleanor B.

economic indicators measure the economic health. Since what constitutes the "good life" involves value judgments, which are difficult to quantify, there is obvious need for new data gathering and processing techniques. Senator Mondale has introduced into Congress a bill to create a Council of Social Advisors to the President, paralleling the powerful Council of Economic Advisors. It would be charged with the responsibility of compiling social statistics in order to formulate policies which would "give every American the opportunity to live in decency and dignity." Attempts to develop social indicators which would measure the quality of life are being carried out by a number of universities and institutions. The concept of "social cost" would presumably aid policy-makers in their planning. The field of pollution, for example, is one in which the cost factor is critical. Would the achievement of clean air be worth the cost if it meant fewer cars, limitations on gasoline sales and use of electricity, fewer consumer goods, and unemployment? Or would it be worth it if the prices of cars, electricity, and fuel should quadruple?

In the field of social services, social costs and cost benefits are harder to assess. Schottland quotes the Finance Minister of one of the developing countries as saying:

> The economists in my country can make a good guess as to the effect of a steel mill if it is established. They can show the increase in the gross national product in monetary terms; they can estimate its effect in raising the level of living and promoting jobs. The educator can demonstrate what an additional year of schooling will mean in terms of additional and measurable skilled manpower. By what right, therefore, can I allocate our limited resources to day care services, counselling services, to strengthen the family, or group work services aimed at "character-building" among our youth?[57]

In the absence of scientifically verifiable, quantified data, social workers rely on limited data and impressions gained from their everyday experience with those who are not living the

---

Sheldon, "Social Indicators," *Encyclopedia of Social Work, 1971,*pp. 1273–1277. See as well R. D. Gastil, "Social Indicators and the Quality of Life," *Public Administration Review*, Vol. 30, No. 6 (June 1970), pp. 596–611; and H. A. Palley and M. L. Palley, "Social Policy Analysis: The Use of Social Indicators," *Welfare in Review*, Vol. 9, No. 2 (March-April 1971), pp. 8–13.

57. Schottland, "Translating Social Needs into Action," p. 9. See pp. 368, 372 for one attempt to justify probation as less expensive than incarceration.

good life. They should make these data available to policy makers as a contribution and possibly a corrective to the delineation of social indicators. An attempt by a reporter to compare the quality of life of a middle-class American family with a similar French family found that the French family was better off in terms of housing, food costs, health costs, and vacation time. Americans in the comparable income bracket have bigger cars and more gadgets but more anxiety, less leisure, and more frustration.[58] Attempting to assign a money value to such differences indicates the lack of precision which is an obstacle in this field. Garn and Flax of the Urban Institute in Washington, D.C. have compiled a series of fourteen "quality of life" indicators. To gauge mental health, they have selected the suicide rate.[59] Any social worker would question whether failure to commit suicide was the equivalent of a good life, just as the absence of a divorce does not automatically indicate a happy marriage.

Social indicators, if perfected, would provide an accurate measure of the extent to which a society's social policies were meeting its social needs. They would make rational planning and resource allocation less random and more systematic. In the absence of such well-defined social indicators, social action comes about as the result of political processes which may or may not be in the best interests of all members of the society. Occasionally there are outbursts of protests by or in behalf of certain segments of the society which call attention to the uneven distribution of power and benefits. The "Great Humanitarian Awakening" of the nineteenth century was a middle-class protest against the inhumanities of industrialization on workers. The Community Action Programs of the 1960s were a similar reaction to the "discovery" of poverty and the black power movements.

SOCIAL ACTION IN THE 1960s

Michael Harrington's *The Other America,* published in 1962, shocked a nation which had regarded the problem of poverty as all but solved. Early action by the Kennedy administration was followed in 1964 by the Economic Opportunity Act, which set up a number of programs with varying degrees of success.

58. See Scott Sullivan, "They Do Live Better," *Newsweek,* July 30, 1973, pp. 30, 31.

59. Robert Reinhold, "Trying to Get Desire on a Graph," *The New York Times,* September 2, 1973, sec. 4, p. 7.

The most controversial were the Community Action Programs (CAP), which attempted to redistribute power in order to meet the social needs of the poor more adequately. A pioneer effort in neighborhood organization was Mobilization for Youth (MFY) in New York City. Organized by voluntary agencies and supported at first by the Ford Foundation, it was financed by the President's Committee on Juvenile Delinquency before being taken over by the Office of Economic Opportunity (OEO).[60]

MFY was located in an area of depressed housing characterized by low incomes and high delinquency rates (it was originally planned as a project to reduce delinquency) and inhabited mostly by blacks and Puerto Ricans. The early effort of MFY was to mobilize the poor for political action, using the techniques of the late Saul Alinsky to organize citizen groups. Alinsky's emphasis on confrontation tactics and union-style bargaining ran counter to methods found acceptable to the social work establishment but were highly influential in many CAPs.[61]

MFY's first concern was with housing, particularly housing code enforcement and tenant education, but the results were discouraging, since the residents not only feared the landlords but felt that income maintenance was a more critical issue for the target population. Consumer education efforts were also unsuccessful in bringing about widespread change. It was in the area of legal services that MFY achieved its greatest success, although in some respects it proved also its undoing. Legal services designed to protect the rights of the area residents as consumers and tenants were increasingly used to force the welfare department to increase grants and treat applicants more equitably. The organizing of welfare recipients led ultimately to the formation of the National Welfare Rights Organization. The strategy of overloading the welfare system in order to force

60. For a comprehensive study of Mobilization for Youth, see Harold H. Weissman, ed., *The New Social Work*, four volumes (New York: Association Press, 1969). For a study which includes the decline of anti-poverty programs since 1970, see Peter Marris and Martin Rein, *Dilemmas of Social Reform: Poverty and Community Action in the United States*, second edition (Chicago: Aldine Publishing Company, 1973).

61. Alinsky's major book was *Reveille for Radicals* (Chicago: University of Chicago Press, 1946); his last work was *Rules for Radicals: A Practical Primer for Realistic Radicals* (New York: Random House, 1971). See also Marion K. Sanders, *The Professional Radical: Conversations with Saul Alinsky* (New York: Harper & Row, 1970). For a critique of Alinsky's position as it was applied to community action in the 1960s, see Robert Pruger and Harvey Specht, "Assessing Theoretical Models of Community Organization Practice: Alinsky as a Case in Point," *Social Service Review*, Vol. 43, No. 2 (June 1969), pp. 123–135.

a guaranteed income was advocated by Richard Cloward, at one time Director of Research at MFY, and Frances Fox Piven, his associate at the Columbia University School of Social Work.[62]

However effective this strategy may have been in providing more adequate welfare grants in New York City and the other parts of the country where OEO-sponsored Legal Aid lawyers went to court against welfare departments on behalf of clients and applicants, it contributed to the mounting hostility to welfare recipients which became instrumental in repressive actions in the 1970s. The propriety of using government funds to attack a branch of government was widely debated, and Legal Aid in many states was constrained, openly or subtly, from proceeding with vigor to support the rights of recipients. The efforts of vested interests and bureaucracies to protect themselves against change made it necessary for many CAPs to revert to more traditional social service patterns.[63]

The literature contains many references to CAPs, to techniques for organizing neighborhoods and citizens groups, to training and using indigenous personnel, and to the role strains this produced in both professionals and nonprofessionals.[64]

A study by Kenneth Clark and Jeannette Hopkins,[65] borne out by many other writers, shows that CAPs were relatively unsuccessful in redistributing power to the target population.

---

62. See Richard A. Cloward and Frances Fox Piven, "A Strategy to End Poverty," *The Nation*, Vol. 202, No. 17 (May 2, 1966), pp. 123–137.

63. See Matthew Dumont, "Variations of Bureaucratic Defensiveness," *Psychotherapy and Social Science Review*, Vol. 7, No. 2 (December 22, 1972), pp. 22–24. See also Dr. Dumont's *The Absurd Healer: Perspectives of a Community Psychiatrist* (New York: Science House, 1968), for a psychiatrist's contribution to social planning.

64. See, among many other possibilities, the following: Si Kahn, *How People Get Power: Organizing Oppressed Communities for Action* (New York: McGraw-Hill Book Company, 1970); Douglas Glasgow, "Black Power Through Community Control," *Social Work*, Vol. 17, No. 3 (May 1972), pp. 59–64; Dale R. Marshall, *The Politics of Participation in Poverty* (Berkeley: University of California Press, 1971); Janice R. Neleigh, Frederick L. Newman, C. Elizabeth Madore, and William F. Sears, *Training Nonprofessional Community Project Leaders* (New York: Behavioral Publications, 1971); Richard E. Edgar, *Urban Power and Social Welfare: Corporate Influence in an American City* (Beverley Hills, Ca.: Sage Publications, 1971); Richard J. Krickus, "Organizing Neighborhoods," *Dissent*, Vol. 19, No. 1 (Winter 1972), pp. 107–117; and Louis Zurcher, *Poverty Warriors: The Human Experience of Planned Social Intervention* (Austin: University of Texas Press, 1970).

65. Kenneth B. Clark and Jeannette Hopkins, *A Relevant War Against Poverty* (New York: Harper & Row, 1969). See also David M. Austin, "Poverty and Organizations of the Poor," *Encyclopedia of Social Work*, 1971, pp. 906–915.

Just because a group is powerless does not mean that it seeks power or that it knows how to use it. This is one of the defects in the Alinsky strategy; Alinsky concentrated on securing power for the poor, assuming that this would enable them to make wise decisions. Schottland notes that there are realistic limits to direct citizen participation in many decisions.[66]

When decisions must be made in haste or when they demand a high degree of expertise, widespread participation may be counterproductive. But social learning is best achieved in situations where the participants feel they have some voice in the conditions under which they live and work. The student movements of the 1960s made that clear for one minority group. How to enable recipients of service to have some measure of control over the quality and conditions of the service is a question which affects every citizen, not just those who were the targets of change in CAPs. The pressure for consumers on health organizing bodies, the concern of citizens over invasion of civil rights by overzealous government officials, and fears of the data banks generated by computers demand citizen participation. If the dialectic analysis made by Gilbert, Rosenkranz, and Specht (see page 480) is correct, participation having been in the ascendancy in the 1960s will be in eclipse in the 1970s. Social action may, in this decade, be achieved by coalitions of power groups such as the National Coalition of Human Needs and Budget Priorities, including the Council on Social Work Education, the National Association of Social Workers, the American Psychiatric Association, the American Nursing Association, and the National Association for Mental Health which brought suit in late 1973 to force the release of impounded funds for the National Institute of Mental Health.

SOCIAL WORKERS AND SOCIAL ACTION

Daniel Thursz raises five significant issues of extreme relevance to social workers in today's political climate:

1. To what degree can social strategies rely on the effectiveness of traditional methods for influencing legislators?
2. To what extent can significant change take place within the present system of government?
3. Can goals be realized by consensus-seeking, or should conflict be increased?
4. Should social action strategy be designed to obtain

---

66. Schottland, "Translating Social Needs into Action," pp. 11, 12.

specific legislative goals in a building-block approach, or should comprehensive change be sought?

5. Should social workers attempt to change the agencies that employ them through public social action and partnerships with clients, or should they limit their efforts to activities within the agency?[67]

Thursz analyzes each one of these issues in detail, stressing the need for accurate information and new skills to make social work expertise more available and acceptable to policymakers. Those who advocate civil disobedience, he points out, cannot expect immunity from legal consequences just because their motives were pure. The Code of Ethics does not permit the professional social worker to use violence or to abrogate the democratic process.

Where social workers have been subjected to reprisals because they have acted as client advocates, they should be supported by the professional association, the National Association of Social Workers. The dilemma of the social worker caught between the demands of the agency which employs him and upon which he may be dependent for his job and his obligations is a difficult one. It may occasionally be necessary to use the mass media to dramatize real injustice, but more constructive change may be secured by attempting to work within the agency structure. Dilemmas such as these are part of the social worker's life. His anger, resentment, or frustration at "the system" must not be expressed in ways which will bring damage to the client.

Another kind of dilemma is whether to support a social change which is grossly inadequate but may represent a first step in a desired direction. Social workers were put in this position when the Family Assistance Plan (FAP) was first announced.[68] While the payment levels were woefully inadequate, FAP did represent a new approach to welfare and was seen by many social workers as a move toward a guaranteed family income. They were reluctant to support so inadequate a proposal but eager to encourage the development of alternatives to the present public assistance program. The conflicting opinions

67. Thursz, "Social Action," p. 1191. Reprinted with the permission of the National Association of Social Workers.

68. See Daniel P. Moynihan, *The Politics of a Guaranteed Income* (New York: Random House, 1973), an account of the rise and fall of the "Nixon Welfare Program."

about FAP are reflected in the editorial comments and lead article in the January 1970 issue of *Social Work*.[69]

The efforts of the profession to raise payment levels for public welfare clients, to minimize the impact of the separation of income maintenance and services on clients, to eliminate racism not just from the society but from the profession (see Chapter 10), to extend services to those groups of potential clients not now being served, and to press for more enlightened and just social policies will engage the efforts of the whole profession. These efforts should be directed by those social workers with skill in community organization and social action. There is urgent need for better public relations in a society that still equates social work with advice-giving or "pushing people around." There is urgent need to document to a cost-conscious public the greater costs of failing to provide adequate service. There is continuing need for flexibility in approach to meet the needs of new kinds of clients rather than following stereotyped notions of "appropriate" staff behavior and "typical" clients.

COMMUNITY ORGANIZATION THEORY

In addition to extending its services into new areas and improving its effectiveness, the field of community organization continues to devote a large part of its attention to attempts to develop an adequate theoretical frame of reference for practice. It is engaged in synthesizing a body of theory derived from sociology, psychology, social anthropology, organization and systems theory, and empiric data derived from its practical experience. Social casework and social group work have gone through the same process, although it was undertaken earlier.

The more verbal of the community organizers are often those most interested in theory formation; hence much of the current literature seems highly abstract and preoccupied with semantic distinctions.[70] A refreshing contrast is Helen Harris Perlman, who comments on the shift from

> . . . co-ordination of existing services to the development of new kinds of structures and functions . . . from consulta-

69. See "Not a Blueprint," pp. 2, 143–144; "Guaranteed Protestant Ethic," pp. 3–4; and Edith G. Levi, "Mr. Nixon's 'Speenhamland'," all in *Social Work*, Vol. 15, No. 1 (January 1970), pp. 7–11. See also "Exit Welfare Reform," an editorial in the *New York Times*, October 5, 1972.

70. Perlman and Gurin, *Community Organization and Social Planning*, devote Chapter 3 to analyzing various authorities' conceptualizations of practice.

tion and standard-setting functions to social planning and action functions . . . Thus the social work method called community organization, which has in the past largely suggested a replenishment and tidying-up within a bounded area of given circumstances and conditions, has stretched and opened to include concepts of community development and planning and action, all with progressive, participant connotations.[71]

Community organization as a field of practice will attract those who enjoy the challenge and stimulus of working with groups of community-minded citizens and with legislative bodies in the area of planned social change. As a field, contemporary community organization demands the integration of background knowledge from the social sciences with social work's skill in understanding and influencing behavior. It also offers excellent opportunities for those who have skill in research and in deriving concepts and building theory as well.[72]

RESEARCH

The critical importance of research has been referred to in every chapter of this book, and much of the content of this volume is derived from research efforts of social workers. The great bulk of social work knowledge was derived empirically and needs to be tested and verified by the usual rigorous techniques of social research. The use of increasingly precise measurement instruments has been paralleled by the use of new tools. Video tape, computerized data retrieval systems, sophisticated research designs, and simulation techniques make possible a degree of scientific precision unimagined in 1949 when the Social Work Research Group was organized. The 1960 NASW statement on the qualifications of the beginning social work research practitioners[73] would seem naive today. In his article on "Research in Social Work," Richard Stuart, after a

71. Helen Harris Perlman, "Social Work Method: A Review of the Past Decade," *Social Work*, Vol. 10, No. 4 (October 1965), pp. 166–178. The quotation is from pp. 172–173 and is used with the permission of the National Association of Social Workers.

72. See William C. Brennan, "The Practitioner as Theoretician," *Journal of Education for Social Work*, Vol. 9, No. 2 (Spring 1973), pp. 5–12.

73. See "Social Work Research Section," NASW *NEWS*, Vol. 5, No. 4 (August 1960), pp. 20, 21.

systematic review of the research process and major social work studies, concludes:

> While it is true that evaluative studies of group work serv-
> ices have lagged behind casework research, vast strides
> have been made in both areas. First, researchers have posed
> and answered questions of great practical importance to
> practitioners. Second, the field is now ready to accept
> rigorously designed experiments. Third, evaluative re-
> searchers have produced reliable and valid means of rating
> outcome and of focusing on the interventive procedures,
> using a combination of control group, comparison groups,
> and single-subjects design.[74]

Stuart also points out that as yet none of social work's important research efforts has been replicated. Replicated findings
form the basis for scientific knowledge. As more and more
social workers have undergraduate and graduate courses in research, it can be expected that the caliber of research efforts
will improve. In 1973 nine graduate schools of social work
offered a concentration in research, and fifty-one students were
enrolled in the concentration. However, of the more than 2,900
enrolled in combined concentrations, administration, and social policy, there are undoubtedly a number whose primary
interest is research.[75] In addition, the typical master's degree
program includes the preparation of a thesis or participation
in a group research project. This emphasizes the importance to
good practice of alertness to research possibilities and a critical
attitude toward published research. The publication of some of
these theses, as well as doctoral dissertations, has added to the
knowledge base of social work. Teaching research methods and
the critical examination of student efforts are major responsibilities of schools of social work.[76] The Council on Social Work

74. Richard B. Stuart, "Research in Social Work: Casework and Group Work," *Encyclopedia of Social Work, 1971,* pp. 1106–1122. The quotation is from p. 1120 and is used with permission of the National Association of Social Workers. See also the preceding article by Norman Polansky, "Research in Social Work," pp. 1098–1106. For a major research effort, see Henry S. Maas, ed., *Research in the Social Services: A Five-Year Review* (New York: NASW, 1971).

75. Lilian Ripple, ed., *Statistics on Graduate Social Work Education in the United States: 1973* (New York: CSWE, 1974), p. 20. See also Melvin N. Brenner, "The Research Field Placement in Social Work," *Social Work Education Reporter,* Vol. 21, No. 2 (April-May 1973), pp. 32–35.

76. A discouraging report comes from a small-scale study in Florida, which showed that both professionals and student social workers are unable to recognize six commonly used statistical symbols. See Patricia Weed and Shayne R.

Education publishes teaching materials and sample research assignments.[77]

Competence in basic research methods is also required for baccalaureate-level graduates of programs accredited by the Council.[78] The Southern Regional Education Board, whose *Core of Competence* has been repeatedly cited in this volume, sponsored a year's workshop on teaching social work at the undergraduate level. The project resulted in the publication of three volumes, describing introductory and methods courses as developed in a number of southern colleges and universities.[79] Examination of the study indicates the commitment to sound research practice in the baccalaureate curriculum. The same commitment is apparent if one examines the report of a Curriculum Building Project conducted at Syracuse University, when the BSW was officially recognized as the beginning professional level.[80]

The improvement of service to clients, the ultimate goal and purpose of social work research, depends on sharpening skills and building an adequate knowledge base for practice. With practitioners increasingly sophisticated about research theory and technique, more rigorous standards for experimental design, data collection, and analysis are possible. As findings become integrated with those from other fields, particularly psychology, public health, and social anthropology, it will be

---

Greenwald, "The Mystics of Statistics," *Social Work,* Vol. 18, No. 2 (March 1973), pp. 113–115.

77. See *Selected Papers in Methods of Teaching Research in the Social Work Curriculum* (1959) and *Aids for Research Teachers* (1969), both (New York: CSWE); the landmark thirteen-volume *Curriculum Study,* published by the Council in 1959, was itself a major research effort. See Volume I, Werner W. Boehm, *Objectives for the Social Work Curriculum of the Future,* for a discussion of the general aims of the study. See also the *Curriculum Policy Statement* for graduate schools of social work accredited by the Council.

78. In its *Standards for the Accreditation of Baccalaureate Degree Programs in Social Work* (June 12, 1973), the Council states, "Preparation for effective social work requires development in the student of an appreciation for social research and an understanding of its impact on and application to practice," (p. 4).

79. Lester I. Levin, ed., *Teaching Social Welfare* (Atlanta: Southern Regional Education Board, 1971). The three volumes are entitled: *Course Content and Teaching Methodology; Field Instruction;* and *Issues and Trends in Curriculum Development.*

80. See Lester J. Glick, ed., *Undergraduate Social Work Education for Practice* (Washington, D.C.: Government Printing Office, 1972), especially the Glossary of Terms, pp. viii and ix, and Part Five, "Task Force on Social Welfare Content," pp. 155–285.

possible to evaluate interventive methods and improve effectiveness. Especially needed are soundly based research efforts to permit anticipating future problems with the aim of mobilizing preventive services. It is more difficult to pinpoint unmet needs than the novice might expect. With the present glorification of quantitative and computerized methods as ultrascientific, too many unsound research designs are being uncritically accepted in many fields. Adequate exposure to sound research methodology and some practice in carrying it out will make social workers more critical consumers of other peoples' research, as well as better potential contributors to the research efforts of the profession.

ADDITIONAL REFERENCES

Bernard, Jessie, *The Sociology of Community* (Glenview, Ill.: Scott, Foresman & Company, 1973). Classic models of the community and how they fail to account for the changing nature of life in modern communities.

Caiden, Naomi, *Planning and Building in Poor Countries* (New York: John Wiley & Sons, 1973). A review of budgetary policies in governments in eighty nations, which demonstrates that traditional methods of financial planning are unworkable in developing countries.

Fellman, Gordon and Brandt, Barbara, *The Deceived Majority: Politics and Protest in Middle America* (New York: E. P. Dutton, 1973). An account of the blue-collar home owners of Cambridge, Massachusetts, and how they organized to fight a proposed highway.

Gil, David G., *Unraveling Social Policy: Theory, Analysis, and Political Action Towards Social Equality* (Cambridge, Mass.: Schenkman Publishing Company, 1973). An analysis of the major components of social policy, with suggestions of more equitable ways to deal with current social problems.

Gilbert, Neil and Specht, Harry, *Dimensions of Social Welfare Policy* (Englewood Cliffs, N.J.: Prentice-Hall, 1974). A framework for social welfare policy analysis with specific illustrations from income maintenance, child welfare, model cities, health, and community action.

Greifer, Julian L., ed., *Community Action for Social Change: A Casebook of Current Projects* (New York: Praeger Publishers, 1974). Describes a variety of programs organized by the Institute for Community Affairs at Lincoln University and similar projects in other cities, including Mobilization for Youth in New York City and Project Crossroads in Washington, D.C.

Grosser, Charles and Goldberg, Gertrude S., eds., *Dilemmas of Social Work Leadership: Issues in Social Policy, Planning, and Organizing* (New York: Council on Social Work Education, 1974). Report of a faculty-student seminar at Columbia University School of Social Work, with comments from a sociologist and a welfare administrator.

Hampden-Turner, Charles, *From Poverty to Dignity: A Strategy for Poor Americans* (Garden City, N.Y.: Doubleday/Anchor Press, 1974). Community development corporations as a method of improving the psychosocial development of all members of our society.

Howard, John R., *The Cutting Edge: Social Movements and Social Change in America* (Philadelphia: J. B. Lippincott Company, 1974). The social movements developed by four minority groups: blacks, women, youth and homosexuals.

Kahn, Alfred J., *Social Policy Issues* (New York: Random House– Alfred A. Knopf, 1973). A clearly written analysis of the basic issues involved in policy decisions about social services.

McCartney, Kenneth H., "Social Services: Idealism, Power, and Money," *Smith College Studies in Social Work*, Vol. 44, No. 1 (November 1973), pp. 1–13. The Dean of the Smith School analyzes the political climate of the 1960s and the early 1970s.

Rainwater, Lee, ed., *Deviance and Liberty: A Survey of Modern Perspectives on Deviant Behavior* (Chicago: Aldine Publishing Company, 1974). A collection of articles on social problems and disabilities with illuminating editorial comment.

Shostak, Arthur B., *Modern Social Reforms: Solving Today's Problems* (New York: The Macmillan Company, 1974). A positive approach to solving problems, using day care and health care as viewed by four major "schools of reform."

Smith, Russell E. and Hester, John N., "Social Services in a Technological Society," *Journal of Education for Social Work*, Vol. 10, No. 1 (Winter 1974) pp. 81–89. The need for American social services to adapt to and benefit from the emergence of technology as a major social institution.

Social Indicators, 1973 (Washington, D.C.: Office of Management and Budget, March 1974). The first social indicators report, showing changes in housing, employment, life and death rates, public safety, education, and leisure time activities.

Weaver, Thomas, ed., *To See Ourselves: Anthropology and Modern Social Issues* (Glenview, Ill.: Scott Foresman & Company, 1973). How anthropology can contribute to the resolution of contemporary social problems, including a section on planned social change.

10

social work
issues

Many of the issues which confront social work in the 1970s have already been mentioned in the preceding chapters of this book. Such questions as national policy toward income maintenance, newer philosophies about prisons, children's rights to equality in education, the better distribution of health care, and the preservation of individual liberties in a mass society—all will influence the social work task of the present and the future. The issues we have selected for discussion do not represent a definitive list but are representative of the concerns of the profession which will involve those preparing for practice in this decade.

RACISM

No issue is more pervasive and troubling than that of racism. The belief that the white, superordinate segment of society is superior to ethnic and minority groups permeates the thinking, on conscious and unconscious levels, of American society. Accustomed to considering itself tolerant and free from prejudice, the social work profession has in recent years been the target of charges of racist attitudes by blacks and other minorities, both inside and outside the profession. Burgest calls attention to the extent to which even social work terms such as "culturally deprived" and "nonwhite" are loaded with negative connotations.[1]

1. See David R. Burgest, "Racism in Everyday Speech and Social Work Jargon," *Social Work*, Vol. 18, No. 4 (July 1973), pp. 20–25.

The extent to which minority group status systematically excludes some groups from full participation in the society has been extensively explored.[2] Every study documents the fact that nonwhite segments of the population have significantly less access to critical resources, including income, education, health, housing, justice, and political power. The extent to which access to these resources is denied to minority groups can be seen by comparing median figures for income, educational attainment, employment (both unemployment rates and occupational level), infant and maternal mortality, life expectancy, and other statistical indices. More difficult to measure but no less real are attitudes of apathy, bitterness, powerlessness, as well as lack of knowledge of resources. What Turner calls "social inertia"[3]—resulting from discriminatory treatment over many years and characterized by lowered self-esteem, a lessened conviction that one has any control over circumstances, a reluctance to risk coupled with an unreadiness to exploit what opportunities are available, and a tendency to withdraw rather than risk failure or rebuff—is learned by minority group children in their socialization. In recognition of the burden of social inertia, some activist groups have been calling for reparation and preferential treatment to help undo the damage that has been done by racism.

THE EFFECTS OF RACISM

Since money represents the single most important resource for acquiring the other indices of success and achievement, a comparison of median incomes of different groups is illuminating. According to the U.S. Bureau of the Census,[4] after a period in which blacks gained (relative to whites) in median income, relative black family income declined in 1972, dropping from 64 to 62 percent of the white median. Black male college graduates earn substantially less than white college dropouts. More black wives work, and their families are more dependent on their earnings than are white families. Some 300,000

---

2. See, for example, Leonard Reissman, *Inequality in American Society: Social Stratification* (Glenview, Ill.: Scott, Foresman & Company, 1973); and H. Schuman, "Sociological Racism" *Trans-action*, Vol. 7, No. 2 (November-December 1969), pp. 44–48.

3. John B. Turner, "Racial and Other Minority Groups, Services for," *Encyclopedia of Social Work, 1971* (New York: National Association of Social Workers [NASW], 1971), pp. 1068–1077.

4. *The Social and Economic Status of the Black Population in the United States, 1972* (Washington, D.C.: Bureau of the Census, July 1973.)

blacks previously above the poverty line fell below it in 1972, while 1,600,000 whites climbed above it. Black unemployment increased faster than white unemployment. Only about one black family in four reached the "intermediate standard of living" ($11,500 annual income for a family of four), and more than a third of all blacks fell below the $4,275 poverty line. The respective figures for whites were one half and 9 percent. In late August 1973, *The New York Times* published a series of articles examining conditions and attitudes in black America ten years after the March on Washington. The series contained discussions of the progress and growing disillusionment of blacks, based on extensive interviews in many parts of the country.[5]

Social workers are more aware than many citizens of the damage done to black children by the discrimination blacks suffer. Less well fed, housed, and educated and receiving less health care, black young people drop out of schools which are largely irrelevant to their experience, and they constitute the largest single group of unemployed (rate estimated at 25 percent). The Joint Commission on Mental Health of Children calls attention to the effects of racism on children and also to the need to teach all children how to recognize propagandistic coloration in the mass media.[6] The effect of bigotry and hatred is not limited to the victims; hatred is corrosive also to the hater. Its effect on the mental health of both blacks and whites is documented in a recent series of essays by leading psychiatrists, educators, sociologists, and other professionals.[7]

In a provocative article, Leon Chestang has characterized three conditions of the "black experience": social injustice, societal inconsistency, and personal impotence.[8] Growing up under these conditions creates in the individual some adaptive

5. *New York Times*, August 26, 1973, pp. 1, 44; August 27, 1973, pp. 1, 23; August 28, 1973, pp. 1, 26; August 29, 1973, pp. 1, 16; August 30, 1973, pp. 35, 54.

6. See these publications by the Joint Commission on Mental Health of Children: *Mental Health: Fron Infancy Through Adolescence* (New York: Harper & Row, 1973), pp. 426–428; and *Crisis in Child Mental Health: Challenge for the 1970s* (New York: Harper & Row, 1969), pp. 13, 44, 216–223, 244–249. See also Barbara E. Shannon, "The Impact of Racism on Personality Development," *Social Casework*, Vol. 54, No. 9 (November 1973), pp. 519–525.

7. See Charles V. Willie, Bernard M. Kraner, and Bertram S. Brown, eds., *Racism and Mental Health* (Pittsburgh: University of Pittsburgh Press, 1973).

8. Leon W. Chestang, *Character Development in a Hostile Environment*, Occasional Paper No. 3 (School of Social Service Administration, University of Chicago, November 1972). See also Judith D. R. Porter, *Black Child, White Child: The Development of Racist Attitudes* (Cambridge: Harvard University Press, 1971).

mechanisms which may be considered abnormal by the majority group. The life style becomes characterized by a duality in which self-deprecation is blended with the "transcendent character." The deprecated character exploits and manipulates the environment to his advantage; the transcendent character displays fortitude and self-control under provocation. Where integration of these two opposing characters is incomplete, one or the other predominates leading either to the stereotyped "typical nigger" or to a "white-nigger or oreo."

The usefulness of the adaptive mechanisms developed by many blacks in response to the hostility of their environment is also documented by Robert Coles.[9] His moving accounts of the resiliency and strength demonstrated by impoverished migrant workers and sharecroppers is a plea to all Americans to stop thinking in stereotypes and treat people of all backgrounds and social statuses as individuals. His plea was echoed by many critics of the Community Action Programs of the 1960s, who pointed out the extent to which staff projected "white" behavior as the ideal toward which blacks should strive.[10]

Black Protest

During the 1960s black dissatisfaction with conditions in urban ghettos led to explosive violence in a number of cities. The Watts riot in 1965[11] and the Detroit uprising in 1967[12] led to the creation of the National Advisory Committee on Civil Disorders,[13] which warned that the United States is moving "toward two societies, one black, one white—separate and un-

---

9. See Robert Coles, *Children of Crisis: A Study of Courage and Fear* (1967); *Migrants, Sharecroppers, Mountaineers* (1971); and *The South Goes North* (1971) (Boston: Atlantic–Little-Brown), which are Vols. 1, 2, and 3 of a series, *Children in Crisis*. See also Arthur E. Hippler, *Hunter's Point: A Black Ghetto in America* (New York: Basic Books, 1974), for an anthropological study of a San Francisco ghetto.

10. See, for example, Thomas J. Hopkins, "The Role of the Agency in Supporting Black Manhood," *Social Work*, Vol. 18, No. 1 (January 1973), pp. 53–58, which points out the negative stereotypes of the black male ghetto resident held by many social agencies. See also Nathan Caplan, "The New Ghetto Man: A Review of Recent Empirical Studies," *Journal of Social Issues*, Vol. 26, No. 1 (Winter 1970), pp. 59–73.

11. See Robert Conot, *Rivers of Blood, Years of Darkness* (New York: Bantam Books, 1967).

12. See Bayard Rustin, "A Way Out of the Exploding Ghetto," *The New York Times Magazine*, August 11, 1967.

13. See *The Report of the National Advisory Commission on Civil Disorders* (New York: Bantam Books, 1968). The quotation is from p. 1.

equal." Up to now, white society has been unwilling to accept that white racism is at the basis of black protest and is more willing to support "law and order" than to deal with the grievances which lead to violence. In urban budgets, police departments find it easier to get enlarged appropriations than welfare departments and housing authorities.

In a provocative study of black protest, Murray Gruber[14] analyzed the allegiance of more than 100 black youths to four types of protest—integrationist, nihilist, pluralist, and separatist—and found attitudes were correlated with belief in how best to attain social mobility upward. The idea of individual mobility is the traditional American ideal, and the individual is supposed to "make it" on his own merits. If his feeling of powerlessness was not too great, the black youth favored an integrationist strategy, if extremely powerless, violence or nihilism. Those favoring collective approaches to upward mobility favored the pluralist approach if they did not feel too powerless, and the separatist protest if they did. Gruber points up the usefulness of this typology in assessing the effectiveness of programs of social reform and welfare organization.

RACISM IN SOCIAL WORK

The reluctance of the profession of social work to acknowledge that its members held racist attitudes and that the whole social work establishment supported white values is demonstrated in the relative recency with which social work literature contained articles on the implications of racism in social work practice. Until the mid 1960s there were few references to race as a factor in practice. Since then, there has been an upsurge of interest, and hardly an issue of any professional journal fails to contain some reference to altering racist attitudes, adapting practice to minority group values, and changing the social service system to make it more just and less oppressive. The May 1970 issue of Social Casework, for example, was devoted to the black experience and written by black social workers. It contained articles on powerlessness among disadvantaged blacks, the growth of the Association of Black Social Workers, white racism, and the need for self-awareness by white social workers.

The implications of white racism as it extends to other minority groups has led to increased concern about American Indians, Chicanos, Asians, Puerto Ricans, and certain other ethnic

14. Murray Gruber, "Four Types of Black Protest: A Study," Social Work, Vol. 18, No. 1 (January 1973), pp. 42–51. Note the extensive bibliography.

groups in areas where they are concentrated. Thus, *Social Work* devoted its May 1970 issue to the topic "Ethnicity and Social Work"; and *Social Casework* entitled its May 1971 issue "La Causa Chicana" and its February 1974 issue "Contra Viento y Marea," both on social work with Puerto Ricans. The Council on Social Work Education (CSWE) has published bibliographies and reports from five special task forces.[15] Each contains a wealth of factual information, references to recent publications, and recommendations to the profession, including the necessity of recruiting minority group students for programs of social work education. The Council also reports each year the ethnic identification of graduate students in social work; beginning in 1972, schools were asked to identify ethnicity of faculty members as well. In 1973, whites accounted for roughly three quarters of all students, blacks for approximately 15 percent, Chicanos for approximately 2.3 percent, and other ethnic groups for less than 2 percent each. Faculty minority group representation is a trifle smaller.[16]

Both because blacks constitute the largest single minority group in the United States and because they have been involved in professional social work to a greater extent than other minorities, the literature on prejudice against blacks as it affects social work practice is more voluminous, and the challenge to social work more vehemently expressed.[17]

There is ample documentation of the pervasiveness of racist feelings in the most tolerant of social workers. Barbara Shannon[18] makes some practical suggestions for the white practitioner who is sincere in his disavowal of prejudice. She feels

15. See the following publications of the Council: *Asians in America* (1971); *Asian America Task Force Report* (1973); *Poverty, Participation, Protest, Power and Black Americans* (1970); *The Forgotten American—American Indians Remembered* (1972); *American Indian Task Force Report* (1973); *The Puerto Rican People* (1973); *Puerto Rican Task Force Report* (1973); *The Chicano Community* (1972); and *Chicano Task Force Report* (1973). See also Bok-Lim C. Kim, "Asian Americans: No Model Minority," *Social Work*, Vol. 18, No. 3 (May 1973), pp. 44–53.

16. Lilian Ripple, ed., *Statistics on Graduate Social Work Education in the United States: 1973* (New York: CSWE, 1974), pp. 12, 13, 36.

17. See, for example, Billy J. Tidwell, "The Black Community's Challenge to Social Work," *Journal of Education for Social Work*, Vol. 7, No. 3 (Fall 1971), pp. 59–65, which suggests that the profession has embraced an integrationist view of society and the black community a "coercion" or conflict view.

18. Barbara E. Shannon, "Implications of White Racism for Social Work Practice," *Social Casework*, Vol. 51, No. 5 (May 1970), pp. 270–276. See also George P. Banks, "The Effects of Race on One-to-One Helping Interviews," *Social Service Review*, Vol. 45, No. 2 (June 1971), pp. 137–146.

that it is dishonest for any white person who has grown up in a racist society to maintain that he remains unaffected, and she asserts that he must take a new look at his assumptions about black pathology, black goals, and the suitability of white value systems. She also feels that white social workers must bear some responsibility for attempting to alter the racist attitudes of white clients, whose anxiety levels may be heightened by racial tensions.

As social workers have had to confront their own repressed racist attitudes, several programs have been developed to attempt to modify them. An essential prerequisite to such attitude change is the willingness to face the extent to which his prejudices may be affecting the worker's view of the client and the interaction between worker and client, as well as assessing the part racism may be playing in the client's problem or his defense against problems. As Fibush and Turnquest put it: "Caseworkers have concentrated a great deal of attention on the black victims of racism. It seems high time that more attention be given its white carriers."[19]

One of the recurrent complaints of black social workers and clients is that so much of social work practice is irrelevant to the black experience. Billingsley and Giovannoni, for example, find that the present system of white planning for black children demonstrates racist attitudes and represents a residual rather than an institutional conception of services to all children.[20] They favor such institutional services as provision for full employment, a guaranteed minimum income, and a doctrine of reparations and preferential treatment for blacks.

The charge of irrelevance is echoed by almost all black social workers. Shirley Better,[21] for example, believes that black social workers cannot work within the system; they should reject the treatment approach and move to vigorous social planning with the objectives of gaining political and economic power. The object of practice should be the social structure, not the individualized client. Ms. Better advocates a separate professional

19. Esther Fibush and BeAlva Turnquest, "A Black and White Approach to the Problem of Racism," *Social Casework*, Vol. 51, No. 8 (October 1970), pp. 459–466. The quotation is from p. 460. See also Lou M. Beasley, "A Beginning Attempt to Eradicate Racist Attitudes," *Social Casework*, Vol. 53, No. 1 (January 1972), pp. 9–13. Both articles contain illustrations from actual experience.

20. Andrew Billingsley and Jeanne M. Giovannoni, *Children of the Storm: Black Children and American Child Welfare* (New York: Harcourt Brace Jovanovich, 1972).

21. Shirley Better, "The Black Social Worker in the Black Community," *Public Welfare*, Vol. 30, No. 4 (Fall 1972), pp. 2–7.

organization and a separate Black Chest for voluntary agency funding.

Another critic of the unresponsiveness of the white social work establishment to the black community is Clarence Funnyé.[22] He points out the extent to which urban development, model cities, and manpower training projects in the War on Poverty benefited white executives, consultants, and staff and how little benefit accrued to black professionals. In addition, according to Funnyé, social work education has based its theories and techniques on a European heritage which may not be relevant to the black community and has ignored any real input from black professionals.

The NABSW and the NASW

The National Association of Black Social Workers (NABSW) owes its origin to a group of black students at the Columbia University School of Social Work who organized in the fall of 1966. Dissatisfaction with the National Association of Social Workers had been expressed earlier in the 1960s and was made explicit in a social action workshop sponsored by the NASW in April 1968 in Washington, D.C., when the organization was attacked by both students and professionals. In May 1968, at the National Conference on Social Welfare in San Francisco, a group of several hundred black social workers protested the irrelevance of the Conference to the needs of the black community. The dissident group protested the lack of representation of blacks on the boards and committees of the NASW and urged reconstruction of the economic, political, and social systems of the nation to make them more relevant to the needs of blacks. They further identified white racism as the leading mental health problem of the nation.[23] The Conference was unresponsive to the protests of this group, which stimulated the formation of the national professional organization. The first annual conference of the National Association of Black Social Workers was held in Philadelphia in February 1969.[24]

At the 1969 National Conference of Social Welfare, the NABSW presented a list of demands for shared power and

22. Clarence Funnyé, "The Militant Black Social Worker and the Urban Hustle," *Social Work*, Vol. 15, No. 2 (April 1970), pp. 5–12.

23. See Pauline Lide, "The National Conference on Social Welfare and the Black Historical Perspective," *Social Service Review*, Vol. 47, No. 2 (June 1973), pp. 171–207.

24. See Charles L. Sanders, "Growth of the Association of Black Social Workers," *Social Casework*, Vol. 51, No. 5 (May 1970), pp. 277–284.

shared decision-making.[25] The NABSW ultimately walked out of the 1969 Conference and set up its own and has had an annual conference each year since. More than eighty chapters of the NABSW have since been formed. In addition to the annual conference *Proceedings*, the organization publishes a journal, *Black Caucus*.

Similar organizations have been formed by American Indian Social Workers, Puerto Rican Social Service Workers, Asian American Social Workers, and Jewish Center Workers. These groups are affiliated with the Council on Social Work Education. To what extent members of these groups may have withdrawn from NASW is not known. The NASW *Manpower Data Bank Study* released in January 1973 indicated that approximately 10 percent of NASW members belong to minority groups (7 percent black). This represents no real increase since 1968, in spite of greatly increased numbers of minority students in schools of social work.[26]

The 1969 NASW Delegate Assembly was also challenged by a militant group of black student social workers, who demanded that racism be the first order of business. Since 1969 the NASW has concentrated its efforts on racism and poverty as priorities for action. In September 1973, the NASW released a progress report listing its activities, publications, and altered emphases in its efforts to meet these program targets. As one indication of the extent of the organization's commitment to fight racism, the minority representation on national office staff has climbed from 15 percent in 1968 to 48 percent in April of 1973.[27] It is apparent that the commitment of NASW to fight racism is being maintained. It is equally apparent that many black social workers do not consider any whites able fully to understand black clients or to free themselves from racist attitudes.

The new militancy of minority groups currently in a disadvantaged position vis-à-vis white America should not lead us to overlook continuing societal bias against groups now considered fully assimilated. In his article, "Ethnic Affirmation, or Kiss Me, I'm Italian," Dean Joseph Vigilante, of the Adelphi University School of Social Work, discusses the increasing resentment of lower-class ethnic groups that so little attention is

25. See T. George Silcott, "Social Welfare Priorities—A Minority View," *Social Welfare Forum, 1970* (New York: Columbia University Press, 1970), pp. 137–146.

26. Data supplied by Grant Loavenbruck, Research-Planning Associate, National Association of Social Workers, February 26, 1974.

27. Chauncey A. Alexander, *NASW—Profession in Progress* (Washington, D.C.: NASW, September 15, 1973), p. 3.

paid to their problems.[28] Nor has anti-Semitism been overcome.[29] Much of what has been brought forcibly to the attention of social workers by the black protest is applicable to a
wide range of social work's clientele.

Social Work Education and Minorities

The growing insistence that only minority group professionals
can adequately serve minority group members is reflected in
the insistence on active recruitment of minority group students
for both graduate and baccalaureate social work education. Thus
Mizio argues that the profession is not taking advantage of the
potential contributions of Puerto Rican professionals.[30] If minority group students are to be recruited into an education program staffed entirely by whites, they are deprived of positive
models with whom to identify. In addition to benefiting from
the insights of the Puerto Rican professional, programs more
relevant to the Puerto Rican client can be developed, and much
of what now seems pathological to the white social worker un-
familiar with Puerto Rican culture will be seen to be adaptive
mechanisms in a hostile and unrewarding situation.[31] Similar
pleas for broadening the understanding of professionals educated in a "white establishment" social work educational system are being made by other minority groups.[32]

28. Joseph L. Vigilante, "Ethnic Affirmation, or Kiss Me, I'm Italian," Social
Work, Vol. 17, No. 3 (May 1972), pp. 10–20.

29. See Jack Rothman, ed., Promoting Justice in the Multigroup Society: A Casebook for Group Relations Practitioners (New York: Association Press and CSWE,
1971), "Political Bigotry and Discrimination: Crisis in Suburbia—A Case of
Political Anti-Semitism," pp. 74–81. The entire book is recommended for its cases
of activities in all aspects of intergroup relations, including intercultural, interracial, and interfaith activities, education, housing, and women's liberation.

30. Emelicia Mizio, "Puerto Rican Social Workers and Racism," Social Casework, Vol. 53, No. 5 (May 1972), pp. 267–272.

31. See Oscar Lewis, La Vida: A Puerto Rican Family in the Culture of Poverty—
San Juan and New York (New York: Random House, 1966). While to the casual
reader the lives of this family may represent pathology, closer scrutiny will un-
cover the underlying strengths of the family system, the adequacy of the coping
mechanisms, and the genuine concern for the welfare of the children. See also
Lloyd H. Rogler, Migrant in the City (New York: Basic Books, 1972), for the history of a group effort by Puerto Rican migrants.

32. See Pei-Ngor Chen, "The Chinese Community in Los Angeles," Social
Casework, Vol. 51, No. 10 (December 1970), pp. 591–598; Gordon N. Keller, "Bi-
cultural Social Work and Anthropology," Social Casework, Vol. 53, No. 8 (October 1972), pp. 455–465, an account of social work among a group of Utah Nava-
hos; and Faustina R. Kroll, "Casework Services for Mexican Americans," Social
Casework, Vol. 52, No. 5 (May 1971), pp. 279–284.

A specific area of dissatisfaction has been the admission and retention of minority group students in social work education. The relative number of minority group students in graduate social work education has already been indicated (see page 504). This is true of educational programs in all the professions, in social work somewhat less than some other professions like medicine or college teaching. Social work has long been recognized as an avenue for upward mobility. However, as long as professional preparation entailed two years of graduate school, it was unattainable by great numbers of minority students. Their inferior prior education and their relative lack of financial resources made admission to graduate schools on any competitive basis virtually impossible. The lack of supportive services to compensate for inferior preparation, the lack of minority group faculty with whom they could identify, and the irrelevance of much of their professional education to their own previous experience was discouraging even to those who gained admission. Thus, the recruitment efforts of the profession must be supplemented by attempts to improve secondary and college education. The emergence of the BSW as a professional degree and the increased sensitivity to racism in baccalaureate education are welcome steps to those wishing to see larger numbers of professionals from all minority groups. Many baccalaureate programs in predominantly black colleges are already accredited by the Council on Social Work Education, and the Council pays particular attention to the curriculum of every school whose program it examines for accreditation, to ensure that course content includes adequate exposure to the injustice of racism and to its insidious influence on the thinking of all students.

The pervasiveness of racist thinking even among social work faculty members, committed as most of them are to the cause of racial equality, is demonstrated by Longres.[33] He points out that not only are there small numbers of nonwhite faculty members in schools of social work, owing to previous patterns of poorer education and discrimination in the educational system, but that the reputation of social workers among nonwhites would hardly encourage them to consider social work as a career. Recruitment efforts are half-hearted (Longres points out how successfully departments of physical education have recruited nonwhites) and are based less on the conviction that minority group students have a contribution to make to the

33. John Longres, "The Impact of Racism on Social Work Education," *Journal of Education for Social Work*, Vol. 8, No. 1 (Winter 1972), pp. 31–41.

profession than on the reluctance to seem unresponsive to the demands of minority groups.

Until very recently, social work education has been centered on psychoanalytic and psychological viewpoints, at the expense of critical examination of the social structure. The social work curriculum has had sequences of courses in psychopathology, child psychology, dynamics of human behavior, and various methods of modifying human behavior but only a token course or two in social structure, economics, or social action. Many of the growth and behavior courses perpetuate myths about nonwhites, who are said to be nonverbal, poorly motivated for education, and unable to postpone gratification. Such beliefs are expressive of white middle-class values, not scientifically verified findings. In their efforts to compensate for possible discriminatory treatment of nonwhite students, faculty may be paternalistic and patronizing. In its struggle to achieve professional respectability, social work education has overemphasized those opportunities which lead to status and better incomes. These are not the jobs which will serve nonwhites and the poor. Working in such service agencies is subtly downgraded in favor of "treatment" opportunities.[34]

The influx of minority students into professional social work education has already had a revitalizing, if disturbing, effect on the social work establishment. Activist students have staged demonstrations, strikes, boycotts and have confronted administrations with "non-negotiable demands." They have also forced new relevance and timeliness into a profession which was in danger of becoming rigidly institutionalized and even smug.[35] Minority group students have challenged long-held stereotypes about race, poverty, pathology, and motivation and have forced new assessment of the coping mechanisms used by the disadvantaged. They have also forced a reordering of priorities for the profession, away from the ivory tower of the academic world and into social action, advocacy, and the development of new techniques.

34. See James W. Grimm and James D. Orten, "Student Attitudes Toward the Poor," *Social Work*, Vol. 18, No. 1 (January 1973), pp. 94–100, for an interesting parallel between attitudes toward the poor and racism. The authors conclude that the importance of environment in forming attitudes has not been adequately recognized.

35. See Arnold J. Auerbach, "Quotas in Schools of Social Work," *Social Work*, Vol. 17, No. 2 (March 1972), pp. 102–105.

Implications for Practice

As is true with all revolutions there have been some over-statements and exaggerated claims. To charge that *all* social work theory and practice are irrelevant to minority groups is patently not true. To insist that no social worker or researcher[36] can deal effectively with clients whose experience he has not shared negates work with unmarried mothers by married mothers, with blind clients by the sighted, with mentally ill patients by those who have never experienced a psychotic episode. Irving Franke reports his discouragement at claims by militant blacks that the white man's social sciences are to be dismissed as biased and inappropriate for the education of blacks. The white professor in a black university would be a nonparticipant—the equivalent to the Shabbath goy being victimized in the interests of black solidarity.[37]

Just as social workers learn to be acutely sensitive to the feelings and past experiences of other clients who have been scarred by what has happened to them, they need to learn from blacks what it is like to grow up in a racist society. The ways in which they will learn this are through dialogue and coalition, not through separatism and rejection. Students should enlarge their understanding by reading how sensitive and perceptive blacks have reacted.[38] Social work practitioners must

36. See Neilson F. Smith, "Who Should Do Minority Research?" *Social Casework*, Vol. 54, No. 7 (July 1973), pp. 393–397.

37. Irving F. Franke, "The Black University and the 'Shabbath Goy'," *Social Work*, Vol. 16, No. 1 (January 1971), pp. 101–102; the 'Shabbath goy' is a gentile who performs tasks in the synagogue and the home that Jews are forbidden to perform on the Sabbath.

38. The bibliography *Poverty, Participation, Protest, Power, and Black Americans* (New York: CSWE, 1970) contains useful references. Especially valuable for enlarging the understanding of white students are the following: Malcolm X, *Autobiography* (New York: Grove Press, 1965); William McCord, et al., *Life Styles in the Black Ghetto* (New York: Norton, 1969); Claude Brown, *Manchild in the Promised Land* (New York: Macmillan, 1965); William Grier and Price Cobbs, *Black Rage* (New York: Basic Books, 1968); Ethridge Knight, *Belly Song* (Detroit: Broadside Press, 1972); Angela Davis, *If They Come in the Morning: Voices of Resistance* (New York: New American Library, 1971); Bobby Seale, *Seize the Time: The Story of the Black Panther Party and Huey P. Newton* (New York: Random House, 1970); James Baldwin, *No Name in the Streets* (New York: Dial Press, 1972); Margaret Mead and James Baldwin, *A Rap on Race* (Philadelphia: J. B. Lippincott Company, 1971); Lee Rainwater, ed., *Black Experience: Soul,* second edition (New York: E. P. Dutton, 1973).

reassess their own techniques and attitudes instead of continuing to claim that bias does not affect the profession.

For many years social work acted as if race differences were nonexistent and insisted that it viewed its clients as individuals and treated them all as individuals. Not until the black protests of the 1960s was social work really able to acknowledge that white social workers were affected by having grown up in a racist society. In their anger and guilt at discovering that their thinking was tinged with racial overtones, social workers may have overreacted and become unrealistic. The paternalism implicit in accepting relaxed standards for black clients, in offering special privileges, or in unrealistic overidentification with the victims of oppression eluded social workers who could not see how they were attempting to compensate for the guilt they felt at being part of the dominant group in a society so shot through with racism. Although they prided themselves on the deftness with which they elicited feelings from clients about other aspects of their lives, they tended to ignore "listening with the third ear" when clients' remarks indicated that racist overtones were present in the worker-client relationship.[39] Many recent writers have commented on the infrequency with which racial feelings are discussed between worker and client. In a useful analysis of white guilt and its consequences in treatment, Shirley Cooper considers the consequences of white guilt on the worker and the distortions in personality of the client as the result of oppression.[40] She urges an awareness of the possibilities of overreaction, of overstressing differences, and of focusing so narrowly on ethnic factors as to lose sight of diagnostic insights which could be clear in white clients. Her illustrations include cases in which such universal phenomena as sibling rivalry in a black man and fear of homosexuality in a Chinese male student were overlooked by workers preoccupied with racial concerns. She concludes with a plea for valuing individuality and maintaining clinical objectivity rather than becoming obsessed with a "cripple psychology."

Other writers stress the need for more dialogue between black and white staff members. Pauline Lide[41] describes the uneasi-

---

39. For a discussion of this point, see Evelyn Stiles et al., "Hear It Like It Is," *Social Casework*, Vol. 53, No. 5 (May 1972), pp. 292–299.

40. Shirley Cooper, "A Look at the Effect of Racism on Clinical Work," *Social Casework*, Vol. 54, No. 2 (February 1973), pp. 76–84.

41. Pauline Lide, "Dialogue on Racism, A Prologue to Action?" *Social Casework*, Vol. 52, No. 7 (July 1971), pp. 432–436.

ness with which both black and white staff members approached discussing their feelings about race and resorted to intellectualization to avoid feeling. Great anxiety was created by open acknowledgement of feelings, and no immediately successful efforts resulted from a five-month seminar, but it was the group's hope that the anxiety would be a mobilizing force for more constructive action. The intensity of the feelings generated was some measure of the extent to which they had been repressed previously, and it illuminated some of the discouraging disparities between social work's ideals and accomplishments. Feelings so insidiously taught in the process of growing up in a white racist society will not be easily dispelled by intellectual knowledge or pious platitudes.

A similar position is taken by Alex Gitterman and Alice Schaeffer, who focus on the relationship between black client and white worker and point out that, realistically, most black clients will continue to be served by white professionals in the foreseeable future.[42] They describe three obstacles to the joint efforts of worker and client: institutional racism, social distance, and mutual unknownness. The greater social mobility available to whites has made it possible for the white social worker to achieve prestige, some power, and some security within the system. The black client is unlikely to have any of these advantages. "Thus separated by race, money, education, social position, power, and lack of real knowledge of and feeling for the other's life experience, the white professional and black client come together."[43]

Inevitably, there are fear and anger in both, and both may make efforts to conceal, rationalize, project, or deny the feelings. However, by the nature of the contract between them, in which the black client is seeking service and the white worker is charged with providing it, they should be viewed as engaged in a mutual process and not in the stereotyped superordinate-subordinate relationship. These authors conclude with a lengthy account of a continued contact between a black mother of seven children, dependent on public assistance, and a young white social worker concerned with her client's feelings and anxious to make the relationship a truly mutual one.

Petro and French discuss a staff development project in an agency where the client population was 90 percent black and

42. Alex Gitterman and Alice Schaeffer, "The White Professional and the Black Client," *Social Casework*, Vol. 53, No. 5 (May 1972), pp. 280–291.
43. *Ibid.*, p. 281.

the staff evenly divided between black and white.[44] The clientele included a large component of middle-class blacks as well as those living in poverty. Thus, their study indicated some of the effects of racism in clients who might have been thought of as "making it." Negative self-images, the necessity of caution and circumspection in all behavior, and the variety of coping mechanisms used by black clients from a wide socioeconomic range raised some provocative questions about the socialization patterns they were using with their children. It appeared that the negative stereotypes which clients had received from the white society were being transmitted to their children. Social work thus has a unique opportunity to intervene in the transmission of racist attitudes,[45] as well as in alerting social workers to become more aware of their own prejudices.

RACISM AND SOCIAL POLICY

It is obvious that the social workers of the 1970s will be confronted with increased demand for more equitable participation in decision-making by minority groups and for social policies which insure more equitable distribution of the rewards of society. The objectives of the professional organization are clearly stated. The 1969 Delegate Assembly of the NASW designated racism and poverty as major program targets. In preparation for entering any field of social welfare, students must become familiar with the problems of institutionalized racism in our society, as well as more alert to their own attitudes. As Romanyshyn puts it:

> The number of blacks who are forced to depend on welfare is symptomatic of and interrelated with the fact that Negroes bear an inequitable share of those conditions defined as social problems: unemployment and subemployment, marginal incomes, family disorganization, inadequate housing, education, and other public services, and most of all systematic exclusion from opportunities for self-respect through positively acknowledged and rewarded social participation. As a consequence they figure not only high on the caseloads of public assistance agencies but also repre-

44. Olive Petro and Betty French, "The Black Client's View of Himself," *Social Casework*, Vol. 53, No. 8 (October 1972), pp. 466–474.
45. See Phyllis Harrison-Ross and Barbara Wyden, *The Black Child: A Parents' Guide* (New York: Peter Wyden, 1973), a discussion of black child-rearing practices by a black child psychiatrist and a white editor.

sent a disproportionate number of clients of a vast array of residual welfare and correctional programs.[46]

All this means that white social workers will be dealing, in every social agency, with victims of an unjust society, whose ability to help themselves is impaired by victimization and negativism. The sharpest skills, the most sensitive awareness, and the utmost in commitment will be required to be of maximum service to clients. The active support of social action efforts to correct unjust social policies must be combined with these services to individuals.[47]

POVERTY

The other top priority of the NASW is the elimination of poverty. Poverty and minority group status are inextricably interwoven, and the two problems must be attacked together. In 1972, 25 percent of all black families were dependent on public assistance, as opposed to only 5 percent of all white families; for unrelated individuals, the percentages are 21 and 6. Even among families receiving public assistance, there is a differential, reflecting lower grants to black families; the median family income of black public assistance recipients is $3,353 as against $4,117 for whites. Female-headed families (usually AFDC recipients) constitute 54 percent of all black families and 21 percent of whites, and the median family income when the female head is black is $2,997 as opposed to $3,298 for a white female-headed family.[48]

The continuation of poverty in an age of affluence is impossible to justify. In previous centuries the poor in America were considered to be starting up the ladder of success. However difficult the present, the future was brighter. Hard work and education made it possible for the successive waves of immigrants from abroad and in-migrants from rural areas to rise out of poverty into middle-class status in two or three generations. The frontier, expanding industrialism, and a rising standard of living made the old poverty a transitory condition.

46. John Romanyshyn, *Social Welfare: Charity to Justice* (New York: © Random House, Inc., 1971), p. 129.
47. See Douglas Glasgow, "Black Power Through Community Control," *Social Work*, Vol. 17, No. 3 (May 1972), pp. 59–64, for a cogent statement of social work's responsibilities by the Dean of the School of Social Work, Howard University.
48. *The Social and Economic Status of the Black Population*, p. 33.

Now we are confronting poverty that is permanent. Upward mobility is much less possible for blacks when prejudice
denies them equal access to education and good jobs. The demand for unskilled labor, the traditional first step on the ladder,
has declined, as machines increasingly replace muscle power.
Suburban rings around large cities prevent their expansion and
trap urban residents in zones of stagnation and deterioration.[49]
High building costs make it increasingly impossible for those
with lower incomes to improve their housing, rural as well as
urban. Above all, the poor see affluence all around them. They
are confronted by the status symbols that connote success and
are systematically denied the opportunity to achieve them.
Where Jane Addams settled in Hull House to permit slum residents to see for the first time how the wealthy lived, every
ghetto resident today knows from the mass media what an
enormous gap exists between his standard of living and that of
the wealthy or even the "typical" American family. Poverty is
no longer a respectable way-station to success; it represents
failure and defeat.

Harrington entitled the book which "rediscovered" poverty in
1962 *The Other America*, to dramatize the extent to which
American poverty differed from the typical American way of
life. He pointed out that it was largely invisible, since the middle class could avoid contact with the poor by using automo-
biles for transportation and living in the suburbs. Invisible the
poor may be, but they are not blind. They see and hear of millions of dollars expended on political exploits of illegal character. They read the advertisements which tell them, "You deserve a treat today," and "You owe it to yourself to own this
fine automobile." They confront a public which lashes out at
"welfare chiselers" and those unwilling to work, which resents
welfare costs and votes down anti-poverty and Legal Aid programs. They feel defenseless and friendless, and their defeatism is one more obstacle between them and any hope of
success.

We have discussed in earlier chapters various groups of the

49. See Martin Kilson, "Black Politics: A New Power," *Dissent*, Vol. 18, No. 4
(August 1971), pp. 333–345, which points out that the concentration of blacks in
urban areas gives them great potential political power. See also W. L. Henderson
and L.C. Ledebur, "Programs for the Economic Development of the American
Negro Community: The Militant Approach," *American Journal of Economics and
Sociology*, Vol. 29, No. 4 (October 1970), pp. 337–351, which advocates black ownership and control of business enterprises in the black ghetto.

poor: the aged, minority group members, ghetto residents, the handicapped. No group among these is so disadvantaged and so neglected as the migrant workers. They epitomize both the problems and the struggles of all those living in poverty.

THE MIGRANTS

Migrant farm workers, approximately 1,000,000 in number, travel in three main streams from the southern edge of the country to the North. Starting in the early spring, they follow the harvest until late fall, when they return to home bases in Florida, Texas, Arizona, and southern California. The California stream is largely composed of Mexican-Americans, as is the western stream, which moves into the North Central, Mountain, and Pacific Coast states. The eastern stream is mostly black and Puerto Rican and works its way up the Atlantic Coast to western New York and into New England.

Migrant farm labor, however deplorable from a social standpoint, is an economic advantage for agri-business and a definitive illustration of the economic forces that generate and perpetuate poverty. Growers of crops which require little hand labor for planting and cultivation but must be harvested by hand cannot find sufficient local agricultural labor for the harvest. They import workers for the few weeks needed and do not have to be concerned with year-round labor costs. Agri-business resists the added costs which would result if protective legislation were enacted and enforced. The cost of hand-harvesting is one of the major incentives toward the development of ever more sophisticated harvest machinery and the breeding of more and more crops which can be picked mechanically.

According to Juan Ramos, to meet the threat of increased costs growers may move their farm operations to Mexico, increase exports, switch to crops which can be harvested mechanically, increase mechanization, or demand subsidies from the federal government.[50] It is apparent that any improvement in the appalling conditions under which migrants travel, live, and work will come as a result of pressure from the public and the development of some kind of power base among the powerless migrants themselves. The success of grape and lettuce boycotts in recent years indicates that there is some public concern waiting to be mobilized for effective action.

---

50. Juan Ramos, "Migrant Farmworkers," *Encyclopedia of Social Work*, 1971 pp. 829–836.

The Migrant Subculture

The truly appalling conditions under which migrant laborers work have been documented. Edward R. Murrow's classic, *Harvest of Shame* was produced on national television in 1960 and aroused some stir, yet a follow-up *Migrant* in 1970 demonstrated that nothing had changed in the decade that featured a War on Poverty. The condition of migrants has been summarized by Solis:

> During harvest periods the families may not be eligible for public assistance or medical care. They continue to live in substandard, dilapidated housing with inadequate sanitation facilities and are exposed to environmental hazards that breed disease. Local educational attitudes of school personnel discourage rather than encourage the participation of the migratory children and youth in the schools. The rate of infant mortality and the incidence of certain disease categories are higher than in any other occupational group. Occupational injuries in agriculture are second only to those in the construction industry.
>
> Migrant workers are usually surrounded by a society that is insensitive to them, to their problems, and to their aspirations, values, and needs. They have no political power because their mobility and economic struggles do not allow them to establish the community cohesiveness that is essential both to organization and to the mobilization of political effort. Migrant farm workers are discriminated against by the dominant group and often by their own ethnic group. Historically, they have been considered desirable as laborers but not as citizens. It is, therefore, difficult for this population to believe that perseverance and hard work will insure financial success.[51]

A particularly good source of information on the lives of migrant workers is the volume edited by William Friedland and Dorothy Nelkin in a series of *Case Studies in Cultural Anthropology*.[52] The study was carried out while both were at the New York State School of Industrial and Labor Relations and is drawn largely from the field notes of black and white students from Tuskegee Institute and Cornell University. These students

51. Faustina Solis, "Socioeconomic and Cultural Conditions of Migrant Workers," *Social Casework*, Vol. 52, No. 5 (May 1971), pp. 308–315. The quotation is from pp. 310, 311.

52. William Friedland and Dorothy Nelkin, *Migrant Agricultural Workers in America's Northeast* (New York: Holt, Rinehart, and Winston, 1971).

became migrant laborers and kept detailed diaries, supplemented by recorded conversations and pictures. They found
three main themes in the life of migrant workers: First, life is
unpredictable and disorganized; it is at the mercy of the grower, the crew leader, and the quality of the crop. Second, the
mode of adaptation to the disorganized character of migrant life
is apathy and escapism. Third, the migrant social system traps
its participants in a self-perpetuating set of social patterns,
which hinders adaptation to new conditions. All these elements in the life style of migrants make it more difficult to provide social and health services which might make it possible
for them to break out of the cycle of poverty, indebtedness to
the grower, and exploitation in which they are trapped.

The willingness of migrant workers to work is attested by
Dr. Robert Coles, who has traveled and talked with hundreds
of migrants and their children. In his testimony before the
Senate Subcommittee on Migratory Labor and in *Migrants, Sharecroppers and Mountaineers,* the second volume of his series
Children in Crisis, Dr. Coles repeatedly calls attention to the industry of these harvesters. It is indeed ironic that their devotion to the work ethic so glorified in America remains so un-
rewarded.

The Migrants and Social Services

The U.S. Senate Subcommittee on Migratory Labor has held
public hearings on the problems of migrants for the last decade.
Some protective legislation has been passed, but there are loopholes in much of it and enforcement is very lax.[53] The hearings
before this Subcommittee have documented the plight of migrant children and adults and the extent to which they are systematically excluded from social services and income maintenance programs.

Child labor laws, for example, establish sixteen as the minimum age for employment in agriculture, but the law applies
only during school hours. Children of any age can work outside school hours and during vacations, and preschool children
can work alongside their parents from dawn to dusk. Because
their families need the added income, parents keep children
in the fields, hiding them from inspectors' infrequent visits.
In California in 1973, there were only fourteen inspectors for

53. See U.S. Congress, Senate Subcommittee on Migratory Labor, *Farmworkers
in Rural America, 1971–1972,* hearings before the Subcommittee, 92nd Congress.

the whole state.[54] An eleven-year-old boy could earn $2.70 a day picking chili peppers. The average family income of families in California's migrant labor camps is just over $3,000 a year, and that can be achieved only by having all members of the family use one Social Security number and fill the same container.

The need to work keeps many children out of school, but the frequent moves of the family also make success in school impossible. In spite of some federal funds for education of migrants, most community schools are reluctant to admit migrant children. They disrupt the routine, are fitted into the school and then move on, are often dirty and poorly clothed, and are subjected to discrimination by pupils and teachers. These are some of the reasons why more than 80 percent of migrant children never go beyond sixth grade. Their lack of education is an increasing handicap, as harvesting becomes more and more technologically sophisticated.

Because they cross state lines in their travels, migrants find themselves ineligible for many local and state programs of health and welfare services. Although residence laws have been repeatedly adjudged illegal by courts, states have substituted an "intent to remain" clause, which excludes migrants. Their mobility makes follow-up visits and provision of services next to impossible. The only effective way to provide social services to these families on the move would be to have social workers travel with them, get to know them well enough to establish relationships, and serve as advocates with health and welfare officials in communities near their camps. It would also be almost impossible for most migrants to follow recommendations of health personnel and social workers under the conditions of their lives. More attention to children, dental care, better diets, rest, improvement of housing, and control over the circumstances under which they live are impossible for families whose stay in any one spot is so brief and whose survival is so dependent on weather or laws and policies in which they have no voice. Long-range recommendations for solving the problems of migrant workers include retraining them and allowing them to settle. Evidence is that many of them would be happy to do so, but they cannot without massive programs of help.

Since most migrants work in several states and are in general excluded from state-supplied services, federal programs are the only solution. At present, participation in Social Security

54. "Sweatshops in the Sun," *Time*, July 30, 1973, p. 56.

requires working for one employer a minimum of twenty days, which excludes many migrants. Minimum wage coverage is lower for farm workers, and they are not eligible for Unemployment Insurance. Special programs and modifications of existing programs are needed for older farm workers, as well as provision for educational and health facilities geared to their special needs. Although there is a federal housing code for migrant camps, it is seldom enforced. Federally supported migrant health projects, set up under the Migrant Health Act of 1962 and as amended in 1965 and 1970, cover at best 350,000 people. Financed by the Office of Economic Opportunity, the Illinois Migrant Council (IMC) carried out a study in 1971 to provide data for planning the settling of migrant workers. Noting that mechanization had resulted in a 12 percent decline in farm laborers hired between 1965 and 1970, the IMC interviewed ex-migrants and migrants. (These workers, while migrants in Illinois, had a home base, often in Texas, to which they had some ties.) Investigators were hampered in their data collection not only by the defeatist attitudes of the respondents but by the refusal of some employers to admit them to migrant camps for fear of exposing the living conditions there. The study found that migrants are not aware of and seldom use community social services. Because of their rural isolation, migrants need multiservice mobile units.

This study concluded that unskilled persons over forty years of age were permanently unemployable and that communities were not likely to welcome and assist migrants who wished to settle there. Non–English-speaking migrants have the lowest chances of employment. The study concludes by recommending a community development program in the home base area, which would include job training, the provision of jobs, and regional federal community development agencies which would buy up land and lease it back for farming cooperatives.[55]

Cesar Chavez and the United
Farm Workers

Since public interest in improving the conditions of living for migrants is sporadic and unorganized, the only real hope for improving their lives is through collective action. Previous attempts by the Agricultural Organizing Committee of the AFL-CIO had been ineffective, and in 1962 Cesar Chavez tried work-

55. Mildred Pratt, "Effect of Mechanization on Migrant Farm Workers," *Social Casework*, Vol. 54, No. 2 (February 1973), pp. 105–113.

ing from within the migrant group and organizing around the daily problems of the workers.[56] His United Farm Workers, up from tiny beginnings, was successful in the first strike against the grape growers, begun in 1965 and dragging on until 1970. In 1966 the UFW merged with the Agricultural Organizing Committee of the AFL-CIO to become the United Farm Workers Organizing Committee (UFWOC), with Chavez as director. The pressure of the nationwide table grape boycott begun in 1967 provided the leverage to compel growers to sign contracts with the union.

These contracts represent a historic first for farm workers who were excluded, because of farm lobby pressures and racism, from the rights to organize and to collective bargaining guaranteed industrial workers in the National Labor Relations Act of 1935. Among the specific targets of the UFWOC were the hiring practices of growers and the health conditions of workers. The 1970 contracts provided for hiring halls, seniority in hiring, no discrimination in hiring or housing, grievance procedures, a medical plan (the Robert F. Kennedy Farm Workers Medical Plan), and health and safety provisions. The latter are particularly needed because of the high rate of poisoning from pesticides used in the fields. With many of the grape growers having signed contracts with the UFWOC, Chavez began trying to organize the iceberg lettuce growers.

The big employers would prefer dealing with the Teamsters Union, as it is more responsive to their interests, and they have consistently tried to promote that union as bargaining agent for the farm workers. In 1973 inter-union rivalry between the Teamsters and the UFW seriously weakened the UFW, even though contracts signed by the growers with Teamsters Unions were voided by Teamster President Frank Fitzsimmons on August 21, 1973.

Charges that unionizing farm workers would so raise the cost of farm products as to make food prohibitive have been denied by UFWOC and its spokesman. In 1973, for example, the cost

---

56. The story of Cesar Chavez is well known. Among the best sources of it are the following: Peter Matthiessen, *Sal Si Puedes—Escape if You Can: Cesar Chavez and the New American Revolution* (New York: Random House, 1969); Joan Levin Ecklein and Armand A. Lauffer, *Community Organizers and Social Planners* (New York: CSWE and John Wiley & Sons, 1972), "La Causa and La Huelga," pp. 31–49, which compiles a number of statements and observations by Cesar Chavez on his own work; Joan London and Henry Anderson, *So Shall Ye Reap: The Story of Cesar Chavez and the Farm Workers' Movement* (New York: Thomas Y. Crowell, 1970).

of picking lettuce added between one and two cents to the price of a head. Doubling pickers' wages would not add appreciably to the cost, which as the housewife knows seems always to advance in ten cent quantum leaps. It is estimated that wages paid farm labor account for less than 5 percent of the retail price of agricultural products.[57]

The unionization of farm labor is an inevitable development in the next decade. Whether Cesar Chavez's effective leadership can be maintained in the power struggles of national union politics is dubious, but a national farm workers union even under other leadership will succeed in forcing growers to close the gap between the incomes of farm workers and unskilled industrial workers. The success of the grape and lettuce boycotts demonstrates a level of support from the general population which will facilitate long-overdue legislation and better enforcement of laws already on the books.

While the long-range trends of unionization, technological obsolescence, and limited social concern inch at a snail's pace toward long-range solutions, the migrants continue to travel, live, and work in substandard conditions, ignored by the public who eats the crops picked in agricultural sweatshops by workers in virtual peonage.

NEW ADMINISTRATIVE APPROACHES TO POLICIES AND PROGRAMS IN THE 1970s

In 1969 the NASW designated the elimination of racism and poverty as its major program targets. We have discussed two of the target groups with which social work services should be particularly concerned in the 1970s. It is obvious that the elimination of these social evils will require massive policy changes by government and attitude changes by the public. Social work is committed to social action to influence policy and attitudes.

The 1971 and 1973 Delegate Assemblies of NASW narrowed the program focus within the anti-racism and anti-poverty priority framework and included the issues of competence, manpower education and training, and service delivery standards. It is apparent that organizational and practice changes can be anticipated in the next decade. Traditional funding is no longer available, with cutbacks in federal support and with inflation

57. Joint Strategy and Action Committee, Inc., *Grapevine*, Vol. 3, No. 6 (January 1973), pp. 5, 6. This publication is put out by a coalition of major Protestant denominations, 475 Riverside Dr., Room 1700A, New York, N.Y., 10027.

eroding the United Way financing structure. New types of personnel will be employed in social work agencies and will require new administrative models. Practice models geared to rehabilitation, development of insight, building of corrective relationships, and open-ended timing will be increasingly replaced by goal-oriented, time-limited, directive counseling on a mutually determined contract basis. Accountability and cost-benefit analysis may be increasingly demanded of the profession, and improved efficiency of operations must be demonstrated if social work is to maintain its societal mandate to deal with social problems.

Some changes in traditional methods of administration of social work have been explored in the preceding chapters of this book. The professionalization of the BSW, use of para- and sub-professionals in service delivery, increased emphasis on social planning, and pressure from consumers of service to alter service delivery methods have all contributed to efforts of the profession to develop new administrative arrangements for meeting the needs of its clientele. There are external pressures as well. The field of social welfare has expanded to include programs in such fields as urban development, manpower training, housing, and health maintenance organizations, among others; these demand of social workers competencies which are far wider than those provided by the traditional graduate and undergraduate educational programs which prepared workers essentially for clinical practice. Social welfare programs may be the largest single item in the public budget, and the resulting publicity gives rise to new pressures from legislators and professional groups, as well as from liberal and conservative social action groups, to modify policies and programs. Social agency administrators, in addition to developing the traditional skills of problem-solving, resource allocation, and staff productivity and morale, must now be experts on public relations, legislative liaison, cost-benefit analysis, and PPBS (Program Planning, Budget Systems) techniques. As Rosemary Sarri sums up the factors making for altered methods of administration, they include increased politicization, more democratic administration, consumer involvement in all aspects of planning and service delivery, and greater flexibility in the face of nonroutine and unpredictable problems, including potentially contradictory goals and mandates.[58]

58. Rosemary Sarri, "Administration in Social Welfare," *Encyclopedia of Social Work, 1971,* pp. 39–48. See also Arthur K. Berliner, "Some Pitfalls in Administrative Behavior," *Social Casework,* Vol. 52, No. 9 (November 1971), pp. 562–566.

ADMINISTRATION AS A SOCIAL WORK METHOD

Social agencies are increasingly complex organizations, bureaucratized and formalized. Some knowledge of organizational theory is essential for understanding how social agencies can be administered and what structures will be most effective. Early social work administration drew heavily on public administration and business management theory, based on the perspectives of Max Weber and Chester Barnard.[59] A bureaucracy, according to Weber's "ideal type," emphasizes rationality and efficiency. Weber's model has three essential characteristics: a hierarchical structure, combining a rational division of labor, a line of responsibility, and a set of written rules; a system of rewards based on salaries, graded by rank; and protection of the rights of individuals through appointment, promotion, limitations of compulsion, and the right of appeals of decisions. Whatever its drawbacks, and they are many, no better alternative for getting done the routine work of society has yet been devised.[60]

Classical theories of bureaucracy minimized the importance of social relations among employees. What has been called "bureaucracy's other face"—the importance of small group behavior, of personal influence, and of motivations other than organization-related—obviously operates in the large-scale organization, sometimes to further its objectives and sometimes to obstruct them. Human relations theories[61] stress how individual satisfactions and morale affect the day-to-day operations of large-scale organizations. Other approaches represent modifications of these positions. Systems theory is useful in understanding the ways in which social agencies are not stable and rigidly institutionalized but are continuously being forced to adapt to changing external and internal pressures.

59. See Max Weber, *The Theory of Social and Economic Organizations*, A. M. Henderson and Talcott Parsons, trans. (Glencoe, Ill.: The Free Press, 1947); and Chester Barnard, *The Functions of the Executive* (Cambridge: Harvard University Press, 1938). For an excellent recent summary of organization theory, see Charles Perrow, *Complex Organizations: A Critical Essay* (Glenview, Ill.: Scott, Foresman & Company), 1972.

60. Perrow, *Complex Organizations*. Chapter 1, "Why Bureaucracy?," explains, illustrates, and defends bureaucracy as a form of organization superior to any others currently known and available to modern societies.

61. The name of Rensis Likert is well known in human relations theory. See his *The Human Organization* (New York: McGraw-Hill Book Company, 1967). Likert contrasts authoritative and exploitative management models with "participative" management, stressing the value of the latter.

SOCIAL WORK: AN INTRODUCTION

..uman service organizations have certain distinctive characteristics, reflecting their societal mandates. Their goals are to
process and change people toward socially approved ends for
new roles or for more effective performance of old roles. In
addition, they operate on theories of human behavior which
are not easily susceptible to cost-benefit accounting. Thus,
fewer decisions can be pre-made, written into manuals of procedure, and delegated to lower-level staff. Service organizations
must operate with continuous and flexible problem-solving,
which demands qualified staff with a good deal of autonomy.[62]

For many years administration has been defined as an area
of social work practice. Arlien Johnson in 1946[63] and John
Kidneigh in 1950[64] so described it. One volume of the 1959
Curriculum Study was devoted to administration as a social work
method.[65] The 1960 *Social Work Yearbook,* predecessor of the
Encyclopedia of Social Work, stated:

> Knowledge and skills, and a philosophy of goals and
> service which are generic to all social work practice, have
> profoundly influenced social agency administration. These
> influences have resulted in an emphasis on good human
> relations in administration, sound personnel policies and
> practices, democratic versus authoritarian structure and
> processes, high recognition of the professional staff com-
> ponent in achieving a quality service, and major attention
> to the content and method of staff supervision and staff
> development.[66]

The 1972 *Encyclopedia* definition of administration builds on the
preceding definitions.

> Administration is defined as a method of practice rather than
> as an area of knowledge or research. It is that method which

62. For a detailed analysis of the work context in social and rehabilitation agencies, see Joseph A. Olmstead, ed., *Organizational Structure and Climate: Implications for Agencies,* Working Papers No. 2 (Washington, D.C.: Social and Rehabilitation Service, February 1973).

63. Arlien Johnson, "The Administrative Process in Social Work," *National
Conference of Social Work, Proceedings* (New York: Columbia University Press,
1946), pp. 249–258.

64. John C. Kidneigh, "Social Work Administration: An Area of Social Work
Practice," *Social Work Journal,* Vol. 31, No. 2 (April 1950), pp. 57–61.

65. Sue Spencer, *The Administration Method in Social Work* (New York: CSWE,
1959).

66. Arthur H. Kruse, "Administration of Social Agencies," *Social Work Yearbook, 1960* (New York: NASW, 1960), p. 79. Reprinted with the permission of
the National Association of Social Workers. See also Herman Stein, "Administration," *Encyclopedia of Social Work, 1965* (New York: NASW, 1965), pp. 58–63.

is concerned primarily with the following activities: (1) translation of societal mandates into operational policies and goals to guide organizational behavior; (2) design of organizational structures and processes through which the goals can be achieved; (3) securing of resources in the form of materials, staff, clients, and societal legitimation necessary for goal attainment and organizational survival; (4) selection and engineering of the necessary technologies; (5) optimizing organizational behavior directed toward increased effectiveness and efficiency; and (6) evaluation of organization performance to facilitate systematic and continuous problem-solving.[67]

The increased attention to "societal mandate" and "legitimation" is apparent and reflects the increasing emphasis on administration as a political process in an atmosphere which may well become more hostile. As Briggs[68] has stated in a section entitled "Withdrawal of Community Support for the Profession," some social workers have been concerned for the last ten years about the dispensability of the social work profession. Unless the profession can define its functions and develop new and effective ways of delivering services, it may well lose its identity and its claim to be the profession best suited to providing service functions. The emergence of the income maintenance specialist as a non-social work position (see page 107) and the abrupt cessation of federal support for social work education in the 1974 budget are ominous signs.

Whether social work will be able to sustain its virtual monopoly on administrative and supervisory positions in the voluntary services is a question. In public agencies, particularly in public welfare and corrections, few administrators are social workers. However, the number of social workers in administrative positions in mental health, psychiatric, and family-child service fields has increased, and the number of students preparing for careers in administration has risen dramatically. In 1965 there were thirty-one students (out of almost 9,000) specializing in administration. In 1973, 520 of 16,099 students were concentrating in administration, and the concentration was offered in twenty-one graduate schools.[69] In addition, undoubtedly many of the 617 post–masters degree students were involved in administration,

67. Sarri, "Administration in Social Welfare," pp. 42, 43. Reprinted with the permission of the National Association of Social Workers.

68. Thomas L. Briggs, "Social Work Manpower: Developments and Dilemmas of the 1970's," Margaret Purvine, ed., *Educating MSW Students to Work with Other Social Welfare Personnel* (New York: CSWE, 1973), pp. 4–31.

69. Ripple, *Statistics*, pp. 20, 26.

although their primary field of specialization is not recorded. The traditional route to administrative positions has been from provision of direct service as a social worker, through supervisory responsibilities, to executive of a small agency, and then to a larger agency. Increasingly, positions will be open for administrators who, in addition to understanding of and experience in social work, possess training and skill in the newer responsibilities involved in program planning, grantsmanship, information system design, and staff development. As social agencies become increasingly politicized, expertise in legislation and lobbying will also be useful in agency administration. Accountability demands training and experience in evaluation,[70] an area in which social work has been slow to develop but which will be of growing importance.

DEPLOYMENT OF MANPOWER

One of the new developments in administration is the need to coordinate the activities of a much wider range of employees than was the case when the staffs of social agencies were composed almost entirely of professional social workers, in many cases MSWs. It will be remembered that in June of 1973, the NASW proposed a six-level classification plan for social work manpower. The two preprofessional levels (social work aide and social work technician) will presumably be working under the supervision of one of the professional levels (social worker—the BSW; graduate social worker—the MSW; certified social worker—the ACSW level; and social work fellow—the DSW or its equivalent in specialized practice). Thus the BSW should be prepared to carry some administrative and supervisory responsibility, although agency executives and chief supervisors will undoubtedly be drawn from those with more advanced preparation and extensive experience.[71]

70. See Howard E. Freeman and Clarence C. Sherwood, *Social Research and Social Policy* (Englewood Cliffs, N.J.: Prentice-Hall, 1970); and Tony Tripodi, Phillip Fellin, and Irwin Epstein, *Social Program Evaluation: Guidelines for Health, Education, and Welfare Administrators* (Itasca, Ill.: F. E. Peacock Publishers, 1971). See also Edward J. Mullen, James R. Dumpson, and associates, *Evaluation of Social Intervention* (San Francisco: Jossey-Bass, Publishers, 1972); and the highly critical review essay by Ralph Garber, in *Social Work*, Vol. 18, No. 5 (September 1973), pp. 109–114.

71. See Florence Whiteman Kaslow and associates, *Issues in Human Services* (San Francisco: Jossey-Bass, 1972), for a review of changing administrative practices, including the potential impact of paraprofessionals and indigenous workers on agencies and staff problems centering around race, class, and ethnic backgrounds.

The Indigenous Worker

The indigenous worker is a staff member recruited from the client population of an agency, either because of cultural affiliation with the client group or because he has shared some experiences with the client group, such as drug addiction, prison, or mental illness. His qualifications are based on life experiences rather than on formal education. It is assumed that he will, by virtue of his experiences, be better able to understand and communicate with the client group of the agency than a middle-class–oriented professional social worker. Indigenous workers were widely used in the War on Poverty, partly to increase social services in a period of manpower shortage and partly to provide new employment opportunities for low-income clients. Although this was heralded as a new departure, it was actually first carried out by the FERA and WPA in the Depression of the 1930s. As Kase points out, some of those who entered the profession by that route are today's leading administrators and social work teachers.[72] The new careers concept dates from 1965 when Arthur Pearl and Frank Riessman published a description of the career ladder in human services, which would provide job opportunities and create needed human services not otherwise available.[73] During the War on Poverty, approximately $35,000,000 was appropriated to employ and train paraprofessionals.

The traditional way to use indigenous paraprofessionals is by integrating them into a team,[74] led by a professional social worker and including various professional and paraprofessional specialists. The entire team is, theoretically, involved in analyzing the client or client group and planning the treatment or intervention model to be used. Stress is laid on coordinating and integrating the various services delivered so that each team member's goals are consistent with those of the others. Emphasis is thus laid on professional attitudes and techniques, and the indigenous worker, both consciously and unconsciously, will adopt these attitudes.

72. Harold M. Kase, "Purposeful Use of Indigenous Paraprofessionals," *Social Work*, Vol. 17, No. 2 (March 1972), pp. 109–110.

73. See Arthur Pearl and Frank Riessman, *New Careers for the Poor: The Nonprofessional in Human Service* (New York: The Free Press, 1965).

74. See Robert Barker and Thomas Briggs, *Using Teams to Deliver Social Services* (Syracuse: Syracuse University Press, 1969).

This leads inevitably to role conflict and strain.[75] The incorporation of social work attitudes, vocabulary, and techniques by indigenous personnel weakens the identification with the client group that was their chief usefulness in service delivery. Their credibility with their constituency is undermined, and they are accused of having "sold out" to the establishment. A similar role conflict and loss of credibility may be observed on college campuses when a student leader is co-opted by the administration or when a faculty member leaves teaching to become an administrator.

Thus, as Kurzman points out, the paraprofessional, once in the agency, becomes neutralized as a source of social change, and hiring him possibly weakens the profession's commitment to social reform by co-opting some of the leadership elements in the community.[76] Although many indigenous workers entered social agencies with the aim of making them more responsive to community needs, they found themselves in a bureaucracy with little power to alter policy decisions. Hardcastle suggests that rather than integrating indigenous workers into a team led by professionals, they be "compartmentalized" into a unit composed entirely or largely of their peers;[77] this would prevent the loss of those very characteristics which make indigenous personnel so valuable—their ability to understand and communicate with lower-class clients. Their loyalties would be directed toward their unit rather than toward the agency as a whole. Precedents already exist in the homemaker units operated by some agencies and in the collaborative efforts of social agencies and health agencies, where the health service desired by the social work agency is specified but no attempt is made to co-opt those delivering the service as part of a social work team. This approach to the use of indigenous workers emphasizes their role as potential contribu-

75. This point is well documented in Louis Zurcher, *Poverty Warriors: The Human Experience of Planned Social Intervention* (Austin: University of Texas Press, 1970).

76. Paul A. Kurzman, "The New Careers Movement and Social Change," *Social Casework*, Vol. 51, No. 1 (January 1970), pp. 22–27.

77. David A. Hardcastle, "The Indigenous Nonprofessional in the Social Service Bureaucracy: A Critical Examination," *Social Work*, Vol. 16, No. 2 (April 1971), pp. 56–63. See also Philip Kramer, "The Indigenous Worker: Hometowner, Striver, or Activist," *Social Work*, Vol. 17, No. 1 (January 1972), pp. 43–49, which categorizes indigenous workers as to attitudes toward education, agency goals, and community problems.

tors of service, rather than as low-income clients being given new employment opportunities.[78]

The Social Work Technician

The second category in the six-level classification scheme of the NASW is the social work technician. Usually he will have been prepared for his position by graduation from a two-year "human services" educational program. He may or may not have come from the client group, but he has made a commitment to the profession and tends to identify with it. Many of these social work technicians have received academic and field instruction preparing them for specific tasks (child care worker, income maintenance specialist, psychiatric aide), and there may be career ladders which lead to supervisory positions in these units of service.

Although the Council on Social Work Education does not formally accredit associate degree programs, it does publish guidelines and stresses the need for linkages with baccalaureate programs in four-year colleges. Accredited baccalaureate programs provide a means for social work technicians to advance to full professional status in two additional years, and many will wish to do so. Colleges offering two-year programs should design their courses for maximum transferability of credit, and four-year programs of social work education should develop flexibility in adjusting requirements, granting academic credit for on-the-job experience, and scheduling on-campus classes when agency employees can take them. Federal funds for educational leaves are severely limited under the 1974 budget, but there are opportunities for in-service training by educational institutions which would carry academic credit, for cooperative work-study programs, and for exchanges between colleges and agencies offering field placements to preprofessional students.

78. For descriptions of agency programs using indigenous personnel as staff aides in teams and in separate units, see the following: Kase, "Purposeful Use of Indigenous Paraprofessionals"; Alice Q. Ayers, "Neighborhood Services: People Caring for People," *Social Casework*, Vol. 54, No. 4 (April 1973), pp. 195–215; Stanley Budner, Robert M. Chazin, and Howard Young, "The Indigenous Nonprofessional in a Multiservice Center," *Social Casework*, Vol. 54, No. 6 (June 1973), pp. 354–359; Robert J. Teare, "Employment of Subprofessionals: Staff and Organizational Adaptability and Implications for Service Delivery," *National Study of Social Welfare and Rehabilitation Workers, Work and Organizational Contexts*, Working Papers No. 1 (Washington, D.C.: Social and Rehabilitation Service, May 1971), 199–266; and Alan Gartner, *Paraprofessionals and Their Performance: A Survey of Education, Health, and Social Service Programs* (New York: Praeger Publishers, 1971).

The Social Worker

This volume has been directed primarily at the student who is preparing to practice as a BSW social worker. While it seems clear that this level will be doing the bulk of direct service delivery in the fairly near future, BSWs as professionals are still too new in the field to have been used to maximum advantage. Functional Job Analysis,[79] which grades the complexity of the task according to a design found useful in industry but also applies in the service field, will be increasingly used to assign BSWs to tasks intermediate in complexity, risk, and difficulty.[80]

The Graduate Social Worker

We should not overlook the potential threat that widespread use of BSWs holds for MSW workers, particularly those whose professional education is several years behind them. The traditional professional role of a one-to-one helping relationship will be increasingly superseded, in agencies using Functional Job Analysis, by such roles as consultant, teacher, planner, and evaluator. The one-to-one contacts will be delegated to BSW and lower levels. Supervisory techniques must now be learned in the graduate schools, since MSWs will be moving immediately into supervisory responsibilities. Some graduate schools are including courses or concentrations in "Social Service Management" and "Manpower Utilization" and providing relevant field experience.[81]

Not all social workers are happy about the trend away from using MSWs for service to troubled families and individuals which is apparent in contemporary education and practice. The growth of state organizations of Clinical Social Workers and the establishment of the National Federation of Societies for Clinical Social Work represent a reaction to what is seen as a threat to the primacy of clinical services. The Federation is concerned about demonstrating the need for clinical social work and safeguarding

---

79. See Robert E. Lewis et al., *A Systems Approach to Manpower Utilization and Training* (Salt Lake City, Utah: Utah Division of Family Services, 1972).

80. For a detailed job analysis based on a four-level manpower scheme, with the BSW considered Level III, see Robert J. Teare and Harold L. McPheeters, *Manpower Utilization in Social Welfare Services* (Atlanta: Southern Regional Education Board, 1970), particularly Part II.

81. The programs at the Jane Addams Graduate School of Social Work and at Portland State University School of Social Work are outlined in Margaret Purvine, ed., *Educating MSW Students*, pp. 63–98. See also Margaret Purvine, ed., *Manpower and Employment: A Source Book for Social Workers* (New York: CSWE, 1972).

the public from inadequately trained mental health practitioners. Its official publication, *The Clinical Social Work Journal*, was established in 1973 to further interest in and support of clinical social work and to insure that mental health services offered by social workers are included in any national health insurance bill.

The question of the linkages between undergraduate and graduate education is of increasing importance, as undergraduate courses now include much of the content formerly limited to the first year of graduate school and undergraduate field experience totals 400 hours. Combined five-year programs have existed for some time at Adelphi, Syracuse, and San Diego. In 1973 at least twenty-eight schools had some arrangements for admitting to advanced standing students with extensive undergraduate education and/or practice experience.[82] In October 1973, The Worden School of Social Service, San Antonio, Texas, announced a twelve-month MSW program open to any graduate of a CSWE-approved baccalaureate program. Other schools are following suit. Even where a graduate school does not make a blanket admissions policy, BSWs will find increasing flexibility of admissions requirements on the basis of evaluation of individual applicants. However, now that the MSW degree is not the only route to a career as a professional social worker, students should be considering whether their interests lie in the provision of direct service or in the advanced specializations open to MSWs. With growing public reluctance to fund costly social services, there may well be fewer openings for MSWs in the future, and the tremendous expansion of graduate schools of the 1960s may be followed by a period of shrinking enrollments and consolidation of MSW programs.

IS CASEWORK DEAD?

Not too many years ago, the profession was shocked by the irreverent query, "Is casework dead?"[83] This principal social work method was accused of preoccupation with psychoanalytic theory at the expense of its traditional responsibility for social reform.[84]

---

82. Ripple, *Statistics*, p. 15.

83. The phrase appears to have been first used by Helen Harris Perlman in her article "Casework Is Dead," *Social Casework*, Vol. 48, No. 1 (January 1967), pp. 22–25. According to Mrs. Perlman, the phrase was suggested by the then fashionable statement "God is dead." (Personal communication from Mrs. Perlman, February 12, 1974.)

84. See Herman Borenzweig, "Social Work and Psychoanalytic Theory: A Historical Analysis," *Social Work*, Vol. 16, No. 1 (January 1971), pp. 7–16. See also Willard C. Richan and Allan R. Mendelson, *Social Work: The Unloved Profession* (New York: Franklin Watts, 1973).

Its critics called attention to its alienation from the poor,[85] its aspects of social control,[86] its irrelevance,[87] its high cost,[88] its complacency in the face of unjust social conditions,[89] and its ineffectiveness.[90]

Those who defend casework as the core of the helping efforts of the social work profession include Helen Harris Perlman, who states:[91]

> I believe in casework. That sounds utterly naive, but I shall explain what I mean by that statement of faith further on. Here I will say only that several of the articles chosen for inclusion in this book articulate my conviction and defense of the human values to be preserved and the human suffering to be lessened in a socially supported mode of help for individual human beings . . . Over the two decades in which

85. See page 14, fn. 15.

86. See Frances Fox Piven and Richard A. Cloward, *Regulating the Poor: The Functions of Public Welfare* (New York: Pantheon Books, 1971); and Betty Mandell, "Welfare and Totalitarianism: Part I. Theoretical Issues," *Social Work*, Vol. 16, No. 1 (January 1971), pp. 17–26, and "Part II. Tactical Guidelines," *Social Work*, Vol. 16, No. 2 (April 1971), pp. 89–96.

87. See Harold Throssell, "Where Have All the Social Workers Gone?" *International Social Work*, Vol. 15, No. 2 (1972), pp. 32–35, an article reprinted from the *Australian Journal of Social Work*, which describes from the vantage point of the year 2000 A.D. the total disappearance of the profession because of its withdrawal from involvement with the real problems of the nation.

88. See, for example, Nina Toren, *Social Work: The Case of a Semi-Profession* (Beverly Hills, Ca.: Sage Publications, 1972), who advocates that group work become the principal method of social work intervention.

89. An articulate exponent of this point of view is Martin Rein, "Social Work in Search of a Radical Profession," *Social Work*, Vol. 15, No. 2 (April 1970), pp. 13–28. He develops a typology of social work goals based on whether they accept or challenge standards of behavior and whether change is believed to occur as a result of individual effort or via changed social conditions. Traditional casework accepts prevailing standards of behavior and expects individuals to change in order to conform to them. Rein advocates a "radical casework" based on challenging the status quo and humanizing the bureaucracies with which clients deal.

90. See Joel Fischer, "Is Casework Effective? A Review," *Social Work*, Vol. 18, No. 1 (January 1973), pp. 5–20, which reviews critically a number of well-known research studies, including the famous *Girls at Vocational High* of Meyer, Borgotta, and Jones, and concludes that there is no clear indication that casework services improved the treated group as compared to a control group and that in some cases the treated group actually deteriorated; see also the critiques of Fischer's position in the two succeeding issues of *Social Work*. See as well "Has Social Work Failed?" *Social Service Review*, Vol. 46, No. 3 (September 1972), pp. 427–431.

91. Helen Harris Perlman, "A Guide to the Reader of This Book," *Perspectives on Social Casework* (Philadelphia: Temple University Press, 1971), p. viii. © 1971 by Temple University. All rights reserved. This volume brings together some twelve essays including the well-known "Casework Is Dead," in which Mrs. Perlman demonstrates convincingly that it is not dead.

these essays were written the professions (and occupations) of "people helpers" have proliferated. Therapists and counselors by various names are ubiquitous, and caseworkers have sometimes had to scramble about trying to find their particular place and special function. At the same time, from within social work itself has come the upsetting experience of a kind of righteous rejection of casework as lacking legitimacy in a profession that must pour its resources, it is said, into societal, not individual change.

In 1970 Mrs. Perlman stated, perhaps overoptimistically, that the worst of the battle was over:[92]

The attackers of casework had—and have—a point; more than that, they have a just cause. Because of many good and bad reasons that cannot be examined here, the casework method for too many years had come to dominate social work and to be mistakenly equated with it. From nationwide governmental programs to two-person family agencies, there was an implicit belief that if only there were enough well-trained caseworkers, people in trouble could be enabled to cope with their social problems. We had banked on the great government programs of income maintenance and medical care to furnish the foundation for a living. We had lost sight of the forces and powers for human ill-being and misery that remained virulent and widespread, and in the wake of which any individual—client or caseworker—was helpless. As the spokesmen for social work, caseworkers had tacitly promised more than could be delivered by *any* one profession, whatever its nature or modes of operations. Those who attacked it, therefore, were attacking our sometimes naive and unwitting pretenses. They were calling for forms of social action based upon reforms of social policy and programs, some that were within social work's long–marked-out (but scarcely scratched) turf, and some that called for social work alliances with popular and political as well as with other professional sources of power.

It is a long needed movement that is sweeping through social work now. With some growing sense of their direction and some lessening of their romanticism, the "social actionists"—whether they are community workers, social program planners and developers, consultants and stimulators to grass roots organizations, or government officials—are directing their energies now toward fighting the real enemy. That real enemy is not casework. It is conditions that pollute social living, not only among the poor—although

92. *Ibid.*, pp. 177, 179. © 1971 by Temple University. All rights reserved.

there the social smog is thickest—but across total communities. . . .

Is there then a place and purpose in social work for a helping process that, in the midst of recognized widespread social "disease," gives attention to individual men and women and children who are in trouble and who ask for or need help? If the answer is no, one stands on the edge of nihilism. If one cannot affirm the worth of the individual man one cannot affirm the worth of that man multiplied into mankind. There is no test of a social system or policy except as a measure of its effect upon individual well-being.

In an effort to prove either that casework is dead or is still alive, to reform it for continued vitality or to produce a more viable replacement, social work theorists have been busy. In 1970 Harriet Bartlett, long one of the most articulate writers in social work, produced a monograph delineating the central core of social work's concern, which she finds in the notion of "social interaction" between individuals attempting to cope with life tasks and environmental demands; she favors replacing the term "treatment," including its negative connotations, with "interventive repertoire," which implies versatility and flexibility on the part of the social worker.[93]

Max Siporin favors the term "social treatment" and defines social casework as a "multifunctional set of procedures" for providing individualized services. Social treatment operates on a problem-person-situation model, which is also found to be a systems model involving both personality and social systems. Siporin feels this model offers the possibility of integrating social work's traditional swings between a primarily individual-oriented rehabilitation emphasis and a social reform orientation.[94]

Carol Meyer, distinguished faculty member of the Columbia University School of Social Work, advocates a generalist position with focus on the impact on individuals of our urban, mass society. By defining the "case" as individuals, dyads, triads, families, and groups, Dr. Meyer enlarges the range of services which can be performed by a "caseworker."[95] Like Rein (see footnote 89, page 534), Meyer is concerned with humanizing the bureaucracies with which individuals must deal in a mass society.

93. Harriet M. Bartlett, *The Common Base of Social Work Practice* (New York: NASW,1970).

94. Max Siporin, "Social Treatment: A New-Old Helping Method," *Social Work*, Vol. 15, No. 3 (July 1970), pp. 13–25.

95. Carol H. Meyer, *Social Work Practice: A Response to the Urban Crisis* (New York: The Free Press, 1970).

A symposium held at the University of Chicago School of Social Service Administration brought together presentations by seven leading theoreticians, including Florence Hollis, Ruth Smalley, and Lydia Rapoport, which indicated that casework is far from dead but that it still lacks rigorously scientific and verifiable practice theory.[96]

In 1971 Ann Hartman echoed Mary Richmond's question from 1922, "What is social casework?"[97] Her article analyzed the writings of a number of casework authorities and concluded that casework may include people-changing or situation-changing or a combination of these. Rather than a single model of casework practice, she envisages casework as a discipline embracing a number of different models, including helping individuals to alter personality characteristics, to deal with concrete problems, or to acquire necessary resources.

Many of the issues in social casework and theory have been examined by Scott Briar, long a critic of traditional casework, and by Henry Miller.[98] The various theories of behavior, the basic values of the profession, and the necessity for scientific methodology are considered. Emphasis is laid on the tasks of social casework, which the authors define as identification of the client, worker-client communication and relationship, diagnosis and assessment, objectives and goals, strategy and tactics of intervention, and termination and outcome. The authors conclude that casework is alive and promising.

Herbert Strean in 1972 suggested a "life model" approach to casework. Here emphasis is laid on the developmental tasks and needs of the individual as he grows and interacts with his environment. Ego-psychology, Erik Erikson's "life cycle," and Bernard and Louise Bandler's "growth models" are incorporated into Strean's paradigm, together with insights from Mary Richmond, Gordon Hamilton, Florence Hollis, and Helen Harris Perlman. Strean cites several cases which demonstrate how social casework can promote progressive trends in the individual. His "life model" approach can be useful with "psychosocial dis-

96. Robert W. Roberts and Robert H. Nee, eds., *Theories of Social Casework* (Chicago: University of Chicago Press, 1970).

97. Mary Richmond, *What Is Social Casework? An Introductory Description* (New York: Russell Sage Foundation, 1922); Ann Hartman, "But What Is Social Casework?" *Social Casework*, Vol. 52, No. 7 (July 1971), pp. 411–419, See also the comments by Sherman Merle and Florence Hollis in Vol. 52, No. 10 (December 1971), pp. 651–653, and Ms. Hartman's rejoinder.

98. Scott Briar and Henry Miller, *Problems and Issues in Social Casework* (New York: Columbia University Press, 1971).

orders," a blanket term which covers intrapersonal, interpersonal, and extrapersonal obstacles to maximum use of the client's progressive trends.[99] This model would seem to have great utility for the professional caseworker, and the case illustrations make it easier for the student than some more theoretical discussions.

In an effort to provide a framework within which all social work practice, including casework, can be incorporated, Allen Pincus and Anne Minahan use a general systems approach to social work practice[100] which they view as a process of goal-oriented planned change. Their model for practice may be used by either generalist or specialist. Eight practice areas which the authors consider essential for practice are delineated and described: assessing problems, collecting data, making initial contacts, negotiating contracts, forming action systems, maintaining and coordinating action systems, exercising influence, and terminating the change effort. Three extended case studies are included and are referred to throughout the volume, and there are numerous practical illustrations incorporated in the somewhat technical discussion. In its review of the literature and its integrative approach, this volume may well represent a landmark in the attempts to redefine and reformulate practice theory, as well as being a useful textbook for the practitioner.

A return to the remarkable insights of the pioneering professional social worker, Mary Richmond, shows how relevant many of her ideas still are today. As Carol Meyer has put it:

> Mary Richmond's conception of social casework, interestingly enough, might be viewed as the most appropriate method of work for our time, as well as being suitable for its own time. The reason for the staying power of her ideas may be derived from her views of the purpose of practice and her brilliant combining of the ideas of personality and environment. Today's social scene and knowledge indicate that this is an idea whose time has come, again.[101]

Mary Richmond foresaw that the new profession would undergo cycles in which concentrated emphasis on helping individuals

99. Herbert S. Strean, "Application of the 'Life Model' to Casework," *Social Work*, Vol. 17, No. 5 (September 1972), pp. 46–53. See also *Social Casework: Theories in Action* (Metuchen, N.J.: Scarecrow Press, 1971), a collection of essays edited by Dr. Strean, with a lengthy introduction describing the various theories.

100. Allen Pincus and Anne Minahan, *Social Work Practice: Model and Method* (Itasca, Ill.: F. E. Peacock Publishers, 1973).

101. Carol H. Meyer, "Purposes and Boundaries—Casework Fifty Years Later," *Social Casework*, Vol. 54, No. 5 (May 1973), p. 269.

would alternate with emphasis on reforming adverse conditions. She termed this "the rhythm of social work"[102] and saw the demands for greater individualization versus generalization as continuous. Muriel Pumphrey put it this way at Fifty Years Later, a symposium celebrating the fiftieth anniversary of the publication of *What Is Social Casework?*:

> She passed her final conclusion on to her successors: Social work had three essential emphases—individualization, research and generalization, and social action. She saw no reason why the three could not occur at the same time. Achieving this balance is today's challenge to social casework.[103]

FINAL NOTE

One of the advantages of a field so eclectic and multifaceted as social work is the opportunity it provides for concerned individuals to serve their fellow men in ways which best fit their own life styles. There is ample room and useful tasks in the field for activists and poets, for radicals and conservatives, for theory builders and pragmatists, for those who prize the rewards of one-to-one helping relationships and those with grandiose and sweeping world views. In ghettos and in remote mountain valleys, in nicely appointed agency offices and in dingy prisons, in legislatures and huge service bureaucracies there are places for the skilled, imaginative, resourceful, courageous, and knowledgeable social worker.

Whether or not one chooses a career in social work, the emergence of institutional social services in the "Age of Anxiety" offers an opportunity for scrutinizing and assessing the vitality of democratic institutions in a period when they are being challenged by conflicting ideologies. As such the social services are worthy fields for study and support.

ADDITIONAL REFERENCES

Anderson, Ralph E. and Carter, Irl E., *Human Behavior in the Social Environment: A Social Systems Approach* (Chicago: Aldine Publishing Company, 1974). A lucid and readable introduction to social systems

---

102. Joanna C. Colcord and Ruth Z. S. Mann, eds., *The Long View: Papers and Addresses by Mary E. Richmond* (New York: Russell Sage Foundation, 1930), p. 589.

103. Muriel W. Pumphrey, "Lasting and Outmoded Concepts in the Caseworker's Heritage," *Social Casework*, Vol. 54, No. 5 (May 1973), p. 267.

theory as applied to human behavior, which provides a useful frame of reference for the social work practitioner.

Council on Social Work Education, *Black Perspectives on Social Work Education: Issues Related to Curriculum, Faculty and Students* (New York: CSWE, 1974). A compilation of seven papers dealing with the need of social work education to incorporate material on strengths, problems, and needs of blacks and other minority groups, as these can enrich social work education.

Goldstein, Howard, *Social Work Practice: A Unitary Approach* (Columbia, S.C.: University of South Carolina Press, 1973). A well-organized account of the purposes and interventive models of social work practice, utilizing systems theory.

Levine, Naomi and Hochbaum, Martin, eds., *Poor Jews: An American Awakening* (New Brunswick, N.J.: Trans-action, 1974). Designed to counteract the stereotyped view that all Jews are successful businessmen, with a description of various poor Jewish groups in New York City.

Pilisuk, Marc and Pilisuk, Phyllis, eds., *How We Lost the War on Poverty* (New Brunswick, N.J.: Trans-action, 1973). A number of authorities examine what went wrong in the War on Poverty and suggest how a more effective campaign might be mounted in the future.

Ross, Bernard and Shireman, Charles, eds., *Social Work Practice and Social Justice* (Washington, D.C.: National Association of Social Workers, 1973). An examination of the barriers to social justice within each of the four major social welfare systems: income maintenance, health care, public education, and juvenile and criminal justice.

Sackheim, Gertrude, *The Practice of Clinical Casework* (New York: Behavioral Publications, 1974). The theory and practice of clinical casework as a distinct form of therapy in its own right.

Townsend, Peter, ed., *The Concept of Poverty: Working Papers on Methods of Investigation and Life-Styles of the Poor in Different Countries* (New York: American Elsevier Publishing, 1970). An interesting comparison of levels of living in a number of countries with policy implications involving the entrenched economic and political interests which generate and perpetuate poverty.

Turner, Francis Joseph, ed., *Social Work Treatment: Interlocking Theoretical Approaches* (Riverside, N.J.: The Free Press, 1974). The theoretical bases of practice, including ego psychology, systems theory, and behavior modification.

Weissman, Harold H., *Overcoming Mismanagement in the Human Service Professions: A Casebook of Staff Initiatives* (San Francisco: Jossey-Bass, Publishers, 1973). Documents the need for reform of maladministration in human service agencies and outlines procedures which workers can use to improve services to the community.

index of authors

Aaron, Henry J., 105
Ackerman, Nathan W., 112, 139, 141
Adams, Dwight S., 467
Adams, Margaret, 457
Addams, Jane, 462
Ahlberg, Leif, 480
Akers, Ronald L., 320
Alexander, Chauncey A., 507
Alford, Robert R., 282
Alinsky, Saul, 489
Altman, Dennis, 457
Amada, Gerald, 142
Amen, Grover, 433
Anderson, Henry, 522
Anderson, Ralph E., 539
Anderson, Robert, 144
Andrews, Ernest E., 162
Arkava, Morton L., 201–203
Atelsek, Frank, 276
Attneave, Carolyn, 112
Auerbach, Aline B., 135
Auerbach, Arnold J., 510
Austin, David M., 490
Ayers, Alice Q., 531

Bacon, Selden D., 436

Baer, Paul E., 447
Bahr, Howard M., 450
Baker, Frank, 466
Baldwin, James, 511
Bandler, Bernard, 314
Banks, George P., 504
Barkan, Theresa W., 301
Barker, Robert L., 12, 529
Barnard, Chester, 525
Barnes, Harry Elmer, 381, 395
Barringer, Richard E., 41
Barry, Herbert, 438
Barten, H. H., 162
Barten, S. S., 162
Bartlett, Harriet M., 3, 536
Barusch, Phyllis, 472
Bauer, Raymond E., 486
Bean, Shirley L., 173
Beasley, Lou M., 505
Beatt, Earl J., 156
Beer, Samuel H., 41
Bell, R. Gordon, 448
Bell, Winifred, 93
Bellacci, Matilda T., 130
Benney, Celia, 341
Bergen, Helen M., 342

Bergler, Edmund, 452
Bergum, Kathleen Holt, 292
Berkman, Barbara Gordon, 125, 290
Berkovitz, Irving H., 199
Berliner, Arthur K., 524
Bernard, Jessie, 497
Berne, Eric, 127
Bettelheim, Bruno, 210
Better, Shirley, 505
Biddle, Loureide, 478
Biddle, William W., 478
Billingsley, Andrew, 110, 147, 505
Birren, James E., 250
Bixby, F. Lovell, 367
Bixby, Lenore E., 246
Black, Bertram J., 278
Blank, Marie Latz, 245
Blau, Zena Smith, 276
Blenkner, Margaret, 255
Blodgett, Harriet E., 457
Blumberg, Abraham S., 394
Boehm, Werner W., 496
Boisvert, Maurice J., 173
Boone, Donald R., 416
Booth, Charles, 474
Borenzweig, Herman, 464, 533
Bowlby, John, 175
Bracey, John H., Jr., 110
Braly, Malcolm, 383
Brandt, Barbara, 497
Brandwein, Ruth, 466
Brechenser, Donn M., 310
Breed, Allen F., 377
Brennan, William C., 372, 494
Brenner, Melvin N., 495
Bressler, Robert, 156
Briar, Scott, 14, 537
Briggs, Thomas L., 12, 527, 529
Brill, Leon, 433, 457
Brill, Naomi, 149–150
Brim, Orville G., Jr., 239
Brody, Elaine, 239, 254
Brody, Stanley J., 268, 480
Brokowski, Anthony, 466
Brown, Bertram S., 501
Brown, Christy, 406
Brown, Claude, 511
Brown, Diana L., 415
Brown, Elliot C., 286
Brown, Malcolm J., 478
Bry, Adelaide, 140
Bryan, Helen, 386

Buck, Pearl, 406
Budner, Stanley, 531
Burgess, Ernest W., 461
Burgest, David R., 499
Burkhart, Kathryn W., 386
Burlingham, Dorothy, 175, 423
Burmeister, Eva E., 206
Burns, Eveline M., 41, 78, 284
Burns, Virginia M., 376
Butler, Robert N., 253, 261, 269
Buxbaum, Carl B., 316

Cahn, Sidney, 442, 444, 450
Caiden, Naomi, 497
Cain, Arthur H., 447
Cain, Lillian Pike, 286
Cantilli, Edmund J., 256
Caplan, Gerald, 352
Caplan, Nathan, 502
Carder, Joan Haley, 135
Carey, Jean Wallace, 259, 268
Carlton, Thomas Owen, 484
Carter, Genevieve W., 471
Carter, Irl E., 539
Casriel, Daniel, 433
Chambers, Carl D., 432
Chapin, Rosemary, 58
Chatterjee, Pranab, 472
Chazin, Robert M., 531
Chen, Pei-Ngor, 508
Chestang, Leon W., 226, 228, 501
Chilman, Catherine S., 169
Chilton, Ronald, 93
Clark, Eleanor, 263
Clark, Kenneth B., 490
Clarke, Helen I., 360
Cloward, Richard A., 14, 141, 453, 490, 534
Cobbs, Price, 511
Cohen, Arthur R., 335
Cohen, Jerome, 114
Cohen, Nathan E., 71
Cohen, Pauline C., 444
Cohen, Ruth G., 272
Colcord, Joanna C., 539
Coles, Robert, 502, 519
Commager, Henry Steele, 70
Conkin, Paul R., 108
Conot, Robert, 358, 502
Conrad, W. G., 326
Cooper, Shirley, 512
Corrigan, Eileen, 444

Costin, Lela B., 179, 180, 190, 219
Coughlin, Bernard J., 229
Cowan, Rachel, 257
Cox, Irene, 110
Criswell, Howard D., Jr., 174
Crystal, David, 159
Cull, John G., 276, 372
Curtin, Sharon R., 276
Custance, John, 44

D'Ambrosio, Richard, 174
Daniels, Robert S., 280
Daniels, Roger, 40
Darden, Donna K., 41
Darden, William R., 41
Daste, Barry M., 395
David, Anne C., 341
Davis, Allen F., 462
Davis, Angela, 511
Davis, Elizabeth B., 450
Davis, William N., 439
Dearing, W. Palmer, 284
de Beauvoir, Simone, 260
De Courcy, Judith, 174
De Courcy, Peter, 174
De Francis, Vincent, 173
de la Cruz, Felix F., 420
Denisoff, R. Serge, 452
Denzin, Norman K., 233
De Saix, Christine, 416
De Schweinitz, Karl, 64
Detre, Thomas P., 312
Deutsch, Albert, 305
Deutsch, Cynthia P., 408
Dole, Vincent, 434
Dolgoff, Ralph, 58
Donahue, Wilma, 236
Dover, Frances T., 428, 429
Downey, John J., 362
Drake, Jack, 311
Driscoll, Chancellor B., 292
Dumont, Matthew, 490
Dumpson, James R., 528
Dunbar, Ellen, 292
Duster, Troy, 431
Dworkin, E. S., 326
Dywasuk, Colette T., 230

Eaton, Joseph W., 152
Ecklein, Joan Levin, 473, 522
Edelstein, Rosalind I., 117
Edgar, Richard E., 490

Edgerton, Robert B., 457
Edwards, Mildred G., 156
Ehrlichman, John, 10
Elias, Albert, 367
Elkin, Robert, 195
Elmer, Elizabeth, 173, 174
Engel, Mary, 233
Engler, Richard E., 228
Epstein, Irwin, 14, 528
Epstein, Norman, 142
Erikson, Erik H., 243

Falk, I. S., 88
Farrow, Frank G., 263
Favazza, Armando, 309, 337
Favazza, B., 337
Feiden, Elaine S., 334
Feldstein, Donald, 12
Fellin, Phillip, 528
Fellman, Gordon, 497
Fellner, Irving W., 228
Fenton, Norman, 400
Ferber, Andrew, 162
Fibush, Esther, 505
Field, Minna, 276
Fine, Eric W., 340
Fine, Reuben, 316
Finkle, Harvey, 268
Fischer, Joel, 374, 534
Fisher, Florence, 230
Fisher, Phyllis K., 204
Fisher, Thais, 341
Flendening, Susan E., 123
Forer, Lois G., 401
Fort, Joel, 316
Fox, Ruth, 442
Fraiberg, Selma, 195–196
Franke, Irving F., 511
Franks, Cyril M., 203, 233
Freedman, Alfred M., 316
Freedman, Joel, 311, 412
Freeman, Henry, 117, 118
Freeman, Howard E., 239, 485, 486, 528
French, Betty, 514
Freud, Anna, 169, 175, 306, 318
Frey, Louise A., 292
Fried, Edward R., 59, 486
Friedland, William, 518
Friedlander, Walter A., 198, 471
Friedman, Jeannette Katz, 259, 268
Fromm, Erich, 322
Funnyé, Clarence, 506

Garber, Ralph, 528
Gardner, Richard A., 195
Gardner, William I., 413
Gartner, Alan, 531
Gastil, R. D., 487
Geis, Gilbert, 431
Geismar, Ludwig L., 136, 162
Gerber, Alex, 352
Gerletti, John D., 378
Gersuny, Carl, 416
Gil, David G., 485, 497
Gilbert, Neil, 480, 497
Gill, Merton, 31
Gilmore, Alden S., 238
Giovannoni, Jeanne M., 110, 147, 505
Gitterman, Alex, 513
Glaser, Daniel, 401
Glaser, G. C., 447
Glasgow, Douglas, 490, 515
Glasser, Melvin A., 54, 281, 283
Glasser, Paul, 146
Glen, Jeffrey E., 361, 362
Glenn, Michael, 353
Glick, Lester J., 496
Glueck, Eleanor, 375
Glueck, Sheldon, 375
Gochros, Harvey L., 260, 454, 455
Goffman, Erving, 238, 373
Goist, Park Dixon, 461
Goldberg, Gertrude S., 497
Goldin, George J., 450
Goldstein, Harriet, 206
Goldstein, Howard, 540
Goldstein, Joseph, 164, 169
Goodman, Walter, 311
Goodwin, Leonard, 94
Gottlieb, Benjamin H., 191
Gottlieb, Lois J., 191
Gottschalk, L. A., 447
Green, Judy Kopp, 203
Green, Richard, 454
Greenberg, Arthur, 214
Greenfield, Josh, 406
Greenspan, Stanley I., 204
Greenwald, Shayne R., 496
Greenwood, Ernest, 19
Gregg, Grace S., 174
Greifer, Julian L., 497
Grier, William, 511
Grimm, James W., 510
Grinker, Roy R., 457
Grinnell, Richard M., Jr., 119

Grinspoon, Lester, 434
Grosser, Charles, 497
Grow, Lillian J., 147
Gruber, Murray, 503
Guerard, Paul A., 214
Gula, Martin, 214
Gurin, Arnold, 408, 459, 473, 481, 483, 493

Haberlein, Bernard J., 210
Hall, Richard N., 19
Halleck, Seymour, 311, 396
Hallowitz, Emanuel, 291
Hampden-Turner, Charles, 498
Handler, Joel, 92
Hansen, Howard, 292
Hardcastle, David A., 530
Hardy, Richard E., 276, 372
Harris, Robert, 105
Harris, Thomas A., 127
Harrison, Bennett, 102
Harrison-Ross, Phyllis, 514
Hartman, Ann, 537
Haselkorn, Florence, 408
Hatterer, Lawrence J., 452
Hawes, Joseph M., 401
Headley, E. B., 447
Hefferin, Elizabeth A., 274
Heilig, S. M., 334
Heineman, Ruth K., 124
Heiniche, Christoph M., 175
Helfer, Ray E., 131, 173
Hemphill, Diana P., 444
Henderson, W. L., 516
Hendry, Charles E., 477
Henry, William E., 335
Heraud, Brian J., 39, 43
Hersch, Alexander, 417
Herzog, Elizabeth, 227
Hester, John N., 498
Hetherington, E. Mavis, 112
Hewett, Sheila, 457
Heyman, Margaret M., 443
Heymann, Irmgard, 228
Hickey, Kathleen M., 288
Hill, William G., 159
Hinton, John, 264
Hippler, Arthur E., 502
Hirsch, Carl, 268
Hirsch, Sidney, 278
Hochbaum, Martin, 540
Hodgson, Godfrey, 353

Hoffman, Adeline M., 276
Hoffman, Martin, 454
Hoffman, Mary Ellen, 117, 118
Hollingshead, August B., 14, 114, 314
Hollingsworth, Ellen J., 92
Hollis, Ernest V., 19
Hollis, Florence, 119, 537
Hopkins, Jeannette, 490
Hopkins, Thomas J., 502
Hopkirk, Howard W., 207
Horton, Paul B., 479
Hostetler, John A., 137
Houy, Julia, 272
Howard, Donald S., 49
Howard, John R., 498
Howell, Joseph T., 108
Hunt, Morton M., 310
Huntington, Gertrude Enders, 137
Hurley, Roger, 106, 404, 408, 410
Huttman, John P., 281

Inker, Monroe L., 170

Jacka, Alan A., 230
Jackson, Bruce, 401
Jackson, Doris Seder, 312
Jackson, George, 385
Jackson, Howard, 292
Jacobs, Jane, 480
Jacobs, Jerry, 457
Jahoda, Marie, 308
James, Dorothy B., 106
Jarecki, Henry G., 312
Jefferson, Lara, 353
Jellinek, E. M., 436
Johnson, Arlien, 526
Johnson, Betty Jo, 376
Johnson, Sheila K., 111, 242
Johnson, Virginia E., 128, 144
Jolowicz, Almeda, 224
Jones, Edmund D., 226
Jones, Ernest, 306
Jones, Wyatt, 473
Jordan, William, 162
Josephson, Eric, 210
Josephson, Mary, 210
Josselyn, Irene, 141
Judge, John J., 450
Judson, Horace F., 431
Jung, Marshall, 484

Kadushin, Alfred, 230

Kahn, Alfred J., 498
Kahn, Si, 490
Kalin, Rudolf, 439
Kallen, David, 102
Kaplan, Harold I., 316
Kase, Harold M., 416, 529, 531
Kaslow, Florence Whiteman, 528
Katz, Arnold J., 106
Katz, Jay, 164
Keehn, J. D., 438
Kellam, Constance E., 269
Keller, Gordon N., 508
Kelley, Jerry L., 180
Kelley, Robert K., 162
Kellogg, Paul U., 474
Kempe, C. Henry, 131, 172
Kennard, Sara Sue, 15
Kerns, Elizabeth, 141, 334
Kesey, Ken, 310
Keyes, Daniel, 410
Khinduka, Shanti K., 372
Kidneigh, John C., 526
Killian, Eldon C., 255
Kilpatrick, Dee Morgan, 234
Kilson, Martin, 516
Kim, Bok-Lim C., 504
Kirk, Stuart A., 455
Kirkland, Marjorie H., 404
Kitano, Harry H. L., 40
Kittrie, Nicholas N., 320, 435
Klein, Philip, 58
Kline, Draza, 233
Kluckhohn, Clyde, 43
Klugman, David J., 334
Knapp, Vrinda S., 292
Knight, Ethridge, 511
Koleski, Raymond A., 472
Konopka, Gisela, 197–198, 199, 373
Korner, Anneliese F., 194
Kosberg, Jordan J., 275
Kramer, Philip, 530
Kraner, Bernard M., 501
Krause, Merton S., 444
Krickus, Richard J., 490
Krimmel, Herman, 441, 442, 445, 446
Kris, Anton O., 342
Kroll, Faustina R., 508
Krosney, Herbert, 484
Kruse, Arthur H., 526
Kuehn, William C., 400
Kullman, Elma, 225
Kunitz, Stephen J., 439

Kunkel, Peter, 15
Kurzman, Paul A., 530

LaBarre, Weston, 231
Lally, Dorothy, 470
Lamott, Kenneth, 127
Lane, James B., 461
Lane, Robert P., 471
Langner, Thomas, 314
Lappin, Ben, 473
Lauderdale, Michael, 301
Lauffer, Armand A., 473, 522
Laughlin, John L., 156
LaVeck, Gerald D., 420
Lawder, Elizabeth, 230
Lawrence, Harry, 128
Leader, Arthur L., 148
Lebeaux, Charles N., 47
Ledebur, L. C., 516
Lee, Kenneth A., 419
Lefton, Mark, 416
Leifer, Ronald, 311
Lemert, Edwin M., 377
Lerner, Barbara, 315
Leslie, Gerald R., 479
Levi, Edith G., 493
Levin, Lester I., 496
Levine, Jo Ann, 145
Levine, Naomi, 540
Levine, Sol, 239
Levy, Charles S., 480, 485
Levy, Jerrold E., 439
Lewis, Howard, 320, 353
Lewis, Martha, 320, 353
Lewis, Myrna I., 261, 269
Lewis, Oscar, 508
Lewis, Robert E., 532
Lide, Pauline D., 506, 512
Lieberman, Louis, 457
Lieberman, Robert, 127
Likert, Rensis, 525
Lindeman, Eduard C., 19
Linden, Maurice E., 269
Lingeman, Richard R., 434
Lipscomb, Harry, 450
Loether, Herman J., 261
Loewenberg, Frank M., 58
London, Joan, 522
Longres, John, 509
Lourie, Norma V., 152
Lowenstein, Edward R., 480
Lowery, John O., Jr., 92

Lubin, A. Harold, 292
Lubove, Roy, 475
Luce, Gay, 304
Lukoff, Irving F., 422
Lum, Doman, 284
Lurie, Abraham, 278

Maas, Henry S., 228, 495
McCaghy, Charles H., 452
McCartney, Kenneth H., 498
McCartt, John M., 384, 399
McClelland, David C., 439
McCord, William, 511
McCorkle, Lloyd W., 367
McGee, Richard K., 353
MacIntyre, Duncan P., 93
McKenzie, Roderick D., 461
McLaney, Martha J., 434
Maclay, David, 237
McNeil, C. F., 466
McNeil, Elton B., 204
McPheeters, Harold L., 12, 13, 18, 21, 22,
   23, 403, 532
Maddox, George L., 238
Madore, C. Elizabeth, 490
Mahaffey, Maryann, 483
Maitra, Promila, 300
Malcolm X, 511
Mandelbaum, Arthur, 414
Mandell, Betty, 534
Mangogna, Thomas J., 384, 399
Mann, James, 334
Mann, Ruth Z. S., 539
Mannoni, Maud, 419
Manser, Ellen P., 157
Maple, Frank F., 234
Margolin, Reuben J., 450
Margolis, Philip M., 309, 337
Marmor, Judd, 454
Marmor, Theodore K., 108
Marris, Peter, 489
Marshall, Dale R., 490
Martin, John Bartlow, 381, 383
Masters, William H., 128, 144
Matthiessen, Peter, 522
Matushima, John, 211
Mayeda, Tadeshi A., 413
Mayer, Morris F., 214
Mayfield, William G., 315
Mead, Margaret, 511
Mechanic, David, 353
Meehan, Thomas, 242

Meier, August, 110
Meier, Gitta, 52, 124
Mendelson, Allan R., 533
Menninger, Karl, 307
Merl, Lawrence, 181
Merle, Sherman, 537
Meyer, Carol, 536, 538
Michael, Stanley, 314
Michener, Charlotte W., 313
Miles, Arthur P., 67
Miller, Dorothy, 102
Miller, Henry, 537
Miller, Peter, 444
Miller, Robert, 181–186
Minahan, Anne, 441, 538
Minuchin, Salvador, 162
Mitchell, Maurine B., 405
Mitford, Jessica, 237, 383
Mizio, Emelicia, 508
Moffett, Arthur D., 432
Mogulof, Melvin B., 486
Montiel, Miguel, 41
Moore, Wilbur E., 19
Morlock, Maud, 156
Morrow, William R., 203
Moynihan, Daniel P., 110, 486, 492
Mueller, John F., 444
Mullen, Edward J., 528
Munroe, Ruth, 316
Murphy, Ann, 292, 417
Murray, Henry A., 43

Nackman, Nathan S., 341
Nagpaul, Hans, 46
Najman, Ronald, 250
Nathan, Harriet, 472
Nathan, Peter E., 438
Navarre, Elizabeth, 146
Nebo, John, 181
Nee, Robert H., 537
Neleigh, Janice R., 490
Nelkin, Dorothy, 518
Newman, Frederick L., 490
Newman, Richard, 31
Newson, Elizabeth, 457
Newson, John, 457
Nichols, Elizabeth R., 132–135
Nicolson, Robert, 276
Nobel, Milton, 301
Noble, John H., Jr., 29
Northrop, F. S. C., 474
Nyswander, Marie, 434

O'Connell, Patricia, 111
O'Connor, Alice L., 341
Odegard, Peter H., 430
O'Donnell, Edward J., 461, 465
Ohlin, Lloyd E., 141, 399
Okum, Arthur M., 108
Olmstead, Joseph A., 526
Olsen, Katharine M., 288
Olsen, Marvin E., 288
Olshansky, Simon, 417
Opler, Marvin, 314
Orlin, Malinda, 46
Orshansky, Mollie, 168
Orten, James D., 510
Overstreet, Helen-Mary, 233
Ovesey, Lionel, 452
Owings, W. A., 108

Padfield, Harland, 41
Palley, H. A., 487
Palley, M. L., 487
Palmer, Stuart, 401
Pappenfort, Donnell M., 234, 399
Parad, Howard J., 334, 417
Parad, Libbie G., 334
Park, Robert E., 461
Parker, Beulah, 168
Parker, William, 453
Pattison, E. Mansell, 447
Pauker, Jerome D., 231
Pavloff, George G., 447
Pearl, Arthur, 114, 529
Pennekamp, M., 234
Pennington, Rita, 309, 315
Perkins, Robert A., 395
Perlman, Helen Harris, 32, 494, 533, 534, 535
Perlman, Robert, 408, 473, 481, 483, 493
Perrow, Charles, 525
Perry, Sally L., 450
Perske, Robert, 411
Peterson, David A., 247
Petro, Olive, 514
Piliavin, Irving, 15
Pilisuk, Mark, 540
Pilisuk, Phyllis, 540
Pincus, Allen, 243, 244, 441, 538
Pins, Arnulf M., 58
Piven, Frances Fox, 453, 490, 534
Piven, Herman, 399
Plascowe, Morris, 164
Plaut, Thomas F. A., 440, 445

Polansky, Norman A., 323, 416, 495
Polier, Shad, 177
Polk, Kenneth, 141
Pollack, Harriet, 437
Pollak, Otto, 54
Popper, Hermine L., 104
Porter, Judith D. R., 501
Porterfield, Austin L., 357
Pounds, Lois, 292
Poussaint, Alvin, 315
Powledge, Fred, 476
Pratt, Mildred, 521
Pruger, Robert, 489
Prunty, Howard, 117, 118
Pueschel, Siegfried M., 417
Pumphrey, Muriel, 539
Pumphrey, Ralph, 3
Pursuit, Dan G., 378
Purvine, Margaret, 58, 472, 527, 532
Pusic, Eugen, 470

Queen, Stuart A., 8
Quigley, Stephen P., 458

Radzinowicz, Lionel, 401
Rainwater, Lee, 498, 511
Ramos, Juan, 517
Rapoport, Roger, 282
Redfield, Robert, 61
Redlich, Frederick C., 14, 31, 114, 314
Rees, Stuart, 470
Rehr, Helen, 125, 290
Reid, Otto M., 461
Reid, William J., 468
Reik, Theodor, 38
Rein, Martin, 480, 489, 534
Reinhold, Robert, 488
Reissman, Leonard, 500
Rennie, Thomas, 314
Reno, Virginia, 246
Rice, Elizabeth P., 285
Rich, Thomas A., 238
Richan, Willard C., 533
Richards, Larry D., 419
Richmond, Mary, 537
Rieger, Wolfram, 395
Riessman, Frank, 104, 114, 191, 529
Riis, Jacob, 461
Ring, Martha D., 88
Riley, James Whitcomb, 66
Ripple, Lilian, 495, 504, 527, 533
Rivlin, Alice M., 59, 486

Roberts, Alvin, 458
Roberts, Nancy, 406
Roberts, Robert W., 234, 537
Robinson, David, 353
Robinson, Ira E., 41
Robison, Sophia M., 357, 360, 370
Roby, Pamela, 234
Rogers, Virginia, 260
Rogler, Lloyd H., 508
Romanyshyn, John M., 48, 147, 192, 482, 515
Rorem, C. Rufus, 88
Rose, Robert G., 361
Rose, Sheldon D., 203
Rosenhan, D. L., 322
Rosenkranz, Armin, 480
Roskies, Ethel, 408
Ross, Bernard, 540
Ross, Robert, 479
Rothman, David J., 396
Rothman, Jack, 472, 473, 508
Rudwick, Elliott, 110
Ruitenbeek, Hendrik M., 306
Rustin, Bayard, 502
Ryan, Robert M., 12, 13, 18, 21, 22, 403
Ryan, William, 314, 404
Ryland, Gladys, 200

Sackheim, Gertrude, 540
Sagarin, Edward, 400, 452, 453
Salmon, Robert, 434
Sanders, Charles L., 506
Sanders, Marion K., 489
Sands, Bill, 400
Sands, Rosalind M., 326
Sandusky, Annie Lee, 227
Sarri, Rosemary, 234, 524, 527
Sarton, May, 276
Sarvis, M. A., 234
Schaeffer, Alice, 513
Schafer, Walter E., Jr., 141
Scherz, Frances H., 129, 137
Schild, Sylvia, 43
Schlesinger, Benjamin, 146
Schmidt, Edith R., 156
Schneider, David, 43
Schneider, Jane, 417
Schorr, Alvin, 168, 169, 486
Schottland, Charles I., 485, 487, 491
Schreiber, Meyer, 419
Schreiber, Paul, 154
Schubert, Margaret, 149

Schulz, David A., 162
Schultze, Charles L., 59, 486
Schuman, H., 500
Schumer, Florence, 408
Schur, Edwin F., 437
Scoles, Pascal, 340
Scotch, Norman A., 239
Seale, Bobby, 511
Sears, William F., 490
Segal, Arthur, 410
Segal, Brian, 453, 454
Segal, Julius, 259, 304, 315
Seidl, Frederick W., 227, 230
Selye, Hans, 318
Sessions, Perry M., 442
Shaffer, Anatole, 483
Shai, A., 326
Shannon, Barbara E., 501, 504
Sharlin, Schlomo A., 416
Sheldon, Eleanor B., 487
Shellhase, Fern E., 419
Shellhase, Leslie J., 419
Sherwood, Clarence C., 485, 528
Sherwood, Robert E., 71
Shipsey, Madeline, 421
Shireman, Charles, 540
Shireman, Joan, 227
Shostak, Arthur B., 498
Shushan, Robert D., 416
Shuttlesworth, Guy E., 301
Sidel, Ruth, 478
Sieder, Violet, 471
Silber, Stanley C., 159
Silcott, T. George, 507
Silliphant, Stirling, 334
Simmons, Leo, 236
Simos, Bertha G., 254
Simpson, Donald F., 263
Sinai, Robert, 474
Siporin, Max, 536
Skarnulis, Ed, 420
Skinner, B. F., 203
Sloane, Homer W., 377
Smith, Alexander B., 437
Smith, Edmund A., 3
Smith, Elizabeth M., 124
Smith, Neilson F., 511
Smith, Robert L., 368, 372
Smith, Russell E., 464, 498
Smith, Winifred, 117, 118
Sobey, Francine, 353
Solis, Faustina, 518

Solnit, Albert, 169
Solomon, Charles, 228
Specht, Harry, 59, 480, 489, 497
Speck, Ross, 112, 139–140
Spencer, Sue, 526
Spencer, William A., 405
Spergel, Irving A., 374
Spiegel, John, 162
Spring, William, 102
Srole, Leo, 114, 314
Staines, Graham L., 479
Stanford, Ann G., 444
Stanton, Esther, 466
Stein, Herman D., 526
Steiner, Claude, 440
Steiner, Gilbert, 76, 90
Stern, Leonard W., 376
Sternback, Jack C., 399
Stewart, James C., Jr., 301
Stiles, Evelyn, 512
Stone, Irving, 306
Stotland, Ezra, 335
Stotsky, Bernard A., 276, 450
Strauss, Anselm L., 353
Strean, Herbert S., 538
Stretch, John J., 45
Stuart, Richard B., 159, 495
Studt, Elliot, 359, 396, 399
Subhadra, V., 300
Sullivan, Scott, 488
Sundel, Martin, 128
Sunley, Robert, 189
Sussman, Marvin B., 111
Sutherland, Edwin S., 356
Swartz, Jacqueline, 142
Szasz, Thomas, 311

Tager, Jack, 461
Taves, Marvin J., 238
Taylor, Alice L., 19
Taylor, Ian, 401
Teague, Doran, 289, 302–303
Teare, Robert J., 23, 531, 532
Teed, Genevieve, 301
Teeters, Nancy H., 59, 486
Teeters, Negley K., 381, 395
Theis, Sophie, 230
Theodore, Carol N., 480
Theodore, Eustace D., 480
Thomas, Edwin J., 203
Thomas, William I., 322
Throssell, Harold, 534

Thursz, Daniel, 483, 484, 491–492
Tibbitts, Clark, 236
Tidwell, Billy J., 504
Tissue, Thomas, 247
Titmuss, Richard M., 353
Tiven, Marjorie B., 250, 251
Tobiessen, J. E., 326
Toren, Nina, 59, 534
Towle, Charlotte, 108
Townsend, Claire, 262, 263, 275
Townsend, Peter, 540
Trattner, Walter I., 108
Trieschman, Albert E., 210
Tripodi, Tony, 528
Turner, Francis Joseph, 540
Turner, John B., 26, 500
Turnquest, BeAlva, 505

Ullmann, Alice, 125

Vasey, Wayne, 41
Vietorisz, Thomas, 102
Vigilante, Joseph L., 508
Vinter, Robert D., 377
Vyas, Ashutosh, 341

Waddell, Jack, 439
Wadel, Cato, 108
Waelder, Elsie M., 119–122
Waite, Florence, 166
Wald, Lillian, 462
Waldman, Nancy, 58
Wallace, Anthony F. C., 43
Walton, Paul, 401
Walzer, Hank, 313
Wanner, Eric, 439
Ward, Mary Jane, 310
Warner, Amos G., 7
Warren, Marguerite, 401
Warren, Roland L., 474
Wasser, Edna, 270
Wasserman, Harry, 55
Waters, William F., 336
Watson, Kenneth W., 227
Weaver, Thomas, 498
Webb, Beatrice, 64
Webb, Sidney, 64
Weber, George H., 210
Weber, J. Robert, 361, 362
Weber, Max, 525
Weed, Patricia, 495

Weinberg, George, 452
Weinberg, Isolde Chapin, 371
Weinberg, Jon, 448
Weinberg, Martin S., 451, 458
Weisman, Avery D., 239
Weisman, Irving, 431
Weissman, Harold H., 466, 489, 540
Westheimer, Ilse, 175
Westhues, Kenneth, 142
Weston, W. R., 397
Whatley, Lydia W., 286
Whitehead, Anthony, 263
Whiteman, Martin, 422
Whittaker, James K., 59, 206, 210
Wicker, Tom, 385
Wiernasz, Michael J., 311
Wigginton, Eliot, 244
Wilensky, Harold L., 47
Williams, Colin J., 451, 458
Williams, Roy, 41
Willie, Charles V., 501
Wilson, A. John, III, 123
Wilson, Gertrude, 200
Wilson, G. Terence, 203, 233
Wilson, James Q., 51
Wilson, Marguerite, 359
Wiltse, Kermit, 19, 72
Wiseman, Jacqueline P., 450
Wolfe, P. H., 301
Wolfgang, Marvin E., 401
Woods, Sister Frances Jerome, 41
Wool, Robert, 398
Wright, Erik, 383
Wurmser, Leon, 434
Wyden, Barbara, 514
Wyss, Dieter, 316

Yablonsky, Lewis, 433
Young, Alma T., 125
Young, Arthur K., 326
Young, Howard, 531
Young, Jack, 401
Young, Leontine, 215–219, 231

Zalba, Serapio Richard, 173
Zald, Mayer N., 14
Zander, Alvin F., 335
Zietz, Dorothy, 464
Zimberg, Sheldon, 450
Zukerman, Jacob T., 231
Zurcher, Louis, 15, 490, 530

index of subject matter

Abortion, 46, 52, 110, 123–125, 301
Academy of Certified Social Workers (ACSW), 12, 528
"Acting out," 37, 319–320
ACTION, 258
Addams, Jane, 42, 305, 462–464, 516
Administration, 22, 274, 523–528, 540
  as social work method, 525–528
  training for, 527–528
Administration on Aging (AoA), 238, 240, 246, 258–259, 266–267, 275
Adolescents, 140–142, 197–199, 214–215, 223, 232, 455; see also Delinquency
Adoption, 110, 146–147, 177–178, 209, 225–230, 232, 233, 386, 452
Advocacy, 3, 15, 55, 107, 115, 268, 273, 275, 292–293, 350, 352, 420, 429, 454, 455, 460, 510
Aging, 235–276
  blindness in, 429
  consumer education for, 265, 273
  developmental approach to, 238, 243–245
  health of, 239, 240, 241, 245, 251–255
  housing for, 248–250
  income levels of, 144, 240, 245–248
  institutions for, 240–241, 254–255, 271–272, 274, 276
  life expectancy, 235, 236
  mental health of, 253–255
  needs of, 245–265, 276
  numbers of, 236, 239–240
  nursing homes for, 254, 261–264, 272, 275, 276
  nutritional services for, 241, 252–253, 259, 273
  retirement communities for, 241–242
  rights of, 238–239, 264, 276
  services to, 256, 259, 265–274, 276
  social attitudes toward, 237–238, 259, 260–261
  social needs of, 257–261
  social work with, 244, 254, 268–275
  taxes on, 248
  transportation problems of, 247–248, 255–257
Aid to the Blind (AB), 85–86, 421
Aid to Families with Dependent Children (AFDC), 52, 55, 89–95, 97, 100, 105, 166, 167, 168, 193, 482, 515
Aid to the Permanently and Totally Disabled (APTD), 84, 86–87

Albany Home for Children, 207–209

Alcohol, Drug Abuse and Mental Health Administration (ADAMHA), 438n

Alcoholics, Skid Row, 435, 442, 448, 450–451
  rights of, 436

Alcoholics Anonymous, 433, 440, 446, 447, 449–450

Alcoholism, 434–451; see also Disabilities
  criminal model, 435–437
  defined, 441–442
  disease model, 437–438
  indirect treatment of, 444–446
  psychodynamic model, 439–440
  research in, 437–438
  resources for, 447–451
  social attitudes toward, 434–435
  social work in, 440–445, 447–449, 451
  treatment of, 438, 442–447, 448–449, 457

Alinsky, Saul, 203, 489, 491

Almoners, 285

American Association of Retired Persons (AARP), 265, 267

American Bar Association, 10

American Correctional Association, 306, 380

American Humane Association, 130, 170, 172, 173

American Medical Association, 10, 88, 172, 284

American National Red Cross, 153–154

American Psychiatric Association, 306, 491

Anxiety, 290, 317–318, 336

Auburn prison system, 380–381

Authority
  in corrections, 392–393
  in medical social work, 287–288
  in protective services, 135

Baccalaureate-level social worker (BSW)
  accreditation of, 1, 496
  core of competence for, 21–24
  deployment of, 24, 124, 271, 325, 351, 528
  education for practice, 3, 8, 12, 16–17, 351, 496–497, 509, 528, 532, 533

Beekman-Downtown Hospital, 299

Beers, Clifford, 305, 308

Behavior
  dynamics of, 107, 179, 316–323
  purposefulness of, 34–37
  theories of, 537, 539–540

Behavior modification, 127, 145, 149, 200–204, 233, 413, 438

Blacks
  adoption of, 226–227
  child rearing of, 501–502
  illegitimacy of, 146
  income levels of, 500–501, 514, 515
  in prison, 384–385
  poverty among, 100, 247, 501, 514

Blindness, 421–430; see also Disabilities
  adjustment to, 427–429
  causes of, 421
  educational programs for, 427
  facilities for, 423–424
  independence, 422–423, 428
  rehabilitation, 421–422, 458
  social attitudes toward, 405, 421–422
  social work with, 423–427
  socialization of, 423

Boarding homes, see Foster care

Bureau of Prisons, 369, 383–384, 386

Bureaucracy, 41, 525, 536

Categorical relief, 65, 83, 97–98

Charity Organization Societies (COS), 6–8, 54, 68, 108, 151, 285, 461–462, 463, 467

Chavez, Cesar, 521–523

Chicanos, 151, 503, 504; see also Mexican-Americans

Child guidance clinic, 323–334
  activities of, 324–325
  application process, 326–327
  development of, 323–324
  referrals to, 325
  staff of, 325
  treatment, 324–325

Child welfare
  child abuse, 172–174, 233–234
  children in own homes, 167–206
  delinquent children, 359–378
  foster care, 178, 206–225, 233
  protective services, 130–135
  trends in, 178–179

Child Welfare League of America (CWLA), 130, 208, 221, 227, 230, 468, 473

Children; *see also* Child welfare; Families; *and* Parent-child relationships
abused, 131, 172–174, 233
black, 501–502, 505
health of, 173, 176–177, 192–193
in boarding homes, 166–167, 233
in institutions, 165, 206–215, 386
in one-parent families, 147–148
in own homes, 112–113, 128–129, 136–142, 167–206
mental health of, 164, 192–195
neglected, 131, 174–178, 228
of migrants, 519–520
"permanently neglected," 177–178, 228
play therapy, 195–197, 327
protective services for, 130–135
removal from parents, 171–172, 175–176
rights of, 163–165, 168, 169, 179, 192, 194, 233, 234
Cities
living conditions in, 475–477, 516
renewal of, 476, 479–480
Client, rights of, 25–27, 42, 45, 51–53, 454, 493
Client-worker relationship, 28–29, 149–151, 505, 511–513
Clinics
aftercare, 335, 340–341
alcoholism, 448
child guidance, 323–334
community mental health, 334–341
medical, 300–301
College mental health programs, 142
Columbia University School of Social Work, 8, 14, 490, 536
Commonwealth Fund, 323
Communications, 126
Community Action Programs (CAPs), 16, 266, 270, 476, 488, 489–491, 502
Community chests, 464–468
Community development, 477–478, 497, 498
Community medical social work, 295–303
Community mental health centers, 159, 254, 312–316, 323
services of, 313, 334–335
staff of, 313, 335–336
Community organization, 459–498
activities of, 473

Community organization, *continued*
as social work method, 459–461, 471–473
defined, 460, 470
national and international, 468–470
qualifications for, 472–473, 494
skills needed in, 36–37, 472–473
theory, 493–494
trends in, 466, 477
Community planning, 22, 352, 474–477, 497
Community psychiatry, 254, 352
Confidentiality, 28–30, 229–230
Consumer education, 46, 116, 265, 273
Correctional services, 355–401; *see also* Prisons
caseload, 371, 397–398
evaluation of, 377–378, 394–399
for women, 385–393
half-way houses, 369, 397–398, 400
institutions, 365–367, 378–385
parole, 368–369, 386, 390–393, 396–399
probation, 364–365, 396–397
training for, 378, 399
Cost-benefit accounting, 160–161, 195, 205–206, 233, 481–482, 493, 524
Council on Social Work Education (CSWE)
accreditation by, 1, 8, 12, 472, 495–496, 509, 531
activities of, 12, 17–18, 269, 491
curriculum study, 471, 496*n*
publications of, 269, 441, 473, 504
Courts
criminal, 393–394
family, 170–171
juvenile, 359–374
Crime
causes of, 355–356, 378
definition of, 355, 358
prevention of, 401
research on, 357, 378, 401
"white-collar," 356
"without victims," 437
Criminals
attitudes toward, 358, 395–396, 398
"white-collar," 356, 394
Crisis intervention, 417
Cultural lag, 40, 66

Day care, 94, 104, 131, 204–206, 233

Deafness
  services for, 457, 458
  social attitudes toward, 405
Death, 236, 238–239, 244, 261–265, 276;
  see also Dying
Defense mechanisms, see Mechanisms
  of defense
"Definition of the situation," 322
Delinquency
  causes of, 355–356, 374, 375
  definitions of, 355, 357
  detention, 362–363
  forestry camps, 366–367
  institutions, 365–368, 372–374
  juvenile court, 359–374
  predictive tables, 375
  prevention, 374–376, 489
  research, 357
  subcultures, 358
  treatment, 364–369, 371–374
Depression of the 1930s, 62, 68–71, 75,
  464, 529
Detention facilities, 362–363
Disabilities
  definition of, 405
  rights of those with, 407
  social attitudes toward, 405–407, 421,
  434–435
  social work with, 403–458
Disability benefits, 80–81
Disaster relief, 153, 403
Divorce, 109, 148
Dix, Dorothea, 67, 305, 308
Drop-in centers, 142
Drug addiction, 430–434; see also Disabilities
  causes of, 431–433
  methadone maintenance, 433–434
  research on, 432
  social attitudes toward, 431
  subcultures, 432–433
  treatment of, 431, 433–434, 457
Dying; see also Death
  care of, 263–264
  emotional needs of, 239, 263–265
  rights of, 238–239, 264, 276

Ecology, 476–477, 478
Education; see also School
  and culturally deprived child, 190–
  192
  child's right to, 179

Education, continued
  consumer, 46, 116, 265, 273
  for mentally retarded, 413–414, 420
  of migrant children, 519–520
  problems with, 187
  social work and, see Social work,
  education for
  social work in, see School social work
Elizabethan Poor Law, 64–66, 67, 165
Elmira reformatory, 381
Employment
  guaranteed, 103–104
  of aging, 236, 237, 246, 257–258
  training for, 103–104; see also WIN
  underemployment, 103, 105
  unemployability, 103–104
  unemployment, 103
Encyclopedia of Social Work, 18, 526–527

Families; see also Parent-child relationships
  effects of poverty on, 114–119
  forms of, 111, 125–128
  functions of, 109–113, 114, 145, 148,
  162
  life cycle of, 123, 128–129, 143
  one-parent, 110, 145–149
Family Assistance Plan (FAP), 104,
  492–493
Family courts, 170–171
Family planning, 43, 52, 92, 123–124
Family Service Association of America
  (FSAA), 53, 156–158, 160, 270, 468
Family social work
  agencies in, 113–114, 151, 178
  evaluation of, 32–34, 160–162
  family therapy, 139–141, 162
  illustrative cases, 119–123
  outpost services, 156
  protective services, 130–136
  with mentally ill, 341
  with unmarried mothers, 230–232;
  see also Illegitimacy
Fathers
  absent, 89, 91, 93
  unemployed, 90
  unmarried, 231
Federal Emergency Relief Administration (FERA), 71–73, 529
Federal government
  budget, 1–2, 41, 104–106, 466, 480

Federal government, *continued*
   funding by, 56–58, 59, 97–99, 267,
     315, 466, 476
   policies of, 485–486, 497, 498
   responsibilities of, 70
   role in public assistance, 2, 29, 69,
     486
Forestry camps, 366–367
Foster care
   boarding homes, 214–225
   for mentally retarded, 411–412
   foster parents, 221–225
   group homes, 208–209, 214–215, 223
   home finding, 166–167, 219–221
   illustrative cases, 215–219
   institutions, 206–214
   problems with biological parents,
     223–224
Freud, Anna, 175, 316
Freud, Sigmund, 303, 306–308, 316

General Assistance (GA), 97–98, 99
Genetic counseling, 43, 123, 301
Group homes, *see* Foster care
Guaranteed income, 104–106

Half-way houses, 369, 397–398, 400
Harrington, Michael, 488, 516
Harrison Act, 430
Hartley-Salmon Clinic, 324
Health and Welfare Councils, 465–467
Health care
   costs of, 88, 279, 282
   delivery of, 277–285, 352
   of aging, 251–255
   of children, 173, 176–177, 192–193
   planning of, 278, 302–303
   preventive, 300
   social workers in, 278, 285–300
Health maintenance organizations
   (HMOs), 283–285
Health services, 277–303
   and poverty, 277–283
   distribution of services, 279–282
   health insurance, 277–278, 283–285
   "secondary gain," 321
   social work in, 285–303
Helping process, 58, 59
   contract, 149
   skills, 28–32, 149–151, 152–153
Highfields, 367
Hill, Octavia, 42, 260

Homemaker service, 154–156, 204
Homosexuality, 404, 451–455, 458; *see
   also* Disabilities
   disease model, 452–453
   Gay Liberation Front, 452, 457
   rights, 452–453, 455
   social work and, 451, 454–455
   subcultures, 452
Hopkins, Harry, 70–71
Hospitals
   medical social work in, 285–300
   mental, *see* Mental hospitals
   psychiatric social work in, 341–351
Housing, 46, 480
Howard, Ebenezer, 474
Hull House, 463, 516

Illegitimacy, 91–92, 110, 125, 146–147,
   162, 226, 230–234
Income maintenance programs
   deficiencies in, 100–102
   separation from social services, 2,
     54–56, 100, 106–107, 486, 493
   types, 78–79, 102–106
Indians (native Americans), 247, 439,
   503, 507
Individual rights
   advocacy of, 116
   of accused, 394
   of aging and dying, 238–239, 264, 276
   of alcoholics, 436
   of disabled, 407
   of homosexuals, 452–453, 455
   of mentally ill, 311–312, 341
   of mentally retarded, 415, 420
   of parents, 163–164, 169, 171–172,
     174–176
   of welfare recipients, 50–53, 490
   to claim minimum physical essen-
     tials, 42
   to make decisions, 25–27
Industrial social work, 46*n*
Industrialized society, 40, 47–48, 57, 72,
   78–79, 106, 108, 111–112, 151–152,
   163, 237, 276, 461, 473–476
Institutions
   child-caring, 206–215
   detention, 362–363
   for adult offenders, 378–396
   for aged, 240–241, 254–255, 261–264,
    271–272, 274–276

Institutions, *continued*
  for juvenile delinquents, 365–368, 372–374
  for mentally retarded, 412, 417–418
  for women offenders, 385–393
  residential treatment center, 209–211
Intelligence quotient (IQ), 408–411, 415
International Council on Social Welfare, 470

Jail, *see* Detention facilities
Jewish social work, 157, 467–468
Joint Commission on Mental Health of Children, 164, 174, 194–195, 205, 210, 309, 315, 420
Joint Commission on Mental Illness and Mental Health, 308, 315
Juvenile courts, 359–374
  appeal from, 176, 363–364
  development of, 359–362, 401
  hearing, 363–364
  philosophy of, 170, 359–362
  probation and parole, 364–365, 367–369, 372
  procedures of, 176–178, 363–367, 401
  social study, 363, 370
  staff of, 363, 365, 369–373
  standards for, 170–172, 363, 366
Juvenile delinquency, *see* Delinquency

Legal Aid, 116, 204, 489–490, 516
Local responsibility, 65, 68, 97–99
"Looking-glass self," 198

McClure, Grace, 260
Manpower in human services, 1, 11, 104, 107, 271, 324–325, 351, 457–458, 528–533
Massachusetts General Hospital, 263, 285
Master of Social Work (MSW), 9, 10, 12, 17–18, 325, 351, 528, 532–533
Mechanisms of defense, 317–319, 428
Medicaid, 52, 77, 87–88, 251, 257, 261–262, 279, 282, 416
Medical care, *see* Health care, *and* Health services
Medical social work
  hospital-based, 285–300
  in community, 295–303
  in health planning, 278, 302–303

Medicare, 50, 57, 77, 82–83, 108, 241, 251–252, 254, 261–262, 264, 266, 270, 279, 280, 282, 286
Mental health
  college programs for, 142
  community centers, 159, 254, 312–316, 323, 334–336
  community model, 312
  definition of, 308–309
  medical model, 309
  of children, 164, 192–195, 233
  of poor, 114, 314–315
  psychodynamic model, 312
  services, 303–353
Mental hospitals, 309–312, 341–351, 353
  admission to, 341–342
  aftercare, 340–341
  personnel, 343
  population of, 310
  services of, 309–312, 341–342
  social workers in, 341–342, 343–351
Mental illness
  attitudes toward, 303, 308, 311
  definitions of, 303–304, 322
  extent of, 315
  rights of those with, 311–312, 341
  treatment of, 304–305, 457
Mental retardation, 404, 405, 407–421, 457; *see also* Disabilities
  causes of, 408
  degrees of, 409–411
  education, 413–414, 420
  facilities, 411–414, 415, 416, 417, 419
  foster homes, 411–412
  institutions, 412, 417–418
  prevention of, 414–415, 420
  rights of those with, 415, 420
  sheltered workshops, 416, 427
  social work in, 414–421
Methadone, 433–434
Mexican-Americans, 247, 508*n*, 517; *see also* Chicanos
Migrants, 151–152, 168, 517–523
Minorities, 151, 499–515; *see also specific group names*
Mobilization for Youth (MFY), 489, 490, 497
Mothers
  AFDC, 90–95, 166–167
  and "suitable home," 92–93, 167, 175–176
  and Work Incentive Program (WIN), 53, 94, 166, 205

Mothers, *continued*
unmarried, 230–232
"Mothers' pensions," 89

Narcotic addiction, *see* Drug addiction
National Advisory Committee on Civil Disorders, 63, 502–503
National Assembly for Social Policy and Development, 266, 469
National Assembly of National Voluntary Health and Social Welfare Organizations, 469
National Association for Mental Health, 305, 491
National Association for Retarded Children, 410, 418
National Association of Black Social Workers, 484, 503, 506–507
National Association of Social Workers (NASW)
activities of, 57, 420, 491
Code of Ethics, 11, 20–21, 483, 492
manpower classification, 11, 528
membership, 1, 2, 8, 11–12, 20–21, 507
policies, 2, 54–55, 57, 506–507, 514–515, 523
publications of, 468–469, 471–472, 494
National Conference of Social Work, 471, 506–507
National Council on Aging, 256, 266
Project FIND, 256, 259
National Council on Crime and Delinquency, 170, 396
National Council on Illegitimacy, 125, 231
National Federation of Societies for Clinical Social Work, 532–533
National Institute on Alcohol Abuse and Alcoholism (NIAAA), 437–438, 448
National Retired Teachers Association (NRTA), 265, 267
Negative income tax, 105
Newburgh, New York, 84
New Deal, 68–70, 464, 485
New Haven, Connecticut, 476
Nursing homes, 254, 261–264, 272, 275, 276

Office of Economic Opportunity (OEO), 15, 52, 84, 420, 488–489, 521

Old Age and Survivors Insurance (OASI), 80–83, 90, 245–246, 247, 266–267, 270
Old Age Assistance (OAA), 72, 81–82, 84–85, 90, 242, 245, 270
Orphans, 66, 67, 165, 206–207; *see also* Adoption, *and* Foster care
Outreach, 116, 268, 272, 350, 429

Paraprofessionals, 11, 13, 15, 23, 274, 302, 336, 351, 353, 451, 529–531
Parent-child relationships, 128–129, 136–137, 162, 163–164, 169–170, 173–174, 178–180, 183, 187, 193–194, 206, 232–233, 321–322, 333; *see also* Families
Parents, *see also* Families, *and* Parent-child relationships
adoptive, 226–230
attitudes of, 128–129, 136–137, 138–139, 189
of children in foster care, 223–224
rights of, 163–164, 169, 171–172, 174–176
treatment of, 173–174, 194
unmarried, 230–232
Parole
adult, 396–399
juvenile, 368–369
of women, 386, 390–393
Penitentiary, 379; *see also*, Prisons
Pennsylvania prison system, 379–380
Philadelphia Prison Society, 379–380
Pierce, Franklin, 67
Play therapy, 195–197, 327
Police, 357–358, 362, 393
Pollak, Otto, 53–54
Poor, *see also* Welfare
and categorical relief, 65, 83, 97–98
and consumer education, 116
deserving vs. undeserving, 63, 65, 83, 87
"maximum feasible participation" of, 15
mental health of, 114, 314–315
pauper's oath, 66
social work's disengagement from, 13–15, 115, 534
Poverty, 515–517
among aging, 246–248
effect on families, 115–119, 169
extent of, 100–102, 108, 168–169, 404, 478, 515

Poverty, *continued*
  health services and, 277–283
  history of, 6–7, 15–16
  mental retardation and, 409–410
  "permanent," 79, 515–516
  social workers and, 14, 312
  War on Poverty, 1, 58, 463, 476, 478,
    480, 484, 506, 529, 540
Prisoners
  black, 384–385
  female, 385–393
  male, 379–384
  stigmatization of, 394–395, 398, 400
  subcultures of, 394
Prisons, *see also*, Correctional services
  alternatives to, 395–396
  description of, 381–383
  development of, 378–381
  evaluation of, 394–396
  for women, 385–393
  homosexuality in, 455
Private agencies, *see* Voluntary agencies
Private practice of social work, 53, 160
Probation
  adult, 396–397
  juvenile, 364–365
Protective services
  for aging, 242, 270–271, 273
  for children, 130–136
Psychiatry, 42, 341–351, 352, 356
  community, 254, 352
  psychiatrist, 158, 313, 325
Psychology, 40, 356
  psychologist, 325
Psychosomatic illness, 320–321, 327
Public assistance
  alternatives to, 102–106
  black recipients of, 514, 515
  categories of, 83–99
  costs of, 2
  eligibility for, 84–89
  federal role in, 2, 29, 69, 84, 486
  history of, 61–78
  personnel, 1–2, 9–11, 56
  public attitudes toward, 47–48, 52–53,
    62–63
  residence requirements for, 152, 520
  separation of payments and services,
    2, 54–55, 100, 107–108, 486
  services in, 55–56, 100
  stigma of, 50–53, 102, 105–106
Puerto Ricans, 151, 503, 504, 507, 508,
  517

Racism, 16, 40–41, 106, 117, 190, 226–
    227, 312, 357–358, 384–385, 404,
    415, 499–515
Recidivism, 373, 398–399
Reformatory, 381
Rehabilitation, 47, 48, 95–96, 118
  of blind, 421–422, 428, 429–430
  of disabled, 406–407, 413
  vocational, 407, 427, 558
Research, 494–497
  in community organization, 481–482
  in health services, 292
  in social casework, 539
  in social work curriculum, 495–497
Residence laws, 152, 520
Residential treatment center, 209–211
Richmond, Mary, 537, 538–539
Rights of individual; *see* Individual
  rights
Riis, Jacob, 305, 461*n*
Roles of social workers, 19, 22, 107,
    272–275, 350–351, 352, 400, 421,
    429, 456–457, 460, 482, 532
Roosevelt, Franklin D., 69, 70, 108
Rusk, Howard, 406

Salvation Army, 450–451
Schenectady Child Guidance Center,
    325–334
School; *see also* Education
  attendance problems, 189–190
  culturally deprived and, 190–192
  drop-outs, 189–190
  functions of, 137–138, 179–181, 191–
    192
  migrants and, 520
School social work, 179–192, 233
  community organization model, 180–
    181, 187–189
  consultant service, 180, 191
  direct service model, 180–187
  functions of, 179–180, 191–192, 234
  illustrative cases, 181–186, 188–189
Schools of social work
  accreditation of, 472
  admission to, 17–18
  curricula of, 414, 421, 472, 527–528, 532
  enrollment of, 472, 495
  field work at, 158
  linkages with BSW, 17–18
  minority groups at, 504, 509–510
  research at, 495–496
Sectarian agencies, 157, 465–466

Self-help, 16, 48–49, 57, 399, 433, 440, 464

Settlement, 65

Settlement house movement, 68, 462–464

Sheltered workshops, 416, 427

Social action, 41, 352, 456, 459, 472–473, 482–493, 497, 498, 523, 539
  in the 1960s, 488–491, 498
  methods of, 483–484, 491–493
  political activity, 484–485

Social casework
  clinical 532–533, 540
  contrasted with behavior modification, 204
  criticisms of, 13–14, 533–534, 537
  defined, 36, 119, 536, 538
  effectiveness of, 14–15, 534–535
  family, 113–114
  history of, 113, 533–538
  in child guidance, 327–334
  in community mental health, 335–341
  in health care, 288–293
  in mental hospitals, 341–351
  in public assistance, 55, 107, 136
  in school setting, 179–187
  need for, 535–536
  with ghetto residents, 117–118
  with parents, 194, 224, 417–419
  with unmarried mothers, 232

Social class, 14, 41, 53, 114, 314, 322

Social control, 63, 355–356, 453

Social group work
  aims of, 197–200
  defined, 36–37
  group therapy, 351–352
  in health settings, 291–292, 294
  in mental health settings, 335
  leadership, 200
  need for, 36, 198, 199
  skills in, 36, 200
  with adolescents, 141–142, 197–198
  with alcoholics, 448
  with blind, 423
  with mentally retarded, 419

Social indicators, 486–488, 498

Social insurance, 75–77, 78, 80–83

Social planning, 250, 274, 478–482
  and research, 481–482

Social policy, 59, 108, 234, 479, 484, 485–486, 497, 498, 514–515

Social reform 67, 274, 464, 472–473, 498, 536, 537

Social sciences, 39–43

Social Security Act, 55, 75–77, 79, 144, 167, 168, 192, 237, 246, 421, 485, 520–521

Social service exchange, 467

Social welfare
  costs of, 2
  definition, 3, 524
  history of, 58, 108
  institutional view of, 47–48, 57–58, 539, 540
  planning, 458, 472, 473–482
  residual view of, 47–48

Social work; *see also* Social workers
  among helping professions, 45–46, 53–54
  and cost-benefit accounting, 160–161, 195, 205–206, 233, 481–482, 493, 524
  and racism, 499, 503–508, 540
  as a profession, 3–5, 18–23, 59
  casework, *see* Social casework
  clientele of, 53; *see also* Client, rights of, *and* Client-worker relationship
  confidentiality in, 28–30, 229–230
  contributions to behavioral sciences, 42–43
  education for, 1, 9, 16–18, 24, 58, 239, 269–270, 325, 351, 372, 495–496, 504, 506, 508–510, 511–514, 527, 533, 540
  estrangement from poor, 13–15, 534
  group work, *see* Social group work
  helping process, 28–32, 58, 59, 149–153
  history of, 5–6, 58, 533–538
  in corrections, 359, 372–373, 377, 385, 396–400
  industrial, 46n
  in genetic counseling, 43, 123, 301
  in health services, 285–303
  in public assistance, 19, 53–55, 106–108, 527
  in teams, 209, 234, 456–457
  Jewish, 157, 467–468
  knowledge base of, 40–42, 540
  manpower in, 1, 11, 23–25, 106–108, 324–325, 351, 528–533
  medical, 278, 285–303
  paraprofessionals, 11, 13, 107, 302, 336, 351, 353, 451, 529–531
  private practice, 53, 160
  public attitudes toward, 8, 10, 53–54, 527

Social work, *continued*
  qualifications for, 9, 12–13, 106–107, 351, 539
  relation to liberal arts, 39–45
  values in, 24–39, 46–47, 107–108, 150–151
  with addicts, 434
  with aging, 268–275
  with alcoholics, 440–445
  with children, 173–191, 193–194, 195–196, 199–200, 202, 209, 211–213, 217–219, 221–224, 229, 232, 233, 324, 326
  with delinquents, 359, 371
  with mentally retarded, 411–412, 414–421
  with migrants, 520
Social Work Research Group (SWRG), 494
Social Work Year Book, *see* Encyclopedia of Social Work
Social workers
  ACSW, 12, 528
  and racism, 499, 503–506, 511–514
  and social action, 482–485, 491–493
  BSW, 1, 3, 8–9, 12, 13, 16–17, 325, 351, 509, 524, 528, 532
  Code of Ethics, 11, 20, 492
  DSW, 12, 528
  in alcoholism, 443, 445
  manpower classification and deployment, 1–2, 11–12, 23–24, 54, 524, 528–533
  MSW, 9, 10, 12, 17–18, 325, 351, 528, 532–533
  prestige of, 53–54
  private practice, 160, 301
  roles of, 19, 22, 107, 272–275, 350–351, 352, 400, 421, 429, 456–457, 460, 482, 532
  skills of, 28, 30–32, 36
  supervision of, 39, 325, 335–336, 528
Socialization, 112–113, 169, 198, 232, 318, 500
Sociology, 40–41, 356
Sonia Shankman Orthogenic School, 210
South Florida State Hospital, 342–351
Southern Regional Education Board (SREB), 12–13, 460
  "core of competence," 22–24, 272, 350
  objectives of social work services, 21–22, 403

  obstacles to effective functioning, 403, 456
Stateville Prison, 381–383
Subcultures
  delinquent, 358
  drug, 432–433
  homosexual, 452
  prison, 394
Supervision, 39, 325, 335–336, 528
Supplemental Security Income (SSI), 83–86, 99, 105, 241–242, 486
Synanon, 433

"Talking out," 31–32, 37, 309, 315, 327
Team social work, 209, 234, 456–457
Toynbee Hall, 462
Transactional analysis, 127, 162, 440*n*
Transients, 151–152; *see also* Migrants
Travelers Aid and International Social Service of America (TAISSA), 151–153, 256
Treatments
  behavior modification, 200–204
  clarification, 119
  environmental manipulation, 119
  play therapy, 195–197
  short-term, 141
  supportive, 119, 159

Underemployment, 102
Unemployability, 103–104
Unemployment, 79, 96, 101, 103–104, 108, 501
Unemployment Insurance (UI), 96–97, 521
United Community Funds and Councils, *see* United Way
United Farm Workers, 522–523
United Nations, 164, 175, 462, 469–470
United Way, 451, 465, 524
Unmarried mothers, *see* Illegitimacy
U.S. Children's Bureau, 89, 95, 170, 171–172, 215, 363, 366, 369
U.S. Department of Health, Education, and Welfare (HEW), 75, 77, 84, 95, 267–268, 283, 430
U.S. Department of Justice, 364, 384, 430
U.S. President's Commission on Law Enforcement and the Administration of Justice, 361, 371, 376, 397, 435

U.S. President's Committee on Mental Retardation, 407, 414, 419
U.S. Senate Committee on Aging, 249, 267
U.S. Senate Subcommittee on Migratory Labor, 519

Veterans, 153, 407
Veterans Administration, 83, 154
Vocational rehabilitation, 407, 427, 558
Voluntary agencies
    coordination of, 469
    funding for, 56, 466–467
    history of, 58
    role in income maintenance, 99–106
    vs. public agencies, 68, 461, 465
Volunteers, 4, 159, 336, 373–374, 378

Wald, Lillian, 462

War on Poverty, 1, 58, 463, 476, 478, 480, 484, 506, 529, 540
Welfare
    abuse, 6, 10, 63, 516
    rights of those on, 50–53, 490
Welfare Rights Organization, 489
Westfield State Farm, 386–390
White House Conferences
    on aging, 248, 256, 260, 266–269, 469
    on children, 89, 164, 192, 469
Whyte, William F., 357
Widows, 81–82, 144–145, 240, 260
WIN (Work Incentive Program), 53, 94, 166, 205
Women's movement, 261
Worden School of Social Service, 533
Work ethic, 5, 48–50, 53, 57, 94, 106, 169, 257, 434, 519
Works Progress Administration (WPA), 73–75, 529